COLLEGE IS **MY OPPORTUNITY**

Helping first-generation college students make their college dreams a reality!

GUIDE TO COLLEGE

an initiative of

striveforcollege.org

2018 EDITION

ImFirst.org

About Strive for College

Strive for College is a 501(c)(3) nonprofit organization that connects aspiring college students with dedicated mentors online to receive one-on-one guidance and support through the college admissions and financial aid application process. Strive also runs ImFirst.org and publishes the *I'm First! Guide to College* to celebrate and support first-generation college students.

For more information or for permission to use material from this text or product, contact Strive for College, Sobrato Center for Nonprofits, 556 Valley Way, Milpitas, CA 95035; or find us online at www.striveforcollege.org and www.ImFirst.org.

For bulk sales to schools, organizations, colleges, and universities, please contact info@striveforcollege.org.

Editors: *Matt Rubinoff, Cara Martin*

Staff Contributors: *Chelsea Jones, Julie Tennie, Terry Roberts*

Cover Design: *Cinda Debbink*

Interior Page Design and Layout: *Cinda Debbink, Valerie Wilmot*

Special thanks to Michael J. Carter

Photo Credits
© Thinkstock *pages 3, 4, 5, 7, 8, 9, 11, 13, 17, 18, 19, 20, 21, 22, 23, 24, 31, 32, 35, 36, 37, 48, 49, 59, 62, 63, 66, 71, 72, 73, 74, 75, 76, 77, 78, 89, 99, 103, 107, 108, 110, 111, 112, 126, 127, 128, 129, 130, 134, 137, 138, 140, 141, 142, 149, 151, 152, 154, 155, 156, 157, 162, 163, 164, 165*

© Shutterstock *pages 38, 46, 68, 69, 90, 94, 100, 101, 143, 144, 148, 158, 159*

© iStock *pages 2, 119, 120, 122, 146, 147, 160, 161, 166*

Printed in the United States of America

10 9 8 7 6 5 4 3 2 1

Contents

A Message from the Editor

Dear Students,

On behalf of Strive for College, thank you for picking up this copy of the *I'm First! Guide to College.*

There's something special about being first. The first in flight, first man on the moon, and the first African-American president. First kisses, first impressions, first place. **Being among the first in your family to attend and graduate from college is special too.**

We developed this Guide to help students like you get to college and succeed. If you feel overwhelmed by the college process, don't worry! There are specific steps you need to take during the college search and application process. This Guide is designed to turn your college dreams into action-oriented goals and simplify the steps to college so you know what to do next.

It's your responsibility to find out which school is right for you. Asking the right questions and knowing what information to seek out is important. To help you get started, the Guide profiles 168 colleges and universities that are committed to helping students like you thrive in college.

Remember too that you are not alone on the path to college. In the Guide, you will read inspiring stories of students who overcame many obstacles to become first-generation college students. They, along with others, share great advice on how you too can make it to and through college.

We wish you the best of luck on this journey to college and hope you find the *I'm First! Guide to College* to be valuable along the way.

Need more assistance with your college search and application process?

Strive for College can connect you with a mentor to help.

Sign up at www.striveforcollege.org

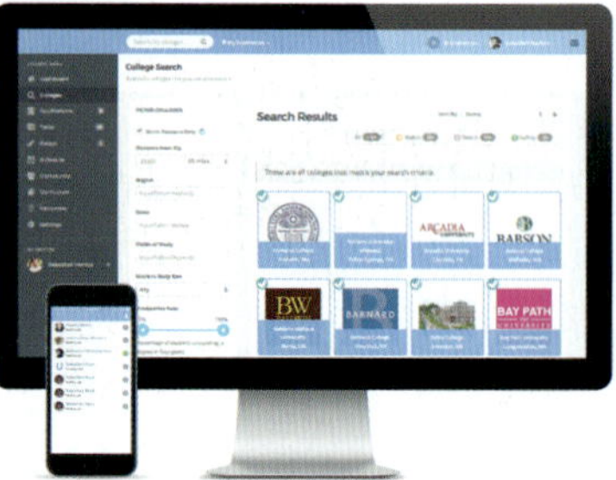

Also visit www.ImFirst.org to find advice and encouragement for first-generation college students. Follow a first-gen student blog and watch video testimonials from first-gen students and graduates.

For counselors, teachers and mentors

The *I'm First! Guide to College,* now with an interactive curriculum and built-in workbook activities and quizzes, is a great resource to use in the classroom or to give to students to call their own.

To purchase additional copies, visit http://store.ImFirst.org.

Contact info@striveforcollege.org to request bulk order discounts.

Unit 1 I'm College Bound

CONTENTS

"The road to reaching your goals begins now. If you wait until tomorrow to begin reaching for them, you might just find it's too late."

Objectives

By the end of this unit, I will...

- understand the benefits of obtaining a college degree.
- identify the characteristics that competitive colleges are looking for in students, both inside and outside of the classroom.
- develop long- and short-term goals which will build toward college success and identify supports that can be used to achieve these goals.

Why College?

With everything you need to do to get ready for college, you may wonder if it's all worth it. Here are four quick (but very important) reasons why:

REASON **1** Every bit of education you get after high school increases the chances you'll earn good pay. Most college graduates earn a lot more money during their working years than people who stop their education at high school.

REASON **2** The more education you get, the more likely it is you will always have a job. According to one estimate, by the year 2028 there will be 19 million more jobs for educated workers than there are qualified people to fill them.

REASON **3** Continuing education after high school is much more important for your generation than it was for your parents' generation. Today most good jobs require more than a high school diploma. Businesses want to hire people who know how to think and solve problems.

REASON **4** Education beyond high school gives you a lot of other benefits, including meeting new people, taking part in new opportunities to explore your interests, and experiencing success.

ON THE SPOT: Do these facts surprise you? How do they affect your decision to apply for college?

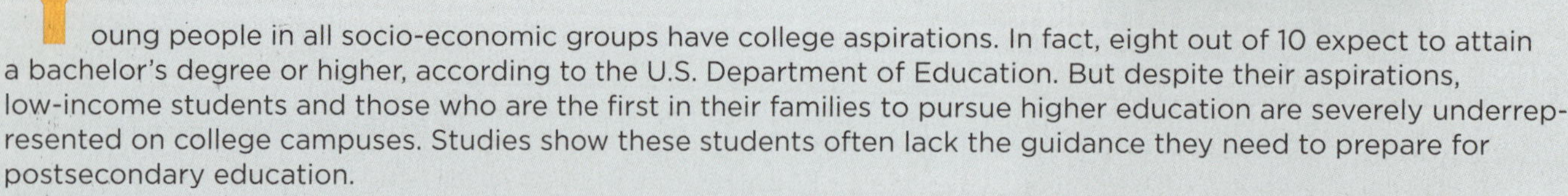

Young people in all socio-economic groups have college aspirations. In fact, eight out of 10 expect to attain a bachelor's degree or higher, according to the U.S. Department of Education. But despite their aspirations, low-income students and those who are the first in their families to pursue higher education are severely underrepresented on college campuses. Studies show these students often lack the guidance they need to prepare for postsecondary education.

In order to turn these students' college dreams into action-oriented goals, the **American Council on Education, Lumina Foundation for Education** and the **Ad Council** launched the KnowHow2GO campaign in 2007. This multi-year, multimedia effort includes television, radio, outdoor public service advertisements (PSAs), and the interactive website KnowHow2GO.org to encourage students to prepare for college using four simple steps.

Throughout the ***I'm First! Guide to College,*** you'll find pages with content and graphics printed with permission from KnowHow2GO. Learn more at KnowHow2GO.org.

SPONSORED BY

Being the FIRST

By Rachel Brody

First things first.
Everyone loves the first.
The first man on the moon, the first African-American president, and the first in flight. First kisses, first impressions, first place.
What is it about the first?

In many ways, it is easier for students who have siblings or parents who took on the big firsts. When it comes to college, students with parents who attended college have a better chance of attending college themselves.

So what does that mean for students who don't have a family history of higher education? These students who enroll in colleges and universities are called first-generation college students.

Yes, being the first can be lonely. Everything feels strange and different the first time. You might worry how your friends and family will see you, the first: "He thinks he is so special because he is first."

But don't hold back on being first. The great thing about being the first one is that it doesn't mean that you will be the last one. By being the first in your family to graduate from college, you open the door for younger siblings, for your children, and their children. College will not be an intimidating unknown because you went first.

OK, maybe the betterment of your imaginary grandchildren isn't the most convincing reason to take on being the first in college. So, think of yourself. College is four years that are all about you. Your discoveries, your achievements, and your firsts. People who attend college live longer, make more money, and vote more often. You will have more opportunities in your lifetime if you go to college.

Although it can be daunting, being the first is an accomplishment. It will make you a stronger and happier person. And that is what really matters. ■

try it Now it's your turn to use what you've learned.
Turn to page 25

BIO Rachel Brody is a former adviser with the National College Advising Corps and past intern with Center for Student Opportunity (now Strive for College).

College Prep Tips

There's an old Chinese saying that goes, "The journey of a thousand miles begins with a single step." But no matter how unsure you feel taking that first step, every single one after that will be a little easier. Here's some helpful tips to get you started.

Plan out a challenging program of classes.

- Colleges care about which courses you're taking in high school. Remember, you will have more options if you start planning now for college and do your best to earn good grades.
- The courses you take in high school show colleges what kind of goals you set for yourself. Are you signing up for advanced classes, honors sections, or accelerated sequences? Are you choosing electives that really stretch your mind and help you develop new abilities? Or are you doing just enough to get by?
- Colleges will be more impressed by respectable grades in challenging courses than by outstanding grades in easy ones.
- Do your high school course selections match what most colleges expect you to know? For example, many colleges require two to four years of foreign language study.
- Your schedule should consist of at least 4 college preparatory classes per year.

Create a file of important documents and notes.

- Copies of report cards.
- Lists of awards and honors.
- Lists of school and community activities in which you are involved, including both paid and volunteer work, and descriptions of what you do.

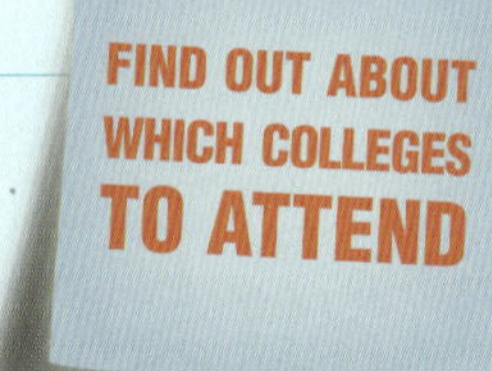

Start thinking about the colleges you want to attend.

- Create list of colleges and universities in which you are interested.
- Discuss the list with your school counselor and narrow it down to your top few.
- Start visiting the campuses.

Find out about honors-level courses at your school.

- Ask if AP or other honors courses are available.
- See if you are eligible for the honors classes you want to take.

OTHER TOP TIPS

- Stay active in clubs, activities, and sports that you enjoy.
- Study, study, study. Colleges look at your permanent academic record for admissions beginning with freshman-year grades.
- Think about an after school or summer job to start saving for college.

KnowHow2GO *Printed with permission from KnowHow2GO. Learn more at KnowHow2GO.org.*

Going Above and Beyond: Taking Rigorous High School Courses

Students are often surprised to learn that many colleges would rather accept a student with okay grades in advanced classes than A's in basic classes.

Course Rigor

The college application process is more competitive now than ever before. So when college admissions officers look at your transcript, they want to see more than just good grades. They are looking for evidence that you are an ambitious student with the skills needed to persevere in a rigorous academic setting. In other words, they want to see that you've taken advanced classes. Students are often surprised to learn that many colleges would rather accept a student with okay grades in advanced classes than A's in basic classes.

It's no wonder that course rigor is important to colleges. Many first-year college students find that the transition from high school academics to college is challenging because college-level work is more difficult and time-consuming than high school work. However, students who have been exposed to college-level classes before arriving on campus are usually better prepared to handle their first-year work load.

> When college admissions officers look at your transcript, they want to see more than just good grades. They are looking for evidence that you are an ambitious student.

AP Courses

Most high schools offer Advanced Placement (AP) courses for their students. AP courses are generally year-long classes offered in a specific content area, from Chinese to Studio Art (a full list of courses available can be found at www.apstudent.collegeboard.org/apcourse). AP courses are designed to offer college-level rigor, and students who take them can sometimes receive credit towards their college degree before they even graduate high school! Sometimes these courses are only available to juniors and seniors. Check with your guidance counselor to see what courses are offered at your school and what eligibility requirements you need to meet to enroll.

In May of each year, most AP students take the national AP exam in their specific subject. The exam is scored on a scale from 1-5. There is a fee to take the exam, but schools are often provided with fee waivers for low-income students. Students earning a score of 3, 4, or 5 on their exams may be eligible for credit towards their college degree, depending on the college they attend. For example, a student who gets a score of 4 on the AP European History Exam might be excused from taking a history course at his/her college. Not all schools will accept AP credit, and some will only accept credit from certain courses, so make sure you check on the school website to see what their policies regarding APs are.

If your school doesn't offer APs, you may be able to find a class online offered through your state's Department of Education or through a local college or university. Ask your guidance counselor for more information!

International Baccalaureate Program

Select schools around the country (and the world) offer the International Baccalaureate Diploma Programme (IB). This program is open to students ages 16 to 19 and offers rigorous instruction which is well recognized among selective colleges and universities.

Most schools are not able to offer IB for their students, and you must be enrolled in an IB school to participate in the program. To find out if your school, or any schools in your area, offer IB, check out www.ibo.org/schools.

continues on next page

continued from previous page

Dual Enrollment and Early College

Increasingly, high schools are partnering with colleges and universities to offer students the chance to take college courses while they are still in high school through dual enrollment programs, sometimes referred to as "early college." In most cases, students who take these classes earn college credit, which may eventually be used towards their college degree.

Taking college courses in high school is a great idea because it shows colleges you are able to succeed in a postsecondary setting. It also helps you get used to learning in a college classroom and being on a college campus before you begin your first year. Many students participate in dual enrollment programs to save themselves money and time by accumulating college credit early.

Dual enrollment programs may be offered through your school, district, or state. Some states require students and their families to pay for dual enrollment courses, but other states offer dual enrollment for free or reduced prices. If your school does not offer dual enrollment, there may be special charter or Early College High Schools in your district that do.

Go Above and Beyond!

No matter what kind of advanced courses your school offers, take advantage! They will help your academic transition to college and can increase your chances of being admitted to a selective college. Remember to be respectful of your own limits. Taking five AP courses in one year might sound impressive, but will probably end up overwhelming you and taking time away from extracurricular activities and SAT/ACT study. ■

try it Now it's your turn to use what you've learned.
Turn to page 26

Required Courses

The chart below gives you a good overview on what courses you need to take in high school to meet standard college entrance requirements. Of course, every college has its own requirements—check with the ones you're interested in to see what they recommend.

SUBJECT	NUMBER OF YEARS	COURSES
English	four or more years	grammar, composition, literature, etc.
Mathematics	three or more years	algebra I and higher—does not include general math, business math, or consumer math
Natural Sciences	three or more years	earth science, biology, chemistry, physics, etc.
Social Sciences	three or more years	history, economics, geography, civics, psychology, etc.
Additional Courses (Some colleges and universities require other classes as prerequisites for admission)	two or more years one or more year	foreign language visual arts, music, theater, drama, dance, computer science, etc.

FACT

Studies show that the more math courses students take in high school, the more likely they are to graduate from college.[4]

[4] *Clifford Adelman, "Mathematics Equals Opportunity" (U.S. Department of Education, 1997).*

GETTING INVOLVED

When it comes time to apply for college, you should be able to show that you've been involved with activities outside of your regular school day. This way, a college can see what you can add to their campus outside of the classroom. Don't wait until senior year to get started—colleges will become suspicious that you simply got involved to make your applications stronger. And remember, choose depth over breadth. Admission officers are more likely to consider an applicant who is deeply committed to one or only a few activities, rather than loosely involved in many activities.

Activity	How to Get Involved	What it Shows About You
COMMUNITY SERVICE 	• Join your school's community service club. • Get involved with service work at your place of worship. • Find a cause you're committed to (like ending animal cruelty) and Google ways to get involved.	Service work shows colleges that you feel a duty to give back to your community. It shows that you care about leaving your world a better place than you found it.
INTERNSHIPS/ JOBS 	• Ask your guidance counselor (or career counselor) for information on internships or jobs that suit your interests. • Draft a résumé and take it to local businesses. • Search the web and ask friends and family for recommendations of businesses that hire teens.	Holding down a job shows colleges that you are consistent, mature, and responsible, particularly if the money from your job goes to help support your family. Securing an internship in an area of interest to you will show colleges you are dedicated to reaching your career goals.
BECOME A LEADER OF A CLUB/TEAM 	• Pay attention to your school building. Lots of times, clubs and teams post flyers about try-outs and meetings, but if you don't keep your eyes peeled, you'll miss them. • Ask your teachers, coaches, and counselors about available clubs. • If you don't see a club you want to join, ask a teacher to sponsor you in founding a new club.	Joining clubs and teams early in high school gives you time to make your mark and work your way up to leadership/captain positions by junior or senior year. Holding a leadership position shows that you are responsible, you get along well with your peers, and you are committed. Founding and growing a club shows initiative, dedication, and perseverance.
DEVELOP A TALENT YOU'RE GOOD AT 	• Ask your guidance counselor for summer enrichment opportunities in a certain skill area. • See if there are groups at your school devoted to developing your specific skill.	If you are a budding author or a first-rate flute player, don't keep these skills to yourself. Finding groups in your community to join and participating in a summer enrichment program will show schools you are serious and passionate about developing your talents.

TRANSFORM THE TRAJECTORY OF YOUR LIFE

SUMMER EXPERIENCES CAN PROPEL YOU TO COLLEGE

By Joni Bissell

Every summer, seniors meet with their mentor and me, as their college advisor, to reflect on their two and a half years participating in Summer Search, a leadership development program providing students with year-round mentoring, life-changing summer experiences, college advising, and a lasting support network. Ninety-one percent of these low-income students head to college each fall, and much of their courage and willingness to take this step is emboldened by the experiences of their summer trips.

During a recent meeting, one senior told me that he never thought he would go to college. He assumed he would work to provide for his siblings; a responsibility that he shouldered from a very young age. His proudest reflection, aside from his college destination, was his recent choice to initiate a family meeting to talk with his siblings about their family's dynamics and history. He was, in effect, passing on responsibility in a thoughtfully mature way, which freed him to find comfort in leaving home for college soon.

We spoke about his first summer wilderness trip and the culminating hike when each student in the group was offered a choice, poetically the "hard road" or the "easy road." He took the "hard road." His second summer trip was an academic program. He fell in love with architecture and was able to experience living with a variety of peers on a college campus. Both experiences, holistically combined with Summer Search mentoring, transformed the trajectory of his life.

Summer experiential programs contribute to student success by providing an opportunity to take healthy risks and experience unfamiliar settings. Students learn to navigate social challenges as these summer experiences often consist of more wealthy, less diverse students, an experience that can be both alienating and intimidating. The courage it takes to be vulnerable in these situations is what defines their immense personal growth. Students return home with new confidence and broader options. They and their families begin to bridge the dramatic distances between college and home life.

Combined with thoughtful mentoring and best possible preparation to ensure success, summer experiences offer students practice for challenges similar to those they will face on campus. In doing so, students develop skills to be resilient leaders and voices in college, their communities and beyond. ■

TIPS for Finding a Summer Experience

Summer Search runs offices in Boston, New York City, North San Francisco Bay, Philadelphia, San Francisco, Seattle, and Silicon Valley. If you're a student in one of these cities, visit **www.summersearch.org** for more information.

If not, here are a few tips for researching and finding the best summer program for you:

Summer Search
where change begins
www.summersearch.org

1. **Start early.** Many programs require an application and have a limited number of spaces available, so the earlier you start the more options you'll have.
2. **Check local colleges and universities.** Many schools offer pre-college initiatives over the summer that give you a chance to preview the school while exploring your academic interests.
3. **Ask your counselor or mentor.** Counselors, community leaders, or mentors may be able to point you to local programs tailored specifically to high school students.
4. **Search online.** Tailor your search to the type of program you are interested in, and the geographic location where you are looking to spend your summer.
5. **Ask for financial aid.** Summer experiential programs cost money, but many will offer financial assistance and scholarships to those who need it. Just ask!

BIO *Joni Bissell is Bay Area College Director for Summer Search San Francisco.*

CHANGE YOUR LIFE IN ONE SUMMER

Lysa Vola
College: Williams College
Hometown: Jensen Beach, FL

You've just made it through a year of high school. So, what are your plans for this summer? What about going to college? Every summer there are programs held on college campuses across the country. They range by various interests, activities, and academic areas. Some are science programs, while others enhance artistic ability or musicality, but all of them are right at your fingertips.

So, now you might be thinking, how can I afford to go to a summer program if I don't have the money? Many summer programs such as MITES (Minority Introduction to Engineering and Science) and QuestBridge affiliated summer programs offer full scholarships for all students accepted into their programs. You could attend a program the summer following your junior or even sophomore year of high school for free!

While these programs may not sound like the most exciting thing to do over your summer, let me share my experience with you.

As a high school junior, I applied to the MITES program on the campus of Massachusetts Institute of Technology (MIT). It is a seven week program in Science and Engineering that is aimed towards helping disadvantaged minorities and/or students from low-income backgrounds excel in the field of science. While at MIT, I was given the chance to complete research in genomics at the Broad Institute of MIT and Harvard. My research team dealt with Single Nucleotide Polymorphisms in genetic disorders such as Cystic Fibrosis and early onset Breast Cancer. Prior to the summer, I had no idea what that even meant!

Besides doing work and taking courses, I also explored the city of Boston on weekends, went to theme parks, dances, and dinners. I spent that summer at MIT living on my own and learned how to balance my time. I got a chance to experience what college might be like before actually getting into college.

My point is not that all of you should apply to the MITES program, but rather that you should consider finding out more information about summer programs like MITES. Summer programs provide you with opportunities to discover what it's like to be in a college setting prior to actually applying to or attending college. Summer programs also offer high school students an edge in the college admissions process. They are looked highly upon, because many of them are a lot of work, and prove your dedication and skill. Completing a program successfully makes you stand out from amongst thousands of high school college applicants who didn't take the opportunity to explore, learn, or take their summer seriously. Most are only a few weeks long, so you will still have time to be home and relax with friends before school starts!

So before you turn away an application to spend your summer away studying, consider how it might change your life, the new adventures you might be able to take, and the people you may meet. Never turn down an opportunity, because they are just that, something that you either take or leave, but ultimately can never be replaced!

LYSA VOLA is an I'm First! scholarship winner. Lysa shares her college experiences and offers advice on the I'm First! student blog.

Visit www.ImFirst.org to follow the student blog and watch video testimonials from first-generation college students and graduates.

HAVE A GOAL-ORIENTED MINDSET

goals

Alexis Montes
College: University of Rochester
Hometown: National City, CA

Three years ago, I struggled to decide which colleges I wanted to apply to. There was no doubt in my mind that I would make my goal of attending college a reality. The question was: where would I apply? As I cracked down on my search and shared my tentative choices with others, a pattern revealed itself. After reading my list of potential schools, one of my teachers declared, "You're undervaluing yourself."

I heard similar statements from everyone who saw my list. I didn't understand what they meant. "I don't think you realize what you have to offer to these schools," my teacher explained. **"They want kids like you. You need to sell yourself efficiently. You have bargaining power through your diversity, so don't be afraid to reach for the stars."**

What my teacher meant was that often times, diverse students don't realize how much colleges value their unique backgrounds and how committed they are to helping first generation and low-income students succeed on their campuses. But what he didn't understand at the time was that this "bargaining power" he spoke of (my low-income status, race, and sexual orientation) was something that I truly saw as a pure disadvantage to my life. The fact that I was poor wasn't a "bargaining power" to me, it was a circumstance that had brought me to feel sorry for myself because of how society perceived people like me. How was I supposed to understand that colleges viewed these same traits as positive aspects that would help bring diversity to their campuses?

Through some soul-searching and meditation, I learned that we create our own realities. If we set goals for ourselves and see ourselves achieving them, then we will. If we undervalue ourselves and set the bar low, we will never reach higher. As diverse students, we are vulnerable to underestimating our capabilities when we are constantly told, for example, that "Latinos, African-American, and other minority groups are less likely to graduate high school." We must be able to create and honor our own realities and acknowledge that existing perceptions created by others may not be correct. This is not to say that systems of inequality do not exist, simply that we as diverse students all have the choice to counter these systems with goal-oriented thinking and view ourselves not as inferior, but as limitless beings.

ON THE SPOT: Have you ever felt as though your potential was being undervalued? What did you do in that situation?

Fortunately, there are people and organizations (like Strive for College and I'm First!) whose sole mission is to challenge and alter our cultural realities to make them fair and equal for those who are systematically disadvantaged because of race, income status, sex, etc. When I realized my potential was quite literally limitless if I refused to accept to the cultural stigmas that were placed upon me for being poor or gay, I was able to allow myself to dream bigger. I was able to accept that I was worthy of attending a prestigious Ivy League school if I chose to do so. In essence, I was able to have a goal-oriented mindset in which I no longer undervalued myself and my merits, but instead set realistic and ambitious goals.

Set goals for you and you only. Don't underestimate yourself by believing in someone else's perception of who you are and who you will be. Instead, set goals tailored around you and your very own reality.

"You might not do as well on a paper as you'd hoped, but it's not the grade that matters, but rather what happens afterward. What did you learn from it? How are you going to adapt and make things better next time? It's a learning process, and you might even learn more from your mistakes than from the things you did right."

– It's a Learning Experience

Maggie Acosta
College: Bowdoin College
Hometown: Kansas City, MO

Samuel Hayes
Northern Arizona University
Hometown: Chandler, AZ

"At first, my priorities were out of whack, and my grades suffered. But a big part of college is maturing and getting your priorities straight. College really makes you grow up fast because you are on your own and your parents aren't there to bail you out."

– Learning Experience

ALEXIS MONTES is an I'm First! scholarship winner. Alexis shares his college experiences and offers advice on the I'm First! student blog.

Visit www.ImFirst.org to follow the student blog and watch video testimonials from first-generation college students and graduates.

Learning to Walk: Effective Goal Setting

Ever heard the expression "you can't learn to walk until you learn how to crawl"? This idiom stresses the necessity of setting short-term goals to help you achieve your long-term goals. We all have big dreams. Maybe yours is to become a doctor, or an engineer, or a politician. No one becomes these things overnight. Ask any lawyer or scientist how they got to where they are today and they'll tell you it took a lot of hard work and discipline.

Short-term goals are tasks we set ourselves to accomplish in a small amount of time, such as one week or one month. Long-term goals are the ambitions that drive and shape our lives—the colleges we want to graduate from, the careers we want to have. But having a long-term goal without having short-term goals to support it is like trying to build a bridge in midair: our goals can't stand without positive foundational habits to support them.

GOALS short-term gets you to long-term

Margarita is a high school senior who is aspiring to become a newspaper journalist. In order to achieve this long-term goal, she set short-term goals for herself:

daily

- Finish all assigned homework
- Read three newspaper articles
- Spend one hour in Spanish tutoring after school

weekly

- Research two colleges
- Write one article for the student paper
- Spend five hours per week studying for the SAT

1 year

- Maintain honor roll grades
- Get accepted to a school with a well-known journalism program
- Obtain an internship at a local newspaper

5 year

- Graduate from college with a Bachelor's degree in Journalism
- Become editor for my college newspaper
- Study abroad to become bilingual in English and Spanish

10 year

- Become a journalist at a leading global newspaper

Without finishing her homework, Margarita could not become an honor roll student. Without being an honor roll student, she might not be able to get into a competitive school to study journalism. And without studying journalism in college, she might not be able to get a job as a reporter once she graduates.

The road to reaching your goals, like Margarita's, begins now. If you wait until tomorrow to begin reaching for them, you might just find it's too late.

try it Now it's your turn to use what you've learned. **Turn to page 27**

L.O.V.E. YOUR PARENTS

Jeremy Harris
College: University of Missouri
Hometown: Chicago, IL

As I look back on my first two years in college, I realize I'm at the halfway point. I'm grateful for the opportunity, but more importantly, I'm grateful for L.O.V.E. The month of February gives me a chance to express my love for those who have been in my corner. February is also a chance to thank those who have my back through whatever and whenever. That would be my parents.

We often take our parents for granted. I realize some may have grandparents or other family members who substitute as their parents. I just want to show some love to my parents because I realize how critical their assistance has been in my life up to this point.

I am pursuing higher learning because I want to achieve a level of success in life which will allow me to have my best life. The main reason I'm here today is because of the values instilled in me by my parents. My parents ensured I was in the right programs and schools in order to position myself for college. I could not have done this alone.

So, it is with love that I write this for them.

L is for the love my parents have consistently given me through the years.

O is for my continuous effort to obey their rules, advice, and guidance as they share their personal experiences with me.

V is for the value of all that love and support - it's priceless and I value them to the highest. And finally,

E is because I encourage them to continue to be a part of my life even though I'm away from home. I call my mom all the time to ask her for advice and direction. I realize that I still need them in my life - now, more than ever.

As you're preparing for college, please never forget what matters most: the L. O. V. E. you share with your parents - it's invaluable and the best thing in life!

JEREMY HARRIS is an I'm First! scholarship winner. Jeremy shares his college experiences and offers advice on the I'm First! student blog.

Visit www.ImFirst.org to follow the student blog and watch video testimonials from first-generation college students and graduates.

Ask People for Help!

By Dr. Tomika Ferguson

When I was younger, I had aspirations to attend the University of Virginia. Despite not having a strong college-going culture in my hometown, opportunities existed for me to accomplish my goals.

Every semester during high school, I signed up for classes that challenged me. I did not always get straight A's, but I did gain skills that prepared me for college. I was not the valedictorian of my high school class, but I was a risk taker.

My parents and I did not understand all of the specifics about applying to college since I was first in our family to do so. I took a personal risk and asked people for advice about the college application process. Asking for help wasn't a sign of weakness, but rather the most important step in following my dream of being accepted at the University of Virginia.

Here are a few people who helped me throughout my college journey.

• **My English teacher** was the best writer I knew, and she helped me to organize my thoughts. I felt very confident in the essays I submitted with my college applications.

• **An older cousin** helped me craft a résumé, and it paid off big time! High school activities demonstrated my capacity for leadership and interests beyond academics.

• **My parents** didn't understand how to fill out the Free Application for Federal Student Aid (FAFSA) but with the help of **my guidance counselor**, we completed it well before the deadline.

As a high school student, you are surrounded by teachers, college counselors, family members and friends who want you to become successful. They will do everything they can to help you reach your goals.

It is hard to admit when you need help, but you have to be brave and take the first step to find people who have the answers you need. Without asking for help, I never would have accomplished my goal of graduating from the University of Virginia. ■

try it Now it's your turn to use what you've learned. **Turn to page 30**

BIO Dr. Tomika Ferguson is an Assistant Professor at Virginia Commonwealth University in the School of Education. Previously, she was an adviser with the National College Advising Corp and an intern with Center for Student Opportunity (now Strive for College).

I really liked working with my mentor. She was always flexible with time, eager to help and reminded me to stay confident in my writing. She helped me with essays and applying for scholarships.

Jazzlyn

I was looking for help regarding my financial aid reward and resources to help me pay for college. My mentor helped me see my options for paying for college.

Morgan

I was accepted by two colleges and needed help choosing the one best for me. My mentor was great! He reviewed the colleges with me so I could make a decision. And I did not have to pay anything!

Stephane

advice

Find advice from real first-generation college students who blog about their college experiences on www.ImFirst.org

SOS: SEEK OUT SUPPORT

Angelica Robinson
College: Dillard University
Hometown: New Orleans, LA

"Being a first-generation college student, it is imperative that I seek guidance, branch out to grasp what I need to succeed in my environment. I've realized that it is true that everyone needs someone in their corner."
- Second Semester Freshman: Through the Storm

Abigail Macias
College: Dartmouth College
Hometown: Sparks, NV

"ASK, ASK, ASK! Don't be afraid to ask questions! You may think that you'll look dumb because your classmates seem to know what they're doing or where they're headed. But, you'll only hurt yourself by not getting the information you need."
- Dumb Questions?

Gina Bolanos
College: University of Rochester
Hometown: Dallas, TX

"I give thanks to my Spanish Teacher, Mrs. Martinez, who has supported me academically/socially for half my life, and of course, my dear and lovely college bound adviser, Ms. Marano, who is the main reason why I even went to college. Each person, event, club, team and aspect of my life has given me the power and confidence to challenge myself and try new things."
- Thankful Blessings

Raquel Diaz
College: Reed College
Hometown: Monterey Park, CA

"College can feel like a maze riddled with trap doors. A mentor is somebody who has traversed the maze, found the exit, and walked back into the maze with a flashlight to help others who have entered the maze."
- The Places You'll Go—Much, Much Further With A Mentor

Jesse Sanchez
College: Harvard University
Hometown: San Diego, CA

"Not having a mentor can leave you without a sense of direction—you need someone there to go to for advice, to keep you motivated, and to help you out in times of need. It is very important to find this person in your life early on so they can help you make the right decisions from the beginning."
- Got Mentors?

blog

Visit www.ImFirst.org to follow the student blog and watch video testimonials from first-generation college students and graduates.

Community and Virtual Supports

Feeling overwhelmed by the prospect of going to college? You're not alone. Fortunately, there are resources in your community and online to help you in your pursuit of college.

Here are some online resources to help you find support in your community:

National College Access Network (NCAN)
www.collegeaccess.org

NCAN builds, strengthens, and empowers communities committed to college access and success by providing nearly 400 member organizations across 49 states and territories with professional development, networking, benchmarking, and news from the field.

National Partnership for Educational Access (NPEA)
www.educational-access.org

There are over 300 organizations across 34 states that comprise NPEA's membership. These organizations all serve underrepresented students with academic preparation, placement services and counseling, and ongoing support to ensure enrollment at and graduation from four-year colleges.

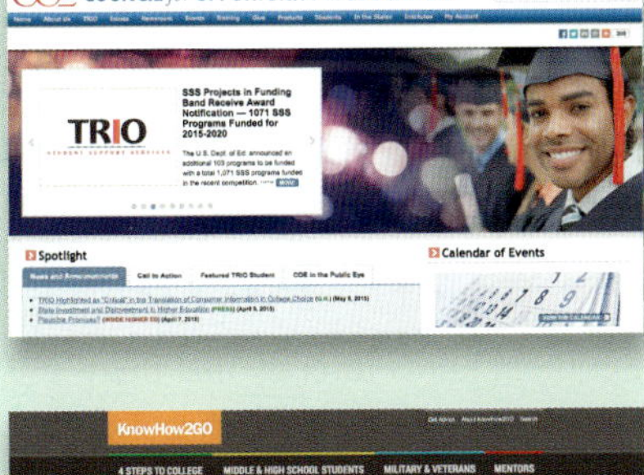

Directory of TRIO and GEAR UP Programs
www.coenet.us

Check out the directory of TRIO and GEAR UP programs hosted by the Council for Opportunity in Education (COE). COE works in conjunction with colleges, universities, and agencies that host TRIO Programs to help low-income students enter college and graduate.

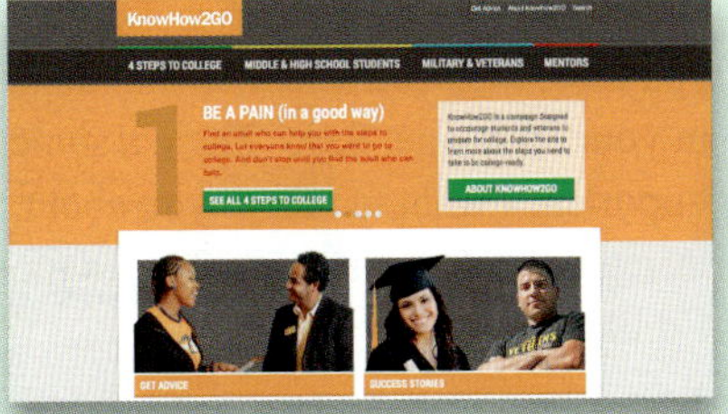

KnowHow2GO
www.knowhow2go.org

The "Useful Links" page offers links to resources in your community.

Get the Conversation Started!

Planning for college isn't something you do by yourself—it's really a team effort. But it's up to you to put together your team. And that means talking to the adults in your life who can help—from your parents, guardian, or other family members to your teachers, coaches, guidance counselor, or religious leader.

YOUR PARENTS

The best way to communicate with parents, or any adult, is to keep talking to them, no matter what. Strong relationships really depend on keeping the lines of communication open. Here are some ways to approach your parents (or any adult) with a specific topic:

Plan what to say.

Think over what you want to say in advance, and write down the two or three most important points you want to make.

Be direct.

Let them know directly that there's something you'd like to discuss. Be sure you have their full attention and be direct in your language. Say, "There's something important I want to talk to you about," instead of "Hey, when you have a moment I'd like to talk."

Pick a good time to talk.

Try to approach them at a time when you know they'll be less busy and more able to focus on you. You may even want to ask if they could talk at a particular time so that you know you have their attention.

Write it down first.

Some people find it easier to put their ideas into a letter. Let the other person read it and then have your discussion.

Disagree without disrespect.

Parents are only human, and they can feel offended when their views are challenged. Using respectful language and behavior is important. Resist the temptation to use sarcasm, yell, or put down your parents and you'll have a much better chance of getting what you want.

OTHER ADULTS

No matter how good your relationship is with your parents or guardian, there will be times when you'll feel more comfortable confiding in other adults. Even if you'd rather talk to friends about certain things, an adult may have more experience, be able to contact the right person, or find the best resources to get help.

Ask for their word.

Most adults will keep your conversations confidential if you ask them to, unless they fear that your health or well-being may be in danger.

ARE YOU READY FOR
COLLEGE
Quiz
Parents are always the best people to talk to about preparing for college.
TRUE
FALSE

Other adults.

Other adults who may be able to help include teachers, your school guidance counselor, or other family members such as an aunt, uncle, or older sibling. Parents of a close friend may also be able to help.

Spiritual leaders.

If you're involved in a church group or belong to a synagogue or mosque, your spiritual or youth group leader may also be a good source of advice.

Extracurricular leaders.

If you're involved in an extracurricular activity, such as sports or drama, you may feel close enough to your coach or advisor to ask him or her about more personal stuff.

FALSE If your parents didn't go to college, chances are there's an adult in your life who did – and would be happy to help you prepare for college.

If you find a subject hard, talk to your teacher right away about extra tutoring. If you find it boring, talk to your teacher about ways to see the subject in a different light.

YOUR TEACHERS

OK, so it may be hard to think of your teachers as real people. But they eat pizza, watch movies, and enjoy sports on the weekends just like you. And they know about more than just their subject matter. Given the chance they can offer you the kind of advice and support that might change your life forever. Here's how to build a connection:

Show some interest.

Obviously, your teachers are really interested in their subjects. Showing the teacher that you care—even if you're not a math whiz or fluent in French—sends the message that you are a dedicated student.

Schedule a conference.

Schedule a private conference during a teacher's free period to get extra help, ask questions, inquire about a career in the subject, or talk about your progress in class. You may be surprised to learn that your teacher is a bit more relaxed one-on-one than when lecturing in front of the whole class.

Be yourself.

Teachers can sense when your only motivation for trying to be a "favorite student" is to get special treatment or a good grade. Just be yourself and forget about trying to show off.

Deal with study problems.

If you find a subject hard, talk to your teacher right away about extra tutoring. If you find it boring, talk to your teacher about ways to see the subject in a different light. For example, you may hate math, but learning how to calculate averages and percentages can help you in everything from sports to leaving a tip.

Show some respect.

Just as teachers need to be fair and treat everyone equally, students have responsibilities too. You don't have to like your teacher or agree with what he or she says, but it is necessary to be polite. ■

KnowHow2GO *Printed with permission from KnowHow2GO. Learn more at KnowHow2GO.org.*

HOW TO Use Your High School Counselor

By Mary Lee Hoganson

School counselors are one of the best sources of support for college-bound students. Whatever grade you are in, now is the time to start helping your counselor get to know you and your college dreams.

Introduce yourself and state clearly that it is your definite goal to attend college. Let your counselor know that, regardless of your test scores or grades to date, you are highly motivated.

Also, make sure to tell your counselor about yourself: your interests, activities, college and career goals, and family background — including what your parents do and whether or not anyone in your family has attended college. With this initial meeting as a good starting point, your counselor can help you plot a successful course for college.

Top 10 items to cover with your counselor:

1) Plan classes that will prepare you for college.
2) Review your academic record and suggest areas that need improvement.
3) Identify the questions you should be asking, like: Do I want to stay near home? Does the college have my major? How important is size?
4) Get information about specific colleges and universities.
5) Identify opportunities like college fairs, weekend or summer programs on college campuses (often free for first-generation or low-income students), internships, or community college classes open to high school students.
6) Register for college admission tests and get fee waivers if your family can't afford to pay for tests.
7) Write a letter of recommendation to colleges or universities.
8) Complete and submit college applications carefully and on time and ask colleges to waive application fees.
9) Figure out how to pay for college.
10) Compare offers of admission and financial aid from all of your colleges.

There are a few other very important things to remember about working with your school counselor:

• Most school counselors have many, many students who they want to help. So make appointments early, show up on time, and submit forms that require counselor completion well in advance of due dates.

• Make backup copies of everything you mail or give to your counselor.

• Make sure that you keep your counselor "in the loop" in terms of what you are hearing from colleges. If there are any problems which arise, your counselor can act as your direct advocate with colleges.

• If you think it would be helpful, try to schedule a meeting with your counselor AND your parent(s). There are parts of the college process that will require additional assistance, such as completing the financial aid applications.

• Be sure to thank your counselor for assistance given. When you have made it successfully through the college selection and admission process, send your counselor a handwritten note (along with any teachers who helped).

BIO Mary Lee Hoganson has over 35 years experience as a high school counselor, 25 of those years focused on college counseling. She served as President of the National Association for College Admission Counseling in 2007.

High School Timelines

The college planning process can be daunting for everyone. It's best to plan ahead and allow plenty of time. It also helps if you have a plan to follow from your freshman year through your senior year—and here it is.

FRESHMEN TIMELINE

START HERE FRESHMEN

FALL

- ❑ Make sure you enroll in geometry or algebra. Colleges require that you take rigorous math courses in high school.
- ❑ Create a college information folder that you can take with you through high school.
- ❑ Start the school year off right by getting organized and practicing good study habits.
- ❑ Meet new people by signing up for extracurricular activities and trying something new!
- ❑ Explore careers on the Web on your home computer or at the library.
- ❑ Find job shadowing opportunities in the community, where you can spend a day shadowing someone at work and watching what he or she does.

SPRING

- ❑ Start to plan your sophomore year.
- ❑ Talk with your parents and counselor about summer vacation. Explore summer programs or camps to attend at local colleges and universities. Look for volunteer or service opportunities in the community. Some may be sponsored by a local church, synagogue or mosque.

SOPHOMORE TIMELINE

SOPHOMORE TIMELINE

FALL

- ❑ Polish your study skills. If you need to improve in some subjects, this is the time to do it. Colleges and future employers look at high school transcripts and are impressed with regular attendance and improving grades.
- ❑ Have you taken a career interest inventory? Ask your counselor or guidance office to give you one. These tests help assess your strengths and weaknesses and can help guide your college search and long-term career plans.
- ❑ Take the Preliminary Scholastic Aptitude test PSAT—the preliminary version of the SAT—or the PLAN, the preliminary version of the ACT. Taking the PSAT now is practice for the PSAT test in junior year which allows you to be considered for a National Merit Scholarship. Find dates and more information about the PSAT from your high school's guidance office.
- ❑ Surf the Web to check out colleges, technical schools, and apprenticeship opportunities.
- ❑ Consider job shadowing to get some work experience and test possible careers.

SPRING

- ❑ Begin exploring financial aid and scholarships options.
- ❑ Use the Internet to explore different careers.
- ❑ Select five to ten colleges to contact for brochures and applications.
- ❑ Visit your school or community Career Center.
- ❑ Plan a productive summer. The summer before 11th grade is a good time to have a part-time job to prepare for a future career.
- ❑ Choose a summer camp or find a volunteer service program to jumpstart your skills.
- ❑ Remember to sign up for the most challenging classes for next year.

KnowHow2GO *Printed with permission from KnowHow2GO. Learn more at KnowHow2GO.org.*

JUNIOR YEAR TIMELINE

August:

- ❑ Start your year off right: Talk with your guidance counselor about your options and your plans. Be sure to ask about test dates for the PSAT, ACT, and SAT. You'll need to register up to six weeks ahead of time.
- ❑ Sign up for courses with your eyes on the prize: college and money to pay for it! A tougher course load may pay off with scholarships and may get you a better chance to get admitted to the school of your choice.
- ❑ Start investigating private and public sources for financial aid. Take note of scholarship deadlines and plan accordingly.
- ❑ Sign up for activities to boost your college applications.

September:

- ❑ Find out about schools you are interested in attending. Treat your school selection process like a research paper: Make a file and gather information about schools, financial aid, and campus life to put in it. Go to college fairs and open houses and learn as much as you can from the Internet about schools.
- ❑ Begin planning college visits. Fall, winter, and spring break are good times because you can observe a campus when classes are going on.

October:

- ❑ Take the PSAT. You'll get the results by Christmas.
- ❑ Sign up for ACT or SAT prep courses.
- ❑ Do your top college picks require essays or recommendations? Now is the time to begin planning your essays and choosing whom you'd like to ask for a recommendation.

November:

- ❑ Sign up for the ACT and SAT, if you haven't already.

December:

- ❑ Begin the application process for service academies (West Point, Annapolis, etc.)
- ❑ Decide if you should take AP exams in May. Investigate the College-Level Examination Program® or CLEP, which grants college credit for achievement in exams covering many different college-level subjects.

January:

- ❑ Meet with your guidance counselor again to develop your senior schedule.
- ❑ Organize your Individual Graduation Plan.

February:

- ❑ Think about lining up a summer job, internship, or co-op.
- ❑ Plan campus visits for spring break.
- ❑ Memorize your Social Security number if you haven't already. It will be your identity on campus.

March/April:

- ❑ Get ready for AP exams next month.
- ❑ Write a résumé.

SENIOR YEAR TIMELINE

August

- ❑ Sign up for the ACT and/or SAT if you didn't take it as a junior, or if you aren't satisfied with your score.
- ❑ Review ACT and/or SAT test results and retest if necessary.

August to December

- ❑ Visit with your school counselor to make sure you are on track to graduate and fulfill college admission requirements. Consider taking courses at a local university or community college.
- ❑ Keep working hard all year; second semester grades can affect scholarship eligibility.
- ❑ Ask for personal references from teachers, school counselors, or employers early in the year or at least two weeks before application deadline.
- ❑ Follow your school's procedure for requesting recommendations.
- ❑ Visit with admissions counselors who come to your high school.
- ❑ Attend a college fair.
- ❑ Begin your college essay(s).
- ❑ Apply for admission at the colleges you've chosen.
- ❑ Avoid common college application mistakes.
- ❑ Find out if you qualify for scholarships at each college where you have applied.
- ❑ Start the financial aid application process.
- ❑ See your school counselor for help finding financial aid and scholarships.
- ❑ Start the financial aid application process. FAFSA (Free Application for Federal Student Aid) opens October 1.

January to May

- ❑ Ask your guidance office in January to send first semester transcripts to schools where you applied. In May, they will need to send final transcripts to the college you will attend.
- ❑ Visit colleges that have invited you to enroll.
- ❑ Decide which college to attend, and notify the school of your decision.
- ❑ Keep track of and observe deadlines for sending in all required fees and paperwork.
- ❑ Notify schools you will not attend of your decision.
- ❑ Continue to look for scholarship opportunities.
- ❑ Keep track of important financial aid and scholarship deadlines.
- ❑ Watch the mail for your Student Aid Report (SAR)—it should arrive four weeks after the FAFSA is filed.
- ❑ Compare financial aid packages from different schools.
- ❑ Sign and send in a promissory note if you are borrowing money.
- ❑ Notify your college about any outside scholarships you received.

June to August

- ❑ Make sure your final transcript is sent to the school you will be attending.
- ❑ Getting a summer job can help pay some of your college expenses.
- ❑ Make a list of what you will need to take with you for your dorm room.
- ❑ If you haven't met your roommate, call, write, or e-mail to get acquainted in advance.
- ❑ Make sure housing documentation is quickly accessible when you move into the dorm.
- ❑ Learn how to get around at your new school. Review a campus map.
- ❑ Wait until after your first class meeting to buy your books and supplies.

KnowHow2GO *Printed with permission from KnowHow2GO. Learn more at KnowHow2GO.org.*

Free Write: Why is College for Me?

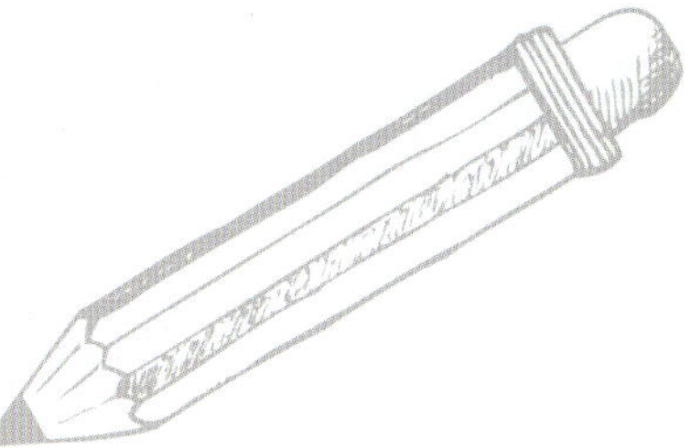

You just read some of the reasons that college is an important step for all students. Take a minute to think about what priorities and goals are important to you personally. Why is college important for you in particular? As you write, you may want to think about:

- How will going to college affect your future career path?
- How will going to college impact your family?
- What might you be exposed to in college (academically and socially) that will help you grow as a person?

Mapping Out Your Courses

The chart on page 6 gives you a good overview of what courses you need to take in high school to meet standard college entrance requirements. Now let's see how you stack up.

List the courses you have taken and those you plan to take before you graduate. You may need to consult your guidance counselor for help.

Subject	Number of Years Required	Example Courses	Courses Taken	Courses You Will Take
English	four or more years	English I, AP English Language, AP English Literature		
Mathematics	three or more years	Algebra I and higher—does not include general math, business math, or consumer math		
Natural Sciences	three or more years	Biology, AP Physics, Environmental Science		
Social Sciences	three or more years	History, economics, psychology, sociology, etc.		
Additional Courses	two or more years two or more years	foreign language visual arts, music, theater, drama, dance, computer science, etc.		

Setting Goals: Planning Backwards to Set Short-Term Goals

You just read about the importance of setting goals, and how setting short-term goals can lead to achieving long-term goals. Now it's time to think about your short- and long-term goals and how they relate. Answer the questions below. As you write, think about how your short-term goals are setting you up for success in your long-term goals.

1. What career goal do you hope to achieve in the next ten years?

2. What goals will you set for yourself to achieve in the next five years?

a)

b)

c)

d)

TIP:

Keep your goal-setting document with you as the year goes on.

Make sure to monitor your progress.

Are you on track to meeting your goals? If not, why?

What can you do to ensure you meet them in the future?

continues on next page

continued from previous page

3. What goals will you set for yourself to achieve by the end of the year?

a)

b)

c)

d)

4. What goals will you set for yourself to achieve every week of this school year?

a)

b)

c)

d)

5. What goals will you set for yourself to achieve everyday of this school year?

a)

b)

c)

d)

Unit 1 Quiz

answers on page 136

Multiple Choice, circle your answer

1. Most colleges require high school students to take at least how many years of Math, Natural Science, and Social Science?

a) two years

b) three years

c) four years

d) most colleges don't have standard entrance requirements

2. My guidance counselor can and should help me with all of the following except:

a) writing a letter of recommendation for college

b) helping me to choose what colleges to apply to

c) completing my college applications

d) sending my high school transcript to colleges

3. Goal-setting is most effective when I:

a) write down my goals

b) revisit my goals often and check my progress

c) create short-term goals which build toward long-term goals

d) all of the above

4. When planning my high school schedule, I should do all of the following except:

a) sign up for rigorous courses, including honors and/or AP classes

b) choose courses that allow me to explore academic fields that interest me

c) balance my schedule to ensure that I have time for extracurricular activities

d) choose easy elective courses to boost my GPA

5. When deciding whether to admit a student, colleges generally consider all of the following except:

a) my standardized test scores

b) my counselor's and teachers' opinions of me

c) my middle school grades

d) whether or not my grades have improved over time

True or False, circle your answer

1. Most college graduates earn a lot more money during their working years than people who stop their education in high school.

T F

2. Going to college was more important for my parents' generation than it is for mine.

T F

3. Colleges care more about how good my grades are than how rigorous my classes are.

T F

4. Involving myself in extracurricular activities can increase my chances of getting into college.

T F

5. If I performed poorly in freshmen and sophomore years, I probably won't get accepted to college.

T F

Fill in the Blank

1. One example of a web-based College Access Program that I can use as a resource in my college journey is ____________________.

2. Most colleges require one to three ____________________ written on my behalf by my high school counselor and teachers.

3. The things I do outside of school, such as clubs, sports, community service, or working, are all ____________________.

4. When setting goals, it is important to set both ____________ and ____________ goals.

5. A ____________ student is a student whose parents have not gone to or graduated from college.

continues on next page

continued from previous page

Open Answer

1. What are some obstacles you expect to face in your journey to college?

What supports can you use to overcome these obstacles?

2. What characteristics of a college-bound student do you already have?

What do you need to improve on before applying to college?

3. List people that may be able to help and support you through your college journey:

Unit 2

How Do I Find the Right Fit?

CONTENTS

I'm First!

"Ultimately, finding the right college fit is also about taking time to think about why you want a college education and what you hope to do with your life."

Objectives

By the end of this unit, I will...

- know the various types of two- and four-year postsecondary institutions.
- evaluate my priorities in order to develop a list of the most important factors in the college search and narrow down a college list.
- understand and integrate information from the various elements of a college profile.
- identify additional ways to obtain information about a college beyond the college profile.

Finding the Right Fit

What should you be looking for?

By Dr. Larry D. Shinn

Surprisingly, more than half of college students who declare a major when they arrive as freshmen change their major one or more times before they graduate! So, selecting a college that has the major you want to study is not a sufficient reason when deciding the best college fit.

There is one consideration that all students should make in deciding the "fit" of a college: its capacity to provide an educational environment that promotes life-long learning. Even if the colleges that you are considering have programs specialized for a specific career path (e.g. fashion design, civil engineering, architecture, or teaching), every one of those professions will require continued learning beyond college.

The best fit is ultimately the college whose learning environment is diverse and where you are challenged to think and grow beyond your current interests. From internships to undergraduate research and study abroad programs, your college experience should expand your abilities and horizons in ways you cannot do yourself. ■

BIO Dr. Larry D. Shinn is retired president of Berea College, a liberal arts college in Berea, Kentucky that provides every admitted student a four-year tuition scholarship and the opportunity to work on campus to assist with costs of room and board.

Get Started!

By Michelle D. Gilliard, Ph.D.

Finding an institution that provides the right fit works best when you take the time to develop a short list of institutions that (1) offer majors in your areas of interest, (2) provide you with multiple opportunities to become actively engaged in your own learning, and (3) are focused on creating an environment where students from a variety of backgrounds and experiences can be successful.

Ultimately, finding the right college fit is also about taking time to think about why you want a college education and what you hope to do with your life. A college that both challenges you and supports your educational and social development is the type of college that will lead to your success. ■

BIO Michelle D. Gilliard, Ph.D. is a partner at Venture Philanthropy Partners.

Find advice from real first-generation college students who blog about their college experiences on www.ImFirst.org

OH SO MANY OPTIONS

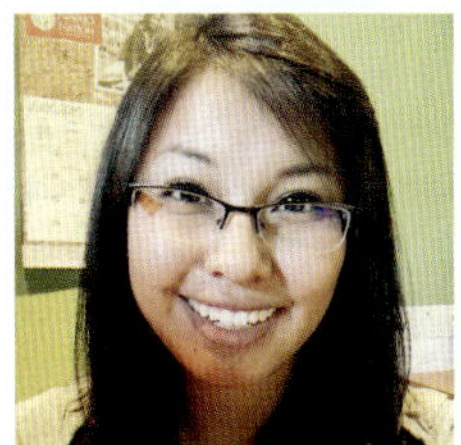
Megan Cooke
College: Whitman College
Hometown: Window Rock, AZ

"Act like a tourist looking at the city. Every place has its gem. If you find yourself lost in the cave, start a new direction because any direction will work as long as you can picture the happiness you'll feel when you finally stumble out."

– I got...

Benjamin Hoertnagl-Pereira
College: Johns Hopkins University
Hometown: Water Mill, NY

"If things do not work out as you would have wished, there will be plenty of opportunities to improve, and you may find that what you once dismissed as a secondary option may be better than expected. If things do work out, congratulations! You deserve it! In either case, enjoy the last few months of high school life, and make memories to cherish and look back on when you have moved on to college."

– Decisions are coming... Game of Groans

ON THE SPOT: Ask someone you know who is in college now why they chose the school they did.

Joseph Dingman
College: Occidental College
Hometown: Pueblo, CO

"When applying to schools listen to others but also think for yourself. What you want is important, and it is your education on the line here."

– Do You Feel Like Time is Running Out?

Leah Jean-Louis
College: Swarthmore College
Hometown: Cambridge, MA

"As for deciding, I can also give you this advice: do you! When trying to decide which option is best or what path to choose, think of yourself and be selfish for once in your life. It's not about what your parents want or how many of your high school friends are going to a specific college."

– Look Ma I'm Going to College

Visit www.ImFirst.org to follow the student blog and watch video testimonials from first-generation college students and graduates.

Types of Colleges

There are thousands of colleges and universities in the United States, and each of them are unique. Generally speaking however, these schools can be broken into two basic categories: Four-Year Schools and Community Colleges.

Four-Year Schools

There are many types of four-year institutions offering Bachelor's degrees: public universities, which are funded by the state, private colleges which are funded privately, or Institutes of Art or Technology, which provide various types of specialized degrees. When it comes to deciding what kind of four-year school to attend, however, most students find themselves choosing between a liberal arts college and a university.

If you're looking for a school with small class sizes where you can try out classes in many different subjects, a liberal arts college might be the place for you. If you're confident in your future career and want to join a fraternity or sorority, you may want to focus your search on universities. Check out the chart for more details.

LIBERAL ARTS COLLEGE	UNIVERSITY
• Has a small student body (usually under 5,000)	• Usually has a large student body (sometimes over 10,000!)
• Usually offers small class sizes and accessible professors	• Larger class sizes, with some classes being taught by teaching assistants rather than professors
• Only offers undergraduate education (no associated graduate schools)	• Generally includes graduate schools and professional programs as well as undergraduate education
• Encourages students to try courses in many areas of study, including math, science, humanities, foreign language, and the arts	• Offers career-specific fields of study for students to focus on and major in
• Usually privately funded	• Some funded privately, some publicly

ON THE SPOT: Do you think you would thrive at a liberal arts college or a university? Why?

Community Colleges

Two-year colleges, more commonly known as community colleges or junior colleges, offer their students the chance to earn an Associate's degree. Community colleges are mostly publicly-funded institutions designed to serve local students of all ages and academic abilities. Almost half of all college students in America attend community colleges. Many are drawn by the affordable prices, others by the open-admissions policy. Most community colleges also offer career-specific training programs for students looking to transition quickly into the workforce.

Many community college students attend community college with the intention of eventually transferring into a four-year institution as college juniors. This can be a good idea for students, especially those who might need some extra support before transitioning into a four-year school, and those who have a weak academic record in high school. However, most community college students do not actually transfer into four-year institutions. If you plan to attend community college and transfer, make sure to speak with an advisor during your first semester so you can make sure you are taking the right courses and on track to meet the transfer requirements.

Almost half of all college students in America attend community colleges.

Specialized Schools

Some colleges were founded to serve specific groups of students. Others strive to instill certain values in their students or prepare them for specific career paths.

Here you'll find a list of specialized schools with a brief blurb about each. For more information and to see lists of schools in each category, check out the appendix!

Historically Black Colleges & Universities

While Historically Black Colleges and Universities (HBCUs) represent only 3% of American institutions of higher learning, they graduate nearly 25% of all African Americans who earn Bachelor's degrees. HBCUs are leaders in training young professionals—especially in the arts, business, and the sciences—who are prepared to address the unique needs of the African American community.
Learn more on Page 120.

ON THE SPOT: What types of specialized schools would you consider applying to? Why?

Hispanic-Serving Institutions

Did you know that over half of all Hispanic undergraduate students in higher education are enrolled in less than 10 percent of institutions in the United States? This concentration of Hispanic enrollment gave way to a federal program designed to support colleges and universities in the United States that assist first-generation, majority low-income Hispanic students, now known as Hispanic-Serving Institutions (HSIs).
Learn more on Page 122.

Tribal Colleges and Native American-Serving Institutions

Tribal Colleges and Universities (TCUs) are institutions chartered by tribal governments to serve and support American Indian students (along with other students as well). They operate more than 75 campuses around the country and offer a range of curricula, from liberal arts to workforce development. There are also many four-year, traditional institutions that are excited to work with Native students and have created programs to attract them to their schools. The nonprofit organization College Horizons partners with over 50 colleges that have made a commitment to recruiting Native students and meeting their full demonstrated financial need.
Learn more on Page 124.

Women's Colleges

Women's colleges are institutions founded in order to provide female scholars with an outstanding education. Most often, these colleges are small and private. Many are also affiliated with a certain faith.
Learn more on Page 127.

Faith-Based Institutions

Faith-based colleges and universities are those related to a faith tradition. In the U.S., this mostly means their heritage is Roman Catholic, Jewish, or Protestant. In only rare cases are there religious requirements to gain admission, and most of these institutions have diverse student bodies.
Learn more on Page 128.

Military Service Academies

Scattered across the United States, military service academies prepare students to become leaders in a specific branch of the armed forces, such as the Air Force or Coast Guard. Generally, students are provided with access to specialized, career-aligned paths of study as well as courses in the liberal arts. Students earn a Bachelor's degree, often at little or no cost.
Learn more on Page 126.

Community College: A Stepping Stone to Higher Education

By Kristie Rueff, M.Ed

There is more than one path to a college degree. For many students, attending a four-year college or university right out of high school is not an option. If you find yourself in this situation and you're thinking your chances of going to college are over, think again!

Depending on your personal situation, a community college can be a great option after high school. They offer the chance to save money on classes while living at home, getting a better idea of what you want to study without committing to a major, and getting some basic class credits out of the way.

Most importantly, after attending and doing well at a community college for two years, you can (and should!) transfer to a four-year college or university to pursue your bachelor's degree. Just because you attend a community college does not mean your education ends there—it should just be the beginning.

Check out Kristie's story about her successful transition from a community college to a four-year university.

BIO *Kristie Rueff is a former Assistant Director for Recruiting and Admissions at the University of Southern California. She holds a Bachelor's degree in English and Master's in Education, both from the University of Southern California.*

Thriving in the Transfer Process

Attending a community college was a choice I made early in life. I attended Fullerton Community College for the accessibility, affordability, and diversity.

Shortly after I enrolled, my mailbox was flooded with invitations to join student organizations. The Transfer Achievement Program (TAP) flyer stood out because the program guaranteed general education courses, student-centered instruction, peer-support, and transfer resources for students interested in transferring to a four-year college or university after they graduated from Fullerton. I immediately phoned the counselor to apply for TAP and was accepted.

I met regularly with my TAP faculty counselor to discuss four-year university options. My heart was set on the University of Southern California (USC). At the time, Fullerton did not provide a general education course list to transfer to USC. So, I took things into my own hands. Every semester I studied the course catalog, Associate of Arts requirements, and an antiquated USC transfer policy to build my class schedule. I highlighted, penned, and notated every resource. Then, in spring 2004 I graduated with my Associates of Arts degree, and in June I was admitted to USC!

As I transitioned from Fullerton to USC, I learned that I needed to take more initiative towards getting involved and reaching my academic goals. A few weeks after classes began at USC, the university hosted an involvement fair. At the fair I signed up for Troy Camp, a local program that recruited undergraduates to mentor children in the area. Working with Troy Camp gave me an opportunity to bond with my peers and foster friendships that became imperative to my support.

I also realized that I would have to become a more active student in order to succeed in my classes. The faculty at USC encouraged students to take initiative versus Fullerton's hands-on approach. I met with faculty during their office hours and asked questions after class.

My experiences at Fullerton and USC were affected by the support systems I cultivated with students and faculty. Fullerton gave me the resources to transfer to a four-year university, and USC taught me to take charge of my future. The colleges were different, yet both positively influenced my future.

Your college search: By the numbers

By Emily Anderer

Eventually, I realized that to understand the strengths and weaknesses of a school I needed to look at its numbers and statistics.

I was woefully uninformed when I began my college search. Living in Utah, I knew about most of the universities in my state but very little about schools elsewhere. I didn't know the difference between a public and a private college or what a liberal arts school was, and I don't think I was even clear on the difference between undergraduate and graduate school. The most difficult part of my college search was struggling to determine the quality of colleges I had never heard about previously.

Eventually, I realized that to understand the strengths and weaknesses of a school I needed to look at its numbers and statistics. This wasn't the most fun part of my college process, but good, solid research helped me to make informed decisions.

While everyone is looking for something different in a college, here are some factors every student should consider, along with how to interpret the relevant numbers and statistics:

Can I Get In?

Admissions rate - The lower a school's admission rate, the more competitive the school is considered to be to get into. For example, many selective schools have admissions rates below ten percent—only one out of ten students who apply will be admitted. It's good to aim high and apply to some schools where the odds are you may not be admitted, but also apply to some schools where the admissions rate is in your favor.

Average GPA, SAT, and ACT range - Looking at the standardized test scores and average grade point averages of admitted applicants is a good way to evaluate the academic ability of the student body. Compare your test scores to the school's median test scores—the 25th to 75th percentile of admitted students—to get the best idea of your odds of getting accepted.

Is It Affordable?

Financial aid - Financial aid is money you get to make up the difference between the cost of attending a college and your family's ability to pay. Look for schools that have need-blind admissions, through which students are admitted regardless of their ability to pay for tuition on their own.

Average loan debt - Some schools may appear to have great financial aid, but they may be providing much of this support through loans which must be paid back. Looking at the average loan debt will give you a sense of the financial burden you'll have to shoulder once you graduate.

Are Students Successful Here?

First-year retention rate - This percentage describes the number of enrolled freshmen who return as sophomores the following year. Be cautious if a high percentage of the student body doesn't return for their second year. Clearly the school is not providing students something they want or need.

Six-year graduation rate - Whether students failed to graduate from a school because they transferred, dropped out, or failed to complete requirements, this is one of the most important clues to understanding whether or not students are successful. If this percentage is low, the school is not adequately supporting students to ensure graduation. Look at the graduation rate for underrepresented minority students as well. If students of color are graduating at significantly lower rates, that should ring warning bells. You can find a full breakdown of graduation rates by race, gender, and other factors at www.collegeresults.org.

Remember that college is an investment. You invest your money in getting a quality education, which will, in turn, allow you to have access to better jobs. But if a school has a high loan debt and a low graduation rate, maybe it is not the wisest investment for you.

Don't just fall into a college because you didn't do enough research. I'm enormously thankful that I put in the time and hard work to research, identify and gain admittance to my dream school—a liberal arts college in upstate New York that none of my family or friends had ever heard of but which was perfect for me. Don't settle on a college just because you are unaware of what else is out there. Use the numbers to help you find a college that fits your interests and needs. You won't regret it!

BIO *Emily Anderer is a graduate of Hamilton College in Clinton, New York and past intern with Center for Student Opportunity (now Strive for College).*

What Size College is "Right" for You

By Karen Gross

Think about what makes you most comfortable, what energizes you . . .

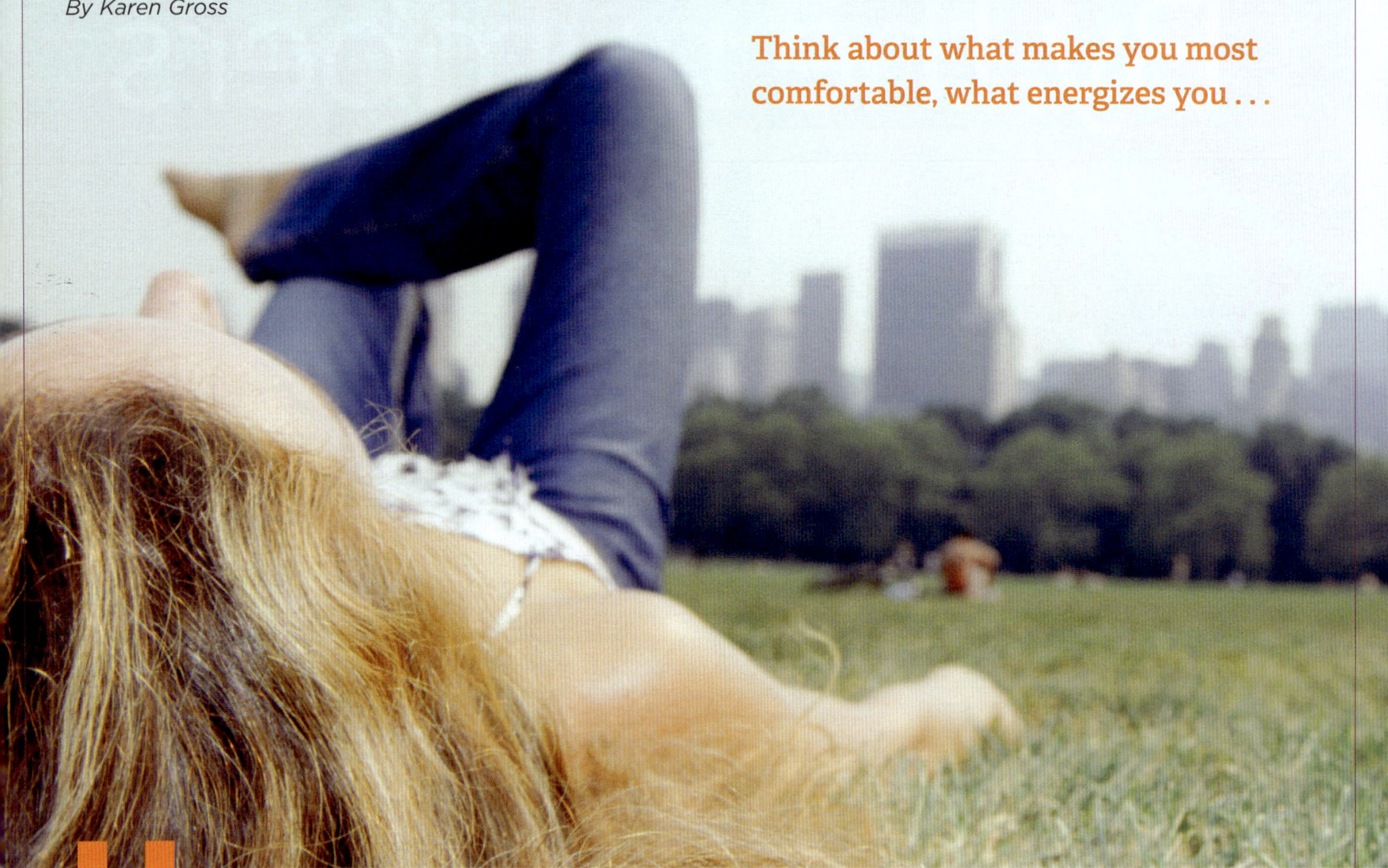

How can you know whether you are better suited to a larger university or a small liberal arts college? Well, instead of looking at size as the central dividing line among colleges, think instead about who you are (and who you will become) – as a person and as a learner. Think about what makes you most comfortable, what energizes you, what environment will enable you to thrive over the next four years.

Let me share with you three prominent myths about college size.

MYTH ONE: YOU MUST GO TO A COLLEGE THAT IS BIGGER THAN YOUR HIGH SCHOOL. FALSE!

The critically important differences between college and high school are NOT based on size. Colleges, whatever their size, are engaged in a different enterprise than high schools. At colleges, the number and breadth of courses is vast and unlike most high school curricula. You will have lots of opportunities over your college career to select among the courses and to specialize in what most interests you.

At college, you get to focus on what most interests you, what most captures your imagination. This can happen in many academic settings, large or small.

MYTH TWO: STUDENTS GET LOST AT LARGE UNIVERSITIES AND BECOME A NUMBER, NOT A NAME. FALSE!

All colleges, regardless of size, work very hard to help their students find niches within their communities. For some students, that "small" feel comes from athletics where student-athletes bond with each other and with the coaching staff. For other students, closeness comes through clubs and organizations. For some, it appears through shared academic interests where students connect with others in courses and projects.

Rather than the size of a college, the more important thing is for you to find ways to connect to other students, to faculty members, to the community. You can do that at all colleges, large and small.

MYTH THREE: SMALL COLLEGES OFFER LIMITED OPPORTUNITIES. FALSE!

Small colleges and large universities all offer amazing opportunities—more opportunities than one student could experience fully in four years. What is important in assessing the opportunities on a college or university campus is not size but the philosophy and vision of the college and its leadership.

So, visit campuses. Walk around without an admissions guide for a while. Make sure you sit in on a class or two. Speak with students in the halls and in the dining facilities. Listen to what is happening when students interact with faculty and staff. Meet coaches. See if you can sense and feel the college's ambition and goals.

... what environment will enable you to thrive

Conclusion

Think about selecting the size of a college this way: If you were shopping for clothing, it is likely that there are many choices, many things that fit at many prices, with many styles, in many colors. But, some of the items selected will just feel right to you. They may not feel right to your friends or parents. But, you will find something you can see yourself wearing.

The same is true for colleges. There are many, many choices. The goal is to choose the places that feel right to you. ■

BIO *Karen Gross is a past President of Southern Vermont College, a small private liberal arts college located in Bennington, Vermont.*

SIZE QUIZ

WHAT SIZE COLLEGE IS OPTIMAL FOR YOU

Use this quiz as a way of thinking about college size. Scoring (and explanations) appear at the end of the quiz. Remember, too, that a quiz is but one of many tools that should be used to help with deciding what college is optimal for you.

1. Do you handle freedom and independence at home and in school maturely and responsibly (e.g. if your teacher leaves your classroom, will you stay on task)?
   ❒ YES ❒ NO ❒ MAYBE
2. When in a difficult situation, do you do best when you have support from teachers, coaches, close friends, and mentors?
   ❒ YES ❒ NO ❒ MAYBE
3. Are you someone who can make independent decisions easily (choosing courses, athletics, after-school activities) and enjoys the decision-making process without adult input?
   ❒ YES ❒ NO ❒ MAYBE
4. Do you take your time and value advice and feedback from others to make a decision? Do you often second-guess your decisions or have trouble making up your mind?
   ❒ YES ❒ NO ❒ MAYBE
5. Are you able to advocate for yourself, identify problems, and ask the right questions to get help when you need it?
   ❒ YES ❒ NO ❒ MAYBE
6. Are you someone who accepts results and situations even if they are not what you wanted? Do you sometimes have trouble standing up for yourself?
   ❒ YES ❒ NO ❒ MAYBE
7. Are you someone who can easily connect and form relationships with peers, older students, and teachers within your school?
   ❒ YES ❒ NO ❒ MAYBE
8. Do you enjoy trying new things, seeking out new activities, and interacting with different social groups?
   ❒ YES ❒ NO ❒ MAYBE

How to score the results:

There are no right or wrong answers to this quiz. Your preference to one environment is not a value judgment about you; instead, it is an assessment of how you function and what might optimize your college success and happiness.

QUESTIONS 1, 3, 5 and 7

"Yes" answers suggest you are likely suited to larger colleges and universities.

"No" answers suggest you may be better suited to smaller colleges and universities.

"Maybe" answers suggest you take a deeper look at whether a large college or university will be a comfortable fit for you—it probably is.

QUESTIONS 2, 4, 6 and 8

"Yes" answers suggest you will likely be well suited to smaller colleges and universities.

"No" answers suggest you may be better suited to larger colleges and universities.

"Maybe" answers suggest you take a deeper look at whether a smaller college or university will be a comfortable fit for you—it probably is.

A combination of answers suggests you think about your personality and how it might relate to different college size to determine the right fit for you.

Truth be told, you can be happy in many environments – even in ones that initially do not seem likely. But, if you can predict which size college or university you are likely to excel in, be happiest at, and progress to graduation from, then you're a step ahead in finding the college home that is optimal for you.

My Priority Factors: What Matters Most to Me?

Before you decide where to apply, it's important to consider what priority factors are most important to you. In other words, what do you need to have in a college?

You should never choose a college just based on its name, location, or reputation.

Think of buying a car. You wouldn't buy one based on the name alone. You would ask yourself: Is it safe? How many people does it seat? How many miles per gallon does it get? What features does it offer? What color do I want?

Below are some of the most common factors students consider when they decide where they want to apply with a list of specific questions to consider. As you read, think about which factors stand out to you as the most important.

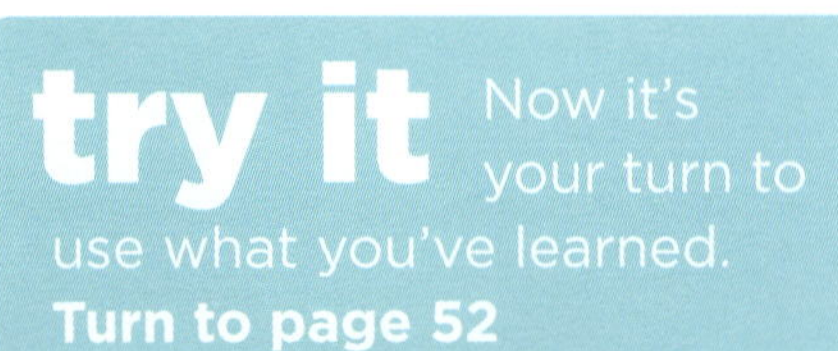

try it
Now it's your turn to use what you've learned.

Turn to page 52

FACTOR	QUESTIONS TO ANSWER
Location	• How far away from home is this school? • How will you travel to and from this school? • What is around the school? Is it rural? In a city? A suburb? • Will you need a car to get around?
Size	• How big is the student body? • What is the average class size? The student/faculty ratio? • How big is the campus? Can you walk from one end to the other?
Financial Aid	• What is the average financial aid package? • What percent of students with need were awarded aid or need-based scholarships? What percent had their need fully met? • What is the average student loan debt on graduation?
Diversity	• What is the racial breakdown of the student body? • How diverse is the faculty at the school? • What is the male/female ratio?
Academics	• What programs of study are offered that interest you? • What are the graduation requirements and required courses? • What is the first-to-second year retention rate? • What is the graduation rate? For underrepresented students?
Supports for First-Generation College Students	• Does the school offer specific supports (student centers, clubs, mentoring, etc.) for first-generation college students? • What percent of the student body is awarded Pell grants? • What is the graduation rate for first-generation college students?
Programs Offered	• Does the school offer study abroad programs? • What clubs/extracurricular activities are offered that you might want to be involved in? • Does the school offer career services for students and alumni?
Campus Life	• What percent of the student body lives on campus? • Is the social scene focused on the Greek system (fraternities and sororities)? • What varsity and club sports are offered? What division do varsity teams play in?

ON THE SPOT:
Find answers to these questions by reading the college profiles in this book and at ImFirst.org. Still can't find what you're looking for? Call the college directly.

Using the College Profile

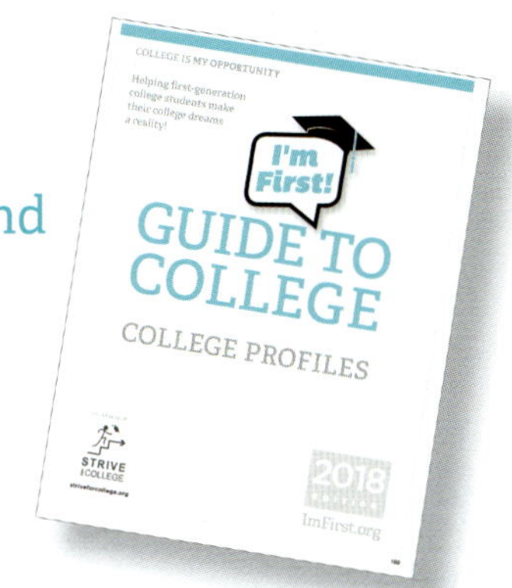
I'm First!
GUIDE TO COLLEGE
COLLEGE PROFILES
2018
ImFirst.org

Starting on page 169, you'll find comprehensive profiles of colleges and universities committed to serving and supporting first-generation college students on their campuses and in their community.

The section is organized by state, with schools presented alphabetically within each state. You are encouraged to continue your research and connect with the colleges profiled here at striveforcollege.org. Our web platform connects aspiring college students with free, one-on-one, online mentoring through the entire college admissions and financial aid application process.

How Can I Use the College Profile?

Think of the college profile as a snapshot. It will provide you with data that can help you get a feel for who attends the school, what academics are like there, how much it costs, and what types of students get accepted. It will also give you an overview of the school's mission and history and the types of support you can expect to receive on campus. What it can't tell you is how it actually feels to be on the college campus and how well you'll fit in. To find out those things, you'll need to dive deeper into the college search.

Criteria for Inclusion

The colleges and universities profiled here do not reflect each and every—or the only—schools that serve first-generation college students. Still, the colleges and universities that are featured exemplify many of the four-year colleges and universities committed to serving and supporting these students and are profiled in light of the unique programs and opportunities they offer.

Profiled colleges and universities partner with Strive for College to build awareness of and improve their institution's efforts on behalf of first-generation college students.

What's Included in Each Profile?

The following pages will give you an idea of the specific information included in each profile, including a breakdown of the data provided and the types of support programs outlined. In general, each profile has four parts shown below.

Note that the profiles use many college access terms which can be confusing to students just starting their search. If you are not yet familiar with what a term means, look it up in the glossary on page 344!

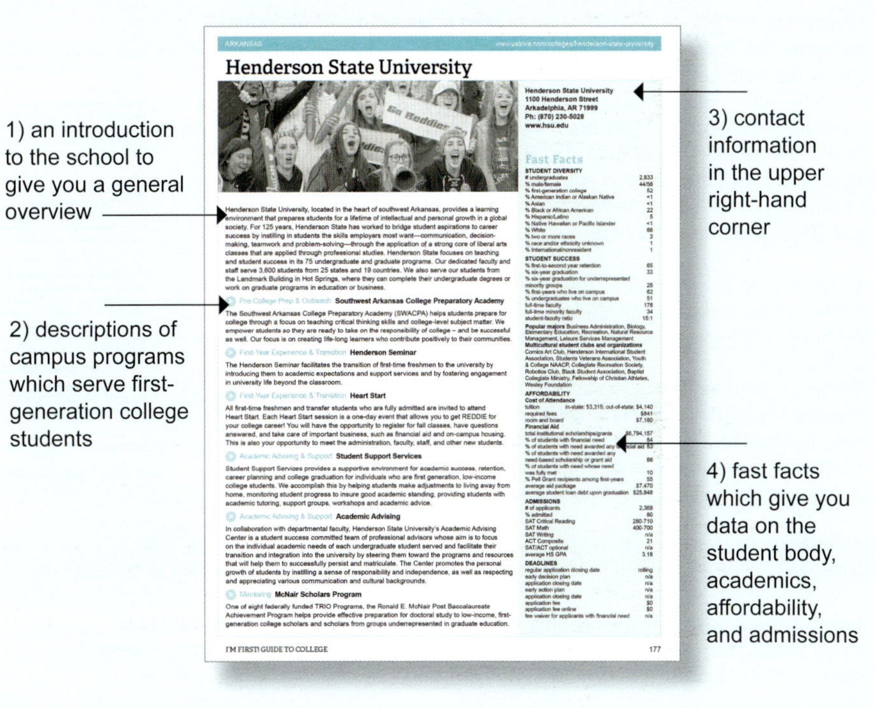
Henderson State University
1) an introduction to the school to give you a general overview
2) descriptions of campus programs which serve first-generation college students
3) contact information in the upper right-hand corner
4) fast facts which give you data on the student body, academics, affordability, and admissions

Compiling the College Profiles

The information and data found in the college profiles is developed by Strive for College staff in collaboration with and approved by the schools themselves. Because of this close editorial process, we believe the information presented to be accurate and up-to-date. If a college did not supply a certain piece of data requested, the information either does not appear or is marked as "n/a" for "not available." We still encourage you to check directly with schools to verify important information on programs, deadlines, tuition and fees, and other data.

We believe that the best way to research and select your future college home is not just by the numbers, but by the important programs and services that will support you academically, socially, and financially through college and to graduation.

Continue your research and to connect with the colleges and universities profiled here at StriveforCollege.org.

ARKANSAS www.ustrive.com/colleges/henderson-state-university

Henderson State University

Henderson State University, located in the heart of southwest Arkansas, provides a learning environment that prepares students for a lifetime of intellectual and personal growth in a global society. For 125 years, Henderson State has worked to bridge student aspirations to career success by instilling in students the skills employers most want—communication, decision-making, teamwork and problem-solving—through the application of a strong core of liberal arts classes that are applied through professional studies. Henderson State focuses on teaching and student success in its 75 undergraduate and graduate programs. Our dedicated faculty and staff serve 3,600 students from 25 states and 19 countries. We also serve our students from the Landmark Building in Hot Springs, where they can complete their undergraduate degrees or work on graduate programs in education or business.

Pre-College Prep & Outreach **Southwest Arkansas College Preparatory Academy**

The Southwest Arkansas College Preparatory Academy (SWACPA) helps students prepare for college through a focus on teaching critical thinking skills and college-level subject matter. We empower students so they are ready to take on the responsibility of college – and be successful as well. Our focus is on creating life-long learners who contribute positively to their communities.

First-Year Experience & Transition **Henderson Seminar**

The Henderson Seminar facilitates the transition of first-time freshmen to the university by introducing them to academic expectations and support services and by fostering engagement in university life beyond the classroom.

First-Year Experience & Transition **Heart Start**

All first-time freshmen and transfer students who are fully admitted are invited to attend Heart Start. Each Heart Start session is a one-day event that allows you to get REDDIE for your college career! You will have the opportunity to register for fall classes, have questions answered, and take care of important business, such as financial aid and on-campus housing. This is also your opportunity to meet the administration, faculty, staff, and other new students.

Academic Advising & Support **Student Support Services**

Student Support Services provides a supportive environment for academic success, retention, career planning and college graduation for individuals who are first generation, low-income college students. We accomplish this by helping students make adjustments to living away from home, monitoring student progress to insure good academic standing, providing students with academic tutoring, support groups, workshops and academic advice.

Academic Advising & Support **Academic Advising**

In collaboration with departmental faculty, Henderson State University's Academic Advising Center is a student success committed team of professional advisors whose aim is to focus on the individual academic needs of each undergraduate student served and facilitate their transition and integration into the university by steering them toward the programs and resources that will help them to successfully persist and matriculate. The Center promotes the personal growth of students by instilling a sense of responsibility and independence, as well as respecting and appreciating various communication and cultural backgrounds.

Mentoring **McNair Scholars Program**

One of eight federally funded TRIO Programs, the Ronald E. McNair Post Baccalaureate Achievement Program helps provide effective preparation for doctoral study to low-income, first-generation college scholars and scholars from groups underrepresented in graduate education.

Henderson State University
1100 Henderson Street
Arkadelphia, AR 71999
Ph: (870) 230-5028
www.hsu.edu

Fast Facts

STUDENT DIVERSITY	
# undergraduates	2,833
% male/female	44/56
% first-generation college	52
% American Indian or Alaskan Native	<1
% Asian	<1
% Black or African American	22
% Hispanic/Latino	5
% Native Hawaiian or Pacific Islander	<1
% White	66
% two or more races	3
% race and/or ethnicity unknown	1
% International/nonresident	1
STUDENT SUCCESS	
% first-to-second year retention	65
% six-year graduation	33
% six-year graduation for underrepresented minority groups	25
% first-years who live on campus	62
% undergraduates who live on campus	51
full-time faculty	178
full-time minority faculty	34
student-faculty ratio	15:1

Popular majors Business Administration, Biology, Elementary Education, Recreation, Natural Resource Management, Leisure Services Management
Multicultural student clubs and organizations Comics Art Club, Henderson International Student Association, Students Veterans Association, Youth & College NAACP, Collegiate Recreation Society, Robotics Club, Black Student Association, Baptist Collegiate Ministry, Fellowship of Christian Athletes, Wesley Foundation

AFFORDABILITY	
Cost of Attendance	
tuition	in-state: $3,315; out-of-state: $4,140
required fees	$841
room and board	$7,180
Financial Aid	
total institutional scholarships/grants	$6,794,157
% of students with financial need	84
% of students with need awarded any financial aid	83
% of students with need awarded any need-based scholarship or grant aid	66
% of students with need whose need was fully met	10
% Pell Grant recipients among first-years	55
average aid package	$7,470
average student loan debt upon graduation	$25,848
ADMISSIONS	
# of applicants	2,368
% admitted	80
SAT Critical Reading	280-710
SAT Math	400-700
SAT Writing	n/a
ACT Composite	21
SAT/ACT optional	n/a
average HS GPA	3.18
DEADLINES	
regular application closing date	rolling
early decision plan	n/a
application closing date	n/a
early action plan	n/a
application closing date	n/a
application fee	$0
application fee online	$0
fee waiver for applicants with financial need	n/a

I'M FIRST! GUIDE TO COLLEGE 177

 Program Categories

Pre-College Prep & Outreach programs include partnerships with local schools and organizations as well as campus-led efforts that assist pre-college students with academic enrichment, mentoring, college preparation, and college guidance.

Pre-College Summer Experience programs provide pre-college students with the opportunity to develop academic and college-readiness skills, explore extracurricular talents, and experience life on a college campus during the summer.

Open House, Fly-in, Visit programs offer prospective or accepted students the opportunity to visit a college campus, sometimes paid for by the college.

Special Admissions Policies include schools that do not require applicants to take the standardized tests (test-optional schools), the opportunity to enroll before you graduate high school, or admission opportunities for students who do not meet all admissions criteria but show promise or have overcome extreme circumstances.

Scholarship & Financial Aid programs provide first-generation, low-income, and minority students with financial options to make it more possible to attend and graduate from college.

Summer Bridge & Orientation programs are offered to incoming college students in the summer before the student enters college to help build college-readiness skills, register for classes, meet and bond with classmates and professors, and transition into the college community.

First-Year Experience & Transition programs are designed specifically for first-year college students to help them adjust academically and socially to college.

Scholars & Leadership programs offer ambitious students the opportunity to excel in academics and extracurricular activities through honors classes, research opportunities, student government, and outreach, etc.

Academic Advising & Support programs provide students with the resources they need to succeed in their college courses. Such support is offered both inside and outside the classroom and between students, staff, and faculty.

Academic Courses & Service Learning programs are academic classes that are unique to the college and opportunities to engage in the community service through your coursework.

Student Life & Support programs provide students with communities and resources on campus that help them feel happy, safe, and at home so they can be successful and persist to graduation.

Peer, Staff or Faculty Mentoring programs involve one-on-one or small group mentoring throughout the year intended to provide students with guidance and community to help them succeed during college.

Fast Facts

This column of data gives a snap-shot of the school's vital statistics (see next page for details).

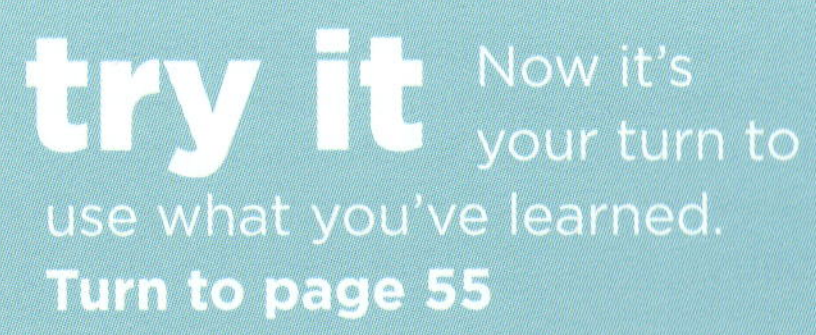
try it
Now it's your turn to use what you've learned.
Turn to page 55

Fast Facts

This data gives a snap-shot of the school's vital statistics. In addition to the program information, this data will help determine if a school is the right fit for you.

STUDENT DIVERSITY

How many students go here? Is it a diverse student body? Does the school serve many students from low-income or first-generation backgrounds?

STUDENT DIVERSITY
\# undergraduates
% male/female
% first-generation college
% American Indian or Alaskan Native

The data here includes number of undergraduate students, the male and female percentages, the first-generation college student percentage, and the racial/ethnic makeup of the student body.

STUDENT SUCCESS

What percent of first-year students return for their second year? What percent of students graduate in six years? What percent of minority students graduate in six years? Will I live on campus? How big will my classes be? What are the most popular majors? What student organizations exist to support minority and first-generation students?

STUDENT SUCCESS
% first-to-second year retention
% six-year graduation
% six-year graduation for underrepresented minority groups

The data here includes the first-to-second year retention rate, percentages of all students and minority students who will graduate within six years, percentage of students who live on campus, the number of full-time faculty, student-faculty ratio, popular majors, and multicultural clubs and student organizations.

AFFORDABILITY

What are the "sticker price" costs of attendance? What do most students actually pay? How many students receive financial aid and what kinds? How much debt do most students have upon graduation?

AFFORDABILITY
Cost of Attendance
tuition in-state: $3,315; out-of-state:
required fees
room and board

The data here includes tuition (academic fees), room and board (housing, meals, etc.) and required fees (books, registration costs, etc.), as well as the percentage of students receiving financial aid, percentage of students receiving need-based scholarship or grant money (money given based on financial need which does not have to be paid back), percentage of students whose need was fully met, the percentage of Pell grant recipients—students who receive federal grant aid for having the greatest financial need—and average financial aid package in dollars, and average student loan debt upon graduation.

ADMISSIONS

How many students apply, and what percent are accepted? What are the median-range test scores? How do I compare to most students academically? When is my application due?

ADMISSIONS
\# of applicants
% admitted
SAT Critical Reading 4
SAT Math 4

The data here includes the number of applicants, percentage of applicants accepted, the middle 50 percent range on the SAT and ACT scores of admitted students, average high school GPA of admitted students, application types, deadlines, fees, and fee waiver availability.

Henderson State University
1100 Henderson Street
Arkadelphia, AR 71999
Ph: (870) 230-5028
www.hsu.edu

Fast Facts

STUDENT DIVERSITY	
# undergraduates	2,833
% male/female	44/56
% first-generation college	52
% American Indian or Alaskan Native	<1
% Asian	<1
% Black or African American	22
% Hispanic/Latino	5
% Native Hawaiian or Pacific Islander	<1
% White	66
% two or more races	3
% race and/or ethnicity unknown	1
% International/nonresident	1

STUDENT SUCCESS	
% first-to-second year retention	65
% six-year graduation	33
% six-year graduation for underrepresented minority groups	25
% first-years who live on campus	62
% undergraduates who live on campus	51
full-time faculty	178
full-time minority faculty	34
student-faculty ratio	15:1

Popular majors Business Administration, Biology, Elementary Education, Recreation, Natural Resource Management, Leisure Services Management

Multicultural student clubs and organizations Comics Art Club, Henderson International Student Association, Students Veterans Association, Youth & College NAACP, Collegiate Recreation Society, Robotics Club, Black Student Association, Baptist Collegiate Ministry, Fellowship of Christian Athletes, Wesley Foundation

AFFORDABILITY	
Cost of Attendance	
tuition	in-state: $3,315; out-of-state: $4,140
required fees	$841
room and board	$7,180
Financial Aid	
total institutional scholarships/grants	$6,794,157
% of students with financial need	84
% of students with need awarded any financial aid	83
% of students with need awarded any need-based scholarship or grant aid	66
% of students with need whose need was fully met	10
% Pell Grant recipients among first-years	55
average aid package	$7,470
average student loan debt upon graduation	$25,848

ADMISSIONS	
# of applicants	2,368
% admitted	80
SAT Critical Reading	280-710
SAT Math	400-700
SAT Writing	n/a
ACT Composite	21
SAT/ACT optional	n/a
average HS GPA	3.18

DEADLINES	
regular application closing date	rolling
early decision plan	n/a
application closing date	n/a
early action plan	n/a
application closing date	n/a
application fee	$0
application fee online	$0
fee waiver for applicants with financial need	n/a

If you're using this Guide, you're off to a great start in finding the information you need to make your college dreams a reality! But this book is just the beginning.

Did you know that you find more advice and encouragement online?

Sign up at **www.StriveForCollege.org**
Visit **www.ImFirst.org**

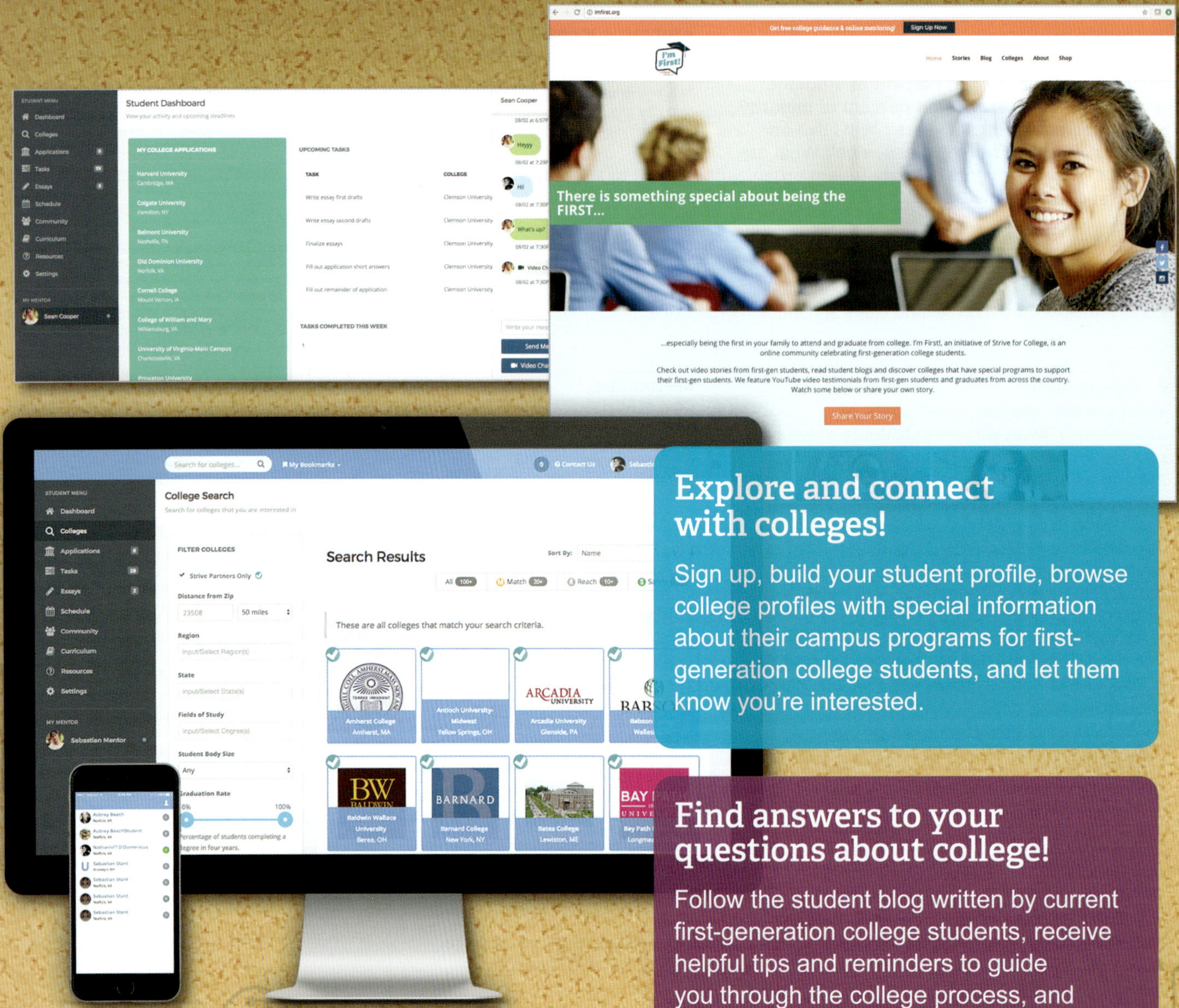

Explore and connect with colleges!

Sign up, build your student profile, browse college profiles with special information about their campus programs for first-generation college students, and let them know you're interested.

Find answers to your questions about college!

Follow the student blog written by current first-generation college students, receive helpful tips and reminders to guide you through the college process, and participate in Twitter chats and Google Hangouts on important topics!

Share your story and be inspired by others!

ImFirst.org is also collecting YouTube video stories from first-generation college students and graduates to inspire and offer advice to the next generation of students who will be first!

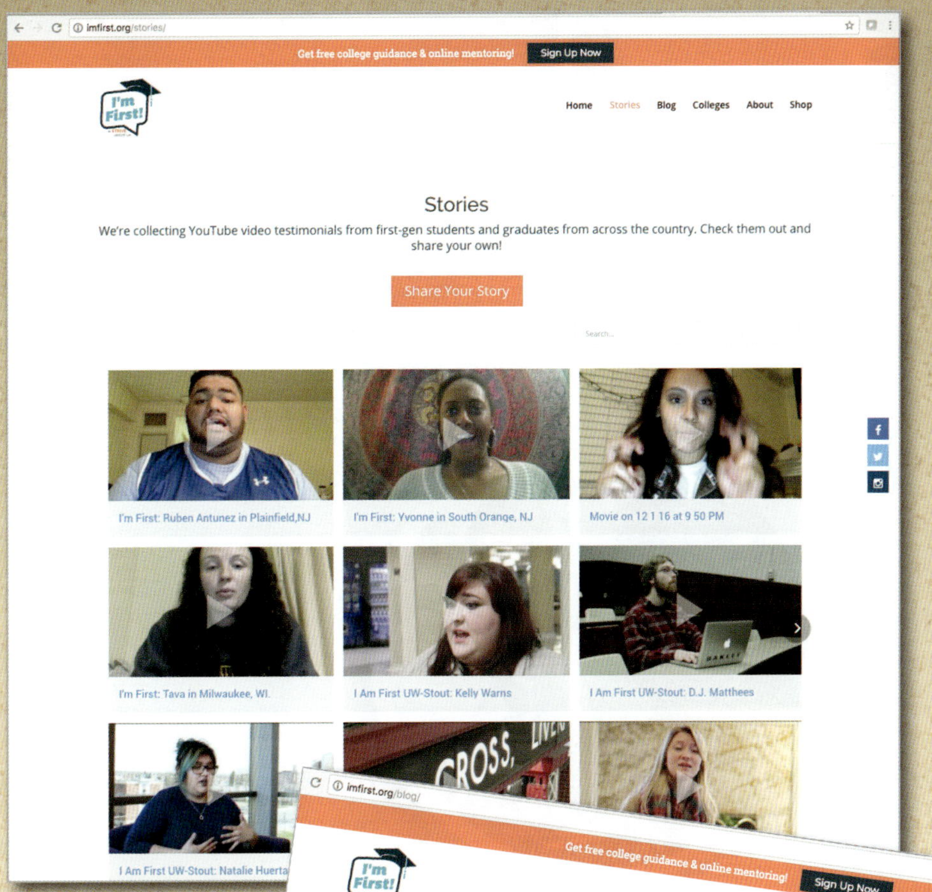

Follow a first-gen student blog

Find advice and inspiration from current first-generation college students as they blog about their college experiences on www.ImFirst.org.

Visiting College FOR FREE!

By Joe Tavares

See about fly-in and special visit programs where schools pay for prospective students with limited financial resources to visit campus.

The biggest question you need to answer before choosing your future college home is "what would it really be like for me at this school?" No matter how much research you do, how many pictures you see, or how many people you speak with, the only way you can find out what it would be like at a school is to spend a few days there.

If you're thinking about going to school away from home, you should be familiar with fly-in and special visit programs where schools pay for prospective students with limited financial resources to visit campus. These programs can give you a unique opportunity to not only visit campus, but to spend a few days there, sit in on classes, and interact with students who may very well be your peers for the next four years.

Where do you start?

You can find out about fly-in and special visit programs by using guidebooks like this, websites like www.ImFirst.org, and checking out schools' websites for information about visiting campus.

Does the school offer tours, on-campus interviews, and overnight stays? Do they have special events for low-income or multicultural students? If you're not sure, call up the school's Admissions Office and let them know who you are, when you want to visit, and if your family has financial difficulties. They may have special programs or transportation stipends for you and your family to visit campus.

Preparing for your visit

Make sure you write down all the questions you have about a school before you go. If you're attending a special visit program, review the agenda beforehand to see if there's anything not included that you want to see or do.

Being on Campus

Make sure you speak with students and professors, look around the library, eat in a dining hall, visit a dorm, and pick up the school newspaper.

How would you fit in at the school? What would you bring to the campus community? Would you feel safe? Is this an environment you would thrive in? Are support services and professors easily accessible?

Campus visits will have a big impact on your college choice, so take advantage of special visit opportunities and fly-in programs that are available for you! ■

BIO *Joe Tavares is a High School Counselor at Jakarta Intercultural School. Previously, he worked at Center for Student Opportunity (now Strive for College).*

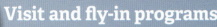

Visit and fly-in programs

Fall is a great time to get out and visit colleges and universities. Many schools host **visit and fly-in programs** during this time of year to expose prospective students to life on their campuses. Some schools will even pay for you to travel to and attend these programs.

Below are a few of the visit and fly-in programs offered by schools profiled in the *I'm First! Guide to College.* For more information on dates and registration/application deadlines, contact the schools directly.

Amherst College (MA) – Page 237
Diversity Open House Weekends

Babson College (MA) – Page 238
Experience Diversity Overnight Program and Multicultural Overnight Experience

Barnard College (NY) – Page 276
Barnard Bound

Bates College (ME) – Page 233
Prologue to Bates

Brandeis University (MA) – Page 242
Students Exploring and Embracing Diversity (SEED)

Bucknell University (PA) – Page 311
Journey to Bucknell

Carnegie Mellon University (PA) – Page 312
Celebration of Diversity Weekend

The Catholic University of America (DC) – Page 211
Visiting Campus

Claremont McKenna College (CA) – Page 182
Preview CMC!

Colorado College – Page 200
Funded Campus Visits

Columbia University in the City of New York – Page 277
Columbia Engineering Experience

Cornell University (NY) – Page 278
Diversity Hosting

Dartmouth College (NH) – Page 265
Native American Fly-In Program & Summer Dartmouth Bound Program

Davidson College (NC) – Page 292
Multicultural Visit Program

Dickinson College (PA) – Page 315
Discover Diversity

Duke University (NC) – Page 293
Blue Devil Days, Black Student Alliance Invitational Weekend, & Latino Student Recruitment Weekend

Emory University (GA) – Page 214
Essence of Emory and CORE (Cultural Overnight Recruitment Experience)

George Washington University (DC) – Page 212
Your GW

Grinnell College (IA) – Page 229
Grinnell Diversity Travel Opportunity (GDTOP)

Hamilton College (NY) – Page 280
Diversity Overnight

Johns Hopkins University (MD) – Page 234
Hopkins Overnight Multicultural Experience (HOME)

Luther College (IA) – Page 231
Fly-In Reimbursement Program

Maryville College (TN) – Page 328
Fly Maryville Program

Missouri University of Science and Technology – Page 261
¡Sí Se Puede!

New York University (NY) – Page 283
Diversity "Pathways" Open House

Northwestern University (IL) – Page 222
Fly-In Program for admitted students

Occidental College (CA) – Page 188
Multicultural Visit Program

Quinnipiac University (CT) – Page 205
Admissions Events/Visit Program

Reed College (OR) – Page 306
Discover Reed Fly-in Program and Junior Scholars Program

Rensselaer Polytechnic Institute (NY) – Page 285
Science, Technology, Arts at Rensselaer (STAR) Program

Skidmore College (NY) – Page 289
Discovery Tour

Smith College (MA) – Page 247
Women of Distinctions

St. John's College (MD & NM) – Pages 235 & 275
St. John's College Fly-In Program

Trinity College (CT) – Page 206
Preview Weekend

Tufts University (MA) – Page 248
Voices of Tufts

University of Notre Dame (IN) – Page 228
Open House/Fly-Ins

University of Pennsylvania – Page 324
Multicultural Preview Programs

University of Rochester (NY) – Page 291
Multicultural Visit Program

University of San Francisco (CA) – Page 196
Discover Diversity

Vanderbilt University (TN) – Page 329
MOSAIC Weekend and Vandy Fan for a Day

Washington University in St. Louis (MO) – Page 264
Discovery Weekend & Multicultural Celebration Weekend

Wellesley College (MA) – Page 250
Discover Wellesley Weekend

Wesleyan University (CT) – Page 208
Transportation Assistance Program

Whitman College (WA) – Page 338
Visit Scholarship Program (VSP)

Willamette University (OR) – Page 309
Access to Excellence

Williams College (MA) – Page 251
Windows on Williams (WOW) & Previews

Worcester Polytechnic Institute (MA) – Page 252
Discover: The Diversity Experience @ WPI

Yale University (CT) – Page 209
Multicultural Open House/Fly-In Program

SNEAK PEAK: THE COLLEGE VISIT

Tyler Lattimore
Emory University
Hometown: Gainesville, FL

"To me, selecting a college is like buying a car. You can look up a car's features, its perks, what it has over another make or model, or even read and listen to others' reviews, but you won't know if it's the right car for you until you drive it."

– Drive It Before You Buy It

Lauren Mayo
College: University of Georgia
Hometown: Marietta, GA

"When I say visit, I am not simply talking about the "drive-by" informal visit. I encourage you to plan a formal and involved visit, complete with information sessions and time to explore the campus, take a tour, and visit a class, if possible."

– Do Not Underestimate The Value of A College Visit

Visit www.ImFirst.org to follow the student blog and watch video testimonials from first-generation college students and graduates.

Visiting Campus

No matter how many brochures you read or websites you visit, nothing tells you more about a college than visiting its campus in person. Plus, you can learn a lot more just by asking questions.

Here's a list to get you started:

Ask your college host:

- What activities and services are available to help students get settled (academically and socially) during their first year?
- How big are the classes?
- What is the total cost of attending the college?
- What types of financial aid does the college offer and how do I apply?
- Are all freshmen assigned to an academic advisor?
- Where do most freshmen live?
- Can I take a tour?
- What activities are available for students?
- Who teaches the courses for first-year students?
- How successful are the college's graduates in finding jobs?
- What services (such as transportation and shopping) are available locally?

Ask any students you meet:

- How easy is it to meet with faculty?
- Are you able to register for the classes you want?
- What is there to do on weekends? Do most students stay or leave campus on weekends?

Can't get to a campus? Go online:

- Visiting a college's website is an invaluable tool to learn everything you need to know about a school. You can find answers to many of the questions above and some college websites even offer a virtual tour for you to get familiar with the campus.
- KnowHow2GO University—accessible at www.KnowHow2GO.org—is a virtual college tour that replicates the experience of being on a real college campus and is designed to help you learn what to expect. By visiting various campus buildings—Admissions, Financial Aid, Academics, Career Center, Student Center, Library, Dormitories, Quad, and the Athletic Complex—you'll learn about the college environment and what it takes to get there. ■

Can't Visit? Don't Stress!

Visiting a college campus is definitely the best way to determine if a school is going to be a good fit for you or not. But that doesn't mean that you shouldn't consider schools that you can't physically visit. Here are some other ways to get to know a school a little better.

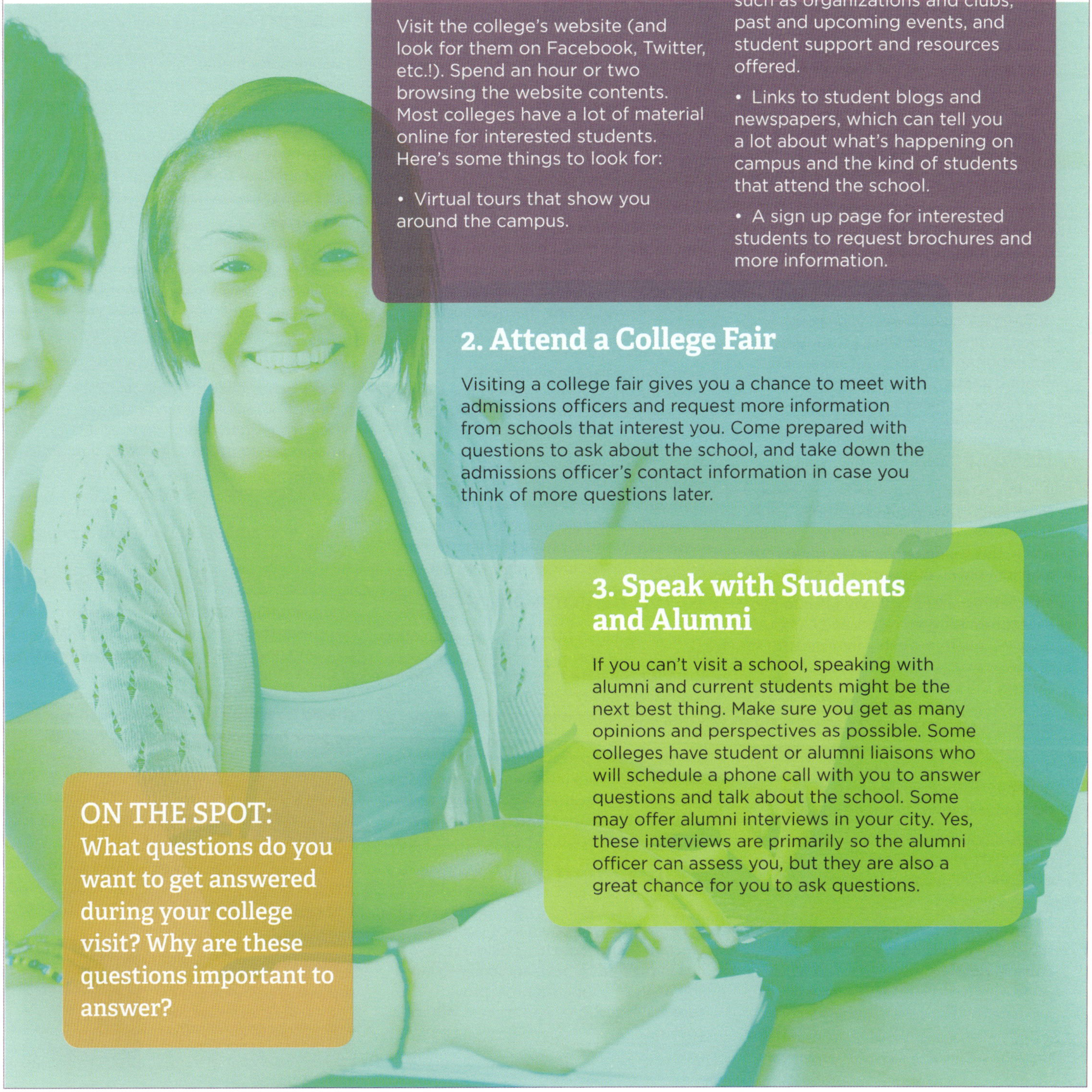

1. Go Online

Visit the college's website (and look for them on Facebook, Twitter, etc.!). Spend an hour or two browsing the website contents. Most colleges have a lot of material online for interested students. Here's some things to look for:

- Virtual tours that show you around the campus.
- Information about campus life, such as organizations and clubs, past and upcoming events, and student support and resources offered.
- Links to student blogs and newspapers, which can tell you a lot about what's happening on campus and the kind of students that attend the school.
- A sign up page for interested students to request brochures and more information.

2. Attend a College Fair

Visiting a college fair gives you a chance to meet with admissions officers and request more information from schools that interest you. Come prepared with questions to ask about the school, and take down the admissions officer's contact information in case you think of more questions later.

3. Speak with Students and Alumni

If you can't visit a school, speaking with alumni and current students might be the next best thing. Make sure you get as many opinions and perspectives as possible. Some colleges have student or alumni liaisons who will schedule a phone call with you to answer questions and talk about the school. Some may offer alumni interviews in your city. Yes, these interviews are primarily so the alumni officer can assess you, but they are also a great chance for you to ask questions.

ON THE SPOT:
What questions do you want to get answered during your college visit? Why are these questions important to answer?

Building Your College List

by Kelly Herrington

Creating a college list can be a daunting process. With so many colleges and factors to consider, how do you start to research and narrow down the schools where you'll apply?

Self-Discovery

You need to know some things about yourself before you can determine the colleges that are right for you. **Ask yourself:** What are my academic strengths? What classes interest me? In what environment do I learn best? There are free personality tests, like the Myers Briggs, on the web that will allow you to understand your personality and learning style. Many of these tests also make career suggestions.

Search Criteria

Before picking colleges, you should first stop to think about what characteristics are important to you in a college. Think about campus size, location, athletic and arts options, student support services, and retention rates.

Resources

It is important to use a variety of resources to research colleges and generate your college list. You've already found a great one in this Guide and can continue your research online at www.ImFirst.org.

Internet resources typically fall into two categories: list generators and campus reviews. You're probably familiar with some of the popular list generators like College Board's Big Future. Campus reviews found on sites like Unigo or College Prowler give a more personal take, but keep in mind that students who post on these sites are typically either really happy or really unhappy at their colleges, so consulting numerous sources is important.

Exploring a college's own website and reading its mission statement is also extremely valuable.

Remember that visiting a college is the best way to determine how well you'll fit in there. See pages 46-48 for more on college visits.

Work in Progress

Your college list is a work in progress and it will probably change. As a high school student, your interests change and, as they do, your college list might too. Be flexible and open minded.

Avoid Stereotyping Perceived Prestige

Try to keep your stereotypes in check and remember that all institutions have strengths and weaknesses. A college education is a powerful tool with wonderful outcomes. There is no one perfect college. Some students thrive at large public universities and others will flourish at smaller private institutions. It is important not to rule out a college based on preconceived notions or perceived prestige.

Your college list may contain colleges that are unfamiliar to you or that differ slightly with your stated preferences, however, an initial list should include colleges that expand your horizons and offer strong programs in disciplines that interest you.

Move Beyond Rankings

College rankings provide some interesting data, but are also highly subjective. Use them for the data they contain, but do not focus too heavily on the numeric rank they assign colleges. I once heard someone say that the true measure of a college is in the students it produces, not what kind it admits. Most rankings focus on input, the criteria to gain admission, but few address output, what students do post college. Most of life, though, is lived after college.

Find a Mentor

As you create your college list, try to find a mentor like your guidance counselor, teacher, friend, coach, or religious leader. It is important to have someone to help you analyze your strengths, provide career suggestions, and discuss potential colleges.

Put Your List Into Three Categories

Predicting admission is never an exact science. Most students apply to between four and eight colleges. Try to put the colleges on your list into one of three categories: "likely," "best fit," and "reach."

"Likely" colleges are ones where your grade point average and test scores are significantly higher than the school's averages and you are therefore likely to be admitted.

For **"best-fit"** colleges, your numbers are on par with the college's statistics, so you have a good chance of being admitted.

"Reach" colleges are ones where your numbers are below average. Your odds of getting into a reach school are not as good as getting into a likely or best-fit college, but that doesn't mean you shouldn't apply at all.

Most students apply to at least two "likely" and "best-fit" schools. Since admission to college hinges largely on the competition in a given year, it is impossible to predict the exact outcome of your applications, especially for highly selective institutions. So, it is extremely important for every student to have an appropriate group of schools within a healthy range of selectivity.

Once you have taken a well-rounded approach to generating your college list by using numerous resources, you will be in great shape when admission decisions are rendered. **Most importantly, you should be happy to attend any college on your final college list.** Good luck!

try it Now it's your turn to use what you've learned. **Turn to page 56**

BIO *Kelly Herrington is Director of College Counseling at University Prep in Seattle, WA and Co-Founder of College Application Wizard.*

What Matters to Me? Worksheet

Now that you've had a chance to review some of the factors that students should consider when deciding on best-fit colleges, it's time for you to identify what's most important to you.

Fill in the chart below, using the guiding questions in "What Matters to Me?" to help you. We provided an example to help you get started.

Priority Factor	**Why is this important?** **What specifically do you need?**
Example: Location	• This is important to me because I know that I want to stay close enough to my family to be able to visit on holidays and long weekends. • I need a school that is: - within a four hour drive - accessible by public transportation (train or bus) - suburban or urban

Free Write: My Dream School

Picture your dream college—consider its setting (urban, suburban, rural), climate, size of the student body, class sizes, diversity, academics, sports and extracurriculars, campus life, etc. Have a group discussion with your peers about what you're looking for in a college or write a description of your dream school.

continued

Reading the College Profile Quiz

1. What percent of first-year students come back for their sophomore year at Trinity College? ______

2. What percent of the student body is Hispanic/Latino at Holy Names University? ______

3. Does California Institute of Technology offer a pre-orientation program for its incoming students? Explain.

4. Find three colleges with six-year graduation rates above 80%:

5. How many full-time minority faculty are on staff at Emory University? ______

6. What percent of students at Reed College have their need fully met? ______

7. Find three colleges where the average loan debt is under $20,000:

8. If you wanted to obtain more information about Central Connecticut State University, what contact information would you use?

9. What is the student-faculty ratio at Sarah Lawrence College? ______

10. Find a school that you are interested in applying to. Explain three reasons you are interested based on the information given in the school profile.

College Comparison Chart

Choose four colleges that you think you are interested in and complete the college comparison chart below using information you find in the Guide's profile pages.

	EXAMPLE	COLLEGE 1	COLLEGE 2	COLLEGE 3	COLLEGE 4
School name	Opportunity College				
Location (city and state, urban, suburban, or rural, and climate)	Bethesda, MD – suburb of Washington, DC; has all four seasons				
Transportation (How will you get to and from school? How much will it cost? How long will it take?)	Red line on DC metro; $2-4 dollars each way, 20 minutes from home				
Website	www.ImFirst.org				
Phone number	(301) 363-4222				
Admissions officer assigned to my region	Mr. First				
STUDENT PROFILE					
# of students	3,000				
% male/female	40/60				
Student diversity	33% African American, 10% Hispanic, 15% Pell Grant recipients				
ACADEMICS					
student-faculty ratio	12:1				
average class size	16				
% first-year retention rate	98				
% graduation rate (6 years)	99				
% underrepresented minorities graduation rate	99				
Popular majors	English, Biology, Journalism, Computer Science				
CAMPUS LIFE					
% live on campus (% freshmen)	65% (100% freshmen)				
Student clubs and organizations you might be interested in	ALANA, Black Student Alliance, Diversity Council				
Athletics	NCAA Division III, intramural teams				
Pre-orientation, orientation, transition, first-year experience programs	Summer Bridge Program – 3 weeks on campus for academic credit First-Year Experience – seminar for entire first year				

	EXAMPLE	COLLEGE 1	COLLEGE 2	COLLEGE 3	COLLEGE 4
Academic advising and mentoring programs	Student Ambassador Program – incoming students assigned upperclass mentor Learning Center and Writing Center – peer tutors and writing coaches				
Other programs or services	Office of Multicultural Affairs – cultural events, lectures, support				
ADMISSIONS					
% of applicants accepted	75%				
SAT Critical Reading range	510-610				
SAT Math range	490-590				
SAT Writing range	500-600				
ACT range	19-23				
Average HS GPA	3.6				
Reach, best fit, or likely school?	Best fit				
Application Deadlines	Early Decision 11/15 Regular Decision 2/1				
Fee waiver for applicants with financial need?	Yes				
Visit programs or open houses	Multicultural Weekend – fly-in program in October Diversity Open House – for admitted students of color in April				
COST & AID					
Tuition	$21,250				
room & board	$7,500				
% of students who receive aid	90				
% receiving need-based scholarship or grant aid	90				
% receiving aid whose need was fully met	100				
Average aid package	$19,975				
Average student loan debt upon graduation	$8,995				
Based on all of the information you have gathered, will you apply to this school?	Yes				
Important scholarships or financial aid opportunities	First-Generation Scholarship - $5,000 if you are first in your family to go to college; apply by 2/1 Opportunity Promise – no loan pledge if income if household income is under $40,000				

Unit 2 Quiz

answers on page 136

Multiple Choice, circle your answer

1. When considering whether or not a college will be a good financial investment, every student should look at all of the following except:

a) how many students attend the school
b) what percentage of students graduate from the shool
c) average financial aid package
d) average loan debt on graduation

2. Liberal arts colleges usually:

a) have large student bodies
b) are public schools
c) offer two-year degrees
d) only serve undergraduate students

3. Community colleges offer:

a) Bachelor's degrees
b) Associate's degrees and professional certificates
c) Master's degrees
d) All of the above

4. The percentage of students who return for their second year at a college is called:

a) graduation rate
b) acceptance rate
c) retention rate
d) matriculation rate

5. The *I'm First! Guide to College* school profiles can tell you all of the following about a college except:

a) how diverse the student body is
b) what percent of the student body are first-generation college students
c) how happy students are who attend the school
d) the percent of students who live on campus

True or False, circle your answer

1. Most students who attend community colleges eventually transfer to four-year schools. T F

2. When applying to college, I should only apply to schools that I know I can get into. T F

3. Going to visit a college is the best way to know whether or not it's a good fit for me. T F

4. I should only consider schools that have the exact major I'm interested in. T F

5. The lower a school's admittance rate, the harder it is to get into. T F

Fill in the Blank

1. A college or university originally founded to serve the Black community is called a/an ______________________.

2. The percent of first-year college students who return for their sophomore year is the ______________.

3. A/an ______________________ is a college or university in which over 25% of the student body is Hispanic.

4. To find out the size of an average class at a college, I should look at the ______________ ratio.

5. I should attend a/an ________________ in my area to meet college representatives and collect information, brochures, etc. from many schools.

Open Answer

1. Do you think you will be a better fit at a university or a liberal arts college? Why?

2. What are three most important priority factors in your best fit college? Why are these things important to you?

Unit 3

CONTENTS

How Do I Apply to College?

"Your GPA and standardized test scores are important in the college admissions process, but you are more than a test score. While many people perceive the college admissions process as a 'numbers game,' most colleges want to know more about the person you are."

Objectives

By the end of this unit, I will...

- understand the importance of each element of the college application and evaluate my own applicant profile in order to determine strengths and areas of growth.
- read and analyze a high school transcript.
- know the differences between the SAT, ACT, and other standardized tests and understand how to register and prepare for these exams.
- write compelling personal statements which showcase unique voice, perspective, and experiences.
- use professional language in order to write letters to request recommendations from teachers and counselors.
- develop a timeline for preparing and submitting college applications.
- understand how to prepare for and complete the college application.

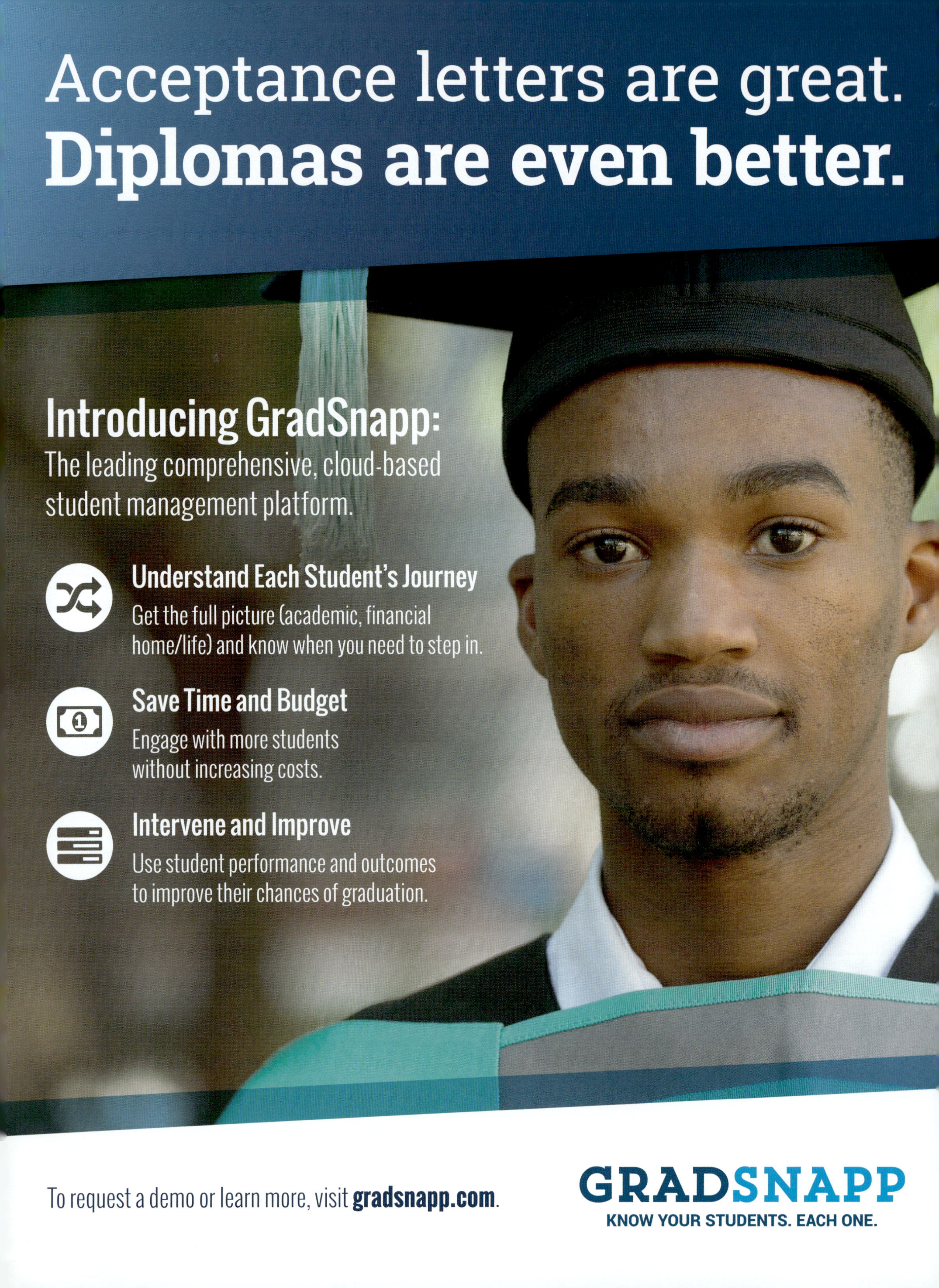
Acceptance letters are great.
Diplomas are even better.
Introducing GradSnapp:
The leading comprehensive, cloud-based student management platform.
Understand Each Student's Journey
Get the full picture (academic, financial home/life) and know when you need to step in.
Save Time and Budget
Engage with more students without increasing costs.
Intervene and Improve
Use student performance and outcomes to improve their chances of graduation.
To request a demo or learn more, visit gradsnapp.com.
GRADSNAPP
KNOW YOUR STUDENTS. EACH ONE.

The Six Things Colleges Most Commonly Consider

Every college has a unique way of assessing applicants and deciding which will be the most successful on their campuses. Some schools look for students who have demonstrated a commitment to service. Others take into account the level of interest a student has shown in their school.

But most four-year colleges use the six following factors as their main criteria for evaluating a student's application.

Element	What It Is	Why It's Important
Transcript 1	An official document issued by your high school which shows your individualized grades, GPA, class rank, etc.	GPA is the best predictor for student success in college, so admissions officers look closely at your grades. They will also be looking for improvement over time, course rigor, and your level of competitiveness with your peers.
Standardized Test Scores 2	Scores you receive from your SAT, ACT, and/or SAT IIs broken down by content area.	Not all high schools were created equal, so using GPA as the sole measure of a student's academic talent can be unfair. Standardized test scores are used by many schools as a way to get a fair and objective baseline of a student's raw skills and knowledge.
Personal Statement 3	A short (usually under 650 words) narrative essay on a subject of the student's choice or assigned by the college.	First-year college students often say that college-level writing is the most difficult thing about their academic transition. Your personal statement allows colleges to gauge your writing level. It also gives admissions officers insight into your personality: what makes you who you are and what you're passionate about.
Extracurricular Activities 4	Any activity you engage in outside of your regular school classes (e.g. sports, clubs, work, community service, etc.).	Colleges want academically motivated students, but they are also looking for well-rounded individuals who will add something to their campus outside the classroom. Your extracurricular involvement gives schools a preview of what you might bring to their campus.
Letters of Recommendation 5	Letters from adults whom you know in a professional capacity, especially teachers and counselors, which are written in support of your character and qualifications as a college student.	Letters of recommendation give colleges a window into how you are perceived by those around you. Well-written letters can add depth and dimension to the picture of you formed by your overall application. Likewise, sub-par letters can detract from the power of your application.
Interviews 6	A meeting with a representative from the college (usually an admissions officer, student, or alumnus) in which you are asked questions about your background, motivations, passions, and interest in a particular college.	Interviews are a great way for you to show your interest in a particular school. They also offer you a forum to give your admissions committee a fuller picture of who you are, why you are qualified to attend, and explain anything on your record that may stick out as a red flag.

Now that you have a glimpse at what factors most colleges consider in the admissions process, we'll explore each of these elements in depth in the following pages.

You Are a Jigsaw Puzzle

By Bruce Poch

College applications are evaluated in most places not by formula but by close readers. The more selective the college, the more likely it is that grades and scores are not where the decision may turn, but rather those numbers may simply open a door to the real conversation that decides your acceptance.

No one single factor can determine whether or not an admissions team will accept you (unless your transcript is riddled with problems). You are more than just your GPA, more than just your test scores, more than just your personal statement or what your teachers have to say about you. You want to show readers who you are, and at the same time, aim to leave the admission officer wanting to know the next chapter in your story.

But mostly, you must be you. College admissions officers understand that. They also know that when they put all these elements together, your individual identity should shine through. That's why it is so important that students are genuine and authentic in their applications.

In a strong application, all your materials will come together to tell a cohesive and compelling story of who you are and give admissions officers a glimpse at what kind of student you'll be on their campuses.

When your application is completed, the finished puzzle should reflect an authentic portrait of who you are.

This is extremely important, especially at residential colleges, where admissions teams are considering your merits not just as a student but as a community member: Will this student be a considerate roommate? Will she be an enthusiastic and supportive teammate? Will he engage in classroom discussion or as a lab partner? Does she have the leadership and responsibility it takes to be a student government representative? How will this student represent my institution after he graduates?

Admissions officers are searching for a union between their college and the students they accept. In answering the "why this college?" question in interviews or supplemental essays, students often generalize too much ("I want a small college," or "I want a big sports atmosphere") rather than directly addressing the individual college's mission, teaching style, or curriculum requirements (or the absence of them). These days, supplements can be at least and sometimes more important than the main Common Application essays.

Admission committees evaluate candidates for learning styles, academic interests and talent. And, in selecting colleges, you should do the exact same for the schools to which you apply. That's why doing your research and carefully examining view books, websites and college guides is so important. Searching for the right college is like searching for a soul mate: you shouldn't pick one based only on its reputation, ranking or its convenient location; it should fit the way you work, think and play. Finding a student who fits in all those ways becomes compelling for admission officers. Properly thought out, an application can lead admission officers to that conclusion.

If you have to stretch reality and package your application to make yourself seem like a suitable candidate for admissions for a certain college, maybe it isn't the right place for you. You should be looking for a school that you believe will appreciate and support your authentic character and value the unique priorities and passions that make you who you are and that offers an environment, faculty and peers who will help you bring out your best.

You've spent the better part of two decades working hard to become who you are, so being disingenuous on your college applications is doing yourself a disservice. Be confident in who you are and what you have achieved. Know you have more to learn and show an eagerness to engage the college, ideas and those around you to move forward. The rest is up to the admissions team.

Your college applications should come together much like a jigsaw puzzle: piece by piece. When your application is completed, the finished puzzle should reflect an authentic portrait of who you are.

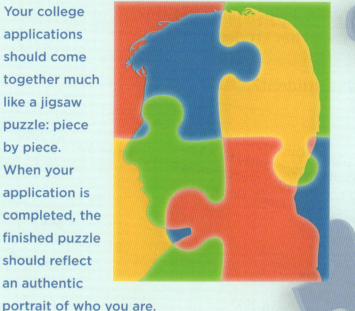

If your résumé reads like Mother Teresa's but your recommenders say nothing about your commitment to community service, admissions officers will become suspicious. If you present yourself in your personal statement as a challenge-seeker and a risk-taker who loves to learn, but your transcript shows you have never taken an advanced or AP course, your application contradicts itself.

If your essay is excessively polished with million-dollar words scattered throughout, but no recommender says you are the next Shakespeare, Mark Twain, or Toni Morrison, you may leave them wondering who wrote what. Most admissions officers read through hundreds (if not thousands) of applications a year, so they get very good at spotting holes or inconsistencies in your story. ■

BIO *Bruce Poch is Dean of Admissions and Executive Director of College Counseling at Chadwick School. He is the former Vice President and Dean of Admissions at Pomona College.*

advice

COLLEGE APPLICATIONS

Steven Shi
Brown University
Hometown: Grove city, PA

"The quality of your applications will forge the next stage of your life (and possibly the rest of it), so do what your limitless self can but remember that your future is now legitimately in your hands and you have unbounded possibilities before you."

– Living In The Present

Gina Bolanos
University of Rochester
Hometown: Dallas, TX

"Something I did while writing my applications, I thought about what is something people haven't said before; what makes you, YOU? Everybody has a story to tell, and it is your chance to let the admission committee know why you're amazing and why they should be happy to have you on their campus."

– On the Road to Success

Visit www.ImFirst.org to follow the student blog and watch video testimonials from first-generation college students and graduates.

Every Transcript Tells a Story

Colleges can tell more about you from your transcript than you think. How are you performing in comparison to the other students at your high school? Has your attendance been consistent? Have you become more or less motivated as a student? Are you challenging yourself? **Take a look at this transcript and we'll help you see what a college admissions officer sees.**

TRANSC

School District: Opportunity Public Schools
School Name: Opportunity High School
School Address: 1000 Graduation Road NE, Washington DC 20000
School Principal: Jane J. Opportunity

Course Title	Mark	Credit Earn
School Year 2010-2011	**Grade: 9**	
English I	A	1.00
Algebra II	B-	1.00
Biology I	B	1.00
Physical Education I	A	0.50
World History I	B+	0.50
World History II	A-	0.50
Studio Art I	B	0.5
JROTC	A-	0.5
2010-2011 GPA: 3.5 **2010-2011 Weighted GPA: 3.5**	**Days Absent: 4** **Days Tardy: 2**	**Credits: 5.**
School Year 2011-2012		**Grade: 1**
English II	B+	
Pre-calculus/Trigonometry	B-	
AP Studio Art	A-	
Physics I	C+	
US Government	B-	
Music Theory I	B-	
JROTC	A-	
2011-2012 GPA: 2.9 **2010-2011 Weighted GPA: 3.1**	**Days Absent: 12** **Days Tardy: 16**	**Cre**

Absences

Many high schools record your absences and tardies on your transcript so colleges can see how consistently you are attending school. A pattern of absences or tardies may be a red flag. If you know this will stand out on your transcript, think about writing a statement (or having a qualified adult write one) explaining the reason for your absences.

Weighted GPA

Your weighted GPA gives more value to your advanced and AP classes. That way, your GPA doesn't suffer because you made the decision to challenge yourself. Not all schools calculate weighted GPAs on your transcript (and some schools *only* calculate weighted GPAS), so check your transcript to see what appears.

Course Rigor

Your transcript will usually show the level of rigor of your courses. AP and advanced classes will be noted so that colleges can see how you are challenging yourself.

Graduation Date: 5/30/2014
Credits Earned: 16.5
Cumulative GPA: 3.3
Class Rank: 24 out of 216

T

…dent Name: John Success
…dent Address: 500 Opportunity Lane SE,
…Washington, DC 20000
…udent Phone: 555-555-5555
…ender: Male
…irthdate: 09/08/1994

Course Title	Grade: 11	Mark	Credit Earned
School Year 2012-2013			
AP English Literature		A	1.0
Calculus I		B+	1.0
AP European History		A-	1.0
Economics I		A-	0.5
Adv. Biology II		A	1.0
Music Theory II		A-	0.5
JROTC		A	0.5

2011-2012 GPA: 3.7
2010-2011 Weighted GPA: 4.0
Days Absent: 2
Days Tardy: 2
Credits: 5.5

Grade: 12

School Year 2013-2014

AP English Language
AP United States History
AP Statistics
Chemistry I
JROTC
Choir

Signature of School Official: ________

Class Rank

Class rank allows colleges to see how competitive you are within your high school. This allows them to understand how you measure up compared to students who likely come from the same community and take similar courses. Again, not all high schools will give out this information.

Electives

Schools look at your electives to get an idea of your talents and passions. This student has been enrolled in JROTC for his entire high school career, so a college might expect him to have a deep commitment to and interest in this area.

Academic Trends

Colleges will be looking at how your grades change over time. This student's grades slipped in his sophomore year, but they improved markedly in his junior year. This raises questions for admissions officers (what caused the slip?) but also shows them your ability to improve over time (the student addressed the problem that caused his grades to fall). Grades that consistently worsen over time are a major red flag.

Your Senior Year

When you apply to college in the fall, your senior grades may not have come in yet, but your currently enrolled courses will appear on your transcript so schools know what you are taking. Some colleges will require you to submit a first semester grade report as well.

try it Now it's your turn to use what you've learned.
Turn to page 80

Standardized Tests: What's in a Score?

Most four-year colleges and universities require students to submit standardized test scores. Primarily, these institutions want to see either SAT or ACT scores, while selective schools may require additional tests as well.

Test	Subjects Tested	When should I take it?	Why is it important?
PSAT	Evidence-Based Reading and Writing • Reading Test • Writing and Language Test Math	Most students take the PSAT in the fall of their sophomore or junior year.	Schools may recruit you based on your scores, and if they are high enough, they may also qualify you for a National Merit Scholarship.
SAT	Evidence-Based Reading and Writing • Reading Test • Writing and Language Test Math Essay (optional)	It's a good idea to take the SAT in the spring of your junior year and in the fall of your senior year.	Most schools require the SAT or the ACT.
SAT Subject Test	Various specific subjects (e.g. U.S. History or Biology) Log onto http://sat.collegeboard.org/about-tests/sat-subject-tests to see the full list of tests available.	Because these tests are content specific, you should try to take them as soon as possible after you take a high school class in the same subject. (e.g. if you take Physics in junior year, you should take the Physics subject test the spring of that same year).	Many selective institutions require one or more subject tests. They show mastery of specific content, and often students can choose to take those tests they will score the best in.
PLAN	English Math Reading Science	PLAN is administered to students in their sophomore year.	PLAN helps you to see where your strengths and gaps are as a test-taker so you can better prepare yourself for the ACT.
ACT	English Math Reading Science	It's a good idea to take the ACT in the spring of your junior year and in the fall of your senior year.	Most schools require the SAT or the ACT.

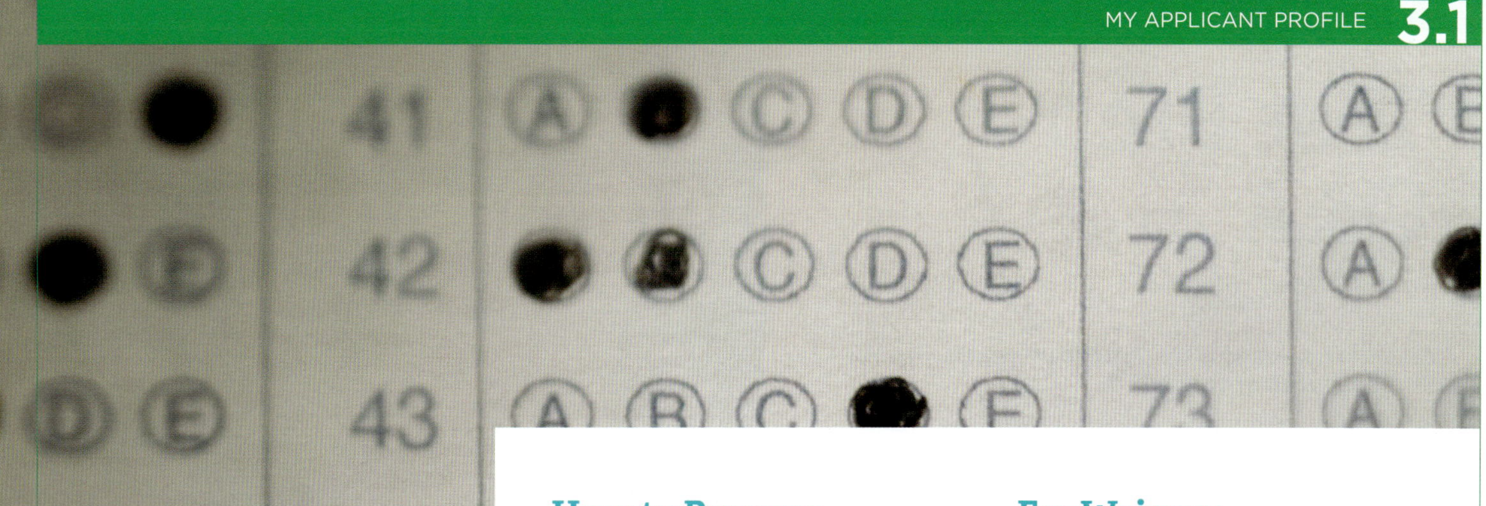

How to Prepare

Just like you should never take a test at school without studying, you shouldn't try to take standardized tests without preparing ahead. It's not uncommon for high school juniors and seniors to spend upwards of eight hours a week studying for their standardized exams months beforehand. Even if other students at your school aren't studying on their own time, that doesn't mean you shouldn't. Remember, when it comes to college admissions, you'll be competing against everybody, not just the students at your school.

On the following page, you'll find more tips on preparing for standardized tests. Remember to also check whether or not your school offers test prep classes for credit or after school.

Register On Time!

You need to register to take standardized tests at least a month beforehand (except for the PSAT, which is usually offered through schools) to avoid paying late registration fees. Many students register for their tests earlier so they can get their preferred testing location. Registering online is the fastest and easiest way to confirm your attendance. The College Board—the organization that administers the SAT—requires that you have a digital photo on hand to submit with your registration.

Fee Waivers

Taking standardized tests costs money, but it doesn't have to. Guidance counselors are provided with fee waivers for the SAT, ACT, and SAT Subject Tests so that students can register and send their scores to their college choices free of charge. Students can use two waivers for each test. Be sure to ask your guidance counselor about obtaining a fee waiver before you register.

What to Bring

On the day of the test, make sure to give yourself half an hour cushion time to ensure you arrive early. Dress in loose, layered clothes so you won't be too hot, too cold, or uncomfortable. Bring:

- Your admissions ticket
- A photo ID
- Number 2 Pencils with erasers
- A bottle of water and a snack for break

Do NOT bring any electronics with you to the test! If you are found to have an electronic, you will be asked to leave the testing site and your scores will be cancelled.

ARE YOU READY FOR COLLEGE Quiz

My high school grades are more important than my standardized test (ACT, PSAT, & SAT) scores.

TRUE FALSE

TRUE Colleges know that your performance in high school is a better predictor of college success than the standardized tests. That does not mean that most colleges will ignore your test scores.

Test Prep Q&A

By Jay Rosner

Q: When should a student start preparing for the SAT and/or the ACT?

A: Some students start as early as freshman year, but I generally suggest that students start planning their preparation for the SAT or ACT the summer between sophomore and junior year. Most students will pick a target SAT or ACT test date occurring in the spring of their junior year, depending on the rest of their schedule. By taking the SAT or ACT in the spring of the junior year, the student has several opportunities to retake the test in the late spring or fall, if that is desirable.

Q: How much time does it take to prepare for these tests?

A: Students should prepare most intensively in the 6-8 weeks immediately prior to their target test date. Students can begin their study of vocabulary and brush up on basic arithmetic, algebra, and geometry skills prior to that intensive test prep period.

Q: Are there low cost ways to prep?

A: There are two primary low-cost options for test prep available to everyone. The first is to use two books: a book featuring methods and techniques for answering test questions (like Princeton Review's Cracking the SAT), along with a book containing lots of real test questions (the College Board's Official SAT Study Guide). Copies of these books can be found in many libraries. The second option is to use one of the several free test prep programs on the internet.

Be careful with online prep — the official SAT (and ACT) are in pencil and paper format, and the online learning and practicing format is different from the actual testing experience. Some students have access to low cost test prep programs provided by their school or in their community.

BIO *Jay Rosner is an admissions test expert. As Executive Director of the Princeton Review Foundation, he specializes in preparing and coaching underrepresented minority students for tests such as the SAT, ACT, GMAT, GRE, MCAT and LSAT.*

Test Optional Admissions

By Bob Schaeffer

Did you know that there are a growing number of "test-optional" colleges and universities that are creating more opportunities for first-generation, low-income, and minority applicants seeking higher education?

There are 850 accredited, bachelor-degree granting schools that do not require all or many applicants to submit SAT or ACT results before making admissions decisions. These schools want to recruit young people with skills and talents that are not measured well by filling in multiple-choice bubbles.

They recognize that teenagers who are from low-income backgrounds or are among the first in their families to consider college often have solid academic records, but not super-high exam scores. Whether the reason is test bias, lack of access to high-priced coaching courses, or simply not testing well, these schools are worth considering in your college search.

Beware of one wrinkle. Some colleges and universities, including a number that are test-optional for admission, do require test scores for some "merit" scholarships. But many make meeting your financial need their top priority.

Test-optional admissions can open additional doors to college and beyond. It's up to you to take advantage of these great opportunities!

To see the full variety of choices available to you in the test-optional universe, check out http://www.fairtest.org/university/optional. There, you can view free lists of colleges and universities that do not need to see your SAT/ACT scores listed in alphabetical, state-by-state, and printable formats.

Be careful to follow the footnotes. Some programs require students to meet requirements, such as ranking in the top quarter of their high school class, posting "B" average grades, or submitting a graded writing project, to qualify for test-optional consideration.

BIO *Bob Schaeffer is the Public Education Director of the National Center for Fair & Open Testing (FairTest). He is coauthor of Standing Up to the SAT and Test Scores Do Not Equal Merit: Enhancing Equity & Excellence in College Admissions by Deemphasizing SAT and ACT Results.*

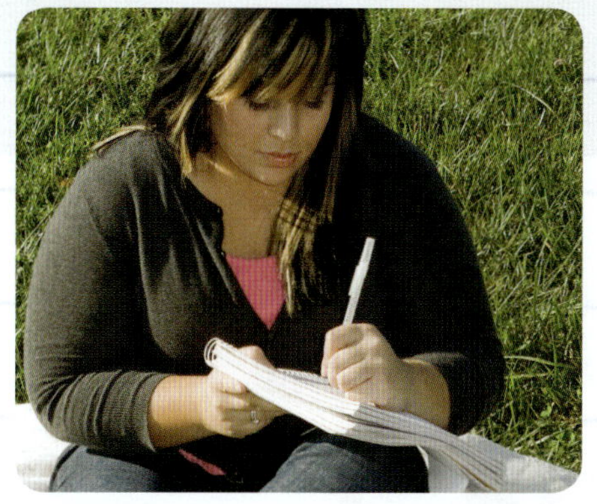

The College Essay

Your GPA and standardized test scores are important in the college admissions process, but you are more than a test score. While many people perceive the college admissions process as a "numbers game," most colleges want to know more about the person you are. They want to admit students who will add diverse perspectives and come with unique life experiences.

Your college essay, often known as a personal statement, is the best (and often only) chance you'll have to show off these aspects of your personality. As a first-generation college student, you have likely overcome obstacles and had experiences that most other college applicants haven't, and the college essay is the best place to express those parts of your personality.

Here are some things you need to know before you begin writing.

- **Narrative:** A personal statement is not the same as an academic essay, so throw out everything you know about thesis statements and supporting evidence. The personal statement is a narrative essay, meaning an essay that tells a story.
- **Voice:** The college essay does not have to be written in a strictly formal language. It should be written from the first person and should portray a strong sense of voice. Your personality should show through your writing; your best friend should be able to read your essay and know who wrote it.
- **Length:** Most personal statements are required to be under 650 words. Pay close attention to your word count before you submit (but don't fret if your first draft is too long), and make every word count!
- **Topic:** Personal statements can be written about almost anything, but they need to be almost microscopic in focus. In other words, anchor your essay to a specific place in time and fill it with lots of concrete details to help your reader relate and visualize. Write your essay on a topic that is unique to your life and shows off positive aspects of your personality.

Supplemental Essays

Many selective schools require their applicants to write more than one essay (even those accepting the Common Application). You should spend just as much time and effort on these essays as you do on your primary essay. The school wouldn't ask you to write it if they weren't going to look closely at your answer.

Often colleges will ask applying students to write an essay about why they want to attend their institution and/or what the student will add to the campus. When answering these questions, be sure to do your research and make your essay as specific as possible. "I am drawn by Best Fit College's cutting edge research facilities and reputation for hands-on learning" sounds better than "Best Fit College has lots of great academic programs."

To give you an idea of what you might be writing about, check out the prompt options for the 2017-18 Common Application (remember, you'll only pick one!):

Common Application Prompts:

1. Some students have a background, identity, interest, or talent that is so meaningful they believe their application would be incomplete without it. If this sounds like you, then please share your story.

2. The lessons we take from obstacles we encounter can be fundamental to later success. Recount a time when you faced a challenge, setback, or failure. How did it affect you, and what did you learn from the experience?

3. Reflect on a time when you questioned or challenged a belief or idea. What prompted your thinking? What was the outcome?

4. Describe a problem you've solved or a problem you'd like to solve. It can be an intellectual challenge, a research query, an ethical dilemma - anything that is of personal importance, no matter the scale. Explain its significance to you and what steps you took or could be taken to identify a solution.

5. Discuss an accomplishment, event, or realization that sparked a period of personal growth and a new understanding of yourself or others.

6. Describe a topic, idea, or concept you find so engaging that it makes you lose all track of time. Why does it captivate you? What or who do you turn to when you want to learn more?

7. Share an essay on any topic of your choice. It can be one you've already written, one that responds to a different prompt, or one of your own design.

The Common Application is a membership organization of over 750 institutions that provides a common, standardized online application for First-year and Transfer Applications.

The College Essay Do's and Don'ts

DO

- Analyze the prompt and rewrite it in your own words before beginning your essay
- Begin with a strong "hook" to pull your reader into your essay
- Write about a subject you are passionate about
- Choose a topic and a subject that is unique to you and displays positive aspects of your personality, such as perseverance, courage, sense of humor, etc.
- Focus your essay on one specific scene or point in time
- Use a rich, vivid vocabulary with lots of figurative language and sensory details
- Write in the first person
- Use dialogue when appropriate
- Show your thinking and learning process throughout the essay
- End with a sense of closure, like a lesson learned
- Proofread your own essay by reading out loud
- Ask others to read your essay and give their feedback

DON'T

- Answer only part of the prompt
- Use clichés to start your essay (or at any point in your essay!)
- Write about a topic because it's easy or obvious
- Choose a subject that many other people can write about
- Try to tell your whole life story in your essay
- Use your essay only to brag about your accomplishments or make excuses for bad grades
- Write "he said," "she said" dialogue
- Use slang, vulgarity, or curse words
- Plagiarize essays or part of essays from any source
- Use a thesaurus extensively to try to make yourself sound smart
- Start every sentence with "I"
- End your essay exactly the way it began
- Go above the specified word count
- Send your essay without proofreading it and having at least three others review it

ON THE SPOT: What strengths do you have as a writer? What areas of growth do you think you'll need to work on in your personal statement?

Steps to Writing Your College Essay

Now that you know what the personal statement is and what you can write on, it's time to start planning your essay. Easier said than done, right?

Follow these steps to get started.

1. Pick your prompt: If you're responding to the Common Application prompts, you'll need to choose which topic to write on. (If you are using an independent school application or writing a supplemental essay, you may not have a choice.) Give yourself time to decide. You may want to narrow it down to two or three prompts and create an outline for each to see which topic you think will make for the best essay. Go with the one that will yield the most original story that tells the most about your personality. Rewrite your chosen prompt in your own words before beginning.

ON THE SPOT: What topic or experience sticks out to you as something you might like to write about? What will this essay show readers about your personality?

try it Check out the Common Application essay prompts. **Turn to page 69**

2. Outline your essay: Once you know what prompt you will write on, it's time to plan your response. Before you write your first draft, you'll need to think about:

- **Tone:** What kind of tone will you establish in your essay? Will it be humorous? Nostalgic? Hopeful?
- **Personality:** What aspects of your personality do you want your essay to highlight? Does your essay show your ability to persevere through tough times? How you have matured over time? Your passion for a certain hobby?
- **Scene:** What scene will you write about? Although college essays can be about a long-term theme or event in your life (for example growing up in foster homes), your reflection on this topic should be anchored in one or two particular scenes (for example your first night in your foster home). This makes the content of your essay more easily accessible to your readers. Make sure you think of sensory details to add to your scene. What do you want readers to be able to feel? Hear? See? Smell?
- **Main Idea:** Personal statements don't necessarily include thesis statements, but they do have some overarching main idea they convey. For instance, if you are writing about your move to America, your main idea might be that integrating into a new culture can be very hard.
- **Conclusion:** Remember that your essay should show some kind of thinking process, so that the main idea you begin with should grow and change with your essay. Often, the conclusion takes the form of a lesson learned or a realization made. For instance, using the example above, your conclusion might be about how although fitting into a new culture is hard, it makes you a stronger and more well-rounded person.

3. Draft your essay: Once you have a strong outline, it's time to draft your essay. Remember to start with a "hook" to grab your readers' attention. Don't spend a lot of time worrying about making everything perfect. Just get your thoughts organized on paper for now.

4. Get feedback and rewrite: Once you have a first draft, share your essay with peers, family, teachers, or mentors—whoever you feel comfortable with. Ask them for their ideas for improvement. Once you have their feedback, write your second draft. Repeat this process until you are happy with your essay.

5. Proofread: Now go through your essay with a fine-toothed comb. Look for grammar, spelling, mechanics, word choice, etc. Have a mentor or teacher proofread with you. Don't submit until you are satisfied that you have done your best and your essay is error-free.

Timeline

You should start planning your personal statements the summer before your senior year. (Wait until the upcoming year's application is released—otherwise you might end up writing on the wrong prompt.) Give yourself at least a month before the essay is due to move through drafting, rewriting, and proofreading process. So if you are applying for a November 1st deadline, start drafting by October 1st.

try it Now it's your turn to use what you've learned. **Turn to page 82**

Let Me Introduce Myself

Your personal statement is likely the best shot you'll get at showing admissions officers your personality, your passions and motivations, and what life experiences have shaped your world perspective.

But all too often, admissions officers are overwhelmed by the number of applications they have to read. The truth is, if your essay doesn't get off to a strong start fast, your application reader may become quickly disinterested and simply skim through the rest of your statement.

That's why it is crucially important to start with a creative hook that will pull your readers in and make them curious to read the rest of your essay: a vivid image, a striking statement, a compelling question, etc. Does your opening sentence cause your reader to ask questions? It should. A simple thesis statement like you might write for your academic essays won't do the trick.

To help you on your way, here are some hooks from actual essays written by Stanford University admitted students.

> Does your opening sentence cause your reader to ask questions? It should.

ON THE SPOT: Which of these hooks is your favorite or the most interesting to you? Why?

"Unlike many mathematicians, I live in an irrational world; I feel that my life is defined by a certain amount of irrationalities that bloom too frequently, such as my brief foray in front of 400 people without my pants."

"I almost didn't live through September 11th, 2001."

"When I was in eighth grade I couldn't read."

"While traveling through the daily path of life, have you ever stumbled upon a hidden pocket of the universe?"

"The spaghetti burbled and slushed around the pan, and as I stirred it, the noises it gave off began to sound increasingly like bodily functions."

"Cancer tried to defeat me, and it failed."

"I have old hands."

"Flying over enemy territory, I took in Beirut's beautiful skyline and wondered if under different circumstances I would have hopped on a bus and come here for my vacation. Instead, I saw the city from the window of a helicopter, in military uniform, my face camouflaged, on my way to a special operation deep behind enemy lines."

"My younger sister, Jessica, arrived home one day reeling about the shirt that her friend had worn to school. It had simply read, "Genocide, Homicide, Suicide, Riverside."

"Some fathers might disapprove of their children handling noxious chemicals in the garage."

"I was paralyzed from the waist down. I would try to move my leg or even shift an ankle but I never got a response. This was the first time thoughts of death ever crossed my mind."

"As an Indian-American, I am forever bound to the hyphen."

"I have been surfing Lake Michigan since I was 3 years old."

"On a hot Hollywood evening, I sat on a bike, sweltering in a winter coat and furry boots."

"I change my name each time I place an order at Starbucks."

Adapted from "Let Me Introduce Myself: First lines from the application essays of Stanford's newest class." Originally published in STANFORD magazine. Reprinted with permission.

Extracurricular Activities

Sure, colleges care about your GPA and SAT scores. They want students who will be able to handle college coursework. But admissions officers are also looking for students who will add something to their school's student body. When they look at your extracurricular involvement, they are looking to see if you might be the next student body president, the next alto soprano in the accapella group, or the next editor of the newspaper.

Keep these tips in mind when you're putting together your list of extracurriculars.

Emphasize Leadership

Have you been a team captain? Student body officer? Club president? Shift manager? Lead counselor? Make sure you emphasize your leadership positions and responsibilities in your description of your extracurricular involvement. It shows colleges you have the potential to become a leader on campus. And if you haven't yet held a leadership position, now is the perfect time to put your name in the running for student government elections, or to tell your coach you'd like some extra responsibility this semester.

Work Experience/Family Responsibilities

Not all students are able to participate in activities like clubs and sports because they have to work or support their family in other ways. Remember that work experience and family responsibilities can be counted as an extracurricular and should definitely be noted on your application. Drawing attention to your work experience or how many hours a week you cared for younger siblings shows colleges why you were not able to participate in other common extracurriculars, but more importantly it shows them that you possess responsibility and maturity.

Show Commitment

Lots of students get involved with numerous extracurricular activities because they think it will make them look like a well-rounded student. In reality, most colleges would rather see a student who has been very committed to a few extracurriculars than one who is a member of ten different clubs but only spends one hour a week with each and quits at the end of the semester.

Highlight Service

Most high schools have some kind of community service requirement for students, and some colleges do as well. If you've completed any volunteer work during your high school career, make sure to list it as an extracurricular. Service work shows that a student wants to give back to their community and will most likely be a productive and responsible member of the student body.

Recommendation Letters

Most four-year colleges require at least two letters of recommendation.

Not sure who to ask to write them or how to ask? See the tips below.

Who to Ask?

Most four-year colleges require at least one letter of recommendation from a counselor and one from a teacher. Selective schools may require three or even four letters. Make sure to pay careful attention to how many letters you need to send to each college, and who needs to write them.

In general, your writers should be adults who have known you in an academic or professional capacity (not your family!) for an extended period of time and who are still involved in your education, work, or extracurricular activities. They can obviously be teachers and counselors, but depending on the school they can also be administrators, coaches, work supervisors, etc.

You should request letters from those adults you have a good relationship with and who have seen the best aspects of your personality. Additionally, your writers should be people you trust to have your best interests and to get the job done right. Adults (like kids!) can be very busy, and if you and your writers don't have a strong relationship, your letter may fall to the bottom of their to-do list, or they may write a sub-par recommendation.

How to Ask?

- **Provide a written request:** A request in writing will show your recommender that you are serious about applying and will help them to remember to complete your letter. Additionally, you can use your request to add in some details about your personal and academic achievements that your recommender might use in their letter.
- **Provide a copy of your résumé:** Along with your request letter, give your recommender your résumé. This will give your recommender more material to write about.
- **Ask in advance:** Respect your recommender's time. Writing an excellent recommendation letter takes time. Request your letter a month in advance of the due date.
- **Remind your recommender:** Your recommender may need a courteous reminder of when the letter is due and how it should be delivered (online, by mail, etc.). While you don't want to be demanding, it is fine to politely ask your recommender for updates and ask that he or she let you know when it has been sent.

try it Now it's your turn to use what you've learned. **Turn to page 84**

The College Interview

Along with the college essay, the college interview is a great venue to show off your personality.

You'll get to meet with someone from the college (or a representative of the college), and tell your story, talk about your passions, and explain your reasons for wanting to attend the college.

Do I Have to Interview?

Many schools don't offer interviews to prospective students at all. Those that do may or may not require students to do interviews. Even if a college doesn't require one, it is recommended. The interview can make your application stand out from the rest and distinguish you as an individual (especially if the college in question has their admissions officers conduct interviews!).

How Do I Schedule an Interview?

Go online and look at the college's website. Under their "Admissions" or "Prospective Students" tab, there should be information about how to schedule an interview.

try it Now it's your turn to use what you've learned.
Turn to page 85

What if I Can't Travel to the School?

Many schools that offer interviews also have the option of doing alumni interviews. If you can't travel to the college, you can often schedule an interview with an alumni in your area. (If you are rural or international, this may be more difficult to do, however some schools are starting to offer interviews via Skype or other interface software. Contact the school's admissions office for further guidance.)

Tips for Your Interview

Here are some helpful tips to keep in mind to make sure your interview goes well:

- **Practice.** Whether it's in the mirror at home or with a trusted teacher or friend, you should practice answering common interview questions beforehand. When you practice with others, you can get feedback on how to improve your answers.
- **Do your research.** The most common interview question is probably "why do you want to attend this school?" Make sure you have scoped out the school extensively (which you should have already done, of course!) and have a detailed answer prepared.
- **Be aware of yourself.** We all have nervous habits. Some people tap their foot when they get anxious. Others bite their nails. Identify your nervous habits so you can make a conscious effort to avoid them during the interview.
- **Dress well.** You know that pair of jeans you've had forever? The ones with all the holes? Now is not the time to drag them out of your closet. You don't have to wear a suit and tie or a formal gown, but you should look professional. Avoid t-shirts, tank tops, jeans, or anything too short or tight.
- **Be polite.** Be courteous during your interview. Remember to say "please" and "thank you" and to send a thank you e-mail or card to your interviewer after the fact.
- **Prepare questions.** There is so much to learn about a college before making your decision to attend, and some of it can't be found online. If you don't have any questions about the school, it shows a lack of interest on your part. Have at least three prepared.
- **Be yourself.** You will likely be nervous in your interview, but try to keep cool. Your interviewer just wants to get to know you, so relax and let your true colors shine through.

Social Media Manners and Etiquette 101

By Chelsea Jones

Follow us on social media @Strive4C @ImFirstGen

High school students today are always on their cell phones texting, tweeting, Facebooking, following, and liking. We know it's fun! However, sharing too much can affect your chances of getting that job or even an acceptance letter to college. More and more, employers and colleges are using social media to scope you out. Here are a few tips to keep your online image fun, yet respectable.

Profile Pictures: Should you be in your Facebook profile picture making an inappropriate gesture or partying? Probably not. Your profile picture is the first encounter someone has with you while browsing your page, and you know that saying, "First impressions are everything"? It is absolutely true. You may be an extremely intelligent and hardworking person, but the Twitter profile picture of you smoking from a hookah will rub admissions officers the wrong way. Try posting a simple and clear headshot of yourself.

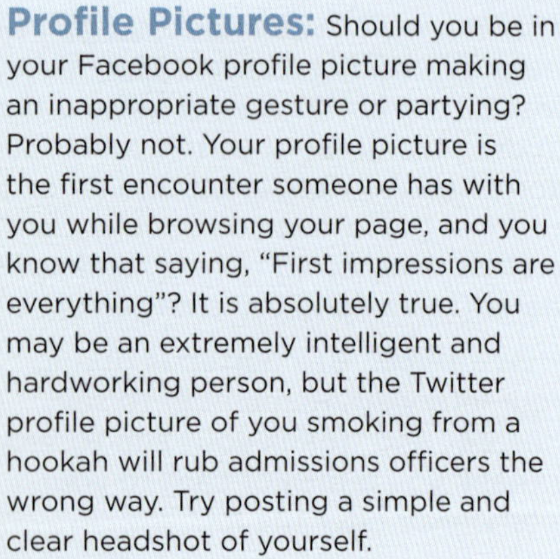

Profanity: You wouldn't use that language in front of your mother, so don't do it on social media! What you say in your Facebook status and in your tweets reflect who you are and how you feel. Potential employers and colleges want an individual who will represent their institution well. What others write on your wall also reflects the type of people you associate with. If your friend Kyle from back home drops an inappropriate comment on your Facebook wall, delete it.

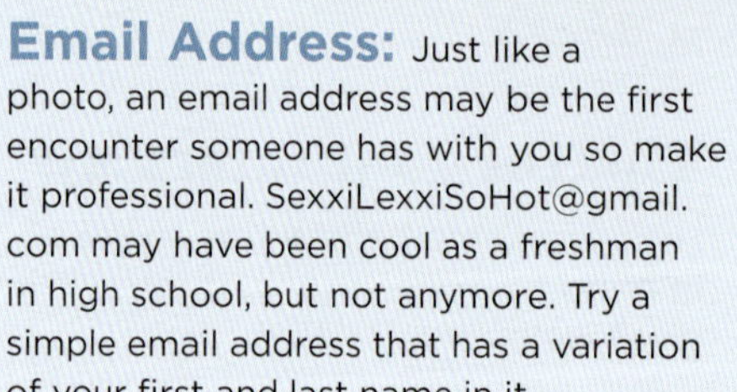

Email Address: Just like a photo, an email address may be the first encounter someone has with you so make it professional. SexxiLexxiSoHot@gmail.com may have been cool as a freshman in high school, but not anymore. Try a simple email address that has a variation of your first and last name in it.

Voicemail: This may not be social media, but it is also very important to have an appropriate voicemail recording. No college recruiter wants to listen to an entire Lady Gaga song before they are able to leave a message on your phone. When setting up a voice message recording on your cell phone or landline, make sure there is no background noise and that you speak clearly and slowly.

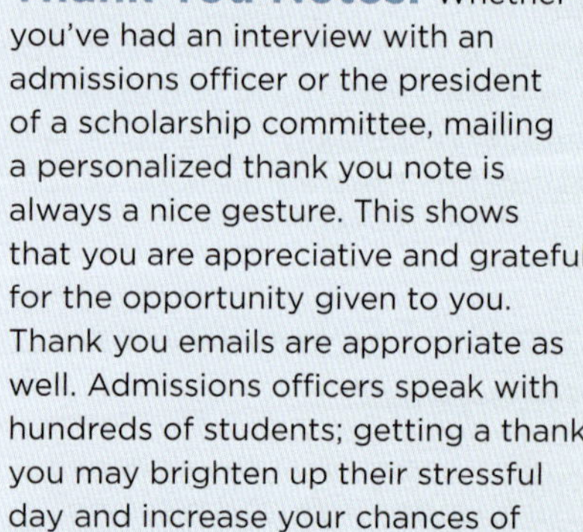

Thank You Notes: Whether you've had an interview with an admissions officer or the president of a scholarship committee, mailing a personalized thank you note is always a nice gesture. This shows that you are appreciative and grateful for the opportunity given to you. Thank you emails are appropriate as well. Admissions officers speak with hundreds of students; getting a thank you may brighten up their stressful day and increase your chances of getting that acceptance letter or scholarship. ■

BIO *Chelsea Jones is a former Community Manager at Strive for College.*

Application Timeline: When to Apply to College

So you've finalized your list of colleges to apply to. Now what?

Before senior year begins (or as soon as possible after!) it's time to plan out your application timeline. Before you do that, however, it's important to be aware of the various types of deadlines colleges use.

Early Decision Deadline

Early decision applications are usually due between October and December of your senior year, and they are binding, which means if you get accepted to a school where you apply early decision, you are contractually obligated to attend. For this reason, you should only apply to an early decision school if you are sure it's your number one choice. If you are accepted, you will be asked to withdraw all your applications at other schools, even if they haven't yet been processed. Be sure to ask your admissions counselor what the school's policy is if you are accepted early decision but are not given enough financial aid to attend.

If you are certain of your choice, however, early decision applications can be a great option. If you receive an acceptance, you will be able to focus your spring semester on applying for scholarships rather than waiting to hear back from schools. Additionally, some colleges have higher acceptance rates for early decision applicants (most schools would rather accept students who will definitely accept their offer than ones who might say no).

Early Action Deadline

Early action applications are usually due between October and December of your senior year, but are non-binding. In other words, you can still decide not to accept the offer if you're admitted. Keep in mind, though, that the deadlines for making your decision are usually earlier than regular decision deadlines, so you may still have to make your decision about the school before you hear back from your other options.

Regular Deadline

While not all schools offer early decision or early action deadlines, most of them have a regular decision deadline. Generally this deadline is sometime between January and April of your senior year, though a handful of schools have deadlines as late as July. This application is non-binding.

Rolling Deadline

If a school offers "rolling" admissions that means it accepts applications throughout a range of dates. Generally, the earlier you apply, the better. Rolling deadline decisions are non-binding, so there's no disadvantage to applying earlier. Applying later in the cycle can put you at a disadvantage when it comes to getting financial aid.

On-Site Admissions

Some schools will offer "on-site" admission to select students during campus open-houses, college fairs, or high school visits. This form of admission can be offered throughout the year. Keep in mind, however, that you should never accept an offer of admission made on the spot (and an admissions officer should never ask you for your decision in the moment). Just because it's easy doesn't mean it's your best option, and you still need time to think and do your research.

try it Now it's your turn to use what you've learned. **Turn to page 86**

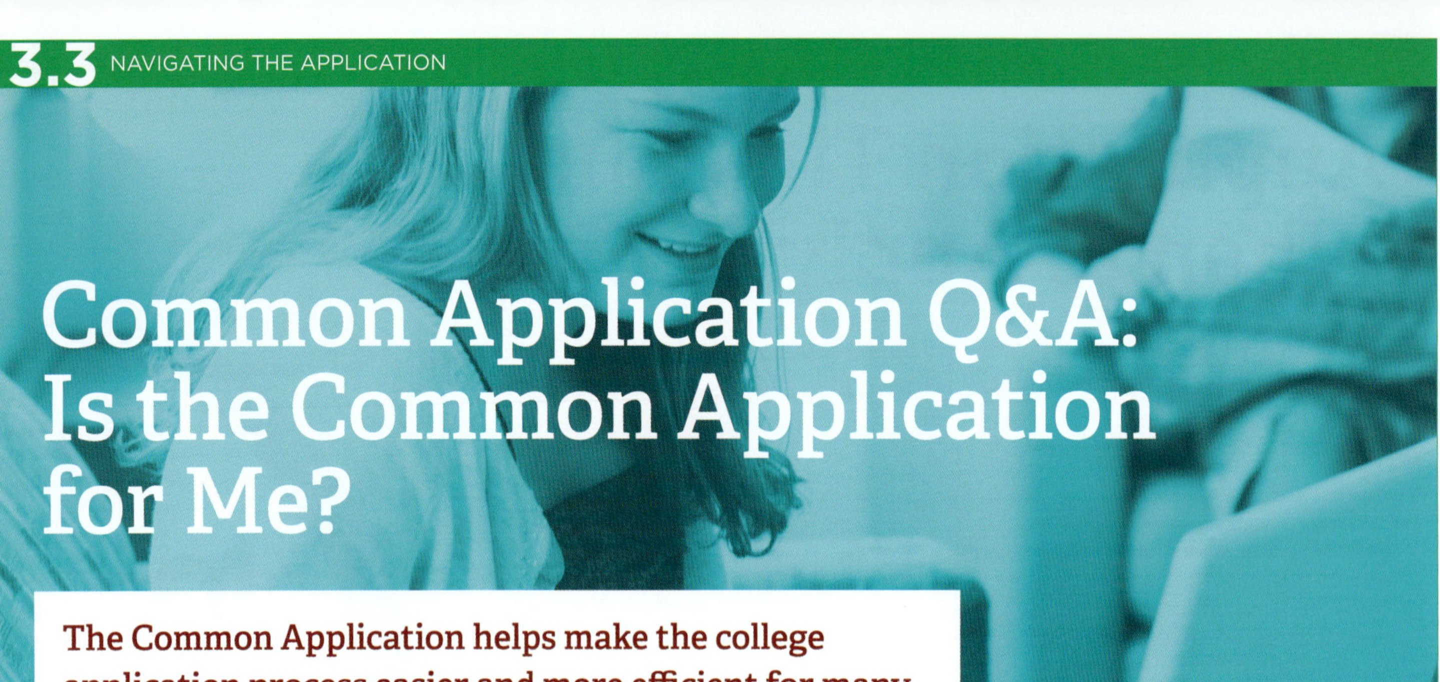

Common Application Q&A: Is the Common Application for Me?

The Common Application helps make the college application process easier and more efficient for many students. Here's everything you need to know:

What is the Common Application?

The Common Application is an online application that is accepted by more than 750 colleges and universities in the United States and around the world. It is also your admissions and financial aid resource hub with free tools on how to prepare and pay for college. The Common App allows you to connect to more schools than any other application system. You enter your applicant information one time and share it across all of your schools.

While colleges use the Common App to make the process of applying to college more straight forward, they also see it as the proven way to reach and support students from all backgrounds, especially students who will be the first in their family to attend college.

As a student, you can create your Common App account at any time. Your account will roll over from year to year, using the same user name and password. Go to commonapp.org to get started and for free resources on planning and paying for college, searching for schools, and successfully completing your applications.

How do I know if a school I'm applying to accepts the Common Application?

You can search for the school by clicking the "Explore Colleges" button on commonapp.org, in addition to finding this information on the college's website.

You can also download Common App onTrack, the free mobile companion to your Common App account (available for both iOS and Android). With Common App onTrack you can search for Common App schools, add them to your college list, see your submission status for each application, and receive push notifications for upcoming deadlines and other important reminders.

The school I'm applying to accepts both the Common Application and their own application. Is there an advantage to doing one over the other?

More and more schools accept the Common App because the platform makes the admissions process more streamlined on both ends. Schools that offer both their own and the Common App do not have a preference.

The Common App also provides you with free 24/7 support for each step of the college admissions process. Contact appsupport.commonapp.org or appsupport@commmonapp.net if you need help with your Common App.

The school that I'm applying to accepts the Common Application but has a supplement. What is that?

Some schools want more information (and particularly additional essays) than required in the Common App. These schools provide their own additional section for you to complete within your Common App. Once you select your schools in the Common App, the individual school supplements will be automatically added onto your application.

What information do I need before I begin the Common Application?

Great question! Here's an overview of information you'll be asked for:

Printed with permission from The Common Application. Learn more at commonapp.org.

The following displays the sections and pages within The Common Application. It is designed to familiarize students with the information they will be asked to report and is not intended to be a comprehensive collection of all questions within the application.

PROFILE

Contacts - *Email address, phone number, mailing address*

Demographics - *Religion, military service, race/ethnicity (all optional)*

Geography - *Birthplace, countries lived in, language proficiency, citizenship*

FAMILY

Household - *Parent marital status, parent(s) with whom you reside*

Parent and/or Guardian - *Name, birthplace, occupation, education, stepparent information*

Siblings - *Age, grade, education*

EDUCATION

School - *Current school, dates attended; counselor name, phone, and email*

History - *Previous schools, dates attended, past/pending education interruptions (e.g. time off, early graduation, gap year, etc.), college courses, college assistance programs*

Academic Information - *GPA, class rank, current year courses, honors and awards*

TESTING

College Entrance - *ACT and SAT*

English For Non-Native Speakers - *TOEFL, IELTS, PTE Academic*

Academic Subjects - *AP, IB, SAT Subject Tests, A-Levels*

Other - *Optional reporting for other relevant 9-12 testing*

ACTIVITIES

Principal Activities/Work - *Years of participation, hours per week, weeks per year, position/leadership held (50 characters), brief description (150 characters). 10 activities maximum.*

WRITING

Personal Essay - *Select one of seven available prompts, 650 Words Maximum; each institution can determine whether to require the Personal Essay*

Disciplinary History - *Explanations regarding school discipline and misdemeanor or felony convictions*

Additional Information - *Relevant circumstances or qualifications not reflected elsewhere in the application*

COLLEGE-SPECIFIC QUESTIONS

General - *Entry term, degree status, housing preference, test-optional preference, scholarship and financial aid preference*

Academics - *Academic interest, program(s) applying to*

(Some colleges may also ask additional questions about your family, state of residence, activities, and general interests.)

COLLEGE WRITING SUPPLEMENTS

Writing Supplement - *Institutions have the option to include additional short answer or essay responses*

Analyzing My Student Profile

Use your transcripts, SAT/ACT scores, and extracurricular history to fill out the following information and start analyzing your applicant profile. When you are done filling out the profile, you will evaluate your own application using the questions on the next page.

I. Academic Qualifications

Freshman Year GPA: __________ Junior Year GPA: __________

Sophomore Year GPA: _________ Senior Year GPA: __________

Overall Unweighted GPA: ___________ Overall Weighted GPA: ______________ Class Rank: ________ out of _________

Advanced/AB/IB/Dual Enrollment Courses Taken	School Year	Score Earned (AP) and/or Grade Earned

List any academic awards earned. Include the year earned and a description of the award.
1.
2.
3.
4.
5.
6.
7.
8.
9.
10.

II. Extracurriculars & Leadership

Activity (club, team, service group, etc.)	Semester(s)/year(s)	Hours per week

Jobs/Internships I've Held (Position/ Employer)	Skills I Learned and Interests I Explored	What months/year(s) did I work here?

Summer Programs I've Participated In	Skills I Learned and Interests I Explored	What summer did I participate?

List any leadership positions that you have held in the above activities. Include the year earned and a description of your position.
1.
2.
3.
4.
5.
6.
7.
8.
9.
10.

III. Test Scores

	Score 1	Score 2	Score 3	Score 4
SAT Math				
SAT Reading				
SAT Writing				
	Score 1	**Score 2**	**Score 3**	**Score 4**
ACT English				
ACT Math				
ACT Science				
ACT Reading				
ACT Writing				

SAT Subject Test Taken	Score 1	Score 2

After completing your profile, go back and read through it as if you were an admissions officer deciding whether or not to accept your application. Answer the questions below in a few sentences.

1. What strengths do I have that will make me an attractive candidate for college admissions? What can I do to capitalize on those strengths?

2. What gaps do I see in my profile that might hold me back from getting into the schools that I want to apply to?

3. What am I going to do to address these gaps in my profile?

College Essay Brainstorming

Once you have chosen a prompt to write on, use the outline below to start brainstorming your college essay.

The main idea I will start with is...

The specific scene I will ground my essay in is...

The conclusion I come to is...

Aspects of my personality that I want to show...

Sensory details that I will use to help tell my story...

My tone will be...

How this essay will be unique from others...

Why this topic is important to me...

Recommendation Letter Request Template

Using the recommendation request template below, fill out your information to use as a rough draft for your letter.

Recommender's Name:

Recommender's Address:

Date:

Your Name:

Your Address:

Dear ____________________,

I hope this letter finds you well. I'm writing to you today because I am applying to college. For my application, I will need a letter of recommendation. I feel you would be the perfect person to write this recommendation letter because ____.

Going to college is important to me because I will be the first in my family to attend and ____.

While I am in college, I hope to study ____________________ and will strive to achieve my goals of ____.

In your letter, you may want to mention the following characteristics, which I feel that I embody: ____.

The letter is due ________, and must be submitted via __________. If you cannot write the letter, please let me know as soon as possible. I appreciate your time and effort in helping me achieve my dreams of becoming a college student.

Best wishes,

____

Practice Interview

The college interview can be one of the most nerve-wracking parts of the college application process, but it doesn't have to be. If you practice your answers ahead of time, you'll be ready for the real interview when the time comes and can let your personality shine!

Grab a partner and take turns asking and answering some of these common interview questions. Switch books and allow your partner to grade your interview and give written feedback in your book.

1. What are the three adjectives that best describe you?
2. What are you passionate about?
3. What's your favorite subject in school? What subject is most challenging for you?
4. What is your greatest achievement?
5. What was the most recent book you read? What did you think of it?
6. What is one current event that matters to you?
7. What did you contribute to your high school community?
8. What would you change about your high school?
9. Why do you want to attend this college?
10. What will you contribute to our campus?
11. What do you plan to study here? Why?
12. What are your future plans after college graduation?

	4 (Strong)	**3 (Good)**	**2 (Fair)**	**1 (Weak)**
Clarity of Answers				
Strength of Answers				
Academic / Professional Language Used				
Non-verbal Communication (eye contact, posture)				
Courteousness				
Things you did well: Things you could do better:				

My Application Timeline & Checklist

Timeline

Each college has different deadlines. Keep your important dates straight so you don't miss the boat on important deadlines!

DEADLINES	EXAMPLE	COLLEGE 1	COLLEGE 2	COLLEGE 3	COLLEGE 4
College Name					
Early Decision Deadline	11/1				
Early Action Deadline	11/1				
Regular Deadline	1/1				
Rolling Deadline	3/1				
Scholarship #1 Deadline	1/15				
Scholarship #2 Deadline	1/15				

Checklist

Have you completed the necessary requirements for applying to each of your potential colleges? Sometimes it can be hard to keep everything straight.

Use the checklist below to check off all of the requirements for your schools. If your potential college has additional requirements, use the blank rows at the bottom to keep track of them.

REQUIREMENTS	COLLEGE 1	COLLEGE 2	COLLEGE 3	COLLEGE 4
College Name				
Application submitted				
Application Supplement (if using Common Application) submitted				
Personal Statement #1 completed				
Personal Statement #2 completed				
Recommendation #1 sent				
Recommendation #2 sent				
Recommendation #3 sent				
Interview				
SAT/ACT scores sent				
SAT Subject Test scores sent				
Transcript sent				
Any additional requirements				

answers on page 136

Unit 3 Quiz

Multiple Choice, circle your answer

1. A great personal statement should always include:

a) reasons why you want to attend a certain school

b) excuses for why you did poorly in specific classes

c) a unique voice that shows off your distinct personality

d) reasons why a school should accept you

2. I should consider all of the following people to write recommendation letters for me except:

a) relatives

b) counselors

c) teachers

d) coaches

3. Extracurricular activities could include all of the following except:

a) sports teams

b) work or internships

c) community service

d) AP courses

4. Which of the following types of schools should all students apply to?

a) best-fit schools

b) likely schools

c) reach schools

d) all of the above

5. A student with a good GPA but low SAT/ACT scores should probably apply to:

a) community colleges

b) test-optional schools

c) liberal arts schools

d) public schools

True or False, circle your answer

1. Some college admissions teams might check my Facebook page or other social media sites.

T F

2. I can take my phone to the SAT/ACTs if I only plan to use for the calculator function.

T F

3. It's fine to submit a personal statement that is a few words over the word limit.

T F

4. Most selective colleges would rather admit a student who has shown commitment to a few extracurricular activities than a student who has dabbled in many extracurricular activities.

T F

5. Interviews are not required by most colleges.

T F

Fill in the Blank

1. The ____________________ is a web-based application accepted by over 700 colleges nationwide.

2. The single most important indicator to predicting student success in college is their ____________.

3. Great college essays begin with a creative ________________ to catch the reader's attention.

4. My GPA relative to other students in my grade at my school is called ____________.

5. The standardized tests that colleges most often require students to take to test knowledge in one specific subject area (e.g. world history) are called ____________.

continues on next page

continued from previous page

Open Answer

1. What extracurricular activity you've been involved in has been the most important to you? Why?

2. Name the six most important elements colleges consider in a student. For each element, list one thing colleges are able to learn about you.

Unit 4

How Will I Pay for College?

CONTENTS

"Pursuing scholarships and financial aid does not happen overnight. Rome was not built in a day, and only on very rare occasions will a student acquire all of the funds necessary to support a college education through one source."

Objectives

By the end of this unit, I will...

- define and compare the various types of financial aid available to me.
- understand the importance of the FAFSA and CSS Profiles and the steps I will need to take to complete them.
- search for and identify potential scholarships.
- know how to borrow for college responsibly.
- read and analyze a financial aid award letter.

Financial Aid: Lots of Options

Financial aid is any type of assistance used to pay college costs that is based on financial need. There are three main types:

Grants and Scholarships

Also called gift aid, grants don't have to be re-paid and you don't need to work to earn them. Grant aid comes from federal and state governments and from individual colleges. Scholarships are usually awarded based on merit. To search for scholarships, visit www.fastweb.com.

Work

Student employment and work-study aid helps students pay for education costs such as books, supplies, and personal expenses. Work-study is a federal program which provides students with part-time employment to help meet their financial needs and gives them work experience while serving their campuses and surrounding communities.

Loans

Most financial aid (54%) comes in the form of loans to students or parents—aid that must be re-paid. Most loans that are awarded based on financial need are low-interest loans sponsored by the federal government. These loans are subsidized by the government so no interest accrues until you begin repayment after you graduate.

Current Average College Costs

Average College Costs Per Year

Public, two-year: $8,928

Public, four-year: $15,022

Private, four-year: $39,173

Did you know that...

- About 60% of students attending public four-year colleges pay less than $6,000 for tuition and fees per year.
- 44% of all students attend two-year colleges. The average two-year public college student receives grant aid that reduces the average tuition to about $400.
- A record $135 billion in financial aid is available to students and their families.
- About 60% of all college students receive grant aid. Grant aid averaged $1,800 per student at two-year public colleges, $3,300 at four-year public colleges, and $9,600 at private four-year colleges.

Statistics for 2012-13. Source: U.S. Department of Education, National Center for Education Statistics (2015). Digest of Education Statistics, 2013 (NCES 2015-011), Table 330.10.

If my parents saved for college, we can still qualify for aid.

TRUE FALSE

TRUE Saving for college is almost always a good idea. Since a lot of financial aid comes in the form of loans, the aid you are likely to receive will need to be repaid.

KnowHow2GO *Printed with permission from KnowHow2GO. Learn more at KnowHow2GO.org.*

What is the FAFSA?

The FAFSA, or Free Application for Federal Student Aid, is the only way to apply for federal student aid (aid that comes from the United States government), like Pell Grants, Federal Loans, and work-study programs.

Individual states and colleges often use the information on your FAFSA to determine whether or not you are eligible for state aid and institutional aid. The FAFSA will ask for information from you about your family's financial history and current status to determine how much they can afford to contribute to your college education. This, in turn, let's federal, state, and institutional financial bodies determine how much financial aid to give you.

Why should I fill out the FAFSA?

Filling out the FAFSA can be a long and complicated process, but it's the single most important thing you can do to help yourself pay for college. Without filling out the FAFSA, you will not be eligible for federal aid, and you may not be eligible for any state or institutional aid either.

How do I know if I'm eligible for the FAFSA?

Most U.S. citizens, (and select non-citizens), are eligible to fill out the FAFSA. Check out www.studentaid.ed.gov eligibility to check out in-detail eligibility requirements.

How do I fill out the FAFSA?

Logon to **www.fafsa.ed.gov** to fill the FAFSA out online.

When should I fill out the FAFSA?

You should aim to submit your FAFSA as soon as possible after October 1 of your senior year to make sure you get the most aid possible. The FAFSA takes time and patience to complete, so it is to your advantage to start gathering the necessary documentation before October. The FAFSA does ask for your tax return information for the current year, which is generally not available until later in the year. You can choose whether or not to wait to supply this information or to use projected estimates from the previous year's tax returns.

Do I need to fill out the FAFSA every year?

Yes. As long as you need financial assistance, you will need to fill out the FAFSA for each year you plan to be a student.

What kind of aid am I eligible for?

The amount of aid you qualify for will depend on your Estimated Family Contribution (EFC). The FAFSA will make you eligible for both grants (which do not have to be paid back) and loans (which do).

continues on next page

Printed with permission from
Federal Student Aid.
Learn more at **fafsa.ed.gov**
Federal Student Aid
An OFFICE of the U.S. DEPARTMENT of EDUCATION

continued from previous page

HERE IS INFORMATION ON THE TYPES OF AID OFFERED:

- **Federal Pell Grants** are usually awarded to undergraduate students who have not yet earned a bachelor's degree. The maximum Federal Pell Grant award for the 2017-2018 award year is $5,920; however, the actual award depends on the student's financial need, the college's cost of attendance, the student's enrollment status, and the length of the academic year in which the student is enrolled.
- **Federal Supplemental Educational Opportunity Grants (FSEOG)** are awarded to undergraduate students with exceptional financial need. The amount of the award is determined by the college's financial aid office, and depends on the student's financial need and the availability of funds at the college.
- **Teacher Education Assistance for College and Higher Education (TEACH) Grants** are awarded to students who intend to teach in a public or private elementary or secondary school that serves students from low-income families. If the service requirement is not fulfilled, it could turn into a loan.
- **Iraq and Afghanistan Service Grants** are awarded to students whose parents or guardians were members of the Armed Forces and died as a result of performing military service in Iraq or Afghanistan after Sept. 11, 2001. To qualify, a student must have been under 24 years of age or enrolled in college at the time of the parent's or guardian's death.
- **Loans** consist of money that the student borrows to help pay for college, and must be repaid (plus interest). There are two federal student loan programs. See "All About Loans" on page 99 for additional information about the types of federal and other loans available.

try it Now it's your turn to use what you've learned. **Turn to page 104**

Printed with permission from Federal Student Aid.
Learn more at **fafsa.ed.gov**

Federal Student Aid
An OFFICE of the U.S. DEPARTMENT of EDUCATION

What's the CSS Profile?

The College Scholarship Service/Financial Aid Profile—usually written as CSS Profile—is required by hundreds of colleges and universities (most of them private) as a supplemental measure of financial need. Just as you must fill out the FAFSA to be eligible for federal aid, many schools require that you fill out the CSS Profile to be eligible for institutional aid—aid that comes directly from the college).

Here are the need-to-knows:

- Check with a college's admissions and/or financial aid team to see if they require or offer the CSS Profile. If so, try to fill it out as soon as possible after the first filing date (sometimes as early as fall of your senior year).
- The CSS Profile allows financial aid offices to examine your financial profile more carefully and thoroughly than just with the FAFSA alone.
- The CSS Profile is even more complex than the FAFSA, so it takes time and organization to fill it out correctly. Get started as soon as possible.
- Unlike the FAFSA, undocumented/immigrant students can and should fill out the CSS Profile.
- There is a small fee for creating the CSS Profile and for submitting it to each college, however, College Board offers a limited number of fee waivers to students from low-income backgrounds. These fee waivers are processed and offered automatically, so there's no need to apply.

While the CSS Profile can be time consuming and in some cases cost money to submit, it is well worth your time. Remember, private schools often have deep pockets, but in order to access the grants and scholarships they offer, you'll need to fill out the CSS Profile correctly and on time.

Learn more and complete the CSS Profile at http://student.collegeboard.org/css-financial-aid-profile

Getting Free Money for College

Now is the time for you to prepare for applying to competitive scholarship programs. Consider these steps:

1 Set goals. Develop short- and long-term goals for your college years and beyond. Scholarship programs want you to have goals to work toward. They lay a foundation for your future.

2 Make the grades. It is important to do well academically. Scholarship programs are looking for students who do well in school. Strong study and note taking skills are keys to academic achievement.

3 Be a leader. Engage in leadership and extracurricular activities. You do not have to limit yourself to being an officer in an established organization. You can also create opportunities for leadership, such as identifying a cause that interests you and developing and implementing a plan.

4 Make a difference. Community service can benefit those you serve and can make you competitive for scholarships. Giving back is a way to enhance your leadership skills, make a difference in the lives of others and support your community.

5 Keep a log. Document your leadership and community service activities. Most scholarship applications require you to provide information from 9th through 12th grade that details the date, activity, and number of hours of your engagement in your activity. Include a description that measures your activities. For instance, "I coordinated a project that provided clothing for over 200 homeless people" is much more convincing than "I participated in a clothing drive effort."

6 Build relationships. A teacher or other educator is often required to support your scholarship application. It is important to start developing relationships early with individuals who know your academic and/or personal achievements.

7 Use your resources. Family members, teachers and community organizations are all a part of your resources. Ask for their assistance in reviewing your work, reading essays for scholarships, and providing tips for success.

8 Make a commitment to succeed. Most scholarship applications have some question(s) that determine your ability to meet challenges. Make the choice to never give up and use those experiences when you are successful to tell your story.

BIO *Mary Williams is Director of Outreach and Recruitment for the Gates Millennium Scholars Program.*

SHOW ME THE MONEY!

Seanna Leath
College: Pomona College
Hometown: N. Little Rock, AR

For many low-income, first-generation students, scholarships and financial aid are crucially important in the college choice process. Personally, one of my top priorities in choosing a college relied on the school's ability to provide financial aid that I could afford to repay after graduation. In my hopes of continuing on to graduate from medical school, four years of undergraduate study is only the beginning. Therefore, scholarships and financial aid were a large focus during senior year. Here are a few things that I wish I'd known beforehand, or that I learned along the way:

1. It is a process. Pursuing scholarships and financial aid does not happen overnight. Rome was not built in a day, and only on very rare occasions will a student acquire all of the funds necessary to support a college education through one source. Instead, students should plan on looking at a variety of sources for financial support, including community, school, and corporation scholarships. Many colleges have available grant money or special scholarships given annually to a select number of students. Also, just as in any process, generous amounts of time should be devoted to seeking and completing scholarship applications. Although some applications may only require demographic information, many require recommendations and essays, all of which require time, attention, and effort.

2. Just do it! Searching for scholarships is an active process of trial and error. Although there are millions of scholarship opportunities out there, many apply to a limited number of people (students born on an Indian reservation or students whose parents work at Wal-Mart). Although a great number might apply to you, there is still the process of weeding out those that don't. Using scholarship search engines can be a great way to find hundreds of opportunities that seem to fit your criteria, but you must still zone in on those that suit you best. Procrastinating is one of the worst things that can be done during this process. Start early and remain diligent.

3. Collaborate and Synthesize Although every scholarship deserves your undivided attention, the reality of being able to write new essays for every application is impractical and could potentially add extra, unnecessary stress to your senior year. Instead, determine if a certain spectacular essay can be applied to more than one scholarship. If three different applications ask about your aspirations for after college, consider writing one original and creative essay to satisfy all three. It is always beneficial to manage time wisely!

"He is able who thinks he is able" -Gautama Siddharta

SEANNA LEATH is an I'm First! scholarship winner. Seanna shares her college experiences and offers advice on the I'm First! student blog.

Visit www.ImFirst.org to follow the student blog and watch video testimonials from first-generation college students and graduates.

Tips for Finding Scholarships to Help Pay for Your College Education

By Amy Weinstein

search and find all kinds of scholarships . . . start early and look everywhere

Did you know scholarships can help you pay for your college education? In fact, the more scholarship money you get, the less you will have to borrow to pay for tuition, room and board, books, and other expenses. Most importantly, unlike loans, scholarships do not need to be repaid and should be an important part of your financial aid package.

You can find scholarships that are industry specific—those that have to do with science, technology, engineering, the arts or mathematics. Additionally, there are scholarships if you have overcome challenging life obstacles. There are a number of scholarships available for students who are gifted academically, artistically, athletically, or musically.

Members from the National Scholarship Providers Association (NSPA) give scholarships and are committed to access, choice, and success. They offered the following tips for finding and applying for scholarships:

Start Early

"If you're a freshmen and sophomore in high school, you should be looking at scholarship applications early on, in order to see what kind of information scholarship providers request. It is overwhelming for many students who begin looking at applications late in their junior year, only to realize that they could have been a bit more proactive in their level of involvement both in their school and in their community." *Patti Ross, Coca-Cola Scholars Foundation*

Look Everywhere

"Remember to look for scholarships at your local community foundation! Other sources include high schools, libraries, employers, civic groups, community organizations, private foundations, and online searches. It's worth spending time to complete these applications. Two hours spent completing applications that can get you a $500 scholarship is like getting $250 per hour for your efforts!" *Dawn Lapierre, Community Foundation of Western Mass.*

"Applying for scholarships is like applying for college. The process is lengthy, and takes commitment on your part to find the best options available. Check with your local area merchants, guidance counselors, and librarians for information on possible opportunities. Search the web. Adhere to all deadlines and information requirements. Applying late or sending incomplete information is not the message you want to send to scholarship providers." *Vanessa Evans, Ron Brown Scholar Program*

"Don't give up. You might be able to find scholarships your freshman year in college to fund the next year. Some scholarships are renewable each year (provided you meet certain requirements). Register on Scholarships.com while you are in high school, the earlier the better." *Kevin Ladd, Scholarships.com*

Be Thorough

"When searching for scholarships using an online matching service like FastWeb.com, try to complete the profile as thoroughly as possible. Students who answer all of the optional questions on average will match twice as many scholarships as students who answer only the required questions. If you have to pay money to get money, it's probably a scam. Never invest more than a postage stamp to obtain information about scholarships or to apply for scholarships." *Mark Kantrowitz, Publisher of FinAid.org and FastWeb.com*

"Earn it. Scholarships are free, but they require effort on your part. Write the topically specific essays first and see if you can "recycle" some of the language for the general essays. Be thorough and polite. Once you begin applying, make sure to read, understand and follow the rules. If you don't follow the rules you could be disqualified." *Kevin Ladd, Scholarships.com*

BIO *Amy Weinstein is Executive Director of the National Scholarship Providers Association (NSPA), the only national organization dedicated solely to supporting the needs of professionals administering scholarships in colleges and universities, non-profits and foundations.*

Scholarship Searches

The following free websites allow you to search for scholarships offering millions of dollars to help you pay for college. You'll find a range of different scholarships; find the ones that suit you best and apply. Good luck!

College Board Scholarship Search, www.collegeboard.org

The College Board Scholarship Search provides users with access to information about more than 2,300 sources of college scholarships, internships, loans, and grants. Results from the site are tailored to students' educational level, talents, and backgrounds; and are acquired through the College Board's Annual Survey of Financial Aid Programs.

FastWeb, www.fastweb.com

FastWeb provides students with a scholarship directory searchable by college, year of study, extracurricular activities, academic interest, and race. Once you create a personal profile, you are matched with scholarships from a database of over 1.5 million scholarships. The site also offers advice on the college admission process, financial aid, and student life; while providing tools such as discussion boards, checklists, and financial aid calculators.

Also check out FastWeb's sister site, FinAid.org, a free wide-ranging source of student financial aid advice, information and tools.

FindTuition, www.findtuition.com

FindTuition is a free search tool through which users can research, target, and manage scholarship opportunities by college, athletic interest, and prospective major. Site services include a free scholarship search from a database containing over $7 billion dollars in aid, a specific loan search, an online college search, and detailed information on thousands of schools.

Scholarships.com, www.scholarships.com

Scholarship.com consists of free scholarship search results and financial aid information resources. The site contains 2.7 million frequently updated scholarships and its own scholarship awards. Many scholarship results are based on characteristics like financial need, intended field of study and community service, rather than academic achievement.

Unigo, www.unigo.com/scholarships

Unigo.com provides students and parents with free and organized scholarship search results without comprising their privacy. These results are customized to match profiles created by student users, and are consistently updated by a team of scholarship researchers that works closely with scholarship providers. The Application Request Tool allows users to request detailed scholarship application information for specific scholarships from their search results.

Chegg, www.chegg.com

Chegg gives students access to 5,000+ school profiles and $2 billion in scholarships. Based on individual student profiles, students are matched with scholarships; and given the opportunity to learn about, interact with, and get recruited by schools from around the world. Chegg also connects students to other students, and provides parents and counselors with free downloadable financial aid information guides.

try it
Now it's your turn to use what you've learned.
Turn to page 105

Scholarships

Don't miss out on applying for these flagship scholarships for low-income, minority, and first-generation college-bound students.

GATES MILLENNIUM SCHOLARS PROGRAM, www.gmsp.org

AWARD AMOUNT: Based on financial need | DEADLINE: January

The Gates Millennium Scholars Program (GMS) is the nation's largest private scholarship program and works to eliminate financial barriers for African American, Asian/Pacific Islander, American Indian/Alaskan Native, and Hispanic American students to further their education especially in the fields of computer science, education, engineering, library science, mathematics, public health, and the sciences—subjects in which these groups are severely underrepresented. Each year GMS selects 1,000 students to receive a four-year scholarship to use at any college or university of their choice, along with academic support and professional guidance throughout their collegiate career.

POSSE FOUNDATION, www.possefoundation.org

AWARD AMOUNT: Four-year, full tuition scholarship
DEADLINE: Nominations are accepted from spring of a student's junior year through the fall of their senior year.

The Posse Foundation is a college access and youth leadership development program that identifies, recruits, and selects student leaders from public high schools in Atlanta, Bay Area, Boston, Chicago, Houston, Los Angeles, Miami, New Orleans, New York and Washington, D.C and sends them in groups called Posses to some of the top colleges and universities in the country. Each Posse is comprised of 10 Scholars who receive four-year, full-tuition leadership scholarships. Students must be nominated by their high school or community-based organization, be a high school senior, and demonstrate leadership and academic potential.

QUESTBRIDGE, www.questbridge.org

AWARD AMOUNT: Up to $200,000 | DEADLINE: September

The **QUESTBRIDGE NATIONAL COLLEGE MATCH SCHOLARSHIP** connects high-achieving low-income high school seniors with admission and full four-year scholarships to some of the nation's leading colleges. To qualify, you must be a high school senior, demonstrate academic achievement, and come from a low-income background. Historically, most awardees come from households earning under $60,000 per year.

AWARD AMOUNT: Varies | DEADLINE: March

The **QUESTBRIDGE COLLEGE PREP SCHOLARSHIP** equips high-achieving low-income students with the knowledge necessary to compete for admission to the nation's most selective colleges. To qualify, you must be a high school junior, demonstrate academic achievement, and come from a low-income background. Historically, most awardees come from households earning under $60,000 per year.

COCA-COLA SCHOLARS, www.coca-colascholarsfoundation.org

AWARD AMOUNT: Up to $20,000 | DEADLINE: October

Each year Coca-Cola Scholars selects 50 students as National Scholars who receive $20,000 scholarships to college, and 200 students as Regional Scholars who receive $10,000 scholarships to college. Students selected as Coca-Cola scholars commit to leadership development and community involvement for their entire collegiate career and for the rest of their lives. In addition, the Coca-Cola First-Generation Scholarship has awarded more than $19 million in scholarships to more than 1,000 students who are the first in their immediate families to go to college at approximately 400 U.S. campuses. Interested students should contact the school you plan to attend to see if the scholarship is offered.

DELL SCHOLARS PROGRAM, www.dellscholars.org

AWARD AMOUNT: $20,000 and technology | DEADLINE: January

The Dell Scholars Program provides students with $20,000 to put towards their college education over six years and support including technology, mentoring, and a network of previous Dell Scholars to assist them through their collegiate career. In order to be eligible, students must have participated in a Michael & Susan Dell Foundation approved college access or college readiness program for at least two years of high school and have demonstrated need.

UNITED NEGRO COLLEGE FUND, www.uncf.org

AWARD AMOUNT: Varies | DEADLINE: Varies

The United Negro College Fund (UNCF) works to help under-represented, low income students attend and graduate from college through scholarship opportunities, active support of HBCUs, and promotion of higher education opportunities for African Americans throughout the community. UNCF awards over 10,000 scholarships to African American students through more than 400 scholarship, internship, fellowships and grants.

HISPANIC SCHOLARSHIP FUND, www.hsf.net

AWARD AMOUNT: Varies | DEADLINE: April

The Hispanic Scholarship Fund (HSF) works to make higher education more accessible to Hispanic Americans. HSF awards scholarships to Hispanic American high school students and community college graduates with plans of attending a full-time undergraduate degree program at an accredited U.S. college or university.

THE ASIAN & PACIFIC ISLANDER AMERICAN SCHOLARSHIP FUND, www.apiasf.org

AWARD AMOUNT: Varies | DEADLINE: January

The Asian & Pacific Islander American Scholarship Fund (APIASF) awards scholarships to Asian and Pacific Islander Americans from disadvantaged backgrounds and/or with significant leadership and community service experience in high school. Once selected, scholars receive individual advising and access to support services and programs, in addition to financial assistance, to help them with the transition from high school to college and throughout their time as college students until graduation.

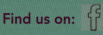

All About Loans

There are many different types of loans, both for students and for parents to take on behalf of their student. Read on for the basics.

Federal Student Loans

Perkins Loans

Perkins Loans are need-based loans and are awarded by the financial aid office to students with the highest need. The interest rate is very low—5 percent—and you don't make any loan payments while in school.

Subsidized Stafford or Direct Loans

Subsidized Stafford Loans are need-based loans with interest rates in the 4-6 percent range. The federal government pays the yearly interest while you're in school. This is why they're called "subsidized" loans.

Unsubsidized Stafford or Direct Loans

Unsubsidized Stafford Loans aren't based on financial need and can be used to help pay the family share of costs. You're responsible for paying interest on the loan while in school. You may choose to capitalize the interest. The advantage of doing this is that no interest payments are required. The disadvantage is that the interest is added to the loan, meaning that you will repay more money to the lender.

Grad PLUS Loans

This is a student loan for graduate students sponsored by the federal government that is unrelated to need. Generally, students can borrow Grad PLUS loans up to the total cost of education, minus any aid received. The advantage of this loan is that it allows for greater borrowing capacity. However, we recommend that students consider lower-interest loans, such as the Subsidized Stafford or Unsubsidized loans prior to taking out a Grad PLUS loan.

Parent Loans

Federal PLUS loans

The PLUS Loan program is the largest source of parent loans. Parents can borrow up to the full cost of attendance minus any aid received, and repayment starts 60 days after money is paid to college.

Private parent loans

A number of lenders and other financial institutions offer private education loans for parents. These loans usually carry a higher interest rate than PLUS Loans.

College-sponsored loans

A small number of colleges offer their own parent loans, usually at a better rate than PLUS. Check each college's aid materials to see if such loans are available.

Other Student Loan Options

Private student loans

A number of lenders and other financial institutions offer private education loans to students. These loans are not subsidized and usually carry a higher interest rate than the federal need-based loans. The College Board private loan program is an example of a private education loan for students.

College-sponsored loans

Some colleges have their own loan funds. Interest rates may be lower than federal student loans. Read the college's financial aid information.

Other loans

Besides setting up scholarships, some private organizations and foundations have loan programs as well. Borrowing terms may be quite favorable. You can use Scholarship Search to find these.

Smart Borrowing for College

By Ann Coles

Paying for college can be very intimidating, but smart borrowing ensures your investment in your education will pay off. Here are some tips to help make going to college affordable.

1. Use scholarships, grants, savings, and work-study earnings before taking out loans

• Grants and scholarships are gift money that you never have to repay. Work-study requires you to earn the money awarded.

• Complete the FAFSA (Free Application for Federal Student Aid) as soon as possible after October 1 and definitely before March 1 of the year you plan to go to college. Some colleges also require you to complete the CSS PROFILE. If your family has limited income, you may be eligible for a fee waiver.

• Search scholarships in online databases and talk to high school counselors, public librarians, community organization and church staff, parents' employers, and college financial aid officers.

• Save as much money for college as you can from after-school and summer jobs.

• Talk to a financial aid officer at the college you want to attend if your family has special financial circumstances that make it difficult for them to help you with college costs.

2. Reduce borrowing by using other options

• Use an interest-free monthly payment plan that allows you to spread the cost of paying for college over the school year. Your college financial aid office can recommend a plan.

• Work part-time but preferably not more than 15 hours a week so that you will have enough time to do well in your studies.

• Consider going to a college that has eliminated or limited loans for most students and gives aid only in grants and scholarships.

3. Borrow wisely

• Borrow only what you need because loans need to be repaid—even if you don't finish college. Never use student loans to pay off other bills or buy things you may want but don't need.

• Carefully compare your financial aid award letters from different colleges. If you don't understand an award letter, call the financial aid office and ask someone to explain it to you.

• Borrow federal student loans first. Federal loans (Perkins and Stafford Loans for students, PLUS loans for parents) have low fixed interest rates and flexible repayment plans. Apply for a private student loan only if federal loans are not enough.

• Consider options for having your student loans forgiven, such as volunteer service (participating in the Peace Corps, VISTA, or AmeriCorps).

4. Never use credit cards to pay for your education

• Credit cards are the most expensive source of funds. If you must borrow, exhaust all federal loan options first and then consider private education loans to pay for expenses.

• If you have an emergency, talk to a financial aid advisor to see if your college has an emergency loan fund or can help you in some other way.

Useful Web Sites

> **Federal Student Aid:** **www.federalstudentaid.ed.gov** provides information about federal grants and loans. You also can complete the FASFA online.

> **FinAid!:** **www.finaid.org/calculators** has calculators you can use to estimate your college costs, compare your financial aid awards from different colleges, compare the cost of borrowing different types of loans, and determine how much to borrow.

> **Project on Student Debt:** **www.projectonstudentdebt.org** features advice to borrowers and a listing of colleges and universities that have decided to eliminate or limit loans from their financial aid award packages for many students.

> **Simple Tuition:** **www.simpletuition.com** allows users to compare student loans from over 90 sources. Remember, featured lenders may not necessarily be the best alternative for you.

ON THE SPOT:

There is much debate over whether or not it is worthwhile for students to take out large loans. Taking out loans can provide a student with access to a college education, but it can also be a long-term financial burden. What do you think about taking out loans?

Important Student Loan Terms

- **APR (Annual Percentage Rate):** the total cost of a loan, including the interest rate and fees, expressed as the percentage of the amount borrowed that you have to pay each year. It is a good way to compare loans from different lenders.
- **Co-borrower or co-signer:** A person who agrees to pay the loan if the primary borrower can not or does not pay. Some lenders require students to get a co-borrower with good credit before they will make a loan.
- **Cost of Attendance:** The total cost of attending a particular college for a year, including tuition and fees, housing costs, food, books and supplies, transportation, and other necessary expenses such as a personal computer and health care.
- **Credit:** Indicates a person's financial strength, which includes a history of having paid bills and the demonstrated ability to repay a future loan.
- **Discount:** A reduction in the interest rate or the fees charged on a loan.
- **Interest:** The money or price paid by the borrower to use someone else's funds. Interest is stated as a percentage of the original amount borrowed.
- **Promissory Note or Credit Agreement:** A legal contract the borrower signs with the lender that details the terms of the loan including how and when it must be repaid.

BIO *Ann Coles has been working on college readiness since the 1960s and currently serves as Senior Fellow for College Access Programs at uAspire, an organization dedicated to ensuring that all young people have the financial information and resources necessary to find an affordable path to—and through—a postsecondary education.*

Sample Financial Aid Letter

No two financial aid offer letters are alike, but here is an example of the information contained in a typical aid letter.

ON THE SPOT:
Will Miya's financial aid package and her family contribution combined be enough to meet the total cost of her first year? If not, what can she do to cover the difference?

Your Expected Family Contribution is the amount of money you and your parents should reasonably be able to put towards your education according to the information on your FAFSA.

Dear Miya,

The Financial Aid Office at Opportunity University is writing in response to your request for financial assistance in the upcoming school year. The amount of the aid offered is based on the information provided by your FAFSA and financial aid applications, from which we have established your Expected Family Contribution is $2,500.

Please see below, where the tuition, room and board, and approximate fees for the upcoming school year are listed. All financial aid you are awarded will be applied toward tuition and fees, room and board. Your aid package may not be applied toward the cost of books and supplies or miscellaneous fees.

Pay attention to what costs your awards can and cannot be used towards.

Tuition & Academic Fees	$41,230
Room & Board	$12,900
Books & Supplies	$1,500
Miscellaneous Fees	$1,200
Total	$56,830

The total approximate value of your first year.

We are able to offer you a financial aid award with the following components:

Award Type	Fall	Spring	Total
Opportunity Merit-Based Scholarship	$4,500	$4,500	$9,000
Opportunity Need-Based Scholarship	$12,000	$12,000	$24,000
Estimated Federal Pell Grant	$2,775	$2,775	$5,500
Federal S.E.O.G.	$2,000	$2,000	$4,000
Federal Direct Subsidized Loan	$3,200	$3,200	$6,400
Work-Study Program	$1,500	$1,500	$3,000
	$25,975	$25,975	$51,950

Remember, scholarships and grants are money given to you that you don't have to pay back.

You must pay loans back upon graduation.

Work-study means you'll be working a part-time job to pay back part of your college fees.

The total amount of money you will receive towards paying your first year of college. Subtract this number from the total cost of your first year to find out what you'll have to pay out of pocket.

Your Federal Direct Loan will be sent directly to the college and will be applied to your account.

Some of your scholarships may be based upon your academic performance and assumed full-time enrollment. Please consult the Opportunity University Financial Aid Guide in order to establish the criteria for which you are accountable upon accepting your aid package. Note that your financial aid package may differ year-to-year.

If you do not wish to accept any part of your offered aid package, you must let the Financial Aid Office know within 30 days. To discuss your aid package or if you have any questions, call the office at (555) 555-1000.

Best,

Opportunity University Financial Aid Office

Most schools offer a financial aid guide book or website which you can use to understand what "strings" are attached to specific scholarships (e.g. you must keep a GPA of 2.5) and whether or not they are renewable.

Just because this is the aid package you receive this year does not mean you will receive the same amount next year, so plan ahead.

What do you need to do to confirm that you accept your offer? Some schools assume acceptance unless told otherwise, while others require you to provide a written confirmation.

If you have questions about your aid offer or want to petition for more aid, the best place to help you is your school's financial aid office.

Understand Your Financial Aid Package

Congratulations, you've been accepted to college!

Now comes the hard part of figuring out how much college is going to cost and how to pay for it. Following are some tips to help you understand your financial aid package and make the decision about how to pay.

Understanding Award Letters. When analyzing your award letters, consider two key categories of information—Gift Aid vs. Self-Help Aid and the Full Cost of Attendance. Gift Aid is money from the government (federal or state), the college, or other sources that does not need to be paid back. Self-Help Aid is money that either needs to be paid back or earned through work study. By comparing these two categories—on a school-by-school basis—you will find how much of the final bill you and your family will be required to foot. The second aspect of your award letter is the Full Cost of Attendance, which includes tuition, fees, room, board, books, transportation, and any miscellaneous charges.

Calculating Need. After figuring out how much school will cost and how much financial aid you'll receive, you can determine the unmet need or gap that you will have to pay. To find your need, take the Full Cost of Attendance and subtract the total amount of aid offered (both Gift Aid and Self-Help Aid). All schools don't cost the same and every financial aid package is different, so it's important to follow this exercise for each college you get into.

Making a Decision. Finances are the number one reason cited by students for not finishing college, so it's very important that you carefully consider cost when choosing a school. Be mindful of how much debt you'll have at graduation because it can impact major life decisions like buying a home or what jobs you can accept. Once you've decided which school is the right fit academically and financially—in the short and long term—then you're ready to decide.

Final Tips.

1. Don't hesitate to call a school's financial aid office if you don't understand your award letter.
2. Remember that the offer you're considering—unless it says differently—is only for the first year, not for all four years!
3. Consider living at home if your college is close by, even for just a year or two. It can save you a lot of money!
4. Search for outside scholarships to help bring down your tuition.
5. A tuition payment plan can help break down your unmet need into small, manageable payments that are interest free!

BIO *Bob Giannino-Racine is Chief Executive Officer at uAspire (formerly known as ACCESS) helping young people find an affordable way to — and through — a postsecondary education.*

FAFSA Checklist

The FAFSA questions ask for information about you (your name, date of birth, address, etc.) and about your financial situation. Depending on your circumstances (for instance, whether you're a U.S. citizen or what tax form you used), you might need the following information or documents as you fill out the application:

- ❑ Your Social Security number (it's important that you enter it correctly on the FAFSA form!)
- ❑ Your parents' Social Security numbers if you are a dependent student
- ❑ Your driver's license number if you have one
- ❑ Your Alien Registration number if you are not a U.S. citizen
- ❑ Federal tax information or tax returns including IRS W-2 information, for you (and your spouse, if you are married), and for your parents if you are a dependent student:
  - IRS 1040, 1040A, 1040EZ
  - Foreign tax return
  - Tax return for Puerto Rico, Guam, American Samoa, the U.S. Virgin Islands, the Marshall Islands, the Federated States of Micronesia, or Palau
- ❑ Records of your untaxed income, such as child support received, interest income, and veterans noneducation benefits, for you, and for your parents if you are a dependent student
- ❑ Information on cash; savings and checking account balances; investments, including stocks and bonds and real estate (but not including the home in which you live); and business and farm assets for you, and for your parents if you are a dependent student

For more information on filling out the FAFSA visit https://studentaid.ed.gov/sa/fafsa/filling-out#documents.

Not sure whether you will need to put your parents' information on the FAFSA?
Check out "Am I Dependent or Independent?" at www.studentaid.ed.gov/pubs or call 1-800-4-FED-AID (1-800-433-3243).

If you file your taxes before filling out your FAFSA online, you might be able to have your tax information automatically retrieved from the Internal Revenue Service and inserted in your FAFSA. The FAFSA will walk you through the process.

Printed with permission from
Federal Student Aid.
Learn more at **fafsa.ed.gov**

Scholarship Tracker

Planning for how to afford college can be tricky. Just like college applications, scholarship applications have hard deadlines and various requirements from essays to recommendation letters to videos and art portfolios.

Keep track of the scholarships you will apply for here, and refer back to this chart often to make sure you are on schedule to complete your scholarship applications on time.

	EXAMPLE	SCHOLARSHIP 1	SCHOLARSHIP 2	SCHOLARSHIP 3	SCHOLARSHIP 4
Scholarship Name	Scholarship Name Here				
Scholarship Amount	$2,000 a year				
Renewable after one year?	Yes				
Eligibility Requirements	• Current high school senior • First-generation college student (neither parent has earned a four-year college degree) • Must be attending an I'm First! partner college				
Application Deadline	Late May				
Where will Application be Submitted?	Online www.address				
Application Requirements	Personal, academic, and extracurricular information Two short essays One letter of recommendation				
Scholarship Notification Date	Winners announced in August				

Unit 4 Quiz

answers on page 136

Multiple Choice, circle your answer

1. Which of the following terms means money given to a student to help pay for college that doesn't have to be repaid?

a) Loans
b) Scholarships
c) Grants
d) B and C

2. A student whose grades are very strong will likely be eligible for a:

a) Merit-based scholarship
b) Need-based scholarship
c) Private loan
d) Federal loan

3. Your financial aid award letter should tell you everything except:

a) How much aid you will receive in loans
b) How much aid you will receive in scholarships
c) How much aid you will receive for your second year in college
d) How much you owe independent of the financial aid package

4. The best way to find scholarships is:

a) By checking with my guidance counselor
b) Using online search engines like fastweb.org
c) Asking at community organizations, such as local businesses and religious organizations
d) All of the above

5. I should not apply for a scholarship if:

a) I don't think I can get it
b) It requires essays to complete
c) I have to pay to apply
d) I am undocumented

True or False, circle your answer

1. I should not submit a FAFSA if I am undocumented.
T F

2. I cannot apply for scholarships until my senior year.
T F

3. Once I receive my financial aid award letter, I can still appeal for more aid. T F

4. I should not use credit cards to pay for all or part of my college tuition/fees. T F

5. If the "sticker price" of a school is high, I probably cannot afford to attend. T F

Fill in the Blank

1. Any amount of money that is taken from schools, banks, or the government which must be repaid is called a __________________.

2. __________________ allows you to maintain a job on your college campus in order to pay for part of your tuition/fees.

3. The ______________ Grant is given by the federal government to help low-income students pay for college.

4. ____________________ is what amount of money my parents or guardians are expected to contribute towards my education.

5. All U.S. citizens hoping to receive assistance in applying to college should fill out the ________ as soon as possible after January 1st of their senior year.

Open Answer

1. One of your friends tells you s/he is thinking of taking out loans to help pay for college. What advice would you give him/her on responsible borrowing?

Unit 5

Making My College Dreams a Reality

CONTENTS

"Being the first person in your family to go to college is a pretty amazing accomplishment. It's a new journey. As you prepare to step foot on campus, you'll experience a whirlwind of emotions. Those feelings are completely natural."

Objectives

By the end of this unit, I will...

- know the necessary steps to enroll in and register for my first year of college.
- be prepared academically and psychologically for arrival on a college campus.
- be able to navigate my college campus and locate on-campus resources.

Packing for College

Plan for the Long Haul

When packing for college, it's important to remember that you are not packing for just a few days or weeks. If your college is far from home, you're likely packing for months. If your college is in a colder climate, that means you need to pack for fall and winter as well as summer. Your shorts may be fine for August, but come November you'll wish you packed your snow coat!

Check your College Guidelines

Most colleges have a list of items which are not allowed in student dorm rooms. Fire hazards like candles, incense, and hot plates are often not allowed. Pets are usually a no-go too. Small refrigerators and microwaves are usually okay, but check your guidelines first. Remember, you can be fined for having prohibited items in your room, so double-check if in doubt.

Wait on the Big Stuff

Dorm rooms vary vastly from college to college. Some may be spacious and well-stocked, while others may be tiny and offer only the bare necessities. Most colleges will supply you with the basics: a bed frame, mattress, desk, chair, and dresser. If you're thinking of bringing extra furniture or large accessories (futons, chairs, refrigerators, microwaves, TVs, etc.), wait until you see the size and layout of your room before purchasing anything. You may want to split the cost of some of these items with your roommate, or you may not be able to fit them in your room at all!

Give Me Specifics!

Packing for college is like packing for life. You know what you need and what you don't. Here are a few items that are specific to college life that you may want to consider adding to your list. Remember, most of these things can be bought once you're on campus too.

- ❑ Bedding—most college dorm room beds take extra long twin sheets
- ❑ Towels
- ❑ Extension cords and power strip/ surge protectors
- ❑ Earplugs/headphones
- ❑ Desk lamp
- ❑ Small fan
- ❑ Iron/miniature ironing board
- ❑ Clothes hangers
- ❑ Flip flops and toiletry caddy for the shower
- ❑ Plastic cutlery and dishes
- ❑ Laundry bag and quarters to operate laundry machine
- ❑ Swim suit
- ❑ Formal/dress clothes for special occasions
- ❑ Umbrella/rain coat
- ❑ Day Planner
- ❑ Notebooks, paper, writing utensils and calculator for your first day of class
- ❑ Laptop computer

Completing Your Paperwork

Are you ready to start college? Between the time you accept your admission offer and the time you arrive for orientation, there are some important steps that must happen. For instance, most colleges require you to send a deposit to hold your spot. You'll also be required to have your guidance counselor send your final official transcript. Over the summer, you'll need to keep up with sending important paperwork, like your registration and housing forms and immunization records.

try it Now it's your turn to use what you've learned. **Turn to page 114**

ON THE SPOT: What is one thing not on this list that you know you can't live without at college? Why?

Find advice from real first-generation college students who blog about their college experiences on www.ImFirst.org

ORIENTATION

ADJUSTING TO A NEW COMMUNITY

Most colleges and universities offer students an orientation experience before they begin their first year. While it is sometimes optional, orientation is a great way to get to know your campus, peers, and faculty. Here's some advice for starting college on the right foot:

Alexa Rodriguez
Wellesley College
Hometown: Compton, CA

"I'm still very new to the college setting, but from my understanding, college is what you make of it. The opportunities are there, trust me. The only difference is that you have to look for them. They are not going to knock on your door and ask you if you want to take them. You've got to stay on your toes and be attentive."
- The Big Leagues

"Trust me, transitioning is difficult, especially if you feel out of place or that you do not belong. If you were accepted into a university, it is because the admission officers believed in your potential. They know that you are going to strive and that you were an important addition to their student body. They wanted you because you are going to contribute to your community and be a successful leader."
- Let's Talk About Transitioning from High School to College

Santiago Montoya
Brandeis University
Hometown: Jackson Heights, NY

Visit www.ImFirst.org to follow the student blog and watch video testimonials from first-generation college students and graduates.

Jordan Lillegard
Univ of Southern California
Hometown: Long Beach, CA

"Get involved in something during your freshman year. That way you won't just be in your room all the time not really experiencing college. I am happy to have made the club baseball team and am looking forward to traveling and playing against other universities."
- 6 Weeks Into My New Life

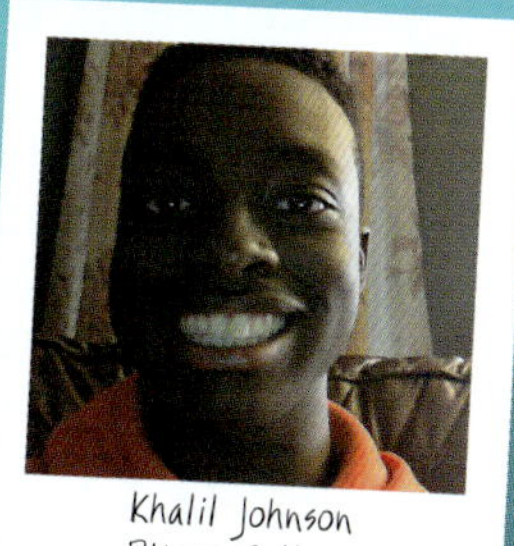

Khalil Johnson
Pitzer College
Hometown: Philadelphia, PA

"As a first-generation college student, we have a little more on our shoulders than anyone else on campus. We also have a little more responsibility than everyone else because we are paving the way for our younger siblings, and even parents. However, we should not crumble under this pressure, but embrace it."
- Embrace the Challenge

"Talk to your folks (whoever it is—family, friends, mentors, etc) regularly. As much as this might be a new transition for you, it is also a transition for the people who love you—a period of adjustment to your absence—and they just want to make sure you're okay. Side note: I video-chatted with my cat today (yes, my cat) and it was glorious."
- Orientation at Wellesley

Omawatie Beharry
Wellesley College
Hometown: Bronx, NY

Dallas Sims
University of Virginia
Hometown: Cape Charles, VA

"My advice to first-generation college students is to find a group of people that seem friendly or intriguing and approach the whole group. Approaching a group can be difficult, but in college, that's what you do. Everyone is in the same boat, trying to make friends and feeling awkward about how to do so."
- Crossing the Bridge: From Friendliness to Friendship

Placement Tests: The Gateway to First-Year Courses

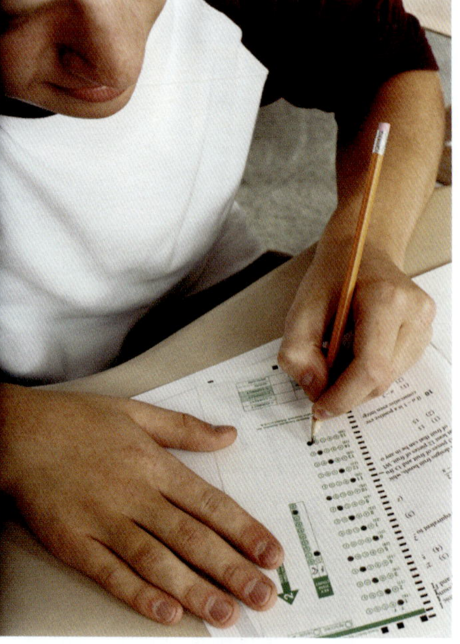

As a high school student, you're probably no stranger to taking tests. Chances are, you've already taken the SAT, PSAT, ACT, PLAN, and SAT IIs, or some combination thereof. But while most students are familiar with these exams and understand their importance, many have never been told about the placement tests they may have to take before they register for first-year college courses.

So what is a placement test?

A placement test is an exam given to new college students in order to determine their academic readiness levels. The results of your placement exam will be used to decide what courses you can take your first year of college.

What happens if I don't pass the placement test?

Students who don't reach "college readiness" levels on their placement tests are generally required to take one or more remedial courses before they can begin (or in some cases while they begin) taking first-year courses. Remedial courses are non-credit bearing courses (courses that don't count towards your degree) intended to provide students with the basic knowledge they need to succeed in college-level courses.

Do all schools require students to take a placement test?

Not every school requires placement tests, but most do. Almost all community colleges require students to take placement tests, and many four-year schools do as well.

Do all schools use the same placement test?

No. Two of the most popular placement tests are College Board's ACCUPLACER and ACT's Compass test. However some schools may create their own exam or use other placement tests.

What is tested on a placement test?

Generally these exams will test your reading and math skills, and possibly your writing skills as well. Some schools require students to take a foreign language test upon admittance as well.

How do I know if my college requires me to take a placement exam?

Simple: ask. Ask your admissions counselor whether or not a placement test is required and which placement test is administered at your college. If your counselor can't tell you, ask him or her to refer you to someone in Academic Affairs who can.

How can I prepare myself for a placement test?

Ask your admissions counselor to put you in contact with someone at your college (a testing site coordinator, a student support specialist, etc.) who can explain to you what is tested on the placement exam. Ask if there are practice tests available, either online or at the college, to take over the summer. (You can easily find study guides and samples of ACCUPLACER and Compass tests online.) Take a practice test and use it as a diagnostic to show you what skills you need to work on before taking your official placement test.

What are the long-term consequences of not passing a placement test?

Because many students lack the funds, time, and motivation to complete remedial coursework, only about one in ten community college students tracked into these classes will graduate within three years, and only about one in three four-year students taking remedial courses will graduate in six.

> Many students have never been told about the placement tests they may have to take before they register for first-year college courses.

So ask the necessary questions to find out whether or not your college requires a placement test and what's tested. Use the answers to prepare yourself adequately for the test ahead!

Survival of the Fittest: Ways to Survive College on a Budget

By Katie Delaney

Look for student discounts. Many shops, restaurants, and businesses around college campuses offer discounts to students, so carry your student ID with you at all times. When you need to go grocery shopping or buy anything, use coupons and daily discounts and compare prices at different stores to ensure you are getting the best price.

Save on college textbooks. Textbooks have become one of the most expensive aspects of college, with book costs ranging from $500-$700 (per semester!). Rather than buying new textbooks, opt for used books at your bookstore, or buy from sites like amazon.com or half.com. When buying from online sellers, just be sure to search for books by ISBN number so you buy the correct edition, and place your order at least a month in advance as shipping can take longer than usual.

Make a spending plan. Keep track of your spending habits, distinguish between needs and wants, and figure out what responsibilities you have financially (bills, food, transportation). Allot a certain amount of money for spending during each week at school to make sure your various "needs" are accounted for, leaving wiggle room for an occasional "want" if possible. If you don't already have one, open a student bank account to deposit your money into. Most banks allow their clients to track their spending and saving habits through online banking. Check with your student center if they have information about opening a bank account.

Use public transportation. Avoid the unnecessary cost of gas if your school offers free shuttles or inexpensive buses. And don't forget the option of walking or biking when you can; it's free and you'll also get some exercise!

Be careful with credit. While credit cards provide students with a way to start building good credit and a safety net in case of emergency, they can also wreak havoc on a student's financial plan and future.

Overspending, making late payments, or forgetting to make payments can do serious damage to your credit score, a number that is very important to your chances of being able to buy a car, buy a home, or even get a job later in life. If you decide to have a credit card, be sure to keep track of your spending and pay off your purchases as soon as you make them.

Get a job. Most colleges and universities offer on-campus jobs to students. Talk to your school's business office, career center, or the department of your academic major about what's available. Jobs in your field of study, such as working as a research assistant in a science lab, serve as easy résumé builders and look great to future employers.

Check out credit unions. Credit unions offer a great alternative to big-name banks for your first credit account. Banks are trying to make money, so they may charge extra to open an account, charge fees to use other banks' ATMs, and have high penalty fees if you overdraw your account. Non-profit credit unions offer lower fees, and many colleges and universities have access to a credit union on campus or nearby in the community.

Beware identity theft. Students are particularly vulnerable to identity theft because they don't think they are likely targets since they generally do not have a lot of money. Identity theft can happen quickly and easily, by someone stealing your personal information via email/phone scams, discarded bank statements, or most commonly through information found in a stolen wallet. Make sure your personal information is protected, and avoid carrying any unnecessary information (social security card, passwords, etc.) in your wallet that you don't absolutely need.

BIO *Katie Delaney is a first-generation college graduate from Franklin & Marshall College and a past intern with Center for Student Opportunity (now Strive for College).*

Finding the Right Support

Being the first person in your family to go to college is a pretty amazing accomplishment. It's a new journey. As you prepare to step foot on campus, you'll experience a whirlwind of emotions.

Excitement. Nervousness. Joy. Hesitation. And that's cool. Those feelings are completely natural.

Let's be honest. No one really preps you for how to maneuver the college life, especially as a first-generation college student. As you transition from being a high school student to a first-generation college student, you don't have the opportunity to ask your mom or dad what their college experiences were like and what to look out for. That doesn't mean that you are at a disadvantage. It just means you will have to work a bit harder to make sure you get the support you need.

> The right support systems are there on campus, and it's in your best interest to find and use them!

You will inevitably face some obstacles and hiccups along the way, but the right support systems are there on campus, and it's in your best interest to find and use them! Here are some tips for taking advantage support on campus:

Identify Supports Early

Most colleges and universities have support systems and programs designed specifically to help first-generation college students (and other student populations) acclimate to the college life, assist you academically, socially, professionally, emotionally, and mentally, and help you persist to graduation. Seek out these programs and resources as you're researching and applying to college. Don't wait until you show up on campus to figure out what supports are available. All of the colleges and universities in this Guide have these programs. You can also continue your research and connect with these schools at www.ImFirst.org.

Leave No Stone Unturned

So, your school doesn't have a support program specific to first-generation students? No worries. You can definitely find support elsewhere! You know your amazing Intro to Philosophy professor who you think is the smartest person on earth? She may have been the first in her family to graduate from college. You never know unless you ask! Be sure to talk to your professors and seek out their encouragement and advice about what college was like for them and how they dealt with certain issues.

Lean on Your Peers

Okay, so maybe you are freaking out about not being able to register for that 8 a.m. class you really wanted and you have no idea what to do next. Chances are, if you call home your family won't understand where you are coming from, and you may not feel comfortable venting to a professor. This is where making friends comes into play! Being able to connect with other students who are also first-generation (and maybe from the same city, state, region, etc. you're from) will give you an outlet and a peer support group. You'll have a place to vent to peers who are facing the same struggles and obstacles as you and can help come up with solutions to your unique challenges as first-generation college students.

As a first-generation college student—just like any college student—you will have ups and downs. There will be days when you question if college is right for you. However, if you surround yourself with the right supports, handling the ups and downs and the second guessing will be a lot more manageable. Remember, take advantage!

try it Now it's your turn to use what you've learned. **Turn to page 115**

ON THE SPOT: What kind of support will you seek out on campus? Who will you turn to for that support and why?

advice

As a first-gen graduate, what would you say to your high school self to better prepare for what's in store in college?

WHAT I WISH I KNEW WHEN...

Khadijah Williams
Harvard University 2013

"College is difficult in ways that you will not expect. Treat it as though you are an explorer in a new foreign country. What would you do to better learn the culture? Would you seek out more advice than if you were in a place you knew well? Of course! Will you make mistakes or feel unsure since this environment is new to you? Of course you will. Will you learn a lot of new and amazing things? Absolutely. Go forth, for you are trailblazer and adventurer, creating a path for others to follow!"

Khadijah Williams, Harvard University '13
Program Associate at the Office of the Ombudsman for Public Education and Office of the Student Advocate for the State Board of Education in Washington, DC

Duylam Nguyen-Ngo
University of Virginia 2013

"I would say to my younger self—explore more. Keep an open mind because the answers you have now will probably change...because the question changes. Don't ask "How do I become rich?" but "What matters most?"

Duylam Nguyen-Ngo, University of Virginia '13
Product Designer in Portland, OR

Lysa Diggins
Williams College 2013

"As a first-gen graduate, I would tell my high school self not to rush through college always set on your career and end goals; try to live in the moment as well! It can be hard when you have your family, or even an entire community relying on you and pushing you to what they believe your full potential is...maybe even telling you that you must become a "doctor" or a "lawyer." But, if that is not where your heart or passions lie, look elsewhere for guidance. Don't ever allow yourself to just settle...for anything: grades, learning, or your career. You've come too far and worked too hard, so make sure you ultimately, do what you love and love what you do; because in the end...that's how you'll find true success!"

Lysa Diggins, Williams College '13
Graduate student pursuing a Master's of Medical Science at Nova Southeastern University to become a Physician Assistant in Davie, FL

Alexis Montes
University of Rochester 2015

"If I could speak to my high school self, I would say be unapologetically bold with your ideas. As a first-generation college student, you are about to become a goldmine of unique ideas and customs in a school that may be inundated with middle and upper-class ideals that don't properly represent America or the world. You have an opportunity to educate an entire campus community on the struggles of the underprivileged. Some people may not like this, but they probably never will. Believe in yourself, because you have overcome intense structural violence, whether you're aware of this or not. There's a reason you are a first-generation college student, it is a gift and something you have earned. Focus on the people who want to listen, want to learn, and who want to make a better world with you. You'll feel more at home then, even if sometimes you don't feel like you belong."

Alexis Montes, University of Rochester '15
Teacher in Houston, TX

Visit www.ImFirst.org to follow the student blog and watch video testimonials from first-generation college students and graduates.

College-Ready Checklist

Many students believe once they have an acceptance letter in hand from a college, they are ready to begin their first year. Actually, there are a few more crucial steps that students must take before they begin college.

Every college has requirements and procedures for students to follow before they enroll. For instance, most schools require students provide up-to-date records of certain vaccinations against illnesses like meningitis.

Use the checklist below to make sure you do everything necessary to start your school year off right. Remember, each college has different requirements. Use the blank row at the bottom of the checklist to for any additional requirements not listed.

Requirement	When?	Check when completed
1. Accept your offer and submit deposit (if required)	Once a school sends you an acceptance letter and you are sure you want to attend. Consult with your family and counselor first. Winter or spring of senior year.	
2. Accept financial aid award	Once your award letter is received and you've looked it over with your counselor in the spring semester of your senior year.	
3. Submit your official final transcript	Once your final grades for spring semester are finalized. Your counselor will need to send this for you.	
4. Submit your housing form indicating your preferences for living on campus	Varies by school. Spring or summer before your first year of college.	
5. RSVP to orientation (if your school provides one)	Varies by school. Spring or summer before your first year of college.	
6. Register for classes	Varies by school. Some colleges have students register for classes during the summer before their first year, while others do not allow first year students to register until they are on campus.	
7. Submit immunization records	Summer before your first year of college. Check with your college's student health office to see what immunizations are required.	
8. Study for placement tests	Spring and summer before your first year of college. Call the school first and ask them what placement tests you'll be required to take.	
9. Reach out to roommate and/or join official social media groups	Pre-orientation.	

Support My College Offers

Colleges are so much more than just classrooms and dorm rooms. Most colleges offer a wide array of support offices and opportunities that serve all students, but especially first-generation college students who will sometimes seek out more help to be successful in college.

Before you get to campus, make sure that you know what supports your school offers so you can take advantage of them. If your college is in this Guide, start by reading their profile or visit the school's website to find what resources are available. Then complete the chart below.

Type of Support	**My School Offers...**	**Important Information**
Ex: Writing center	*John. G. Opportunity Writing Center*	*Writing support offered by peer mentors. Open 8am to 5pm Monday-Friday. Appointment needed.*
For African American students		
For Asian students		
Career services		
Counseling		
For students of faith		
Financial aid office		
First-generation college students		
For Hispanic students		
For LGBTQ+ students		
Mentoring groups		
For Native students		
Student health		
Student life		
Tutoring		
For Women		
Writing		

Unit 5 Quiz

answers on page 136

Multiple Choice, circle your answer

1. Only students planning to live on campus must submit their:

a) Immunization records
b) Housing forms
c) Registration choices
d) Final high school transcripts

2. As soon as I arrive on campus, I should make sure I know where to find:

a) The classrooms where my courses are being held
b) The student health center
c) The writing/tutoring center
d) All of the above

3. Which of the following is generally allowed in dorm rooms?

a) Small pets
b) Refrigerators
c) Candles
d) All of the above

4. During the summer before my first year of college, I should:

a) Call campus every day to see if my dorm room and roommate have been assigned
b) Not read or study at all so I can give my brain a break before classes start
c) Find out what placement tests I will need to take and study for them beforehand
d) None of the above

5. If I have a disagreement with my roommate when I arrive on campus, I should first:

a) Talk to the resident/hall assistant or a representative from student life
b) Explain to him/her the reasons why I am right
c) Try to find a new place to live
d) Talk with him/her about the problem and hear his/her point of view

True or False, circle your answer

1. At most colleges, I must submit proof of immunizations against certain illnesses like meningitis before beginning my freshman year.

T F

2. If I perform poorly in the spring semester of my senior year, colleges may withdraw my acceptance.

T F

3. Once I receive my financial aid award letter, I automatically receive the financial aid specified.

T F

4. Many colleges require freshmen to take specific, pre-determined courses in their first semester, or even year, of college.

T F

5. When I get to college, I should only try to find people with similar backgrounds and life experiences to my own to hang out with.

T F

Fill in the Blank

1. An exam I take which determines what classes I can take in my first year is called a ________________ test.

2. It is important to know when I can ____________ for my classes so that I can get into the classes I want and/or need to take.

3. Attending ______________ before classes begin is a great way to get to know my classmates and become familiar with my new community.

4. Before buying my ____________ for classes, I should look online and compare prices, so I can get the best deal possible.

5. After I graduate, my guidance counselor must submit a copy of my ______________ to my college.

continues on next page

continued from previous page

Open Answer

1. Adapting to new communities can be challenging, but ultimately rewarding. What challenges do you think you will face as a first-year student, and how will you overcome them?

2. Why is it important for you to save money during college? What are three ways you plan on saving money?

Celebrate First-Generation College Students on November 8, 2018

The Council for Opportunity in Education (COE), in partnership with NASPA — Student Affairs Administrators in Higher Education and other higher education organizations, invites college access and success professionals to join with TRIO's McNair Postbaccalaureate Achievement and Student Support Services programs across the country for the Second Annual First-Generation College Celebration on **November 8, 2018**—the 53rd Anniversary of the Higher Education Act of 1965.

This event will celebrate the achievements of young people and adults who are in the first-generation of their families to attend college and encourage colleges to expand offerings to address the obstacles that first-generation students face.

The Council for Opportunity in Education (COE) is a non-profit organization whose membership includes more than 1,100 colleges and community-based organizations with a particular commitment to expanding college opportunity. COE, which was incorporated in 1981, is the only national organization with affiliates in all 50 states, the Caribbean, and the Pacific Islands focused on assuring that low-income and first-generation students have a realistic chance to prepare for, enter, and graduate from college.

NASPA is the leading association for the advancement, health, and sustainability of the student affairs profession. We serve a full range of professionals who provide programs, experiences, and services that cultivate student learning and success in concert with the mission of our colleges and universities. Established in 1918 and founded in 1919, NASPA is comprised of over 15,000 members in all 50 states, 25 countries, and 8 U.S. Territories. Through the financial support of the Suder Foundation, NASPA is home to the Center for First-generation Student Success.

Appendix

CONTENTS

What HBCUs offer 21st Century Students

By Keisha L. Brown

Many students—African Americans and non-blacks alike—are choosing HBCUs for the unique educational experience.

Historically Black Colleges and Universities (HBCUs) have played a crucial role in America's higher education system by educating African Americans who were denied access to white institutions of higher learning in the late nineteenth and early twentieth centuries.

Today, African American students have access to a wide range of post-secondary institutions, especially since an increasing number of schools are actively recruiting minority students. But despite having more options for higher education than ever before, many students—African Americans and non-blacks alike—are choosing HBCUs for the unique educational experience they offer.

Ethnic and Racial Diversity

In the 21st century, HBCUs aren't just for black students anymore. Colleges know that in order to be competitive and train students who are prepared to succeed in the global community, they need diversity. More and more HBCUs, especially public HBCUs, are recruiting white and Hispanic students to add to their campuses' rich ethnic diversity.

Even schools whose student bodies are totally African American exhibit remarkable diversity as students from all over the country bring a bit of their regional culture to the campus mix. Some HBCUs boast an impressive international student population too, with students hailing from Africa, the Caribbean, South America and, in some cases, as far away as the Middle East.

A Legacy of Academic Excellence and Success

While HBCUs represent only 3% of American institutions of higher learning, they graduate nearly 25% of all African Americans who earn Bachelor's degrees. HBCUs are leaders in training young professionals—especially in the arts, business, and the sciences—who are prepared to address the unique needs of the African American community.

HBCUs also provide African American and minority students the opportunity to work with mentors who share the same cultural background as themselves and are successful in their respective fields. The extensive support networks available at HBCUs help students excel in academically rigorous programs. Furthermore, a substantial number of HBCU graduates go on to pursue advanced degrees, often being recruited by elite schools seeking to diversify their graduate programs.

Opportunities for Real World Experience

Every year, numerous national organizations partner with HBCUs to create programs that increase minority, particularly African American, participation in underrepresented fields such as engineering, business, and medicine among others. Businesses and corporations that are committed to increasing diversity often look first to students enrolled in HBCUs to fill internships and part-time positions that offer real world experience and develop leadership skills.

Also, many HBCUs offer students the opportunity to spend a semester or two at other leading universities through domestic exchange programs, which allow students to experience a different academic environment and network with distinguished professionals in a different region of the country.

Choosing between a HBCU or a TWI

Many students struggle with the decision to attend either a HBCU or a traditionally white institution (TWI). While both HBCUs and TWIs provide academically challenging and personally rewarding collegiate experiences, the social dynamics of HBCUs and TWIs are markedly different.

Your college experience can provide you excellent opportunities to break outside of your comfort zone and to grow and adapt in a new environment. Students who went to predominantly white high schools can benefit from the cultural exposure of an HBCU. Also, some HBCUs can be cheaper to attend than TWIs in the same region but still offer students the same solid academic instruction.

You will be spending the next four years of your life at the college you attend, so put the time, effort and research into finding the school that's right for YOU. The decision you make can result in one of the most rewarding experiences of your life.

BIO *Keisha L. Brown is a graduate of Howard University and a past intern with Center for Student Opportunity (now Strive for College).*

HBCUs

United Negro College Fund (UNCF)

Thirty-seven historically black colleges and universities belong to the United Negro College Fund network of member institutions. UNCF provides these colleges and universities with a range of support—operating resources, student scholarships and institutional improvement support—that enables them to keep their academic programs strong and their tuitions affordable: more than 30 percent lower on average than tuition at comparable institutions.
www.uncf.org

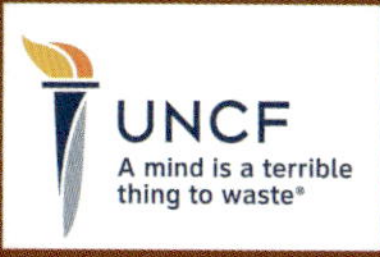

Allen University (SC)
Benedict College (SC)
Bennett College for Women (SC)
Bethune-Cookman University (FL)
Claflin University (SC)
Clark Atlanta University (GA)
Dillard University (LA)
Edward Waters College (FL)
Fisk University (TN) – Page 327
Florida Memorial University (FL)
Huston-Tillotson University (TX)
Interdenominational Theological Center (GA)
Jarvis Christian College (TX)
Johnson C. Smith University (NC)
Lane College (TN)
LeMoyne-Owen College (TN)
Livingstone College (NC)
Miles College (AL)
Morehouse College (GA)
Morris College (SC)
Oakwood University (AL)
Paine College (GA)
Philander Smith College (AR)
Rust College (MS)
Saint Augustine's University (NC)
Shaw University (NC)
Spelman College (GA)
Stillman College (AL)
Talladega College (AL)
Texas College (TX)
Tougaloo College (MS)
Tuskegee University (AL)
Virginia Union University (VA)
Voorhees College (SC)
Wilberforce University (OH)
Wiley College (TX)
Xavier University of Louisiana (LA)

Thurgood Marshall College Fund

The Thurgood Marshall College Fund is proud to be a partner of the *public* HBCUs. Public HBCUs have been helping to develop outstanding leaders for more than 160 years. They provide the world with young men and women distinguishable by their characteristics—confident, accomplished, productive, and innovative leaders who are socially and economically responsible.
www.tmcf.org

Alabama A&M University
Alabama State University
Albany State University (GA)
Alcorn State University (MS)
Bluefield State College (WV)
Bowie State University (MD)
Central State University (OH)
Cheyney University of Pennsylvania
Chicago State University (IL)
Coppin State University (MD)
Delaware State University
Elizabeth City State University (NC)
Fayetteville State University (NC)
Florida A&M University
Fort Valley State University (GA)
Grambling State University (LA)
Harris-Stowe State University (MO)
Howard University (DC)
Jackson State University (MS)
Kentucky State University
Langston University (OK)
Lincoln University (MO)
Lincoln University of Pennsylvania
Medgar Evers College (NY)
Mississippi Valley State University
Morgan State University (MD)
Norfolk State University (VA)
North Carolina A&T State University
North Carolina Central University
Prairie View A&M University (TX)
Savannah State University (GA)
South Carolina State University
Southern University and A&M College (LA)
Southern University at New Orleans (LA)
Southern University at Shreveport-Bossier City (LA)
Tennessee State University
Texas Southern University
Tuskegee University (AL)
University of Arkansas at Pine Bluff
University of the District of Columbia
University of Maryland Eastern Shore
University of Virgin Islands
Virginia State University
West Virginia State University
Winston-Salem State University (NC)
York College (NY)

Check out the **United Negro College Fund (UNCF)** at www.uncf.org to learn about all Historically Black Colleges and Universities (HBCUs) and the many scholarships available to African American students.

Hispanic-Serving Institutions

Did you know that over half of all Hispanic undergraduate students in higher education are enrolled in less than 10 percent of institutions in the United States?

This concentration of Hispanic enrollment gave way to a federal program designed to support colleges and universities in the United States that assist first-generation, majority low-income Hispanic students, now known as Hispanic-Serving Institutions (HSIs).

What are HSIs?

What defines HSIs is not necessarily their mission, but their Hispanic enrollment. Unlike HBCUs and women's colleges, most HSIs were not founded with the purpose of primarily serving a specific demographic.

In 1992, the Hispanic Association of Colleges and Universities (HACU) took the lead in lobbying Congress for official recognition and federal funding for institutions of higher education with large Hispanic populations. That year HSIs were defined under federal law as accredited and degree-granting public or private nonprofit institutions of higher education with 25% or more total undergraduate Hispanic enrollment. Additionally, a minimum of 50% of the Hispanic students attending HSIs must be from low-income backgrounds.

In 1995, Congress appropriated $12 million in grants to HSIs under the Higher Education Act. Federal funding for HSIs from the Department of Education has increased sharply since then, with $117.4 million being appropriated in 2010. These grants are used for the development and improvement of academic programs, endowment funds, academic tutoring, counseling programs, student support services, and more. The continual increase in government funding demonstrates a growing dedication to the advancement of higher education for Hispanic students.

Why choose an HSI?

In addition to the benefits afforded by government grants, there are many reasons why prospective college students choose to attend HSIs. Most are located in areas with large Hispanic populations such as California, Texas, and New Mexico. The proximity of HSIs to these areas facilitates the transition to college life for many Hispanic students, who are able to attend an HSI close to home. HSIs also have lower tuitions, on average, than non-HSI institutions of a similar caliber.

Making a Decision

With the growing Hispanic college-age population in the United States, more and more colleges and universities are becoming HSIs by virtue of their increased Hispanic enrollment. An ever-increasing group of schools are known as "emerging HSIs," meaning that between 15 and 24 percent of their respective student populations are Hispanic. When choosing a college or university, don't write off a school for not being an HSI now; it might be in a couple of years.

Ultimately it is good to keep in mind that HSIs are, their large Hispanic populations notwithstanding, regular institutions designed to serve students from all ethnicities and walks of life. Just because you may not be Hispanic or low-income does not necessarily mean an HSI is not right for you; on the flip side, don't limit yourself to attending an HSI just because you fall within the target demographic.

Looking for scholarships, resources, and mentoring?

Check out the Hispanic Scholarship Fund at www.hsf.net and Hispanic College Fund at www.hispanicfund.org

Check out ¡Excelencia!

in Education at www.edexcelencia.org to learn about their work to accelerate higher education success for Latino students by identifying programs that positively impact Latino college enrollment and graduation.

HSIs in the *I'm First! Guide to College*

Hispanic-Serving Institutions (HSIs) are defined in Title V of the Higher Education Act as not-for-profit institutions of higher learning with a full-time equivalent (FTE) undergraduate student enrollment that is at least 25 percent Hispanic.

Learn more about other institutions committed to serving Hispanic students that are members of the Hispanic Association of Colleges & Universities. Visit HACU at **www.hacu.net**.

EMPTY ROOMS AND CARDBOARD BOXES

The melodies of The Killers play in the living room as I stand in the middle of my bedroom. Scattered around me lie five cardboard boxes, each hopefully holding everything I will need during my first year of college. The excitement of going to college is suddenly met with the nostalgia of packing. Who knew putting your life into cardboard boxes would be so difficult?!

Irvin Gomez
College: Dartmouth College
Hometown: Waukegan, IL

As I admire the sight of what used to be my room, I can't help but feel a bit of sadness creeping in. This house has witnessed my successes in high school as well as my coming of age. I will leave all of this behind in just a few days and it will forever be a part of my past. I am sure that as you begin to pack, you will experience similar emotions. This is totally natural and expected.

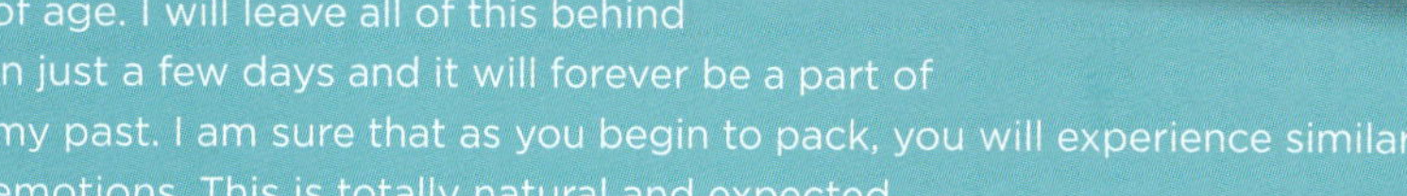

Many of my friends were happy to leave home and had no second thoughts about it. I, on the other hand, had mixed emotions about leaving. Yes, I want to be at Dartmouth as much as my future classmates, but I am going to miss home. My advice to those like me is the following: enjoy every moment that you have left with your family. Hug them while you are close because you will be missing those hugs when you are miles away. Share your excitement with them since I am sure that they are as excited as you are for college.

Lastly, do not let the feelings of sadness overcome the feelings of excitement and expectation. You should be excited. I know I am. Yes, it is hard to see most of your life being placed in boxes and to hear what the future use of your room will be, but over the horizon lies a more exciting picture. Those cardboard boxes are temporary containers of your life and soon you will be standing in an empty room wondering how to make that room your home.

I will end with a few words my dad said in our conversation about leaving home: "No matter how far away you are going, we, as a family will always be together in mind and in spirit." With these words in mind, I will embark on my journey to Dartmouth knowing that I am taking more than five cardboard boxes. I am also bringing my family along for the voyage.

IRVIN GOMEZ is an I'm First! scholarship winner. Irvin shares his college experiences and offers advice on the I'm First! student blog.

Visit www.ImFirst.org to follow the student blog and watch video testimonials from first-generation college students and graduates.

Dancing the Circle

By Jarrid Whitney

An Indigenous Perspective on College Admissions

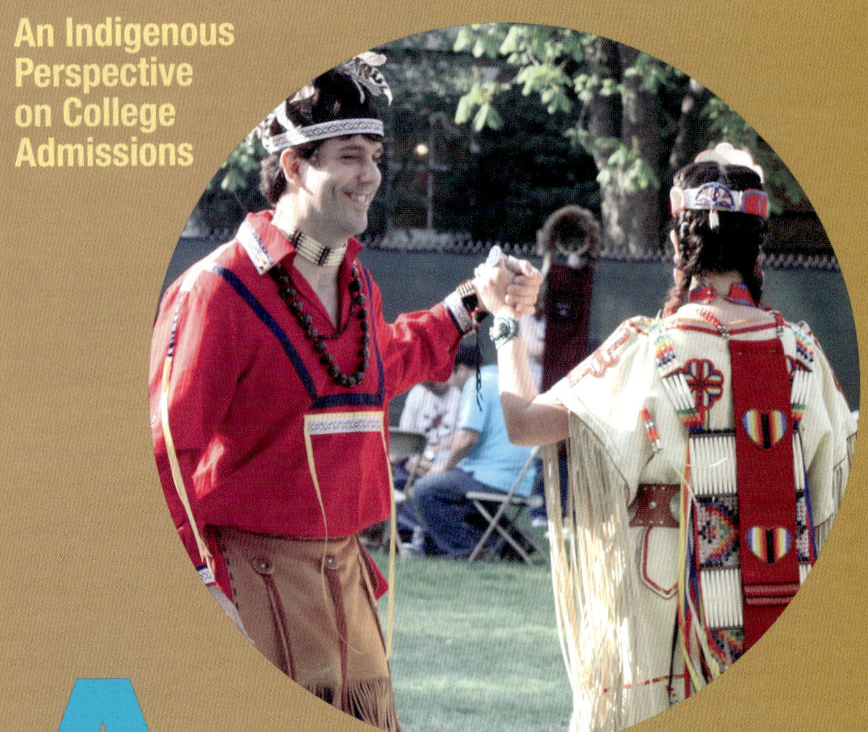

As a first-generation Native American raised in upstate New York, I never really considered attending college until my senior year. Now reflecting back after working in college admissions for the last 15 years, I often make the analogy that applying to college is like a dance since it is an important form of expression for many American Indians, and most teenagers in general.

First Steps

To this day, I distinctly remember attending my first Iroquois Social Dance and feeling like I didn't belong. It seemed that everyone already knew all the right moves, which only made me feel that much more intimidated to enter the dance ring.

Similarly, many Native American and first-generation high school graduates are scared off by college. And if they do apply, they stick with what's familiar—applying only to local colleges or those that are very well known. I'm not suggesting you apply to more than 15 colleges, but it is wise to apply to a range of schools that offer varying programs and opportunities. Don't let fear hold you back.

Learning the Beat

Before I first started dancing, I needed time to listen carefully to the beat so I could coordinate my steps appropriately. Once a high school student gets over the fear of applying to a range of colleges, the next step is understanding how to interpret the beat.

Prospective applicants must research each school they are interested in and keep track of each school's application process and deadlines.

Some schools offer rolling admission or open enrollment opportunities. But if a college offers such a program, it is still best to apply as early as possible, as on-campus housing or scholarship opportunities can sometimes be limited and are often awarded on a first-come, first-serve basis.

Expressing Uniqueness

Just like most Native American dances, especially competitive powwows, there is always room for individualized self-expression.

Once a student knows which colleges he wants to apply to, the next step is actually filling out the applications. Prospective students need to understand that although they have to follow the application guidelines, they should also take some liberty in expressing their identity.

The best way students can showcase their special talents, culture and heritage is through the personal essays, extracurricular lists, and even letters of recommendation. Even though ceremonial dances or making pottery are not high school functions, they can still be noted as extracurricular activities and expressed in an essay. Colleges seek to maintain a diverse student body and value those who are willing to share their life experiences with others.

Selecting Your Dance Partner

Once you have mustered up the courage to enter the dance ring, the most fun part is finding the right dance partner. But choosing a dance partner is a two-way street. To successfully dance with someone, the person you ask to dance must accept your invitation first.

Similarly, in the college admissions process, an applicant won't be able to fully control who a college will admit. But if your application and essays are representative of the best of your abilities, there will still be plenty of options.

When picking the right school to attend, it really does come down to personal fit. Each student and their family has to evaluate the academic offerings, location, size, support programs, and especially financial aid opportunities before a final "partner" can be chosen. Always try to visit before making the final decision. Often times, colleges offer specialized fly-in or open house programs for underserved populations.

Completing the Circle

Entering the dance circle of college admissions will not be easy but the outcome of a college education far outweighs any challenges. My advice to students is to enjoy the experience but never forget your roots.

Adapted from original article published in Winds of Change 15th Annual College Guide, 2008-09

BIO *Jarrid Whitney, Six Nations Cayuga, is Director of Undergraduate Admissions at California Institute of Technology.*

Charles Barry/SCU

College Pride, Native Pride

By Carmen Lopez

When selecting a college to attend, Native American, Alaska Native, and Native Hawaiian students have more choices than ever. There are over 300 colleges and universities that offer academic, social, cultural, and community services, programs, and student spaces to support and enhance the unique needs of Native students on campus.

Finding the right fit is especially important for Native students, who bring a unique perspective and indigenous experience, to feel comfortable in the place they will live, study, and grow in for four years. As a Native student you don't want to just survive college, you want to thrive—so make sure the college you attend provides the support and environment that will help you succeed as a student AND as a Native student.

Be proud of yourself for getting into college and show your Native Pride in college too!

Did you know that there are colleges out there that are excited to work with Native students and have created programs to attract them to their schools?

College Horizons partners with over 50 colleges that have made a commitment to recruiting Native students and meeting their full demonstrated financial need.

Learn more at www.collegehorizons.org

Questions to Ask a College

- What is the Native student enrollment?
- What percentage of Native students graduate in 4 years and in 5 years?
- What student support services do you offer Native students?
- Are there academic programs on Native Studies or Indigenous Studies?
- How many faculty teach courses in Native Studies?
- Are there any Native faculty or Native staff at the college?
- Are Native alumni active with the college?
- What percentage of Native students go onto graduate school?

COLLEGE HORIZONS

BIO Carmen Lopez is Executive Director of College Horizons, a pre-college program for Native American high school students open to sophomores and juniors. Each summer students work with college admissions officers, college counselors, essay specialists, and other educators in a week-long "crash course" on the college application process.

College Horizons College & University Participants

Amherst College (MA) – Page 237
Bard College at Simon's Rock (MA)
Bates College (ME) – Page 233
Bowdoin College (ME)
Brown University (RI)
California Institute of Technology (CA) – Page 178
Carleton College (ME)
Colby College (ME)
Colorado College (CO) – Page 200
Columbia University (NY) – Page 277
Cornell University (NY) – Page 217
Dartmouth College (NH) – Page 265
Dickinson College (PA) – Page 315
Duke University (NC) – Page 293
Emory University (NY) – Page 214
Fort Lewis College (CO)
Franklin & Marshall College (PA)
Guilford College (NC)
Hamilton College (NY) – Page 280
Hanover College (IN)
Harvard University (MA) – Page 244
Johns Hopkins University (MD) – Page 234
Kenyon College (OH)
Lawrence University (WI)
Lehigh University (PA)
Linfield College (OR)
Massachusettes Institute of Technology (MA)
New York University (NY) – Page 283
Northeastern University (MA) – Page 246
Northland College (WI)
Northwestern University (IL) – Page 222
Oberlin College (OH)
Occidental College (CA) – Page 188
Phillips Academy Andover (MA)
Pomona College (CA)
Princeton University (NJ) – Page 269
Reed College (OR) – Page 306
Rice University (TX)
Smith College (MA) – Page 247
St. Lawrence University (NY)
St. Edwards University (TX)
Stanford University (CA) – Page 193
Susquehanna University (PA)
Swarthmore College (PA)
Trinity College (CT) – Page 206
Tufts University (MA) – Page 248
University of California, Irvine (CA)
University of Chicago (IL) – Page 223
University of Denver (CO) – Page 203
University of Michigan (MI) – Page 258
University of Notre Dame (IN) – Page 228
University of Oregon (OR)
University of Pennsylvania (PA) – Page 324
University of Portland (OR)
University of Redlands (CA) – Page 194
University of Rochester (NY) – Page 291
University of San Francisco (CA) – Page 196
Ursinus College (PA)
Vanderbilt University (TN) – Page 329
Washington University in St. Louis (MO) – Page 264
Wellesley College (MA) – Page 250
Wesleyan University (CT) – Page 208
Whitman College (WA) – Page 338
Williams College (MA) – Page 251
Yale University (CT) – Page 209

Military Service Academies

Each year thousands of cadets and midshipmen enter our nation's service academies. They come from all walks of life and bring with them a variety of experiences.

Their common aim is to be challenged at the highest levels and serve our country in the most noble of professions. Cadets and midshipmen at America's service academies accept a lifestyle that is both unique and demanding. Though they differ in terms of their histories and missions, the military academies have more in common than most people think.

Range of Opportunities

Service academies all offer a rigorous four-year program. Their main focus is on developing leaders of character to serve our nation both in peace and during conflict. Tuition, room, and board are paid by the federal government. Every academy graduate receives a Bachelor of Science Degree and a commission as an officer in the uniformed services. Each academy is a top-rated undergraduate college offering majors in Engineering, Math, Science, and the Humanities. When cadets and midshipmen graduate, they have made lasting friendships through bonds forged under intense pressure and high moral and ethical standards demanded by our service academies. They are prepared to rely on each other to get the job done.

> Tuition, room and board is paid by the federal government. Every academy graduate receives a Bachelor of Science Degree and a commission as an officer in the uniformed services.

The healthy balance of these assets is considered by our Admissions Boards. Cadets and midshipmen are taught by men and women who are at the top of their fields. The ratio of students to teachers is among the lowest in the nation. The primary mission for instructors and professors is classroom teaching. Equipment is start-of-the-art and the unique challenges are unmatched. No other schools offer the range of opportunities available at a service academy.

Training and Leadership

Our academies are focused not only on providing a first-class education, but on training and leadership. Cadets and midshipmen are part of a very special team—America's Team. These young men and women are the ones we turn to to maintain our national defense. It's a big job, but these academy graduates are very well prepared. We look for well-rounded candidates: individuals with character, academic prowess, physical toughness, and the potential not only to excel at the academies but also as officers and leaders in the Air Force, Army, Navy, Marine Corps, Coast Guard, or Merchant Marine.

The principle rule of conduct is based on honor. Cadets and midshipmen do not lie, cheat, or steal. Just as they learn to use the most advanced technology in the world, these young men and women also develop an inner confidence that keeps them on the path of honor and integrity. In the process cadets and midshipmen join a long and distinguished line of academy graduates. These graduates thrive on the strength of their vision and the courage of their team.

MILITARY SERVICE ACADEMIES

The United States Air Force Academy, CO – Page 201

The United States Coast Guard Academy, CT

The United States Merchant Marine Academy, NY

The United States Military Academy at West Point, NY

The United States Naval Academy, MD

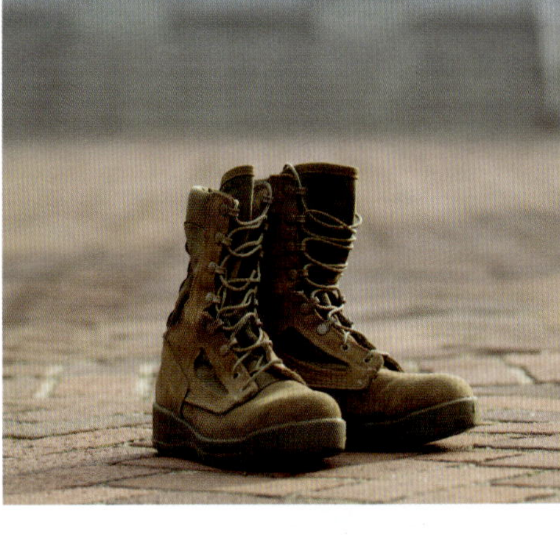

Service academy graduates excel in every sphere of influence. For those who want to reach their potential, they have the help they need to find it at any one of the five service academies.

This article was prepared and approved by the United States Air Force Academy, United States Military Academy, United States Naval Academy, United States Coast Guard Academy, and United States Merchant Marine Academy

A Women's College Might Be for You

By Susan E. Lennon

"Women not only see things differently from men, but they see different things."

– Ret. Lt. Gen. Claudia J. Kennedy

Why does this matter in your education and in your college search? Finding the right fit in a college is all about you. Why might a women's college be the right fit for you? Take a look at what matters in college—because what matters in college matters after college. And it matters in the college selection process.

Women's colleges are focused on you—your dreams and aspirations, your education, your personal and professional development for the many different roles you will assume in life, and your advancement in the ever-changing global economy. Each women's college has its own distinctive identity and culture.

From the east coast to the west coast, from the Midwest to the south, women's colleges are in the hearts of cities and deep in the country. Students come from all socioeconomic, ethnic, racial, and religious groups, from across the country and around the world. What women's college have in common is an unequivocal commitment to your education and advancement.

Research shows that a women's college education:

- Enables students to engage with top faculty and resources.
- Creates leaders, communicators, and persuaders.
- Develops critical skills for life and career.
- Proves its value over a lifetime.

Take a look at women's colleges—they're about you!

Women's Colleges in the *I'm First! Guide to College*

Barnard College (NY) – Page 276
Bay Path College (MA) – Page 239
Cedar Crest College (PA) – Page 313
Meredith College (NC) – Page 294
Mills College (CA) – Page 186
Saint Mary's College (IN) – Page 227
Smith College (MA) – Page 247
Wellesley College (MA) – Page 250

Check out the Women's College Coalition and learn more about other women's colleges at **www.womenscolleges.org**.

BIO *Susan E. Lennon is past President of the Women's College Coalition, an association of women's colleges and universities—public and private, independent and church-related, two- and four-year—in the United States and Canada whose primary mission is the education and advancement of women.*

Astronomer, teacher, lawyer...person of faith

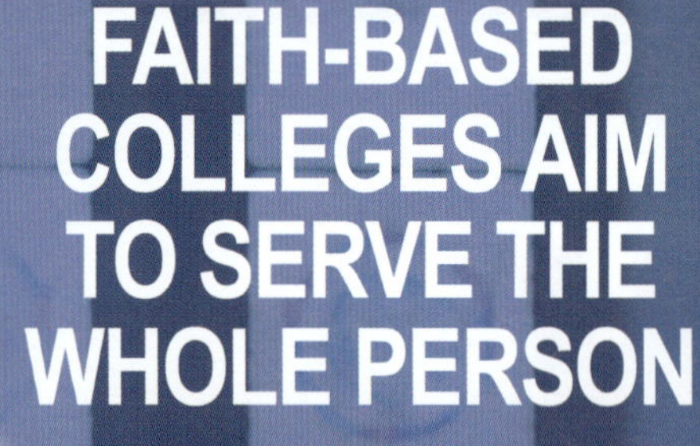

FAITH-BASED COLLEGES AIM TO SERVE THE WHOLE PERSON

Everyone knows that college is about more than earning a degree and choosing a career. Most students also use their college years to explore issues of spirituality, and faith-based institutions are good places to undertake this journey.

Faith-based colleges and universities are those related to a faith tradition. In the U.S., this usually means their heritage is Roman Catholic, Jewish, or Protestant. In only rare cases are there religious requirements to gain admission, and most of these institutions have diverse student bodies. While some of these colleges are for persons of a particular faith or denominational background, most aim to support all students in their spiritual quests.

Our nation's first colleges were founded by church groups, and most have a long tradition of providing access to underrepresented groups and those with limited financial resources. Since faith-based institutions are private, it may surprise you that these institutions use financial aid to enroll some students who have little or no family financial support.

Choosing a faith-based institution is about more than just spiritual growth. These institutions offer academic and student life programs with a point of view. Their programs of general education—the part of your academic program which is common for all students—represents their faculties' views of the world. And student life programs abound with service learning opportunities. There's nothing generic about faith-based colleges, so if you consider them you'll want to ask about their general education or core program as well as student life. Your first year at a faith-based college will be a unique experience!

Because these institutions are small by comparison, students in faith-based colleges have the advantage of getting to know their professors. You'll find rich opportunities for one-on-one learning.

The faculty members who choose to teach in a faith-based college are intentional about that decision, and they bring a deep passion for teaching in this environment as well as a desire to focus on undergraduates and teaching. They are going to get to know you and they will lend a helping hand when necessary. When one thinks about it, that's what one would expect of people working in a faith-based institution.

The research is clear, too. Alumni of faith-based institutions give their education higher marks, and the experience shows in lives of service to their communities and world.

BIO *William E. Hamm is a former president of the Lutheran Educational Conference of North America (LECNA)*

Pursuing College in Rural America

By Dreama Gentry

I'm lucky. I grew up in rural America. After going away to college and then to law school, I returned to make my home in rural Kentucky at the edge of the Appalachian Mountains. In this familiar setting, I work closely with students, teachers, and families from rural Appalachia to ensure that more rural students build the skills and structures necessary to take advantage of postsecondary opportunities and prepare themselves for collegiate success.

While nationally, rural schools have better high school graduation rates than suburban and urban schools, rural schools have lower college-going rates. Rural America must send more young people to college.

So how can a student from a small rural area get ready for college?

So how can a student from a small rural area get ready for college?

You have advantages:

- The teachers and counselors in your school know you well. In some community schools, like my son's school, students spend all of their school years in a single building. Take advantage of this. Find a teacher or counselor and form a meaningful mentoring relationship with them.
- Students in small schools have more opportunities to participate in athletics, academics, and extra-curricular activities. Get involved. Participate in a variety of activities and develop a breadth of skills.
- In most small towns, the businesses, county governments and civic organizations are looking for young people that want to be involved. Volunteer, find an internship, and offer your time and talents.

Growing up in a small town does involve limitations. Here are some ways to overcome them:

- Your school may have limited rigorous courses, such as Advanced Placement courses. Talk to your guidance counselor and do some research. Many state departments of education and community colleges offer online AP courses or first year college courses. Guidance counselors can often find funds to cover the fees for these courses if you ask.
- The closest college or university may be hours away. I was a junior in high school before I ever visited a college campus. See if there are college access programs like Upward Bound and GEAR UP that serve your school. These programs can help you prepare for college and provide you with opportunities to visit college campuses.
- The internet opens a world of possibilities to students from rural America. If you cannot visit a campus, participate in the online campus tours. You can experience the campus, hear from current students, and get a feel for what the campus is like.
- Many rural areas lack diversity. Seek out opportunities to meet and interact with people from different backgrounds and cultures. Talk with your family about hosting an international student, or participate in clubs and organizations that provide opportunities to interact with diverse groups of people.

When I came to college, I found that my campus was very similar to the small town where I grew up. The skills that I developed growing up in rural America helped me find my place. The campus community became my support network, much like my family and small town had been my support system back home.

BIO *As Executive Director for the Partners for Education program at Berea College, Dreama Gentry leads educational outreach initiatives in rural Appalachian Kentucky.*

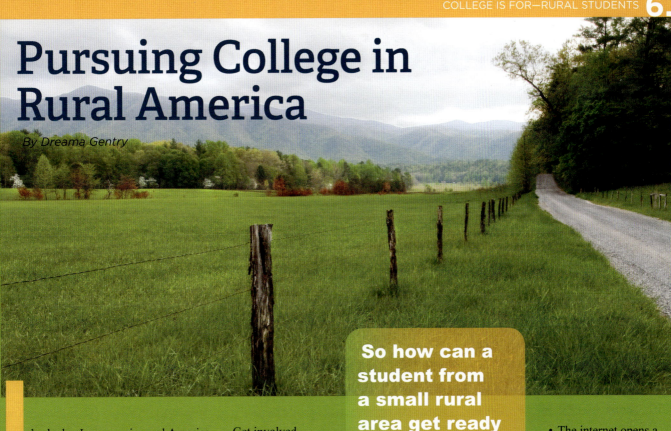

From Foster Care to College

By John Emerson

> Graduating from college meant that I won. Most of all, it meant that I would gain the knowledge to use my experience in foster care to help other people. College meant freedom from my past and the ability to choose my future.
>
> *–Maria, 2007 college graduate*

Graduating from college provides lifelong benefits, such as increased earning power, health benefits, career satisfaction, and a large supportive network of friends, mentors, and professors. And for students raised in foster care, college is often an essential step toward a better life. As Niki, a current college sophomore formerly raised in foster care, reflects, "College offered me the opportunity to break the negative cycle of my upbringing and make a better life for myself. I can take a negative experience and turn it into something positive with all the opportunities in front of me."

So why do so few young adults from foster care ever enroll in or graduate from college? The reasons are varied, but lack of stable guidance is all too common.

This trend seems to be changing. More and more students from foster care are now attending college and finding success. "Coming from the system is no excuse to do poorly in school," says Orlando, a college junior. "We have to break the cycle of living in poverty. Forget about the statistics against you and make something out of your lives. College is the only thing in your life that cannot be taken from you." A growing number of colleges are reaching out to this underserved population, and welcoming them into their programs.

On-campus support services that address their housing, academic, health, and career development needs are increasing. And financial aid resources from a variety of public and private sources are now making it possible for students coming from foster care to attend college without overwhelming loan obligations. Some states also offer good educational benefits for students who choose to stay in foster care until age 21.

BIO *John Emerson is the Postsecondary Education Advisor at Casey Family Programs. Casey Family Programs is the nation's largest operating foundation entirely focused on foster care.*

ADVICE FOR STUDENTS IN FOSTER CARE

What can you do to successfully prepare for college? How do you silence avoidable fears and concerns? Here are a few tips from successful college students who were formerly in foster care:

Problem: Foster care students don't dream about or plan for college, as they have experienced so much disappointment and trauma in their lives.

Solution: "When I learned that there was a section on college applications where you could write about 'extenuating circumstances,' it changed everything. Use this area of the application to talk about the difficulties and challenges you faced growing up in the foster care system." *Margaret*

Problem: Foster care students rarely have a stable educational advocate, mentor or "college coach" on their side to guide and encourage them to succeed.

Solution: "Sign up for college visits, financial aid events, and whatever else you can find. Become friendly with the person who runs the college office. Begin visiting colleges as soon as you can, because things really start piling up your junior and senior years, and you want to have time to fill out applications and write essays for scholarships." *Renee*

Problem: Foster care students change schools frequently; which results in lost records, credit deficiencies, repeated classes, and inconsistent high school and college advising.

Solution: "Talk to your counselor to make sure you have the classes needed for the college you want to attend." *Malcolm*

"Have a calendar or binder where you keep all of your college information in chronological order; that way everything will go smoothly." *Candice*

Problem: Colleges are usually unaware of foster care students' unique support needs and of the various issues they face.

Solution: "Use the free counseling and health center that most campuses offer. Don't be afraid to talk about any problems you may be facing." *Damon*

Problem: Foster care students don't know how or where to get enough financial aid to pay for their college careers.

Solution: "Get to know professors, financial aid advisors, counselors, and support staff throughout campus. They want to help you!" *Nicki*

Problem: Foster care students don't know who to ask for advice or who to turn to for support.

Solution: "Go and sign up for some clubs! By joining extracurricular activities you will begin building friendships and have an outlet for the pressures of college." *Renee*

"Find a study group and stick with them. They really help you get better grades." *Brigit*

Free Online Resources

Foster Care to Success (FC2S)

www.fc2success.org

FC2S provides scholarships for college and post-secondary education, as well as internships, virtual mentoring, care packages, and critical resources to guide foster teens to success.

Foster Care Alumni of America (FCAA)

www.fostercarealumni.org

Founded and led by alumni of the foster care system, FCAA connects the alumni community and transforms foster care policy and practice, ensuring opportunity for people in and from foster care.

Foster Club: The National Network for Young People in Foster Care

www.fosterclub.com

Foster Club has chapters and resources available in most states that can assist you and help provide a network of support. Just click on the "State-by-State" tab.

California Youth Connection (CYC)

www.calyouthconn.org

Guided, focused and driven by current and former foster youth with the assistance of other committed community members, CYC promotes the participation of foster youth in policy development and legislative change to improve the foster care system. CYC has chapters in counties throughout California.

California College Pathways

www.cacollegepathways.org

The goal of the California College Pathways is to increase the number of foster youth in California who enter higher education and achieve an academic or training outcome by expanding access to campus support programs. You can find out about resources, supports and college preparation opportunities.

HOMELESSNESS and COLLEGE EDUCATION aren't often discussed in the same sentence, and it is rarely positive.

Khadijah Williams
College: Harvard University
Hometown: Los Angeles, CA

For low-income students like us, it's enough of a challenge to get through high school. Being homeless presents its own crazy challenges. Your transcript reads like the CIA's most wanted, except, instead of moving from country to country, you move from city to city, county to county, or even state to state, often within the span of weeks or days. How is education even in the cards?! You don't even have steady food or shelter.

I don't remember even participating in the first grade, or finishing the second grade, 5th grade is a blur, 6th grade was a one month stint, 7th grade was speckled with absences, tardies, and unsatisfactories for late work or no work. In middle school, teachers thought I could care less about my education, and I let them believe that. I didn't want them to know I was homeless. But I wanted to learn, I loved to learn, I needed to learn.

But there was hope. It's not as easy as saying, "I'm homeless, let me in your college." I had to fight feelings of insecurity and anxiety, not to mention not knowing what the college process entailed. I didn't know where and how to apply. I applied to two colleges without knowing what the heck I was doing. I didn't know what kind of recommendations I needed, or if my teachers, who only knew me a couple of semesters, knew enough about me. I didn't have a computer to apply to college! Often, it was the lack of these few resources that made my college process suffer.

It can be done though. The key is to seek help. You DO NOT have to do the college application process alone. Seek programs and resources designed to help low income kids. Ask your school about college prep programs. Upward Bound is one of many great programs that you can apply to as early as 9th grade. Find people who you admire, who went to college, and ask for their help. You wouldn't believe how helpful people can be once they know you want to go to college. I got where I am today because of two things—my inner drive and the help from caring adults who I looked up to as role models. Good, caring people will want to see you succeed, and they'll go out of their way to help you if you let it be known that you will do whatever it takes to succeed.

KHADIJAH WILLIAMS is an I'm First! scholarship winner. Khadijah shares her college experiences and offers advice on the I'm First! student blog.

Visit www.ImFirst.org to follow the student blog and watch video testimonials from first-generation college students and graduates.

Undocumented Students *Can* Attend College

By Jose Arreola

KNOW WHERE YOU STAND Don't know your immigration status? Immigration is tricky, but it's crucial that you know your status before you begin applying to college and filling out financial aid forms. So double-check with your parents or family members. Let them know why it's important that you know this information.

Growing up in the United States, I always knew that I was undocumented, even though I didn't understand what my status truly meant. I only knew that I was somehow different than other people because I was born in a different country—Mexico. But as I grew older, I began to confront what being undocumented in the US actually meant. It meant my family and I could be forcibly deported at any moment. It meant that I did not have access to the same benefits, protections and rights as U.S. citizens. And it meant that a higher education would be far more difficult to obtain—if not impossible. I was fortunate because I was able to connect with mentors and educators who provided me with accurate information, access to resources and a sense of hope that college could be a reality. I am the beneficiary of the efforts of many dedicated activists, community leaders and a deeply resilient family.

Though we have seen a significant improvement regarding support and resources for undocumented students, college access and completion remains a challenge.

Here are some pieces of advice and guidance for undocumented youth looking to further their education:

Believe

I was told many times growing up that college was not a reality for me because I was poor and brown and undocumented. And after a while, the message became so pervasive and overwhelming that I even found myself believing it. The fact is, thousands of undocumented youth have been able to overcome remarkable challenges go to college and graduate! Before beginning your journey, you must believe that it's possible- despite any obstacle!

Know Where You Stand

Don't know your immigration status? Immigration is tricky, but it's crucial that you know your status before you begin applying to college and filling out financial aid forms. So double-check with your parents or family members. Let them know why it's important that you know this information.

Applying to College

All students, regardless of immigration status, can apply to college—unless a state/institution formally prohibits it. Your college application will be processed even if you don't provide your social security number, citizenship, and residency status.

The confidentiality of your educational records—application and financial aid forms—is guaranteed by the Family Educational Rights and Privacy Act (FERPA), which covers both high schools and colleges.

Scholarships and Financial Aid

We have seen a tremendous amount of movement over the past couple of years with regard to financial aid being made available to undocumented students. We now have 20 states or state university systems that have enacted laws or policies to allow eligible undocumented students to pay in-state tuition. Six states have enacted policies permitting DACA grantees to establish residency for tuition purposes and receive some tuition benefits.

These states allow undocumented/immigrant students to receive in-state tuition. Research your own state policies to see if you are eligible.

Alabama*	Nebraska
Arizona*	New Hampshire*
California	New Jersey
Colorado	New Mexico
Connecticut	New York
Florida	Ohio*
Hawaii	Oklahoma
Illinois	Oregon
Kansas	Rhode Island
Maryland	Texas
Massachusetts*	Utah
Michigan	Virginia*
Minnesota	Washington

**state allows DACA beneficiaries to get in-state tuition*

Last updated January 2017

Other Ways to Make College Affordable

• While immigration status may prohibit us from accessing federal financial aid, there are plenty of private scholarships which are open to undocumented youth. Start searching early and keep it going. We have seen many private and community scholarship providers either begin accepting undocumented students or significantly increase their support to undocumented students. One example is TheDream.US—a multi-million dollar national scholarship exclusively for undocumented students.

• Even if undocumented young people aren't eligible to fill out the FAFSA, we can still fill out the CSS Profile for participating schools to receive aid from individual institutions.

• Research private colleges and universities and local community colleges. Private institutions often have more flexibility to fund undocumented students than public schools.

Community college could be a more affordable way to get your education started. In fact, a large percentage—if not the majority—of undocumented college students starts in community college and then transfer to a 4-year university.

Deferred Action for Childhood Arrivals

I am the beneficiary of a Department of Homeland Security program called Deferred Action for Childhood Arrivals or DACA. The program provides eligible undocumented young people between the ages of 15 and 30 with a two-year work authorization and protection from deportation. There are hundreds of thousands of undocumented young people who are currently eligible, but have not yet applied. With my DACA approval, I was able to receive a social security number and a driver's license. And for the first time—even if it may only be temporarily—I do not have to worry about getting deported from the United States.

This program has provided close to a million undocumented students with the ability to access employment, study abroad through advance parole, and other educational benefits!

Connect to Legal Services

Due to the cost or accessibility of credible immigration legal services, many undocumented students are not able to get their immigration case reviewed. The distrust that stems from experiences with fraudulent individuals and "notarios," further complicates access to legal services. And because of this, undocumented young people often cannot take advantage or existing immigration remedies or programs such as DACA. If you have the opportunity, I would highly recommend getting your immigration case reviewed!

Connect to Group and the Movement

One of the hardest things about being undocumented is the isolation. I could not be open about my immigration status because of fear for my own safety and the safety of my family. It wasn't until college that I found a group of undocumented students who shared the same passions and aspirations as me. We were able to share stories, offer support, share resources, and confront problems collectively. As we see more and more student groups like this emerging, we have seen a higher level of awareness for the importance of emotional and mental health support for undocumented people, given our experiences with violent enforcement, loss, isolation, and stigma.

BIO *Jose Arreola is Outreach & Organizing Manager for Educators for Fair Consideration (E4FC). Jose was born in Durango, Mexico and came to the United States when he was four years old. He attended Santa Clara University, where he received a full scholarship. As an undocumented student himself, Jose utilizes his experiences to help empower and support other undocumented students across the country.*

ABOUT EDUCATORS FOR FAIR CONSIDERATION (E4FC)

Educators for Fair Consideration (E4FC) is a San Francisco-based non-profit organization that empowers undocumented young people to pursue their dreams of college, career, and citizenship in the United States. We address the holistic needs of undocumented young people through direct support, leadership development, community outreach, and advocacy. For more information, please visit www.e4fc.org.

WHAT DOES IT MEAN TO BE AN UNDOCUMENTED STUDENT?

Luis Espino
College: Pomona College
Hometown: Napa, CA

This was a question I grew to ponder, especially at the peak of college applications. I came to the realization that for most of my life, I really downplayed my underprivileged position as undocumented. I remember having a conversation with my cousin and telling him that I did not feel as if being undocumented had been a major obstacle in my life up to that point, specifically because it had not affected me directly or prevented me from doing what I had wanted to do (academically) up to that point.

Well, this conversation took place before I began to delve deep into the college admissions process, and before it dawned on me how many schools I couldn't apply to, either because they did not accept undocumented students or because they were federally funded, meaning I was not eligible for financial aid. I realized that although I had not been detained or I had not been prevented from getting a driver's license (Deferred Action for Childhood Arrivals (DACA) had been enacted by that time), I was at a severe disadvantage compared to other students in terms of mere opportunities that were available for me.

This same conversation, in hindsight, prepared me for the trek ahead of me, and gave me something to hold in those desperate weeks of college applications. I remember my cousin asking me, "Think about it Luis, if you weren't undocumented, would you be where you are today?"

Truthfully, I don't know where I would be if I didn't grow up seeing my family's constant state of vulnerability. If my parents did not have to work long hours in miserable conditions, if they did not have a family to provide for in Mexico, if my parents had a stable job, decent wages, retirement benefits, and every other privilege that is more attainable with being a citizen of this country, I don't know if I would have faced challenges with the same urgency that I have to date.

In the same way that it is easy to take for granted the privilege of being documented in America, I took for normal the underprivileged position I am in, and failed to see the privilege it had afforded me in being able to turn my undocumented status into a driving force.

To anyone undocumented, who may feel intimidated, afraid, or belittled by the thought of college, I encourage you to look at your situation, acknowledge your struggle, and see the value of your story. Seek out people who can see it for you even when you can't and who will encourage you to keep trekking. Know that there are resources, that there are schools looking for more than GPA and SAT scores, and that more of your perspective is needed in college institutions.

Here are **a few resources and opportunities** for undocumented students (a couple of which include a full ride!) that I have found useful. Best of luck!

The Dream.US - www.thedream.us
Golden Door Scholars - www.goldendoorscholars.org
Educators for Fair Consideration (E4FC) - www.e4fc.org
MALDEF Scholarship Resources - www.maldef.org
QuestBridge - www.questbridge.org

LUIS ESPINO is an I'm First! Scholarship winner. Luis shares his college experiences and offers advice on the I'm First! student blog.

Visit www.ImFirst.org to follow the student blog and watch video testimonials from first-generation college students and graduates.

I AM A SINGLE TEEN MOM AND I AM ENROLLED FULL-TIME AT COLLEGE WHILE WORKING FULL-TIME.

Tereza Ponce de Leon
College: Augsburg College
Hometown: Saint Paul, MN

That is a statement that you do not hear often. As most already know, when you get pregnant in high school everyone automatically assumes that you are not going to graduate high school, let alone go on to college. I am proud to say that I am still pursing my dreams and going to college.

In my opinion, getting pregnant does not prevent you from doing anything. I can take the same road as everyone else does; my road is just a little bumpier. Is it hard? Yes, it is hard, but it is worth it.

Since my mom did not go to college and my father did not even finish high school, I came from a place where my parents struggled with money every day to raise my brother and me. I do not want that type of life for my son. I want him to be able to have a better life and have more opportunities than I had. I know that none of that can be possible if I do not go to college to get an education to better myself. Once you have a child everything you do affects your child too, and I know that bettering myself is what is best for him.

To be able to go to college full-time, work full-time, and be a mom full-time takes a lot of time management skills. Basically every minute of every day I am busy doing something. At times, it can be a bit stressful, but I just have to keep thinking about the reward at the end. To be less stressed you have to try your best to not procrastinate and keep up with your school work. If you let your school work pile up on you then it will add stress to your life that you do not need.

I hope that more teen moms realize that they can still go to college because it is not an impossible dream. It just takes hard work and determination, and in the end, it will benefit you and your child more than you know.

TEREZA PONCE DE LEON is an I'm First! scholarship winner. Tereza shares her college experiences and offers advice on the I'm First! first-generation student blog.

Visit www.ImFirst.org to follow the student blog and watch video testimonials from first-generation college students and graduates.

Did you know that several colleges offer special housing and educational programs for single parents?

Having a child during high school or college does not have to deter your pursuit of a college degree. In fact, a handful of schools across the country offer residential, social, and academic programs for women and their children.

Here are 20 schools with single parent programs to consider:

Baldwin Wallace University (OH) – Page 298
Berea College (KY)
Brigham Young University (UT)
Champlain College (VT)
College of Saint Mary (NE)
Eastern Michigan University
Endicott College (MA)
Ferris State University (MI) – Page 253
Mills College (CA) – Page 186
Minnesota State University
Misericordia University (PA)
Mount Holyoke College (MA)
Saint Paul's College (MN)
Smith College (MA) – Page 247
St. Catherine University (MN)
Texas Woman's University
University of Iowa
University of Massachusetts, Amherst
University of Wisconsin-Eau Claire
Wilson College (PA)

Wilson College also houses the **National Clearinghouse for Single Mothers in Higher Education**, a clearinghouse of information to assist single parent women in the process of becoming successful college students, as well as mothers.

Check out www.wilson.edu/helpful-resources-0

IF YOU'RE LGBTQ+

Abigail Macias
Dartmouth College
Hometown: Reno, NV

College provides students with the opportunity to explore their identity inside and outside the classroom. For some, this may mean challenging a previously steadfast ideal of theirs or discovering a new passion. For others, this may also include exploring their sexuality and/or gender.

During my freshman year, I found myself in the latter group; I had met men *and* women whom I found attractive but felt ashamed of admitting it. Was there a word for what I was feeling? Were these feelings solely due to my newfound environment or were they reflective of something else? Had others experienced something similar? Because I was raised in a conservative Mexican household, I felt that it was better to ignore this internal conflict rather than face a potentially hurtful response from my parents. It would eventually go away, right?

Wrong. Self-denial rapidly became a detrimental source of stress. Would I ever be able to truly share this experience with those who motivated me to come to college in the first place if I couldn't even tell them that I'm queer? I wrestled with this question for many weeks until one of my professors noticed and asked me to stop by her office hours.

Our conversation reassured me that I wasn't the first—or last—person to question my sexuality, and she directed me to the LGBTQ+ (Lesbian, Gay, Bi-Sexual, Transgender, Queer) and Ally Life Office. There, I discovered an experienced advisor ready to provide the support I deeply needed as well as many other campus resources, which included weekly facilitated discussion groups and community building events open to all students. I attended a few and gradually developed the invaluable friendships that gave me the confidence to come out to my family as a queer woman. My siblings were incredibly supportive and, although my parents took a bit longer in coming around, they have since tried to be as understanding as possible; I'm finally at peace.

If you are questioning your sexuality or wondering how to become an ally, remember that there are people on campus who have had similar experiences and are more than willing to help you. **Your college is more than likely to also have a LGBTQ+ information center** and to provide some of the following resources to help you find the support you need:

- LGBTQ+ advisor
- confidential counseling through advisor and/or health services
- designated "safe zones"
- educational and sexual health workshops
- student organizations and conferences
- peer, faculty, and alumni mentoring

If you feel uncomfortable asking a professor or peer about campus LGBTQ+ resources, you could also visit your school's website (usually under "Student Life" or similar heading) and directly contact the individuals you'd feel most at ease talking to. Surround yourself with positive, considerate people and your journey of self-discovery will continue despite whatever roadblocks you find along the way.

ABIGAIL MACIAS is an I'm First! scholarship winner. Abigail shares her college experiences and offers advice on the I'm First! student blog.

Visit www.ImFirst.org to follow the student blog and watch video testimonials from first-generation college students and graduates.

Quiz Answer Key

Unit 1 Quiz Answer Key

Multiple Choice:

1. a
2. c
3. d
4. d
5. c

True or False:

1. True
2. False: more jobs now than ever require a college degree.
3. False: most schools would rather see a student who has tried to challenge herself than one who has a perfect GPA but has only taken easy courses.
4. True
5. False: colleges look for an upwards trend in students' grades. So if your grades are better in junior and senior year, your transcript will show improvement over time.

Fill in the Blank:

1. Multiple Answers: Strive for College's *I'm First!* Website, The National College Access Program Directory, National Partnership for Educational Access, Council of Opportunity in Education.
2. Letters of recommendation
3. Extracurricular activities
4. Short, long
5. First-generation

Unit 2 Quiz Answer Key

Multiple Choice:

1. a
2. c
3. b
4. a
5. c

True or False:

1. False: Though many students enter community college with the intention of transferring to a four-year university, most never do.
2. False: Along with "likely" schools, every student should apply to best-fit and reach schools.
3. True
4. False: Most students who choose their major freshman year will eventually change it, so only considering schools that have a specific major is probably not in your best interest.
5. True

Fill in the Blank:

1. Historically Black College or University (HBCU)
2. Retention Rate
3. Hispanic Serving Institution
4. Student/Faculty
5. College fair

Unit 3 Quiz Answer Key

Multiple Choice:

1. c
2. a
3. d
4. d
5. b

True or False:

1. True
2. False: You may not have any electronics with you when you take the SAT/ACTs.
3. False: You should always adhere to the word limit assigned.
4. True.
5. True.

Fill in the Blank:

1. Common Application
2. GPA
3. Hook
4. Class Rank
5. SAT Subject Tests

Unit 4 Quiz Answer Key

Multiple Choice:

1. d
2. a
3. c
4. d
5. c

True or False:

1. True
2. False: There are many scholarships available to younger students, so you should start looking for scholarships as early as the ninth grade.
3. True
4. True
5. False: Some schools that have high sticker prices have great financial aid resources, making the out-of-pocket price very affordable.

Fill in the Blank:

1. Loan
2. Work-Study
3. Pell
4. Expected Family Contribution
5. FAFSA

Unit 5 Quiz Answer Key

Multiple Choice:

1. b
2. d
3. b
4. c
5. d

True or False:

1. True
2. True
3. False: You must officially accept your offer letter either online or by mail (depending on the school).
4. True
5. False: College is all about opening yourself up to new people and new experiences, so push yourself out of your comfort zone.

Fill in the Blank:

1. Placement
2. Register
3. Orientation
4. Textbooks
5. Transcript

Padres y Mentores en Español página 151

PARENTS & MENTORS

Whether you're a parent, guardian, teacher, mentor, or other caring adult, chances are there's a teen in your life who wants to go to college. You can help your teen succeed by taking time to learn about college planning and financing. Together, you and the teen you care about can share this important goal and achieve it.

MENTORS: Why College?

Q

"Why should I get a college degree?" Has the teen in your life ever asked you this question? Whether you're a parent, guardian, or other caring adult, you need convincing, practical answers to share with your teen. Here they are:

A

"You'll gain greater understanding and skills to help you be successful in our complex world."

College enables you to:

- Expand your knowledge and skills.
- Express your thoughts clearly in speech and in writing.
- Grasp abstract concepts and theories.
- Increase your understanding of the world and your community.
- Gain more financial security.

"You'll find a greater range and a number of job opportunities."

In our changing world, more and more jobs require education beyond high school. College graduates have more jobs to choose from than those who don't pursue education beyond high school.

"You'll earn more money—a lot more."

A person who goes to college usually earns more than a person who doesn't. According to the U.S. Census Bureau, on average, someone with a bachelor's degree earns $51,206—almost double the $27,915 earned annually by someone with only a high school diploma.

KnowHow2GO *Printed with permission from KnowHow2GO. Learn more at KnowHow2GO.org.*

Planning for College: Ten Steps

10

Step One

Save money as early as possible to help pay for your teen's education.

Step Two

Encourage your teen to make high school count, preparing academically for higher education.

Step Three

Discuss with your teen his or her skills and interests, career options and schools he or she is interested in attending.

Step Four

Meet with the high school guidance counselor to determine what schools match your teen's academic abilities.

Step Five

Gather information about the schools your teen is interested in attending, including information on financial aid.

Step Six

Take your teen to visit a college campus and ask the right questions.

Step Seven

Help your teen apply for admission. To apply for financial aid, help your child complete the FAFSA.

Step Eight

Consider scholarships, grants, and work-study programs. Complete any necessary applications or forms and submit them before the deadline.

Step Nine

Consider the loan programs available to you and your child.

Step Ten

Learn more about tax credits, deductions, and other considerations for education expenses.

Talking to Your Teen

It may not always be easy to talk with your teen. But it's important that you support your teen throughout their college planning—help them organize the process, meet deadlines, and talk with the right people. Here are a few tips to consider:

Listen.
Be receptive to and listen when your teen wants to discuss career and/or college plans.

Explore.
Have your teen explore career and college options and collect as much information as possible.

Encourage.
Encourage them to capture their ideas on paper. One idea is to create a scrapbook of their plans for career and college.

Be aware.
Be aware of various deadlines for applications to colleges and financial aid. Put them on a calendar that both you and your teen can look at.

Step in.
Suggest that your teen meet with a school counselor at least once a year, beginning in the 10th grade, to learn more about college and career planning.

Step out.
Give your teen the space *and* support to set some goals and take steps to reach them.

Be supportive.
Be supportive of your teen, and meet with their counselor if you sense that he or she needs additional help.

Connect to career.
Encourage your teen by helping them see the connection between college and career. Emphasize the importance of selecting a major that helps them prepare for a career.

Research.
If your teen is undecided about a career direction, do not try to fix it. Let them look into all the possibilities.

Conversation-Starters

We know that it is often difficult to break the ice with students and get them talking about the steps they need to take to go to college. Think about asking your student the following questions to encourage him or her to turn college dreams into a college plan.

Which adults in your life do you know who went to college?

What excites you about going to college?

What are the reasons you want to go?

I know you want to go to college. Who else have you told about your college plans?

Which adults do you turn to for help when you have a problem you need to solve?

STEP 1 BE A PAIN

Students know that colleges require certain courses, but they often don't know which ones or find out too late into high school to take them all. Get your student thinking about the courses required for college admission by asking some of the following questions:

What courses are you taking this year?

Which courses do you find easiest?

Which do you find the hardest?

Have you thought about which courses are required for certain majors or careers?

Does your high school offer Advanced Placement courses?

How can you sign up?

STEP 2 PUSH YOURSELF

KnowHow2GO *Printed with permission from KnowHow2GO. Learn more at KnowHow2GO.org.*

Conversation-Starters

It is often hard for students to visualize the many postsecondary options available to them. But finding the right fit is an important factor in ensuring a student enjoys and completes college. Use the following questions to get your student thinking about the type of school that's right for him or her.

When you think about college …

Do you have thoughts on what you'd like to study?

Are you interested in going away to school or going to school close to home?

Do you like the idea of a big campus with a lot of students or a smaller campus?

Are you interested in participating in activities like sports? Music? Community service?

Would you like to be in an urban environment or somewhere more rural?

Do you want to live in a campus dorm or commute from home?

STEP 3 FIND THE RIGHT FIT

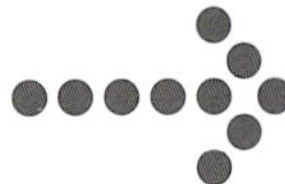

It's hard to talk about money, especially with middle or high school students who may not understand their family's financial situation. Here are some ways to start the conversation and get your student thinking about preparing financially for college.

What courses are you taking this year?

Do you know that the government provides loans to students who can't afford college?

Have you talked with your parents about how you might pay for college?

Where would you look first for information about loans and scholarships? Is there an adult at school who would know where to look?

Do you have questions about how much college costs?

STEP 4 PUT YOUR HANDS ON SOME CASH

By Jaye Fenderson

Getting Your Child To College – No Degree Required!

It all begins with knowing when to get started and how to find the information you need.

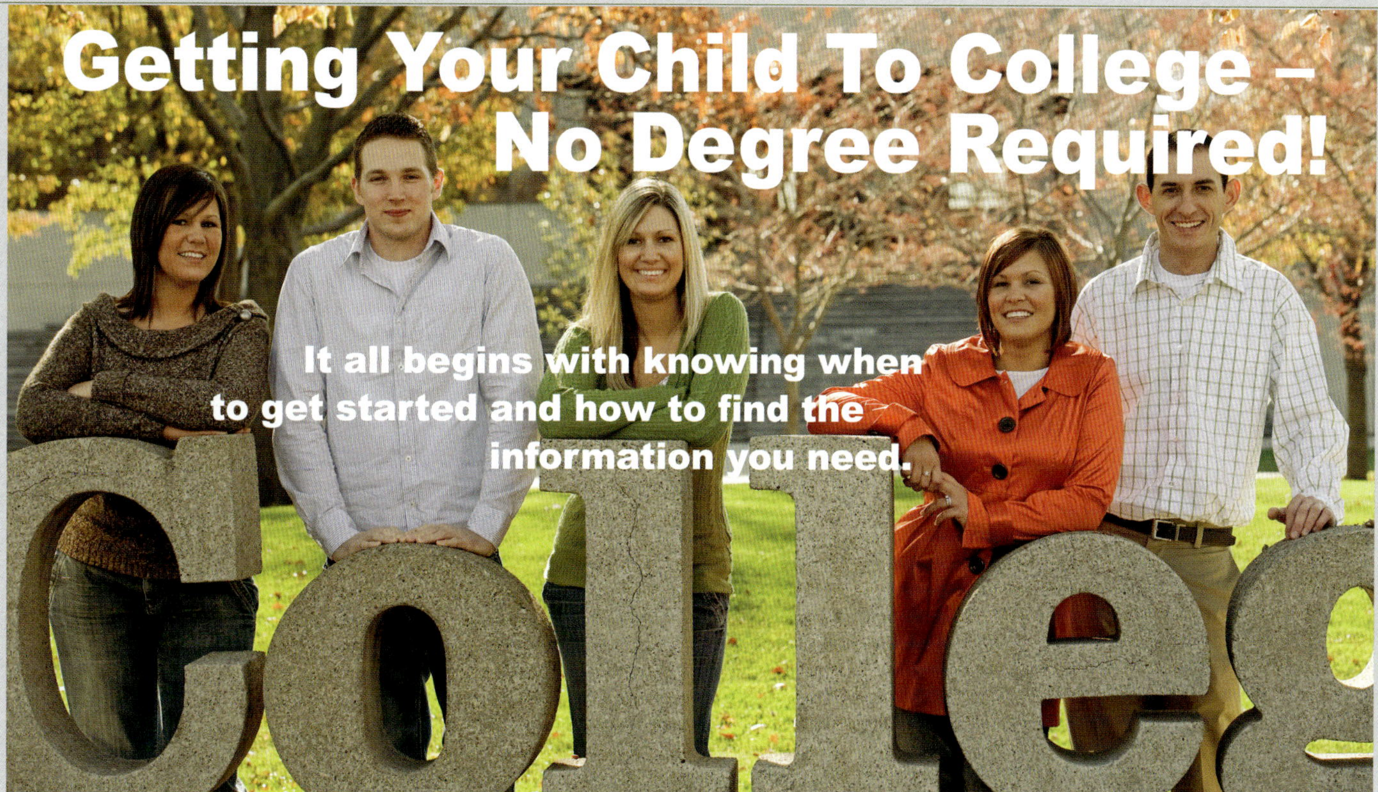

For many parents the idea of their son or daughter going to college is exciting but also overwhelming.

There's a lot to think about and plan for even if you're a parent that graduated from college. But the good news is that there is a wealth of information about how to prepare and apply for college, so even if this is your first time going through the process, rest assured that there are resources to help you and your teenager find the best college fit at an affordable price.

It all begins with knowing when to get started and how to find the information you need.

Start Early – Get a College Mindset

Many students wait until senior year before they start thinking about their college plans, but the truth is that students should actually start planning for college in middle school or junior high. Why so early, you might ask? Well, that's because colleges take into consideration all four years of high school (9th-12th) including the classes a student takes, his or her GPA, as well as any activities, leadership or awards received.

Get Organized

You'll soon receive a flood of information in the form of college brochures, scholarship and financial aid forms, and notifications from your child's guidance office. If you don't have a way to organize all this information, it can be overwhelming or worse yet, you might end up losing track of important papers.

So help your teen create a simple filing system with dividers labeled for college brochures, scholarships, financial aid, as well as one for your child's awards and accomplishments. By the time senior year rolls around, you'll easily be able to access the information you need to help your teen apply for college. You should get in the habit of keeping a calendar on the refrigerator or in your teen's bedroom that lists important college admission dates and deadlines.

Know Where to Look

Visit the high school's college and career center—this is the most important resource where you'll find information about financial aid, local scholarships, and college deadlines and requirements—and meet with your teen's counselor at the beginning of high school.

Attend a college night or college fair—most school districts will typically hold some kind of college information session where admission representatives from schools across the country will attend to share information about their programs and how to apply.

Don't Be Afraid to Ask

One of the best resources you have is the power of asking. If you're unsure about an admissions requirement, the cost of applying, or how to fill out the college or financial aid forms, talk to your teen's college counselor, call the college admissions or financial aid office, or find someone—another parent or a current college student—who has recently been through the college admissions process and may be able to answer your question.

So don't be afraid to ask for help – and once you've been through the process yourself, you'll be able to lend a hand to another family. ■

BIO *Jaye Fenderson is the author of Seventeen's* Guide to Getting Into College *and the producer of First Generation, a documentary about students who are first in their families to go to college.*

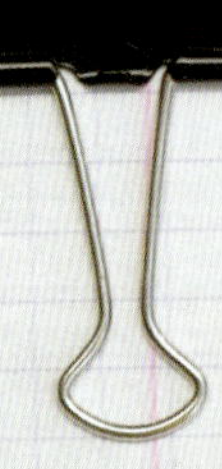

You've probably heard, and might believe, some of these common MYTHS about college. Read on for the REALITIES.

MYTH: Anyone can get into a public university, but it's hard to get into a private college.

REALITY: Some public universities are among the most competitive to get into, while other public universities are required to take nearly all applicants. It's true that some private colleges are very selective, but others take students who wouldn't even be admitted to a home state public university. Check with the colleges you are considering to learn more about the average academic credentials of its students and its admission policies.

MYTH: The college with the lowest price will be the most affordable.

REALITY: Not necessarily! Some of the colleges with a high "sticker price" have raised significant amounts of money for scholarships from their graduates and friends. As a result, they have more money to give to students in the form of scholarships, which reduces the "sticker price." After taking financial aid into consideration, a seemingly more expensive college may be more affordable than a college with a lower list price. Tip: Find out what kinds of scholarship options are available at the colleges you are considering.

MYTH: My teen can make a good living without a college education.

REALITY: There is no doubt that some people have done well without a college degree. However, a college graduate will earn on average about a million dollars more than a high school graduate in his/her lifetime. For most people, college pays.

MYTH: Courses and grades in the spring of senior year aren't important because students already have been accepted by a college by the time those courses are done.

REALITY: Most colleges make statements in their admissions materials that they will look at a senior's spring grades. If the student's academic performance has dropped off substantially, colleges have been known to cancel an offer of admission.

MYTH: To make it in today's world you need a four-year college degree.

REALITY: Someone with a four-year degree may have more career options, but there are many satisfying and good-paying jobs that are possible with certain technical or two-year degrees. Your teen should start with the fields that are of interest to him and learn what kind of education is required and what the job opportunities are in those areas. Then get the degree he needs for the type of career he wants.

MYTH: I don't have the money and my teen can't afford to take out loans to pay for college, even if she wanted to go.

REALITY: Almost all students today can get low-rate education loans to help them pay for college, and education loans typically don't have to be paid back until a student is out of school. The average loan debt of undergraduate students today is roughly $20,000 – that's less than the cost of most new cars! A car lasts a few years. A college education lasts a lifetime.

KnowHow2GO *Printed with permission from KnowHow2GO. Learn more at KnowHow2GO.org*

MYTH: It really doesn't matter if I wait a year or two to go to college.

REALITY: Many students who don't go to college right after high school never get around to it. Others bring great experience to the college when they enroll because of what they did with the time off from school. It is wise for a student to apply to colleges of interest during senior year just like any other student. She can then ask a college to defer enrollment for a year or two, if the student needs the time away. Most colleges will hold the offer of admission, especially if the student has plans that will ultimately make the student even more interesting or valuable as a member of the campus community.

Caution: If the student works during this time away, the income of the student (if substantial) may hinder her/his need-based financial aid eligibility when s/he goes back to school. Because the student will in many cases still qualify as a dependent student, only a small amount of income will be protected under the federal formula. Amounts beyond that can hurt financial aid eligibility.

MYTH: You need to start planning for college during your junior year of high school.

REALITY: While some students may wait this late to do certain things like visiting potential colleges or taking the SAT's, there are other things that should never wait this long. For example, high school course selections and grades represent the single most important consideration in most colleges' admissions decisions. High school course decisions are made sometimes as early as the middle school years. Financial planning, saving for college, and finding out which colleges will be affordable also should be done well before the junior year.

MYTH: No one in my family has gone to college – why should my teen be the first?

REALITY: After high school, your teen may have 40 or 50 years of employment ahead. Many changes will occur in the job market during this time. A college education will certainly give him more options for the long term. Many of today's jobs which require only a high school diploma may no longer exist a few years from now. His education should prepare him for the job market of the future, not the present.

MYTH: Students today have so much loan debt that it doesn't make sense to pay a lot to go to college.

REALITY: Most students who have huge loan debt usually have either done a poor job of finding a college where their family's financial aid works well, or they made a conscious decision to take on that kind of loan debt so they can attend a particular college. (Remember, the average loan debt of undergraduate students today is roughly $20,000 – that's less than the cost of most new cars!) The goal for most families is to find in advance schools that will be financially reasonable for them, usually by using a published financial aid estimator to understand where they stand under the federal formula for financial aid.

MYTH: There isn't a lot of financial aid available, and what is available only goes to a few of the very best students.

REALITY: During the 2002-03 academic year, over $105 billion dollars in financial aid was awarded. The vast majority of this money was doled out by the federal government through grant, loan and work-study programs, while colleges' own grants and scholarships accounted for almost 20% of all financial aid. States helped too by contributing over $5.5 billion to the pot. That's a lot of money for a lot of students. In fact, over 70% of students nationally receive some kind of financial aid.

KnowHow2GO *Printed with permission from KnowHow2GO. Learn more at KnowHow2GO.org.*

Visit the Campus

The best reason to visit a college campus is to get a personal feeling for the quality of education being offered there. While on a campus visit, you and your teen should ask questions that will reveal a school's commitment to providing the best educational environment. The questions that follow can help:

Level of academic challenge?

Challenging intellectual and creative work is central to maintaining a quality learning environment.

- To what degree is studying and spending time on academic work emphasized?
- Do faculty hold students to high standards?
- How much time do students spend on homework each week?
- How much writing is expected?
- How much reading is expected?

Active and collaborative learning?

Students learn more when they are directly involved in their education and have opportunities to collaborate with others in solving problems or mastering difficult material.

- How often do students discuss ideas in class?
- How often are topics from class discussed outside of the classroom?
- Do students work together on projects—inside and outside of class?
- How often do students make class presentations?
- How many students participate in community-based projects in regular courses?
- How many students apply their classroom learning to real life through internships or off-campus field experiences?
- Do students have opportunities to tutor or teach other students?

Student-faculty interaction?

In general, the more contact students have with their teachers, the better. Working with a professor on a research project or serving with faculty members on a college committee or community organization lets students see first-hand how experts identify and solve practical problems.

- Are faculty members accessible and supportive?
- How many students work on research projects with faculty?
- Do students receive prompt feedback on academic performance?

KnowHow2GO *Printed with permission from KnowHow2GO. Learn more at KnowHow2GO.org.*

- How often do students talk with their teachers about what they are learning in class?
- How often do students talk with advisors or faculty members about their career plans?
- Do students and faculty members work together on committees and projects outside of course work?

Enriching educational experiences?

Educationally superior colleges offer a variety of learning opportunities inside and outside the classroom that compliment the goals of the academic program. One of the most important is exposure to students and faculty from diverse backgrounds.

- What types of honors courses, learning communities, and other distinctive programs are offered?
- In what ways do faculty use technology in their classes?
- How often do students interact with peers with different social, political, or religious views?
- How often do students interact with peers from different racial or ethnic backgrounds?
- How many students study in other countries?
- Do students participate in activities that enhance their spirituality?
- What percentage of students do community service?
- What kinds of activities are students involved in outside of the classroom?
- What kinds of events does the campus sponsor?
- Is a culminating senior year experience required?

Supportive campus environment?

Students perform better and are more satisfied at colleges that are committed to their success—and that cultivate positive working and social relationships among different groups on campus.

- How well do students get along with other students?
- Are students satisfied with their overall educational experience?
- How much time do students devote to co-curricular activities?
- How well do students get along with administrators and staff?
- To what extent does the school help students deal with their academic and social needs?

By Maria Carvalho

Be a Safety Net

How to Support Your Child During the College Application Process

Remember the feeling you had when you dropped your child off for the first day of school? I was surprised when that feeling came back years later as I helped my son and daughter navigate the college application process.

Even though they were a lot older, the experience was just as momentous. Going to college is one of the most significant transitions in a young person's life. The ultimate decision about which college is the best fit belongs to him or her, but your support as parents is critical during this complex journey.

It is important to familiarize yourself with the steps your child must take to complete the application process successfully. Serious preparation for college begins in 9th grade as students move into high school. Things really heat up in their junior and senior years. Speaking as a parent of two children who are currently in college, and as a professional in the college-readiness field, I'd like to share a few valuable tips and strategies that got me through this daunting and intense time.

THE RIGHT FIT – Be involved!

• **Get your child thinking.** The more research your child does during junior year, the more informed a decision he or she will be able to make. Ask your child questions about possible majors and career interests. What colleges would be best for those? What about college size and location?

• **Read college handbooks.** Many print resources are available to assist with the college search. Congratulations for reading one right now!

• **Do Internet research.** Websites offer many options to assist students in narrowing down their college choices. You can sort and arrange by campus type, majors, size, and setting. ImFirst.org and StriveForCollege.org will get you started.

• **Visit campuses.** April vacation of the junior year is a great time to tour campuses with your child. College visits allow young people to feel the energy of a school and determine if it is a good match. It's an opportunity to explore, evaluate, and get firsthand information.

• **Check academic entrance requirements.** Be sure your child is on track to meet all college/university requirements before applying: college entrance exams, GPA, required high school course load, and so on.

THE TOOLS – Be organized!

• **Get a school year planner.** Have your child record all deadlines (application and financial aid) in a planner. It's a great visual tool!

• **Use an accordion file folder.** Assign one pocket for each application.

THE DEADLINES – Be ahead of the curve!

• **Request applications early in the senior year.** Most colleges and universities have an online application system. Your child can also receive applications by postal mail.

• **Be considerate of busy educators.** Give teachers and guidance counselors enough time to provide recommendations and transcripts. Encourage your child to request appointments with school staff as soon as possible in senior year to get the ball rolling.

• **Help your child prepare a résumé.** Colleges want to know about your child's extracurricular activities because it helps them see what kind of person he or she is. Make a list together of everything noteworthy: work experience, honors and achievements, major responsibilities (even babysitting), and hobbies.

• **Set a schedule for essay writing.** Many students find the personal essay section of the application a difficult task and are tempted to procrastinate. Don't let your child wait to get started till the day before the application is due. And remind him or her to proofread! An English teacher is often happy to help.

• **Organize your income taxes in December.** The federal financial aid form, or FAFSA, can be completed after January 1. Have your taxes prepared early, so your child won't have to file an updated FAFSA later on.

THE EMOTIONS – Be calm!

• **Be prepared for tears.** Your child may not always appreciate it when you pester him or her about deadlines. It's natural reaction. Just keep the communication open.

• **Stand back but stand by.** Remember that many decisions in this journey belong to your child. Learn how to let go. Know your role, and be a safety net. All the hard work will be worth it when those college acceptances arrive! ■

BIO *Maria Carvalho is Director for Postsecondary Transition and Success Rhode Island, where she oversees high school college-readiness programs and manages a team of full-time Advisors who interact daily with hundreds of students in the state's urban high schools.*

Concerns About College

For teens, going off to college represents a huge change in their lives. But this change can affect the parents and guardians just as much. While you are proud and excited about their accomplishments, there can also be a feeling of loss and separation. Dealing with these mixed emotions can be difficult, but are normal. Handling these changes can be easier if you keep these tips in mind:

Stay connected.

There can be some truth to "absence makes the heart grow fonder" but parents or guardians may worry that "out of sight means out of mind." So you and your student need to determine ways to stay involved in each other's lives and remember to say and do the little things that matter. Cards sent home, care packages sent to school, pictures of events that were missed, and email and phone calls do provide a way to stay connected and involved.

Adjust to a new relationship.

As you play a new role in your teen's life, try to adjust to the new adult-to-adult aspect of the parent-child relationship. Children always need parents, but the relationship may become more peer-like.

Expect ups and downs.

One minute college students are the models of independence, the next they call in tears. This back and forth is natural and expected, as both students and parents become more comfortable and confident in the ability of students to handle situations on their own.

Redirect your time and energy to new activities.

With your parenting time now free time, taking stock of personal interests and assets will reveal areas of your life that may have been neglected. It can be time to develop, reawaken, and pursue old and new hobbies, leisure activities, and careers.

Allow for mistakes.

You should encourage and accept the child's ability to make independent decisions. Both the college student and the parents must realize mistakes will be made along the way—it's called life. Learning from mistakes is just another type of learning.

Guide rather than pressure.

Communicating educational goals and expectations should be done in a manner respectful of your student's own style and interests. College students need to pursue their own passions. Although parental input can be useful, children should not be expected to live out their parents' dreams.

Tips from the NYU Child Study Center, www.aboutourkids.org

By Barbara Sanders

WHO ARE YOU? AND WHAT HAVE YOU DONE WITH MY SON?

I am the mother of Jeremy Harris. May he rest in peace.

No, Jeremy did not die, but the former Jeremy has been replaced by someone who is a stranger to me. I guess that goes with the territory of going off to college.

In Jeremy's junior year, we realized that he needed a game plan or a goal for his life after high school. As a parent, you're excited and proud of your child and know that the sky is the limit for them. You realize that it's going to take hard work on your part as well to ensure that your student meets all of the graduation requirements, pays all the necessary fees, narrows down their many options. It can be quite overwhelming.

Mom and me
Hometown: Chicago, IL

I always tell new parents that being a parent is like having your heart outside of your body. On the move-in date for college, my tears were fierce. I didn't want to leave my son alone to face his new world without me; but I knew that I must.

Jeremy Harris
College: University of Missouri
Hometown: Chicago, IL

In his first year of college, Jeremy learned what he needs to do to be successful, and I learned how to be a "hands-off" mom. While they're away, you try not to be too worried about how they're coping. I'll always be there as his safety net, but sometimes we have to step back and let our children experience life for themselves. I checked in periodically with Jeremy and was relieved to know that he was doing well without me.

I couldn't wait for the breaks. Over Thanksgiving break, Jeremy really seemed happy to be home. He missed me and familiarity of home. Then Spring break came and Jeremy appeared to have broken away from his old self and became someone foreign to me. He was more mature and calm; he had a new set of friends. It was a pleasure to see his growth after a year of college.

As the old adage goes, "No one can prepare you for what heights you will soar until you spread your wings."

JEREMY HARRIS is an I'm First! scholarship winner. Jeremy shares his college experiences and offers advice on the I'm First! student blog.

Visit www.ImFirst.org to follow the student blog and watch video testimonials from first-generation college students and graduates.

PADRES Y MENTORES

Ya sea usted padre, tutor, maestro, mentor u otro adulto afectuoso, es probable que en su vida haya un adolescente que desea ir a la universidad. Puede ayudarlo a triunfar si toma el tiempo para aprender sobre la planificación y el financiamiento de la educación superior. Juntos, usted y el adolescente por el que se interesa pueden compartir esta importante meta y alcanzarla.

"¿Para que ir la Universidad?"

Q

¿Le ha hecho alguna vez el adolescente en su vida esta pregunta? Ya sea usted padre, tutor u otro adulto a cargo, necesita respuestas convincentes y prácticas para compartir con su adolescente. Aquí las tiene:

A

"Vas a lograr un mayor entendimiento y habilidades que te ayudarán a triunfar en este mundo complejo".

La educación superior te permite:

- Ampliar tus conocimientos y habilidades.
- Expresar claramente tus pensamientos, en forma oral y escrita.
- Captar conceptos y teorías abstractas.
- Aumentar tu comprensión del mundo y de tu comunidad.
- Obtener más seguridad financiera.

"Vas a encontrar mayor variedad y cantidad de oportunidades de trabajo".

En nuestro mundo cambiante, más y más trabajos requieren una educación posterior a la de la escuela secundaria. Los graduados de una institución de nivel superior tienen más trabajos para elegir que los que no continúan con su educación luego de la secundaria.

"Ganarás más dinero, mucho más".

La gente con educación superior generalmente gana más que la que no la tiene. Según la Oficina de Censos de los EE. UU., como promedio, la persona con un título universitario gana $51,206, casi el doble que los $27,915 que gana por año la persona que sólo tiene el título de secundaria.

Planificación para la Universidad: Diez Pasos

10

Paso Uno

Comience a ahorrar dinero lo más pronto posible para ayudar al pago de la educación de su adolescente.

Paso Dos

Aliente a su adolescente a darle importancia a la escuela secundaria, preparándose desde el punto de vista académico para la educación superior.

Paso Tres

Analice con su adolescente sus aptitudes e intereses, sus opciones de carreras e instituciones educativas a las que le interesa asistir.

Paso Quatro

Reúnase con el consejero de orientación de la escuela secundaria para determinar qué instituciones se ajustan a las capacidades académicas de su adolescente.

Paso Cinco

Recopile información sobre aquellas a las que su adolescente tiene interés en asistir, incluso información sobre asistencia financiera.

Paso Seis

Lleve a su adolescente a visitar un campus y formule las preguntas adecuadas.

Paso Siete

Ayúdelo a solicitar la admisión. Para solicitar asistencia financiera, ayude a su hijo a completar la Solicitud Gratuita de Ayuda Financiera (Free Application for Federal Student Aid, FAFSA).

Paso Ocho

Considere becas, subsidios y programas de estudio-trabajo. Complete todas las solicitudes o formularios necesarios y preséntelos antes de la fecha límite.

Paso Nueve

Considere programas de préstamos disponibles para usted y su hijo.

Paso Diez

Obtenga más información sobre créditos fiscales, deducciones y otros factores para gastos de educación.

Como hablar con su adolescente

No siempre es fácil hablar con su adolescente. Pero es importante que lo respalde a lo largo de su planificación para la universidad: ayúdelo a organizar el proceso, a cumplir con las fechas y a hablar con las personas adecuadas. Aquí presentamos algunos consejos para considerar:

- Sea receptivo y escúchelo cuando su adolescente desee analizar planes de carrera o de educación superior.
- Hágalo que explore opciones de carrera e institución educativa superior y que recopile toda la información posible.
- Anímelo a que registre sus ideas en papel. Por ejemplo, puede hacer un libro de recortes con sus planes de carrera y de educación superior.
- Esté consciente de las diversas fechas límites para presentar las solicitudes de admisión a las instituciones educativas y para asistencia financiera. Póngalas en un calendario que tanto usted como su hijo puedan mirar.
- Sugiérale que se reúna con un consejero escolar al menos una vez al año, a partir del 10mo grado, para aprender más sobre la educación superior y la planificación de su carrera.
- Bríndele su apoyo y reúnase con su consejero si le parece que su hijo necesita ayuda adicional.
- Anime a su adolescente ayudándole a ver la conexión entre la educación superior y la carrera. Enfatice la importancia de seleccionar una asignatura principal (un "major") que lo ayude a prepararse para una carrera.
- Si el joven está indeciso sobre la orientación de su carrera, no trate de decidir por él. Déjelo que explore todas las posibilidades.

Costos Ayuda Financiera

No hay forma de escapar al hecho de que los costos de la educación superior están creciendo. Según los últimos informes divulgados, la mayoría de los estudiantes y sus familias pueden esperar pagar, en promedio, de $112 a $1,190 más que el año pasado en concepto de matricula y costos este año, de acuerdo al tipo de institución educativa.

Sin embargo, hay buenas noticias. La asistencia financiera disponible es más alta que nunca: más de $135,000 millones. Y a pesar de todos los aumentos en los costos, la educación superior sigue siendo una opción accesible para la mayoría de las familias. Haga clic en los signos de "más" para ver más información:

"Precio de lista" vs. Accesibilidad

Si bien los precios de algunas de las instituciones de educación superior que se oyen pueden ser desalentadores ($30,000 anuales o más por matricula y costos), la mayoría de ellas cuesta mucho menos. Por ejemplo, ¿sabía usted que alrededor del 60 por ciento de los estudiantes que asisten a instituciones de grado de cuatro años pagan menos de $6,000 en concepto de matricula y costos? Luego de tomar en cuenta los subsidios, el precio neto que el estudiante de grado promedio paga por su educación es significativamente menor que la cifra publicada para matricula y costos. Y recuerde, la asistencia financiera puede reducir aún más el monto que su familia pagará en realidad.

La asistencia financiera hace que la universidad le resulte más accesible

La asistencia financiera pretende compensar la diferencia entre lo que su familia puede costear y el costo de la universidad. Más de la mitad de los estudiantes actualmente inscritos en instituciones de educación superior reciben algún tipo de asistencia financiera para ayudar a pagar sus costos.

El sistema de asistencia financiera se basa en la meta del acceso igualitario: que todos puedan tener educación superior, independientemente de sus circunstancias financieras. El sistema funciona así:

- Se espera que el esudiante y su familia contribuyan al costo de la educacion superior en la medida de sus posibilidades.
- Si la familia no puede aportar la totalidad del costo, hay asistencia financiera disponible para cerrar la brecha.

La contribución familiar esperada lo favorece a usted

El monto que su familia puede contribuir es comúnmente conocido como "contribución familiar esperada" (Expected Family Contribution, EFC). La cifra la determina quien quiera que otorga la asistencia; en general, el gobierno federal o cada universidad o institución de educación superior.

El gobierno federal y las oficinas de asistencia financiera utilizan "fórmulas de necesidad" para analizar las condiciones financieras de su familia (elementos como ingresos, activos y tamaño de familia) y las compara en términos de proporción con las condiciones financieras de otras familias.

La mayoría de las familias simplemente no pueden afrontar la EFC sólo con sus ingresos corrientes. Las fórmulas asumen que las familias cumplirán con su contribución a través de una combinación de ahorros, ingresos corrientes y préstamos. Verifique con las instituciones educativas para averiguar de qué modo se espera que satisfaga la EFC.

No descarte a las instituciones de educación superior de mayor costo

Por ejemplo su EFC es de $5,000. En una institución educativa con un costo total de $8,000, usted sería elegible para un máximo de $3,000 en asistencia financiera. En otra institución educativa con un costo total de $25,000, usted sería elegible para un máximo de $20,000 en asistencia financiera. En otras palabras, su familia deberá aportar la misma suma en ambas.

Conocimientos básicos de asistencia financiera

La asistencia financiera es cualquier tipo de asistencia que se utilice para pagar los costos de la educación superior y que se base en necesidad financiera. Hay tres tipos principales:

Subsidios y becas

También denominada donación para asistencia, los subsidios no deben reintegrarse y no se debe trabajar para ganarlos. Los subsidios provienen del gobierno federal y estatal y de las instituciones de educación superior individuales. Las becas en general se otorgan en función del mérito. Para buscar becas, visitewww.fastweb.com.

Trabajo

El empleo estudiantil y la asistencia de trabajo y estudio ayuda a que el estudiante pague por costos educativos como libros, insumos y gastos personales. El programa de trabajo y estudio es un programa federal que proporciona empleos de tiempo parcial a los estudiantes, de modo de ayudarlos a cubrir sus necesidades financieras, y les brinda experiencia laboral a la vez que atienden a sus campus y a las comunidades circundantes.

Préstamos

La mayor parte de la asistencia financiera (54%) se presenta en forma de préstamos a los estudiantes o padres y es una asistencia que debe reembolsarse. La mayoría de los préstamos otorgados en función de las necesidades financieras son préstamos de bajo interés, patrocinados por el gobierno federal. Estos préstamos están subsidiados por el gobierno, de modo que no se acumula interés hasta que comienzan a ser reembolsados, una vez que el estudiante se ha graduado.

Costos Promedio de La Educación Superior

Costos promedio de la educación superior por año

Institución pública, dos años: $8,928

Institución pública, cuatro años: $15,022

Institución privada, cuatro años: $39,173

¿Sabía usted...?

- Alrededor del 60% de los estudiantes que asisten a instituciones públicas de educación superior de cuatro años pagan menos de $6,000 anuales por matricula y costos.

- 44% de todos los estudiantes asisten a instituciones de educación superior de dos años. El estudiante promedio en una institución de educación superior pública de dos años recibe un subsidio de asistencia financiera que reduce los costos de matricula promedio a alrededor de $400.

- Hay un monto récord de $135,000 millones en asistencia financiera disponible para los estudiantes y su familia.

- Alrededor del 60% de todos los estudiantes universitarios reciben asistencia financiera. En 2004-05 la asistencia promedio por estudiante fue de $1,800 en las instituciones públicas de dos años, de $3,300 en las públicas de cuatro años, y de $9,600 en las privadas de cuatro años.

Estadísticas de 2012-2013
Source: U.S. Department of Education, National Center for Education Statistics (2015). Digest of Education Statistics, 2013 (NCES 2015-011), Table 330.10.

KnowHow2GO *Printed with permission from KnowHow2GO. Learn more at KnowHow2GO.org.*

Más información sobre préstamos

Hay distinto tipos de préstamos, para estudiantes y para padres que los toman en nombre de sus hijos. Siga leyendo para conocer la información básica.

Préstamos para padres

Préstamos federales PLUS

El programa de préstamos PLUS es la mayor fuente de préstamos para padres. Los padres pueden tomar hasta el costo total de asistencia menos cualquier asistencia recibida y el reembolso comienza a los 60 días de haber pagado el dinero a la institución educativa.

Préstamos privados para padres

Algunas instituciones financieras y de préstamos ofrecen préstamos privados para educación para padres. Estos préstamos en general tienen una tasa de interés más alta que los préstamos del programa PLUS.

Préstamos patrocinados por las instituciones educativas

Un pequeño número de instituciones de educación superior ofrecen sus propios préstamos para padres, en general con una mejor tasa de interés que el programa PLUS. Verifique los materiales sobre asistencia de cada institución educativa para ver si cuentan con ese tipo de préstamos.

Préstamos federales para estudiantes

Préstamos Perkins

Los préstamos Perkins son préstamos en función de la necesidad, que son otorgados por la oficina de asistencia financiera a aquellos estudiantes que más lo necesitan. La tasa de interés es muy baja (5%) y no se hace ningún pago durante el curso de los estudios.

Préstamos directos o Stafford subsidiados

Los préstamos Stafford subsidiados son préstamos en función de la necesidad, con tasas de interés en el orden del 4-6 por ciento. El gobierno federal paga los intereses durante el curso de los estudios. Por eso se los llama préstamos "subsidiados".

Préstamos directos o Stafford no subsidiados

Los préstamos Stafford no subsidiados no surgen de la necesidad financiera y pueden utilizarse para ayudar a pagar la porción de costos a cargo de la familia. Usted es responsable del pago de los intereses durante el curso de los estudios. Puede optar por capitalizar los intereses. La ventaja de hacerlo es que no se requiere ningún pago de intereses. La desventaja es que los intereses se suman al préstamo, lo que implica que debe reintegrarle más dinero al acreedor.

Préstamos Grad PLUS

Se trata de préstamos para estudiantes graduados, patrocinados por el gobierno federal, que no están vinculados a la necesidad. En general, los estudiantes pueden solicitar préstamos Grad PLUS por el costo total de la educación, menos cualquier asistencia recibida. La ventaja de este préstamo es que permite una mayor capacidad de endeudamiento. Sin embargo, recomendamos que los estudiantes consideren los préstamos de bajo interés, como los Stafford subsidiados o no subsidiados antes de tomar un préstamo Grad PLUS.

Otras opciones de préstamos para estudiantes

Préstamos privados para estudiantes

Algunas instituciones financieras y de préstamos ofrecen préstamos privados para educación para los estudiantes. Estos préstamos no están subsidiados y en general conllevan una mayor tasa de interés que los préstamos federales en función de las necesidades. El programa de préstamos privados del College Board es un ejemplo de préstamos educativos privados para estudiantes.

Préstamos patrocinados por las instituciones educativas

Ciertas instituciones de educación superior cuentan con sus propios fondos para préstamos. Las tasas de interés pueden ser menores que las de los préstamos federales para estudiantes. Lea la información sobre asistencia financiera de la institución.

Otros préstamos

Además de establecer becas, ciertas organizaciones y fundaciones privadas también cuentan con programas de préstamos. Los términos del endeudamiento pueden ser muy favorables. Puede utilizar Búsqueda de Becas para encontrarlos.

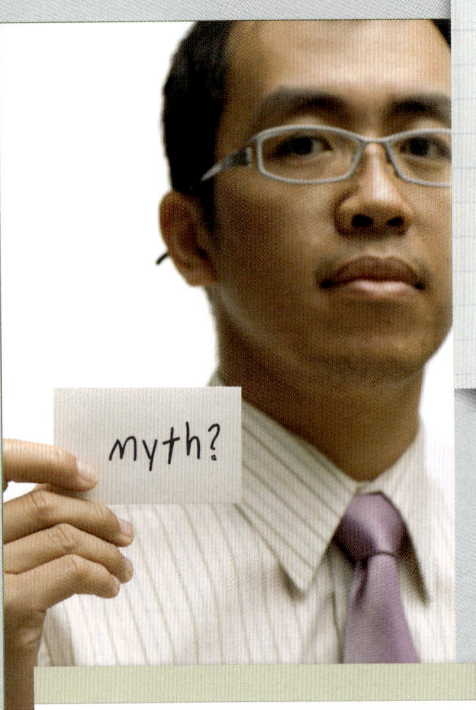

Probablemente haya oído, y tal vez crea, algunos de estos MITOS comunes sobre la educación superior. Siga leyendo para ver cuál es la REALIDAD.

MITO: cualquiera puede entrar a una universidad pública, pero entrar a una institución superior privada es muy difícil.

REALIDAD: algunas universidades públicas están entre las más competitivas en términos de admisión, mientras que otras están obligadas a aceptar prácticamente a todos los solicitantes. Es verdad que algunas instituciones educativas privadas son muy selectivas, pero otras aceptan a estudiantes que ni siquiera serían aceptados en la universidad pública de su estado. Verifique con las instituciones que esté analizando, para saber más sobre los rendimientos académicos promedio de sus estudiantes y sus políticas de admisión.

MITO: la institución educativa de menor precio será la más accesible.

REALIDAD: no necesariamente. Ciertas instituciones educativas de mayor costo han recolectado sumas de dinero significativas para becas de sus graduados y amigos. Como consecuencia, cuentan con más dinero para ofrecer a los estudiantes en la forma de becas, lo que reduce ese precio. Tras tomar en cuenta la asistencia financiera, es posible que la institución aparentemente más costosa sea más accesible que otra con un menor precio de lista. Consejo: averigüe qué tipos de opciones de becas hay disponibles en las instituciones educativas que estén analizando.

MITO: mi adolescente puede tener buenos ingresos sin educación superior.

REALIDAD: sin dudas a algunas personas les ha ido bien sin un título de grado. Sin embargo, en el curso de su vida la persona con un título de grado en promedio ganará un millón de dólares más que un graduado de secundaria. Para la mayoría de la gente, la educación superior paga.

MITO: los cursos y las notas del período de primavera del último año no son importantes porque a los estudiantes ya los han aceptado en alguna institución superior para la época en que esos cursos se llevan a cabo.

REALIDAD: la mayoría de las instituciones de educación superior incluyen notas en sus materiales de admisión donde manifiestan que tomarán en cuenta las notas de primavera del estudiante de último año. Si el rendimiento académico del estudiante muestra una caída sustancial, se sabe de instituciones que han cancelado la oferta de admisión.

MITO: para subsistir en el mundo actual se necesita un título de grado de cuatro años.

REALIDAD: la persona con un título de cuatro años puede tener más opciones de carrera, pero existen muchos trabajos satisfactorios y bien pagos que pueden obtenerse con ciertos títulos técnicos o de dos años. Su adolescente debe comenzar en las áreas que sean de su interés, y averiguar qué tipo de educación se requiere y cuáles son las oportunidades laborales en esas áreas. Y luego procurar el título que necesite para el tipo de carrera a la que aspira.

MITO: no tengo el dinero y mi adolescente no puede permitirse tomar préstamos para pagar la universidad, incluso si quisiera ir.

REALIDAD: actualmente casi todos los estudiantes pueden conseguir préstamos a tasas bajas para ayudarlos a pagar la educación superior y los préstamos para educación típicamente no deben reembolsarse hasta que el estudiante no se haya graduado. El préstamo promedio de un estudiante de grado actualmente es de alrededor de $20,000; menos que el costo de la mayoría de los autos nuevos. Un auto dura unos años. La educación superior dura toda la vida.

MITO: en realidad no importa si espero uno o dos años para ir a la universidad.

REALIDAD: muchos estudiantes que no van a la universidad inmediatamente después de la secundaria nunca se deciden a hacerlo. Otros llevan consigo una gran experiencia cuando se inscriben, gracias a lo que hicieron en el tiempo en que no estudiaron. Es sensato que el estudiante se postule a las instituciones educativas que le interesan durante el último año, como cualquier otro. Luego puede pedirle a la institución que posponga su inscripción por un año o dos, si el estudiante necesita el tiempo. La mayoría de las instituciones de educación superior acepta mantener la oferta de admisión en suspenso, en especial si el estudiante tiene planes que en definitiva lo harán más interesante o valioso como miembro de la comunidad del campus.

Precaución: si el estudiante trabaja durante ese tiempo, sus ingresos (si son grandes) pueden deteriorar su elegibilidad para asistencia financiera en función de la necesidad al retomar los estudios. Como el estudiante en muchos casos todavía calificará como estudiante dependiente, sólo un pequeño monto de ingresos estarán protegidos por la fórmula federal. Los montos que la excedan pueden afectar su elegibilidad para asistencia financiera.

MITO: se debe empezar a planificar para la universidad durante el penúltimo año de secundaria.

REALIDAD: si bien algunos estudiantes pueden esperar hasta este punto para hacer ciertas cosas como visitar las posibles instituciones educativas o tomar el SAT, hay otras que jamás deben dejarse para tan tarde. Por ejemplo, las selecciones y notas de los cursos de secundaria representan la consideración individual más importante en las decisiones de admisión de la mayoría de las instituciones de educación superior. Las decisiones de los cursos de secundaria se toman mucho antes, incluso en los años de escuela media. La planificación financiera, el ahorro para la educación superior y averiguar qué instituciones educativas se podrán costear son actividades que también deben llevarse a cabo antes del penúltimo año.

MITO: los estudiantes hoy en día tienen tanta deuda por los préstamos que no tiene sentido pagar mucho para ir a la universidad.

REALIDAD: la mayoría de los estudiantes con deudas inmensas normalmente no hicieron un buen trabajo al buscar una institución de educación superior donde la asistencia financiera de su familia funcionara bien o tomaron una decisión consciente de asumir ese tipo de deuda a fin de poder asistir a una universidad en particular. (Recuerde, la deuda promedio de los estudiantes de grado actualmente es de alrededor de $20,000; menos que el costo de la mayoría de los autos nuevos). La meta para la mayoría de las familias es encontrar por anticipado las instituciones educativas que sean razonables para ellas desde el punto de vista financiero, normalmente mediante el uso de un estimador de asistencia financiera publicado a fin de entender cuál es su posición según la fórmula federal para asistencia financiera.

MITO: la asistencia financiera disponible no es mucha, y la que hay va a unos pocos de los mejores estudiantes.

REALIDAD: durante el año académico 2002-2003, se otorgaron más de $105,000 millones de dólares en asistencia financiera. La mayor parte de este dinero fue entregado por el gobierno federal a través de subsidios, préstamos y programas de estudio y trabajo, en tanto los subsidios y becas propios de las instituciones de educación superior totalizaron casi el 20% de toda la asistencia financiera. Los estados aportaron lo suyo, contribuyendo con más de $5,500 millones al pozo. Esto es mucho dinero, para muchos estudiantes. De hecho, más del 70% de los estudiantes de todo el país reciben algún tipo de asistencia financiera.

MITO: nadie de mi familia ha ido a la universidad; ¿por qué mi hijo debería ser el primero?

REALIDAD: al terminar la secundaria, su adolescente puede tener 40 ó 50 años de trabajo por delante. Durante ese tiempo pueden ocurrir muchos cambios en el mercado laboral. Una educación superior ciertamente le dará más opciones en el largo plazo. Es posible que muchos de los trabajos actuales que sólo exigen un diploma de secundaria ya no existan en unos pocos años. Su educación lo preparará para el mercado laboral del futuro, no el actual.

Preguntas para su visita al campus

El mejor motivo para visitar el campus de una institución de educación superior es tener una impresión personal de la calidad de educación que allí se ofrece. Durante la visita al campus, usted y su adolescente deben hacer preguntas que revelen el compromiso de la institución para brindar un ambiente educativo óptimo. Las siguientes preguntas pueden ser útiles:

¿Nivel de exigencia académica?

Un trabajo creativo e intelectual exigente es fundamental para mantener un ambiente educativo de calidad.

- ¿Hasta qué punto se enfatiza el estudio y la dedicación de tiempo al trabajo académico?
- ¿El cuerpo de profesores impone parámetros elevados a los estudiantes?
- ¿Cuánto tiempo dedican los estudiantes a las tareas cada semana?
- ¿Cuánto se espera que escriban?
- ¿Cuánto se espera que lean?

¿El aprendizaje es activo y cooperativo?

Los estudiantes aprenden más cuando participan en forma directa en su educación y tienen oportunidades de colaborar con otros para resolver problemas o dominar materiales difíciles.

- ¿Con qué frecuencia los estudiantes discuten ideas en clase?
- ¿Con qué frecuencia los temas de la clase se discuten fuera de ella?
- ¿Los estudiantes trabajan en grupo en proyectos, dentro y fuera de la clase?
- ¿Con qué frecuencia los estudiantes hacen presentaciones ante la clase?
- ¿Cuántos estudiantes participan en proyectos de base comunitaria en cursos regulares?
- ¿Cuántos estudiantes aplican lo aprendido en clase a la vida real, a través de pasantías o experiencias de campo fuera del campus?
- ¿Tienen los estudiantes oportunidades de actuar como tutores o de enseñar a otros estudiantes?

¿Hay interacción entre profesores y estudiantes?

En general, mientras más contacto tienen los estudiantes con sus profesores, mejor. Trabajar con un profesor en un proyecto de investigación o trabajar junto con los miembros del cuerpo de profesores en un comité universitario u organización comunitaria permite que los estudiantes vean de forma directa cómo los expertos identifican y resuelven problemas prácticos.

- ¿Son los miembros del cuerpo de profesores accesibles y alentadores?
- ¿Cuántos estudiantes trabajan en proyectos de investigación con profesores?

- ¿Reciben los estudiantes comentarios inmediatos sobre su desempeño académico?
- ¿Con qué frecuencia hablan los estudiantes con sus profesores sobre lo que aprenden en clase?
- ¿Con qué frecuencia hablan los estudiantes con consejeros o miembros del cuerpo de profesores sobre sus planes de carrera?
- ¿Trabajan juntos los profesores y estudiantes en comités y proyectos fuera del trabajo académico?

¿Hay experiencias educativas enriquecedoras?

Las instituciones que son superiores desde el punto de vista educativo ofrecen diversas oportunidades de aprendizaje dentro y fuera del aula, que complementan las metas del programa académico. Una de las más importantes es la exposición a estudiantes y profesores de diversos orígenes.

- ¿Qué tipos de cursos honorarios, comunidades de aprendizaje y otros programas distintivos se ofrecen?
- ¿De qué forma los profesores utilizan la tecnología en clase?
- ¿Con qué frecuencia interactúan los estudiantes con pares de distintas opiniones sociales, políticas o religiosas?
- ¿Con qué frecuencia interactúan los estudiantes con pares de distintos orígenes raciales o étnicos?
- ¿Cuántos estudiantes estudian en otros países?
- ¿Participan los estudiantes en actividades que aumentan su espiritualidad?
- ¿Qué porcentaje de estudiantes prestan servicios comunitarios?
- ¿En qué tipo de actividades participan los estudiantes fuera del aula?
- ¿Qué tipo de eventos auspicia el campus?
- ¿Se requiere una experiencia de culminación del último año?

¿Hay un ambiente de apoyo en el campus?

Los estudiantes rinden más y están más satisfechos en las instituciones educativas que se comprometen con su éxito y que cultivan relaciones laborales y sociales positivas entre los distintos grupos del campus.

- ¿Qué tan bien se llevan los estudiantes unos con otros?
- ¿Están los estudiantes satisfechos con su experiencia educativa en general?
- ¿Cuánto tiempo dedican los estudiantes a actividades cocurriculares?
- ¿Qué tal se llevan los estudiantes con los administradores y el personal?
- ¿En qué medida la institución ayuda a los estudiantes a manejar sus necesidades académicas y sociales?

Pasos para la Universidad

El proceso de planificación para los estudios superiores puede ser atemorizante para cualquiera, de modo que es mejor planificar por adelantado y contemplar mucho tiempo. De hecho, es una buena idea comenzar las conversaciones sobre la educación superior cuando el adolescente está aun en la escuela media.

Ayude a orientar al joven a través del proceso de planificación para la educación superior. Haga clic en los signos de "más" a continuación para ver los pasos básicos en cada grado. También le recomendamos leer los consejos específicos para estudiantes haciendo clic en los niveles de grado (por ej., Primer año) en la barra de navegación principal y luego en "Pasos hacia la universidad".

CRONOGRAMA: 9NO GRADO

OTOÑO

- ❑ Consulte al consejero escolar para asegurarse que el estudiante esté asistiendo a los cursos preparatorios para la universidad, comenzando por álgebra.
- ❑ Ayude al joven a crear una carpeta de información para su educación superior.
- ❑ Comience el año escolar correctamente ayudando al joven a organizarse y a poner en práctica buenos hábitos de estudio.
- ❑ Aliente al estudiante a conocer gente nueva mediante la inscripción en actividades extracurriculares e intentando algo nuevo.
- ❑ Explore carreras por Internet, en la computadora de su casa o en la biblioteca.
- ❑ Ayude a su adolescente a encontrar oportunidades de aprendizaje por observación del trabajo en la comunidad, donde pasan el día siguiendo de cerca a una persona mientras trabaja y observan lo que la persona hace.

PRIMAVERA

- ❑ Siéntese con su estudiante para planificar el segundo año.
- ❑ Hable sobre las vacaciones de verano. Explore los programas o campamentos de verano a los que puede asistir en universidades e instituciones de educación superior locales. Busque oportunidades de servicio o voluntarias en la comunidad. Algunas pueden ser patrocinadas por una iglesia, sinagoga o mezquita local.

10MO GRADO CRONOGRAMA

CRONOGRAMA: 10MO GRADO

OTOÑO

- ❑ Apoye a su estudiante para que se prepare y tome todos los exámenes necesarios para completar los requisitos de graduación de la escuela secundaria.
- ❑ Haga que su estudiante comience el segundo año puliendo sus aptitudes de estudio. Aconseje a su hijo o hija que si necesita mejorar en ciertos temas, éste es el momento de hacerlo. Refuerce la idea de que las universidades y los futuros empleadores se fijan en certificados analíticos de la escuela secundaria y se impresionan con asistencia regular y mejoras en las calificaciones.
- ❑ Aliente al joven a hacer un inventario de intereses de carrera.
- ❑ Los estudiantes deben tomar el examen de Prueba Preliminar de Aptitud Escolar (Preliminary Scholastic Aptitude, PSTA), la versión preliminar del Examen de Aptitud Escolástica (Scholastic Aptitude Test, SAT) o el PLAN, versión preliminar del Examen Estadounidense para la Universidad (American College Test, ACT). Dar el PSAT ahora es práctica para el PSAT del penúltimo año, que permite que a su estudiante se lo considere para una beca nacional de mérito. Obtenga las fechas e información adicional sobre el PSAT en la oficina de orientación de su escuela secundaria.
- ❑ Navegue por Internet junto con el estudiante para investigar oportunidades de universidades, escuelas técnicas y aprendizajes.
- ❑ Anime al estudiante a comenzar o a seguir aprendiendo sobre carreras.

PRIMAVERA

- ❑ Comience a explorar las opciones de asistencia financiera y becas.
- ❑ Anime a su estudiante a preguntar a sus amigos, colegas y líderes de la comunidad sobre distintas carreras o use Internet para explorar distintas carreras.
- ❑ Ayude al estudiante a seleccionar de cinco a diez instituciones de educación superior a las cuales pedir folletos y solicitudes de ingreso.
- ❑ Arregle con él para visitar un centro de carreras en la zona.
- ❑ Planifique un verano productivo para su adolescente. Si todavía no tiene un trabajo en el verano anterior al 11mogrado, es un buen momento de buscar uno que lo ayude a prepararse para una futura carrera.
- ❑ Elija un campamento de verano o ayúdelo a encontrar programas de servicio voluntario para incentivar las aptitudes de su adolescente.
- ❑ Recuerde a su adolescente que se inscriba en las clases más exigentes para el próximo año.

CRONOGRAMA: 11MO GRADO

11MO GRADO CRONOGRAMA

OTOÑO

- ❑ Verifique que su estudiante esté encaminado hacia la educación superior y tómese tiempo para analizar intereses universitarios.
- ❑ Anime a su estudiante a comenzar una carpeta de información sobre instituciones educativas de nivel superior.
- ❑ Durante el receso de otoño, visiten universidades.
- ❑ Aliente a su adolescente a tomar el examen PSAT para prepararse para el SAT y calificar para el programa de becas nacional de mérito.
- ❑ Participe en noches universitarias y ferias universitarias en la escuela o centros comunitarios locales.
- ❑ Durante el receso de invierno, sugiera reuniones con amigos que estén de regreso de la universidad y arregle visitas a campus.

PRIMAVERA

- ❑ Vuelva a verificar que su adolescente esté inscrito para dar el SAT o ACT. Busque libros para ayudarlo a prepararse. Considere qué universidades deben recibir los puntajes. Reúnase con el consejero escolar de su estudiante para saber qué universidades y becas están disponible según los resultados del examen.
- ❑ Comience una búsqueda activa de becas y asistencia financiera.
- ❑ Continúe animando a su estudiante para que mantenga el rumbo a fin de completar todos los cursos necesarios para la graduación, más cualquier otro curso requerido para la admisión a la universidad.
- ❑ Anímelo a hacer más visitas a universidades durante el verano y hable con los consejeros de admisión con respecto a lo que puede hacerse para aumentar las posibilidades de ser admitido.
- ❑ Si no puede viajar, los sitios web de las universidades e instituciones educativas de nivel superior pueden proporcionarle gran cantidad de información y recorridos en línea.
- ❑ Para adquirir una impresión de la vida universitaria y explorar posibles carreras, anímelo a participar en un programa de verano preuniversitario.

KnowHow2GO Printed with permission from KnowHow2GO. Learn more at KnowHow2GO.org.

12VO GRADO CRONOGRAMA

CRONOGRAMA: 12VO GRADO

OTOÑO

- ❑ Si los hay disponibles, aliente al estudiante a inscribirse en cursos que ofrezcan créditos para la universidad, como los denominados "Advance Placement" o "AP" (equivalencia universitaria) y "Dual Enrollment" (matrícula doble).
- ❑ Ayúdelo a ir reduciendo el abanico de posibilidades de instituciones educativas y a recopilar las correspondientes solicitudes. Haga una lista de verificación con los requisitos de admisión, certificados analíticos, costos de la solicitud, puntajes de los exámenes, cartas de recomendación, ensayos y solicitudes de asistencia financiera.
- ❑ Haga que su estudiante de último año prepare una lista de todos sus servicios escolares y comunitarios junto con sus clases y premios de la secundaria. Esta lista lo ayudará al momento de comenzar a llenar las solicitudes de admisión.
- ❑ Haga que su estudiante practique el llenado del formulario y la escritura del ensayo de admisión a la universidad. Procure recomendaciones para las admisiones y becas universitarias.
- ❑ Visite las instituciones educativas que su estudiante esté considerando. Llame por anticipado para fijar citas con los funcionarios de admisión y de asistencia financiera.
- ❑ Lleve un control de las fechas límite para las solicitudes.
- ❑ Trabaje junto al estudiante a fin de completar las solicitudes aproximadamente dos semanas antes de la fecha límite. Ofrézcase a revisarlas. Verifique que la oficina de orientación escolar esté enviando los certificados analíticos y los puntajes de los exámenes a las instituciones educativas que su estudiante haya elegido.
- ❑ Si el joven no está satisfecho con los puntajes del SAT, sugiérale que tome el SAT o el ACT por segunda vez. Verifique las políticas de cada institución educativa. Muchas oficinas de admisión se concentran sólo en los mejores puntajes.
- ❑ Asista a todas las ferias universitarias y talleres de asistencia financiera que pueda.
- ❑ Ayude a su adolescente a buscar becas e información general sobre temas de asistencia financiera por Internet. La Solicitud Gratuita de Asistencia Federal Para Estudiantes (Free Application for Federal Student Aid, FAFSA) completa a partir del 1 de octubre.

INVIERNO

- ❑ Ayude a su estudiante a llenar la Solicitud Gratuita de Asistencia Federal para Estudiantes (Free Application for Federal Student Aid, FAFSA), que se requiere a todos los solicitantes de asistencia financiera. Este formulario determinará su elegibilidad para subsidios y préstamos con miras a ayudar a cubrir los costos universitarios.

PRIMAVERA

- ❑ Verifique que se envíen las notas de mediados de año, de ser necesario, a las instituciones educativas seleccionadas. Pídale al consejero escolar del estudiante que las envíe.
- ❑ Festeje las cartas de aceptación junto a su estudiante, y empiece los planes para su primer año. Recuérdele mantener buenas notas y asistencia.
- ❑ Minimice las cartas de rechazo, y anímelo a concentrarse en la meta real: ir a la universidad.
- ❑ Repase y evalúe las ofertas de asistencia financiera. Una vez que el estudiante tome la decisión definitiva con respecto a la selección de institución educativa, verifique las fechas límites para el envío del depósito, la solicitud de alojamiento y todos los demás elementos que ésta exija. Notifique a las otras instituciones que su hijo o hija no asistirá a ellas.
- ❑ Ayude a su adolescente a empezar a buscar un trabajo para el verano.

VERANO

- ❑ Verifique que se envíen las notas finales de su estudiante a la institución educativa seleccionada.
- ❑ Ayúdelo a planificar el próximo año en la universidad, haciendo un presupuesto, un horario y una lista de números telefónicos de servicios y apoyos importantes.

KnowHow2GO *Printed with permission from KnowHow2GO. Learn more at KnowHow2GO.org.*

Desafios

Para los adolescentes, la ida a la universidad representa un enorme cambio en sus vidas. Pero este cambio puede afectar en la misma medida a los padres y tutores.

Si bien con seguridad usted está orgulloso y entusiasmado con sus logros, también puede aparecer un sentimiento creciente de pérdida y separación. Afrontar esta mezcla de emociones puede ser difícil, pero son normales.

El manejo de estos cambios puede hacerse más fácil si tiene en cuenta estos consejos:

Manténgase en contacto.

Puede haber algo de verdad en el dicho de que la distancia aviva los sentimientos, pero los padres o tutores tal vez se preocupen de que "ojos que no ven, corazón que no siente". De modo que usted y su estudiante deben acordar las formas de seguir participando en las vidas del otro y recordar decir y hacer esas pequeñas cosas importantes. El envío de tarjetas a casa, los paquetes que se envían a la universidad, las fotos de los eventos a los que no se pudo asistir y las llamadas de teléfono y mensajes de correo electrónico son ciertamente un modo de mantenerse en contacto y participar.

Amóldese a una nueva relación.

A medida que juega un nuevo papel en la vida de su adolescente, trate de amoldarse al nuevo aspecto de adulto a adulto en la relación padre e hijo. Los hijos siempre necesitan a los padres, pero la relación puede transformarse más en una entre pares.

Espere altos y bajos.

Un día los estudiantes son un modelo de independencia y al día siguiente llaman entre llantos. Este ida y vuelta es natural y esperable, a medida que tanto estudiantes como padres se sienten más cómodos y van tomando confianza en la capacidad de los estudiantes de manejar las situaciones por sí mismos.

Reoriente su tiempo y energía hacia nuevas actividades.

Ahora que su tiempo de paternidad se ha transformado en tiempo libre, hacer un inventario de sus intereses y activos personales le revelará áreas de su vida que tal vez tenía descuidadas. Puede ser el momento de desarrollar, volver a despertar y atender viejas y nuevas aficiones, actividades placenteras y carreras.

Contemple que se cometerán errores.

Debe apoyar y aceptar la capacidad de su hijo para tomar decisiones independientes. Tanto el estudiante como los padres deben aceptar que se cometerán errores en el camino; eso es la vida. Aprender de los errores es simplemente otro tipo de aprendizaje.

Guíe sin presionar.

La comunicación de las metas y expectativas educativas debe hacerse de una manera respetuosa hacia el propio estilo e intereses de su estudiante. Los estudiantes deben perseguir sus propias pasiones. Si bien la opinión de los padres puede ser útil, no se debe esperar que los hijos hagan realidad los sueños de los padres.

Consejos del Centro de Estudios sobre los Hijos (Child Study Center) de la Universidad de Nueva York, www.aboutourkids.org

¿QUE SIGNIFICA SER UN ESTUDIANTE INDOCUMENTADO?

Luis Espino
College: Pomona College
Hometown: Napa, CA

Esta es la pregunta en la que llegué a reflexionar, especialmente al llegar el tiempo de aplicar para el colegio. Entonces me di cuenta que por la mayoría de mi vida, le avía dado poca importancia a la posición desfavorecida en la que estoy, siendo indocumentado. Recuerdo haber hablado con uno de mis primos, y recuerdo decirle que no sentía como que el ser indocumentado me haiga perjudicado en mi vida. Específicamente por que asta ese punto en mi vida, el ser indocumentado nunca me había prevenido alcanzar mis metas (en la escuela por lo menos). Pues, esta conversación sucedió antes de que empezara mis aplicaciones para el colegio, y antes de que me diera cuenta a cuantas escuelas no pude aplicar, debido a que no admiten a estudiantes indocumentados, o a que la ayuda financiara que ofrecen viene de el gobierno, y no soy elegible para recibirla.

Me di cuenta que aunque no haiga sido detenido, o aunque no me previnieron agarrar mi licencia (ya habían pasado el programa de DACA para ese entonces), tenia que enfrentar muchas desventajas que la mayoría de los otros estudiantes no tuvieron, simplemente por mi estatus migratorio.

Ahora puedo ver que el tener esta conversación con mi primo me preparo y me dio algo de sostén, para las dificultades que iba a enfrentar al tiempo de aplicar para el colegio. "Piénsalo Luis, si no fueras indocumentado, tu crees que estuvieras en el mismo lugar en el que estas hoy?" me pregunto mi primo. En verdad, no se si estuviera en el mismo lugar si nunca hubiera llegado a ver la constante vulnerabilidad en el que estuvieron mis jefes. Si mis padres no tuvieran que trabajar largas horas en el calorón y en las condiciones duras del campo, si no tuvieran una familia que mantener en México, si mis padres tuvieran un trabajo estable, pago amplio, beneficios, pensión, y cada otro privilegio que se le da a una persona por ser considerado "ciudadano" en los ojos de la ley de este país, no se si pudiera haber enfrentado los retos que tuve con el mismo apuro y con las mismas agallas. En la misma manera en la que es fácil de tomar en vano el privilegio que viene con ser ciudadano de este país, yo mismo tome en vano mi posición desventajada de ser un estudiante indocumentado. También no pude ver el privilegio que esta misma situación me había dado, al poder usar cada obstáculo que se me venia adelante debido a mi estatus migratorio como una fuente de motivación.

Para cualquier persona todavia luchando por recibir sus merecidos papeles, cualquier persona que se sienta intimidada, se sienta menos con simplemente pensar en el colegio, te animo a que mires tu situación, reconoce tus dificultades como inmigrante, pero también reconoce toda la fuerza y la lucha que tuviste que tener para seguir adelante a pesar de todo, y reconoce el valor de tu historia. Acércate a las personas que puedan verlo en ti cuando tu no puedes, y a aquellas que te empujaran a seguir adelante. Ten en mente que hay ayuda, hay recursos, y hay colegios a los que no simplemente tienes oportunidad de entrar, si no que están buscando a personas como tu. Buscan a estudiantes no por sus puntos de GPA o de el examen SAT, si no por su historia. Estas maneras superficiales de medir como un estudiante sabe tomar exámenes salen sobrando a comparación de tu historia, tu vida, y tus experiencias, que siempre tendrán mas valor. Esto es lo que se necesita mas en los colegios de los Estados Unidos, nuestras perspectivas únicas.

Abajo están algunas oportunidades y recursos para estudiantes indocumentados que é encontrado útiles. Algunas son becas completas para atender colegios completamente gratis. Algunas ya cerraron, pero abren nuevamente cada año. Todo esto es alcanzable, simplemente es de intentar. **Suerte, y a seguir adelante!**

The Dream.US - www.thedream.us
Golden Door Scholars - www.goldendoorscholars.org
Educators for Fair Consideration (E4FC) - www.e4fc.org
MALDEF Scholarship Resources - www.maldef.org
QuestBridge - www.questbridge.org

LUIS ESPINO es un ganador de la beca de I'm First! (Soy el Primero). Luis comparte sus experiencias de la universidad y ofrece consejos en el blog de estudiantes de primera generación de I'm First! (Soy el Primero).

Visite a www.ImFirst.org para seguir el blog de estudiantes y ver testimonios en video de estudiantes y graduados universitarios de primera generación.

COLLEGE IS **MY OPPORTUNITY**

Helping first-generation college students make their college dreams a reality!

GUIDE TO COLLEGE

COLLEGE PROFILES

an initiative of

striveforcollege.org

2018 EDITION

ImFirst.org

continue your research, connect with the colleges profiled in this guide, and much more at

www.ImFirst.org

striveforcollege.org

College Profiles

In the following pages, you'll find comprehensive profiles of colleges and universities committed to serving and supporting first-generation college students on their campus and in their community.

The section is organized by state, with schools presented alphabetically within each state. You are encouraged to continue your research and to connect with the colleges and universities profiled here on Strive for College's free online platform. Sign up at www.striveforcollege.org.

How Can I Use the College Profile?

Think of the college profile as a snapshot. It will provide you with data which can help you get a feel for who attends the school, what academics are like there, how much it costs, and what types of students get accepted. It will also give you an overview of the school's mission and history and the types of supports you can expect to receive on campus. What it can't tell you is how it actually feels to be on the college campus and how well you'll fit in. To find out those things, you'll need to dive deeper into the college search.

Criteria for Inclusion

The colleges and universities profiled here do not reflect each and every—or the only—schools that serve first-generation college students. Still, the colleges and universities that are featured exemplify many of the four-year colleges and universities committed to serving and supporting these students and are profiled in light of the unique programs and opportunities they offer.

Profiled colleges and universities partner with Strive for College to build awareness of and improve their institution's efforts on behalf of first-generation college students.

For more detailed information 'Explaining the College Profile' see page 41

Compiling the College Profiles

The information and data found in the college profiles is developed by Strive for College staff in collaboration with and approved by the schools themselves. Because of this close editorial process, we believe the information presented to be accurate and up-to-date. If a college did not supply a certain piece of data requested, the information either does not appear or is marked as "n/a" for "not available." We still encourage you to check directly with schools to verify important information on programs, deadlines, tuition and fees, and other data.

What's Included in Each Profile?

Page 41 gives a detailed explanation of the college profile, including a breakdown of the data provided and the types of support programs outlined. In general, each profile has three parts:

1) an introduction to the school to give you a general overview;

2) descriptions of campus programs which serve first-generation college students;

3) fast facts which give you data on the student body, academics, affordability, and admissions.

Additionally, each school supplies its contact information in the upper right-hand corner.

Note that the profiles use many college access terms which can be confusing to students just starting their search. If you are not yet familiar with what a term means, look it up in the glossary starting on page 360!

College Profile List by Name

College Profile List by **State**

University of Arizona

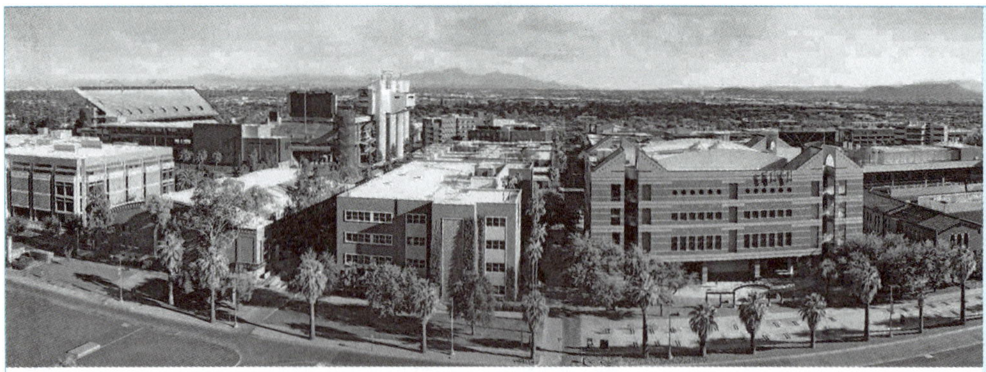

Established in 1885, the University of Arizona, the state's super land-grant university with two medical schools, produces graduates who are real-world ready through its 100% Engagement initiative. Recognized as a global leader and ranked 16th for the employability of its graduates, UA is also a leader in research, bringing more than $580 million in research investment each year, and ranking 19th among all public universities. UA is advancing the frontiers of interdisciplinary scholarship and entrepreneurial partnerships, and is a member of the Association of American Universities, the 62 leading public and private research universities.

Pre-College Prep & Outreach **New Start**

New Start is a comprehensive, six-week summer bridge program designed to help incoming freshmen succeed in the transition from high school to college.

Pre-College Prep & Outreach **Early Academic Outreach**

The mission of the Office of Early Academic Outreach at The University of Arizona is to increase the number of ethnic minority, low-income, and first-generation college-bound students who are eligible to enter a degree program at a university. This mission is accomplished by providing services to K - 12 students throughout southern Arizona. Some of the programs and services offered by Early Academic Outreach include: Mathematics, Engineering, Science Achievement (MESA), Native American Science & Engineering Program (NASEP) and College Academy for Parents.

Scholarship & Financial Aid **Arizona Assurance**

The Arizona Assurance Scholars Program at The University of Arizona is a financial aid program for low-income students in the state of Arizona. The program is designed to assist students by providing both financial aid and support services. The Arizona Assurance Program partners with college and departments on campus to provide scholars with comprehensive programming from their freshmen year through their senior year, so that they are able to have a smooth transition into and out of the University. The mission of Arizona Assurance is achieved through first-year transition programming, mentoring, leadership, and career development, graduate/professional school preparation, and cultural enrichment.

Academic Advising & Support **Think Tank**

The Think Tank is a student support center for Math and Science tutoring, Writing assistance, Weekly Course Reviews, Supplemental Instruction, Academic Skills tutoring and so much more! The Think Tank provides both free and fee based services to all UA students.

Academic Advising & Support **Writing Skills Improvement Program**

The Writing Skills Improvement Program (WSIP) was established over 30 years ago in order to help students at the University of Arizona improve their writing skills and achieve academic success. These writing coaches work one-on-one with students, staff, and faculty across all majors and degree programs. WSIP also offers regular writing workshops, custom workshops, and summer writing institutes.

University of Arizona
PO BOX 210073
Tucson, AZ 85721
Ph: (520) 621-3237
admissions@arizona.edu
www.arizona.edu

Fast Facts

STUDENT DIVERSITY

# undergraduates	35,123
% male/female	48/52
% first-generation college	26
% American Indian or Alaskan Native	1
% Asian	5
% Black or African American	4
% Hispanic/Latino	26
% Native Hawaiian or Pacific Islander	<1
% White	51
% two or more races	4
% race and/or ethnicity unknown	1
% International/nonresident	6

STUDENT SUCCESS

% first-to-second year retention	83
% six-year graduation	63
% six-year graduation for underrepresented minority groups	n/a
% first-years who live on campus	70
% undergraduates who live on campus	21
full-time faculty	1,559
full-time minority faculty	294
student-faculty ratio	22:1

Popular majors n/a

Multicultural student clubs and organizations
African Americans in Life Science (AALS), American Indian Science & Engineering Society, Loans Across Borders (LAB), Many Voices (MV), Professional Women in Business Association (PWBA), Society of Advancing Hispanic/Chicanos and Native Americans in Science (SACNAS), The Tohono O'odham Student Association at The University of Arizona (TOSA), The University of Arizona Enactus

AFFORDABILITY

Cost of Attendance

tuition	in-state: $12,200; out-of-state: $35,700
required fees	$694
room and board	$12,550

Financial Aid

total institutional scholarships/grants	$182,520,970
% of students with financial need	52
% of students with need awarded any financial aid	96
% of students with need awarded any need-based scholarship or grant aid	88
% of students with need whose need was fully met	9
% Pell Grant recipients among first-years	29
average aid package	$12,278
average student loan debt upon graduation	$23,635

ADMISSIONS

# of applicants	37,662
% admitted	76
SAT Critical Reading	n/a
SAT Math	n/a
SAT Writing	n/a
ACT Composite	24
SAT/ACT optional	yes
average HS GPA	3.4

DEADLINES

regular application closing date	5/1
early decision plan	no
application closing date	n/a
early action plan	no
application closing date	n/a
application fee	$50 (AZ); $80 (non-resident)
application fee online	n/a
fee waiver for applicants with financial need	yes

Henderson State University

Henderson State University, located in the heart of southwest Arkansas, provides a learning environment that prepares students for a lifetime of intellectual and personal growth in a global society. For 125 years, Henderson State has worked to bridge student aspirations to career success by instilling in students the skills employers most want—communication, decision-making, teamwork and problem-solving—through the application of a strong core of liberal arts classes that are applied through professional studies. Henderson State focuses on teaching and student success in its 75 undergraduate and graduate programs. Our dedicated faculty and staff serve 3,600 students from 25 states and 19 countries. We also serve our students from the Landmark Building in Hot Springs, where they can complete their undergraduate degrees or work on graduate programs in education or business.

Pre-College Prep & Outreach **Southwest Arkansas College Preparatory Academy**

The Southwest Arkansas College Preparatory Academy (SWACPA) helps students prepare for college through a focus on teaching critical thinking skills and college-level subject matter. We empower students so they are ready to take on the responsibility of college – and be successful as well. Our focus is on creating life-long learners who contribute positively to their communities.

First-Year Experience & Transition **Henderson Seminar**

The Henderson Seminar facilitates the transition of first-time freshmen to the university by introducing them to academic expectations and support services and by fostering engagement in university life beyond the classroom.

First-Year Experience & Transition **Heart Start**

All first-time freshmen and transfer students who are fully admitted are invited to attend Heart Start. Each Heart Start session is a one-day event that allows you to get REDDIE for your college career! You will have the opportunity to register for fall classes, have questions answered, and take care of important business, such as financial aid and on-campus housing. This is also your opportunity to meet the administration, faculty, staff, and other new students.

Academic Advising & Support **Student Support Services**

Student Support Services provides a supportive environment for academic success, retention, career planning and college graduation for individuals who are first generation, low-income college students. We accomplish this by helping students make adjustments to living away from home, monitoring student progress to insure good academic standing, providing students with academic tutoring, support groups, workshops and academic advice.

Academic Advising & Support **Academic Advising**

In collaboration with departmental faculty, Henderson State University's Academic Advising Center is a student success committed team of professional advisors whose aim is to focus on the individual academic needs of each undergraduate student served and facilitate their transition and integration into the university by steering them toward the programs and resources that will help them to successfully persist and matriculate. The Center promotes the personal growth of students by instilling a sense of responsibility and independence, as well as respecting and appreciating various communication and cultural backgrounds.

Mentoring **McNair Scholars Program**

One of eight federally funded TRIO Programs, the Ronald E. McNair Post Baccalaureate Achievement Program helps provide effective preparation for doctoral study to low-income, first-generation college scholars and scholars from groups underrepresented in graduate education.

Henderson State University
1100 Henderson Street
Arkadelphia, AR 71999
Ph: (870) 230-5028
www.hsu.edu

Fast Facts

STUDENT DIVERSITY

# undergraduates	2,833
% male/female	44/56
% first-generation college	52
% American Indian or Alaskan Native	<1
% Asian	<1
% Black or African American	22
% Hispanic/Latino	5
% Native Hawaiian or Pacific Islander	<1
% White	66
% two or more races	3
% race and/or ethnicity unknown	1
% International/nonresident	1

STUDENT SUCCESS

% first-to-second year retention	65
% six-year graduation	33
% six-year graduation for underrepresented minority groups	25
% first-years who live on campus	62
% undergraduates who live on campus	51
full-time faculty	178
full-time minority faculty	34
student-faculty ratio	15:1

Popular majors Business Administration, Biology, Elementary Education, Recreation, Natural Resource Management, Leisure Services Management

Multicultural student clubs and organizations Comics Art Club, Henderson International Student Association, Students Veterans Association, Youth & College NAACP, Collegiate Recreation Society, Robotics Club, Black Student Association, Baptist Collegiate Ministry, Fellowship of Christian Athletes, Wesley Foundation

AFFORDABILITY

Cost of Attendance

tuition	in-state: $3,315; out-of-state: $4,140
required fees	$841
room and board	$7,180

Financial Aid

total institutional scholarships/grants	$6,794,157
% of students with financial need	84
% of students with need awarded any financial aid	83
% of students with need awarded any need-based scholarship or grant aid	66
% of students with need whose need was fully met	10
% Pell Grant recipients among first-years	55
average aid package	$7,470
average student loan debt upon graduation	$25,848

ADMISSIONS

# of applicants	2,368
% admitted	80
SAT Critical Reading	280-710
SAT Math	400-700
SAT Writing	n/a
ACT Composite	21
SAT/ACT optional	n/a
average HS GPA	3.18

DEADLINES

regular application closing date	rolling
early decision plan	n/a
application closing date	n/a
early action plan	n/a
application closing date	n/a
application fee	$0
application fee online	$0
fee waiver for applicants with financial need	n/a

California Institute of Technology

Founded in 1891, California Institute of Technology has a long history of tackling the most challenging, fundamental problems in science and technology. With world-class scholars as their faculty mentors and access to incredible research facilities, students prepare to become leaders in the scientific community. As part of a deliberately small undergraduate population of under 1,000, students are surrounded by extraordinarily talented classmates with whom they collaborate regularly. Caltech has a unique culture that combines a passion for innovation and intense intellectual curiosity with a tradition of practical jokes and pranks for which the school is widely renowned. At Caltech, it is relatively easy for one to find their niche and develop strong working relationships with both their professors and their fellow students.

Scholarship & Financial Aid **QuestBridge Partner**

QuestBridge is a non-profit program that links bright and motivated low-income students with educational and scholarship opportunities at some of the nation's most selective colleges and universities. QuestBridge is the provider of the National College Match Program and the College Prep Scholarship. Caltech partnered with QuestBridge to connect and provide access to high-achieving, low-income students who are looking for exceptional science, math and engineering undergraduate experiences.

Open House, Fly-in, Visit **Caltech Up Close**

High school seniors from a historically underrepresented background with an interest in math, science, and/or engineering are invited to apply to the Caltech Up Close program. Selected students participate in a 3-day, 2-night, all-expenses paid visit to Caltech's campus. The program provides an exciting opportunity for prospective students to experience life in the student houses, explore labs and on-campus research facilities, and learn to navigate the Caltech application and financial aid processes.

Summer Bridge & Orientation **Freshman Summer Research Institute (FSRI)**

Incoming freshmen are selected to participate in the Freshman Summer Research Institute (FSRI) program, designed to bolster the transition from high school to a research-based education and to assist students in developing skills that will enhance their success at Caltech. Participants conduct research with mentors, write research papers, and give professional research presentations.This fully-funded program also provides group field trips, excursions, and social activities in Pasadena and the Greater Los Angeles Area.

Student Life & Support **Caltech Center for Diversity (CCD)**

The mission of the Caltech Center for Diversity is to provide education, advocacy, and allyship in order to increase institutional and personal capacity for diversity, ensuring a community committed to equity and inclusive excellence. The CCD offers proactive academic monitoring with appropriate follow-up, advising, referrals, graduate school guidance, and activities to foster a sense of community among underrepresented groups on campus. The CCD also holds workshops, trainings, and social events for students and members of Caltech community.

California Institute of Technology
Caltech Undergraduate Admissions
383 S. Hill Avenue, MC 10-90
Pasadena, CA 91125
Ph: (626) 395-6341
ugadmissions@caltech.edu
www.caltech.edu

Fast Facts

STUDENT DIVERSITY

# undergraduates	961
% male/female	55/45
% first-generation college	n/a
% American Indian or Alaskan Native	<1
% Asian	45
% Black or African American	2
% Hispanic/Latino	12
% Native Hawaiian or Pacific Islander	<1
% White	28
% two or more races	5
% race and/or ethnicity unknown	n/a
% International/nonresident	8

STUDENT SUCCESS

% first-to-second year retention	98
% six-year graduation	94
% six-year graduation for underrepresented minority groups	n/a
% first-years who live on campus	100
% undergraduates who live on campus	86
full-time faculty	336
full-time minority faculty	64
student-faculty ratio	3:1

Popular majors Computer Science, Engineering, Physics, Mathematics, Biological/Life Sciences

Multicultural student clubs and organizations Caltech Center for Diversity, Black Students of the California Institute of Technology (BSCIT)/The National Society of Black Engineers, Caltech Latino Association of Students in Engineering and Sciences (CLASES)/The Society of Hispanic Professional Engineers, Black Ladies Association of Caltech (BLAC), Mellon Mays Undergraduate Fellowship

AFFORDABILITY

Cost of Attendance

tuition	$48,111
required fees	$1,797
room and board	$14,796

Financial Aid

total institutional scholarships/grants	$19,064,382
% of students with financial need	52
% of students with need awarded any financial aid	n/a
% of students with need awarded any need-based scholarship or grant aid	52
% of students with need whose need was fully met	100
% Pell Grant recipients among first-years	12
average aid package	$46,095
average student loan debt upon graduation	$18,219

ADMISSIONS

# of applicants	7,339
% admitted	8
SAT Critical Reading	740-800
SAT Math	770-800
SAT Writing	730-790
ACT Composite	34-35
SAT/ACT optional	no
average HS GPA	n/a

DEADLINES

regular application closing date	1/3
early decision plan	n/a
application closing date	n/a
early action plan	yes
application closing date	11/1
application fee	$75
application fee online	$75
fee waiver for applicants with financial need	yes

California Lutheran University

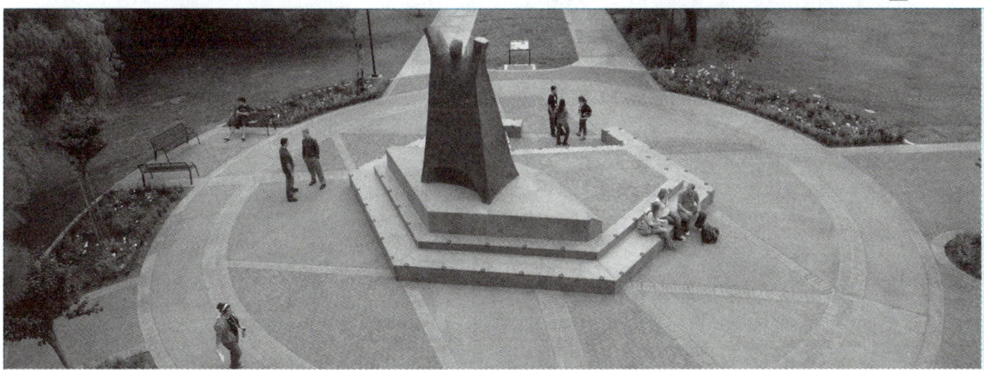

At California Lutheran University, helping students achieve academic excellence is the beginning of what we do to create outstanding graduates. Our dedicated, accomplished faculty works with small classes of undergraduate and graduate students who are open-minded about ideas, people, and faith, and who are seeking to grow as individuals while they excel academically. Both in the classroom and outside of it, everyone at Cal Lutheran is committed to helping each student pursue their passions to discover their purpose and follow that purpose to transform their community and the world.

Pre-College Prep & Outreach **Upward Bound**

The Upward Bound program is dedicated to providing quality academic and personal development services to high school students from low-income and/or first-generation families. Beyond increasing the rate at which high school graduates pursue post secondary education, the Cal Lutheran Upward Bound program strives to increase participants' competency in English, mathematics, science, social science and foreign language. Participants receive tutoring, counseling and mentoring, as well as opportunities to attend cultural enrichment events.

First-Year Experience & Transition **Summer Orientation to Academic Resources**

Incoming first-generation college freshmen are invited to attend this orientation program. The program gives participants an orientation to the college environment and provides them with opportunities to connect with other first-generation students. In addition, the program assists participants in the process of academic exploration by introducing them to relevant resources, challenging them to examine their values and interests and facilitating their transition to Cal Lutheran. During the academic year, students participate in the Student Support Services program that offers a holistic range of services including academic counseling and personal support to assist first-generation students in successfully completing their degree.

California Lutheran University
60 West Olsen Road
Thousand Oaks, CA 91360
Ph: (805) 493-3135
admissions@callutheran.edu
www.callutheran.edu

Fast Facts

STUDENT DIVERSITY

# undergraduates	2,963
% male/female	43/57
% first-generation college	29
% American Indian or Alaskan Native	<1
% Asian	5
% Black or African American	4
% Hispanic/Latino	32
% Native Hawaiian or Pacific Islander	<1
% White	45
% two or more races	8
% race and/or ethnicity unknown	3
% International/nonresident	4

STUDENT SUCCESS

% first-to-second year retention	85
% six-year graduation	71
% six-year graduation for underrepresented minority groups	72
% first-years who live on campus	70
% undergraduates who live on campus	47
full-time faculty	190
full-time minority faculty	46
student-faculty ratio	16:1

Popular majors Business, Biology, Psychology, Exercise Science, Communication

Multicultural student clubs and organizations Black Student Union, CLU French Club, Kupa'a Hawai'I Club, Latin America Student Organization, PRIDE, Prospanica, Saudi Club at CLU, Scandinavian Student Club, United Students of the World

AFFORDABILITY

Cost of Attendance

tuition	$40,880
required fees	$483
room and board	$13,320

Financial Aid

total institutional scholarships/grants	$54,483,100
% of students with financial need	71
% of students with need awarded any financial aid	100
% of students with need awarded any need-based scholarship or grant aid	100
% of students with need whose need was fully met	15
% Pell Grant recipients among first-years	30
average aid package	$35,170
average student loan debt upon graduation	$26,150

ADMISSIONS

# of applicants	5,251
% admitted	73
SAT Critical Reading	540-620
SAT Math	520-610
SAT Writing	n/a
ACT Composite	21-27
SAT/ACT optional	yes
average HS GPA	3.7

DEADLINES

regular application closing date	1/1
early decision plan	n/a
application closing date	n/a
early action plan	yes
application closing date	11/1
application fee	$25
application fee online	$25
fee waiver for applicants with financial need	yes

California Polytechnic State University

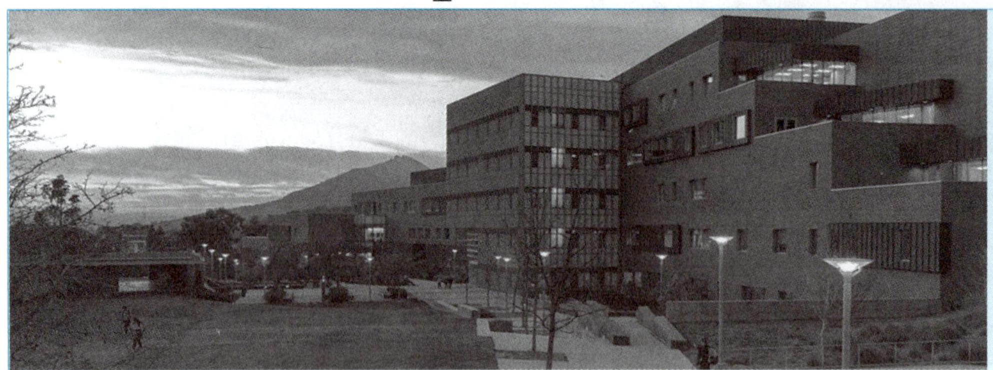

Cal Poly is a nationally ranked, four-year, comprehensive public university located in San Luis Obispo, halfway between San Francisco and Los Angeles on California's Central Coast. It is a distinctive learning community offering academically focused students a hands-on educational experience that prepares them for today's scientific and technical world.

Pre-College Summer Experience **Engineering Possibilities in College (EPIC)**

EPIC is a one-week summer program for middle and high school students (7th-12th) to learn about engineering and experience hands-on labs in a university atmosphere.

Summer Bridge & Orientation **Summer Institute (SI)**

SI is an academic orientation program held for newly admitted freshmen. Through SI, you will have the opportunity to participate in a three-week residential program geared at helping you make a successful transition from high school to college. Summer Institute will provide you with a mini-quarter of academic and social activities to help you succeed in your transition.

First-Year Experience & Transition **Week of Welcome (WOW)**

WOW is a week-long orientation event for first-year or transfer students. It is a balanced combination of excitement, learning, and new experiences during which you will participate in activities, events and presentations introducing you to the campus and community. WOW provides a thrilling environment for you to meet new people, become familiar with Cal Poly and San Luis Obispo, and prepare to start your college career.

Academic Advising & Support **Student Academic Services (SAS)**

Through SAS, students can utilize academic services, advisors, and activities to help you excel and to enhance your learning skills. We provide academic and personal advising, as well as a wide range of other services to support your personal growth and academic achievement. SAS offers support to students from backgrounds that have been traditionally underrepresented by income and/or disability to ensure all have an equal opportunity for success and graduation.

Academic Advising & Support **Multicultural Engineering Program (MEP)**

MEP is an academic support program designed to recruit, retain, and graduate underrepresented students in engineering, computer science disciplines. We build an academic support community and provides the necessary bridges for academic and professional success.

Academic Advising & Support **Educational Opportunity Program (EOP)**

The primary goals of the EOP are to improve the access, retention and graduation of students who have been historically, economically and/or educationally disadvantaged. EOP assists students by providing comprehensive academic support services. EOP will help ease the transition from your current school to Cal Poly, San Luis Obispo and provides services in the following areas to help you succeed at this campus: admissions, financial assistance, orientation, academic support, as well as academic and personal advising.

Student Life & Support **MultiCultural Center (MCC)**

The MCC cultivates a campus-wide community that represents and celebrates the diversity of Cal Poly's student body. The MCC empowers students to grow beyond their personal barriers, strengthen their understanding of diversity and social responsibility, and develop leadership skills, while fostering a sense of belonging. Through cross-cultural dialogues and examining the issues relevant to diversity and social justice, we hope to nurture a generation of ethical and knowledgeable leaders who contribute to a global society.

California Polytechnic State University
1 Grand Avenue Admissions Office #206
San Luis Obispo, CA 93407
Ph: (805) 756-2311
www.calpoly.edu

Fast Facts

STUDENT DIVERSITY

# undergraduates	20,426
% male/female	53/47
% first-generation college	n/a
% American Indian or Alaskan Native	<1
% Asian	13
% Black or African American	<1
% Hispanic/Latino	16
% Native Hawaiian or Pacific Islander	<1
% White	56
% two or more races	7
% race and/or ethnicity unknown	5
% International/nonresident	2

STUDENT SUCCESS

% first-to-second year retention	95
% six-year graduation	83
% six-year graduation for underrepresented minority groups	68
% first-years who live on campus	99
% undergraduates who live on campus	35
full-time faculty	1,318
full-time minority faculty	220
student-faculty ratio	19:1

Popular majors Mechanical Engineering, Computer Science, Psychology, Business Administration, Architecture, Biological Sciences, Animal Science

Multicultural student clubs and organizations Pride Center, Gender Equity Center, Multicultural Center, Multicultural Engineering Program, Society of Black Engineers and Scientists, Society of Hispanic Professional Engineers, Society of Women Engineers, Thai Vietnamese Student Assoc., United Sorority and Fraternity Council, Chinese Students Assoc., Black Student Union, and more!

AFFORDABILITY

Cost of Attendance

tuition	in-state: $5,742; out-of-state: n/a
required fees	$3,603
room and board	$12,507

Financial Aid

total institutional scholarships/grants	$23,848,533
% of students with financial need	42
% of students with need awarded any financial aid	94
% of students with need awarded any need-based scholarship or grant aid	88
% of students with need whose need was fully met	8
% Pell Grant recipients among first-years	15
average aid package	$10,141
average student loan debt upon graduation	$22,413

ADMISSIONS

# of applicants	48,162
% admitted	29
SAT Critical Reading	560-660
SAT Math	590-700
ACT Composite	28
SAT/ACT optional	n/a
average HS GPA	3.9

DEADLINES

regular application closing date	11/30
early decision plan	no
application closing date	n/a
early action plan	n/a
application closing date	n/a
application fee	$55
application fee online	$55
fee waiver for applicants with financial need	yes

*Data/Program Info from Fall 2016 Fact Book & 2016-2017 Common Data Set

Chapman University

Chapman University was the first private college or university in California to enroll students of all races and socio-economic backgrounds in the early part of the 20th century, a tradition to which the University firmly subscribes today. In an effort to continue its legacy of enrolling a diverse student population, Chapman has historically offered funding for students who would be the first from their family to attend college; this funding represents an additional opportunity beyond traditional need-based financial aid and merit and talent-based scholarship programs.

Scholarship & Financial Aid **Thurgood Marshall Scholarship**

The Thurgood Marshall Scholars program is designated for admitted students who are the first from their immediate family to attend college. Recipients should display strong leadership and community service involvement. Scholarship amounts vary, but average approximately $8,000 annually, and are designed to complement a financial aid or scholarship package by alleviating gaps or loans.

Academic Advising & Support **Promising Futures Program**

The Promising Futures Program is the optional support program for first-generation college students at Chapman University through the Provost's Office. Each year about 20% of the incoming student population identifies as first-generation college students. The mission of the Promising Futures Program is to develop a sense of community among first-generation students and to support their academic success through programming including: general meetings, study sessions, workshops, and social events. Two of the hallmarks of the Promising Futures Program is our mentoring program and summer bridge program for new first-generation college students at Chapman. The First-Generation Summer Bridge Program is a two-day program prior to new student orientation which provides students with resources and knowledge to be successful in college and gives our students an opportunity to connect to their fellow first-generation peers prior to the start of their academic career at Chapman.

Academic Courses & Service Learning **Global Citizens Cluster**

As part of the general education program, Chapman University requires all students to take a course focusing on human diversity and world cultures. Courses are designed to help students address contemporary and historical issues that affect underrepresented groups and to understand their implications and consequences. The diversity requirement ensures that all students study different cultures, and promotes the importance of diversity and differing perspectives in our society.

Student Life & Support **Office of Student Engagement**

The Office of Student Engagement helps fulfill Chapman's mission of molding tomorrow's leaders by providing the necessary resources and inspiration for Chapman students to discover, define, and develop their personal leadership identities through critical thinking, community building and social responsibility. Opportunities for student leadership include paid and volunteer positions in student civic engagement, diversity and equity initiatives, student organizations, student union management and marketing.

Chapman University
1 University Drive
Orange, CA 92866
Ph: (714) 997-6711
admit@chapman.edu
www.chapman.edu

Fast Facts

STUDENT DIVERSITY

# undergraduates	6,410
% male/female	40/60
% first-generation college	20
% American Indian or Alaskan Native	<1
% Asian	12
% Black or African American	2
% Hispanic/Latino	15
% Native Hawaiian or Pacific Islander	<1
% White	53
% two or more races	6
% race and/or ethnicity unknown	5
% International/nonresident	6

STUDENT SUCCESS

% first-to-second year retention	89
% six-year graduation	79
% six-year graduation for underrepresented minority groups	73
% first-years who live on campus	92
% undergraduates who live on campus	34
full-time faculty	459
full-time minority faculty	60
student-faculty ratio	14:1

Popular majors Business Administration, Psychology, Communication Studies, Strategic and Corporate Communication, Integrated Educational Studies (Education)

Multicultural student clubs and organizations Diversity & Equity Initiatives, Social Justice Council, Chinese Cultural Club, Hispanic Student Assoc., Japanese Club, Korean Student Assoc., Movimiento Estudiantil Chicano de Aztln, Asian Pacific Student Assoc., Black Student Union, Pua'ikeana, Queer Straight Alliance, Vietnamese Student Assoc.

AFFORDABILITY

Cost of Attendance

tuition	$50,210
required fees	$384
room and board	$14,910

Financial Aid

total institutional scholarships/grants	$109,135,414
% of students with financial need	61
% of students with need awarded any financial aid	99
% of students with need awarded any need-based scholarship or grant aid	87
% of students with need whose need was fully met	11
% Pell Grant recipients among first-years	20
average aid package	$29,909
average student loan debt upon graduation	$25,959

ADMISSIONS

# of applicants	15,677
% admitted	57
SAT Critical Reading	550-650
SAT Math	560-650
SAT Writing	560-660
ACT Composite	28
SAT/ACT optional	no
average HS GPA	3.76

DEADLINES

regular application closing date	1/15
early decision plan	yes
application closing date	11/1
early action plan	yes
application closing date	11/1
application fee	$70
application fee online	$70
fee waiver for applicants with financial need	yes

Claremont McKenna College

Since its inception in 1946, Claremont McKenna College has been committed to providing its students with a robust and rigorous world-class liberal arts education. Education at CMC is rooted in the interplay between the double helix of theory and action: this is the place where the world of ideas and the world of events come together as one. Today, CMC ranks among the nation's premier liberal arts colleges, enrolling 1300 young men and women who are eager to engage in intellectually stimulating discussions, seek to develop practical solutions to today's challenges and needs and who expect to make significant contributions to their communities. With a need blind policy—students are admitted without regard to their family's financial resources—and pledge to meeting 100% of demonstrated financial need for all admitted US citizens and permanent residents, CMC is committed to ensuring diversity in its student body.

Open House, Fly-in, Visit **PREVIEW CMC!**

Claremont McKenna hosts a Preview program in the fall, funding travel, meals and accommodations for multicultural and first generation students interested in exploring all that CMC has to offer. The program grants prospective applicants an inside look into the life of a CMC student by attending classes, connecting with students and professors, exploring campus resources, all while enjoying the perks of that Southern California sun! For inquiries, email preview@cmc.edu.

Pre-College Prep and Outreach **Multicultural Advisory Council (M.A.C.)**

M.A.C. are current students who serve as Admission ambassadors, these students represent diverse cultural and socio-economic backgrounds and are committed to providing insight and support to prospective students as they navigate through the admission application process and learn more about academic, pre-professional, and extracurricular opportunities at CMC.

Scholarship & Financial Aid **Need-Blind, Scholarships, Scholar Community**

CMC is committed to being need-blind for our US citizens and permanent residents and meeting 100% of the student's determined need. We are proud to be a Questbridge College Partner and Chicago Scholars Platinum Partner. We also partner with other community based organizations around the country as well as offer merit scholarships. Students selected for our Scholar Community are provided with the means and support to pursue their specific interests through experiential learning in a variety of disciplines and fields.

First Year Experience & Transition **Welcome Orientation Adventure (W.O.A.)**

Claremont McKenna's orientation program is a 10-day experience where new students will connect with first-year guides who are upperclassmen and who will lead, guide, and mentor them through their first year. All new students participate in a W.O.A. trip and attend sessions on course planning and a host of CMC resources. Students are also assigned a faculty mentor who will advise them on course curriculum.

Student Life & Support **The C.A.R.E. Center (Civility, Access, Resources, Expression)**

The C.A.R.E. Center (Civility, Access, Resources, Expression) is a major catalyst on our campus for creating an environment to help foster learning about our own identity, respecting others, and making the community a more inclusive place. This happens through weekly education workshops, dialogues, and identity-based discussions as well as a rotation of on-campus and Claremont College resources that offer office hours in the Center. The Queer Resource Center, Office of Black Student Affairs, Student Disability Resource Center, Chicano/Latino Resource Center and the Chaplains office each rotate office hours within the center so students can connect with the external resources they need.

Claremont McKenna College
888 Columbia Avenue
Claremont, CA 91711
Ph: (909) 621-8088
admission@cmc.edu
www.cmc.edu

Fast Facts

STUDENT DIVERSITY

# undergraduates	1,347
% male/female	51/49
% first-generation college	n/a
% American Indian or Alaskan Native	<1
% Asian	10
% Black or African American	5
% Hispanic/Latino	14
% Native Hawaiian or Pacific Islander	<1
% White	42
% two or more races	6
% race and/or ethnicity unknown	6
% International/nonresident	17

STUDENT SUCCESS

% first-to-second year retention	93
% six-year graduation	93
% six-year graduation for underrepresented minority groups	n/a
% first-years who live on campus	100
% undergraduates who live on campus	97
full-time faculty	142
full-time minority faculty	22
student-faculty ratio	9:1

Popular majors Economics, International Relations, Government, Psychology, Biology

Multicultural student clubs and organizations Asian Pacific American Mentoring Program (APAM), Brothers and Sisters Alliance, Edunoia, Mi Gente!, Queer, Questioning & Allied Program, Black Student Affairs, Chicano Latino Student Affairs

AFFORDABILITY

Cost of Attendance

tuition	$50,700
required fees	$745
room and board	$15,740

Financial Aid

total institutional scholarships/grants	$19,646,530
% of students with financial need	39
% of students with need awarded any financial aid	100
% of students with need awarded any need-based scholarship or grant aid	98
% of students with need whose need was fully met	100
% Pell Grant recipients among first-years	12
average aid package	$46,129
average student loan debt upon graduation	$23,375

ADMISSIONS

# of applicants	6,342
% admitted	11
SAT Critical Reading	650-740
SAT Math	670-750
SAT Writing	670-750
ACT Composite	31-33
SAT/ACT optional	no
average HS GPA	n/a

DEADLINES

regular application closing date	1/5, 12/1 for merit consideration
early decision plan	yes
application closing date	11/1, 1/1
early action plan	no
application closing date	n/a
application fee	$70
application fee online	$70
fee waiver for applicants with financial need	yes

Fresno Pacific University

Fresno Pacific University
1717 S. Chestnut Ave.
Fresno, CA 93702
Ph: (559) 453-2039
ugadmis@fresno.edu
www.experiencefpu.com

See what's possible when you have everything you ever needed to do everything you always wanted. At Fresno Pacific University, you'll join others who are united by a passion for knowledge. By fellowship and faith. And by a commitment to tackling the big questions that reverberate far beyond the classroom. Discover what inspires you as you dive into your field of study. See God in our diverse campus environment and get closer to Him as you learn. Develop the bonds that will last a lifetime through relationships with classmates and faculty. Express yourself via Sunbird athletics or our vibrant arts community. Find the support you need through our extensive financial aid options. And do it all right here in California's beautiful central valley; rich with culture, food and fun. Fresno Pacific University. Possible happens here.

Academic Advising & Support **The ALAS Program**

The ALAS Program is committed to helping first-generation students successfully graduate from college in just four years. Our free, personal services help you achieve a university degree and become an FPU Sunbird for life. Academic counselors will help you: Design a personalized education plan targeted toward graduating in four years, connect you with student tutors who can answer your questions about classes, teachers and other issues and learn which courses are required to graduate. Career counselors will help you: Assess your skills, abilities, interests and goals to choose a major that is right for you, write a resume/Curriculum Vitae (CV) and cover letter to personalize your presentations, and provide information about opportunities in your field or interest and prepare you to pursue a career or graduate school. The ALAS Program gives you access to computers and printers for classwork and homework at no cost. There is also a friendly staff and information about other matters pertaining to academics and the community.

Summer Bridge & Orientation **STEM Summer Bridge Program**

The STEM bridge summer program aims to give students a leg-up academically as they prepare to enter their first year of college. Students entering STEM disciplines will meet and bond during a one-day event held on FPU's campus and will remain connected online for 4 weeks in the summer. Students can expect to gain early access to some of the general education courses that, once the semester begins, will allow them to be better prepared for academic success. Additionally, they will walk onto campus the first day of classes with a group of students who they have already established personal and academic relationships with that will hopefully last their entire time while at FPU.

Pre-College Prep & Outreach **Dreamer's Workshop**

This annual college informational workshop is for DACA, Dreamer or AB-540 eligible students and their families to receive key information and resources on how to get the most out of their benefits. They interact with counselors and representatives from local colleges and organizations that aim to aid these students in their college-going efforts. Scholarship information and application support is also provided.

Scholarship & Financial Aid **The Samaritan Scholarship Program**

The Samaritan scholarship is for undocumented, academically prepared, first-time freshman or transfer students who have completed their high school education in California. The Samaritan scholarship program provides leadership development, mentoring, career internship opportunities and cultural events/conferences that scholars can lead and attend. Qualifications: Must be an undocumented student, must have attended and graduated from a high school in California, demonstrated Christian commitment, must have filed and submitted the California Dream Act Application.

Fast Facts

STUDENT DIVERSITY

# undergraduates	1,053
% male/female	38/62
% first-generation college	53
% American Indian or Alaskan Native	1
% Asian	5
% Black or African American	5
% Hispanic/Latino	43
% Native Hawaiian or Pacific Islander	1
% White	38
% two or more races	2
% race and/or ethnicity unknown	3
% International/nonresident	2

STUDENT SUCCESS

% first-to-second year retention	75
% six-year graduation	56
% six-year graduation for underrepresented minority groups	n/a
% first-years who live on campus	n/a
% undergraduates who live on campus	50
full-time faculty	125
full-time minority faculty	n/a
student-faculty ratio	13:1

Popular majors Kinesiology, Liberal Studies, Psychology, Communication, Criminal Justice

Multicultural student clubs and organizations Amigos Unidos, Asian Flavor, Colors of India, DREAMers, IMAGES, International Club

AFFORDABILITY

Cost of Attendance

tuition	$29,998
required fees	$460
room and board	$8,400

Financial Aid

total institutional scholarships/grants	$2,000,000
% of students with financial need	91
% of students with need awarded any financial aid	97
% of students with need awarded any need-based scholarship or grant aid	n/a
% of students with need whose need was fully met	n/a
% Pell Grant recipients among first-years	58
average aid package	n/a
average student loan debt upon graduation	n/a

ADMISSIONS

# of applicants	1,004
% admitted	n/a
SAT Critical Reading	n/a
SAT Math	n/a
SAT Writing	n/a
ACT Composite	n/a
SAT/ACT optional	n/a
average HS GPA	n/a

DEADLINES

regular application closing date	rolling
early decision plan	n/a
application closing date	n/a
early action plan	n/a
application closing date	n/a
application fee	$40
application fee online	$40
fee waiver for applicants with financial need	yes

Holy Names University

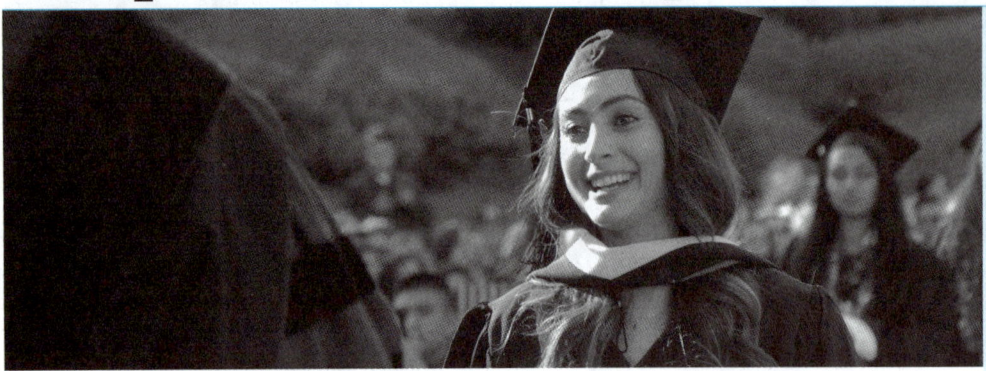

Holy Names University
3500 Mountain Blvd.
Oakland, CA 94619
Ph: (510) 436-1351
admissions@hnu.edu
www.hnu.edu

For nearly 150 years, Holy Names University has been educating students from throughout the California Bay Area and the world. As one of the most ethnically diverse college campuses in the country, HNU believes in the value of a varied student body, faculty and staff who come together to share ideas, challenge, and support each other. With over 30 percent of our student body the first in their family to go to college, the environment is one of growth and discovery through academics, leadership and pursuit of social justice. Four years at HNU isn't just about the time spent in the classroom with world class faculty. It's about shared ideas, development of the whole person and understanding your place in the global community.

Pre-College Prep and Outreach **Early Admit Program**

The Early Admit Program at HNU seeks to provide students from partner high schools in underserved communities with access to college by offering students admission to HNU on contract beginning their freshman year of High School. Through this initiative, students are supported throughout their four years of high school, including mentor support each semester, to make sure each student is staying on track and meeting the necessary academic requirements.

Scholarship & Financial Aid **Cal Grant A/B**

Through the California Student Aid Commission, HNU accepts two types of federal grants specifically for California residents. Cal Grant A offers up to $9,084 annually to in-state students based on their financial aid and academic achievement. Cal Grant B is awarded to first-year college students from disadvantaged backgrounds in California. Recipients of Cal Grant B receive $1,670 for their first year of college, then an additional $10,754 in the following years.

First Year Experience & Transition **HNU Connections Project**

The HNU Connections Project, HNU's first year experience program, provides new students support to help ease the transition to college life, both academically and socially. Embedded in the program is a commitment to academic skill-building and an introduction to college culture. Upon admission, first-year students are assigned to a learning community, common reading project and student Mentor. Because so many of HNU students are first-generation college attendees, many of the program Mentors are the first in their family to go to college.

Academic Advising & Support **Student Success**

All students are provided access to advising and learning resources from their first year to graduation. At HNU, every student is paired with an academic adviser. In addition, free tutoring, test prep, career counseling, job skill building and psychological counseling and support is available. Through these services, HNU demonstrates its commitment to support students during their first year and throughout college, as well as to provide assistance transitioning to work and life beyond.

Fast Facts

STUDENT DIVERSITY

# undergraduates	526
% male/female	36/64
% first-generation college	34
% American Indian or Alaskan Native	<1
% Asian	10
% Black or African American	21
% Hispanic/Latino	42
% Native Hawaiian or Pacific Islander	3
% White	17
% two or more races	2
% race and/or ethnicity unknown	3
% International/nonresident	4

STUDENT SUCCESS

% first-to-second year retention	74
% six-year graduation	45
% six-year graduation for underrepresented minority groups	43
% first-years who live on campus	58
% undergraduates who live on campus	65
full-time faculty	42
full-time minority faculty	11
student-faculty ratio	12:1

Popular majors Business, Psychology, Pre-Biology, Criminology, Liberal Studies

Multicultural student clubs and organizations
Associated Students of Holy Names University (Student Government), Black Student Union (BSU), Dance Force, Darlings, Freaks and Geeks, Hawks Student Athletic Advisory Committee (HSAAC), HNU All Stars, Latinos Unidos, Model United Nations (M.U.N.), Pacific Islanders Club, Peace and Justice Club, PROUD, Student Veteran Alliance

AFFORDABILITY

Cost of Attendance

tuition	$36,574
required fees	$500
room and board	$12,224

Financial Aid

total institutional scholarships/grants	$10,465,092
% of students with financial need	97
% of students with need awarded any financial aid	99
% of students with need awarded any need-based scholarship or grant aid	98
% of students with need whose need was fully met	11
% Pell Grant recipients among first-years	47
average aid package	$41,193
average student loan debt upon graduation	$46,900

ADMISSIONS

# of applicants	872
% admitted	48
SAT Critical Reading	447
SAT Math	463
SAT Writing	441
ACT Composite	18
SAT/ACT optional	n/a
average HS GPA	3.20

DEADLINES

regular application closing date	rolling
early decision plan	yes
application closing date	n/a
early action plan	n/a
application closing date	n/a
application fee	$20
application fee online	n/a
fee waiver for applicants with financial need	yes

*Statistics reflect the 2016–2017 school year.

Loyola Marymount University

Loyola Marymount University
1 LMU Drive
Los Angeles, CA 90045
Ph: (310) 338-2750
www.lmu.edu

Loyola Marymount University, the University of Silicon Beach, is ranked in the top 12 percent of higher education institutions nationally by The Wall Street Journal. Founded in 1911, LMU is a Catholic, Jesuit, and Marymount university with more than 6,100 undergraduate students and more than 3,000 graduate and law students. LMU offers 58 undergraduate majors and 53 minor programs, along with 46 master's degree programs, one education doctorate, one juris doctorate, one doctorate of juridical science and 13 credential/authorization programs. LMU's intercollegiate athletics teams compete in the West Coast Conference with 22 Division I and varsity sports.

Pre-College Summer Experience **Summer Program**

Summer pre-college programs are an engaging opportunity for motivated high school students to get a sneak peek at college life through a unique two-week experience designed to challenge students' critical and creative ways of thinking. More than summer school, this transformative program provides students with the opportunity to explore academic passions, evolve as individuals, and discover what it means to have the heart of an LMU Lion.

Pre-College Summer Experience **Pathway to College**

Undergraduate Admission invites students and families to campus for a free event to learn about the college admission and financial aid process. The day includes an optional tour and a first-generation student panel.

Scholarship & Financial Aid **Financial Aid/LAA/AAAA**

The Financial Aid Office is dedicated to providing sound stewardship of more than 200 million dollars in university, government and private funds that are utilized by our students to finance their LMU education. We offer various resources and scholarship opportunities including the California Dream Act, the African American Alumni Association, Latino Alumni Association, Yellow Ribbon (for veterans and veteran dependents), academic merit-based and the Gates Millennium Scholarship.

First-Year Experience & Transition **First To Go (FTG)**

The FTG program offers students valuable resources and opportunities for academic, professional, and personal growth. It is our mission to emphasize the unique cultural capital first-generation college students bring into the university in an attempt to create a community that will help our students thrive during their tenure at LMU.

Academic Advising & Support **Academic Resource Center (ARC)**

The mission of the ARC is to promote engaged academic citizenship and to provide opportunities for students to become more fully integrated into the rich and diverse culture of the university. The ARC offers content tutoring for gateway courses in subjects such as chemistry, economics, and modern languages. Certified ARC peer tutors provide one-on-one writing support for papers in any class and lead a wide variety of writing workshops.

Student Life & Support **Ethnic and Intercultural Services (EIS)**

EIS assists students in creating a dynamic understanding of themselves in relation to others and cultivating university citizens and leaders. In service to the university and broader community, EIS engages in strategic alliances that enhance the understanding of race, ethnicity, gender, culture and religious belief and its impact on the community.

Fast Facts

STUDENT DIVERSITY

# undergraduates	6,126
% male/female	44/56
% first-generation college	13
% American Indian or Alaskan Native	n/a
% Asian	11
% Black or African American	6
% Hispanic/Latino	21
% Native Hawaiian or Pacific Islander	n/a
% White	44
% two or more races	8
% race and/or ethnicity unknown	n/a
% International/nonresident	10

STUDENT SUCCESS

% first-to-second year retention	90
% six-year graduation	78
% six-year graduation for underrepresented minority groups	n/a
% first-years who live on campus	95
% undergraduates who live on campus	52
full-time faculty	561
full-time minority faculty	192
student-faculty ratio	11:1

Popular majors Marketing, Communication Studies, Psychology, Finance, Film/TV Production, English

Multicultural student clubs and organizations First to Go Community, Ethnic and Intercultural Services, Office of Black Student Services, Chicano Latino Student Services, Asian and Pacific Student Services, Jewish Student Life, Office for International Students and Scholars

AFFORDABILITY

Cost of Attendance

tuition	$44,230
required fees	n/a
room and board	$13,808

Financial Aid

total institutional scholarships/grants	$110,000,000
% of students with financial need	n/a
% of students with need awarded any financial aid	85
% of students with need awarded any need-based scholarship or grant aid	n/a
% of students with need whose need was fully met	n/a
% Pell Grant recipients among first-years	18
average aid package	$27,849
average student loan debt upon graduation	$30,487

ADMISSIONS

# of applicants	13,288
% admitted	51
SAT Critical Reading	550-640
SAT Math	560-660
SAT Writing	n/a
ACT Composite	n/a
SAT/ACT optional	n/a
average HS GPA	3.8

DEADLINES

regular application closing date	1/15
early decision plan	yes
application closing date	11/1
early action plan	yes
application closing date	11/1
application fee	n/a
application fee online	n/a
fee waiver for applicants with financial need	n/a

Mills College

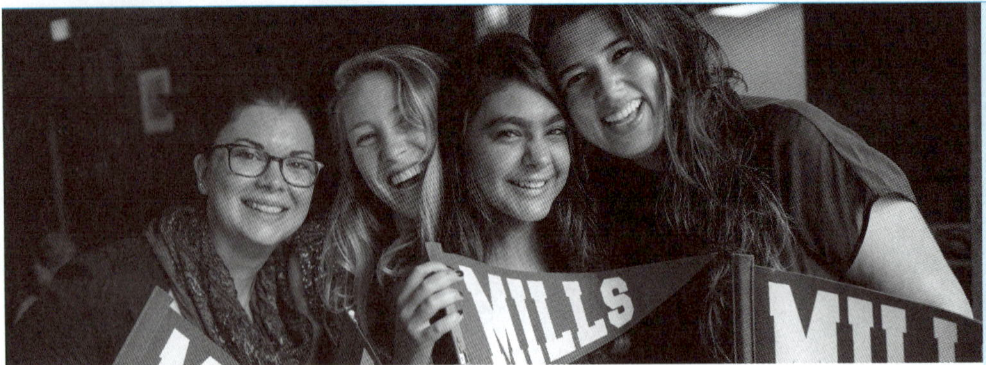

At Mills, we're breaking barriers to a high-quality education by reducing undergraduate tuition by $16,000 beginning in fall 2018. Our goal is to provide access to students so you can experience a life-changing education that prepares you to be a leader in your career and community. You'll join a diverse, inclusive community of women at Mills—32% of our undergraduates are first-generation college students and 57% identify as people of color. Our supportive learning environment encourages discussion and inspires students to put their passions into practice. You'll be encouraged to stand out, emboldened to think big, and empowered to make a statement.

Pre-College Prep & Outreach **Federal TRIO Programs (Upward Bound and Mills Educational Talent Search)**

Mills College is engaged in two Federal TRIO programs: Upward Bound and Mills Educational Talent Search (METS). Upward Bound assists low-income and first-generation college-bound high school students with academic tutoring and opportunities that continue through college. METS connects low-income, first-generation students with academic advisors who offer personalized college planning and access to numerous resources.

Scholarship & Financial Aid **Merit and Need-Based Scholarships**

Ninety-six percent of Mills students receive some portion of their aid directly from the College. Mills offers merit and need-based scholarships and provides additional support for first-generation students. Scholarships can total up to $10,000 for first-year students and transfer students.

Summer Bridge & Orientation **Summer Academic Workshop (SAW)**

Mills prepares first-generation college students for success through the Summer Academic Workshop for Leaders and Scholars, an intensive four-week residential program. Every summer, 15-20 students live in residence halls with advisors and tutors, studying a range of subjects such as English, computer science, math, sociology, and social justice.

First-Year Experience & Transition **Themed Housing Communities**

First-year, traditional-age students at Mills have the benefit of living in themed housing communities that focus on diverse topics such as Bay Area exploration, graphic novels and fandom, STEM, or social justice. Themed housing communities are a great way for first-generation students to build deep connections at Mills while making new friends and exploring activities on and off campus.

Academic Advising & Support **One-on-One Advising with Faculty**

First-year students are paired with faculty members who work with them one-on-one to customize a schedule to their interests and needs. The diversity of the Mills faculty ensures that first-generation college students are immersed in a supportive environment.

Student Life & Support **Being the First**

The Being the First Program provides support and community-building opportunities for first-generation students throughout their college experience at Mills. The program focuses on connecting students with the resources they need to meet their academic, personal, and career goals. Being the First offers specialized study sessions with access to peer tutoring, weekly peer advising services, and an annual speaker series.

Mills College
5000 MacArthur Blvd.
Oakland, CA 94613
Ph: (800) 87-MILLS
admission@mills.edu
www.mills.edu

Fast Facts

STUDENT DIVERSITY

# undergraduates	762
% male/female	0/100
% first-generation college	32
% American Indian or Alaskan Native	<1
% Asian	10
% Black or African American	10
% Hispanic/Latina	29
% Native Hawaiian or Pacific Islander	<1
% White	41
% two or more races	9
% race and/or ethnicity unknown	1
% International/nonresident	1

STUDENT SUCCESS

% first-to-second year retention	78
% six-year graduation	75
% six-year graduation for underrepresented minority groups	75
% first-years who live on campus	89
% undergraduates who live on campus	64
full-time faculty	82
full-time minority faculty	33
student-faculty ratio	9:1

Popular majors English, Psychology, Sociology, Economics, Biology

Multicultural student clubs and organizations Asian Pacific Islander Student Alliance, Black Student Collective, El Club de Español, Indigenous Women's Alliance, Jewish Student Collective, Latinx Student Collective, Mandarin Club, Unión Salvadoreña de Estudiantes Universitarios de Mills College

AFFORDABILITY

Cost of Attendance (2018–19)

tuition	$28,765
required fees	$1,492
room and board	$13,448

Financial Aid (2017–18)

total institutional scholarships/grants	$20,400,000
% of students with financial need	84
% of students with need awarded any financial aid	84
% of students with need awarded any need-based scholarship or grant aid	78
% of students with need whose need was fully met	11
% Pell Grant recipients among first-years	57
average aid package*	$42,594
average student loan debt upon graduation	$26,517

ADMISSIONS

# of applicants	1,329
% admitted	77
SAT Critical Reading	500-630
SAT Math	460-600
SAT Writing	470-630
ACT Composite	27
SAT/ACT optional	yes
average HS GPA	3.55

DEADLINES

regular application closing date	1/15
early decision plan	yes
application closing date	n/a
early action plan	yes
application closing date	11/15
application fee	$50
application fee online	$50
fee waiver for applicants with financial need	yes

*Due to our 36% tuition reduction, the average aid package for 2018–19 will be lower than the 2017–18 average.

Notre Dame de Namur University

Established in 1851, Notre Dame de Namur University (NDNU) is a Catholic, not-for-profit, coeducational institution serving approximately 1,700 students from diverse backgrounds. The historic 50-acre campus is located in Belmont, CA on the San Francisco peninsula in Silicon Valley, the heart of one of the country's most exciting regions for professional growth and personal enrichment.

NDNU is the third oldest college in California and the first authorized to grant the baccalaureate degree to women. NDNU maintains a strong commitment to academic excellence, and fostering social justice and community engagement and strives for new ways to open doors to all students who are driven to grow through higher education. We are committed, above all else, to individual learning- giving each of our students the tools, knowledge and inspiration to successfully engage and expand their talents.

Academic Advising & Support **Student Success Center**

The goal of the Student Success Center is to support students in all aspects of their academic careers at NDNU by offering free integrated learning and support services. The staff engages in a partnership with students to help them achieve their goals. Professional staff members, peer tutors and faculty work together to promote a supportive learning environment.

Academic Advising & Support **Tutorial Center**

With the goal of helping students become independent and effective learners, we provide friendly and free learning support services to all NDNU students. Our services range from building basic study skills to preparing for admission to graduate school. We also facilitate academic success workshops and tutorial assistance in many lower and upper division courses.

Student Life & Support **Career Resource Center**

Career Services provides career counseling, for-credit classes, information resources, and on-campus events aimed at the career development of students and alumni. Career Services strives to:

- Help students to develop competence and confidence in the career planning and job search process.
- Empower students to discover their unique talents, skills, and values.
- Foster career exploration and decision-making through experiential learning activities.
- Provide appropriate up-to-date career-related information and resources.
- Develop and maintain relationships with organizations that offer community engagement and career opportunities to students and alumni.

Notre Dame de Namur University
1500 Ralston Avenue
Belmont, CA 94002
Ph: (650) 508-3600
www.ndnu.edu

Fast Facts

STUDENT DIVERSITY

# undergraduates	927
% male/female	67/33
% first-generation college	71
% American Indian or Alaskan Native	0
% Asian	11
% Black or African American	6
% Hispanic/Latino	50
% Native Hawaiian or Pacific Islander	1
% White	22
% two or more races	5
% race and/or ethnicity unknown	2
% International/nonresident	3

STUDENT SUCCESS

% first-to-second year retention	68
% six-year graduation	49
% six-year graduation for underrepresented minority groups	28
% first-years who live on campus	79
% undergraduates who live on campus	44
full-time faculty	49
full-time minority faculty	16
student-faculty ratio	11:1

Popular majors Business Administration, Biological Sciences/Kinesiology, Psychology, Liberal Studies

Multicultural student clubs and organizations American Desis, Black Student Union, The International Student's Club, and Latinos Unidos

AFFORDABILITY

Cost of Attendance

tuition	$33,926
required fees	$270
room and board	$13,656

Financial Aid

total institutional scholarships/grants	$13,394,767
% of students with financial need	95
% of students with need awarded any financial aid	100
% of students with need awarded any need-based scholarship or grant aid	100
% of students with need whose need was fully met	n/a
% Pell Grant recipients among first-years	52
average aid package	$28,002
average student loan debt upon graduation	$32,743

ADMISSIONS

# of applicants	2,053
% admitted	80
SAT Critical Reading	460-560
SAT Math	360-528
SAT Writing	n/a
ACT Composite	15-22
SAT/ACT optional	n/a
average HS GPA	3.11

DEADLINES

regular application closing date	rolling
early decision plan	n/a
application closing date	n/a
early action plan	yes
application closing date	12/1
application fee	$55
application fee online	n/a
fee waiver for applicants with financial need	yes

Occidental College

Founded in 1887, Occidental College fully integrates the liberal arts and sciences with the cultural and intellectual resources of one of the world's great cities. Situated on a 120-acre residential campus in Los Angeles' Eagle Rock community, our location serves as a springboard for putting theory into practice and ideas into action. Students benefit from our small-classroom environment with stimulating faculty, who take their teaching as seriously as their research. Our distinctive interdisciplinary approach will give you the chance to explore new ideas and see the world from a new perspective. With more than 40 majors and minors, exemplary one-of-a-kind programs and our emphasis on research, Occidental provides its students with a compelling intellectual adventure. Academic rigor is enhanced by internships and community partnerships across Los Angeles. Uncommonly inclusive and consciously collaborative, our students seek to embrace difference and make a difference in the world. Occidental is reinventing the liberal arts and sciences for a new generation of problem solvers, creators, and thinkers.

Open House, Fly-In, Visit **Multicultural Visit Program**

The Multicultural Visit Program (MVP) is a two-day visit to campus for high school seniors from underrepresented backgrounds. MVP is designed for underrepresented students to meet other prospective applicants and current Oxy students and professors while gaining an understanding of Oxy's campus and its relationship to Los Angeles. Students stay overnight in a residence hall, participate in classes, interact with current students and professors, attend information sessions on admission and financial aid and go on an excursion to Downtown L.A.

Scholarship & Financial Aid **Need-Based Scholarships**

Occidental College is committed to meeting the full demonstrated need of all enrolled students. We extend financial aid through merit scholarships, need-based grants and scholarships, work-study and student loans to meet the various needs and circumstances of our students. Our aid programs often make Oxy's cost comparable to those of public institutions. If you are interested in Oxy, we encourage you to apply for financial aid—regardless of your financial circumstances.

Summer Bridge & Orientation **Multicultural Summer Institute (MSI)**

Occidental College chooses up to 50 admitted students each year to participate in a co-curricular program called the Multicultural Summer Institute. This four-week residential summer program takes place before students begin their first year at Occidental and prepares students for their academic career by acquainting them with the campus experience and offering classes related to social justice. Students are awarded four course credits upon successful completion of the program.

Student Life & Support **Intercultural Community Center (ICC)**

The Intercultural Community Center is the co-curricular resource for diversity education and social justice programming. The center fosters an inclusive, democratic community, so that socially responsible and diverse leaders can improve both leadership and communication skills. The center collaborates with student organizations, academic departments, residence halls and members of the surrounding community to sponsor programs that examine, celebrate and appreciate identity, pluralism and democracy. The ICC spearheads key initiatives, including the First Generation College Success Program.

Occidental College
1600 Campus Road
Los Angeles, CA 90041
Ph: (323) 259-2700
admission@oxy.edu
www.oxy.edu

Fast Facts

STUDENT DIVERSITY

# undergraduates	2,055
% male/female	42/58
% first-generation college	12
% American Indian or Alaskan Native	<1
% Asian	14
% Black or African American	5
% Hispanic/Latino	14
% Native Hawaiian or Pacific Islander	<1
% White	51
% two or more races	8
% race and/or ethnicity unknown	2
% International/nonresident	7

STUDENT SUCCESS

% first-to-second year retention	91
% six-year graduation	90
% six-year graduation for underrepresented minority groups	85
% first-years who live on campus	100
% undergraduates who live on campus	82
full-time faculty	173
full-time minority faculty	47
student-faculty ratio	10:1

Popular majors Economics, Diplomacy & World Affairs, Media, Arts & Culture, Biology and Sociology, Urban & Environmental Policy

Multicultural student clubs and organizations Asian Pacific Americans for Liberation, Black Student Association, Beauty Beyond Color, Chinese Culture Club,I Ka Poli O Hawaii, International Stduents Organization, Jewish Student Union, Korean-American Student Association, People of Color in STEM, Queer Student Alliance, South Asian Student Association

AFFORDABILITY

Cost of Attendance

tuition	$52,260
required fees	$578
room and board	$14,968

Financial Aid

total institutional scholarships/grants	n/a
% of students with financial need	57
% of students with need awarded any financial aid	100
% of students with need awarded any need-based scholarship or grant aid	57
% of students with need whose need was fully met	100
% Pell Grant recipients among first-years	16
average aid package	$45,873
average student loan debt upon graduation	$32,008

ADMISSIONS

# of applicants	6,775
% admitted	40
SAT Evidence-Based Reading & Writing	680
SAT Math	680
ACT Composite	30
SAT/ACT optional	no
average HS GPA	3.68

DEADLINES

regular application closing date	1/15
early decision plan	yes
application closing date	11/15 and 1/1
early action plan	n/a
application closing date	n/a
application fee	$65
application fee online	$65
fee waiver for applicants with financial need	yes

Otis College of Art and Design

Established in 1918, Otis College of Art and Design offers undergraduate and graduate degrees in a wide variety of visual and applied arts, media, and design. Core programs in liberal arts, business practices, and community-driven projects support the College's mission to prepare diverse students to enrich the world through their creativity, skill, and vision.

Open House, Fly-in, Visit **Open House**

At Open House, students and their families and friends can participate in art and design workshops, meet current students, faculty and department chairs, and receive one-on-one counseling about Admissions and Financial Aid. First generation students will also have the opportunity to learn about the full range of student services offered at the college.

Student Life & Support **Your Creative Future**

Your Creative Future is an initiative at the core of every Otis College experience. It helps students make the jump from college to career through professional development courses, on-campus internship and job fairs that link students to the professional industries, individualized career mentoring, and much more. A great fact for first-generation students to know is that 92% of the graduating class of 2016 are currently employed within a year of graduating!

Pre-College Summer Experience **Summer of Art**

Summer of Art is a four-week intensive pre-college experience for students ages 15+ that includes hands-on studio courses in a variety of disciplines. Students typically create enough work in the program to develop a full portfolio. Scholarships are available to students based on financial need and merit, and first-generation students are encouraged to apply!

Pre-College Prep & Outreach **Portfolio Preparation Courses**

Otis College offers weekend courses focused on portfolio development. They are a great way for students in the L.A. region to come to the campus weekly to boost their creative skills. First-generation students can apply for scholarships to cover the cost of tuition if admitted.

Academic Advising & Support **Student Learning Center (SLC)**

First generation students can partner with our SLC anytime throughout their studies. Our SLC tutors offer support for students to grow as individuals, scholars, and artists. Students are also assigned to one-on-one peer and academic mentors to ensure their success at the college. Any help or support students need, we have someone on-campus to help them out.

Scholarship & Financial Aid **Scholarships and Financial Aid**

Otis College offers various resources and scholarship opportunities including merit-based scholarships for academic and artistic achievement, need-based grants, Yellow Ribbon (for veterans and veteran dependents) benefits, and more. 87% of our current students are receiving scholarships from the college! First-generation students receive one-on-one counseling by Admissions and Financial aid Counselors.

First-Year Experience & Transition **The Core**

The Core experience begins in the first year at Otis College. Students of diverse backgrounds come together to pursue the Foundation Program, a dedicated year of experimenting, skill building, and ultimately choosing their major. Throughout the 4-year experience, students take Liberal Arts and Sciences courses, as well as a community-based arts engagement program called Creative Action. Students are able to work in teams on real-world issues, often interfacing with communities directly to promote positive change.

Otis College of Art and Design
9045 Lincoln Blvd
Los Angeles, CA 90045
Ph: (800) 527-OTIS
admissions@otis.edu
www.otis.edu/admissions

Fast Facts

STUDENT DIVERSITY

# undergraduates	1,090
% male/female	33/67
% first-generation college	n/a
% American Indian or Alaskan Native	1
% Asian	29
% Black or African American	4
% Hispanic/Latino	10
% Native Hawaiian or Pacific Islander	<1
% White	24
% two or more races	6
% race and/or ethnicity unknown	4
% International/nonresident	22

STUDENT SUCCESS

% first-to-second year retention	79
% six-year graduation	62
% six-year graduation for underrepresented minority groups	53
% first-years who live on campus	30
% undergraduates who live on campus	n/a
full-time faculty	55
full-time minority faculty	11
student-faculty ratio	4:1

Popular majors Visual and Performing Arts, Architecture

Multicultural student clubs and organizations Identity Gay/Straight Alliance, Under the Baobab Tree

AFFORDABILITY

Cost of Attendance

tuition	$42,370
required fees	$2,050
room and board	$14,690

Financial Aid

total institutional scholarships/grants	$11,595,379
% of students with financial need	94
% of students with need awarded any financial aid	100
% of students with need awarded any need-based scholarship or grant aid	100
% of students with need whose need was fully met	10
% Pell Grant recipients among first-years	40
average aid package	$24,098
average student loan debt upon graduation	$33,694

ADMISSIONS

# of applicants	1,160
% admitted	91
SAT Critical Reading	430-560
SAT Math	440-590
SAT Writing	n/a
ACT Composite	22
SAT/ACT optional	yes
average HS GPA	3.16

DEADLINES

regular application closing date	rolling
early decision plan	no
application closing date	n/a
early action plan	no
application closing date	n/a
application fee	$50
application fee online	$50
fee waiver for applicants with financial need	yes

Pepperdine University

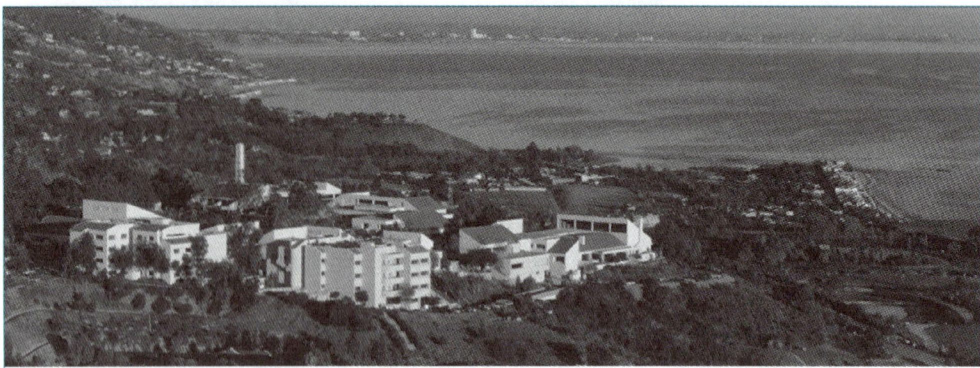

Founded in 1937, Pepperdine is a private Christian university committed to the highest standards of academic excellence and Christian values, where students are strengthened for lives of purpose, service and leadership. Each year over 3,300 undergraduates from every state of the union and from more than 80 countries attend Seaver College, situated on the University's stunning Malibu campus overlooking the Pacific Ocean. Renowned for its high academic standards, its nationally acclaimed Division I Athletics program, and its internationally ranked study abroad programs, Pepperdine is a unique community that is committed to serving the needs of each and every student.

Scholarship & Financial Aid **Scholarships**

Pepperdine University does its best to be financially accessible for all qualified students. There are numerous scholarship opportunities available to Pepperdine students ranging from grant funds awarded based on the eligibility of your FAFSA (Federal Application for Federal Student Aid) to university and private funds based on specific criteria.

Summer Bridge & Orientation **Pepperdine Summer Preview (PSP)**

The Pepperdine Summer Preview (PSP) program is a three-day pre-orientation experience organized by the Office of Admission for a select group of admitted first-generation students. Staying in a residence hall with a cohort of other first-generation students, participants meet with various departments on campus, learn about available resources, and acclimate early to the Pepperdine community.

Student Life & Support **Intercultural Affairs Office**

The Intercultural Affairs Office serves as one of the many avenues on campus where students can gain the awareness, knowledge and skills necessary to become culturally competent. The office facilitates and sponsors a variety of workshops, seminars, excursions, forums, debates and convocation programs throughout the year in order to promote intercultural awareness and understanding between and amongst students.

Pepperdine University
24255 Pacific Coast Highway
Malibu, CA 90263
Ph: (310) 506-4392
admission-seaver@pepperdine.edu
seaver.pepperdine.edu/admission

Fast Facts

STUDENT DIVERSITY

# undergraduates	3,300
% male/female	40/60
% first-generation college	19
% American Indian or Alaskan Native	<1
% Asian	11
% Black or African American	5
% Hispanic/Latino	14
% Native Hawaiian or Pacific Islander	<1
% White	49
% two or more races	5
% race and/or ethnicity unknown	5
% International/nonresident	11

STUDENT SUCCESS

% first-to-second year retention	90
% six-year graduation	87
% six-year graduation for underrepresented minority groups	n/a
% first-years who live on campus	98
% undergraduates who live on campus	60
full-time faculty	377
full-time minority faculty	72
student-faculty ratio	13:1

Popular majors Business Administration, Psychology, Sports Medicine, Economics, and Biology

Multicultural student clubs and organizations Armenian Student Association, Black Student Association, Chinese Student Association, Crossroads, Cultural Italian American Organization, Pasa Pakikisama, Indian Student Organization, Jewish Culture Club, Muslim Student Association, Korean Student Association, Latino Student Association, (PASA), Pepperdine Native American Student Organization, Hawai'i Club, Japan Club

AFFORDABILITY

Cost of Attendance

tuition	$51,740
required fees	$252
room and board	$14,870

Financial Aid

total institutional scholarships/grants	$72,293,181
% of students with financial need	59
% of students with need awarded any financial aid	84
% of students with need awarded any need-based scholarship or grant aid	n/a
% of students with need whose need was fully met	n/a
% Pell Grant recipients among first-years	20
average aid package	$28,300
average student loan debt upon graduation	$32,220

ADMISSIONS

# of applicants	12,417
% admitted	38
SAT Reading & Math	1250-1380
ACT Composite	27-32
SAT/ACT optional	no
average HS GPA	3.61-3.94 unweighted

DEADLINES

regular application closing date	1/5
early decision plan	n/a
application closing date	n/a
early action plan	n/a
application closing date	n/a
application fee	$65
application fee online	$65
fee waiver for applicants with financial need	yes

Sacramento State University

Sacramento State has a diverse student body of 30,510 and a highly knowledgeable faculty, with 98 percent of our full-time professors holding the highest degree in their fields. Each year, our seven colleges award 6,500 degrees to students who pick from 58 undergraduate majors and 41 master's degrees, six post-baccalaureate certificates and two doctoral degrees. Miles of pedestrian and bicycle trails stretch along the nearby American River Parkway, linking our campus and student housing with recreational areas such as Folsom Lake. What makes Sacramento State unique is our focus on tailoring our services to first generation students. Overseen by Student Academic Success and Educational Equity Programs (SASEEP) we have a myriad of resources that address first generation students' needs to foster enrollment and success throughout the college years.

Summer Bridge & Orientation **DEGREES Project**

The DEGREES Project (Dedicated to Educating, Graduating and Retaining Each and Every Student) is designed for first generation students and students who need support along their college journey.

Summer Bridge & Orientation **EOP First Year Orientation/ EOP Summer Bridge Academy**

EOP First Year Orientation is designed to help new EOP students get off to the right start by learning about academic requirements, learning more about EOP and learning about campus programs and services. Students cannot register for classes unless they attend Orientation. In addition, all incoming EOP admitted first year students are required to participate in the EOP Summer Bridge Academy. The Summer Bridge Academy is a unique six-week program that takes place in the summer for students in the EOP Program.

Academic Advising & Support **SASEEP – Student Academic Success & Educational Equity Programs**

SASEEP is the overarching program consisting of many of our equity programs: Educational Opportunity Program (EOP), the College Assistance Migrant Program (CAMP), and much more.

Mentoring **First-Year Experience (FYE)**

FYE is a consortium of campus-wide programs that are administered by representatives from both Academic Affairs and Student Affairs. The Director of FYE (faculty) and the FYE Coordinator (student affairs professional) oversee first year seminars and university learning communities. FYE consists of the University Learning Community Program (LCOM), First Year Seminar Courses (FSEM), and Peer Mentors. FYE consists of special programs to help aid the transition from high school to college. A parallel FYE program is also offered in EOP through Learning Communities offered in the first and second year.

Mentoring **PARC- Peer Academic Resource Center**

PARC delivers a long-awaited goal of fostering student success. This faculty-guided, student-led Center not only strives to increase student retention and graduation rates, but also prepares students for their future professional success through the provision of academic support.

First-Year Experience & Transition **CAMP**

CAMP is a unique educational program that helps students from migrant and seasonal farm worker backgrounds succeed at Sacramento State. CAMP facilitates transition from high school to college and offers first-year support services to help students develop the skills necessary to graduate from college. CAMP strives to be "a home away from home" for its program scholars.

Sacramento State University
Lassen Hall 1102
6000 J Street
Sacramento, CA 95819-6068
Ph: (916) 278-7766
admissions@csus.edu
www.csus.edu

Fast Facts

STUDENT DIVERSITY

# undergraduates	30,510
% male/female	44/56
% first-generation college	27
% American Indian or Alaskan Native	<1
% Asian	22
% Black or African American	6
% Hispanic/Latino	21
% Native Hawaiian or Pacific Islander	<1
% White	37
% two or more races	5
% race and/or ethnicity unknown	5
% International/nonresident	<1

STUDENT SUCCESS

% first-to-second year retention	82
% six-year graduation	48
% six-year graduation for underrepresented minority groups	45
% first-years who live on campus	28
% undergraduates who live on campus	4
full-time faculty	686
full-time minority faculty	191
student-faculty ratio	28:1

Popular majors Criminal Justice, Nursing, Biology, Psychology, and Communication Studies

Multicultural student clubs and organizations n/a

AFFORDABILITY

Cost of Attendance

tuition	$16,632 or in-state $5,472
required fees	$1,130
room and board	$10,370

Financial Aid

total institutional scholarships/grants	$3,701,937
% of students with financial need	87
% of students with need awarded any financial aid	93
% of students with need awarded any need-based scholarship or grant aid	85
% of students with need whose need was fully met	4
% Pell Grant recipients among first-years	n/a
average aid package	$10,722
average student loan debt upon graduation	$4,551

ADMISSIONS

# of applicants	23,944
% admitted	71.9
SAT Critical Reading	n/a
SAT Math	420-540
SAT Writing	410-520
ACT Composite	20
SAT/ACT optional	n/a
average HS GPA	3.25

DEADLINES

regular application closing date	11/30
early decision plan	n/a
application closing date	n/a
early action plan	yes
application closing date	n/a
application fee	$55
application fee online	$55
fee waiver for applicants with financial need	yes

Soka University of America

Soka University of America provides students with a global and personal college experience. Soka is founded on the belief that student-centered education is the best way to promote peace and human rights by fostering a global humanistic perspective on the world in which we live. Soka, which means "to create value," has established a tradition of humanistic scholarship and growth. The university requires a semester of study abroad in the junior year for all students (included in tuition.) With an 8:1 student/faculty ratio and an average class size of 12, about 60% of Soka's students are from the US and about 40% are international (over 50 countries have been represented). Full tuition Soka Opportunity Scholarships assist admitted B.A. students whose annual family income is $60,000 or less.

Pre-College Prep & Outreach **Soka Club Outreach**

Soka University of America has over 35 clubs devoted to arts, dance, music, sports and community outreach. Club members visit local elementary, middle and high schools to share international cultures and to discuss the college experience.

Open House, Fly-In, Visit **Lions Roar Open House and Campus Days**

Lions Roar is offered two times in the fall to high school juniors and seniors. It includes workshops with faculty, admission and financial aid information, student-led campus tours and a free lunch in the Soka Bistro. RSVP online at www.soka.edu/lionsroar. In addition, campus tours are available Monday through Friday at 10 am and 2 pm, check website for details and registration.

Scholarship & Financial Aid **Soka Opportunity Scholarships**

Full tuition Soka Opportunity Scholarships are available to admitted B.A. students whose family's annual income is $60,000 or less. Additional SUA scholarships are also available for higher family incomes. Merit-based and athletic scholarships are also available.

Summer Bridge & Orientation **Orientation**

First-year students come onto campus in mid-August for orientation and for their first Core I classes. They have the entire campus to themselves for three and a half weeks so they can become comfortable with campus life and support each other.

Student Life & Support **Opportunities for Multicultural Study**

Close to half of Soka University of America's students are international, hailing from more than 50 countries. All undergraduate students study a non-native language and every student participates in a semester abroad during their junior year. Soka also offers a master's program in Educational Leadership and Societal Change.

Soka University of America
Admission Office
1 University Drive
Aliso Viejo, CA 92656
Ph: (888) 600-7652
admission@soka.edu
www.soka.edu

Fast Facts

STUDENT DIVERSITY

# undergraduates	412
% male/female	38/62
% first-generation college	n/a
% American Indian or Alaskan Native	0
% Asian	13
% Black or African American	4
% Hispanic/Latino	10
% Native Hawaiian or Pacific Islander	<1
% White	20
% two or more races	7
% race and/or ethnicity unknown	2
% International/nonresident	43

STUDENT SUCCESS

% first-to-second year retention	94
% six-year graduation	90
% six-year graduation for underrepresented minority groups	n/a
% first-years who live on campus	99
% undergraduates who live on campus	99
full-time faculty	46
full-time minority faculty	16
student-faculty ratio	8:1

Popular majors Liberal Arts, with concentrations in Environmental Studies, Humanities, International Studies or Social and Behavioral Sciences

Multicultural student clubs and organizations Ghungroo (Indian Dance), Global Brigades, Humanism in Action, Josho Daiko Club (Taiko Drums), Ka'Pilina Ho'olokahi (Hawaiian Dance), Keep Soul (Hip Hop Dance), Youth in Politics, Queeriosity, Sualseros (Salsa Dance), Soul Wings (Acapella Group)

AFFORDABILITY

Cost of Attendance

tuition	$30,106
required fees	$1,670
room and board	$12,166

Financial Aid

total institutional scholarships/grants	$13,500,000
% of students with financial need	87
% of students with need awarded any financial aid	100
% of students with need awarded any need-based scholarship or grant aid	100
% of students with need whose need was fully met	100
% Pell Grant recipients among first-years	20
average aid package	$31,704
average student loan debt upon graduation	$22,409

ADMISSIONS

# of applicants	500
% admitted	37
SAT Evidence-Based Reading & Writing	580-660
SAT Math	590-720
ACT Composite	26-30
SAT/ACT optional	no
average HS GPA	3.96

DEADLINES

regular application closing date	1/15
early decision plan	no
application closing date	n/a
early action plan	yes
application closing date	11/1
application fee	$45
application fee online	$30
fee waiver for applicants with financial need	yes

Stanford University

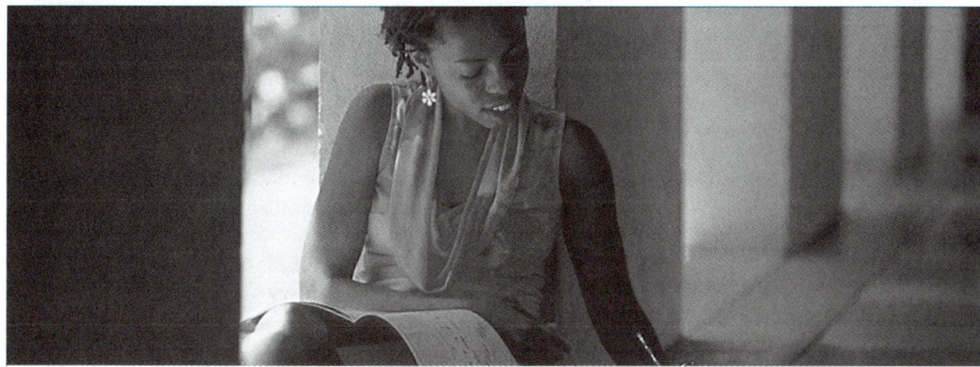

As a respected leader in both the sciences and the humanities, Stanford brings together extraordinary faculty members and students in the pursuit of excellence. Opportunities for discovery begin in the classroom and extend into the rich research life of campus laboratories, libraries, studios and beyond. Learning outside the classroom is also supported by a vibrant residential system that emphasizes service and community. Students may choose to participate in a vast array of educational opportunities, including undergraduate research programs, departmental honors programs and overseas study programs. Stanford has a strong commitment to diversity—about half of the Class of 2021 is made up of students of color and 17% of the incoming freshmen are the first in their families to attend college.

Pre-College Prep & Outreach **Office of Undergraduate Admission**

Partnering with various local and regional community-based organizations, the Office of Undergraduate Admission provides guided campus tours and college information sessions designed to help students think about and prepare for the transition to higher education. The Office of Undergraduate Admission also offers college preparatory workshops in partnership with the following annual Stanford community conferences and programs: the American Indian Science and Engineering Society's (AISES), College Life and Undergraduate Education for Interested Natives (CLUE-IN) Day, the Black Student Union & Black Community Services Center Youth Empowerment Conference, the Stanford Hmong Outreach Program Promoting Education (SHOPPE), MEChA de Stanford's Raza Day, Project Motivation and the Pilipino American Student Union's (PASU) Kapatid mentoring program.

Student Life & Support **The Diversity and First Gen Office**

Our mission is to support students as they evolve into leaders in a pluralistic world. Specifically, the Diversity and First Gen Office supports both the campus and academic life of first generation and/or low-income students through office initiatives and campus partnerships. It also offers leadership in the integration of socioeconomic issues into campus diversity programs. Our efforts focus on creating leaders who will thrive in a pluralistic world, integrating their own multiple identities and negotiating status differences.

Student Life & Support **Diversity at Stanford**

In addition to the faculty advisers that the Undergraduate Advising and Research (UAR) department assigns to all freshmen, Expanded Advising Programs work in conjunction with campus community centers. Stanford's four ethnic community centers, including the Asian American Activities Center, Black Community Services Center, El Centro Chicano y Latino and the Native American Cultural Center, assist students in their success by offering additional resources and support networks. Stanford's ethnic-themed houses—Ujamaa, Casa Zapata, Muwekma-tah-ruk and Okada—all serve to further these networks as well.

Stanford University
Office of Undergraduate Admission
355 Galvez Street
Stanford, CA 94305
Ph: (650) 723-2091
admission@stanford.edu
www.stanford.edu

Fast Facts

STUDENT DIVERSITY

# undergraduates	7,032
% male/female	52/48
% first-generation college	15
% American Indian or Alaskan Native	1
% Asian	21
% Black or African American	6
% Hispanic/Latino	16
% Native Hawaiian or Pacific Islander	1
% White	36
% two or more races	10
% race and/or ethnicity unknown	n/a
% International/nonresident	11

STUDENT SUCCESS

% first-to-second year retention	98
% six-year graduation	94
% six-year graduation for underrepresented minority groups	92
% first-years who live on campus	100
% undergraduates who live on campus	96
full-time faculty	1,589
full-time minority faculty	359
student-faculty ratio	4:1

Popular majors Computer Science, Biology, Engineering, Economics, Science, Technology & Society

Multicultural student clubs and organizations
Asian American Student Association, Black Student Union, Hmong Student Union, Hui 'O Hawai'i, MEChA de Stanford, Pilipino American Student Union, Queer Straight Alliance, Stanford American Indian Organization, Multiracial Identified Community at Stanford, Stanford Society of Chicano/Latino Engineering Scientists, Kaorihiva Polynesian Dance Group, First Generation Low Income Partnership

AFFORDABILITY

Cost of Attendance

tuition	$48,987
required fees	$630
room and board	$15,112

Financial Aid

total institutional scholarships/grants	$144,165,756
% of students with financial need	49
% of students with need awarded any financial aid	98
% of students with need awarded any need-based scholarship or grant aid	97
% of students with need whose need was fully met	100
% Pell Grant recipients among first-years	16
average aid package	$49,220
average student loan debt upon graduation	$21,238

ADMISSIONS

# of applicants	n/a
% admitted	n/a
SAT Evidence-Based Reading & Writing	n/a
SAT Math	n/a
ACT Composite	n/a
SAT/ACT optional	no
average HS GPA	n/a

DEADLINES

regular application closing date	1/2
early decision plan	n/a
application closing date	n/a
early action plan	yes
application closing date	11/1
application fee	$90
application fee online	$90
fee waiver for applicants with financial need	yes

University of Redlands

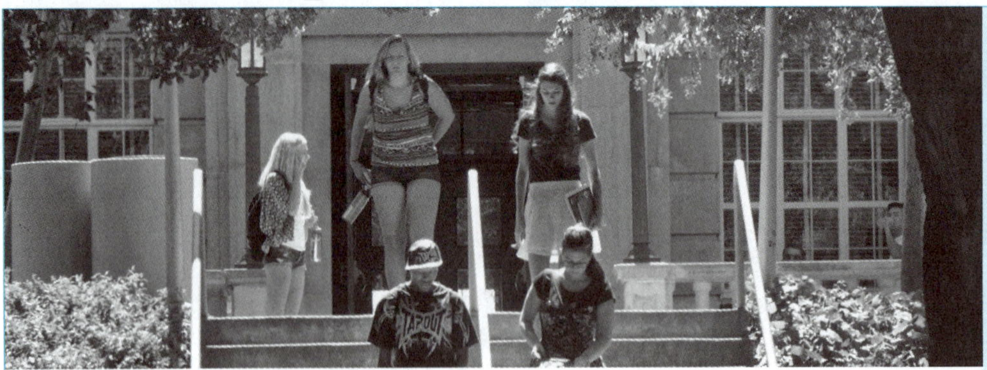

Where your dreams become aspirations and your aspirations become achievements, that is the Redlands experience. Since our founding in 1907, we've fulfilled our promises to providing a transformative education in an environment of academic rigor and personal responsibility, where you can blend what you learn in the classroom with life skills to create positive change in the world.

We are Redlands, where curiosity finds inspiration; where selflessness becomes service; where small classes encourage debate and debate sparks insight; where creativity and innovation open doors and change lives; and where diversity enriches us all.

We are Redlands, where we care more about who you will become rather than who you used to be; where we take good students and turn them into great people.

Pre-College Prep & Outreach **I'm Going To College**

The "I'm Going to College" Program is an initiative of the Office of Campus Diversity and Inclusion geared to educate first-generation and underrepresented students about higher education. Our mission is to work with children from a young age to plant the idea of college so that by the time they are high school students, they are already preparing for their college career. This program addresses the lack of awareness among first-generation college students about their opportunity to gain a first class, individualized education at the University of Redlands and similar institutions.

Pre-College Prep & Outreach **Supporting, Educating & Empowering Diverse Students**

The Supporting, Educating and Empowering Diverse Students (S.E.E.D.S.) Mentorship Program is a collaborative initiative between local high schools and the University of Redlands. U of R students started this program after visiting a local high school campus and finding a lack of support for students from first-generation and under-served communities. U of R student mentors work with sophomores and juniors to enhance their academic abilities and social skills.

First-Year Experience & Transition **Students Together Empowering Peers**

Students Together Empowering Peers (STEP), formerly known as PUEDE, is one of the most highly efficient mentoring programs offered at the University of Redlands. The mission of the STEP program is to provide resources and support for first semester, first-generation college students in order to ease their transition into higher education.

First-Year Experience and Transition **Summer Bridge**

Summer Bridge is a five-day, intensive program designed to facilitate the immersion into collegiate life for first-generation and/or Cal Grant recipient students. During Summer Bridge, students connect with their peers and professors, while being introduced to resources and opportunities available at the University. Of students who participate in this program, 91% are retained and graduate within four years.

Student Life & Support **Book Lending Program**

The Book Lending Program is an initiative to ensure the academic success of every student. Funded through alumni donations, this program provides books for students who could not otherwise afford to purchase them. Books are returned at the end of the course, to be used by other students the next semester. When needed, the program may cover other classroom necessities, such as lab fees. The program works alongside the library and faculty members to ensure the availability of books and classrooms materials.

University of Redlands
Office of Admissions
1200 E Colton Ave. P.O. Box 3080
Redlands, CA 92373
Ph: (800) 455-5064
admissions@redlands.edu
www.redlands.edu

Fast Facts

STUDENT DIVERSITY

# undergraduates	2,452
% male/female	42/58
% first-generation college	34
% American Indian or Alaskan Native	<1
% Asian	6
% Black or African American	3
% Hispanic/Latino	25
% Native Hawaiian or Pacific Islander	<1
% White	51
% two or more races	5
% race and/or ethnicity unknown	6
% International/nonresident	3

STUDENT SUCCESS

% first-to-second year retention	87
% six-year graduation	74
% six-year graduation for underrepresented minority groups	n/a
% first-years who live on campus	89
% undergraduates who live on campus	66
full-time faculty	169
full-time minority faculty	n/a
student-faculty ratio	13:1

Popular majors Business Administration, Johnston Center for Integrative Studies (individualized degree), Psychology, Communication Sciences & Disorders, Music

Multicultural student clubs and organizations First Generation Student Programs, LGBTQ Programs, Gender Programs, Religious and Cultural Programs, Multicultural Center, Women's Center, Pride Center, Office of International Students & Scholars

AFFORDABILITY

Cost of Attendance

tuition	$49,154
required fees	$350
room and board	$14,278

Financial Aid

total institutional scholarships/grants	n/a
% of students with financial need	n/a
% of students with need awarded any financial aid	90
% of students with need awarded any need-based scholarship or grant aid	n/a
% of students with need whose need was fully met	n/a
% Pell Grant recipients among first-years	35
average aid package	n/a
average student loan debt upon graduation	n/a

ADMISSIONS

# of applicants	5,157
% admitted	73
SAT Critical Reading	590
SAT Math	570
SAT Writing	optional
ACT Composite	25
SAT/ACT optional	no
average HS GPA	3.65

DEADLINES

regular application closing date	1/15
early decision plan	yes
application closing date	11/15
early action plan	yes
application closing date	11/15
application fee	$50
application fee online	$50
fee waiver for applicants with financial need	yes

University of San Diego

The University of San Diego is a Roman Catholic institution committed to advancing academic excellence, expanding liberal and professional knowledge, creating a diverse and inclusive community and preparing leaders dedicated to ethical conduct and compassionate service. The university is a nationally ranked, co-educational and residential university serving students of diverse backgrounds from across the country and around the world. USD supports the belief that academic excellence requires inclusive engagement with diverse groups and varying perspectives, and it recognizes that the benefits of a rich, diverse learning community are most likely realized when institutions demonstrate high levels of commitment to inclusion and diversity. USD actively supports recruitment and retention of under-represented students, staff, faculty and administrators in pursuit of the compositional diversity required to achieve excellence.

Pre-College Prep & Outreach **Upward Bound**

The University of San Diego's Upward Bound program strives to create an educational and multicultural learning community of students who demonstrate a strong desire to participate in higher education. Students, families and staff involved in USD Upward Bound engage in a highly motivational, relevant, challenging and empowering curriculum which promotes a deeper personal and cross-cultural understanding.

Academic Advising & Support **Student Support Services**

Student Support Services is a federally funded grant by the US Department of Education to serve 160 eligible undergraduates at USD. The program provides opportunities for academic development, assists students with college requirements, and serves to retain and motivate students toward successful completion of their postsecondary education at USD. Services provided include: academic counseling/advising, tutoring, career counseling, personal counseling, faculty/student mentoring, cultural activities, grant aid, FAFSA assistance, Summer Bridge Program, time management techniques, note-taking techniques, test-taking techniques, essay writing improvement, reading strategies and graduate school application assistance.

Student Life & Support **Student Outreach and Recruitment Club**

The Student Outreach and Recruitment Club (SOAR) is a student organization that specifically focuses on and is committed to engaging in diversity recruitment, outreach and retention efforts at the University of San Diego. Members of SOAR participate, coordinate and assist with multicultural recruitment events such as our fly-in overnight visit program and other activities geared toward making the University of San Diego a more diverse and inclusive campus community.

University of San Diego
5998 Alcala Park
San Diego, CA 92110
Ph: (619) 260-4506
admissions@sandiego.edu
www.sandiego.edu

Fast Facts

STUDENT DIVERSITY

# undergraduates	5,774
% male/female	46/54
% first-generation college	20
% American Indian or Alaskan Native	1
% Asian	7
% Black or African American	4
% Hispanic/Latino	20
% Native Hawaiian or Pacific Islander	1
% White	51
% two or more races	6
% race and/or ethnicity unknown	2
% International/nonresident	9

STUDENT SUCCESS

% first-to-second year retention	87
% six-year graduation	77
% six-year graduation for underrepresented minority groups	72
% first-years who live on campus	95
% undergraduates who live on campus	44
full-time faculty	440
full-time minority faculty	100
student-faculty ratio	14:1

Popular majors Business, Communication Studies, Mechanical Engineering, Behavioral Neuroscience, Psychology

Multicultural student clubs and organizations
Asian Students Association (ASA), Black Student Union (BSU), Chaldean American Student Association, Filipino Ugnayan Student Organization (FUSO), International Student Organization (ISO), Jewish Student Union (JSU), Movimiento Estudantil Chicano de Aztlan (MEChA), Muslim Student Association (MSA), Native American Student Organization (NASO), People of the Islands (POI), Phi Beta Sigma Fraternity, PRIDE, Sigma Theta Psi Sorority, Taiwan Student Association (TSA)

AFFORDABILITY

Cost of Attendance

tuition	$47,100
required fees	$608
room and board	$12,630

Financial Aid

total institutional scholarships/grants	$83,600,936
% of students with financial need	51
% of students with need awarded any financial aid	98
% of students with need awarded any need-based scholarship or grant aid	95
% of students with need whose need was fully met	14
% Pell Grant recipients among first-years	14
average aid package	$33,737
average student loan debt upon graduation	$30,854

ADMISSIONS

# of applicants	14,739
% admitted	49
SAT Middle 50% Admitted	1210-1350
ACT Composite	27-31
SAT/ACT optional	n/a
average HS GPA	3.75-4.19

DEADLINES

regular application closing date	12/15
early decision plan	n/a
application closing date	n/a
early action plan	n/a
application closing date	n/a
application fee	$55
application fee online	$55
fee waiver for applicants with financial need	yes

University of San Francisco

The University of San Francisco welcomes students from different cultures, lifestyles, and beliefs, making us the third-most diverse school in the country, according to U.S. News and World Report. But we aren't diverse for the sake of rankings. By creating a world on a campus, we create the ideal incubator for learning and for fresh ideas. As a result, our students graduate prepared to meet the challenges and opportunities of a rapidly changing planet. At USF, our Jesuit values inspire us to build a truly inclusive community. Our campus is varied and vibrant, enriched by people of different abilities, ages, colors, creeds, faiths, sexual orientations, cultures, nationalities, and family backgrounds. One-third of USF students are the first in their families to attend college. USF students include U.S. military veterans and students from more than 96 countries. They are lifelong learners returning to school and undergraduates just beginning their journeys. They are united by a passion to make a difference. They are a lot like you.

Open House, Fly-in, Visit **Discover Diversity**

The Discover Diversity event, held one day each November, gives underrepresented high school students and their parents a chance to experience our campus community. Our program introduces the resources and opportunities at USF, highlighting the multicultural student experience on campus, in the classroom, and beyond. Come see how we build community and support students on their way to success in college and in life after college.

Summer Bridge & Orientation **Muscat Scholars Program**

The Muscat Scholars Program, a two-week summer session, gives incoming first-generation first-year students both an academic and social preparation for their first year and beyond at the University of San Francisco. Participants live on campus for two weeks and receive an orientation to San Francisco as well as to the university. They are awarded two units toward graduation.

Student Life & Support **Diversity Engagement**

The USF Office of Diversity Engagement and Community Outreach seeks to promote a campus climate and culture that values diversity in all its forms through inclusive dialogues, interpersonal experiences, and intercultural appreciation.

Student Life & Support **Cultural Centers**

The Cultural Centers at USF bring students together to increase their understanding, and embrace their roles, as members of a diverse community on the local and global levels. The Cultural Centers include the Gender & Sexuality Center and the Intercultural Center. The centers serve as physical spaces on campus where students build community, and as outlets for student-run programs that explore social issues and identity.

Academic Advising & Support **Academic Advising and Support Centers**

The Center for Academic and Student Achievement (CASA) supports all students on their academic and personal paths. At CASA, students find their university advisers, get guidance on completing forms, and get connected to all kinds of resources, from mentoring to tutoring to career tips.

PACT is a support program for undergraduate men of color. In this program, men help each other, hold each other accountable, and promote the following: personal and leadership development, community engagement, programs that enhance the campus climate for men of color, and opportunities to interact with and invite middle-school men of color to the USF campus.

University of San Francisco
2130 Fulton Street
Office of Admission
San Francisco, CA 94117
Ph: (415) 422-6563
www.usfca.edu

Fast Facts

STUDENT DIVERSITY

# undergraduates	6,754
% male/female	37/63
% first-generation college	34
% American Indian or Alaskan Native	<1
% Asian	22
% Black or African American	4
% Hispanic/Latino	21
% Native Hawaiian or Pacific Islander	<1
% White	28
% two or more races	6
% race and/or ethnicity unknown	1
% International/nonresident	17

STUDENT SUCCESS

% first-to-second year retention	83
% six-year graduation	71
% six-year graduation for underrepresented minority groups	n/a
% first-years who live on campus	94
% undergraduates who live on campus	32
full-time faculty	497
full-time minority faculty	158
student-faculty ratio	14:1

Popular majors Biology, Nursing, Business, International Studies, Psychology

Multicultural student clubs and organizations
Arab Student Union, Asian Entrepreneurs Club, Baile Folklorico de San Pancho, Black Student Union, Brother Connection, Delta Sigma Theta Sorority, Hui 'O Hawai'i, Indian Student Organization, Organization, Jewish Student Organization, Kasamahan at USF, Latinas Unidas, MEChA de USF, Queer Alliance

AFFORDABILITY

Cost of Attendance

tuition	$44,040
required fees	$454
room and board	$13,990

Financial Aid

total institutional scholarships/grants	$75,000,000
% of students with financial need	55
% of students with need awarded any financial aid	98
% of students with need awarded any need-based scholarship or grant aid	85
% of students with need whose need was fully met	6
% Pell Grant recipients among first-years	39
average aid package	$28,715
average student loan debt upon graduation	$25,000

ADMISSIONS

# of applicants	15,360
% admitted	64
SAT Critical Reading	530-620
SAT Math	540-640
SAT Writing	520-620
ACT Composite	24-28
SAT/ACT optional	no
average HS GPA	3.63

DEADLINES

regular application closing date	1/15
early decision plan	yes
application closing date	11/15
early action plan	yes
application closing date	11/15
application fee	$65
application fee online	$65
fee waiver for applicants with financial need	yes

University of Southern California

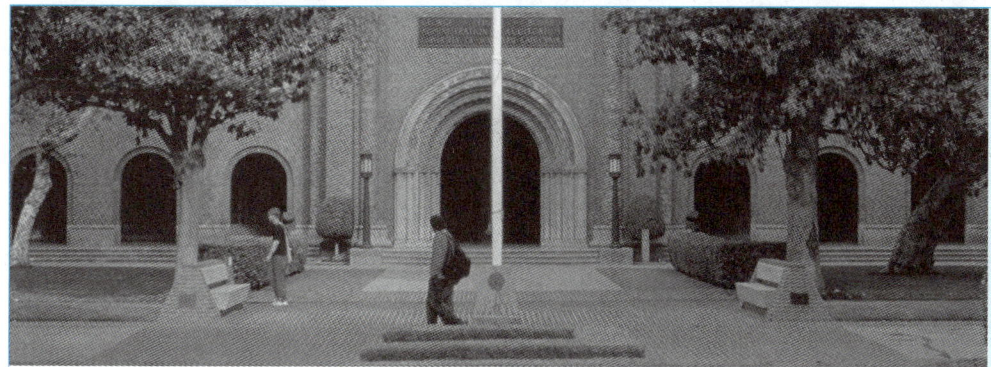

The University of Southern California continues to be recognized as one of the most culturally diverse campuses in the United States. The Office of Admission actively recruits students from all backgrounds and socioeconomic statuses. This includes first-generation college goers from lower income families who may need additional support as they continue on to college. The University partners with a number of organizations to ensure their students' continued academic success and that a top-tier education remains available and affordable to all students, regardless of background or ability to pay.

Scholarship & Financial Aid **QuestBridge Partner College**

USC is a partner with QuestBridge, a non-profit organization that connects low-income students with educational and scholarship opportunities at 30 top colleges and universities throughout the U.S. Through the QuestBridge National College Match Program, USC has enrolled low-income students from diverse geographical areas in the U.S.

Scholars & Leadership **Norman Topping Student Aid Fund (NTSAF)**

NTSAF offers financial support to students who demonstrate an extraordinary level of community awareness in their pursuit of higher education at USC. Primary consideration is given to applicants from neighborhoods surrounding the University Park and Health Science.

Scholars & Leadership **Black Alumni Association (BAA)**

A primary alumni resource providing tuition assistance to African American students at USC, the Black Alumni Association was founded in 1976 by the late Reverend Dr. Thomas Kilgore, Jr., a peer of Martin Luther King, Jr., and special advisor to USC President John Hubbard. The BAA has provided over $1.7 million to 1,600 USC students. BAA scholarships are awarded annually based on financial need and academic merit. BAA scholarship funds are matched 2:1 for undergraduate students.

Scholars & Leadership **Latino Alumni Association (LAA)**

USC boasts one of the nation's leading Latino alumni associations devoted to the academic advancement and development of Latino students attending USC. LAA is one of the few Latino alumni associations in the country with a $3 million endowment fund.

Pre-College Prep & Outreach **Neighborhood Academic Initiative (NAI)**

The USC Neighborhood Academic Initiative offers a comprehensive college-preparation program for local middle-school students. Students also have the chance to earn a full scholarship to USC.

University of Southern California
850 West 37th Street
Los Angeles, CA 90089
Ph: (213) 740-2311
admitusc@usc.edu
www.usc.edu

Fast Facts

STUDENT DIVERSITY

# undergraduates	17,414
% male/female	49/51
% first-generation college	17
% American Indian or Alaskan Native	2
% Asian	21
% Black or African American	5
% Hispanic/Latino	15
% Native Hawaiian or Pacific Islander	<1
% White	38
% two or more races	7
% race and/or ethnicity unknown	<1
% International/nonresident	14

STUDENT SUCCESS

% first-to-second year retention	97
% six-year graduation	90
% six-year graduation for underrepresented minority groups	88
% first-years who live on campus	n/a
% undergraduates who live on campus	n/a
full-time faculty	3,400
full-time minority faculty	n/a
student-faculty ratio	9:1

Popular majors Cinematic Arts, Business, Music, Engineering, Communications

Multicultural student clubs and organizations Center for Black Cultural and Student Affairs, El Centro Chicano, Asian Pacific American Student Services, Black Student Assembly, Latino Student Assembly, M.E.Ch.A. de USC, 100 Black Men of USC, Vietnamese Student Association

AFFORDABILITY

Cost of Attendance

tuition	$54,323
required fees	n/a
room and board	$14,886

Financial Aid

total institutional scholarships/grants	$192,300,000
% of students with financial need	n/a
% of students with need awarded any financial aid	100
% of students with need awarded any need-based scholarship or grant aid	60
% of students with need whose need was fully met	100
% Pell Grant recipients among first-years	16
average aid package	n/a
average student loan debt upon graduation	$30,217

ADMISSIONS

# of applicants	56,675
% admitted	16
SAT Reading & Writing	650-730
SAT Math	650-770
ACT Composite	32
SAT/ACT optional	yes
average HS GPA	3.8

DEADLINES

regular application closing date	1/15
early decision plan	no
application closing date	n/a
early action plan	no
application closing date	n/a
application fee	$80
application fee online	$80
fee waiver for applicants with financial need	n/a

University of the Pacific

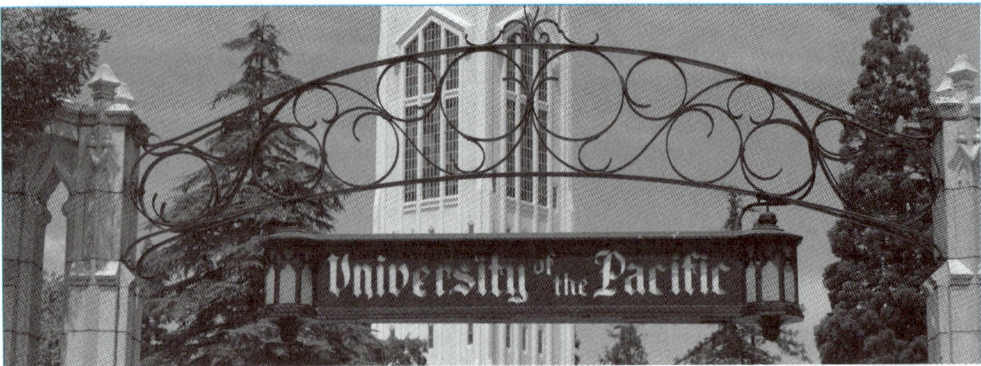

University of the Pacific is a nationally-ranked university providing students with personalized learning that prepares them to live and lead with purpose. Our three campuses serve the northern California region and our students join Pacific from 20+ states and 30 countries. Pacific's 80 programs of study and small class sizes (average of 19 students) provide students with opportunities for meaningful classroom experiences as they pursue their interests. In 2016, *Wall Street Journal*, *U.S. News & World Report*, and *White House College Scorecard* rankings all placed Pacific among the top 10 private California universities.

Pre-College Prep & Outreach **Latino Community Outreach**

The Latino Community Outreach Office (LCO) represents the University during college nights, career fairs, school visits, and other informational programs. Raymond lodge is a home away from home for Latino/a, Chicano/a and Hispanic students, as well as on-campus student clubs.

Pre-College Prep & Outreach **Beyond Our Gates**

Through the Beyond Our Gates initiative, University of the Pacific is working collaboratively to improve the social and economic health of our region. Embracing the Collective Impact model, the University is working alongside local individuals and organizations to prepare more of our young people for a successful future.

- The Tomorrow Project: To lift college-attendance rates in the Valley, we have joined a number of community partners to offer specialized academies that deliver the skills, resources and sustained support elementary and high school students need to prepare for higher education.
- The Beyond Our Gates Community Council: To help guide Pacific's ongoing community engagement priorities, the council is an advisory body made up of local leaders from fields spanning business, education, non-profit, media, government and faith.

Student Life & Support **Students Emerging as Pacificans (STEPs)**

STEPs assists incoming African-American students through their transition to college life. Pacific faculty, staff, current students, and alumni work directly with STEPs participants, introducing them to University and community resources to enhance their academic and personal success. STEPs begins with a 2-day residential, pre-college program that continues through the entire academic year.

Student Life & Support **Community Involvement Program (CIP)**

CIP is a comprehensive, need-based scholarship program for first-generation college students from the Stockton community who have demonstrated community awareness and service, along with the potential for responsible leadership. In addition to financial support, each cohort of CIP students forms a learning community.

Student Life & Support **SUCCESS Program**

The SUCCESS Program provides academic and support services to low-income, first generation or disabled college students to increase retention and graduation rates and foster an institutional climate supportive of their success. The program includes: tutoring; assistance with course selection based on factors such as graduation and general education requirements; financial and economic literacy workshops; career development assistance in conjunction with the Career Resource Center; peer mentoring; academic workshops, and graduate and professional school advising.

University of the Pacific
3601 Pacific Avenue
Stockton, CA 95211
Ph: (209) 946-2211
admission@pacific.edu
www.pacific.edu

Fast Facts

STUDENT DIVERSITY

# undergraduates	3,536
% male/female	46/54
% first-generation college	n/a
% American Indian or Alaskan Native	<1
% Asian	36
% Black or African American	3
% Hispanic/Latino	20
% Native Hawaiian or Pacific Islander	1
% White	23
% two or more races	7
% race and/or ethnicity unknown	3
% International/nonresident	7

STUDENT SUCCESS

% first-to-second year retention	85
% six-year graduation	68
% six-year graduation for underrepresented minority groups	67
% first-years who live on campus	78
% undergraduates who live on campus	49
full-time faculty	441
full-time minority faculty	n/a
student-faculty ratio	12:1

Popular majors Business Administration, Pre-pharmacy, Health, Exercise and Sport Science, Biological Sciences, Pre-dentistry, Mechanical Engineering, Psychology, Computer Science, Education, Biochemistry

Multicultural student clubs and organizations Black Student Union, Hawaii Club, International Club, Kilusan Philipino, Me.Ch.A, Student Associations: Cambodian, Hmong, Indian, Korean, South Asian, Vietnamese, United Cultural Council

AFFORDABILITY

Cost of Attendance

tuition	$46,446
required fees	$520
room and board	$12,802

Financial Aid

total institutional scholarships/grants	$47,952,230
% of students with financial need	69
% of students with need awarded any financial aid	87
% of students with need awarded any need-based scholarship or grant aid	89
% of students with need whose need was fully met	9
% Pell Grant recipients among first-years	36
average aid package	$22,641
average student loan debt upon graduation	$23,370

ADMISSIONS

# of applicants	13,115
% admitted	65
SAT Critical Reading	490-620
SAT Math	520-660
SAT Writing	490-630
ACT Composite	24
SAT/ACT optional	n/a
average HS GPA	3.54

DEADLINES

regular application closing date	rolling
early decision plan	n/a
application closing date	n/a
early action plan	yes
application closing date	11/15
application fee	$35
application fee online	$35
fee waiver for applicants with financial need	yes

Vanguard University

Welcome to Vanguard! We like to think we've come up with the perfect mix—unbeatable academic training, a caring community where lifelong friendships are born every day, a beautiful campus near Southern California's beaches and cultural attractions, and a strong spiritual foundation that puts Christ at the center of it all. Let us show you how we go beyond scholarship, beyond the classroom, beyond the expected, equipping you to lead the story God has for you.

Open House, Fly-in, Visit **Fall Pre-VU**

Discover what Vanguard University has to offer and see why we're a top-ranked school. Meet our faculty, eat in the Café and get a taste of college life. You'll see why we've got it all—an excellent education, authentic community and a great location—at Fall Pre-VU! High school seniors, juniors, transfer students and family members are welcome to come! Cost is free for all attendees and you can register online.

Open House, Fly-in, Visit **Schedule A Personal Day Visit**

We are open for appointments on weekdays from 8 a.m.-5 p.m., except holidays. A standard visit includes a 30 minute appointment with an Admissions Counselor and a 1 hour campus tour. We have set campus tour times at 11 a.m. and 3 p.m. Overnight visit opportunities are available on Monday and Wednesday with a one-night maximum and must be requested two weeks in advance.

Scholarship & Financial Aid **Scholarships and Grants**

Vanguard University offers a number of different scholarships and grants for undergraduate students: Academic Scholarships, Talent Scholarships, Federal and State Grants, and Institutional Grants and Scholarships. Vanguard also accepts other outside scholarships.

First-Year Experience & Transition **First Year Transition**

ADJUSTING TO COLLEGE LIFE Each of you will experience the freedom of college life in a different way. For some, there will be a period of time where you will miss what you left immensely. For others, you could not be more excited to begin this new stage of life. The majority of you will shift between these two extremes. Some of you may even find yourself standing in the middle, not sure of which one you want to embrace more. Regardless of where you are at, we want you to know that what you are going through is completely normal. We are here to support you!

Academic Advising & Support **Tutorial Center**

The Tutorial and Math Learning Centers offer a unique approach to academic intervention in that they are programs for the students, of the students and by the students.

Vanguard University
55 Fair Drive
Costa Mesa, CA 92626
Ph: (714) 966-5496
www.vanguard.edu

Fast Facts

STUDENT DIVERSITY

# undergraduates	1,787
% male/female	35/64
% first-generation college	46
% American Indian or Alaskan Native	<1
% Asian	5
% Black or African American	7
% Hispanic/Latino	47
% Native Hawaiian or Pacific Islander	1
% White	62
% two or more races	7
% race and/or ethnicity unknown	2
% International/nonresident	<1

STUDENT SUCCESS

% first-to-second year retention	75
% six-year graduation	56
% six-year graduation for underrepresented minority groups	n/a
% first-years who live on campus	77
% undergraduates who live on campus	63
full-time faculty	58
full-time minority faculty	15
student-faculty ratio	15:1

Popular majors Business, Psychology, Kinesiology, Communication, and Religion

Multicultural student clubs and organizations Asian Pacific Islander Club (APIC), Black Student Union (BSU), El Puente (Latin American Club), Live2Free (Human Rights Club), and many more!

AFFORDABILITY

Cost of Attendance

tuition	$31,980
required fees	$450
room and board	$9,690

Financial Aid

total institutional scholarships/grants	$18,201,230
% of students with financial need	72
% of students with need awarded any financial aid	99
% of students with need awarded any need-based scholarship or grant aid	60
% of students with need whose need was fully met	n/a
% Pell Grant recipients among first-years	49
average aid package	$20,755
average student loan debt upon graduation	n/a

ADMISSIONS

# of applicants	3,088
% admitted	47
SAT Critical Reading	480
SAT Math	460
SAT Writing	n/a
ACT Composite	21
SAT/ACT optional	yes
average HS GPA	3.25

DEADLINES

regular application closing date	8/1
early decision plan	n/a
application closing date	n/a
early action plan	yes
application closing date	12/1
application fee	$45
application fee online	$45
fee waiver for applicants with financial need	yes

Colorado College

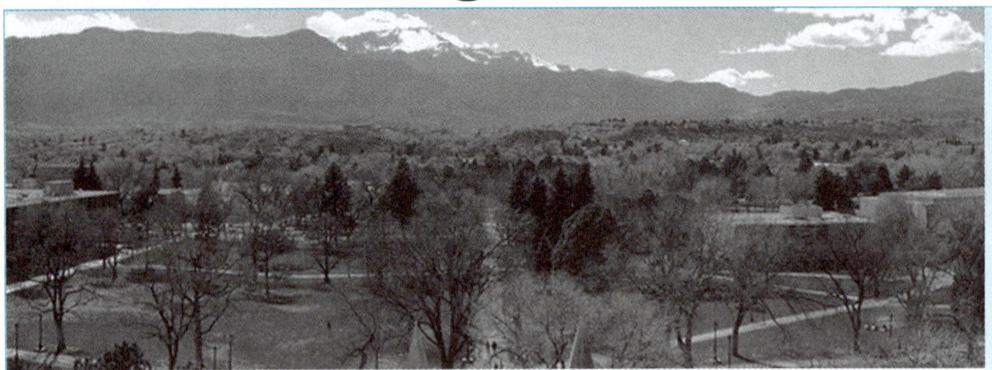

Founded in 1874, Colorado College is a selective liberal arts college located in the heart of the Rocky Mountain West at the foot of Pikes Peak in Colorado Springs. Colorado College provides rigorous and experiential learning opportunities through a unique academic schedule: the Block Plan. Dividing the year into eight three-and-a-half week blocks, during which students take one course at a time, the plan provides students with the opportunity to fully immerse themselves in subject matter through a wide array of learning experiences.

Pre-College Prep & Outreach **Friends of CC Host Family Program**

Friends of CC is an outreach program which pairs minority, international and first-generation students with friends in the community for events several times a year both on and off-campus.

Open House, Fly-In, Visit **Funded Campus Visits**

Colorado Colleges offers two funded campus visit programs in the fall. The first program provides a travel grant for high school seniors, which funds attendance at the Fall Open House in early October. The second program is a grant for high school seniors to travel to CC at the end of October for an overnight program. Both programs provide funds for an accompanying parent or counselor, as well as an exciting opportunity for prospective students to experience life at Colorado College. The visit includes a campus tour, class visit, overnight stay on campus, and more information about applying to CC.

First-Year Experience & Transition **Bridge Scholars Program**

The Bridge Program is a unique learning experience which is dedicated to helping incoming freshmen successfully transition academically and socially from high school to college. Students invited to participate— typically graduates of under-resourced high schools, members of historically underrepresented populations at CC, or first-generation college students—have the opportunity to improve writing, reading and critical thinking skills while establishing a support group of invaluable relationships with CC faculty, staff, and peers.

Student Life & Support **The Butler Center**

The Butler Center at Colorado College supports cross-cultural inclusion and success through various advising and mentorship programs, including the First Generation Program, which provides support to students who are the first in their families to attend a four-year college or university. In conjunction with Residential Life, the Butler Center also provides advising and support to the Glass House, a multicultural themed house located on the East Campus, as well as the Enclave, an experimental learning community for students interesting in understanding "ethnic enclaves" and "safe spaces" in higher education and the community.

Colorado College
14 E. Cache La Poudre Street
Colorado Springs, CO 80903
Ph: (800) 542-7214
admissions@coloradocollege.edu
www.coloradocollege.edu

Fast Facts

STUDENT DIVERSITY

# undergraduates	2,101
% male/female	46/54
% first-generation college	11
% American Indian or Alaskan Native	<1
% Asian	4
% Black or African American	3
% Hispanic/Latino	9
% Native Hawaiian or Pacific Islander	0
% White	65
% two or more races	9
% race and/or ethnicity unknown	1
% International/nonresident	8

STUDENT SUCCESS

% first-to-second year retention	96
% six-year graduation	87
% six-year graduation for underrepresented minority groups	89
% first-years who live on campus	100
% undergraduates who live on campus	75
full-time faculty	186
full-time minority faculty	46
student-faculty ratio	10:1

Popular majors Biology, English, Economics, International Political Economy, Environmental Science

Multicultural student clubs and organizations Artists and Makers of Undying Nobility, Asian Student Union, Black Student Union, Chinese Student Assoc., FemCo, Korean American Student Assoc., Minority Assoc. for Pre-Health Students, MOSAIC, Native American Student Union, Queer People of Color Collective, Muslim Student Assoc., Black Women at CC, EQUAL, Multi-Racial Affinity Group, SOMOS, Ubuntu African Group

AFFORDABILITY

Cost of Attendance

tuition	$52,380
required fees	$438
room and board	$12,076

Financial Aid

total institutional scholarships/grants	$29,484,608
% of students with financial need	33
% of students with need awarded any financial aid	100
% of students with need awarded any need-based scholarship or grant aid	95
% of students with need whose need was fully met	100
% Pell Grant recipients among first-years	13
average aid package	$46,960
average student loan debt upon graduation	$20,742

ADMISSIONS

# of applicants	8,222
% admitted	15
SAT Critical Reading	680
SAT Math	690
SAT Writing	670
ACT Composite	32
SAT/ACT optional	no
average HS GPA	n/a

DEADLINES

regular application closing date	1/15
early decision plan	yes
application closing date	11/10, 1/15
early action plan	yes
application closing date	11/10
application fee	$60
application fee online	$60
fee waiver for applicants with financial need	yes

United States Air Force Academy

The U.S. Air Force Academy is one of the five federal military service academies. The mission of the U.S. Air Force Academy is to educate, train and inspire men and women to become officers of character motivated to lead the United States Air Force in service to our nation. This institution is a four-year immersive college experience and offers unique opportunities and programs, including aviation programs. There is no tuition, room, or board cost to attend. Graduates receive a Bachelor of Science degree in their major and earn a commission as a Second Lieutenant in the U.S. Air Force. Upon commissioning, our graduates agree to serve as an Air Force officer for a minimum of five years.

Academic Advising & Support **Student Academic Affairs**

The U.S. Air Force Academy offers 27 liberal arts and STEM-focused majors. Majors include several engineering programs as well as multiple offerings in humanities and social science. *US News & World Report* ranks the U.S. Air Force Academy as the nation's #3 Public School and the #2 Aerospace / Aeronautical / Astronautical Engineering Program. It's a demanding curriculum, but the Academy has programs in place to help cadets succeed. The Student Academic Affairs office offers cadets self-improvement services, which include study skills, graduate school program assistance and reading and writing assistance. In addition, the campus has a full collegiate library and tutors available to help. Our low student-to-faculty ratio (8:1) ensures our faculty is available to cadets. *Princeton Review* regularly ranks the U.S. Air Force Academy in the top 5% for Most Accessible Faculty.

Student Life & Support **Campus Life**

All U.S. Air Force Academy students, called Cadets, are federal employees whose job is to earn their degree while training to be officers in the Air Force. Cadets live on campus at the U.S. Air Force Academy for all four years of their intensive education and military training program. Housing and meals are provided at no cost to the Cadet. As Cadets are federally employed, they receive a monthly salary and full medical and dental benefits. Athletic, entertainment, and professional development programs are also available to Cadets on campus to enhance their experience.

Pre-College Prep & Outreach **U.S. Air Force Academy Preparatory School & Falcon Foundation Scholarships**

All congressional districts, states and territories are given the opportunity to be represented at the U.S. Air Force Academy. Though school systems across our nation do not provide equivalent college preparation, all students have an opportunity to apply for an appointment. Applicants whose school systems did not prepare them adequately to be academically successful at the Air Force Academy may be considered for participation in one of our preparatory school programs. To be considered for one of these programs, students must apply for admission to the United States Air Force Academy. Successful completion of one of our preparatory school programs improves chances for appointment, but does not guarantee an appointment.

Pre-College Summer Experience **Summer Seminar Program**

The Summer Seminar Program allows selected high-performing high school students to spend a week at the Academy during the summer to gain insight into life as a Cadet. The application window for applying to attend Summer Seminar is December 1st – January 15th. Attendees live on campus, attend academic seminars and compete in intramural sports. Summer Seminar gives students an opportunity to be exposed to academic facilities and research labs, military structure and a glimpse of cadet life.

United States Air Force Academy
2304 Cadet Drive, Suite 2400
USAF Academy, CO 80840
Ph: (800) 443-9266
rr_webmail@usafa.edu
www.academyadmissions.com

Fast Facts

STUDENT DIVERSITY	
# undergraduates	4,316
% male/female	74/26
% first-generation college	16
% American Indian or Alaskan Native	1
% Asian	9
% Black or African American	8
% Hispanic/Latino	9
% Native Hawaiian or Pacific Islander	2
% White	63
% two or more races	2
% race and/or ethnicity unknown	6
% International/nonresident	1
STUDENT SUCCESS	
% first-to-second year retention	94
% six-year graduation	81
% six-year graduation for underrepresented minority groups	79
% first-years who live on campus	100
% undergraduates who live on campus	100
full-time faculty	550
full-time minority faculty	n/a
student-faculty ratio	8:1

Popular majors Management, Systems Engineering, Economics, Behavioral Sciences, Biology

Multicultural student clubs and organizations Los Padrinos, Native American Heritage Club, Prior Enlisted Cadet, Way of Life, Pacific Rim, International Club, Tuskegee Airmen

AFFORDABILITY*	
Cost of Attendance	
tuition	$0
required fees	n/a
room and board	$0
Financial Aid	
total institutional scholarships/grants	n/a
% of students with financial need	<1
% of students with need awarded any financial aid	100
% of students with need awarded any need-based scholarship or grant aid	100
% of students with need whose need was fully met	100
% Pell Grant recipients among first-years	<1
average aid package	n/a
average student loan debt upon graduation	$0

**All cadets receive taxable pay which can be used to pay for textbooks and uniforms, free room and board, and pay no tuition or fees*

ADMISSIONS	
# of applicants	10,202
% admitted	12
SAT Critical Reading	600-690
SAT Math	620-720
SAT Writing	n/a
ACT Composite	30
SAT/ACT optional	no
average HS GPA	3.8
DEADLINES	
regular application closing date	12/31
early decision plan	n/a
application closing date	n/a
early action plan	yes
application closing date	12/31
application fee	$0
application fee online	$0
fee waiver for applicants with financial need	n/a

University of Colorado Colorado Springs

At the University of Colorado Colorado Springs we value students and never forget that students are our reason for being. We consider students and student outcomes in all the decisions we make. We provide a supportive environment in order to create lasting and significant educational experiences for every student. We are committed to our students and their success.

Special Admissions Policy **MOSAIC Gateway Program**

The MOSAIC Gateway program provides holistic admission review and learning communities for students who face particular academic and social challenges but show strong potential to succeed in college. Nominations to the program are made by UCCS admissions committees upon review of a UCCS application and required support documents. A limited number of students are admitted to the program on a case-by-case basis and are required to participate in the MOSAIC Gateway learning community their first semester. The learning community is designed to provide added layers of support needed to promote academic and social success for MOSAIC Gateway Scholars. MOSAIC Gateway is coordinated by Anthony Cordova, Director of MOSAIC (Multicultural Office for Student Access, Inclusiveness and Community). MOSAIC provides support with admission, academic coaching, mentoring, and college transition for all students. MOSAIC serves all UCCS students and specializes in supporting students who are ethnically diverse, international, LGBTQ, first generation, and/or non-traditional.

International Social Support **International Social Support**

MOSAIC ISS provides International Students with assistance and support in adjusting to life in Colorado Springs and in navigating campus life at UCCS. We provide opportunities throughout the academic year for students to engage in social activities and events aimed at providing opportunities for International Students to connect with each other as well as with domestic students. Our goal is to help create a positive and supportive campus environment and an overall productive and meaningful experience for all International Students visiting our campus from around the world.

International Social Support **LGBT Resource Center**

The LGBT Resource Center @ MOSAIC exists as part of the University of Colorado Colorado Springs' on-going commitment to fostering a positive and inclusive atmosphere for everyone on campus. As part of the Multicultural Office for Student Access, Inclusiveness, and Community (MOSAIC), the LGBT Resource Center is designed to provide resources and information to LGBT students, advocate for LGBT+ interests throughout campus, conduct outreach and education, and ensure LGBT+ voices are represented among the campus at large.

University of Colorado Colorado Springs
1420 Austin Bluffs Parkway
Colorado Springs, CO 80918
Ph: (719) 255-3084
www.uccs.edu

Fast Facts

STUDENT DIVERSITY

# undergraduates	10,187
% male/female	47/53
% first-generation college	29
% American Indian or Alaskan Native	<1
% Asian	3
% Black or African American	4
% Hispanic/Latino	17
% Native Hawaiian or Pacific Islander	1
% White	65
% two or more races	8
% race and/or ethnicity unknown	2
% International/nonresident	1

STUDENT SUCCESS

% first-to-second year retention	69
% six-year graduation	47
% six-year graduation for underrepresented minority groups	35
% first-years who live on campus	65
% undergraduates who live on campus	14
full-time faculty	1,100
full-time minority faculty	92
student-faculty ratio	15:1

Popular majors Business, Biology, Psychology, Communication, Engineering, Nursing

Multicultural student clubs and organizations El Circulo de Espanol, German Club, Hawai'i Club, Indian Student Alliance, International Buddy Program, Japanese Language Club, Native American Student Union, Latino Student Union, Black Student Union, etc.

AFFORDABILITY

Cost of Attendance

tuition	$8,280
required fees	$1,582
room and board	$11,000

Financial Aid

total institutional scholarships/grants	n/a
% of students with financial need	67
% of students with need awarded any financial aid	77
% of students with need awarded any need-based scholarship or grant aid	n/a
% of students with need whose need was fully met	n/a
% Pell Grant recipients among first-years	32
average aid package	$12,057
average student loan debt upon graduation	$16,780

ADMISSIONS

# of applicants	12,000
% admitted	92
SAT Critical Reading	540-n/a
SAT Math	530-n/a
SAT Writing	n/a
ACT Composite	23
SAT/ACT optional	n/a
average HS GPA	3.42

DEADLINES

regular application closing date	rolling
early decision plan	n/a
application closing date	n/a
early action plan	n/a
application closing date	n/a
application fee	$50
application fee online	n/a
fee waiver for applicants with financial need	yes

University of Denver

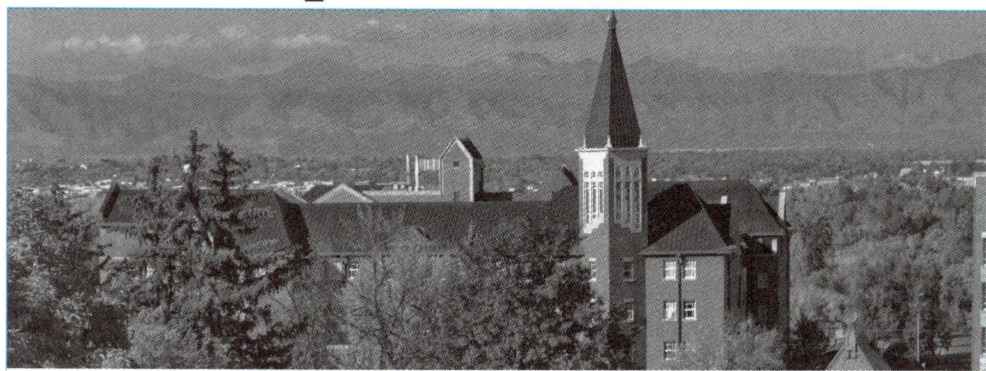

The University of Denver offers a dynamic learning environment that prizes innovation, interdisciplinary exploration, inclusive excellence and important learning partnerships between students and faculty. Our students discover purpose through their own paths and enjoy meaningful and life-changing interactions with professors, newfound friends and campus mentors. With a student-faculty ratio of 11:1, this rewarding relationship with professors continues through the undergraduate experience, with students collaborating with faculty members on research projects, fieldwork and creative endeavors. With the personal attention offered at a small liberal arts college and the resources of a large research institution, the University of Denver is the perfect choice for students looking to join other adventurous learners.

Pre-College Prep & Outreach **Volunteers in Partnership (VIP)**

VIP collaborates with students, parents, faculty and staff from Denver West Campus, Abraham Lincoln High School, Pinnacle Charter School, the Denver Center for International Studies, the Denver School of Science & Technology, South High School, Hinkley High School and Kepner Middle School. VIP is committed to the promotion of self-esteem in students, to encouraging students to complete high school, to assisting with the transition into higher education and to providing scholarship funding to DU when possible.

Pre-College Summer Experience **Pioneer Prep Leadership Institute**

A three-day summer campus experience, the Pioneer Prep Leadership Institute is designed for high-achieving African American and Latino/a high school juniors and seniors to have a dynamic learning opportunity on the University of Denver campus. Travel stipends are available. Participants who are admitted and enroll at DU will receive a DU Pathways Scholarship valued at a maximum of $7,500 per year for four years.

First-Year Experience & Transition **Excelling Leaders Institute**

Students complete one week of on-campus training focusing in the areas of academic preparation, interacting with faculty, learning the campus physical layout, meeting as many individuals and resources on campus as possible and most importantly, creating a tightly knit community of support for themselves and other incoming students. Participants are also offered a wide range of benefits not offered to all students.

First-Year Experience & Transition **1GenU and Equity in Science, Technology, Engineering and Math (E-STEM)**

1GenU is a one-year development and community-building program designed for first-generation students. It begins with a three-day pre-orientation that connects students with faculty, staff, continuing students, and other campus resources to assist in navigating available support systems on campus as well as support their academic and personal success at DU. 1GenU provides programs that address academic success, personal growth, and social engagement. Our newest academic program, Equity in Science, Technology, Engineering and Math (E-STEM), aims to nurture the strengths of incoming undergraduates from historically underrepresented backgrounds who elect to major in STEM subjects, helping them successfully transition to the college environment and navigate STEM paths at DU.

Student Life & Support **Cherrington Global Scholars Study Abroad Program**

Currently ranked the #3 university in the nation for the percentage of students who study abroad, international initiatives are an integral part of the DU experience. Through the Cherrington Global Scholars Program, eligible juniors and seniors can study abroad at no additional charge to the cost of studying on campus in Denver.

University of Denver
2199 S. University Blvd.
Denver, CO 80208
Ph: (303) 871-2036
admission@du.edu
www.du.edu

Fast Facts

STUDENT DIVERSITY

# undergraduates	5,754
% male/female	41/59
% first-generation college	20
% American Indian or Alaskan Native	1
% Asian	4
% Black or African American	2
% Hispanic/Latino	10
% Native Hawaiian or Pacific Islander	<1
% White	69
% two or more races	4
% race and/or ethnicity unknown	2
% International/nonresident	8

STUDENT SUCCESS

% first-to-second year retention	87
% six-year graduation	79
% six-year graduation for underrepresented minority groups	n/a
% first-years who live on campus	93
% undergraduates who live on campus	47
full-time faculty	723
full-time minority faculty	130
student-faculty ratio	11:1

Popular majors Business, Social Sciences, Biology, Communications, Visual and Performing Arts

Multicultural student clubs and organizations Asian Student Alliance (ASA), Belay, Black Student Alliance (BSA), Latino Student Alliance (LSA), Native Student Alliance (NSA), Out for Business, Pi Lambda Chi Latina Sorority, Inc., Pioneer Veteran Students, Queer Straight Alliance, Sigma Lambda Beta International Fraternity, Inc.

AFFORDABILITY

Cost of Attendance

tuition	$47,520
required fees	$1,149
room and board	$12,612

Financial Aid

total institutional scholarships/grants	$94,513,237
% of students with financial need	41
% of students with need awarded any financial aid	99
% of students with need awarded any need-based scholarship or grant aid	98
% of students with need whose need was fully met	35
% Pell Grant recipients among first-years	15
average aid package	$37,109
average student loan debt upon graduation	n/a

ADMISSIONS

# of applicants	20,322
% admitted	53
SAT Critical Reading	550-660
SAT Math	560-650
SAT Writing	520-618
ACT Composite	28
SAT/ACT optional	n/a
average HS GPA	3.72

DEADLINES

regular application closing date	1/15
early decision plan	yes
application closing date	ED I: 11/1, ED II: 1/15
early action plan	yes
application closing date	11/1
application fee	$65
application fee online	$65
fee waiver for applicants with financial need	yes

Central Connecticut State University

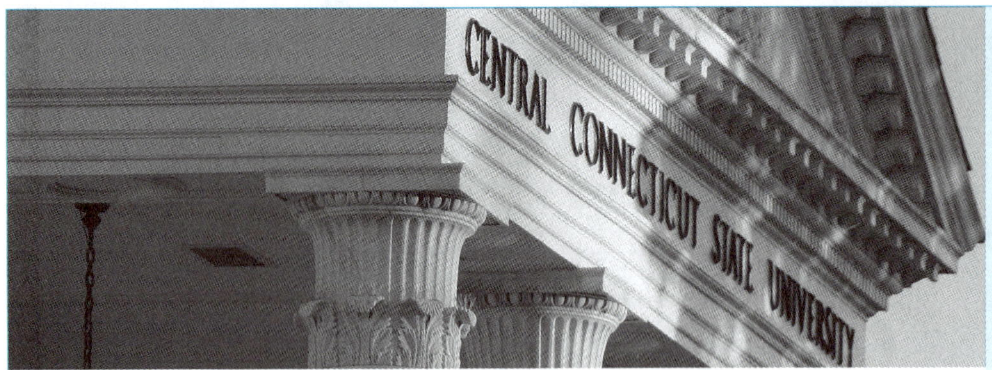

CCSU is a leading comprehensive public university. Excellent professors and a wide array of academic programs prepare students for success in whatever field they choose. Nearly one third of our students are the first in their family to attend college. The University is committed to both access and excellence and offers a campus that warmly welcomes and supports all. We believe diversity is a strength. CCSU's educational excellence has been nationally recognized. Among our many honors, the Education Trust ranks CCSU 17th in the nation among public institutions in closing the academic achievement gap for African American students, and 23rd in the nation for improvement in African American student graduation rates.

Pre-College Prep & Outreach **Pre-Collegiate and Access Services Department**

The Pre-Collegiate and Access Services Department's mission is to provide a diverse population of first generation and low-income students with access to higher education by preparing them to meet high academic, personal and social standards.

Pre-College Summer Experience **TRiO Educational Talent Search (ETS)**

The TRiO ETS program provides high students with academic assistance and support, college preparation and exposure, career development, and cultural enrichment. The program ensures that students will expand their knowledge and grow personally through career exploration activities that will help them succeed beyond secondary school. The program identifies and assists 500 students in grades 6-12, who are enrolled in the Consolidated School District of New Britain. TRiO ETS students must be from populations traditionally underrepresented in postsecondary education (i.e., first generation potential college and low-income students).

Special Admissions Policy **Educational Opportunity Program (EOP)**

The Educational Opportunity Program is a five-week summer program designed for students who have the potential and the desire to do college-level work, but do not meet CCSU's regular admissions standards. EOP students live on campus in CCSU residence halls during the summer with all expenses paid. Graduates of the summer program are admitted to CCSU as full-time matriculated students.

Scholars & Leadership **Honors Program**

Undergraduates with strong academic skills who are looking for further challenges are encouraged to consider the Honors Program. Students receive a half scholarship (half in state tuition and fees) upon entry, with the possibility for upgrade (based on academic performance) after completing one year in the program.

Academic Advising & Support **Career Success Center**

The Career Success Center provides students with resources and opportunities which assists in the development and implementation of career plans and goals. We help students achieve career readiness with 1-on-1 Career Coaching, Resume/Cover Letter Critiques, Internship, Co-op, and Job Search Strategies, Interview Preparation and Practice, Career Development Workshops, Networking with Employers, and Career Fairs.

Central Connecticut State University
Davidson Hall, Room 115
1615 Stanley Street
New Britain, CT 06050
Ph: (860) 832-2278
admissions@ccsu.edu
www.ccsu.edu

Fast Facts

STUDENT DIVERSITY

# undergraduates	9,538
% male/female	54/46
% first-generation college	n/a
% American Indian or Alaskan Native	<1
% Asian	4
% Black or African American	11
% Hispanic/Latino	12
% Native Hawaiian or Pacific Islander	<1
% White	65
% two or more races	3
% race and/or ethnicity unknown	3
% International/nonresident	2

STUDENT SUCCESS

% first-to-second year retention	78
% six-year graduation	58
% six-year graduation for underrepresented minority groups	42
% first-years who live on campus	70
% undergraduates who live on campus	23
full-time faculty	434
full-time minority faculty	104
student-faculty ratio	16:1

Popular majors Business, Social Sciences, Education, Psychology, Criminology, Engineering & Technology, BS Nursing

Multicultural student clubs and organizations Black Student Union, Diversity Advocates, Ebony Choral Ensemble, Habitat for Humanity, Hillel Jewish Student Organization, Latin American Student Organization, Muslim Student Association, NAACP - CCSU Chapter Association, NAACP - CCSU Chapter, PPRIDE, United Caribbean Club

AFFORDABILITY

Cost of Attendance

tuition	in-state: $10,225; out-of-state: $22,914
required fees	n/a
room and board	$11,816

Financial Aid

total institutional scholarships/grants	$59,000,000
% of students with financial need	73
% of students with need awarded any financial aid	94
% of students with need awarded any need-based scholarship or grant aid	78
% of students with need whose need was fully met	4
% Pell Grant recipients among first-years	24
average aid package	$7,951
average student loan debt upon graduation	$26,000

ADMISSIONS

# of applicants	7,719
% admitted	64
SAT Critical Reading	460-540
SAT Math	460-550
SAT Writing	460-550
ACT Composite	22
SAT/ACT optional	no
average HS GPA	3.1

DEADLINES

regular application closing date	5/1
early decision plan	n/a
application closing date	n/a
early action plan	n/a
application closing date	n/a
application fee	$50
application fee online	$50
fee waiver for applicants with financial need	yes

Quinnipiac University

On a scenic campus of 600 acres in southern Connecticut, Quinnipiac University offers students a range of opportunities, including access to state-of-the-art facilities, a multitude of student organizations and activities, counseling and academic support services, small classes, individual attention from your professors, individualized career planning and much more. Quinnipiac is a private, coeducational university offering 58 undergraduate majors and 25 graduate programs in Business, Engineering, Communications, Health Sciences, Nursing, Liberal Arts and Sciences, Education, Law and Medicine. Multicultural education is a key component of the Quinnipiac experience. At Quinnipiac University, we believe that diversity enriches the educational experiences of all students and promotes personal growth and a healthy society.

Pre-College Prep and Outreach **Middle School College Awareness Program**

The Office of Admissions hosts groups of area middle school students on campus for its 'College Awareness Program,' designed to foster a "college-going" mindset, to demystify the college environment and to help students view a college education as a beneficial and attainable path for their future.

Open House, Fly-In, Visit **Admissions Events/Visit Program**

The Office of Undergraduate Admissions hosts individual interviews, group information sessions, campus tours and Open House programs throughout the year for college-bound students and their families. Admissions also offers newly admitted students the opportunity to participate in a day visit program.

First-Year Experience & Transition **First-Year Experience (FYRE)**

FYRE is designed to help all first-year students have a positive transition to college life at Quinnipiac. The experience helps our students build meaningful relationships with residents in their hall and make lasting connections with the campus community. Quinnipiac's Global Living Community is a residential interest community for first-year students interested in learning about inclusion, cultural diversity and individual identity through domestic and international immersion programs and experiences.

Scholars & Leadership **The University Honors Program**

A number of Quinnipiac undergraduates are looking for a unique and particularly sophisticated academic experience. These students share a common desire to excel in their studies and to learn by discussing and sharing new ideas. The University Honors Program helps Quinnipiac's most academically talented students get the most from their education—with special seminar courses, close relationships with professors, leadership opportunities and great opportunities for enrichment.

Academic Courses & Service Learning **Serving to Learn & Learning to Serve**

Service Learning is a teaching and learning strategy that integrates meaningful community service with instruction and reflection to enrich the learning experience, teach civic responsibility and strengthen communities.

Mentoring **Office of Multicultural and Global Education**

The Office of Multicultural and Global Education provides advocacy for the cultivation of a sustainable campus environment that is supportive of a diverse student body. The Quinnipiac University Enriching Student Transitions (QUEST) program provides a means for first-year underrepresented and first-generation students to connect directly with peer and professional mentors to aid in their success and adjustment to college.

Quinnipiac University
275 Mount Carmel Avenue
EC-UGR
Hamden, CT 06518
Ph: (800) 462-1944
admissions@qu.edu
www.qu.edu

Fast Facts

STUDENT DIVERSITY

# undergraduates	7,305
% male/female	39/61
% first-generation college	14
% American Indian or Alaskan Native	<1
% Asian	3
% Black or African American	4
% Hispanic/Latino	9
% Native Hawaiian or Pacific Islander	<1
% White	76
% two or more races	2
% race and/or ethnicity unknown	3
% International/nonresident	3

STUDENT SUCCESS

% first-to-second year retention	88
% six-year graduation	76
% six-year graduation for underrepresented minority groups	80
% first-years who live on campus	95
% undergraduates who live on campus	75
full-time faculty	351
full-time minority faculty	52
student-faculty ratio	16:1

Popular majors Marketing, Engineering, Finance, Psychology, Biology, Communications, Public Relations, Nursing, Health Science Studies, Game Design & Development, Occupational Therapy

Multicultural student clubs and organizations African & Caribbean Student Union, Asian & Pacific Islander Student Assoc., Black Student Union, International Club, Italian Cultural Society, Latino Cultural Society, Quinnipiac Collegiate Chapter NAACP, Quinnipiac Hellenic Society, Irish Club, South Asia Society

AFFORDABILITY

Cost of Attendance

tuition	$44,420
required fees	$2,360
room and board	$14,190

Financial Aid

total institutional scholarships/grants	$131,858,841
% of students with financial need	64
% of students with need awarded any financial aid	63
% of students with need awarded any need-based scholarship or grant aid	62
% of students with need whose need was fully met	10
% Pell Grant recipients among first-years	15
average aid package	$28,707
average student loan debt upon graduation	$48,894

ADMISSIONS

# of applicants	23,456
% admitted	69
SAT Critical Reading	550
SAT Math	568
SAT Writing	559
ACT Composite	24
SAT/ACT optional	n/a
average HS GPA	3.40

DEADLINES

regular application closing date	2/1
early decision plan	yes
application closing date	11/1
early action plan	n/a
application closing date	n/a
application fee	$65
application fee online	$65
fee waiver for applicants with financial need	yes

Trinity College

Trinity College is a small private liberal arts college in the heart of Connecticut's capital city of Hartford. Trinity's urban location and global reach drive students to engage the liberal arts with a spirit of innovation and independence, all while preparing to face the world boldly and become leaders in their fields. The College is committed to a vibrant multicultural community, offering programs and resources that support and help give voice to a diverse student body. Though they come from 44 states and 63 countries, Trinity students are united by their independence, curiosity, and an insatiable desire to engage with the world around them–on campus, in Hartford, and around the world.

Open House, Fly-in, Visit **Preview Weekend**

Preview Weekend is an overnight program designed to give seniors in high school an opportunity to explore both the academic and social aspects of the Trinity community, with a focus on the experiences of our students of color, first-generation college students, and international students. Visiting students enjoy observing classes, meeting faculty and students, attending campus events, and interviewing with a member of our staff at the preeminent liberal arts college in an urban setting.

Scholarship & Financial Aid **Posse University Partner**

Trinity is a partner institution with the Posse Foundation, a non-profit organization that identifies students with extraordinary academic and leadership potential who may be overlooked by the traditional college section process. Posse students come to campus to pursue their academic interests and promote cross-cultural communication. They share a collaborative support system with a special mentor to adjust to campus and college life. Trinity's Posse Scholars hail from New York City and Chicago.

Scholarship & Financial Aid **First-Generation Fee Waiver**

In an effort to tear down a barrier between first-generation students and educational opportunities, Trinity College has eliminated application fees for first-generation students. Applicants automatically qualify for the fee waiver by checking a box in the Common Application indicating that they would be the first in their family to earn a bachelor's degree.

First Year Experience & Transition **First-Year Seminars**

Our first-year seminars are small, discussion-rich classes where students and their professor engage one another and wrestle intellectually with a topic. The seminars cultivate curiosity, introducing students to academic habits of mind. Students practice critical reading and analysis, use writing as a mode of learning, and develop skills in research and documentation. The intimacy of these seminars prepares students for becoming active participants in their own learning, fostering the capacity to communicate effectively and collaboratively.

First Year Experience & Transition **The Bantam Network**

Trinity's Bantam Network is designed to support you from your first days on campus through a unique network of individuals and experiences. Designed by students for students, the Bantam Network is at the heart of Trinity's first-year experience, helping you get to know other students and faculty and staff, offering the support that new students want, and allowing you to become more deeply acquainted with Trinity and Hartford.

Trinity College
300 Summit Street
Hartford, CT 06106
Ph: (860) 297-2180
admissions.office@trincoll.edu
www.trincoll.edu

Fast Facts

STUDENT DIVERSITY

# undergraduates	2,174
% male/female	50/50
% first-generation college	14
% American Indian or Alaskan Native	<1
% Asian	4
% Black or African American	6
% Hispanic/Latino	8
% Native Hawaiian or Pacific Islander	<1
% White	65
% two or more races	3
% race and/or ethnicity unknown	3
% International/nonresident	12

STUDENT SUCCESS

% first-to-second year retention	90
% six-year graduation	86
% six-year graduation for underrepresented minority groups	82
% first-years who live on campus	99
% undergraduates who live on campus	91
full-time faculty	207
full-time minority faculty	37
student-faculty ratio	9:1

Popular majors Political Science, English, History, Human Rights, Engineering, Neuroscience

Multicultural student clubs and organizations Asian-American Student Association, Caribbean Students Association, Elemental Movement Dance Crew, Latin Dance Club, La Voz Latina, Men of Color Alliance, Muslim Students Association, Shondaa Steppers, Temple of Hip Hop, Trinity College Black Women's Organization

AFFORDABILITY

Cost of Attendance

tuition	$52,280
required fees	$2,490
room and board	$14,200

Financial Aid

total institutional scholarships/grants	$49,800,000
% of students with financial need	48
% of students with need awarded any financial aid	100
% of students with need awarded any need-based scholarship or grant aid	100
% of students with need whose need was fully met	100
% Pell Grant recipients among first-years	16
average aid package	$45,859
average student loan debt upon graduation	$25,855

ADMISSIONS

# of applicants	6,085
% admitted	34
SAT Critical Reading	600-680
SAT Math	570-700
SAT Writing	620-690
ACT Composite	28-32
SAT/ACT optional	yes
average HS GPA	n/a

DEADLINES

regular application closing date	1/1
early decision plan	yes
application closing date	11/15
early action plan	n/a
application closing date	n/a
application fee	$65
application fee online	$65
fee waiver for applicants with financial need	yes

University of Bridgeport

University of Bridgeport
126 Park Ave
Bridgeport, CT 06604
Ph: (800) EXCEL-UB
admit@bridgeport.edu
www.bridgeport.edu

The University of Bridgeport was founded in 1927 as the Junior College of Connecticut—the first junior college chartered by any legislature in the northeastern states. In the words of its founders, the college's purpose was to develop in students "a point of view and a habit of mind that promotes clear thinking and sound judgment in later professional and business experience." Although UB has changed in many ways since then, its commitment to student preparation and community service remains central to its mission. The University maintains its primary commitments and holds fast to its values. Academic programs are offered through twelve schools, colleges, and institutes. Concern for student development and support predominate. A career-oriented focus in academic programs is complemented at the undergraduate level with a state-of-the-art core curriculum that helps students secure competencies for lifelong learning and knowledge about our world.

Scholars & Leadership **The Honors Program**

Recent UB Honors Program grads have gone on to some of the best colleges and universities in the world for graduate study and have also gone on to assume important roles in Fortune 500 companies and international organizations such as the United Nations. The program's learning environment utilizes both multi- and inter-disciplinary approaches to key topics to prepare you with skills to succeed in today's society. Team teaching, seminar moderation, and course material evaluation are conducive to the multi-faceted competencies and expertise of Honors Program faculty, who have extensive research backgrounds.

Academic Advising & Support **Academic Resource Center**

The mission of the Colin "Ben" Gunn Academic Resource Center at the University of Bridgeport is to support undergraduate classroom instruction and provide academic assistance to our undergraduate students through tutoring, workshops, and study groups. The Academic Resource Center offers tutoring, group study sessions, study skills workshops and other valuable services to ensure student success.

Academic Advising & Support **Tutoring and Learning Center**

The Tutoring and Learning Center works with full-time and part-time undergraduate students who need and want assistance with their courses. Although we offer supportive services, such as tutoring and workshops, a tutor is not a substitute for a professor's instruction of the course content. There is no fee for using the center. Professional and peer tutors are available for both individual and group sessions. We do take walk-ins if a tutor is available. Appointments can be made by calling us or stopping by the center. We are located on the 5th floor of the library building.

Academic Advising & Support **eTutoring**

eTutoring is another free service offered by the University of Bridgeport to undergraduate students. Students must log in on the eTutoring website to receive tutoring services. Online tutors work for various colleges and universities in the Northeast. As participants in eTutoring, students have access to the following: Online Writing Lab, Live Tutoring, and Offline Questions.

Student Life & Support **Center for Career Development**

The Center for Career Development is a comprehensive career counseling and resource center dedicated to empowering students as active participants in their own career development. Through career exploration and experiential opportunities, students are motivated to expand their knowledge of themselves and the world of work in a dynamic global community.

Fast Facts

STUDENT DIVERSITY

# undergraduates	2,941
% male/female	38/62
% first-generation college	n/a
% American Indian or Alaskan Native	<1
% Asian	3
% Black or African American	25
% Hispanic/Latino	11
% Native Hawaiian or Pacific Islander	1
% White	33
% two or more races	2
% race and/or ethnicity unknown	n/a
% International/nonresident	24

STUDENT SUCCESS

% first-to-second year retention	64
% six-year graduation	29
% six-year graduation for underrepresented minority groups	n/a
% first-years who live on campus	n/a
% undergraduates who live on campus	60
full-time faculty	130
full-time minority faculty	n/a
student-faculty ratio	16:1

Popular majors n/a

Multicultural student clubs and organizations
The university offers more than 60 active clubs and organizations, including co-ed intramural sports, fraternities and sororities.

AFFORDABILITY

Cost of Attendance

tuition	$31,630
required fees	n/a
room and board	$13,320

Financial Aid

total institutional scholarships/grants	n/a
% of students with financial need	n/a
% of students with need awarded any financial aid	96
% of students with need awarded any need-based scholarship or grant aid	n/a
% of students with need whose need was fully met	n/a
% Pell Grant recipients among first-years	n/a
average aid package	$24,000
average student loan debt upon graduation	n/a

ADMISSIONS

# of applicants	n/a
% admitted	60
SAT Critical Reading	500
SAT Math	500
SAT Writing	500
ACT Composite	n/a
SAT/ACT optional	no
average HS GPA	3.0

DEADLINES

regular application closing date	rolling
early decision plan	no
application closing date	n/a
early action plan	n/a
application closing date	11/15, 1/1
application fee	$25
application fee online	$25
fee waiver for applicants with financial need	yes

Wesleyan University

Wesleyan University is a highly selective private liberal arts university that attracts a diverse student body from all over the world. It is dedicated to the outreach and support of under-represented students in the United States and beyond. Approximately 35% of undergraduates are students of color and 15% are first-generation college students. Wesleyan University will meet 100% of demonstrated financial need. Located in the small New England city of Middletown, Connecticut, Wesleyan extends to students the flexibility of an open liberal arts curriculum at a top-notch research university. Campus can be described as a vibrant intellectual atmosphere populated by students that champion inclusivity and differences in thought and engagement.

Open House, Fly-In, Visit **Transportation Assistance Program & Admission Workshops**

The Transportation Assistance Program (TAP) encourages first-generation, low-income, and other under-represented students to consider Wesleyan among their top college choices during their senior year of high school. For the students selected, Wesleyan arranges and subsidizes transportation to the University for those students unable to afford a visit to campus. The office of admission also works closely with guidance counselors and community-based organizations to administer admission workshops throughout the country during the fall and spring travel season.

Academic Advising & Support **Pathways to Inclusive Excellence (PIE)**

The purpose of PIE is to increase a sense of community amongst students, faculty, and staff. The goal is to remove obstacles along the pathways to secondary and post-secondary education for a wide range of education seeking students. Wesleyan also offers programs to support Wesleyan students during and following their time at Wesleyan. PIE provides support for students who come from historically under-represented backgrounds.

Together, these five communities make up the Pathways to Inclusive Excellence (PIE): Wesleyan Mathematics and Science Scholars Program; The Upward Bound Math-Science Program; Ronald E. McNair Post-baccalaureate Program; Mellon Mays Undergraduate Fellowship; and Posse Veteran Scholars Program. To learn more, please visit our website at: http://www.wesleyan.edu/inclusion/PIE.html

Summer Bridge & Orientation **First Things First: The First-Generation Pre-Orientation**

"First Things First" is a pre-orientation pilot program designed to familiarize first-generation students with the college experience and the Wesleyan community. Up to thirty students from the Class of 2021 will be selected for the fall 2017. The program will begin on August 27 with a dinner featuring university leaders. The following two days will feature a variety of workshops that will connect students to resources on campus and help them develop strategies for success.

Student Life & Support **First-Generation Programming**

There are student groups (such as First Class), a program house (called Haven), different campus programs (such as SuitUP!, a meal points program, etc.) and a FGLI task force made up of students, faculty and staff.

Wesleyan University
70 Wyllys Avenue
Middletown, CT 06459
Ph: (860) 685-3000
admission@wesleyan.edu
www.wesleyan.edu

Fast Facts

STUDENT DIVERSITY

# undergraduates	2,971
% male/female	46/54
% first-generation college	15
% American Indian or Alaskan Native	<1
% Asian	7
% Black or African American	7
% Hispanic/Latino	10
% Native Hawaiian or Pacific Islander	<1
% White	55
% two or more races	5
% race and/or ethnicity unknown	5
% International/nonresident	10

STUDENT SUCCESS

% first-to-second year retention	94
% six-year graduation	91
% six-year graduation for underrepresented minority groups	88
% first-years who live on campus	100
% undergraduates who live on campus	100
full-time faculty	372
full-time minority faculty	78
student-faculty ratio	8:1

Popular majors Psychology, Economics, English Language and Literature, Political Science and Government, Biology

Multicultural student clubs and organizations
Wesleyan students have over 200 groups, including 35 based on identity, some of which are listed here: Ajua Campos (Latino Students Assoc.), Ujamaa (Black Student Assoc.), Shakti (South Asian Students Assoc.), Freeman Asian Scholars Assoc., Invisible Men, PINOY (Fillipino Student Assoc.), Women of Color Collective, Student of Color Coalition, African Students Assoc., and Middle Eastern Student Union

AFFORDABILITY

Cost of Attendance

tuition	$52,174
required fees	$300
room and board	$14,466

Financial Aid

total institutional scholarships/grants	$56,587,164
% of students with financial need	44
% of students with need awarded any financial aid	44
% of students with need awarded any need-based scholarship or grant aid	42
% of students with need whose need was fully met	100
% Pell Grant recipients among first-years	17
average aid package	$50,280
average student loan debt upon graduation	$22,930

ADMISSIONS

# of applicants	12,453
% admitted	16
SAT Reading & Writing	720-770
SAT Math	720-790
ACT Composite	33
SAT/ACT optional	yes
average HS GPA	n/a

DEADLINES

regular application closing date	1/1
early decision plan	yes
application closing date	11/15
early action plan	n/a
application closing date	n/a
application fee	$55
application fee online	$55
fee waiver for applicants with financial need	yes

Yale University

Yale is one of the world's great research universities, with a total student population of more than 11,000 in Yale College and thirteen graduate and professional schools. Yale College alone educates 5,300 young men and women each year from all 50 states in the U.S. and from more than 80 other countries. For all its size and scope, Yale holds firmly to its traditional emphasis on undergraduate life and teaching. If you are considering Yale, please do not hesitate to apply because you fear the cost will exceed your family's means. Yale College admits students on the basis of academic and personal promise and without regard to their ability to pay. All aid is need-based. Once a student is admitted, Yale will meet 100% of that student's demonstrated financial need. This policy, which applies to U.S. citizens and to international students alike, helps to ensure that Yale will always be accessible to talented students from the widest possible range of backgrounds.

Open House, Fly-In, Visit **Multicultural Open House/Fly-In Program**

The Multicultural Open House is a one-day fall program that introduces prospective students to Yale's academic programs, campus life, admissions process and financial aid resources. The Fly-In Program is for admitted students who demonstrate significant financial need. Students who qualify for the Fly-In Program are provided a travel stipend to attend the admitted student weekend in the spring.

First-Year Experience & Transition **Cultural Connections (CC)**

In the Cultural Connections program (CC), freshmen participate in a week of activities intended to facilitate their transition to Yale. CC is designed to introduce freshmen to Yale's cultural resources as well as to explore the diversity of student experiences on the Yale campus, with emphasis on the experiences of traditionally underrepresented students and issues related to racial identity. CC is open to any freshman regardless of race or ethnicity. Activities include discussions with faculty experts in the concepts of ethnicity, nationality, and race; panels on academic expectations by faculty; presentations on campus life by students; and group visits to local points of interest such as the Yale College cultural centers, local and University museums and parks.

Scholars & Leadership **Science, Technology and Research Scholars (STARS)**

The Science, Technology and Research Scholars (STARS) Program is designed to support women, minority, economically underprivileged, and other historically underrepresented students in the sciences, engineering, and mathematics. The STARS program provides undergraduates an opportunity to combine course-based study, research, mentorship, networking, and career planning in the fields of science and technology. The program seeks to improve student performance and persistence rates in any of Yale's natural sciences and engineering majors.

Academic Advising & Support **Residential College Dean and Head of College**

Residential college deans serve as the chief academic and personal advisers to students in their colleges. The Head of College is the chief administrative officer and the presiding faculty presence in each residential college. He or she is responsible for the physical well-being and safety of students in the residential college, and for fostering the cultural and educational character of the college. During the year, he or she hosts lectures, study breaks (especially during finals) and College Teas'—intimate gathering during which students have the opportunity to engage with renowned guests from the academy, government, or popular culture.

Yale University
38 Hillhouse Avenue
New Haven, CT 06511
Ph: (203) 432-9300
www.yale.edu

Fast Facts

STUDENT DIVERSITY

# undergraduates	5,400
% male/female	50/50
% first-generation college	14
% American Indian or Alaskan Native	3
% Asian	23
% Black or African American	11
% Hispanic/Latino	12
% Native Hawaiian or Pacific Islander	<1
% White	68
% two or more races	6
% race and/or ethnicity unknown	2
% International/nonresident	12

STUDENT SUCCESS

% first-to-second year retention	98
% six-year graduation	97
% six-year graduation for underrepresented minority groups	97
% first-years who live on campus	100
% undergraduates who live on campus	83
full-time faculty	1,171
full-time minority faculty	232
student-faculty ratio	6:1

Popular majors Economics, Political Science, History, Psychology, Biology

Multicultural student clubs and organizations African Student Association, American Indian Science and Engineering Society, Asian American Students Alliance, Association of Native Americans at Yale, Black Student Alliance, Chinese American Students Association, International Students Organization, Latin American Student Organization, Mexican Student Organization

AFFORDABILITY

Cost of Attendance

tuition	$51,400
required fees	n/a
room and board	$15,500

Financial Aid

total institutional scholarships/grants	$137,289,116
% of students with financial need	64
% of students with need awarded any financial aid	100
% of students with need awarded any need-based scholarship or grant aid	100
% of students with need whose need was fully met	100
% Pell Grant recipients among first-years	18
average aid package	$44,000
average student loan debt upon graduation	$14,853

ADMISSIONS

# of applicants	32,900
% admitted	6
SAT Critical Reading	710-800
SAT Math	710-800
SAT Writing	710-790
ACT Composite	32-35
SAT/ACT optional	no
average HS GPA	n/a

DEADLINES

regular application closing date	1/1
early decision plan	n/a
application closing date	n/a
early action plan	yes
application closing date	11/1
application fee	$80
application fee online	$80
fee waiver for applicants with financial need	yes

University of Delaware

At the University of Delaware, you'll be more than a student. You'll be a scholar. An explorer. An innovator. And the connections you will make here—with ideas, professors and alumni—will enrich your classroom experience and your future. Whichever one of our 150+ undergraduate majors you choose, you'll find our University is designed for collaboration—thanks to our medium-sized campus, abundance of undergraduate research opportunities and faculty committed to connecting with you. UD is committed to embracing a diverse and inclusive campus, promoting respect and equity for people of different backgrounds.

Pre-College Prep & Outreach **College Readiness Scholars Institute (CRSI)**

The College Readiness Scholars Institute is a program exclusive to first-generation high school juniors and seniors from Delaware, immersing them in an academic experience that will transform the way they understand campus and college culture. CRSI is a two-week program that provides an introduction to college life and an understanding of scholarship and leadership.

Pre-College Prep & Outreach **Upward Bound Classic and Math/Science**

UD's Upward Bound programs are federally funded TRIO programs that provide exciting educational opportunities that prepare area students for college and beyond. Both Upward Bound Classic and Upward Bound Math/Science are year-round programs that provide free college prep workshops, summer academic courses, academic advisement and tutoring for first-generation students and students from modest income households.

Student Life & Support **The First Gen Network**

The First Gen Network, supported through Residence Life and Housing, is a collection of resources on campus seeking to connect first-generation college students to each other and to the broader University of Delaware student body. The First Gen Network provides a space for first-generation college students to share their stories, about both their upbringing and their success. Each month they host a workshop that focuses on community building, skill development and storytelling. The First Gen Network gives students the option of in-person campus meetings and for students to participate in online workshops.

Student Life & Support **We're First**

We're First is a student-run organization that is designed to be a support network for first-generation college students. It exposes peers to on-campus resources and mentorship, and creates a space for students to forge a community with one another.

Student Life & Support **U-First Living Learning Community**

First-generation students have the option of residing together in U-FIRST LLC, a living-learning community on campus for first-generation students. The goal of the U-FIRST LLC is to help students engage socially and academically, allowing them to get the full benefit of their time in college. Our faculty and staff teams mentor students to ensure they take advantage of all the University has to offer. Our mentors assist students in finding and using student services, student organizations, undergraduate research and internships.

University of Delaware
210 South College Avenue
Newark, DE 19716
Ph: (302) 831-8123
admissions@udel.edu
www.udel.edu/admissions

Fast Facts

STUDENT DIVERSITY

# undergraduates	18,144
% male/female	42/58
% first-generation college	13
% American Indian or Alaskan Native	<1
% Asian	5
% Black or African American	5
% Hispanic/Latino	8
% Native Hawaiian or Pacific Islander	<1
% White	72
% two or more races	3
% race and/or ethnicity unknown	1
% International/nonresident	5

STUDENT SUCCESS

% first-to-second year retention	91
% six-year graduation	83
% six-year graduation for underrepresented minority groups	76
% first-years who live on campus	92
% undergraduates who live on campus	40
full-time faculty	1,198
full-time minority faculty	252
student-faculty ratio	13:1

Popular majors Finance, Nursing, Marketing, Biological Sciences, Exercise Science, Psychology, Mechanical Engineering, Elementary Teacher Education, Accounting, Criminal Justice

Multicultural student clubs and organizations We're First, Multicultural Fraternities and Sororities, ASPIRA at University of Delaware Student Chapter, Caribbean Student Alliance, Delaware African Student Association (DASA), HOLA, Black Student Union, Asian Student Association (ASA)

AFFORDABILITY

Cost of Attendance

tuition	in-state: $11,870; out-of-state: $31,860
required fees	$1,290
room and board	$12,332

Financial Aid

total institutional scholarships/grants	$95,184,383
% of students with financial need	48
% of students with need awarded any financial aid	98
% of students with need awarded any need-based scholarship or grant aid	83
% of students with need whose need was fully met	11
% Pell Grant recipients among first-years	15
average aid package	$12,963
average student loan debt upon graduation	$33,150

ADMISSIONS

# of applicants	27,800
% admitted	63
SAT Critical Reading	540-650
SAT Math	550-650
SAT Writing	540-640
ACT Composite	23-29
SAT/ACT optional	n/a
average HS GPA	3.70

DEADLINES

regular application closing date	1/15
early decision plan	n/a
application closing date	n/a
early action plan	n/a
application closing date	n/a
application fee	$75
application fee online	$75
fee waiver for applicants with financial need	yes

The Catholic University of America

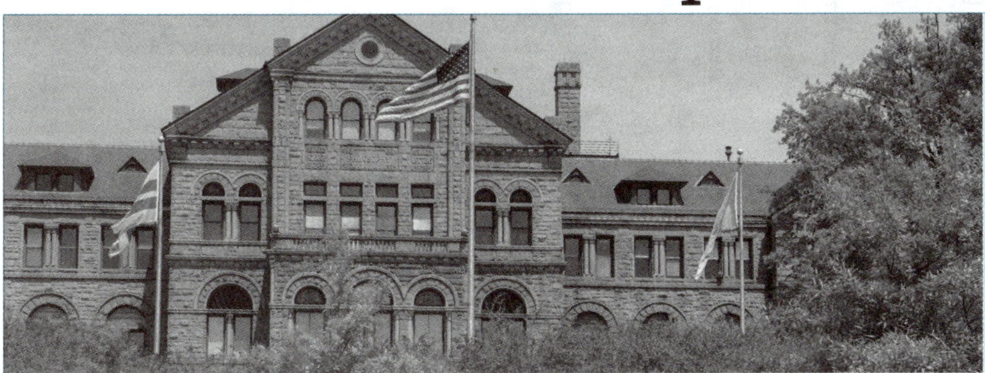

At the Catholic University of America, we are proud of our distinctive identity as the national university of the Catholic Church, where all the advantages of a large research university are combined with the nurturing feel of a smaller undergraduate arts college. Our location in the heart of Washington, D.C., offers students from all faith backgrounds unparalleled opportunities to learn both in and out of the classroom. World-class museums and scientific institutions are a short Metro ride away, and our students have a front row seat to American politics that no other city can offer. Catholic University is a place where the search for truth ranges across 12 schools, 120 disciplines, and every continent.

Open House, Fly-In, Visit **Visiting Campus**

We host on-campus information sessions and offer campus tours throughout the week. Information sessions and tours are offered at both 10 a.m. and 2 p.m., Monday through Friday, during much of the academic year, as well as most Saturday mornings throughout the fall. There are also Open Houses and special programs for students interested in particular areas such as architecture, engineering, music, or social work. If you're unable to attend one of our scheduled sessions, call us—we may be able to accommodate you and your family for a personalized tour! We also offer financial support for travel expenses for admitted students from distant locations to visit our campus.

Scholarship & Financial Aid **Catholic University Grants and Scholarships**

Catholic University offers financial aid to eight out of every 10 full-time students, based on both need and academic potential. Many unique scholarships for undergraduate students are available, including The Catholic University Merit Scholarship, ranging from $10,000 to $25,000, and the Parish Scholarship. Need-based grants currently range from $1,000 to $39,000.

First-Year Experience & Transition **First-Year Experience**

To help students make the transition from high school to college, we offer a unique First-Year Experience. In small learning communities, first-year students take a sequence of four core classes in philosophy, theology, and English; take part in service activities; enjoy excursions into Washington, D.C.; learn from a series of guest speakers; and benefit from one-on-one academic advising.

Academic Advising & Support **Center for Academic Success**

We want all students to succeed! Whether you need help with one of your classes, a bit of academic advice, or an opportunity to get you excited about your future, the Center for Academic Success is here to help make it happen. We offer a wide range of academic services designed to help students of all abilities become even more successful.

Academic Advising & Support **Undergraduate Advising Center**

Sometimes putting all the pieces of your education together can seem like assembling a giant puzzle. We can help you with course advice; provide guidance as you ponder education abroad opportunities; offer assistance with the nuts and bolts of registration; and much more.

The Catholic University of America
620 Michigan Ave., N.E.
Washington, DC 20064
Ph: (202) 319-5305
cua-admissions@cua.edu
www.catholic.edu

Fast Facts

STUDENT DIVERSITY

# undergraduates	3,318
% male/female	46/54
% first-generation college	n/a
% American Indian or Alaskan Native	<1
% Asian	4
% Black or African American	5
% Hispanic/Latino	13
% Native Hawaiian or Pacific Islander	<1
% White	65
% two or more races	5
% race and/or ethnicity unknown	3
% International/nonresident	6

STUDENT SUCCESS

% first-to-second year retention	87
% six-year graduation	70
% six-year graduation for underrepresented minority groups	56
% first-years who live on campus	93
% undergraduates who live on campus	56
full-time faculty	413
full-time minority faculty	55
student-faculty ratio	7:1

Popular majors Politics, Psychology, Nursing, Architecture, Engineering (Mechanical), Business

Multicultural student clubs and organizations Center for Cultural Engagement, Black Student Alliance, Chinese Club, CUA Student Organization of Latinos, Filipino Organization of Catholic Students, Indus Valley Association, Society of Hispanic Professional Engineers, and more

AFFORDABILITY

Cost of Attendance

tuition	$43,300
required fees	$760
room and board	$14,316

Financial Aid

total institutional scholarships/grants	$57,000,000+
% of students with financial need	65
% of students with need awarded any financial aid	100
% of students with need awarded any need-based scholarship or grant aid	83
% of students with need whose need was fully met	80
% Pell Grant recipients among first-years	13
average aid package	$27,895
average student loan debt upon graduation	$45,210

ADMISSIONS

# of applicants	6,068
% admitted	82
SAT Critical Reading	560-680
SAT Math	540-640
SAT Writing	560-680
ACT Composite	23-29
SAT/ACT optional	yes*
average HS GPA	3.4

DEADLINES

regular application closing date	1/15
early decision plan I and II	yes
application closing date	11/15 or 1/15
early action plan	yes
application closing date	11/1
application fee	$55
application fee online	$55
fee waiver for applicants with financial need	yes

*SAT/ACT scores are not required for admission, but are required should you choose to enroll.

George Washington University

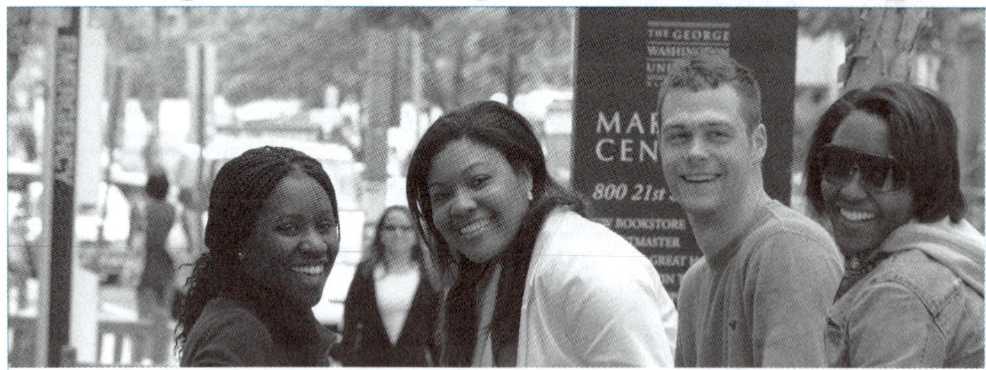

The George Washington University is a diverse, motivated and active community, in which the leaders of today nurture the leaders of tomorrow. The university enrolls undergraduates from all 50 states, the District of Columbia, Puerto Rico, the Virgin Islands, and more than 130 countries worldwide. GW offers an array of classroom experiences, academic resources, and expert faculty. GW students put knowledge into action every day through internships, research, service, and study abroad opportunities.

Pre-College Prep & Outreach **GW Pre-College Programs**

GW Pre-College provides a transformative introduction to college life. College Intensive programs offer rising juniors and seniors the opportunity to earn college credit by engaging in challenging undergraduate-level courses in 3- or 6-week sessions. Summer Immersion includes both one- and two-week full-day noncredit options for rising sophomores, juniors, and seniors. Participants attend lectures with guest speakers as well as experiential and applied activities. Both programs provide a challenging academic environment where high school students benefit tremendously from the resources found at GW and in Washington, D.C.

Scholarship & Financial Aid **Need-Based Scholarship and Grant Aid**

The university offers a notable Fixed Tuition plan for the duration of students' undergraduate studies to provide families with financial assurance and flexibility when planning for college. The tuition an entering student pays remains fixed for the entire undergraduate program, taking the uncertainty out of what the future might bring. In addition, all applicants to GW are automatically considered for scholarships as part of the admissions process, and no scholarship application is required.

Student Life & Support **Multicultural Student Services Center**

The Multicultural Student Services Center is the George Washington University's center for multicultural communication, community building and leadership. The MSSC hosts workshops, and programs each semester such as cultural heritage celebrations, the Black Men's Initiative, which offers activities to advance the mission of supporting the academic, social, intellectual, and spiritual growth of black male students. The LGBT Resource center also lives within the MSSC.

Open House, Fly-in, Visit **Your GW**

Each fall, GW invites high school seniors from around the country to campus for Your GW - An Overnight Program Celebrating Diversity and Inclusion. The program allows students to see firsthand how GW puts knowledge into action while learning about the diversity and cultural opportunities within the Colonial community.

George Washington University
2121 I Street, NW
Suite 201
Washington, DC 20052
Ph: (202) 994-6040
gwadm@gwu.edu
www.gwu.edu

Fast Facts

STUDENT DIVERSITY

# undergraduates	10,541
% male/female	40/60
% first-generation college	13
% American Indian or Alaskan Native	<1
% Asian	10
% Black or African American	6
% Hispanic/Latino	10
% Native Hawaiian or Pacific Islander	<1
% White	54
% two or more races	4
% race and/or ethnicity unknown	5
% International/nonresident	12

STUDENT SUCCESS

% first-to-second year retention	91
% six-year graduation	84
% six-year graduation for underrepresented minority groups	77
% first-years who live on campus	99
% undergraduates who live on campus	75
full-time faculty	1,279
full-time minority faculty	294
student-faculty ratio	13:1

Popular majors International Affairs, Political Science, Finance, Economics, Psychology

Multicultural student clubs and organizations Black Student Union, George Washington Williams House, Asian Student Alliance, Organization of Latino American Students, Racially and Ethnically Mixed Student Association, Multicultural Greek Council, Organization of African Students, GW Raas, GW Bhangra

AFFORDABILITY

Cost of Attendance

tuition	$53,435
required fees	n/a
room and board	$13,000

Financial Aid

total institutional scholarships/grants	$196,927,072
% of students with financial need	46
% of students with need awarded any financial aid	99
% of students with need awarded any need-based scholarship or grant aid	93
% of students with need whose need was fully met	49
% Pell Grant recipients among first-years	14
average aid package	$45,233
average student loan debt upon graduation	$33,305

ADMISSIONS

# of applicants	25,554
% admitted	40
SAT Critical Reading	580-690
SAT Math	600-700
SAT Writing	600-700
ACT Composite	27-32
SAT/ACT optional	yes
average HS GPA	n/a

DEADLINES

regular application closing date	1/5
early decision plan	yes
application closing date	11/1
early action plan	no
application closing date	n/a
application fee	$75
application fee online	$75
fee waiver for applicants with financial need	yes

University of Florida

The University of Florida is a leading research institution and is ranked in the top 10 of U.S. public universities. We offer more than 100 undergraduate and 200 graduate degree programs. UF students come from all 50 states and 131 nations. We have a rich student life program that offers nearly 1,000 student organizations. The University of Florida is interested in admitting students who will enrich and broaden the education of all students. We hope to build a community of leaders, learners, and thinkers whose education will be enhanced by a wide range of experiences.

Pre-College Prep & Outreach **Student Science Training Program**

The SSTP is a seven week residential research program for selected rising juniors and seniors who are considering STEM careers. The program emphasis is research participation with a UF faculty research scientist and his or her research team. Students engage in the ongoing research of the faculty-mentor for 28 hours each week, attend a lecture series on current research topics, and participate in a UF honors seminar class. Students enrolled in a Florida high school have the option to earn dual credit enrollment credit.

Pre-College Prep & Outreach **College Reach Out Program**

The College Reach-out Program (CROP) is a statewide project designed to increase the number of students who successfully complete a postsecondary education. Its primary objective is to strengthen the educational motivation and preparation of low-income and educationally disadvantaged students in grades 6-12 who otherwise would be unlikely to seek admission to a community college, state university or independent postsecondary institution without special support and recruitment efforts.

Pre-College Summer Experience **Health Care Summer Institute**

The Office for Diversity and Health Equity and the University of Florida Area Health Education Centers (AHEC) co-sponsor a 4-week summer camp for minority high school students with career interests in health professions who live within the University of Florida AHEC service areas. Participants shadow several health care professions and attend workshops on study skills and test taking, including a preparatory course for the SAT.

Scholarship & Financial Aid **Machen Florida Opportunity Scholars Program**

The Machen Florida Opportunity Scholars Program is an initiative to ensure first-generation Florida resident students from economically disadvantaged backgrounds have the resources they need to be academically successful at the University of Florida. The goal of the program is to retain these students and have them graduate at rates equal to or greater than the undergraduate population at large.

First-Year Experience & Transition **Transition Orientation Program**

The OAS Summer and Fall Transition Programs are programs targeted to first generation and/or underrepresented students accepted to UF. Students that participate in these programs will receive more intensive and individualized academic support. Students are also made aware of opportunities beyond the classroom. The programs connect students to campus resources and services that foster academic and professional success.

Mentoring **University Minority Mentoring Program (UMMP)**

UMMP supports first-year students in their transition to the University of Florida campus community by pairing them with a faculty/staff mentor. In addition to having a mentor, mentees are invited to participate in several activities that will expose them to various aspects of campus life.

University of Florida
201 Criser Hall
PO Box 114000
Gainesville, FL 32611
Ph: (352) 392-1365
freshman@ufl.edu
www.admissions.ufl.edu

Fast Facts

STUDENT DIVERSITY

# undergraduates	34,554
% male/female	46/54
% first-generation college	n/a
% American Indian or Alaskan Native	<1
% Asian	7
% Black or African American	6
% Hispanic/Latino	17
% Native Hawaiian or Pacific Islander	<1
% White	54
% two or more races	3
% race and/or ethnicity unknown	3
% International/nonresident	9

STUDENT SUCCESS

% first-to-second year retention	97
% six-year graduation	87
% six-year graduation for underrepresented minority groups	n/a
% first-years who live on campus	82
% undergraduates who live on campus	24
full-time faculty	2,472
full-time minority faculty	568
student-faculty ratio	20:1

Popular majors Biology, Psychology, Political Science, Finance, Mechanical Engineering

Multicultural student clubs and organizations Asian American Student Union, Black Student Union, Hispanic Student Organization, Islam on Campus, Jewish Student Union

AFFORDABILITY

Cost of Attendance

tuition	in-state: $6,381; out-of-state: $28,658
required fees	n/a
room and board	$9,910

Financial Aid

total institutional scholarships/grants	$24,209,572
% of students with financial need	73
% of students with need awarded any financial aid	98
% of students with need awarded any need-based scholarship or grant aid	66
% of students with need whose need was fully met	25
% Pell Grant recipients among first-years	32
average aid package	$13,430
average student loan debt upon graduation	$21,603

ADMISSIONS

# of applicants	33,153
% admitted	41
SAT Critical Reading	637
SAT Math	652
SAT Writing	635
ACT Composite	29
SAT/ACT optional	no
average HS GPA	4.33

DEADLINES

regular application closing date	11/1
early decision plan	n/a
application closing date	3/1
early action plan	n/a
application closing date	n/a
application fee	n/a
application fee online	$30+$5 processing fee
fee waiver for applicants with financial need	yes

Emory University

One of Emory University's greatest strengths lies in the diversity of its students, faculty and staff. As a campus community, Emory collectively believes that the intellectual and social energy that stems from a wide variety of perspectives is one of its best assets. The richness of Emory's diversity extends beyond race, religion, and sexual orientation to include a wide range of socioeconomic backgrounds, intellectual interests, social causes, nationalities, political affiliations and the like. The diversity of Emory University's campus organizations and programming further supports students as they discover their own unique identities. Regardless of individual interests and background, Emory students find a diverse group of people with whom to share their ideals.

Open House, Fly-In, Visit **CORE (Cultural Overnight Recruitment Experience)**

CORE is designed to support talented, high-achieving high school seniors from underrepresented backgrounds. Students invited to participate are traditionally either first-generation college students or they are from an underrepresented cultural or socioeconomic background. Students invited to CORE explore campus, attend classes, interact with current students, stay overnight in residence halls, and engage with faculty and staff. CORE runs from Thursday early-afternoon through Saturday early-afternoon in mid-October.

Open House, Fly-In, Visit **Essence of Emory**

Essence of Emory is an event in April for underrepresented students who have been admitted to Emory. This program allows students to experience Emory University firsthand and meet current students, faculty and administrators prior to making a decision about enrolling. Students spend two nights in a residence hall, attend classes, eat in the dining hall, explore the beautiful campus and have the chance to meet with members of various multicultural groups.

Scholarship & Financial Aid **QuestBridge Partner College**

The QuestBridge program helps low-income high school seniors gain admission and full four-year scholarships to partner colleges like Emory. Students matched with Emory through QuestBridge are awarded with scholarships that cover full tuition, fees and room and board.

Scholarship & Financial Aid **Emory Advantage**

Emory Advantage is a financial aid initiative for students from families with annual total incomes of $100,000 or less with demonstrated financial need. The program reduces the amount of money borrowed to pay for school and can include a combination of Loan Replacement Grants (for families with total incomes of $50,000 or less) and Loan Caps (for families with total incomes between $50,000 and $100,000) capping the cumulative Federal Subsidized Stafford Loan debt at $15,000 followed by grants to replace the Federal Subsidized Stafford Loan.

Summer Bridge & Orientation **Emory Crossroads Retreat**

The Emory Crossroads Retreat is held for incoming freshmen of any racial or ethnic background one week prior to their arrival on Emory's campus. Participants praise the program for easing the transition into college, creating lasting friendships and providing a memorable experience through a ropes course, community-building games and story circles.

First-Year Experience & Transition **MORE (Multicultural Outreach and Resources Mentoring Program)**

The Multicultural Outreach and Resources Mentoring Program at Emory assists first-year students with the social and academic transition to Emory through one-on-one mentoring relationships with upperclassmen. The organization also engages in a number of group activities including the Fall Carnival and other social and academic-related programs.

Emory University
1390 Oxford Rd NE
3rd Floor
Atlanta, GA 30322
Ph: (800) 727-6036
admission@emory.edu
apply.emory.edu

Fast Facts

STUDENT DIVERSITY

# undergraduates	6,937
% male/female	41/59
% first-generation college	n/a
% American Indian or Alaskan Native	<1
% Asian	19
% Black or African American	8
% Hispanic/Latino	9
% Native Hawaiian or Pacific Islander	<1
% White	41
% two or more races	4
% race and/or ethnicity unknown	2
% International/nonresident	17

STUDENT SUCCESS

% first-to-second year retention	93
% six-year graduation	91
% six-year graduation for underrepresented minority groups	85
% first-years who live on campus	100
% undergraduates who live on campus	65
full-time faculty	1,031
full-time minority faculty	215
student-faculty ratio	9:1

Popular majors Biology, Business, Economics, Nursing, Psychology, Neuroscience and Behavioral Biology, Chemistry, Political Science, Human Health, International Studies

Multicultural student clubs and organizations African Student Association, All Mixed Up, Black Student Alliance, Brotherhood of Afrocentric Men, Indian Cultural Exchange, International Association, Latino Student Organization, Multicultural Council, Multicultural Yearbook, Students in Alliance for Asian American Concerns

AFFORDABILITY

Cost of Attendance

tuition	$48,690
required fees	$702
room and board	$13,894

Financial Aid

total institutional scholarships/grants	$96,802,871
% of students with financial need	45
% of students with need awarded any financial aid	100
% of students with need awarded any need-based scholarship or grant aid	92
% of students with need whose need was fully met	100
% Pell Grant recipients among first-years	19
average aid package	$44,155
average student loan debt upon graduation	$28,186

ADMISSIONS

# of applicants	23,747
% admitted	22
SAT Evidence-Based Reading & Writing	690-760
SAT Math	690-780
ACT Composite	31-34
SAT/ACT optional	no
average HS GPA	3.75-3.98

DEADLINES

regular application closing date	1/1
early decision plan	yes
application closing date	11/1
early action plan	n/a
application closing date	n/a
application fee	$75
application fee online	$75
fee waiver for applicants with financial need	yes

Georgia Institute of Technology

Georgia Institute of Technology
225 North Avenue, NW
Atlanta, GA 30332
Ph: (404) 894-2000
admission@gatech.edu
www.gatech.edu

Students at the Georgia Institute of Technology enjoy the best of both worlds—living in the dynamic city of Atlanta, while studying at one of the world's top technological universities. Georgia Tech recruits, enrolls, supports and graduates students from diverse geographic, ethnic and socioeconomic backgrounds who go on to great success locally, regionally, nationally and throughout the world. While Georgia Tech is a top producer of African-American, Hispanic and female engineers, we also consistently graduate students who pursue and thrive in fields such as Architecture, Business, Computing, Liberal Arts and Sciences. In one day at Tech you can hear a world-class lecture, participate in ground-breaking research, cheer on a Division I ACC sports team and eat at one of the country's finest restaurants.

Scholarship & Financial Aid **G. Wayne Clough Georgia Tech Promise Program**

The G. Wayne Clough Georgia Tech Promise Program is intended to assist Georgia students whose families have an annual income of less than $33,300. Awards from the Tech Promise Program are combined with other scholarships, grants, and a Federal Work Study job opportunity to meet the student's financial need associated with the cost of attendance, which includes tuition, fees, books, on-campus housing, and a meal plan.

Summer Bridge & Orientation **Challenge**

Challenge is a five-week program held every summer for incoming Georgia Tech freshmen. In Challenge, students are immersed in the Georgia Tech environment; they live in a freshman dorm, take classes taught by Georgia Tech professors, and participate in social and academic workshops provided by upperclass Tech students. During the five weeks, Challenge students take core courses that simulate a typical student's freshman year. The courses are taught in the same manner and pace as a real Georgia Tech course. This allows students to become familiar with Georgia Tech academics as well as understand strategies that will help them be successful in their first year.

First Year Programs and Transition **GT 1000 Freshman Seminar**

GT 1000 is Tech's freshman seminar course. The course is taught by academic faculty and university administrators with advanced degrees, and upperclass students volunteer to serve as Team Leaders (or TLs) in each class. TLs facilitate small groups within the class and offer mentoring, advice and support to freshmen. Many students who have successfully completed GT 1000 report that the friendships that form with their fellow students and team leaders last well beyond the completion of the course. Additionally, students who take a GT 1000 course have proven to hold higher GPAs that those who do not take this course.

Student Life & Support **Individualized Tutoring**

Individualized tutoring is available to assist students with time management, study skills, and course content and preparation. Peer-led supplemental instruction, peer tutoring, academic coaching, and other services provide the skills and strategies to help our students excel.

Mentoring **Team Coach Program**

The Team Coach Program is a peer mentoring program that supports Tech freshmen, dual degree, and transfer students academically and socially throughout their first year. Upperclassmen, serving as coaches, mentor participants as they acclimate to the new responsibilities and challenges of Georgia Tech.

Fast Facts

STUDENT DIVERSITY

# undergraduates	14,766
% male/female	63/37
% first-generation college	n/a
% American Indian or Alaskan Native	<1
% Asian	20
% Black or African American	7
% Hispanic/Latino	7
% Native Hawaiian or Pacific Islander	<1
% White	50
% two or more races	4
% race and/or ethnicity unknown	3
% International/nonresident	10

STUDENT SUCCESS

% first-to-second year retention	97
% six-year graduation	85
% six-year graduation for underrepresented minority groups	78
% first-years who live on campus	97
% undergraduates who live on campus	53
full-time faculty	1,075
full-time minority faculty	317
student-faculty ratio	20:1

Popular majors Engineering, Business/Marketing, Computer and Information Sciences, Biological/Life Sciences, Physical Sciences

Multicultural student clubs and organizations Black Student Recruitment Team, Hispanic Recruitment Team, Women's Recruitment Team, GTIA, African American Student Union, National Pan-Hellenic Council, Georgia Tech Society of Black Engineers, AIPFA, GT Society of Hispanic Professional Engineers, GT Society of Women Engineers

AFFORDABILITY

Cost of Attendance

tuition	in-state: $10,008; out-of-state: $30,604
required fees	$2,410
room and board	$11,492

Financial Aid

total institutional scholarships/grants	$38,543,137
% of students with financial need	49
% of students with need awarded any financial aid	94
% of students with need awarded any need-based scholarship or grant aid	91
% of students with need whose need was fully met	24
% Pell Grant recipients among first-years	14
average aid package	$13,854
average student loan debt upon graduation	$32,169

ADMISSIONS

# of applicants	30,529
% admitted	26
SAT Critical Reading	640-730
SAT Math	680-770
SAT Writing	640-730
ACT Composite	32
SAT/ACT optional	no
average HS GPA	4.03

DEADLINES

regular application closing date	1/1
early decision plan	no
application closing date	n/a
early action plan	yes
application closing date	10/15
application fee	$75
application fee online	$75
fee waiver for applicants with financial need	yes

Georgia State University

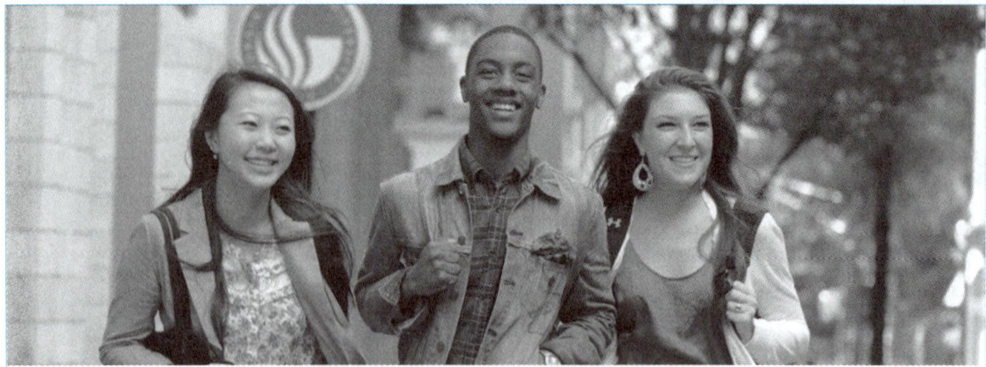

Georgia State University
PO Box 4009
Atlanta, GA 30302
Ph: (404) 413-2500
admissions@gsu.edu
www.gsu.edu

With seven campuses throughout metro Atlanta, the university provides its world-class faculty and more than 50,000 students with unsurpassed connections to the opportunities available in one of the 21st century's great global cities. A national leader in graduating students from diverse backgrounds, Georgia State provides a rich experience with award-winning housing, hundreds of student clubs and organizations, and one of the most diverse student bodies in the country. Students, faculty and alumni enjoy a unique campus personality and culture based on ambition, hard work, dedication and perseverance. At Georgia State's Perimeter College, students can enjoy one of Perimeter's five community campuses or choose an online experience. Perimeter has over 30 pathways to earn an associate degree.

Special Admissions Policy **Perimeter College at Georgia State University**

Perimeter College consists of five campuses in the metro Atlanta area. The college is the major provider of associate degrees and student transfer opportunities in Georgia and a gateway to higher education, easing students' entry into college-level study.

Through the college, Georgia State serves the largest number of dual enrollment, international, online, transfer and first-time freshman students in the University System of Georgia.

Scholarship and Financial Aid **Georgia State Scholarships**

Georgia State students are eligible for a number of scholarships, including:

Centennial Merit - These awards range from $500 to $3,000. No application is required. Students who apply to Georgia State's Atlanta Campus no later than March 1 are automatically considered.

Goizueta Scholarships - These scholarships are for students of Hispanic/Latino origin who attend Georgia State University. Each year, 24 students from the Atlanta Campus will receive a $10,000 scholarship, renewable for up to four years and 24 students from Perimeter College will receive a $3,600, renewable for up to two years. Students must first apply to Georgia State on or before February 6 and then apply for this scholarship on or before February 13.

First Year Programs and Transition **Student Success Programs**

Georgia State has the staff, resources and systems to help students grow, learn and achieve their goals. See why U.S. News and World Report ranked Georgia State No. 4 in the nation, behind only Arizona State, Stanford and Massachusetts Institute of Technology, for the innovations it has made to give all students an outstanding learning experience.

To learn more, go to: http://success.students.gsu.edu.

Student Life and Support **Clubs and Athletics**

With over 400 student organizations, Georgia State has many ways for students to get involved. The Multicultural Center offers many programs to promote student success. To learn more, go to http://multicultural.gsu.edu.

The Latino Student Services and Outreach (LASSO) is a very popular group that is a unit under the area of Student Retention and Undergraduate Studies at Georgia State University. The primary function of LASSO is to promote an inclusive community that enhances the success of Latino students.Learn more at: http://success.students.gsu.edu/latino-outreach.

To learn more about all of the clubs and activities, go to: http://campuslife.gsu.edu.

And to learn more about Georgia State's new Football Stadium and the Athletics Department, go to: http://georgiastatesports.com

Fast Facts

STUDENT DIVERSITY

# undergraduates	44,485
% male/female	42/58
% first-generation college	25
% American Indian or Alaskan Native	<1
% Asian	14
% Black or African American	43
% Hispanic/Latino	10
% Native Hawaiian or Pacific Islander	<1
% White	32
% two or more races	6
% race and/or ethnicity unknown	4
% International/nonresident	2

STUDENT SUCCESS

% first-to-second year retention	83
% six-year graduation	53
% six-year graduation for underrepresented minority groups	54
% first-years who live on campus	55
% undergraduates who live on campus	20
full-time faculty	1,336
full-time minority faculty	389
student-faculty ratio	21:1

Popular majors Biological Science, Computer Science, Psychology, Nursing, Interdisciplinary Studies, Psychology, Marketing, Political Science, Criminal Justice and Sociology

Multicultural student clubs and organizations African Students Association, Chinese Student Union, Filipino Student Association, Haitian Student Association, Indian Student Association, Latin American Student Association, Progress Organization of Liberian Students, Saudi Student Association, Turkish Cultural and Student Association and more.

AFFORDABILITY

Cost of Attendance

tuition	$8,730
required fees	$2,128
room and board	$9,394

Financial Aid

total institutional scholarships/grants	$7,859,431
% of students with financial need	73
% of students with need awarded any financial aid	94
% of students with need awarded any need-based scholarship or grant aid	84
% of students with need whose need was fully met	8
% Pell Grant recipients among first-years	52
average aid package	$13,276
average student loan debt upon graduation	$29,606

ADMISSIONS

# of applicants	18,981
% admitted	52
SAT Critical Reading	500-590
SAT Math	500-590
SAT Writing	n/a
ACT Composite	25
SAT/ACT optional	no
average HS GPA	3.5

DEADLINES

regular application closing date	3/1
early decision plan	n/a
application closing date	n/a
early action plan	yes
application closing date	11/15
application fee	$60
application fee online	$60
fee waiver for applicants with financial need	yes

Columbia College Chicago

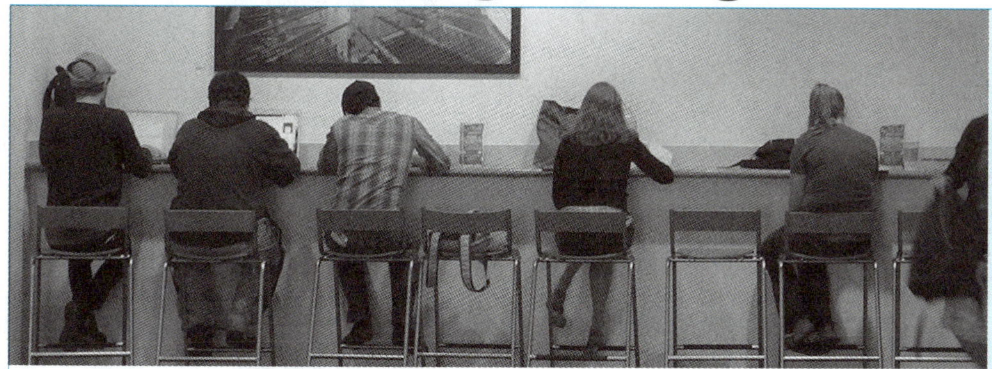

Columbia College Chicago is a creative liberal arts college focused on rigorous academics, hands-on learning, collaboration and career preparation. With more than 120 years of deep experience, we encourage students to take creative risks, develop an authentic voice and author the culture of their time. Columbia offers an inclusive learning community and an educational philosophy that weds theory with practice. Columbia gives students the opportunity to practice and perfect their craft from day one while grounding them in a liberal arts curriculum. Our location in Chicago—one of the most vibrant, forward-thinking cities in the world—provides students access to an array of cultural and professional experiences, and our award-winning faculty of working professionals prepare graduates for successful careers and leadership roles in their field.

Pre-College Prep & Outreach **Center for Community Arts Partnerships**

The Center for Community Arts Partnerships, which has played an integral role at Columbia since 1998, oversees a variety of college-community partnerships in the arts. Two of its initiatives, Project AIM and Community Schools, are committed to building meaningful, sustainable partnerships by uniting the college, public schools, and the local community. It is through these unique relationships that all partners are able to create innovative arts programming that builds stronger schools and neighborhoods. Under the auspices of the Center for Community Arts Partnerships, Columbia College also offers a graduate concentration in Arts in Youth and Community Development.

Scholarship & Financial Aid **Scholarships**

Columbia offers a number of scholarships to both incoming and continuing students. Each of these scholarships is awarded based on a unique set of criteria which may include some combination of financial need, academic achievement and creative merit.

Columbia College Chicago
600 S. Michigan Ave.
Chicago, IL 60605
Ph: (312) 369-7130
admissions@colum.edu
www.colum.edu

Fast Facts

STUDENT DIVERSITY

# undergraduates	7,312
% male/female	42/58
% first-generation college	n/a
% American Indian or Alaskan Native	<1
% Asian	4
% Black or African American	13
% Hispanic/Latino	14
% Native Hawaiian or Pacific Islander	<1
% White	54
% two or more races	4
% race and/or ethnicity unknown	5
% International/nonresident	5

STUDENT SUCCESS

% first-to-second year retention	70
% six-year graduation	45
% six-year graduation for underrepresented minority groups	n/a
% first-years who live on campus	n/a
% undergraduates who live on campus	34
full-time faculty	374
full-time minority faculty	n/a
student-faculty ratio	12:1

Popular majors Film & Video, Art & Design, Photography, Theatre, Writing

Multicultural student clubs and organizations Asian Student Organization, Black Student Union, Common Ground, Latino Alliance, Black Actors Guild,National Association of Hispanic Journalists,Hillel, American Sign Language Club

AFFORDABILITY

Cost of Attendance

tuition	$25,580
required fees	$372
room and board	$13,630

Financial Aid

total institutional scholarships/grants	$40,400,000
% of students with financial need	79
% of students with need awarded any financial aid	90
% of students with need awarded any need-based scholarship or grant aid	n/a
% of students with need whose need was fully met	n/a
% Pell Grant recipients among first-years	n/a
average aid package	$14,152
average student loan debt upon graduation	n/a

ADMISSIONS

# of applicants	9,509
% admitted	92
SAT Critical Reading	n/a
SAT Math	n/a
SAT Writing	n/a
ACT Composite	23
SAT/ACT optional	yes
average HS GPA	3.28

DEADLINES

regular application closing date	rolling
early decision plan	n/a
application closing date	n/a
early action plan	n/a
application closing date	n/a
application fee	$50
application fee online	$50
fee waiver for applicants with financial need	yes

Elmhurst College

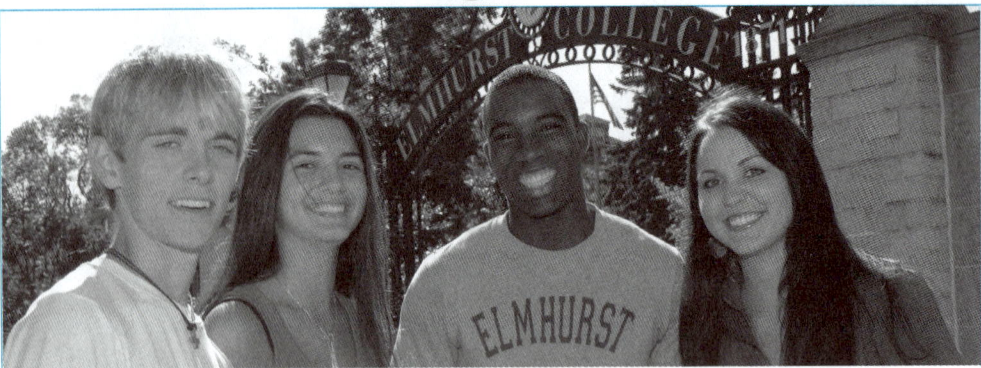

Located in suburban Chicago, Elmhurst College combines the close-knit community of a small school with the unlimited opportunities of a world-class city a short train ride away. Elmhurst is among the top colleges and best values in the Midwest, according to college guides like *U.S. News & World Report* and *Money* magazine. And we make college affordable by awarding some type of financial aid to 100% of our new students.

Scholarship & Financial Aid **Scholarships**

Elmhurst is committed to making the Elmhurst Experience an affordable option. That's why 100% of our new students receive financial aid, including grants and scholarships that don't have to be repaid. We even offer a $2,000 grant, the American Dream Grant, to first-generation college students (and can be added to a merit scholarship).

Student Life & Support **Student Success**

Elmhurst supports your success in the classroom and beyond. Academic support services include tutoring in subjects like math, writing and study skills, while the Steps to Success program provides guidance for students who are having academic difficulty. The Office of Intercultural Education promotes an awareness of different cultural perspectives through art exhibits, lectures, retreats and more. And our career-focused centers will connect you with professional opportunities like internships to prepare you for a dynamic career.

Elmhurst College
190 Prospect Avenue
Elmhurst, IL 60126
Ph: (630) 617-3400
admit@elmhurst.edu
www.elmhurst.edu

Fast Facts

STUDENT DIVERSITY

# undergraduates	2,856
% male/female	46/54
% first-generation college	28
% American Indian or Alaskan Native	<1
% Asian	6
% Black or African American	5
% Hispanic/Latino	16
% Native Hawaiian or Pacific Islander	<1
% White	67
% two or more races	3
% race and/or ethnicity unknown	n/a
% International/nonresident	1

STUDENT SUCCESS

% first-to-second year retention	84
% six-year graduation	74
% six-year graduation for underrepresented minority groups	51
% first-years who live on campus	61
% undergraduates who live on campus	40
full-time faculty	149
full-time minority faculty	17
student-faculty ratio	14:1

Popular majors Business, Education, Health Sciences, Nursing, Music, Psychology, Biology
Multicultural student clubs and organizations Black Student Union, H.A.B.L.A.M.O.S., International Organizations, Asian Club, Let's Talk About Gender, Muslim Student Association, NAACP, Queer Straight Alliance

AFFORDABILITY

Cost of Attendance

tuition	$36,370
required fees	$475
room and board	$10,326

Financial Aid

total institutional scholarships/grants	$45,000,000
% of students with financial need	75
% of students with need awarded any financial aid	100
% of students with need awarded any need-based scholarship or grant aid	100
% of students with need whose need was fully met	n/a
% Pell Grant recipients among first-years	27
average aid package	$25,830
average student loan debt upon graduation	$26,000

ADMISSIONS

# of applicants	3,528
% admitted	70
SAT Critical Reading	460-600
SAT Math	450-630
SAT Writing	450-590
ACT Composite	23
SAT/ACT optional	no
average HS GPA	3.4

DEADLINES

regular application closing date	rolling
early decision plan	n/a
application closing date	n/a
early action plan	yes
application closing date	11/1
application fee	$0
application fee online	$0
fee waiver for applicants with financial need	n/a

Illinois State University

Illinois State University
Campus Box 4000
Normal, IL 61790
Ph: (309) 438-8393
Admissions@IllinoisState.edu
www.illinoisstate.edu

Illinois State University is a top-100 public university located in a top-ranked college town that offers students the resources of a large institution with the personalized focus of a small school community. As a university that focuses on individual attention, we are committed to meeting the needs of our diverse student body by fostering an inclusive environment characterized by cultural understanding, ethical behavior, and social justice. Illinois State University is committed to building bridges between groups and to celebrate diversity within our faculty, staff, and students.

Open House, Fly-In, Visit **You Can Do ISU**

Bring your family and explore how you'll learn, how you'll find your community, and how you'll find success as a member of our Illinois State family. Hear from campus leaders and current students, learn about scholarships and financial aid, and tour our beautiful campus. See yourself as a Redbird, and meet other future Redbirds from underrepresented and/or first generation backgrounds.

Special Admissions Policy **Application Fee Waiver**

Our $50 application fee will be waived for students who qualify for an economic hardship waiver.

Pre-College Summer Experience **Preview**

Preview is Illinois State University's two-day summer orientation program required for all incoming freshmen. While attending Preview, students will have the opportunity to meet with their academic advisor, register for classes, meet current Illinois State students and their future classmates, interact with faculty and staff from various academic departments, and receive their Redbird ID card. In addition, students will have the chance to discover the various opportunities provided at Illinois State including involvement in student organizations, volunteer opportunities, support services, and many other aspects of being a Redbird.

Academic Advising & Support **Academic Advising**

You've got questions, they've got answers! Academic advisors are here to help you navigate your intended academic path while at Illinois State University. They are a great resource that can help you plan a course schedule and choose a major, and also provide referrals to other resources and services on campus.

First-Year Experience & Transition **First Year LinC**

The First Year Learning in Communities (LinC) Seminar is an 8-week one-credit course designed to assist incoming freshman in their transition to the University in the Fall semester by providing tools to help them succeed at Illinois State. The course focuses on assisting students in their transition to college, helping students identify majors and careers, and introducing students to opportunities for campus and community involvement.

Scholarship & Financial Aid **University Scholarship**

This is a minimum $24,000 award (minimum $6,000 per year, renewable for up to four years) for new freshmen from traditionally underrepresented groups or first-generation college students who have overcome hardship in achieving their academic goals. The minimum credentials required to be invited to apply are an ACT score of at least 25 (or equivalent SAT) and a cumulative high school GPA of at least 3.4 on a 4.0 scale.

Fast Facts

STUDENT DIVERSITY

# undergraduates	18,643
% male/female	43/56
% first-generation college	n/a
% American Indian or Alaskan Native	<1
% Asian	2
% Black or African American	8
% Hispanic/Latino	10
% Native Hawaiian or Pacific Islander	<1
% White	75
% two or more races	3
% race and/or ethnicity unknown	<1
% International/nonresident	<1

STUDENT SUCCESS

% first-to-second year retention	81
% six-year graduation	72
% six-year graduation for underrepresented minority groups	62
% first-years who live on campus	98
% undergraduates who live on campus	32
full-time faculty	877
full-time minority faculty	137
student-faculty ratio	18:1

Popular majors Business/Marketing, Education, Health Professions, Social Sciences, Communications/Journalism

Multicultural student clubs and organizations Asian Pacific American Coalition, Association of Latin American Students, Black and Latin Male Movement, Black Student Union (BSU), COLORS International, Hellenic Student Association, Indian Student Association, My Brotha's Keeper, My Sister's Keeper, National Association of Colored Women's Club

AFFORDABILITY

Cost of Attendance

tuition	in-state: $11,107.50; out-of-state: $22,215
required fees	$2,455.70
room and board	$9,850

Financial Aid

total institutional scholarships/grants	$16,600,000
% of students with financial need	61
% of students with need awarded any financial aid	95
% of students with need awarded any need-based scholarship or grant aid	75
% of students with need whose need was fully met	9
% Pell Grant recipients among first-years	30
average aid package	$10,177
average student loan debt upon graduation	$23,938

ADMISSIONS

# of applicants	13,095
% admitted	80
SAT Critical Reading	n/a
SAT Math	n/a
SAT Writing	n/a
ACT Composite	24
SAT/ACT optional	n/a
average HS GPA	3.36

DEADLINES

regular application closing date	4/1
early decision plan	no
application closing date	n/a
early action plan	no
application closing date	n/a
application fee	$50
application fee online	$50
fee waiver for applicants with financial need	yes

MacMurray College

Founded in 1846, MacMurray College is a four-year, independent, residential, baccalaureate college with a strong liberal arts tradition. For the past 170 years, MacMurray has been committed to preparing graduates for satisfying and productive professional careers, providing the tools needed for effective leadership, and encouraging individual growth throughout one's education and future endeavors. MacMurray College is a place where you will matter.

Open House, Fly-In, Visit **Campus Visits**

At MacMurray, campus visits matter. Visiting allows you to make connections, explore your interests, and get a glimpse of what it means to be a Highlander. Students may join us for one of our Open House events or schedule a personalized campus visit. Students should contact the Office of Admissions to schedule a visit or online at www.mac.edu/visit.

Scholarship & Financial Aid **Academic Achievement Scholarships**

Academic Achievement Scholarships range from $12,000 to $20,000 per year based on high school academic achievement. Students in the top 1%, valedictorians, and salutatorians with a 30 ACT are eligible for full-tuition. Eagle Scouts, Gold Award recipients, Summit Award recipients, and youth and young adult leaders of the United Methodist Church qualify for one scholarship level higher.

Summer Bridge & Orientation **Highlander Orientation**

All first-year students who plan to attend MacMurray College will attend Highlander Orientation during the summer prior to the start of their first semester. At Highlander Orientation, students meet their future classmates, learn what it means to be a Highlander and member of the MacFam, get their Mac ID, meet with an academic advisor, are introduced to the Mac360 program, and walk away with their fall class schedule.

First-Year Experience & Transition **First-Year Program & Seminar**

The First-Year Program encourages new students to get involved in the intellectual and social community of the College. As a part of the program, each first-year student is enrolled in a First-Year Seminar that introduces the essential elements of college coursework. In this course students write, speak, perform research, work with appropriate media, and interact with professors and fellow students at a college level performance. First-Year Seminar encourages students to develop a greater sense of intellectual and social community through engaged learning.

MacMurray College
Office of Admissions
447 East College Avenue
Jacksonville, IL 62650
Ph: (217) 479-7056
admissions@mac.edu
www.mac.edu

Fast Facts

STUDENT DIVERSITY

# undergraduates	552
% male/female	50/50
% first-generation college	n/a
% American Indian or Alaskan Native	<1
% Asian	<1
% Black or African American	10
% Hispanic/Latino	6
% Native Hawaiian or Pacific Islander	<1
% White	76
% two or more races	3
% race and/or ethnicity unknown	5
% International/nonresident	<1

STUDENT SUCCESS

% first-to-second year retention	67
% six-year graduation	33
% six-year graduation for underrepresented minority groups	n/a
% first-years who live on campus	94
% undergraduates who live on campus	74
full-time faculty	39
full-time minority faculty	3
student-faculty ratio	13:1

Popular majors Criminal Justice, Business, Nursing, Biology, Social Work

Multicultural student clubs and organizations American Sign Language Club (ASL), Belles Lettres, BACCHUS, Business Club, Campus Activities Board, Council for Exceptional Children, Newman Club, Student Nurses Association, etc.

AFFORDABILITY

Cost of Attendance

tuition	$25,340
required fees	$760
room and board	$8,925

Financial Aid

total institutional scholarships/grants	$6,033,000
% of students with financial need	90
% of students with need awarded any financial aid	100
% of students with need awarded any need-based scholarship or grant aid	99
% of students with need whose need was fully met	20
% Pell Grant recipients among first-years	49
average aid package	$21,500
average student loan debt upon graduation	$40,497

ADMISSIONS

# of applicants	1,238
% admitted	58
SAT Critical Reading	n/a
SAT Math	n/a
SAT Writing	n/a
ACT Composite	21
SAT/ACT optional	no
average HS GPA	3.42

DEADLINES

regular application closing date	rolling
early decision plan	n/a
application closing date	n/a
early action plan	n/a
application closing date	n/a
application fee	n/a
application fee online	n/a
fee waiver for applicants with financial need	no

Monmouth College

Monmouth College
700 East Broadway
Monmouth, IL 61462
Ph: (800) 747-2687
admissions@monmouthcollege.edu
www.monmouthcollege.edu

Founded in 1853 by pioneering Presbyterians, Monmouth College is dedicated to serving students from all backgrounds, including first generation college students. Currently, 29% of our students identify as first generation college students. As an institution, we believe our mission statement supports our efforts to continually improve the success of our students. We believe Monmouth College offers a high-quality and engaging environment that prepares first generation college students to excel in learning, leadership, and service. Through a variety of measures, students receive the challenge and support to succeed academically and socially at Monmouth.

Scholars & Leadership **Summer Opportunity for Intellectual Activity (SOFIA)**

SOFIA is a unique opportunity for incoming students to gain substantive undergraduate research experience through highly personalized mentoring by Monmouth College faculty members. There are opportunities to deepen focus within your major and discover new interests through engagement in cross-disciplinary collaboration with students and faculty members in an intensive on-campus setting. You will present the research in poster sessions and oral presentations giving you an accelerated start to your academic and intellectual future at Monmouth College. Spanning a variety of academic departments, some recent SOFIA projects include Mathematical Modeling with High-Speed Imagery, Social Behavior in Urban and Rural Coffee Shops, Mapping Lightning, Sensory Abilities of Brown Recluse Spiders, and many more. Students earn a $500 stipend, as well as room and board for three-weeks of SOFIA work.

Scholars & Leadership **The James and Sybil Stockdale Fellows Program**

The James and Sybil Stockdale Fellows Program is the most prestigious scholarship, leadership and enrichment program at Monmouth College. Stockdale Fellows participate in a comprehensive four-year leadership development program that includes the following program components: Stockdale Fellows Leadership Retreat, Stockdale Fellows Leadership Training Program, Curricular and co-curricular involvement, Scots Mentoring Program, Service to the local community, Service to the larger community, and Educational enrichment opportunities.

Academic Advising & Support **Teaching and Learning Center**

The Teaching and Learning Center's mission is to promote intellectual engagement, cultivate critical thinking and foster academic success. Students have access to tutoring services, academic coaching, and writing assistance.

Mentoring **Scots Success Mentoring Program**

Our Scots Success Mentoring Program offers the opportunity for new students to partner with a peer mentor. Students communicate with their mentor throughout the entire year as they acquire the skills needed to become successful in college. This program aims to educate students about on and off campus resources, help students network, enable students to feel comfortable and successful on campus, and to allow students to make a home at Monmouth College.

Fast Facts

STUDENT DIVERSITY

# undergraduates	1,100
% male/female	49/51
% first-generation college	29
% American Indian or Alaskan Native	<1
% Asian	2
% Black or African American	10
% Hispanic/Latino	10
% Native Hawaiian or Pacific Islander	<1
% White	61
% two or more races	3
% race and/or ethnicity unknown	6
% International/nonresident	7

STUDENT SUCCESS

% first-to-second year retention	71
% six-year graduation	59
% six-year graduation for underrepresented minority groups	56
% first-years who live on campus	98
% undergraduates who live on campus	95
full-time faculty	88
full-time minority faculty	4
student-faculty ratio	11:1

Popular majors Business Administration, Exercise Science, Psychology, Elementary Education, Biology/Biochemistry

Multicultural student clubs and organizations Umoja (Unity), ColorfulVoices of Praise (CVoP), Gospel Choir International Club, Raíces, LGBTQIA-Spectrum

AFFORDABILITY

Cost of Attendance

tuition	$36,400
required fees	$195
room and board	$8,620

Financial Aid

total institutional scholarships/grants	$9,626,393
% of students with financial need	81
% of students with need awarded any financial aid	99
% of students with need awarded any need-based scholarship or grant aid	81
% of students with need whose need was fully met	n/a
% Pell Grant recipients among first-years	38
average aid package	n/a
average student loan debt upon graduation	$32,500

ADMISSIONS

# of applicants	2,700
% admitted	60
SAT Critical Reading	490-540
SAT Math	470-510
SAT Writing	480-570
ACT Composite	23
SAT/ACT optional	n/a
average HS GPA	3.34

DEADLINES

regular application closing date	rolling
early decision plan	n/a
application closing date	rolling
early action plan	n/a
application closing date	rolling
application fee	$0
application fee online	$0
fee waiver for applicants with financial need	n/a

Northwestern University

Northwestern a world-class, private, research university is committed to excellent teaching, innovative research, and the personal and intellectual growth of its students. Northwestern's international reputation and open community draw talented students from diverse social, ethnic, and economic backgrounds. Six undergraduate schools offer over 190 academic majors, minors, certificates and concentrations and more than 4,100 undergraduate courses. Northwestern's 8,000 undergraduates experience a vibrant student life with more than 450+ organizations to choose from and 19 Big Ten athletic teams to cheer for. Committed to college affordability and access, Northwestern offers need-based financial aid, meeting 100% of demonstrated need for admitted students throughout four years of college.

Student Life & Support **Student Enrichment Services (SES)**

Student Enrichment Services (SES) works with low-income and first-generation students to enhance their academic success, personal development, and professional growth. Through campus-wide partnerships, SES builds an inclusive Northwestern community by engaging students and their allies with programming and dialogue.

Student Life & Support **Quest Scholars (first gen. network)**

The Quest Scholars Network has a two-fold mission: to both create a community of low-income students on campus and to help give opportunities to low income students at Northwestern and in high schools.

Summer Bridge & Orientation **McCormick School of Engineering - EXCEL**

EXCEL is a five-week program that recruits incoming engineering freshmen who have demonstrated a commitment to diversity issues and encourages group bonding. The program's purpose is to build a cultural community of support among future leaders in the field of engineering. During their five weeks on campus, the students live in dorms and attend specialized academic classes and participate in leadership activities.

Summer Bridge & Orientation **Summer Academic Workshop (SAW)**

Multicultural Student Affairs and the Associate Provost for Undergraduate Education present a two-week program that provides new students with an opportunity to strengthen writing skills across the university curriculum and develop a supportive social network for the next four years. Since 1966, SAW has invited over 1,400 students to campus.

First-Year Experience & Transition **1st year experience**

The First-Year Experience area within the Office of New Student and Family Programs is responsible for providing programs, processes, and communication that will help to enrich the first year for students at Northwestern. In collaboration with various departments, offices, and academic areas, Northwestern strives to support students throughout their transition to the community, including social and academic transition.

Scholarship & Financial Aid **Special admission policy need based aid**

Northwestern University offers financial assistance to students on the basis of demonstrated need. Northwestern is among a small group of private institutions that continue to meet 100% of demonstrated institutional financial need of applicants.

Open House, Fly-in, Visit **Fly-In Program for admitted students**

Each year, the Office of Undergraduate Admissions provides the opportunity to a select group of students allowing them to visit campus during one of the Open House events for admitted students. Students visit campus, stay overnight and learn about university life.

Northwestern University
633 Clark St
Evanston, IL 60208
Ph: (847) 491-3741
ug-admission@northwestern.edu
www.northwestern.edu

Fast Facts

STUDENT DIVERSITY

# undergraduates	8,353
% male/female	50/50
% first-generation college	10
% American Indian or Alaskan Native	<1
% Asian	18
% Black or African American	8
% Hispanic/Latino	12
% Native Hawaiian or Pacific Islander	<1
% White	49
% two or more races	5
% race and/or ethnicity unknown	2
% International/nonresident	10

STUDENT SUCCESS

% first-to-second year retention	98
% six-year graduation	94
% six-year graduation for underrepresented minority groups	n/a
% first-years who live on campus	100
% undergraduates who live on campus	53
full-time faculty	1,479
full-time minority faculty	267
student-faculty ratio	7:1

Popular majors Economics, Psychology, Journalism, Engineering, Theater, Music, Computer Science

Multicultural student clubs and organizations
For Members Only: Black Student Alliance, Alianza: Hispanic/ Latino Student Alliance, Rainbow Alliance, Mixed Race Student Coalition, Soul4Real, Muslim-Cultural Students Association, Northwestern University Quest Scholars Network, ReFresh Dance Group, Promote 360, Out Da Box Improvisation Group

AFFORDABILITY

Cost of Attendance

tuition	$54,219
required fees	$446
room and board	$16,653

Financial Aid

total institutional scholarships/grants	$132,151,807
% of students with financial need	44
% of students with need awarded any financial aid	100
% of students with need awarded any need-based scholarship or grant aid	100
% of students with need whose need was fully met	100
% Pell Grant recipients among first-years	19
average aid package	$45,100
average student loan debt upon graduation	$17,896

ADMISSIONS

# of applicants	37,259
% admitted	9
SAT Critical Reading	690-760
SAT Math	710-800
SAT Writing	n/a
ACT Composite	32-34
SAT/ACT optional	no
average HS GPA	n/a

DEADLINES

regular application closing date	1/1
early decision plan	yes
application closing date	11/1
early action plan	n/a
application closing date	n/a
application fee	$75
application fee online	$75
fee waiver for applicants with financial need	yes

University of Chicago

The University of Chicago is known for its emphasis on open and rigorous inquiry. The strength of our intellectual traditions—intense critical analysis, free and lively debate, creative solutions to complex problems—rests on the students and faculty who comprise our community. Our students further their intellectual development through small seminar-style classes, research opportunities, and a 5:1 student-faculty ratio. With a strong tradition of scholarship (90 Nobel Prize winners have been affiliated with UChicago, the largest number of any American university), as well as a close community feel, UChicago is a place where bright and talented students of all backgrounds find a college home.

Pre-College Prep & Outreach **Collegiate Scholars Program**

The three-year Collegiate Scholars Program offers college-level classes and enrichment seminars free of charge to high-achieving students in Chicago public high schools. Designed to prepare students for high achievement in college, the program offers summer courses in the Humanities, Social Sciences, Mathematics, Biological Sciences, Physical Sciences, Entrepreneurship, and the Arts. During the school year, the program includes courses and events that prepare students for college, develop students' understanding of other cultures, and involve students in their communities.

Scholarship & Financial Aid **QuestBridge Partner College**

QuestBridge National College Match helps talented, low-income high school seniors gain admission and full four-year scholarships to some of the nation's most selective colleges and universities. These scholarships include zero parent contribution and meet 100% of students' demonstrated need without the use of loans. The Questbridge application is free of charge. Selection for the program is competitive and based on the applicants' academic achievement, essays, and letters of recommendation.

Scholarship & Financial Aid **Odyssey Scholarships**

The Odyssey Scholarship is awarded to students from lower income backgrounds or who are the first in their families to attend college. This scholarship meets 100% of students' financial need through grants and scholarships, without the use of loans. Odyssey Scholars also receive a summer internship or research opportunity after their first year in the College.

Academic Advising & Support **Office of Multicultural Student Affairs (OMSA)**

The Office of Multicultural Student Affairs supports the academic success of students of color at the University of Chicago, and works to build an inclusive campus community. OMSA provides students with academic support services, information on summer internships, scholarships, and fellowships for students of color. OMSA's programs focus on enriching students' experiences and encouraging cross-cultural dialogue on campus. OMSA executes its mission in collaboration with other departments within the University of Chicago.

Academic Advising & Support **Center for College Student Success**

The CCSS is committed to helping students think strategically to plan ahead and also troubleshoot the unexpected. The Center provides early academic exposure, transition support, and ongoing advising and resources to students in the College, especially those who are first in their family to attend college, who are from lower-income or under-resourced backgrounds, or who may be undocumented. CCSS Advisers help students navigate campus resources and foster an inclusive and supportive campus community that facilitates student success.

University of Chicago
5801 South Ellis Avenue
Chicago, IL 60637
Ph: (773) 702-8650
collegeadmissions@uchicago.edu
collegeadmissions.uchicago.edu

Fast Facts

STUDENT DIVERSITY

# undergraduates	5,941
% male/female	52/48
% first-generation college	n/a
% American Indian or Alaskan Native	<1
% Asian	18
% Black or African American	3
% Hispanic/Latino	11
% Native Hawaiian or Pacific Islander	<1
% White	44
% two or more races	4
% race and/or ethnicity unknown	6
% International/nonresident	12

STUDENT SUCCESS

% first-to-second year retention	99
% six-year graduation	94
% six-year graduation for underrepresented minority groups	89
% first-years who live on campus	100
% undergraduates who live on campus	56
full-time faculty	1,323
full-time minority faculty	265
student-faculty ratio	5:1

Popular majors Economics, Biological Sciences, Political Science, Mathematics, English Language/ Literature

Multicultural student clubs and organizations African and Caribbean Students Assoc., Asian Students Union, Movimiento Estudiantil Chicano de Aztlán, Muslim Students Assoc., Native American Student Assoc., Org. of Black Students, Org.n of Latin American Students (OLAS), Puerto Rican Students Org., Queers & Associates (Q&A), Students Promoting Interracial Networks (SPIN)

AFFORDABILITY

Cost of Attendance

tuition	$53,292
required fees	$1,533
room and board	$15,726

Financial Aid

total institutional scholarships/grants	$124,220,049
% of students with financial need	43
% of students with need awarded any financial aid	100
% of students with need awarded any need-based scholarship or grant aid	100
% of students with need whose need was fully met	100
% Pell Grant recipients among first-years	11
average aid package	$49,967
average student loan debt upon graduation	$23,852

ADMISSIONS

# of applicants	31,484
% admitted	8
SAT Critical Reading	730-800
SAT Math	700-800
SAT Writing	n/a
ACT Composite	32-35
SAT/ACT optional	no
average HS GPA	n/a

DEADLINES

regular application closing date	1/2
early decision plan	yes
application closing date	11/1
early action plan	yes
application closing date	11/1
application fee	$75
application fee online	$75
fee waiver for applicants with financial need	yes

University of Illinois at Chicago

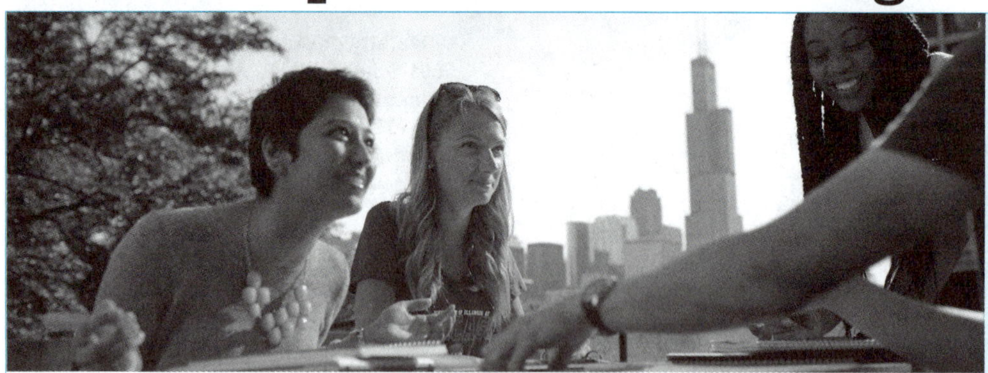

The University of Illinois at Chicago is Chicago's university—big, diverse and alive. UIC is a real campus community embedded in some of Chicago's most interesting neighborhoods. Consistently ranked among the nation's most diverse and welcoming campuses, UIC is home to more than 30,000 students. UIC students have the advantage of studying in 15 different academic colleges alongside a superb faculty that discovers what others teach. This university offers a challenging, career-building education and a life-changing college experience through hundreds of academic and success programs.

Pre-College Prep and Outreach **UIC CHANCE**

The UIC - CHANCE Program was formed in 2004 to assist the campus with recruitment, retention, and graduation rates of underrepresented students. Our comprehensive programming addresses the needs of our student-body through face-to-face and online workshops which are facilitated by the (Blackboard Learning Management System). The CHANCE Program is committed to providing academic, personal, and professional assistance to students with demonstrated academic and personal needs.

Pre-College Prep and Outreach **UIC TRIO**

The goal of TRIO/ASP is to help increase the retention and graduation of low-income, first-generation college students and to foster an institutional climate supportive of their success. We seek to accomplish these goals through supportive services that foster academic achievement, personal growth and development, self-actualization, self-confidence, and leadership.

Pre-College Summer Experience **Summer College**

As a UIC Summer College student, you'll get individualized attention in small classes taught by experienced instructors. You'll improve your skills in math, writing, creative arts, computer literacy, science, studying and note-taking, and more. You'll meet other new students, make friends and study partners, connect with faculty and advisors, learn your way around the UIC campus, and discover UIC's many student resources.

Scholarship & Financial Aid **Presidential Award Program**

The PAP Scholars Program is a four-year scholarship program that promotes student success and academic excellence in collaboration with the entire UIC community. PAP Scholars participate in the PAP Academy which is comprised of Summer College and a First Year Experience. In addition, students are encouraged to participate in many opportunities, such as undergraduate research, a study abroad experience, specialized seminars facilitated by faculty liaisons, and career and graduate/professional school preparation.

Scholarship & Financial Aid **PAP Honors Scholars Program**

The PAP Honors Scholars Program is a four-year residential scholarship program that provides opportunities for academic engagement and mentoring as a member of the UIC Honors College. The PAP Honors Scholars Program promotes academic excellence within and beyond the Honors College community, connects students with Honors College Faculty Fellows and other faculty members, and fosters civic engagement and leadership. The scholarship covers four years of tuition and housing, a week-long Summer College orientation program, and a new laptop computer. Students must apply separately to the Honors College for consideration.

University of Illinois at Chicago
1200 West Harrison Suite 1100
Chicago, IL 60607
Ph: (312) 996-4350
www.uic.edu

Fast Facts

STUDENT DIVERSITY

# undergraduates	19,448
% male/female	52/48
% first-generation college	44
% American Indian or Alaskan Native	<1
% Asian	21
% Black or African American	8
% Hispanic/Latino	33
% Native Hawaiian or Pacific Islander	<1
% White	30
% two or more races	3
% race and/or ethnicity unknown	<1
% International/nonresident	5

STUDENT SUCCESS

% first-to-second year retention	81
% six-year graduation	60
% six-year graduation for underrepresented minority groups	n/a
% first-years who live on campus	39
% undergraduates who live on campus	17
full-time faculty	1,941
full-time minority faculty	465
student-faculty ratio	18:1

Popular majors Biological and Life Sciences, Psychology, Accounting, Computer Science, Kinesiology

Multicultural student clubs and organizations Asian American Students In Alliance, Black Student Union, Chinese Students and Scholars Association, Confederation of Latin American Students, DESIgn Movement, Fearless Undocumented Alliance, Filipinos in Alliance, Hellenic Students Association, Hindu Students Council, Pride

AFFORDABILITY

Cost of Attendance

tuition	in-state: $10,584; out-of-state: $23,440
required fees	$4,272
room and board	$11,342

Financial Aid

total institutional scholarships/grants	$14,775,392
% of students with financial need	85
% of students with need awarded any financial aid	75
% of students with need awarded any need-based scholarship or grant aid	85
% of students with need whose need was fully met	6
% Pell Grant recipients among first-years	58
average aid package	$14,210
average student loan debt upon graduation	$18,750

ADMISSIONS

# of applicants	19,295
% admitted	74
SAT Combined (Middle 50%)	1080-1320
ACT Composite	21-27
SAT/ACT optional	no
average HS GPA	3.1-3.7

DEADLINES

regular application closing date	1/15
early decision plan	no
application closing date	n/a
early action plan	yes
application closing date	11/1
application fee	$60
application fee online	$60
fee waiver for applicants with financial need	yes

Anderson University

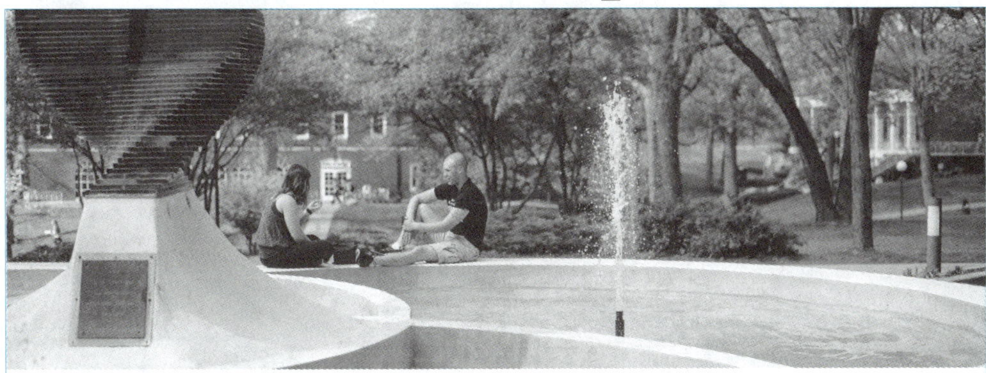

Anderson University is a private Christian college in Anderson, Indiana. Founded in 1917 by the Church of God, the university remains affiliated with its founding church and values its heritage and history. Today about 2,200 students call Anderson University home while enrolled in more than 50 undergraduate majors, as well as graduate programs in business, theology, and music education.

First-Year Experience & Transition **First-Year Experience**

The FYE program includes Raven 101, orientation, two academic courses, and a mentoring program. Each mentor group consists of 15-17 freshman students and is led by a faculty mentor as well as a student peer mentor. Mentors work with students during the first and second semester through the First-Year Seminar and the Critical Thinking Seminar to make sure that students have the most success during their First-Year Experience.

Open House, Fly-in, Visit **Discover AU**

Discover what we're all about as you walk through campus, meet faculty and staff, and learn about our programs inside the classroom and beyond. We strive to be a home base for our students, a firm foundation for whatever opportunities come their way. Find out what it feels like here and picture yourself as a Raven!

Academic Advising & Support **Educational Support Services**

Educational Support Services seeks to help students understand and negotiate the institution's academic rules, regulations, and requirements. Our Educational Support Services staff also coordinates with the Kissinger Learning Center, which offers FREE group and individualized tutoring programs to help in writing, reading, and learning strategies.

Scholarship & Financial Aid **Student Financial Services**

Never assume that you can't afford a school based on the price tag alone. Our Student Financial Services staff are eager to assist you regarding all federal, state, and university scholarships, grants, and loans you may be eligible to receive. Over 98% of AU students receive financial aid.

Mentoring **Career and Calling**

The Center for Career and Calling is here to support the university's mission to educate students for a life of faith and service in the church and society. Our staff assists in providing the tools and guidance necessary to explore, discover, and plan for a meaningful career after graduation day because getting a great education in the classroom is only part of the Anderson University student experience.

Anderson University
1100 E. Fifth Street
Anderson, IN 46012
Ph: (800) 428-6414
info@anderson.edu
www.anderson.edu

Fast Facts

STUDENT DIVERSITY	
# undergraduates	1,883
% male/female	40/60
% first-generation college	n/a
% American Indian or Alaskan Native	1
% Asian	2
% Black or African American	13
% Hispanic/Latino	2
% Native Hawaiian or Pacific Islander	0
% White	76
% two or more races	0
% race and/or ethnicity unknown	3
% International/nonresident	2
STUDENT SUCCESS	
% first-to-second year retention	78
% six-year graduation	58
% six-year graduation for underrepresented minority groups	50
% first-years who live on campus	91
% undergraduates who live on campus	63
full-time faculty	116
full-time minority faculty	13
student-faculty ratio	12:1

Popular majors Business, Nursing, Education, Dance, Athletic Training

Multicultural student clubs and organizations Asian Student Association, Anderson University Gospel Choir, Black Student Association, Global International Student Association, Hispanic Latino Student Association, PAK Men's Social Club

AFFORDABILITY	
Cost of Attendance	
tuition	$28,510
required fees	$150
room and board	$9,550
Financial Aid	
total institutional scholarships/grants	n/a
% of students with financial need	n/a
% of students with need awarded any financial aid	n/a
% of students with need awarded any need-based scholarship or grant aid	n/a
% of students with need whose need was fully met	n/a
% Pell Grant recipients among first-years	n/a
average aid package	n/a
average student loan debt upon graduation	n/a
ADMISSIONS	
# of applicants	2,650
% admitted	66
SAT Critical Reading	450-550
SAT Math	460-560
SAT Writing	n/a
ACT Composite	22
SAT/ACT optional	required for FR
average HS GPA	3.364
DEADLINES	
regular application closing date	rolling
early decision plan	n/a
application closing date	n/a
early action plan	n/a
application closing date	n/a
application fee	$0
application fee online	$0
fee waiver for applicants with financial need	n/a

Indiana Wesleyan University

Indiana Wesleyan University (IWU) is an evangelical Christian comprehensive institution committed to liberal arts and professional education. *U.S. News & World Report* ranks Indiana Wesleyan University as number seven on their list of "Best Value Schools", and Affordableschools.net ranks IWU as number three on their "30 Most Inviting Yet Affordable College Dorms in America." Indiana Wesleyan University stands ready—with the resources and the passion—to equip future generations of learners with skills they will need to meet the challenges of our rapidly changing world. At IWU, diversity and inclusion are not just values; they are interwoven into the academic and social threads of our community. We are a Christ-centered academic community committed to changing the world by developing students in character, scholarship and leadership. We seek to increase access for first generation and historically underserved ethnic-minority groups through scholarship opportunities and innovative programs and initiatives. At IWU you will find community. With a 15:1 student to faculty ratio, professors are attentive to every student's academic needs. Come home to IWU!

Pre-College Prep & Outreach **IWU Near You Pre-College Programming**

The purpose of IWU Near You is to expose high school students—and their parents—to the necessary Pre-college survival skills needed to ensure college entry and first year success. IWU Near You serves as a resource for local constituents, ensuring that students and parents can navigate the college search environment successfully. The modules will address: financial aid literacy, keys to navigating college environments, admissions 101, and an orientation to college academics.

First-Year Experience & Transition **TRIO Student Support Services**

The Indiana Wesleyan University TRiO Student Support Services (SSS) Program supports eligible students in transition from high school through college graduation, by motivating them toward academic, personal, and social self-determination. TRIO supports students by providing financial assistance, one-on-one tutoring, free printing, and a personal advising counselor. TRIO also offers workshops that address studying skills, time management, financial management, and more.

Scholars & Leadership **Luther Lee Scholars**

The Luther Lee Scholars is a cohort based learning community open to first generation students, low-income, or racial/ethnic minority students. Together, scholars engage in an immersive academic and co-curricular experience that develops them as leaders in reconciliation and justice. Selected recipients receive full tuition scholarships to fund their education. Through engagement with the LLS community, faculty and staff, students receive opportunities to grow together as intercultural leaders both at IWU and in their own communities.

Apply and learn more at: indwes.edu/luther-lee-scholars

Indiana Wesleyan University
4201 S. Washington St.
Marion, IN 46953
Ph: (866) 468-6498
www.indwes.edu

Fast Facts

STUDENT DIVERSITY	
# undergraduates	n/a
% male/female	33/67
% first-generation college	21
% American Indian or Alaskan Native	<1
% Asian	<1
% Black or African American	17
% Hispanic/Latino	3
% Native Hawaiian or Pacific Islander	<1
% White	77
% two or more races	1
% race and/or ethnicity unknown	n/a
% International/nonresident	n/a
STUDENT SUCCESS	
% first-to-second year retention	84
% six-year graduation	65
% six-year graduation for underrepresented minority groups	60
% first-years who live on campus	97
% undergraduates who live on campus	n/a
full-time faculty	163
full-time minority faculty	16
student-faculty ratio	14:1

Popular majors Nursing, Education, Business, Psychology, Social Work, Ministry
Multicultural student clubs and organizations
n/a

AFFORDABILITY	
Cost of Attendance	
tuition	$24,102
required fees	n/a
room and board	n/a
Financial Aid	
total institutional scholarships/grants	$30,855,562
% of students with financial need	78
% of students with need awarded any financial aid	99
% of students with need awarded any need-based scholarship or grant aid	69
% of students with need whose need was fully met	n/a
% Pell Grant recipients among first-years	35
average aid package	$20,995
average student loan debt upon graduation	n/a
ADMISSIONS	
# of applicants	3,589
% admitted	66
SAT Critical Reading	480-590
SAT Math	480-590
SAT Writing	460-580
ACT Composite	21-26
SAT/ACT optional	no
average HS GPA	3.3
DEADLINES	
regular application closing date	rolling
early decision plan	no
application closing date	n/a
early action plan	no
application closing date	n/a
application fee	$0
application fee online	$0
fee waiver for applicants with financial need	no

Saint Mary's College

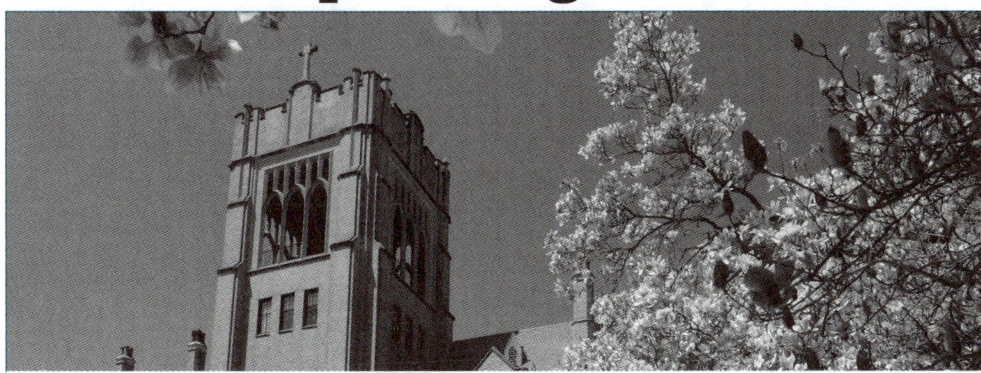

Saint Mary's College, a private, Catholic, residential college, has been educating women in the liberal arts tradition for over 170 years. As one of the nation's oldest women's colleges, Saint Mary's is an academic community in which women develop their talents and prepare to make a difference in the world. Founded by the Sisters of the Holy Cross in 1844, Saint Mary's seeks to provide academic, social and spiritual growth. Located near the city of South Bend and directly across the street from the University of Notre Dame, the Saint Mary's community includes 1,496 students from 40 states and 10 foreign countries.

Scholarship & Financial Aid **Holy Cross Grants**

Saint Mary's offers Holy Cross grants, ranging up to $5,000/year, to Pell eligible, first generation students. They also offer merit-based scholarships to 100% of incoming students that range from $10,000 to $25,000 per year.

Summer Bridge & Orientation **Belles Connect**

Student Involvement and Multicultural Programs offers Belles Connect, a unique opportunity for incoming first year students to ease into campus life. The program introduces students to Saint Mary's before the official Welcome Week that precedes the start of classes. Participants learn how to navigate the campus, explore Saint Mary's extraordinary heritage, and are introduced to support services.

Academic Courses & Service Learning **College Academy of Tutoring Program (CAT)**

CAT was formed in 2006 to meet the needs of at-risk students in the South Bend area. Saint Mary's students partner with Title 1 elementary schools; working as tutors, teacher's assistants, reading partners and special program coordinators. The program also provides the partner school with physical resources (school supplies, clothing, software and more), training and cultural events for parents, staff and community members.

Student Life & Support **Offices of Student Involvement and Multicultural Programs**

The Offices of Student Involvement and Multicultural Programs provide solid evidence of Saint Mary's commitment to supporting the inclusion of women of all races, ethnicities and cultures. SIMS advances the understanding of diversity at all levels by providing educational programs and services, and serving as a support network for all students. The office maintains a resource library of novels, scholarship information, art, films and literature on multicultural topics. It works with faculty and Academic Affairs to help ensure each student's successful academic and social adjustments to Saint Mary's. The Offices provide a social and professional gathering place.

Saint Mary's College
122 Le Mans Hall
Notre Dame, IN 46556
Ph: (574) 284-4587
admission@saintmarys.edu
www.saintmarys.edu

Fast Facts

STUDENT DIVERSITY

# undergraduates	1,496
% male/female	0/100
% first-generation college	n/a
% American Indian or Alaskan Native	<1
% Asian	2
% Black or African American	2
% Hispanic/Latino	11
% Native Hawaiian or Pacific Islander	<1
% White	77
% two or more races	3
% race and/or ethnicity unknown	3
% International/nonresident	2

STUDENT SUCCESS

% first-to-second year retention	86
% six-year graduation	80
% six-year graduation for underrepresented minority groups	72
% first-years who live on campus	98
% undergraduates who live on campus	88
full-time faculty	144
full-time minority faculty	17
student-faculty ratio	10:1

Popular majors Elementary Education and Teaching, Nursing Science, Biology, Communication Studies, Business, Psychology

Multicultural student clubs and organizations Around the World Club, Black Student Union, Chinese Cultural Club, Diverse Student Leadership Conference, Korean Club, La Fuerza, Pacific Islanders and Asian Club (PAC), SMC Irish Club, Straight and Gay Alliance

AFFORDABILITY

Cost of Attendance

tuition	$39,980
required fees	$820
room and board	$12,100

Financial Aid

total institutional scholarships/grants	$34,000,000
% of students with financial need	57
% of students with need awarded any financial aid	99
% of students with need awarded any need-based scholarship or grant aid	55
% of students with need whose need was fully met	19
% Pell Grant recipients among first-years	23
average aid package	$29,850
average student loan debt upon graduation	$32,898

ADMISSIONS

# of applicants	1,830
% admitted	78
SAT Critical Reading	520-630
SAT Math	500-630
SAT Writing	510-620
ACT Composite	26
SAT/ACT optional	no
average HS GPA	3.76

DEADLINES

regular application closing date	rolling
early decision plan	yes
application closing date	11/15
early action plan	n/a
application closing date	n/a
application fee	n/a
application fee online	n/a
fee waiver for applicants with financial need	n/a

University of Notre Dame

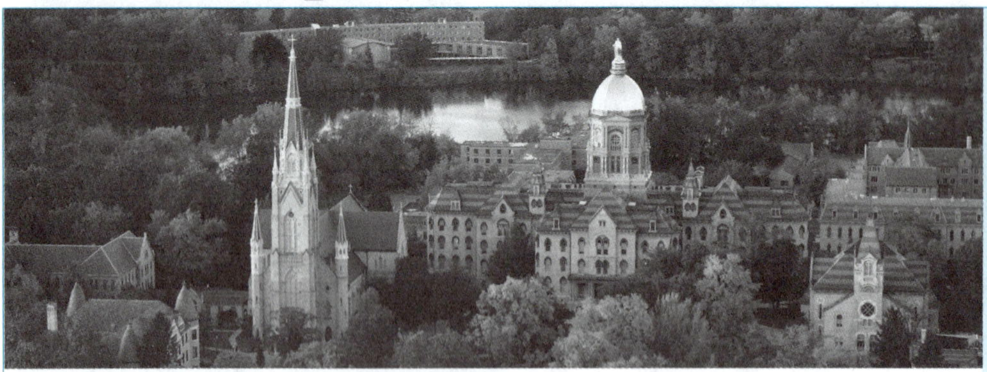

Notre Dame is a place where faith is treasured and diverse traditions are shared and respected. Our students represent all 50 states and over 74 countries. Our campus community is rich in diversity and committed to inclusion. Students travel from around the country and the world, seeking the academic excellence for which Notre Dame is known. What they find is a place where they can learn about other cultures, beliefs, and perspectives. They find a place where they can engage with peers, be supported by mentors, and conduct research with some of the foremost scholars in the world. Students are welcomed into a community where they can come together in large group activities or find the friends and space to call their own. Our students are becoming culturally competent, global citizens while studying in a community that is growing more diverse.

Pre-College Summer Experience **Notre Dame Leadership Seminars**

Notre Dame Leadership Seminars explore topics affecting the global community. The courses are centered on vibrant discussion and a robust exchange of ideas. This creates a context in which students are encouraged to examine their own conclusions and hone their own leadership capacities by improving their communications and analytical skills. Expenses for students accepted to Leadership Seminars—including transportation to and from Notre Dame—will be paid for by the University. Approximately 100 students are admitted to Leadership Seminars each year, and students are eligible to receive one college credit upon completion of the program.

Open House, Fly-In, Visit **Open House/Fly-Ins**

Notre Dame's Open House and Fly-In weekends are an opportunity for some of the most promising and talented students in the country to experience Notre Dame. These special weekends provide opportunities for students to visit Notre Dame's campus and learn more about the University, as well as the admissions and financial aid process. Students will be assigned a student host, have the opportunity to go to classes, meet students and faculty, attend workshops, and find out more about the campus community.

Special Admissions Policy **Need-Blind Admissions**

Notre Dame has a need-blind admissions policy for all U.S. citizens and permanent residents. A student's financial situation is not considered in the evaluation of his or her application. Notre Dame is committed to meeting 100% of each family's demonstrated financial need in its need-based financial aid process, which is completely separate from its admissions process.

Scholars & Leadership **AnBryce Scholars Initiative**

The AnBryce Scholars Initiative provides intellectual and social opportunities for underserved youth. Selected scholars are the first in their families to attend college. They also have demonstrated great promise in the face of challenging socioeconomic circumstances. AnBryce Scholars are offered enrichment programming that includes opportunities to connect with professionals and faculty from a range of fields.

Scholars & Leadership **Latino Studies Scholars Program**

This merit-based, leadership scholarship is designed to attract and shape key leaders working to support and empower Latino communities. The scholarship was created by the Institute for Latino Studies (ILS) as part of its mission to advance the understanding of the fastest growing and youngest population in the United States and the Catholic Church. ILS strengthens Notre Dame's mission to prepare transformative leaders in education, the professions, the arts, economic and civic participation, faith, and family life among Latinos and all members of our society.

University of Notre Dame Admissions
220 Main Building
Notre Dame, IN 46556
Ph: (574) 631-7505
www.nd.edu

Fast Facts

STUDENT DIVERSITY

# undergraduates	8,530
% male/female	53/47
% first-generation college	22
% American Indian or Alaskan Native	<1
% Asian	5
% Black or African American	4
% Hispanic/Latino	11
% Native Hawaiian or Pacific Islander	<1
% White	69
% two or more races	5
% race and/or ethnicity unknown	<1
% International/nonresident	6

STUDENT SUCCESS

% first-to-second year retention	98
% six-year graduation	95
% six-year graduation for underrepresented minority groups	n/a
% first-years who live on campus	100
% undergraduates who live on campus	79
full-time faculty	1,126
full-time minority faculty	194
student-faculty ratio	10:1

Popular majors Aerospace Engineering, Biology, Biochemistry, Chemical Engineering, Economics, Finance, Management Consulting, Marketing, Mechanical Engineering, Neuroscience, Political Science, Pre-Professional/Pre-Health Studies

Multicultural student clubs and organizations Asian American Association, Black Student Association, Chinese Culture Society, Diversity Council, La Alianza, Organizacion Latino Americana, Korean Student Association, Native American Student Association, Vietnamese Student Association

AFFORDABILITY

Cost of Attendance

tuition	$49,178
required fees	$507
room and board	$14,358

Financial Aid

total institutional scholarships/grants	$138,187,774
% of students with financial need	45
% of students with need awarded any financial aid	100
% of students with need awarded any need-based scholarship or grant aid	94
% of students with need whose need was fully met	100
% Pell Grant recipients among first-years	11
average aid package	$44,507
average student loan debt upon graduation	$27,237

ADMISSIONS

# of applicants	19,505
% admitted	19
SAT Critical Reading	670-760
SAT Math	680-780
SAT Writing	650-750
ACT Composite	32-35
SAT/ACT optional	no
average HS GPA	n/a

DEADLINES

regular application closing date	12/31
early decision plan	n/a
application closing date	n/a
early action plan	yes
application closing date	11/1
application fee	$75
application fee online	$75
fee waiver for applicants with financial need	yes

Grinnell College

Grinnell College
1103 Park Street
Grinnell, IA 50122
Ph: (641) 269-3600
admission@grinnell.edu
www.grinnell.edu

Founded in 1846, Grinnell College is a private, co-educational, liberal arts college that seeks to educate its students in the liberal arts through free inquiry and the open exchange of ideas. Grinnell provides a lively academic community of students and teachers of high scholarly qualifications from diverse social and cultural backgrounds. The college aims to graduate women and men who can think clearly, who can speak and write persuasively and eloquently, who can evaluate critically both their own and others' ideas, who can acquire new knowledge and who are prepared to use their knowledge and abilities to serve the common good.

Open House, Fly-In, Visit **Grinnell Diversity Travel Opportunity (GDTOP)**

Grinnell offers a fall fly-in opportunity through the Grinnell Diversity Travel Opportunity. Through GDTOP, selected students of color and/or first-generation college students are provided a fully-funded opportunity to experience life as "Grinnellians." Grinnell also invites select students of color and first-generation college students to fly-in, free of charge, to its April Admitted Student Programs.

Special Admissions Policy **Need-Blind Admission**

Grinnell is committed to need-blind admission and accessibility for academically qualified students, and thus offers significant financial aid. Grinnell meets 100 percent of demonstrated need, and awards over $30 million in financial aid every year.

Summer Bridge & Orientation **Grinnell Science Project**

Grinnell has a program for traditionally underrepresented students in the sciences called the Grinnell Science Project (GSP). This program, developed in the early 1990s to prevent students of color and/or first-generation college students from abandoning academic goals in the sciences, brings students to campus one week before New Student Orientation to introduce them to the study of science at Grinnell College.

Summer Bridge & Orientation **Peer Connections Pre-Orientation Program**

Once students deposit they are invited to participate in the Peer Connections Pre-Orientation Program (PCPOP). PCPOP introduces students to the variety of services available at Grinnell College, tutoring opportunities and pairs PCPOP participants with a currently enrolled student mentor and a faculty or staff mentor.

Student Life & Support **Office of Social Commitment**

Grinnell's Office of Social Commitment provides volunteer opportunities throughout the city of Grinnell for current students. Grinnell partners with local schools, after-school centers and programs, and with our local head start program. In addition, Grinnell assists students in seeking out and completing applications for post-graduate service opportunities with organizations such as Teach for America, AmeriCorps, Grinnell Corps and the Peace Corps.

Fast Facts

STUDENT DIVERSITY

# undergraduates	1,702
% male/female	47/53
% first-generation college	16
% American Indian or Alaskan Native	0
% Asian	7
% Black or African American	6
% Hispanic/Latino	8
% Native Hawaiian or Pacific Islander	0
% White	51
% two or more races	4
% race and/or ethnicity unknown	5
% International/nonresident	19

STUDENT SUCCESS

% first-to-second year retention	96
% six-year graduation	86
% six-year graduation for underrepresented minority groups	86
% first-years who live on campus	100
% undergraduates who live on campus	88
full-time faculty	213
full-time minority faculty	47
student-faculty ratio	9:1

Popular majors Economics, Political Science, Computer Science, Biology, English, Mathematics

Multicultural student clubs and organizations African Students Union, Asia and Asian American Association, Asian Media and Culture Club, Chalutzim, Concerned Black Students, International Students Organization, Queer People of Color, Student Organization of Latinx, Vietnamese Student Organization

AFFORDABILITY

Cost of Attendance

tuition	$50,264
required fees	$450
room and board	$12,400

Financial Aid

total institutional scholarships/grants	$48,579,289
% of students with financial need	65
% of students with need awarded any financial aid	65
% of students with need awarded any need-based scholarship or grant aid	65
% of students with need whose need was fully met	100
% Pell Grant recipients among first-years	17
average aid package	$47,561
average student loan debt upon graduation	$19,392

ADMISSIONS

# of applicants	5,850
% admitted	29
SAT Evidence-Based Reading & Writing	640-740
SAT Math	670-770
ACT Composite	30-34
SAT/ACT optional	no
average HS GPA	n/a

DEADLINES

regular application closing date	1/15
early decision plan	yes
application closing date	11/15
early action plan	n/a
application closing date	n/a
application fee	n/a
application fee online	n/a
fee waiver for applicants with financial need	yes

Loras College

Loras College
1450 Alta Vista Street
Dubuque, IA 52001
Ph: (563) 588-7236
www.loras.edu

Relating the rich liberal arts tradition to a changing world, Loras College strives to develop active learners, reflective thinkers, ethical decision makers and responsible contributors in their diverse professional, social, and religious roles. Housed on a safe, scenic campus nestled high atop the majestic bluffs of the Mississippi River in Dubuque, Iowa, Loras College offers a wide array of academic programs, extracurricular offerings, and opportunity for personal growth. We would be proud to welcome you into our circle of loyal Duhawks who will forever call our Dubuque campus home. In alignment with our social responsibility we work with students and families of first generation backgrounds to ensure all who would like to pursue higher education, are able to, and supported towards success.

Scholarship & Financial Aid **First Generation Scholars Program**

The First Generation Scholars Program offers a $1,500 scholarship and strives to support first-generation college students and their families and promote engagement, study skills, and experiential opportunities for the student to have as they successfully progress toward graduation. This program is designed to recruit and retain first-generation students (your parent(s) or guardian(s) has/have no bachelor's degree). First-generation students who opt to participate in the program are eligible for additional funds beyond their initial acceptance award. Awards are renewable with continued program participation.

Summer Bridge & Orientation **REACH Orientation**

REACH stands for Respect, Empathize, Appreciate, Connect, and Help. REACH is an early move-in orientation program for domestic students of color, first generation students, and international students. Students are welcomed to move in early before other students to meet faculty, staff, and upperclass students to help ease their transition to college.

First-Year Experience & Transition **Modes of Inquiry First Year Experience**

Modes of Inquiry (MOI) is a first year student semester long seminar experience that aids students in their transition to college. Students are grouped together and particpate in a semester long course after experiencing Launch into Loras together. Launch into Loras is a weekend long team building, and community service oriented first year welcome experience. Each MOI group is led by a faculty member and have thier coursework based off a common reading and faculty selected topics.

Academic Advising & Support **Lynch Learning Center**

Loras recognizes the dignity of persons with disabilities and challenges them to grow in our supportive environment while developing the skills associated with active learners, reflective thinkers, ethical decision makers and responsible contributors. The Lynch Learning Center offers three levels of service for students with diagnosed disabilities.

Student Life & Support **Intercultural Programs Office**

Loras College strives towards an inclusive and challenging learning environment for students, staff, and faculty by actively engaging the educational, spiritual, academic, cultural, and social fabric of campus and Dubuque community to achieve social justice. The Intercultural Programs Office administers and supports a variety of programs, as well as interpersonal activities that facilitate the adjustment of students from marginalized backgrounds to college.

Fast Facts

STUDENT DIVERSITY

# undergraduates	1,397
% male/female	52/48
% first-generation college	25
% American Indian or Alaskan Native	<1
% Asian	1
% Black or African American	2
% Hispanic/Latino	8
% Native Hawaiian or Pacific Islander	<1
% White	81
% two or more races	2
% race and/or ethnicity unknown	5
% International/nonresident	2

STUDENT SUCCESS

% first-to-second year retention	79
% six-year graduation	71
% six-year graduation for underrepresented minority groups	74
% first-years who live on campus	95
% undergraduates who live on campus	65
full-time faculty	100
full-time minority faculty	4
student-faculty ratio	13:1

Popular majors Sports Management, Accounting, Marketing, Public Relations, Elementary Education

Multicultural student clubs and organizations Black Student Union, Loras Intercultural Student Association, Spanish Club, LGBTQ Alliance

AFFORDABILITY

Cost of Attendance

tuition	$32,524
required fees	$1,660
room and board	$8,275

Financial Aid

total institutional scholarships/grants	$28,988,704
% of students with financial need	78
% of students with need awarded any financial aid	78
% of students with need awarded any need-based scholarship or grant aid	78
% of students with need whose need was fully met	90
% Pell Grant recipients among first-years	23
average aid package	$27,644
average student loan debt upon graduation	$34,775

ADMISSIONS

# of applicants	1,161
% admitted	95
SAT Critical Reading	n/a
SAT Math	n/a
SAT Writing	n/a
ACT Composite	23
SAT/ACT optional	n/a
average HS GPA	3.41

DEADLINES

regular application closing date	rolling
early decision plan	n/a
application closing date	n/a
early action plan	n/a
application closing date	n/a
application fee	$25
application fee online	n/a
fee waiver for applicants with financial need	yes

Luther College

Luther College
700 College Drive
Decorah, Iowa 52101
Ph: (563) 387-1287
admissions@luther.edu
www.luther.edu

Located in the vibrant town of Decorah in northeastern Iowa, Luther College is an undergraduate liberal arts college affiliated with the Lutheran Church (ELCA). Luther offers more than 60 majors and preprofessional programs leading to the bachelor of arts degree. By asking students to learn in many disciplines, a liberal arts education produces graduates who are aware, perceptive, critical, and creative, and it gives them the tools they need to thrive in an ever-changing world. The mission of Luther College explicitly affirms the educational, social, and civic benefits of diversity. As a community we see diversity as essential to learning. It stimulates new questions and perspectives by challenging accustomed ways of thinking and responding.

Open House, Fly-In, Visit **Fly-In Reimbursement Program**

High school seniors who have applied for admission to Luther College may qualify for our Fly-In Reimbursement Program. This includes up to $300 in air travel reimbursement, on-campus overnight accommodations with a current student, complimentary meal passes for the duration of your stay, and transportation to and from the Minneapolis-St. Paul International Airport during our fly-in visit events.

Scholarship & Financial Aid **Scholarships and Awards**

All academic scholarships and awards are based on a student's cumulative grade point average, college entrance exam scores (ACT or SAT), and class rank (if applicable). There is no separate application for these awards. Scholarships are awarded automatically to eligible students upon admission. The total amount of Luther College scholarships offered to a student are capped at the cost of tuition.

First-Year Experience & Transition **New Student Immersion Program**

The New Student Immersion orientation experiences are designed to give incoming Luther students the opportunity to build community while engaging in the natural world through experiential learning and outdoor adventure. Trips foster personal development and ease the transition to college life. Each group will be led by two current Luther students. A faculty guest will support each trip.

Academic Advising & Support **Student Academic Support Center**

The Student Academic Support Center (SASC) helps students develop confidence in their abilities and achieve their academic potential. SASC provides support to all Luther College students, responding to the individual needs through a variety of services in the context of a community committed to faith, learning, service, and the liberal arts. All services are available to all students free of charge.

Mentoring **Connect for Success**

Connect for Success is an annual, semester long program that begins with an intensive 3.5 day series of workshops that orient students to Luther's academic and campus culture. Connect for Success is designed to assist first year students in the social, personal, and academic acclimation to Luther by pairing them with outstanding sophomore, junior, and senior students who will be their mentors formally through the fall semester and informally beyond this time.

Student Life & Support **TRIO Achievement Program**

TRIO is a federally-funded student retention program that provides participating students with holistic, individualized support and comprehensive programming that promotes their academic success, personal development, and sense of community. Eligibility is based on family income and/or first generation status.

Fast Facts

STUDENT DIVERSITY

# undergraduates	2,008
% male/female	45/55
% first-generation college	20
% American Indian or Alaskan Native	<1
% Asian	1
% Black or African American	2
% Hispanic/Latino	5
% Native Hawaiian or Pacific Islander	<1
% White	81
% two or more races	2
% race and/or ethnicity unknown	0
% International/nonresident	8

STUDENT SUCCESS

% first-to-second year retention	83
% six-year graduation	79
% six-year graduation for underrepresented minority groups	65
% first-years who live on campus	100
% undergraduates who live on campus	93
full-time faculty	175
full-time minority faculty	20
student-faculty ratio	11:1

Popular majors Business/Marketing, Visual and Performing Arts, Biological/Life Sciences, Social Sciences, Foreign Languages, Literatures, and Linguistics

Multicultural student clubs and organizations Black Student Union, HOLA-Enlaces Hispanic Org Latinos Y Amigos, Asian Student Association and Allies (ASAA), Men of Color, Beta Theta Omega (BTQ), Ethnic Beats, International Student and Allies Association (ISAA), PRIDE, Zeta Tau Psi

AFFORDABILITY

Cost of Attendance

tuition	$41,950
required fees	$340
room and board	$9,460

Financial Aid

total institutional scholarships/grants	$38,244,440
% of students with financial need	89
% of students with need awarded any financial aid	100
% of students with need awarded any need-based scholarship or grant aid	100
% of students with need whose need was fully met	44
% Pell Grant recipients among first-years	21
average aid package	$35,228
average student loan debt upon graduation	$35,642

ADMISSIONS

# of applicants	4,288
% admitted	65
SAT Evidence-Based Reading & Writing	503-640
SAT Math	520-665
ACT Composite	23-28
SAT/ACT optional	no
average HS GPA	3.71

DEADLINES

regular application closing date	rolling
early decision plan	no
application closing date	n/a
early action plan	no
application closing date	n/a
application fee	$0
application fee online	$0
fee waiver for applicants with financial need	n/a

Centre College

Centre College is a top-50 liberal arts college that attracts bright, highly motivated students from around the country. It's the kind of school that provides extras (leadership training, real-world preparation for career success, a global perspective) that cause our students to lead the nation in loyalty. Current students will share: a Centre education isn't just an accomplishment, it's an experience. Learning both inside and outside of the classroom, collaborating with faculty and other students, and traveling around the world are just the beginning of the uniquely intense and immersive brand of education Centre is famous for. Centre graduates have more than a diploma after commencement—they also boast a global perspective, career experience, and research skills, making them real-world-ready in ways other college grads aren't. With 97 percent of students employed or in advanced study within ten months of graduation, it's safe to say that Centre degrees don't just put extra words on a resume—they put graduates to work. Centre is a place where first-generation students thrive. According to the National Survey of Student Engagement, first-gen students at Centre hold more leadership positions (proportionally) on campus than continuous-generation, and they graduate at a higher rate as well. In the class of 2017, 90% of the first-generation students graduated in four years!

Scholars & Leadership **Grissom Scholars Program**

Available to first-year applicants, the Grissom Scholars Program offers ten high-achieving, first-generation college students a full-tuition scholarship and $5000 in educational enhancement funds to pursue special opportunities such as study abroad, independent research, and academic internships. Grissom Scholars participate in a unique summer orientation focused on personal growth and team building. Each scholar receives personal guidance from the program director and a first-generation peer mentor. Over the course of four years, each cohort of ten student scholars meet regularly for fun activities and personal development.

Scholars & Leadership **Brown Fellows Program**

In partnership with the James Graham Brown Foundation, Centre launched the Brown Fellows Program in 2009. The initiative is the premier scholarship and enrichment program in Kentucky and is one of the nation's elite fellowship programs. The program was established as an individualized course of development for outstanding students to build leadership skills through independent study, community service, and experiential learning. Brown Fellows are awarded "full-ride-plus" scholarships and are provided four summer enrichment experiences, around themes of service, research, international study, and leadership, beginning the summer before their first year at Centre.

Scholars & Leadership **Lincoln Scholars Program**

Lincoln Scholars are exceptional young people who aspire to pursue lives of work and service to change our world for the better. Each scholar's experience will be an intentional, self-initiated journey toward the accumulation of knowledge and a deep understanding of the human condition. Ten scholars will be selected from each entering class and will receive a full-ride scholarship as well as individual mentoring from the program director and three fully funded summer enrichment experiences.

Academic Advising & Support **New Student Orientation**

The Academic Advising Office coordinates academic advising and partners with the Student Life Office to implement new student orientation. New student orientation includes summer mailings, basic skills and placement testing, the fall orientation program, and special programs for students during the fall term.

Centre College
600 West Walnut St.
Danville, KY 40442
Ph: (800) 423-6236
admission@centre.edu
www.centre.edu

Fast Facts

STUDENT DIVERSITY

# undergraduates	1,450
% male/female	49/51
% first-generation college	17
% American Indian or Alaskan Native	n/a
% Asian	12
% Black or African American	5
% Hispanic/Latino	5
% Native Hawaiian or Pacific Islander	n/a
% White	76
% two or more races	3
% race and/or ethnicity unknown	3
% International/nonresident	8

STUDENT SUCCESS

% first-to-second year retention	91
% six-year graduation	82
% six-year graduation for underrepresented minority groups	n/a
% first-years who live on campus	100
% undergraduates who live on campus	97
full-time faculty	130
full-time minority faculty	15
student-faculty ratio	11:1

Popular majors Biology, Economics, Behavioral Neuroscience

Multicultural student clubs and organizations CentreFirsts (for first-generation college students, Centre Queers & Allies, Chinese Club, Diversity Student Union, International Student Union, Japanese Club, Muslim Student Association, Latin American Student Organization

AFFORDABILITY

Cost of Attendance

tuition	$40,500
required fees	n/a
room and board	$10,180

Financial Aid

total institutional scholarships/grants	$30,008,340
% of students with financial need	60
% of students with need awarded any financial aid	100
% of students with need awarded any need-based scholarship or grant aid	99
% of students with need whose need was fully met	39
% Pell Grant recipients among first-years	17
average aid package	$34,441
average student loan debt upon graduation	$20,545

ADMISSIONS

# of applicants	2,521
% admitted	75
SAT Critical Reading	638
SAT Math	654
SAT Writing	n/a
ACT Composite	26-31
SAT/ACT optional	n/a
average HS GPA	3.62

DEADLINES

regular application closing date	1/15
early decision plan	yes
application closing date	11/15
early action plan	yes
application closing date	12/1
application fee	$0
application fee online	$0
fee waiver for applicants with financial need	yes

Bates College

Since 1855, Bates College has been dedicated to the emancipating potential of the liberal arts. Bates educates the whole person through creative and rigorous scholarship in a collaborative residential community. With ardor and devotion, "Amore ac Studio," we engage the transformative power of our differences, cultivating intellectual discovery and informed civic action. Preparing leaders sustained by a love of learning and a commitment to responsible stewardship of the wider world, Bates is a college for coming times.

Bates was founded in 1855 by people who believed strongly in freedom, civil rights, and the importance of a higher education for all who could benefit from it. Bates has always admitted students without regard to race, sex, religion, or national origin. Great efforts were made in designing the institution to ensure that no qualified student would be turned away because he or she could not afford the cost of a Bates education. Although they met with considerable criticism from other colleges, the founders held fast to their commitment to admit both men and women: Bates was New England's first coeducational college and one of the first coeducational colleges in the United States.

Open House, Fly-In, Visit **Prologue to Bates**

Seniors may spend three days on us to enjoy a slice of what Bates College has to offer. During the overnight program, designed by the Bates Office of Admission for first-generation-to-college and/or students from diverse backgrounds, you will: attend a class of your choosing, stay with current Bates students, meet Bates faculty and staff, tour Bates' beautiful, 109-acre campus, catch an information session, participate in an admission interview and attend academic, athletic, cultural and co-curricular events.

Student Life & Support **Office of Intercultural Education**

Providing all of our students from underrepresented backgrounds a "space to be apart," while providing the resources and opportunities for the entire Bates community to experience "time to be together" is the hallmark of our work.

Student Life & Support **Purposeful Work**

Work is fundamental to our lives. It helps define who we are and who we will become. At Bates, enabling students to lead lives of meaningful work lies at the heart of our liberal arts mission.

Purposeful Work is a college-wide initiative that helps students identify and cultivate their interests and strengths and acquire the knowledge, experiences and relationships necessary to pursue their aspirations with imagination and integrity. Purposeful Work encourages collaboration and risk-taking. It supports failure and reinvention. When coupled with a liberal arts education, Purposeful Work prepares students for success in the modern economy.

Bates College
23 Campus Ave
Lindholm House
Lewiston, ME 04240
Ph: (855) 228-3755
admission@bates.edu
www.bates.edu

Fast Facts

STUDENT DIVERSITY

# undergraduates	1,780
% male/female	50/50
% first-generation college	14
% American Indian or Alaskan Native	<1
% Asian	4
% Black or African American	6
% Hispanic/Latino	8
% Native Hawaiian or Pacific Islander	<1
% White	70
% two or more races	4
% race and/or ethnicity unknown	<1
% International/nonresident	7

STUDENT SUCCESS

% first-to-second year retention	95
% six-year graduation	88
% six-year graduation for underrepresented minority groups	n/a
% first-years who live on campus	100
% undergraduates who live on campus	95
full-time faculty	169
full-time minority faculty	27
student-faculty ratio	10:1

Popular majors Economics, Political Science, English, Psychology, Biology

Multicultural student clubs and organizations AASIA - Asian-American Students in Action, African Club, Arabic Club, CSA - Caribbean Student Association, Latinos Unidos, Men Against Sexual Violence, OUT Front, Sankofa, The Women of Color Club, Women's Advocacy Group

AFFORDABILITY

Cost of Attendance

tuition	$50,310
required fees	n/a
room and board	$14,190

Financial Aid

total institutional scholarships/grants	$32,519,543
% of students with financial need	43
% of students with need awarded any financial aid	43
% of students with need awarded any need-based scholarship or grant aid	43
% of students with need whose need was fully met	100
% Pell Grant recipients among first-years	n/a
average aid package	$45,494
average student loan debt upon graduation	$13,171

ADMISSIONS

# of applicants	5,356
% admitted	22
SAT Critical Reading	630-720
SAT Math	630-710
SAT Writing	640-710
ACT Composite	31
SAT/ACT optional	yes
average HS GPA	n/a

DEADLINES

regular application closing date	1/1
early decision plan	yes
application closing date	11/15; 1/1
early action plan	n/a
application closing date	n/a
application fee	$60
application fee online	$60
fee waiver for applicants with financial need	yes

Johns Hopkins University

Johns Hopkins University is a place where ambitious, talented, and creative students thrive. Since the university's start in 1876, students in all majors have embraced a spirit of learning through exploration and discovery. Campus life outside the classroom is active and dynamic, with more than 300 student groups—from dance, a cappella, and cultural groups to international service organizations. Hopkins values diversity in all forms. All students have the opportunity to develop independent critical thinking, gain cultural competencies, and flourish on a socially diverse campus. With help from the Center for Diversity and Inclusion and the Center for Student Success, the holistic development of students is promoted by providing direct services to underrepresented populations, including first generation students.

Open House, Fly-In, Visit **Discovery Days**

The Discovery Days program connects admitted underrepresented minority students to the clubs, organizations, and resources that bring together our multicultural community. Students are hosted on campus for a three-day, two-night experience in April, during which they learn about multicultural life at Johns Hopkins, explore Baltimore, and spend the night with current student hosts.

Open House, Fly-In, Visit **Hopkins Overnight Multicultural Experience (HOME)**

HOME is a fly-in, three-day, two-night program for underrepresented minority students. Prospective students experience multicultural life at Hopkins and are hosted overnight by current students. This program coincides with the Fall Open House program. HOME requires an application; information is available via high school counselors and an invitation from the university.

Scholarship & Financial Aid **Meeting 100% of Financial Need**

Hopkins is committed to helping students make their college decision without being limited by family financial circumstances. A variety of financial support programs are available to undergraduates and the university meets 100% of demonstrated financial need for students for all four years of study.

First-Year Experience & Transition **Hop-In**

The Hop-In program supports incoming freshmen who are the first in their family to go to college, had limited opportunities for advanced course work in high school, or who may have significant time constraints with their coursework during the first year on campus in the transition from high school to college. Students continually receive personal and academic development through resource workshops, social events, and individual advising.

Student Life & Support **The Center for Diversity and Inclusion**

The center cultivates an environment of inclusiveness and has established specific aims to support underrepresented populations. The Office of Multicultural Affairs; the Interfaith Center; the Office of Lesbian, Bisexual, Transgender, and Questioning Life; and the Office of Gender and Equity are all housed within The Center for Diversity and Inclusion.

Student Life & Support **The Center for Student Success**

The Center for Student Success provides ongoing support through academic and student services programming. Several initiatives and programs serve underrepresented students, such as Mentoring Assistance Peer Program (MAPP) and Johns Hopkins Underrepresented in Medical Professions (JUMP).

Johns Hopkins University
3400 North Charles Street
Baltimore, MD 21218
Ph: (410) 516-8171
gotojhu@jhu.edu
apply.jhu.edu

Fast Facts

STUDENT DIVERSITY

# undergraduates	5,366
% male/female	49/51
% first-generation college	n/a
% American Indian or Alaskan Native	<1
% Asian	25
% Black or African American	6
% Hispanic/Latino	14
% Native Hawaiian or Pacific Islander	<1
% White	37
% two or more races	5
% race and/or ethnicity unknown	4
% International/nonresident	10

STUDENT SUCCESS

% first-to-second year retention	97
% six-year graduation	94
% six-year graduation for underrepresented minority groups	88
% first-years who live on campus	95
% undergraduates who live on campus	48
full-time faculty	708
full-time minority faculty	127
student-faculty ratio	10:1

Popular majors Public Health, Engineering, Social Sciences, Biological/Life Sciences, Psychology, Writing Seminars

Multicultural student clubs and organizations Johns Hopkins Underrepresented in Medical Professions, Mentoring Assistance Peer Program, Students Educating and Empowering for Diversity, Black Student Union, Organizacion Latino Estudiantil, African Students Association, National Society of Black Engineers, Hopkins Organization for Minority Engineers and Scientists, Multicultural Student Volunteers, Caribbean Culture Society

AFFORDABILITY

Cost of Attendance

tuition	$52,170
required fees	$500
room and board	$15,410

Financial Aid

total institutional scholarships/grants	$90,000,000+
% of students with financial need	48
% of students with need awarded any financial aid	99
% of students with need awarded any need-based scholarship or grant aid	94
% of students with need whose need was fully met	100
% Pell Grant recipients among first-years	13
average aid package	$35,792
average student loan debt upon graduation	$23,627

ADMISSIONS

# of applicants	26,578
% admitted	12
SAT Critical Reading	680-760
SAT Math	710-790
SAT Writing	680-770
ACT Composite	34
SAT/ACT optional	no
average HS GPA	3.92

DEADLINES

regular application closing date	1/3
early decision plan	yes
application closing date	11/1
early action plan	n/a
application closing date	n/a
application fee	$70
application fee online	$70
fee waiver for applicants with financial need	yes

St. John's College (Maryland)

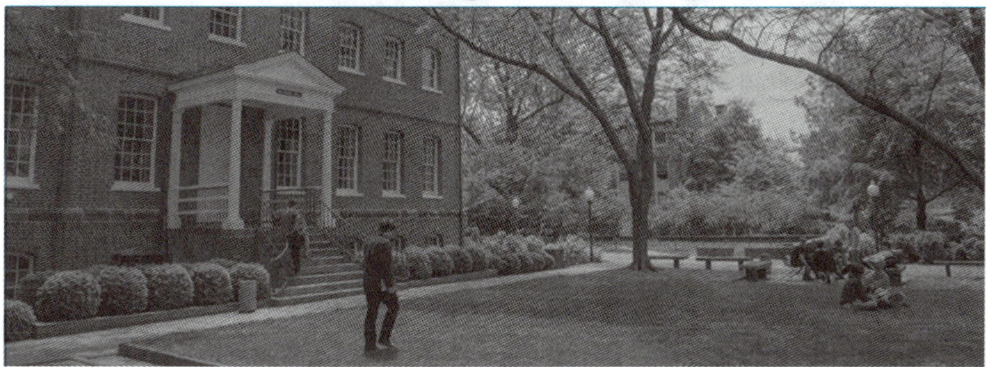

St. John's College (Maryland)
60 College Avenue
Annapolis, MD 21401
Ph: (410) 626-2522
www.sjc.edu

At St. John's College, great books—and great discussions—are the heart of the college's distinctive liberal arts program. At the college's two campuses in Annapolis, MD and Santa Fe, NM, every class consists of 14-20 students discussing the greatest books of Western civilization across disciplines that include literature, philosophy, math, science, language, and music. The college's coeducational community, free of religious affiliation, takes an open-minded approach to ideas of all kinds. Rather than being told how and what to think about what they're reading, St. John's students are asked to reach their own conclusions through deep thinking, critical analysis, and intense discussion. Every part of the program aims to raise essential questions that have been the subject of human inquiry since the beginning of time. Most students live on campus in a socially and academically supportive community, where diversity of mind and thought are valued and encouraged.

Pre-College Summer Experience **The St. John's College Summer Academy**

The St. John's College Summer Academy is a pre-college, residential program that shows students the possibilities of a liberal arts education. Students explore works by some of the greatest thinkers of Western culture in discussion-based classes. They also participate in an array of extra-curricular activities—from poetry writing to improv techniques to yoga and pottery—and enjoy excursions to museums and historic sites. Financial assistance is available.

Open House, Fly-in, Visit **St. John's College Fly-In Program**

St. John's College encourages prospective students to visit campus to see our distinctive education in action. Students can schedule a campus tour or a day or overnight visit throughout the year, including during the summer. To make visiting accessible for accepted students, the college offers a fly-in program that covers travel expenses. Two admitted student events are scheduled in 2018: the first runs from Sunday, March 25 to Monday, March 26; the second from Sunday, April 22 to Monday, April 23.

First-Year Experience & Transition **First-Year Support**

St. John's hires student assistants in every subject studied at the college. These assistants, having experienced the program themselves, provide invaluable academic and social support to first-year students. Resident Assistants, current students trained to provide support in the dorms, also help students with their college transition. Through the Assistant Dean's office, academic tutoring and personal counseling can be arranged. Students are encouraged to build relationships with professors by participating in the college's "Take a Professor to Lunch" program.

Fast Facts

STUDENT DIVERSITY

# undergraduates (Maryland campus)	458
% male/female	53/47
% first-generation college	n/a
% American Indian or Alaskan Native	<1
% Asian	4
% Black or African American	2
% Hispanic/Latino	6
% Native Hawaiian or Pacific Islander	<1
% White	64
% two or more races	3
% race and/or ethnicity unknown	<1
% International/nonresident	22

STUDENT SUCCESS

% first-to-second year retention	87
% six-year graduation	67
% six-year graduation for underrepresented minority groups	n/a
% first-years who live on campus	94
% undergraduates who live on campus	85
full-time faculty	102
full-time minority faculty	9
student-faculty ratio	7:1

Popular majors Liberal Arts

Multicultural student clubs and organizations
Black Student Union, Inter-sectional Feminist Group, Pangea (International Student Club), Pink Triangle (LGBTQ+ Alliance Group), Shammai (Jewish Student Club), Chinese Teahouse (Eastern Authors study group).

AFFORDABILITY

Cost of Attendance

tuition	$51,200
required fees	$470
room and board	$11,486

Financial Aid

total institutional scholarships/grants	$3,942,772
% of students with financial need	79
% of students with need awarded any financial aid	100
% of students with need awarded any need-based scholarship or grant aid	100
% of students with need whose need was fully met	84
% Pell Grant recipients among first-years	23
average aid package	$37,870
average student loan debt upon graduation	$25,400

ADMISSIONS

# of applicants	1,175
% admitted	58
SAT Evidence-Based Reading & Writing	610-800
SAT Math	510-800
ACT Composite	22-35
SAT/ACT optional	yes
average HS GPA	3.5

DEADLINES

regular application closing date	rolling
early decision plan	n/a
application closing date	n/a
early action plan	yes
application closing date	11/15
application fee	n/a
application fee online	n/a
fee waiver for applicants with financial need	n/a

*Data reported is combined for St. John's College's two campuses in Maryland and New Mexico, unless otherwise noted.

St. Mary's College of Maryland

St. Mary's College of Maryland
47645 College Drive
St. Mary's City, MD 20686
Ph: (240) 895-2000
www.smcm.edu

St. Mary's College of Maryland, the Public Honors College, for over 175 years has provided a quality, liberal arts-based education for the citizens of Maryland and beyond. Our 'Public' mantra means access and inclusion are hallmarks that the College takes very seriously. We strive for greater diversity among our students, faculty and staff and work towards equity in all its forms. The 'Honors' mantra means that St. Mary's attracts intellectually ambitious students who want to engage in a rigorous academic environment where they have the chance to connect with faculty, staff and other students who have the same desire to thrive in a diverse learning community. In the end, St. Mary's prepares students to become responsible and thoughtful global citizens.

Open House, Fly-in, Visit **Campus Visits**

A campus visit is a good way to get a sense of St. Mary's College of Maryland. 'Can you see yourself as a student here?' The best way to begin that process is by visiting the college. Students have the opportunity to sit in on an information session, take a tour of the campus, and if they choose, have an informational interview with an Admissions counselor. If you cannot make it to campus, a phone or Skype interview could be set up.

First-Year Experience and Transition **The Core Curriculum**

Being a liberal arts institution, St. Mary's provides students with a broad based education. Students need to think critically, communicate effectively, use reasoning skills, intellectual and ethical skill sets, and develop a curiosity about the world around them. Through the Core Curriculum of studies, students will develop these abilities across all disciplines ranging from creative production in the fine arts to original student research in the sciences.

Scholarship & Financial Aid **Office of Financial Aid**

Financing a college education involves much more than just the college's "Cost of Attendance" (COA). Financial Aid bridges the gap between the cost of attending the institution and what a student/parents can reasonably pay on their own. All students that apply to St. Mary's will be considered for any of the College's merit (academic) based awards. Students are also highly encouraged to apply for federal/state aid by filling out a FAFSA form. (The College's FAFSA ID# is 002095).

Student Life & Support **Office of Student Activities**

"Outside of the classroom," the Office of Student Activities offers students a chance to develop leadership skills and be a change agent through close to 100 clubs and organizations, campus wide civic engagement opportunities and giving back to the community.

Academic Advising & Support **Office of Student Support Services**

Advising is an on-going process to help students progress towards graduation. Each St. Mary's student is assigned an academic adviser to develop a student's academic goals, career-interest and/or graduate school plans and understand the value of a liberal arts education.

Scholars & Leadership **DeSousa-Brent Scholars Program**

St. Mary's 'DeSousa-Brent Scholars Program' prepares a select group of St. Mary's students for academic and leadership. Students selected for this program become campus leaders by promoting diversity and inclusiveness. The program seeks out students with great leadership potential who belong to underrepresented college-going groups on campus

Fast Facts

STUDENT DIVERSITY

# undergraduates	1,618
% male/female	43/57
% first-generation college	25
% American Indian or Alaskan Native	<1
% Asian	4
% Black or African American	9
% Hispanic/Latino	9
% Native Hawaiian or Pacific Islander	<1
% White	69
% two or more races	5
% race and/or ethnicity unknown	4
% International/nonresident	<1

STUDENT SUCCESS

% first-to-second year retention	87
% six-year graduation	79
% six-year graduation for underrepresented minority groups	79
% first-years who live on campus	96
% undergraduates who live on campus	83
full-time faculty	141
full-time minority faculty	20
student-faculty ratio	10:1

Popular majors Social Sciences, Psychology, Biological/Life Sciences, English, Visual and Performing Arts

Multicultural student clubs and organizations African Student Association (ASA), Asian Pacific American Club (APAC), Association of Computing Machinery for Women and Minorities (ACM-WAM), Black Student Union, Cultural Dance Club, Latinos Unidos, Minority Association of Pre-Medical Students (MAPS), Minority Students in the Social Sciences Association (MSSA), Transgenda

AFFORDABILITY

Cost of Attendance

tuition	$11,418
required fees	$2,774
room and board	$12,442

Financial Aid

total institutional scholarships/grants	$5,903,127
% of students with financial need	65
% of students with need awarded any financial aid	99
% of students with need awarded any need-based scholarship or grant aid	90
% of students with need whose need was fully met	7
% Pell Grant recipients among first-years	25
average aid package	$13,772
average student loan debt upon graduation	$24,218

ADMISSIONS

# of applicants	1,767
% admitted	80
SAT Critical Reading	510-640
SAT Math	490-610
SAT Writing	490-600
ACT Composite	26
SAT/ACT optional	no
average HS GPA	3.34

DEADLINES

regular application closing date	1/15
early decision plan	no
application closing date	n/a
early action plan	yes
application closing date	11/1
application fee	$50
application fee online	$50
fee waiver for applicants with financial need	yes

Amherst College

Founded in 1821 as a nonsectarian institution for "the education of indigent young men of piety and talents," Amherst College is now widely regarded as one of the premier liberal arts colleges in the nation, enrolling nearly 1,800 young men and women. Diversity, defined in its broadest sense, is fundamental to Amherst's mission. The college enrolls students from nearly every state and from more than 50 countries, and for the past several years approximately 45 percent of Amherst's students have been students of color. Amherst is one of the few truly need-blind colleges in the nation; students are admitted without regard to financial need, and each admitted student is guaranteed financial aid equal to demonstrated financial need. The college's financial aid packages are consistently among the most generous in the nation, and among its peer universities and colleges Amherst is exceptionally economically diverse. By any measure of accessibility and quality, Amherst is consistently ranked among the top schools in the country. Its outstanding resources, dedicated faculty and rigorous academic life allow the college to enroll students with an extraordinary range of talents, interests and commitments.

Pre-College Prep & Outreach **Telementoring Program**

Amherst College offers a telementoring program in which current students use e-mail and other technological mediums to help high-school students locate and gain acceptance to colleges and universities. The telementoring program matches 25 Amherst students from disadvantaged socio-economic backgrounds with talented high school students from underserved schools across the nation to aid in their college search.

Pre-College Prep & Outreach **The A Better Chance (ABC) Tutoring and Mentoring Program**

Amherst students assist young male participants with homework and general activities in preparation for college level work. The goals of ABC are to offer support and aid in any subjects being taken by the participants, and to promote diversity by providing the opportunity for Amherst students to form meaningful relationships with students of different backgrounds.

Open House, Fly-In, Visit **Diversity Open House Weekends**

Amherst hosts two Diversity Open House Weekends each fall in which the College funds travel for multicultural and first-generation students to spend three days exploring the community. Students attend classes, cultural events and admission workshops during their stay. Fourteen current students work as diversity interns and help organize and coordinate the Open House weekends. The diversity interns also serve as liaisons and mentors to students.

Summer Bridge & Orientation **Access to Amherst**

Matriculated students from disadvantaged backgrounds who are interested in the sciences are eligible for the Summer Science Program, while those interested in the humanities and social sciences are eligible for the Summer Humanities and Social Science Program. The two three-week courses occur before first-year orientation. Approximately 20 members of the incoming class participate in each program and gain assistance transitioning between high school and college. Participants in the science program gain further assistance in learning various approaches to math and science while those in the humanities and social science program develop writing and study skills.

Amherst College
P.O. Box 5000
220 S. Pleasant Street
Amherst, MA 01002
Ph: (413) 542-2328
admission@amherst.edu
www.amherst.edu

Fast Facts

STUDENT DIVERSITY

# undergraduates	1,849
% male/female	50/50
% first-generation college	15
% American Indian or Alaskan Native	<1
% Asian	14
% Black or African American	12
% Hispanic/Latino	14
% Native Hawaiian or Pacific Islander	0
% White	43
% two or more races	5
% race and/or ethnicity unknown	3
% International/nonresident	9

STUDENT SUCCESS

% first-to-second year retention	96
% six-year graduation	93
% six-year graduation for underrepresented minority groups	90
% first-years who live on campus	100
% undergraduates who live on campus	98
full-time faculty	209
full-time minority faculty	43
student-faculty ratio	8:1

Popular majors Economics, English, Mathematics, Political Science, Psychology

Multicultural student clubs and organizations Black Student Union, African & Caribbean Student Union, La Causa, Asian Students Association, Asian Culture House, Pride Alliance, International Students Association, Muslim Students Association, Hillel, South Asian Students Association, Native American Students Organization

AFFORDABILITY

Cost of Attendance

tuition	$51,620
required fees	$856
room and board	$13,710

Financial Aid

total institutional scholarships/grants	$50,891,149
% of students with financial need	52
% of students with need awarded any financial aid	100
% of students with need awarded any need-based scholarship or grant aid	100
% of students with need whose need was fully met	100
% Pell Grant recipients among first-years	22
average aid package	$52,877
average student loan debt upon graduation	$14,490

ADMISSIONS

# of applicants	8,406
% admitted	14
SAT Critical Reading	680-780
SAT Math	680-780
SAT Writing	680-780
ACT Composite	32
SAT/ACT optional	no
average HS GPA	n/a

DEADLINES

regular application closing date	1/1
early decision plan	yes
application closing date	11/1
early action plan	no
application closing date	n/a
application fee	$65
application fee online	$65
fee waiver for applicants with financial need	yes

Babson College

The Babson curriculum emphasizes hands-on, experiential learning, and is infused top to bottom with Entrepreneurial Thought and Action®. So, whether your interests include marketing or accounting, finance or technology, the arts or athletics, founding new companies or directing nonprofits, you'll gain both a business skill set and an entrepreneurial mindset. Babson provides students opportunities to work hands-on all four years: in fact, the college gives all first-year students (grouped in teams) $3,000 in start-up loans to conceive, launch, manage, and eventually liquidate a real business or organization, with all profits donated to a local community service agency. Babson is a living/learning laboratory where you'll discover something new about leadership-and yourself-every day. At Babson, everything is real. Real businesses. Real experiences, Real impact.

Pre-College Prep & Outreach **Network for Teaching Entrepreneurship Conference (NFTE)**

Babson currently hosts the northeast regional conference of the Network for Teach Entrepreneurship. This organization, which provides both training to students and teachers, helps you people from low-income communities build skills and unlock their entrepreneurial creativity. In addition, Babson offers a NFTE Scholarship, a four year, full tuition scholarship.

Pre-College Prep & Outreach **Babson's Summer Study**

Babson provides a living/learning laboratory for high school students to focus on applying and advancing their knowledge in business and entrepreneurship. Students earn college credit and learn from top-ranked faculty in a challenging and ambitious campus atmosphere. They will differentiate themselves from their peers for college applications and have the opportunity to build their network in meeting with business leaders and industry experts, engaging with real time business challenges, and launching a venture by the end of the program.

Open House, Fly-In, Visit **Multicultural Overnight Experience**

This fall program will provide prospective seniors with the opportunity to experience our diverse, multicultural, and inclusive community, through engaging with current students, faculty, and staff and learning more about residence halls, classes, and many other resources. Travel scholarships are available.

Open House, Fly-In, Visit **Experience Diversity Overnight Program**

Held in conjunction with Babson's annual admitted student day in April, the Experience Diversity Overnight Program allows admitted seniors to learn more about the Babson experience and resources available, interact with other admitted students, and connect with current students, faculty, and staff.

Scholarship & Financial Aid **Diversity Leadership Award**

The Diversity Leadership Award is a four-year full tuition scholarship awarded to students with the greatest potential for leadership in creating a diverse community. Scholars receive student mentoring, are provided with unique leadership development opportunities, and are able to participate in distinct academic, social, and cultural activities and events.

Scholarship & Financial Aid **Posse University Partner**

Babson College participates in the Posse Foundation, a program that brings talented inner city youth to campus to pursue their academics ad to help promote cross-cultural communication.

Babson College
231 Forest Street
Lunder Admission Center
Babson Park, MA 02457
Ph: (781) 239-5522
ugradadmission@babson.edu
www.babson.edu

Fast Facts

STUDENT DIVERSITY

# undergraduates	2,342
% male/female	52/48
% first-generation college	15
% American Indian or Alaskan Native	<1
% Asian	12
% Black or African American	5
% Hispanic/Latino	11
% Native Hawaiian or Pacific Islander	<1
% White	37
% two or more races	2
% race and/or ethnicity unknown	5
% International/nonresident	28

STUDENT SUCCESS

% first-to-second year retention	96
% six-year graduation	93
% six-year graduation for underrepresented minority groups	n/a
% first-years who live on campus	100
% undergraduates who live on campus	80
full-time faculty	177
full-time minority faculty	36
student-faculty ratio	11.5:1

Popular majors Business

Multicultural student clubs and organizations
AMAN, Association of Latino Professionals in Finance and Accounting, Babson African Student Organization, Babson Asian Pacific Student Association, Babson Korean Student Association, Babson Thai Student Association, Japanese International Circle,Origins of Necessary Equality (O.N.E.) Tower, Chinese Student Association (CSA), Hong Kong Student Association (HKSA)

AFFORDABILITY

Cost of Attendance

tuition	$49,664
required fees	$0
room and board	$15,838

Financial Aid

total institutional scholarships/grants	$37,000,000
% of students with financial need	40
% of students with need awarded any financial aid	100
% of students with need awarded any need-based scholarship or grant aid	95
% of students with need whose need was fully met	100
% Pell Grant recipients among first-years	14
average aid package	$42,799
average student loan debt upon graduation	$35,013

ADMISSIONS

# of applicants	7,122
% admitted	24
SAT Critical Reading	644
SAT Math	672
SAT Writing	n/a
ACT Composite	31
SAT/ACT optional	no
average HS GPA	n/a

DEADLINES

regular application closing date	1/2
early decision plan	yes
application closing date	11/1
early action plan	yes
application closing date	11/1
application fee	$75
application fee online	$75
fee waiver for applicants with financial need	yes

Bay Path University

A Bay Path University education empowers undergraduate women and graduate women and men to become leaders in their careers and communities with an innovative approach to learning that prepares students to flourish in a constantly changing world. The Bay Path experience is nothing less than transformational. Our women-only undergraduate programs and our coeducational graduate programs are offered both on campus and online, providing a flexible, 21st-century education for learners at all stages of life and career. Bay Path students find a supportive and diverse community, close mentoring, and rigorous preparation for success in a complex and globally interdependent society. Students graduate with the applied knowledge, portable skillset, and confidence to thrive in their professions, identify and realize their dreams, and make a lasting difference in the world.

Scholarship & Financial Aid **Scholarships**

Bay Path University is dedicated to ensuring college remains accessible and affordable to young women regardless of their level of financial need. Upon completion of the admissions application, students are automatically considered for one of Bay Path's merit scholarships, which do not have to be repaid, and are based on your academic performance and renewable contingent upon full time enrollment and maintaining satisfactory academic progress.

Academic Advising & Support **The Bashevkin Center for Academic Excellence**

The Bashevkin Center for Academic Excellence assists all Bay Path University students in becoming more independent and successful learners, equipped with the knowledge of their own abilities in order to gain a deeper educational experience. The Center assists students in strengthening understanding of various content areas and in developing vital skills in time management and learning strategies. The Center provides free, on ground tutoring and 24/7 online tutoring to students. The Center welcomes students of all abilities and serves as an initial contact for those with learning differences.

Academic Courses & Service Learning **Women in STEM Honors Program**

Housed within the Center of Excellence for Women in STEM, the Bay Path University Women in STEM Honors Program (WiSH) offers a four year curriculum consisting of integrated and advanced study and research for dedicated future women scientists. Within this program students will experience hands-on project-based research and link science to real world applications. WiSH uniquely prepares women to not only enter scientific fields and excel within them, but to truly impact them. Research has shown that women thrive in environments that encourage hands-on project-based research, include female mentoring and role models, and link science to real world applications. WiSH students also receive great scholarship support through a renewable annual $2,500 scholarship!

Academic Courses & Service Learning **Women as Empowered Learners and Leaders (WELL) Program**

WELL is a one of a kind program devoted to helping students find and use tools that will lead to their success in academics, in beginning a rewarding career, and in building a fulfilling life. Students in the WELL program are supported from their transition into college life to graduation. Students tap into their strengths, challenge themselves to step out of their comfort zone, and think about their role as a leader, all while receiving the guidance and support of WELL faculty, advisors, and a peer mentor. Through activities in and out of the classroom, students are prepared for public speaking, communications, internships and understanding what it means and what it takes to be a successful woman in today's complex world.

Bay Path University
588 Longmeadow Street
Longmeadow, MA 01106
Ph: (413) 565-1331
admiss@baypath.edu
www.baypath.edu

Fast Facts

STUDENT DIVERSITY

# undergraduates	677
% male/female	0/100
% first-generation college	41
% American Indian or Alaskan Native	0
% Asian	4
% Black or African American	10
% Hispanic/Latino	15
% Native Hawaiian or Pacific Islander	0
% White	60
% two or more races	3
% race and/or ethnicity unknown	7
% International/nonresident	1

STUDENT SUCCESS

% first-to-second year retention	70
% six-year graduation	61
% six-year graduation for underrepresented minority groups	n/a
% first-years who live on campus	72
% undergraduates who live on campus	43
full-time faculty	63
full-time minority faculty	8
student-faculty ratio	11:1

Popular majors Digital Forensics, Forensic Psychology, Forensic Science, Pre-Occupational Therapy Studies

Multicultural student clubs and organizations Black Student Union, ALANA Leaders, Essence Step Team, Motherland, Women of Culture

AFFORDABILITY

Cost of Attendance

tuition	$33,557
required fees	n/a
room and board	$12,799

Financial Aid

total institutional scholarships/grants	n/a
% of students with financial need	92
% of students with need awarded any financial aid	92
% of students with need awarded any need-based scholarship or grant aid	77
% of students with need whose need was fully met	10
% Pell Grant recipients among first-years	60
average aid package	$27,274
average student loan debt upon graduation	n/a

ADMISSIONS

# of applicants	1,470
% admitted	63
SAT Critical Reading	500-550
SAT Math	430-550
SAT Writing	420-550
ACT Composite	23
SAT/ACT optional	yes
average HS GPA	3.4

DEADLINES

regular application closing date	8/18
early decision plan	yes
application closing date	8/1
early action plan	n/a
application closing date	n/a
application fee	$25
application fee online	$0
fee waiver for applicants with financial need	yes

Bentley University

Bentley University is a top ten business university in the nation. At Bentley, we know a modern education has to prepare you for today's complex business world. We've designed the Bentley curriculum to give you more: Business plus the arts and sciences; Classroom learning plus real-world experience; World-class technology plus global perspective. The community encourages hands-on learning through corporate partnerships, internships, service-learning and study abroad. We offer the strength of a university with the values and student focus of a small college. Bentley is committed to ensuring social and cultural diversity in all aspects of campus life.

Summer Bridge & Orientation **MOSAIC Experience**

The MOSAIC Experience is a two-day program for all incoming Asian American, Latino/a, African American, Native American and Multiracial students. The program gives students the opportunity to network through a series of workshops, information sessions and social events before orientation to acclimate to life at the university. Staff and upperclassmen help guide students in gathering the tools needed for success at Bentley University.

First-Year Experience & Transition **Summer Transition Education Program (STEP)**

The Summer Transition Education Program (STEP) provides college admission support for high potential students who may have faced academic, socioeconomic, and/or personal challenges beyond their control. The program's support system includes mentoring and monitoring each student's academic progress and providing academic advising, counseling, and referrals. Realizing the importance of support at home, the STEP staff collaborates with students' families and guardians. Students also attend a six-week summer residential program, upon the completion of which they earn credit for two Bentley courses.

Student Life & Support **The Multicultural Center**

The Multicultural Center serves as a home for many ALANA students at Bentley University. The center serves to further the retention and success of the ALANA students through academic mentoring, guidance, leadership development, advocacy and personal support services. There is a committed staff that helps students with personal, academic and career counseling. Additionally, the Multicultural Center serves as the campus-wide resource for promotion, exploration and celebration of the University's diversity mission. It organizes a full calendar of events in collaboration with all cultural organizations.

Mentoring **The Peer2Peer Program**

The Peer2Peer program pairs first-year students with upperclassmen mentors to create a support system for navigating life at Bentley while promoting academic, personal, and social development.

Bentley University
175 Forest Street
Waltham, MA 02452
Ph: (781) 891-2244
ugadmission@bentley.edu
www.bentley.edu

Fast Facts

STUDENT DIVERSITY

# undergraduates	4,222
% male/female	49/51
% first-generation college	n/a
% American Indian or Alaskan Native	0
% Asian	8
% Black or African American	3
% Hispanic/Latino	7
% Native Hawaiian or Pacific Islander	1
% White	61
% two or more races	2
% race and/or ethnicity unknown	3
% International/nonresident	15

STUDENT SUCCESS

% first-to-second year retention	92
% six-year graduation	91
% six-year graduation for underrepresented minority groups	84
% first-years who live on campus	99
% undergraduates who live on campus	78
full-time faculty	284
full-time minority faculty	47
student-faculty ratio	12:1

Popular majors Marketing, Computer Sciences, Accounting, Finance

Multicultural student clubs and organizations
Asian Students' Association, Association of Latino Professions in Finance and Accounting, Association of Chinese Students, Black United Body, International Students' Association, La Cultura Latina, National Association of Asian American Professionals, National Black MBA Association, South Asian Student Association, Vietnamese Students Association

AFFORDABILITY

Cost of Attendance

tuition	$46,370
required fees	$1,630
room and board	$15,720

Financial Aid

total institutional scholarships/grants	$75,329,000
% of students with financial need	74
% of students with need awarded any financial aid	100
% of students with need awarded any need-based scholarship or grant aid	98
% of students with need whose need was fully met	42
% Pell Grant recipients among first-years	12
average aid package	$31,974
average student loan debt upon graduation	$31,046

ADMISSIONS

# of applicants	8,867
% admitted	44
SAT Evidence-Based Reading & Writing	590-670
SAT Math	620-710
ACT Composite	27-30
SAT/ACT optional	no
average HS GPA	n/a

DEADLINES

regular application closing date	1/7
early decision plan	yes
application closing date	11/15
early action plan	no
application closing date	n/a
application fee	$75
application fee online	$75
fee waiver for applicants with financial need	yes

Boston University

Boston University is the alma mater of Dr. Martin Luther King, Jr., and Dr. Solomon Carter Fuller, the first African American psychiatrist in the United States. It was the first university in the nation to award a Ph.D. to a woman and to award a medical degree to a Native American student. It is a world-recognized, private, teaching and research university offering more than 250 programs of study in the liberal arts and professions. Students are prepared for success through rigorous academics, cutting-edge research with faculty, and internships in the U.S. and abroad. At BU, students experience the city of Boston as an extension of the campus; and can explore the world through global curriculum and faculty, and more than 100 study abroad opportunities.

Student Life & Support **First Gen Connect**

First Generation Connect serves as a resource for students to ensure a smooth and successful transition from high school to college life and beyond. First Gen Connect hosts events at the start of each semester to welcome new and continuing students to campus. Throughout the academic year, First Gen Connect sponsors workshops and social events for students who are the first in their families to go to college. Learn more about First Gen Connect at bu.edu/usc/g1.

Student Life & Support **The Howard Thurman Center for Common Ground**

The Howard Thurman Center for Common Ground builds a sense of community for students through cultural, social, and academic networks on campus. Along with dynamic programming throughout the year, the Center holds a mandatory workshop for all first-year students during University Orientation to educate all students about the teachings Dr. Howard Thurman (mentor to Dr. Martin Luther King, Jr.) on discovering our shared humanity.

Scholarship & Financial Aid **Trustee and Presidential Scholarships**

The Presidential Scholarship is a $20,000 tuition scholarship awarded to the best and brightest freshmen from around the globe. High school seniors who have been chosen as National Merit finalists may also be eligible for the $20,000 Presidential Scholarship. The Trustee Scholarship is BU's most prestigious merit-based award, recognizing students with extraordinary academic and leadership abilities and covers full tuition and student fees. Applications must be received by December 1 to be considered for both scholarships.

Scholarship & Financial Aid **National Hispanic Recognition Program**

The National Hispanic Recognition Program offers academic recognition to Hispanic students who have received high scores on the PSAT/NMSQT taken during their junior year in high school, and who have a 3.0 GPA or higher. The program sends a list of recognized students to subscribing colleges. National Hispanic Recognition Program finalists with exceptional academic records who are admissible to BU will be considered for a four-year, $20,000 Presidential Scholarship.

Pre-College Summer Experience **Summer Pathways**

Summer Pathways is a program for female high school students who demonstrate promise in the fields of science and engineering. The Summer Pathways program seeks students from Boston Public Schools who would not otherwise have the opportunity to attend a summer enrichment program. Summer Pathways students learn about the wide range of academic and career opportunities in science and engineering.

Boston University
233 Bay State Road
Boston, MA 02215
Ph: (617) 353-2300
admissions@bu.edu
www.bu.edu

Fast Facts

STUDENT DIVERSITY

# undergraduates	16,239
% male/female	40/60
% first-generation college	19
% American Indian or Alaskan Native	<1
% Asian	14
% Black or African American	4
% Hispanic/Latino	11
% Native Hawaiian or Pacific Islander	<1
% White	41
% two or more races	4
% race and/or ethnicity unknown	4
% International/nonresident	22

STUDENT SUCCESS

% first-to-second year retention	93
% six-year graduation	87
% six-year graduation for underrepresented minority groups	84
% first-years who live on campus	99
% undergraduates who live on campus	75
full-time faculty	1,798
full-time minority faculty	257
student-faculty ratio	10:1

Popular majors Business Administration/ Management, Communications, International Relations, Pre-Medical Studies, Psychology, Biomedical Engineering

Multicultural student clubs and organizations 450+ Clubs, including the African Students Organization, Alianza Latina, Asian Student Union, Brazilian Association, Chinese Students and Scholars Association, India Club, Japanese Student Association, Korean Student Association, Russian American Cultural Club, Thai Student Association, and more.

AFFORDABILITY

Cost of Attendance

tuition	$50,980
required fees	$1,102
room and board	$15,270

Financial Aid

total institutional scholarships/grants	$180,922,199
% of students with financial need	36
% of students with need awarded any financial aid	100
% of students with need awarded any need-based scholarship or grant aid	100
% of students with need whose need was fully met	21
% Pell Grant recipients among first-years	18
average aid package	$39,725
average student loan debt upon graduation	$27,000

ADMISSIONS

# of applicants	60,815
% admitted	25
SAT Critical Reading	670-750
SAT Math	690-770
SAT Writing	n/a
ACT Composite	32
SAT/ACT optional	no
average HS GPA	3.8

DEADLINES

regular application closing date	1/2
early decision plan	yes
application closing date	ED 1: 11/1, ED 2: 1/2
early action plan	n/a
application closing date	n/a
application fee	$80
application fee online	$80
fee waiver for applicants with financial need	yes

Brandeis University

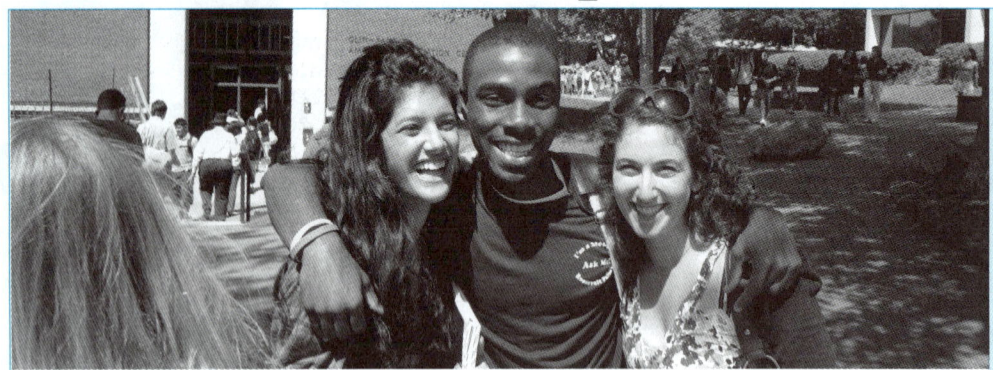

Brandeis University
415 South Street
Waltham, MA 02453
Ph: (781) 736-3500
admissions@brandeis.edu
www.brandeis.edu

A student-centered, mid-sized research university nestled in Waltham, a suburb of the greater Boston area, Brandeis University opened its doors in 1948 with the founding principle of inclusivity. Founders created the school as a place of learning, research, and community-building that was free of discriminatory admissions practices during an era when other colleges were placing quotas on applicants based on religious, gender, and/or racial identities. The community is illuminated by values rooted in Jewish history and experience, with focuses in reverence for higher learning and academic excellence, a robust engagement in critical thinking, and a commitment to making the world a better place. With a flexible curriculum allowing for interdisciplinary approaches and unparalleled access to world-class faculty who are personally invested in their students, Brandeis is rooted in the passionate pursuit of first-rate education, groundbreaking research, and innovative global outreach.

Brandeis is dedicated to making first-rate education affordable by working hard to meet demonstrated financial need and awarding merit scholarships, awarding more than $51 million in scholarships and grants each year to undergraduate students. Below are some of the opportunities offered in support of its scholars' academic pursuits:

Open House, Fly-In, Visit **Students Exploring and Embracing Diversity (SEED)**

The Students Exploring and Embracing Diversity program is an opportunity for prospective students to connect with current students, the Brandeis Intercultural Center and racial identity groups on campus. All meals are provided, and full and partial travel scholarships are available to cover students' transportation costs to and from Brandeis. Because space is limited, students interested in attending SEED are asked to complete a mini-application for the program, and they will be notified on a rolling basis about the status of their application.

Scholarship & Financial Aid **Posse University Partner**

Brandeis Posse is a merit-based scholarship program founded by Brandeis alumna Debbie Bial, '87. Brandeis Posse Scholars are selected for their academic, leadership and communication skills. They are expected to not only demonstrate strong academic abilities but also outstanding interpersonal and problem-solving skills. These students receive four-year full tuition leadership scholarships.

Scholarship & Financial Aid **Martin Luther King, Jr. Scholarship**

The Dr. Martin Luther King Jr. Fellowship is awarded to entering first-year students on the basis of academic performance and extracurricular participation in secondary school, outstanding community involvement and demonstrated financial need. Approximately 10-15 students receive the scholarship each year. MLK Fellows are generally under-represented in college as first-generation college students, students of color, and/or have high demonstrated financial need.

First-Year Experience & Transition **Myra Kraft Transitional Year Program (MKTYP)**

Established in 1968, Brandeis University's Myra Kraft Transitional Year Program (MKTYP) is an integral part of the institution's enduring commitment to social justice. Small classes and strong support systems in the first year help Myra Kraft TYP students apply the focus, energy, perseverance and maturity developed through leadership practiced in their life experiences to rigorous studies at the postsecondary level. Students admitted through the program are outstanding students who often have not had access to AP courses and honors courses in their previous schooling experiences. The program enables this group of young people, who otherwise may not have had access, the opportunity to explore new possibilities for their lives. The deadline to apply for the Myra Kraft Transitional Year Program is February 1, 2018.

Fast Facts

STUDENT DIVERSITY

# undergraduates	3,608
% male/female	43/57
% first-generation college	17
% American Indian or Alaskan Native	<1
% Asian	13
% Black or African American	5
% Hispanic/Latino	8
% Native Hawaiian or Pacific Islander	<1
% White	46
% two or more races	3
% race and/or ethnicity unknown	4
% International/nonresident	21

STUDENT SUCCESS

% first-to-second year retention	94
% six-year graduation	90
% six-year graduation for underrepresented minority groups	88
% first-years who live on campus	99
% undergraduates who live on campus	78
full-time faculty	361
full-time minority faculty	47
student-faculty ratio	10:1

Popular majors Economics, Business, Biology, Neuroscience, Chemistry, Psychology, Politics, History, PreHealth and PreLaw Programs

Multicultural student clubs and organizations Black Student Organization, Arab Culture Club, Chinese Cultural Connection, Society for the Advancement of Chicanos and Native Americans in Science, Students Organized Against Racism, Muslim Student Association, African Students Organization, Diverse City, Brandeis Zionist Alliance, Asian American Students Association

AFFORDABILITY

Cost of Attendance

tuition	$51,460
required fees	$2,077
room and board	$14,744

Financial Aid

total institutional scholarships/grants	$70,051,957
% of students with financial need	50
% of students with need awarded any financial aid	99
% of students with need awarded any need-based scholarship or grant aid	94
% of students with need whose need was fully met	69
% Pell Grant recipients among first-years	18
average aid package	$41,876
average student loan debt upon graduation	$32,922

ADMISSIONS

# of applicants	11,351
% admitted	33
SAT Critical Reading	610-710
SAT Math	660-770
SAT Writing	n/a
ACT Composite	31
SAT/ACT optional	yes
average HS GPA	3.88

DEADLINES

regular application closing date	1/1
early decision plan	yes
application closing date	11/1, 1/1
early action plan	n/a
application closing date	n/a
application fee	$80
application fee online	$80
fee waiver for applicants with financial need	yes

Framingham State University

Located just 20 miles west of Boston, Framingham State University offers small, personalized classes to undergraduate and graduate students on a beautiful, 78 acre, traditional New England campus. Framingham prides itself on its friendly, family-style community and provides freshman transition programs, as well as well-developed honors programs for exceptional students. Diversity among faculty, staff, the student body and curriculum contribute to the community's understanding of the multicultural world and enhance the quality of the learning experience on campus. Framingham State University is known for its outstanding academic reputation, interesting course offerings, exciting location, sense of community spirit and affordable cost.

Summer Bridge & Orientation **Orientation**

The Orientation Program provides an introduction to student life at the University. At orientation, new students meet faculty advisors from their academic departments; learn about courses, majors, and academics works at Framingham State University; meet current student leaders and other new students; learn about campus life and available support resources for students; and become familiar with the Framingham State University campus.

First-Year Experience & Transition **Relevant Advice & Mentoring for Multicultural Students (R.A.M.2S)**

The R.A.M.2S Program is designed to assist first-year students of color in the achievement of academic and life skills. It accomplishes its mission through connections with the University in three distinct areas: academic excellence; interpersonal connections; and personal awareness. Students are taught to eliminate the stigma associated with seeking out academic assistance and tutoring, and achieve academic success through individual mentor teams and the development of study skills. Participants in the program also learn the value of social involvement and are guided to explore career paths and life success.

Academic Advising & Support **Center for Academic Success and Achievement (CASA)**

CASA is a free resource for all current students, for those wishing to maintain good grades to those who are struggling academically. Services include tutoring in math and writing, seminar rooms that serve as meeting places, workshops on academic success, a networked computer lab with a printer and individual study carrels for quiet study.

Academic Advising & Support **GenerationOne**

GenerationOne is a support group that brings first-generation faculty, staff and students together for activities such as special programming and social gatherings. The trademark is a G1 logo that can be found all around campus, allowing for easy identification of other first-generation faculty, staff and students. When students see the sticker, they know they have an ally who may understand or relate to their experience as a first-generation student. There are also youth mentoring opportunities available to first-generation college students, allowing them to engage in a meaningful way with the campus and community.

Student Life & Support **Center for Inclusive Excellence**

The Center for Inclusive Excellence at Framingham State University is a Brave Space dedicated to creating and supporting an environment that reflects a collective commitment to promoting equity, advocating social justice and making excellence inclusive. As a guiding principle, Inclusive Excellence is meant to include and engage the rich diversity of students, staff, faculty, administrators, alumni and community constituents in authentic learning which often requires embracing the brave qualities of challenge, risk and difficulty. Thus, we recognize this work to be a journey of discovery and transformation for every aspect and level of the university.

Framingham State University
100 State Street
Framingham, MA 01701
Ph: (508) 626-4500
admissions@framingham.edu
www.framingham.edu

Fast Facts

STUDENT DIVERSITY

# undergraduates	4,337
% male/female	41/59
% first-generation college	48
% American Indian or Alaskan Native	<1
% Asian	3
% Black or African American	11
% Hispanic/Latino	14
% Native Hawaiian or Pacific Islander	<1
% White	65
% two or more races	4
% race and/or ethnicity unknown	2
% International/nonresident	1

STUDENT SUCCESS

% first-to-second year retention	76
% six-year graduation	54
% six-year graduation for underrepresented minority groups	52
% first-years who live on campus	80
% undergraduates who live on campus	48
full-time faculty	197
full-time minority faculty	39
student-faculty ratio	14:1

Popular majors Psychology, Business Administration, Food and Nutrition, Criminology, Elementary Education, Communication Arts, Fashion Design and Retailing, Biology, Sociology

Multicultural student clubs and organizations Black Student Union, The Pride Alliance Club, FSU Veterans Association, M.I.S.S (Motivation. Intersectionality. Solidarity. Sisterhood), Student Leaders in Diversity (SLID), Brother to Brother (B2B)

AFFORDABILITY

Cost of Attendance

tuition	$16,000 or in-state: $9,920
required fees	n/a
room and board	$11,820

Financial Aid

total institutional scholarships/grants	$2,800,000
% of students with financial need	65
% of students with need awarded any financial aid	100
% of students with need awarded any need-based scholarship or grant aid	51
% of students with need whose need was fully met	53
% Pell Grant recipients among first-years	40
average aid package	$11,775
average student loan debt upon graduation	$29,493

ADMISSIONS

# of applicants	5,210
% admitted	65
SAT Critical Reading	460-550
SAT Math	460-550
SAT Writing	440-540
ACT Composite	21
SAT/ACT optional	no
average HS GPA	3.1

DEADLINES

regular application closing date	2/15
early decision plan	n/a
application closing date	n/a
early action plan	yes
application closing date	11/15
application fee	$50
application fee online	$50
fee waiver for applicants with financial need	yes

Harvard University

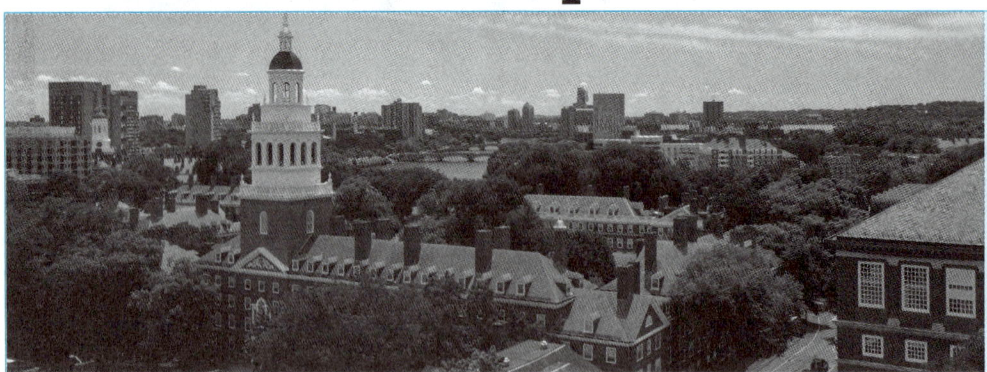

From world-renowned professors to world-class friendships, students at Harvard find a community that welcomes them, challenges them, and exposes them to new ideas daily. With so many opportunities afforded to our students, the Harvard experience is unique for every undergraduate. With over 450 student organizations to join, 49 concentrations to study, 17 freshman dorms and 12 upperclass houses to live in, in addition to hundreds of faculty members and more than 6600 students to befriend, each student experiences a different piece of Harvard College over the course of four years here. While Harvard is renowned for its academic excellence, we strongly believe that one of our greatest strengths is the exceptional diversity within the student body. We are committed to ensuring all admitted students have the opportunity to attend Harvard, regardless of the economic obstacles they may have encountered.

Pre-College Prep & Outreach **Harvard College Recruitment Coordinators**

The Admissions and Financial Aid Office sponsors several initiatives designed to encourage talented students from all backgrounds to learn more about Harvard. Through these programs, prospective students can get in touch with current Harvard students to hear about their experiences and to ask questions about admissions and financial aid.

The Harvard First Generation Program (HFGP) focuses on directing college awareness to future first generation college students and shares information about first generation student life at Harvard. Email: firstgen@fas.harvard.edu.

The Harvard Financial Aid Initiative (HFAI) serves as a touchstone for those looking to learn more about the application and financial aid process and raises awareness about college affordability for students interested in all kinds of colleges. Email:hfai@fas.harvard.edu.

The Undergraduate Minority Recruitment Program (UMRP) helps to expand the diversity of incoming classes by encouraging minority students to consider applying to Harvard College. Email: umrp@fas.harvard.edu.

Scholarship & Financial Aid **The Harvard College Griffin Financial Aid Office**

Harvard is committed to meeting 100 percent of demonstrated financial need. For many families, the expected parent contribution is between zero and 10 percent of family income, with no contribution for parents with incomes under $65,000 a year. One-hundred percent of students can graduate debt-free. For low-income students, there is additional assistance through the Student Events Fund and the Winter Coat Fund, as well as for paying for tutoring costs and helping with the expenses of starting college.

Student Life & Support **First Generation Programs**

Harvard First Generation Student Union (FGSU)

FGSU is a student organization that seeks to ease the transition to college, to build community, and to advocate for first-gen students on campus. FGSU not only hosts fun study breaks to bring the first-gen community together, they also collaborate with many Harvard offices (the Office of Career Services, the Bureau of Study Counsel, the Freshman Dean's Office and the Financial Aid Office) to host events for and to provide resources to first-gen students.

First Generation Harvard Alumni

The First Generation Harvard Alumni Mentor Program pairs first-generation students with alumni mentors who were the first in their family to graduate from college. Alumni mentors add to the existing advising network for first-year students, who all have assigned academic advisors, residential advisors, and peer advisors to support them as they transition to college.

Harvard University
Office of Admissions and Financial Aid
86 Brattle Street
Cambridge, MA 02138
Ph: (617) 495-1551
college@fas.harvard.edu
www.college.harvard.edu

Fast Facts

STUDENT DIVERSITY

# undergraduates	6,650
% male/female	51/49
% first-generation college	15
% American Indian or Alaskan Native	1
% Asian	19
% Black or African American	7
% Hispanic/Latino	10
% Native Hawaiian or Pacific Islander	1
% White	42
% two or more races	7
% race and/or ethnicity unknown	2
% International/nonresident	11

STUDENT SUCCESS

% first-to-second year retention	98
% six-year graduation	97
% six-year graduation for underrepresented minority groups	97
% first-years who live on campus	100
% undergraduates who live on campus	98
full-time faculty	1,020
full-time minority faculty	335
student-faculty ratio	7:1

Popular majors Economics, Government, History and Literature, Biological Sciences

Multicultural student clubs and organizations Asian American Association, Black Students Association, Act on a Dream, Fuerza Latina, Native Americans at Harvard College, South Asian Association, Black Men's Forum, Latinos in Health Careers, International Women's Rights Collective, and many more

AFFORDABILITY

Cost of Attendance

tuition	$44,990
required fees	$3,959
room and board	$16,660

Financial Aid

total institutional scholarships/grants	$177,000,000
% of students with financial need	55
% of students with need awarded any financial aid	100
% of students with need awarded any need-based scholarship or grant aid	100
% of students with need whose need was fully met	100
% Pell Grant recipients among first-years	18
average aid package	$50,650
average student loan debt upon graduation	$15,114

ADMISSIONS

# of applicants	39,506
% admitted	5
SAT Evidence-Based Reading & Writing	700-800
SAT Math	710-800
ACT Composite	32-35
SAT/ACT optional	no
average HS GPA	top 10%

DEADLINES

regular application closing date	1/1
early decision plan	no
application closing date	n/a
early action plan	yes
application closing date	11/1
application fee	$75
application fee online	$75
fee waiver for applicants with financial need	yes

Lasell College

An innovator in education since 1851, Lasell College located 8 miles from Boston in suburban Newton, MA is a challenging environment; where self-expression and academic exploration are promoted; where dedicated faculty deliver a diverse curriculum through *Connected Learning*, Lasell's unique undergraduate teaching method; and where our students immerse themselves in academic, civic, and career-relevant areas, so they are ready to succeed in a diverse and complex world. Every Lasell student completes at least one professional internship prior to graduation; earning Lasell College recognition as a national leader in experiential learning and earning Lasell graduates employment and graduate school success.

Open House, Fly-In, Visit **Schedule your visit at lasell.edu/visitus**

Each year, the Office of Undergraduate Admission sponsors two College-wide Open House Programs for prospective students and families. Open House is an excellent opportunity to explore Lasell's academic programs, 17 division III varsity athletic programs, 70 plus student clubs and organizations, and to learn more about Lasell's unique teaching method: *Connected Learning*. In addition, the Office of Undergraduate Admission offers tours of campus Monday-Friday and select Saturdays during the year.

Special Admissions Policy **Lasell is Test Optional**

Lasell College reviews complete applications for entry to the Fall and Spring terms. Early Action candidates for the Fall semester must submit applications by November 15 and are informed of decisions beginning December 1. Regular Admission candidates for the Fall and Spring semesters are reviewed on a deadline-free rolling basis and are informed of decisions beginning December 15 (for the Fall entry term) and September 15 (for the Spring entry term). Students are encouraged to complete their applications as soon as possible.

Lasell College is Test Optional and holistically evaluates applicants emphasizing their scholastic record, extracurricular involvement, personal essay and interview. Students who believe the results from the SAT or ACT support their candidacy for admission, are encouraged to submit their scores. SAT and ACT scores are not used in consideration of merit scholarships. All undergraduate candidates are considered for the College's merit scholarships. Admitted students are also encouraged to submit the FAFSA for potential financial assistance.

Academic Advising & Support **One to One Professional Advising**

Lasell provides all first-year students with a full-time, professional advisor. Advisors assist students with developing educational and career goals, succeeding academically, planning internships and meeting graduation requirements. Lasell also recognizes the individuality of each student's learning style, as a result the Academic Achievement Center provides free academic support services through a variety of programs.

Academic Courses & Service Learning **Top-10 for required Internships**

Lasell College offers nearly 40 undergraduate majors, a challenging Honors Program, Fifth-Year Option (4+1) graduate degree, a Three-year degree option, credit-bearing ESL, and the Lasell Works Program (a cost-savings initiative that provides students with the ability to earn a Lasell College bachelor's degree at a declining tuition rate).

Lasell College recently earned The Carnegie Foundation's classification for excellence in community engagement, a distinction awarded to fewer than 10% of institutions nationally, and Lasell was named with distinction for 5 consecutive years by the President's Community Service Honor Roll. Lasell's commitment to service and global awareness is supported by the College's Center for Community-based Learning and over 75 study-abroad programs.

Lasell College
1844 Commonwealth Avenue
Newton, MA 02466
Ph: (617) 243-2225
info@lasell.edu
www.lasell.edu

Fast Facts

STUDENT DIVERSITY	
# undergraduates	1,696
% male/female	36/64
% first-generation college	43
% American Indian or Alaskan Native	0
% Asian	2
% Black or African American	7
% Hispanic/Latino	9
% Native Hawaiian or Pacific Islander	0
% White	69
% two or more races	2
% race and/or ethnicity unknown	4
% International/nonresident	7

STUDENT SUCCESS	
% first-to-second year retention	73
% six-year graduation	54
% six-year graduation for underrepresented minority groups	43
% first-years who live on campus	92
% undergraduates who live on campus	74
full-time faculty	93
full-time minority faculty	17
student-faculty ratio	13:1

Popular majors School of Business, School of Communication & the Arts, School of Fashion, School of Health Sciences, School of Social Sciences, Humanities, & Education

Multicultural student clubs and organizations Multicultural Student Union, Latin America Culture Club, Lasell College Chapter of Niños de Veracruz, International Club, Saudi Students Association, PRIDE, She's the First, Relay for Life, Habitat for Humanity, Student Government Association

AFFORDABILITY	
Cost of Attendance	
tuition	$33,300
required fees	$1,300
room and board	$14,800
Financial Aid	
total institutional scholarships/grants	$31,481,313
% of students with financial need	77
% of students with need awarded any financial aid	100
% of students with need awarded any need-based scholarship or grant aid	99
% of students with need whose need was fully met	13
% Pell Grant recipients among first-years	39
average aid package	$32,700
average student loan debt upon graduation	$40,600

ADMISSIONS	
# of applicants	3,822
% admitted	80
SAT Critical Reading	500-590
SAT Math	490-580
SAT Writing	n/a
ACT Composite	21
SAT/ACT optional	yes
average HS GPA	3.0

DEADLINES	
regular application closing date	rolling
early decision plan	n/a
application closing date	n/a
early action plan	yes
application closing date	11/15
application fee	$40
application fee online	waived
fee waiver for applicants with financial need	yes

Northeastern University

Northeastern University is a leader in integrating rigorous classroom studies with experiential learning opportunities, anchored by the nation's largest, most innovative cooperative education (co-op) program. In addition to the signature co-op program, in which students alternate between classroom learning and work experience, Northeastern offers students several other experiential learning opportunities, including student research, service learning and global learning experiences. All of this takes place on a vibrant, 73-acre campus located in the heart of Boston, which offers modern academic, residential and recreational facilities.

Scholarship & Financial Aid **$263.6 Million in Financial Aid**

Northeastern is committed to making college accessible and affordable for all students interested in pursuing their passions. The university offers more than $263 million in grant and scholarship assistance, participates in federal aid programs and offers information on the Northeastern payment plan as well as private educational loans. In addition, Northeastern offers a number of scholarships that are awarded to students who are well prepared for success in college and demonstrate strong leadership and community values.

Scholarship & Financial Aid **Torch Scholars Program**

The Torch Scholars Program is a bold and innovative scholarship initiative awarded to individuals who have overcome exceptional odds and who demonstrate the potential to excel academically. Torch Scholars receive full tuition, fees and room and board, as well as significant personal and academic support throughout their undergraduate careers.

Student Life & Support **Diverse University Community**

Reflecting the city of Boston and the world beyond, Northeastern is a rich blend of cultures, languages, religions and traditions. The university supports and celebrates these characteristics through many centers, institutes and programs including the John D. O'Bryant African-American Institute, Asian American Center, Latino/a Student Cultural Center, LGBT Community, Hillel Jewish Community, Catholic Center, Spiritual Life Center, Center for Intercultural Engagement, and Office of Global Services.

Student Life & Support **Diversity Initiatives**

Northeastern is a community that is comprised of students, faculty and staff from a diversity of backgrounds and experiences. The university values the contributions of all its members and works to support its under-represented populations through a network of active cultural centers and mentoring programs. In recruiting students, Northeastern reaches out to a wide variety of geographically distant locations, nationally and internationally, and works closely with a host of support programs such as Upward Bound, Gear UP and Kids to College.

Mentoring **Legacy Mentoring/Retention Program**

The Legacy Mentoring Program provides a sense of belonging, retention and academic success for the black and Latino/a community. This active program includes events such as Black and Latino New Student Orientation, a study abroad forum, financial aid and professional development workshops, community service projects and many social outings.

Northeastern University
360 Huntington Avenue
Boston, MA 02115
Ph: (617) 373-2200
admissions@northeastern.edu
www.northeastern.edu

Fast Facts

STUDENT DIVERSITY

# undergraduates	18,107
% male/female	49/51
% first-generation college	n/a
% American Indian or Alaskan Native	<1
% Asian	17
% Black or African American	5
% Hispanic/Latino	10
% Native Hawaiian or Pacific Islander	<1
% White	62
% two or more races	5
% race and/or ethnicity unknown	6
% International/nonresident	20

STUDENT SUCCESS

% first-to-second year retention	97
% six-year graduation	86
% six-year graduation for underrepresented minority groups	n/a
% first-years who live on campus	99
% undergraduates who live on campus	n/a
full-time faculty	1,400
full-time minority faculty	n/a
student-faculty ratio	14:1

Popular majors Business/International Business, Engineering, Health Services/Allied Health

Multicultural student clubs and organizations Asian Student Association, Black Student Association, Choral Society, Females' Center of Excellence and Leadership, FIRST Robotics, Latin-American Student Organization, Northeastern News, NUBiLAGA, Resident Student Association, Student Government Association

AFFORDABILITY

Cost of Attendance

tuition	$48,560
required fees	$937
room and board	$15,660

Financial Aid

total institutional scholarships/grants	$263,600,000
% of students with financial need	48
% of students with need awarded any financial aid	100
% of students with need awarded any need-based scholarship or grant aid	98
% of students with need whose need was fully met	100
% Pell Grant recipients among first-years	14
average aid package	$39,320
average student loan debt upon graduation	n/a

ADMISSIONS

# of applicants	54,206
% admitted	27
SAT Evidence-Based Reading & Writing	680-750
SAT Math	690-770
ACT Composite	32-34
SAT/ACT optional	no
average HS GPA	4.0-4.4

DEADLINES

regular application closing date	1/1
early decision plan	yes
application closing date	11/1
early action plan	yes
application closing date	11/1
application fee	$75
application fee online	$75
fee waiver for applicants with financial need	yes

Smith College

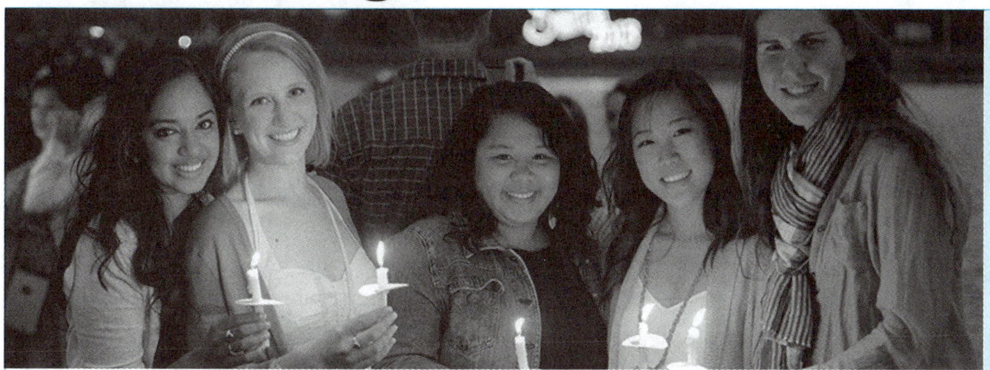

Smith College educates women of promise for lives of distinction. Smith links the power of the liberal arts to excellence in research and scholarship, developing leaders for society's challenges. Smith is distinguished by a diverse student body, a culturally vibrant surrounding area and participation in the Five College Consortium. The rigorous academic program "anchored in the sciences, the humanities and arts"is demanding yet flexible, with course offerings in more than 50 areas of study. A host of unique study abroad programs, the first engineering program offered at a women's college and a growing roster of "concentrations" which allow students to organize unique combinations of intellectual and practical experiences, are signature offerings of the college.

Pre-College Summer Experience **Summer Programs**

High school students from around the globe participate in a month-long summer program in science and engineering. Funding is available for low-income students. Students and teachers also come to Smith's campus for enrichment programs and professional development workshops. Additional summer programs include: Field Studies for Sustainable Futures, Discovering Women's History and Young Women's Writing Workshop.

Open House, Fly-In, Visit **Women of Distinction**

The Women of Distinction program for high school seniors highlights the opportunities at Smith for African American, Asian American, Latina and Native American students. Participants in the three-day program live in campus houses, experience academic life and attend panels and workshops on student life and the college admission process. There is a required application, and students are chosen on the basis of academic and personal qualities. All expenses are covered by Smith.

Scholarship & Financial Aid **Springfield and Holyoke Partnership**

Through this partnership, four graduates from the Springfield and Holyoke, Massachusetts public schools are selected to receive a full-tuition scholarship for each of their four undergraduate years at Smith. Students are selected based on their academic record and leadership potential and are automatically considered by applying to Smith.

Academic Courses & Service Learning **Urban Education Initiative**

The Urban Education Initiative is a service-learning program that brings Smith students to elementary, middle and high schools in New York City, Chicago and nearby Springfield, Massachusetts. Urban Education Fellows spend three weeks in January at one of the partner schools providing one-on-one tutoring and classroom assistance.

Student Life & Support **Student Support Groups**

Support groups for underrepresented and first-generation students include: The Minority Association of Pre-health Students, Union of Underrepresented Students in the Sciences, AEMES (Achieving Excellence in Mathematics, Engineering and Sciences) and FIGS (First-Generation Student Alliance of Smith College).

Smith College
7 College Lane
Northampton, MA 01063
Ph: (413) 585-2500
admission@smith.edu
www.smith.edu

Fast Facts

STUDENT DIVERSITY

# undergraduates	2,521
% male/female	1/99
% first-generation college	18
% American Indian or Alaskan Native	<1
% Asian	12
% Black or African American	6
% Hispanic/Latino	10
% Native Hawaiian or Pacific Islander	<1
% White	45
% two or more races	5
% race and/or ethnicity unknown	9
% International/nonresident	14

STUDENT SUCCESS

% first-to-second year retention	90
% six-year graduation	88
% six-year graduation for underrepresented minority groups	85
% first-years who live on campus	100
% undergraduates who live on campus	96
full-time faculty	270
full-time minority faculty	54
student-faculty ratio	9:1

Popular majors Sciences, Foreign Languages, Area, Ethnic, Cultural, Gender, and Group Studies, Psychology, Visual and Performing Arts, Social Sciences, Government, Economics, English

Multicultural student clubs and organizations Asian Students' Assoc., Black Students' Alliance, Chinese Interregional Student Org., South Asian Student Assoc, Indigenous Smith Students, International Students' Org., Korean Students' Assoc., Multiethnic Interracial Smith College, Nosotras, African and Caribbean Students' Assoc., Vietnamese Students' Assoc.

AFFORDABILITY

Cost of Attendance

tuition	$49,760
required fees	$284
room and board	$16,730

Financial Aid

total institutional scholarships/grants	$69,189,392
% of students with financial need	62
% of students with need awarded any financial aid	100
% of students with need awarded any need-based scholarship or grant aid	99
% of students with need whose need was fully met	100
% Pell Grant recipients among first-years	20
average aid package	$51,046
average student loan debt upon graduation	$24,501

ADMISSIONS

# of applicants	5,432
% admitted	32
SAT Critical Reading	650-740
SAT Math	630-750
SAT Writing	620-720
ACT Composite	31
SAT/ACT optional	yes
average HS GPA	4.0

DEADLINES

regular application closing date	1/15
early decision plan	yes
application closing date	ED 1 – 11/15, ED 2 – 1/1
early action plan	n/a
application closing date	n/a
application fee	$0
application fee online	$0
fee waiver for applicants with financial need	n/a

Tufts University

Tufts University
Bendetson Hall
Medford, MA 02155
Ph: (617) 627-3170
undergraduate.admissions@tufts.edu
www.tufts.edu

Located less than five miles outside of downtown Boston, Tufts University is a world-class research institution offering undergraduate degrees in liberal arts and engineering. As a midsize university, Tufts offers the chance to join a close-knit community that supports students' desire to take intellectual risks and challenge conventional wisdom, all in a beautiful campus setting with easy access to one of America's most exciting cities.

Pre-College Prep & Outreach **Early College Awareness Initiative**

Tufts' Office of Undergraduate Admissions runs an Early College Awareness Initiative, which brings Boston area middle and early high school students to campus regularly to expose them to college life.

Open House, Fly-In, Visit **Voices of Tufts**

The Voices of Tufts program invites high school seniors interested in the diversity that exists at Tufts to visit the campus for a two-day, fly-in program each fall that provides a multicultural perspective on attending the university.

Special Admissions Policy **Questbridge**

Tufts is a partner school with QuestBridge, a national non-profit organization that connects high-achieving, low-income students with some of the best universities. Tufts also has an active Quest Scholars network chapter which supports QuestBridge students at Tufts.

Scholarship & Financial Aid **Loan Replacement Policy/Financial Aid**

Tufts' Loan Replacement Policy replaces loans with scholarship grants for all undergraduates whose annual family income is below $60,000. Tufts meets 100% of demonstrated need for all students admitted no matter their citizenship status.

Summer Bridge & Orientation **Bridge to Engineering Success at Tufts (BEST Scholars Program)**

The BEST Scholars Program is a six-week residential summer bridge program for a select group of incoming engineering students. The program is designed to give nominated students an opportunity to take two Tufts University courses and participate in workshops to assist incoming first-year students transition from high school to college.

Summer Bridge & Orientation **Bridge to Liberal Arts Success at Tufts (BLAST Scholars Program)**

The BLAST Scholars Program is a six-week residential summer bridge program for a select group of incoming liberal arts students. The program is designed to give nominated students an opportunity to take two Tufts University courses, and participate in workshops to help students transition from high school to college.

First-Year Experience & Transition **Promoting Retention in Science and Engineering**

This program is an advising program designed to create a sense of community, build a supportive cohort and acquaint students with academic resources.

Student Life & Support **First Generation College Student Council**

The Tufts First Generation College Student Council's mission is to bridge the gap between Tufts' resources and first-generation college students. The council serves as a networking opportunity for support and empowerment for all students who self-identify as first-generation-to-college.

Fast Facts

STUDENT DIVERSITY

# undergraduates	5,459
% male/female	50/50
% first-generation college	10
% American Indian or Alaskan Native	<1
% Asian	12
% Black or African American	4
% Hispanic/Latino	7
% Native Hawaiian or Pacific Islander	<1
% White	56
% two or more races	5
% race and/or ethnicity unknown	6
% International/nonresident	10

STUDENT SUCCESS

% first-to-second year retention	97
% six-year graduation	94
% six-year graduation for underrepresented minority groups	94
% first-years who live on campus	100
% undergraduates who live on campus	65
full-time faculty	674
full-time minority faculty	136
student-faculty ratio	9:1

Popular majors Computer Science, Biology, Economics, Engineering, International Relations, Psychology, English

Multicultural student clubs and organizations
African Student Assoc. (ASO), Arab Students Assoc., Asian American Alliance (AAA), Assoc. of Latin American Students (ALAS), Assoc. of South Asians (ASA), Baha'I Student Assoc., Caribbean Club, Chinese Students Assoc., Black Student Union, Hindu Students Council, International Club, Muslim Students Assoc., Hillel, Pan-African Alliance (PAA), Assoc. of Multiracial People at Tufts (AMPT)

AFFORDABILITY

Cost of Attendance

tuition	$53,152
required fees	$1,166
room and board	$14,054

Financial Aid

total institutional scholarships/grants	$80,855,639
% of students with financial need	39
% of students with need awarded any financial aid	100
% of students with need awarded any need-based scholarship or grant aid	91
% of students with need whose need was fully met	100
% Pell Grant recipients among first-years	12
average aid package	$43,518
average student loan debt upon graduation	$26,185

ADMISSIONS

# of applicants	21,101
% admitted	15
SAT Evidence-Based Reading & Writing	700-760
SAT Math	710-780
ACT Composite	33
SAT/ACT optional	no
average HS GPA	n/a

DEADLINES

regular application closing date	1/1
early decision plan	yes
application closing date	11/1 and 1/1
early action plan	n/a
application closing date	n/a
application fee	$75
application fee online	$75
fee waiver for applicants with financial need	yes

University of Massachusetts Lowell

UMass Lowell is a comprehensive, public, national research university. Its 125-acre campus is located along the banks of the Merrimack River in the culturally rich city of Lowell, 25 miles north of Boston. We are committed to preparing students for work in the real world by providing an affordable, high-quality education. Our students are more successful than ever thanks to accredited programs, a focus on hands-on learning and personal attention from accomplished faculty and dedicated staff.

Scholarship & Financial Aid

Scholarships are gift aid that does not need to be repaid. Most scholarships are awarded based on merit, financial need or both. Although not required for all scholarships, we recommend all students fill out the FAFSA. The specific amounts and number of scholarships offered to students are based on available funding each year. UMass Lowell does not use separate applications for the selection of most merit and need-based scholarships.

First-Year Experience & Transition **Strategies for Success**

Strategies for Success is designed to prepare incoming first year students for college success. The program enables students to develop academic skills and the motivation needed for effective learning. Program highlights include faculty-led classroom experiences, a session with current UMass Lowell students, study skills enrichment, college transition techniques, a goal setting session and more. Previous track options have included: Find Your Hidden Potential, Conquer College Challenges or Make Connections in Class and Beyond.

First-Year Experience & Transition **Centers for Learning and Academic Support Services (CLASS)**

Our mission is to enhance the educational experience by easing the transition into UMass Lowell. We create a climate of collegiality, a sense of community and collaboration among students, faculty and staff in an environment that fosters and encourages creativity, growing independence and academic success.

Scholars & Leadership **DifferenceMaker**

Do you want to help shape the future? Do you thrive in a supportive or collaborative environment? If so, get involved! The DifferenceMaker program sponsors workshops and holds contests that award money to the best projects, helping students fund their ideas as they learn how to solve problems through innovative and entrepreneurial action. DifferenceMakers come from all majors and the program provides various resources such as training, alumni mentoring, faculty advising and funding to help students pursue their ideas.

Academic Courses & Service Learning **Co-ops and Internships**

Want to test drive a job? UMass Lowell's partnerships with key employers provide improved quality and depth of education and experience through meaningful, sometimes even paid, work in a real-world environment. Internships are available for students in any major and can lead to full-time employment after graduation. We hear it all the time: Employers love UMass Lowell students.

Academic Courses & Service Learning **Service Learning**

Service learning gives students the opportunity to work with community organizations, tackling real life issues and gaining course credit in the process. Projects range from developing a business plan for a local not-for-profit, working with foster children to creating energy solutions for a village in Peru.

University of Massachusetts Lowell
University Crossing, 220 Pawtucket St., Suite 420
Lowell, MA 01854-2874
Ph: (978) 934-3931
admissions@uml.edu
www.uml.edu

Fast Facts

STUDENT DIVERSITY

# undergraduates	10,854
% male/female	63/37
% first-generation college	23
% American Indian or Alaskan Native	<1
% Asian	9
% Black or African American	6
% Hispanic/Latino	9
% Native Hawaiian or Pacific Islander	0
% White	60
% two or more races	3
% race and/or ethnicity unknown	5
% International/nonresident	10

STUDENT SUCCESS

% first-to-second year retention	85
% six-year graduation	56
% six-year graduation for underrepresented minority groups	49
% first-years who live on campus	80
% undergraduates who live on campus	37
full-time faculty	576
full-time minority faculty	148
student-faculty ratio	17:1

Popular majors Business Administration and Management, Criminal Justice/Safety Studies, Psychology, Computer and Information Sciences, Engineering, Health Sciences

Multicultural student clubs and organizations Assoc. of Latino Professionals for America, Assoc. of Students of African Origin, Cambodian American Student Assoc., Haitian American Student Assoc., International Student Club, Latin American Student Assoc., Society of Hispanic Professional Engineers, Southeast Asian Student Assoc., Vietnamese Student Assoc., Student Assoc. of Chinese Americans

AFFORDABILITY

Cost of Attendance

tuition	In-state: $14,350; Out-of-state: $31,415
required fees	$450
room and board	$12,496

Financial Aid

total institutional scholarships/grants	$34,327,992
% of students with financial need	61
% of students with need awarded any financial aid	100
% of students with need awarded any need-based scholarship or grant aid	88
% of students with need whose need was fully met	51
% Pell Grant recipients among first-years	25
average aid package	$15,393
average student loan debt upon graduation	$31,432

ADMISSIONS

# of applicants	13,182
% admitted	65
SAT Critical Reading	520-620
SAT Math	550-640
SAT Writing	500-590
ACT Composite	24-29
SAT/ACT optional	yes
average HS GPA	3.59

DEADLINES

regular application closing date	2/1
early decision plan	yes
application closing date	n/a
early action plan	yes
application closing date	11/1
application fee	$60
application fee online	$60
fee waiver for applicants with financial need	yes

Wellesley College

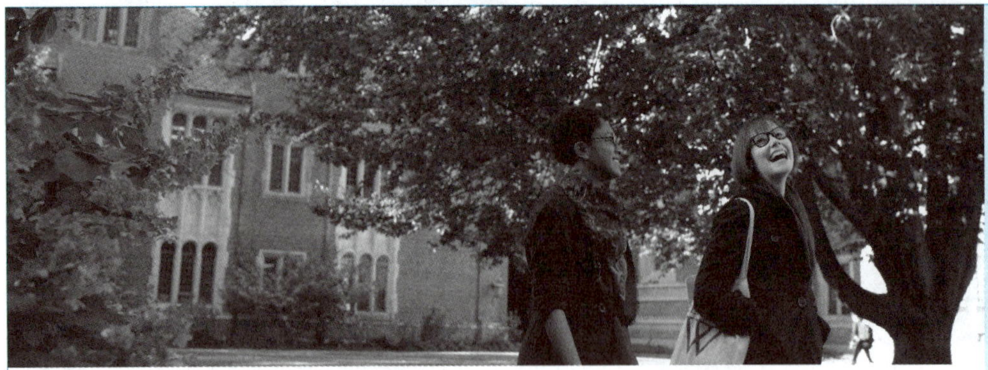

Wellesley College
106 Central Street
Wellesley, MA 02481
Ph: (781) 283-2270
admission@wellesley.edu
www.wellesley.edu

On Wellesley's scenic residential campus, just 12 miles west of Boston, students enjoy the best of both worlds: a great sense of community in a breathtakingly beautiful setting and easy access to Boston, an academic, medical, cultural, and historic hub and one of the largest college cities in the world. Ranked among the top liberal arts and sciences colleges, Wellesley has a deep tradition of educating women who make a difference in the world. In addition to 1,000+ classes and 54 majors, Wellesley offers pre-medical and pre-law advisory programs, and cross-registration with MIT and others. Wellesley professors are accessible and known for their outstanding commitment to teaching and academic career advising. Multiculturalism is a way of life within the College's welcoming community, which includes students from all 50 states and more than 80 countries. Due to its need-blind admission policy for U.S. citizens and permanent residents, generous financial aid, and low student-loan levels, Wellesley is also considered one of the most socio-economically diverse colleges in the nation. Classes are discussion based so students have the opportunity not only to learn from the professor, but also each other. With a rich history, an established reputation for academic excellence, and state-of-the-art resources, Wellesley provides its students with the skills and experiences necessary to be successful in today's global environment.

Open House, Fly-In, Visit **Discover Wellesley Weekend**

Wellesley fully funds a select number of travel grants for talented high school seniors from lower socioeconomic and first-generation backgrounds to attend Discover Wellesley Weekend in October. Visitors spend time with current students overnight, attend classes, engage with student clubs, and get an insider's view of the campus and community. The annual priority deadline for the fall travel grant application is June 30th. The final application deadline occurs in mid-August. Wellesley also selects and funds travel for admitted students for Spring Open Campus.

Scholarship & Financial Aid **Financially Possible**

Wellesley is able to use its substantial endowment to meet the financial needs of it students. Wellesley admits U.S. Citizens and U.S. Permanent Residents based on their personal and academic merits alone, without any regard for their ability to pay. Once admitted, Wellesley guarantees to meet 100 percent of every student's demonstrated financial need. The College keeps packaged loan levels very low, even eliminating loans to students from families with incomes under $60,000. Financial aid packages are portable to the more than 160 approved study abroad programs, and funding is also available for research and service projects.

Academic Advising & Support **Mentors Abound**

Wellesley's more than 35,000 alumnae and 2,300 students make up one of the world's most powerful women's networks. Wellesley's new Career Education model for the liberal arts is designed to prepare and inspire every Wellesley student to craft a lifetime of opportunity and reach her full potential. Through an individually tailored, holistic approach to career education, Wellesley students develop strategies to pursue their goals in any field, and receive continued support through all stages of their lives and all stages of the career development process. Additionally, students have access to the Hive; designed exclusively for Wellesley, this platform lets students and alumnae interact to ask questions, seek guidance, and coach and inspire each other, and as well as find paths toward their professional goals. Cultural advisors also work closely with both students and faculty. Individualized peer tutoring is available to all students at no extra cost. In addition, Wellesley Plus, a voluntary transition program for first year students, and the First Generation Network are programs designed to support and connect students that are the first in their families to attend college.

Fast Facts

STUDENT DIVERSITY	
# undergraduates	2,300
% male/female	0/100
% first-generation college	17
% American Indian or Alaskan Native	<1
% Asian	22
% Black or African American	7
% Hispanic/Latino	13
% Native Hawaiian or Pacific Islander	<1
% White	36
% two or more races	7
% race and/or ethnicity unknown	1
% International/nonresident	13

STUDENT SUCCESS	
% first-to-second year retention	96
% six-year graduation	93
% six-year graduation for underrepresented minority groups	94
% first-years who live on campus	100
% undergraduates who live on campus	98
full-time faculty	293
full-time minority faculty	75
student-faculty ratio	7:1

Popular majors Economics, Political Science, English, Psychology, Neuroscience, Biological Sciences, Computer Science

Multicultural student clubs and organizations African Students' Assoc., Asian Student Union, Chinese Students Assoc., Club Filipina, Ethos (Women of African Descent), First Generation Network, Korean Students Assoc., Mezcla (Women of Latinx Descent), Native American Student Org., Slater International Assoc., Spectrum (LGBTQA), Taiwanese Cultural Org., United World Colleges, Assoc. for South Asian Cultures

AFFORDABILITY	
Cost of Attendance	
tuition	$50,840
required fees	$308
room and board	$15,836
Financial Aid	
total institutional scholarships/grants	$57,587,172
% of students with financial need	63
% of students with need awarded any financial aid	100
% of students with need awarded any need-based scholarship or grant aid	100
% of students with need whose need was fully met	100
% Pell Grant recipients among first-years	20
average aid package	$47,527
average student loan debt upon graduation	$13,415

ADMISSIONS	
# of applicants	5,703
% admitted	22
SAT Reading & Writing	660-750
SAT Math	650-750
ACT Composite	30-33
SAT/ACT optional	no
average HS GPA	n/a

DEADLINES	
regular application closing date	1/15
early decision plan	yes
application closing date	ED 1: 11/1, ED 2: 1/1
early action plan	n/a
application closing date	n/a
application fee	$0
application fee online	$0
fee waiver for applicants with financial need	n/a

Williams College

Williams College
995 Main Street
Williamstown, MA 01267
Ph: (413) 597-2211
admission@williams.edu
www.williams.edu

As one of the trailblazing schools that launched American higher education, Williams has path-breaking originality in its DNA. Williams believes in undergraduates. Remarkable freedom and resources are at your disposal so that you may explore widely and deeply and grow as an individual and as a citizen of a global society. With a committed and accomplished faculty, a 7:1 student to faculty ratio, 63 areas of study across the humanities, natural sciences, and social sciences, a breathtaking campus and one of the most generous financial aid programs imaginable, Williams is regarded as one of the finest liberal arts colleges in the country.

Open House, Fly-In, Visit **Windows on Williams (WOW) & Previews**

Each fall, Windows on Williams (WOW) offers approximately 200 high school seniors the opportunity to spend three all-expenses paid days at Williams. WOW participants stay in dorms with current students, attend classes, meet with professors, and learn about Williams' admission process and extraordinary financial aid program. WOW is a selective program open to high school seniors in the U.S. and Puerto Rico; preference is given to high-achieving students who couldn't otherwise afford to visit Williams.

In April, approximately 150 admitted students from low-income backgrounds have the opportunity to visit campus for two all-expenses paid days during Williams Previews. Questions? Please contact wow@williams.edu.

Summer Bridge & Orientation **Summer Humanities and Social Sciences and Summer Science Program**

Summer Humanities and Social Sciences (SHSS) and the Summer Science Program (SSP) are two programs for incoming first-years who are passionate about their studies, interested in spending five weeks of the summer on campus doing academic work, and who are first-generation college students and/or come from groups historically underrepresented in higher education. Both programs include four classes taught by Williams professors and sessions on study skills, time management, and the many resources available to Williams students, as well as field trips, cultural activities, and some time for fun. The goal of these programs is to offer students a preview of the Williams experience and for students to consider leadership roles, research, or careers in these fields.

Student Life & Support **First-Generation Initiatives**

Under the direction of the Dean of First-Generation Initiatives, Williams provides a series of programs that engage first-generation college students by connecting them with the resources and support needed in order to have a successful transition into the college environment. Events and programs occur throughout the year in collaboration with other offices, departments at the college, and the student-led First-Gen Advisory Board. First-Generation Student Orientation occurs before the start of the school year to build community amongst first-generation students. To learn more about Williams First-Generation Initiatives visit dean.williams.edu/first-generation-students.

Scholarship & Financial Aid **Financial Aid**

Williams meets 100% of the demonstrated need for all students and is need-blind in the admission process for U.S. citizens, permanent residents, DACA-status students, and undocumented students. Students receive $50 million in financial aid every year at Williams and the average financial aid package for a student is $55,000. To get an estimate of what your family might be expected to pay within three minutes, visit admission.williams.edu/costestimator.

Fast Facts

STUDENT DIVERSITY	
# undergraduates	2,193
% male/female	53/47
% first-generation college	16
% American Indian or Alaskan Native	1
% Asian	16
% Black or African American	12
% Hispanic/Latino	11
% Native Hawaiian or Pacific Islander	n/a
% White	49
% two or more races	n/a
% race and/or ethnicity unknown	5
% International/nonresident	8
STUDENT SUCCESS	
% first-to-second year retention	97
% six-year graduation	94
% six-year graduation for underrepresented minority groups	89
% first-years who live on campus	100
% undergraduates who live on campus	93
full-time faculty	278
full-time minority faculty	60
student-faculty ratio	7:1

Popular majors Math, Biology, Art/Art History, Economics, English, History, Psychology

Multicultural student clubs and organizations Asian American Students in Action, Black Student Union, Chinese-American Student Organization, International Club, Koreans of Williams, Muslim Student Union, Queer Student Union, South Asian Student Association, Students of Caribbean Ancestry, Vista (Latina/o Organization), Williams African Student Organization, Williams College Jewish Association, Women's Center

AFFORDABILITY	
Cost of Attendance	
tuition	$53,240
required fees	$310
room and board	$14,150
Financial Aid	
total institutional scholarships/grants	$49,569,275
% of students with financial need	50
% of students with need awarded any financial aid	100
% of students with need awarded any need-based scholarship or grant aid	100
% of students with need whose need was fully met	100
% Pell Grant recipients among first-years	22
average aid package	$55,200
average student loan debt upon graduation	$15,700
ADMISSIONS	
# of applicants	8,593
% admitted	14
SAT Evidence-Based Reading & Writing	710-780
SAT Math	690-780
ACT Composite	31-34
SAT/ACT optional	no
average HS GPA	n/a
DEADLINES	
regular application closing date	1/1
early decision plan	yes
application closing date	11/15
early action plan	no
application closing date	n/a
application fee	$65
application fee online	$65
fee waiver for applicants with financial need	yes

Worcester Polytechnic Institute

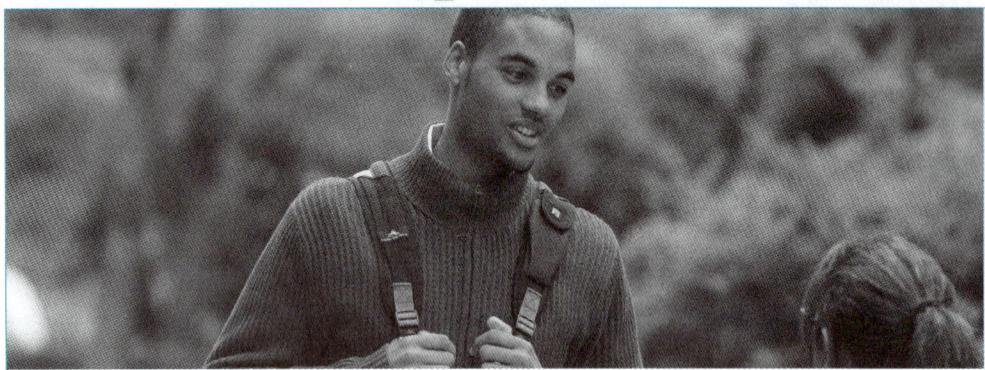

Dedicated to researching and teaching cutting-edge science, math, engineering and technology, Worcester Polytechnic Institute has developed a reputation for innovation and preparing students for successful careers. WPI graduates have invented life-altering technologies such as stainless steel, the airbag safety system and the catalytic converter. WPI's project-based curriculum emphasizes hands-on learning, and teamwork instead of competition, fostering an environment of collaboration among students. The only test-optional techie school, WPI prepares students to imagine anything and innovate everything.

Inside the classroom and beyond, WPI is committed to creating and fostering an inclusive campus community. The WPI community includes a broad range of backgrounds, cultures, religions, opinions, and orientations, creating a rich, dynamic learning—and living—environment. In recent years, WPI's enrollment of women and student of colors has risen dramatically, and is expected to continue to grow. The result is a welcoming and supportive community where anyone can find their place and everyone feels at home.

Pre-College Prep & Outreach **Frontiers**

The university offers one of the nation's preeminent university-based K-12 STEM outreach programs to students. Frontiers, for grades 11-12, is a residential program that challenges students across the country and around the globe to explore the outer limits of their knowledge across a wide spectrum of disciplines. A full schedule of activities, including meeting current WPI students, evening workshops, field trips, movies, and tournaments, ensures that this is not just an academic experience at WPI. Learn more at wpi.edu/+frontiers.

Open House, Fly-In, Visit **Discover: The Diversity Experience @ WPI**

Discover: The Diversity Experience at WPI is a special overnight program for African American, Latino, and Native American students, as well as students interested in diversity, to spend the night on campus. When students visit, they experience the diversity on campus, eat in dining halls, connect with current students, participate in social activities, explore WPI's vast academic options, and much more. The Discover Program is held annually in November. Travel scholarships are available to those who qualify. Learn more at wpi.edu/+discoverdiversity.

First-Year Experience & Transition **Connections**

Connections is a comprehensive network of support services for WPI students to help make a transition to college for first generation students, and in particular underrepresented students of African, Latino and American Indian descent. Connections begins with a pre-orientation program that extends throughout the academic year. The program empowers students by helping them establish a solid academic and personal development foundation to increase their potential for college success. It also promotes academic excellence, leadership and community service.

Student Life & Support **Diversity and Inclusion**

There are many opportunities on campus for students to connect with others who share their interests and experiences through programming and events and student-run organizations. WPI students have access to a wide variety of different initiatives, programs, and resources that celebrate culture and identity.

Examples include a religious center, LGBTQ+ support, and the Office of Multicultural Affairs (OMA). OMA promotes social justice, equity, and multicultural awareness through a wide variety of initiatives, programs, and support services. Students receive tools and resources needed to achieve their academic, professional, and personal goals, and become responsible and productive global citizens.

Worcester Polytechnic Institute
100 Institute Road
Worcester, MA 01609
Ph: (508) 831-5286
admissions@wpi.edu
www.wpi.edu

Fast Facts

STUDENT DIVERSITY

# undergraduates	4,337
% male/female	64/36
% first-generation college	n/a
% American Indian or Alaskan Native	<1
% Asian	3
% Black or African American	3
% Hispanic/Latino	9
% Native Hawaiian or Pacific Islander	0
% White	64
% two or more races	2
% race and/or ethnicity unknown	8
% International/nonresident	11

STUDENT SUCCESS

% first-to-second year retention	95
% six-year graduation	89
% six-year graduation for underrepresented minority groups	84
% first-years who live on campus	96
% undergraduates who live on campus	49
full-time faculty	373
full-time minority faculty	66
student-faculty ratio	14:1

Popular majors Biomedical, Mechanical, Chemical, and Electrical Engineering, Biology, Computer Science, Game and Interactive Media Design

Multicultural student clubs and organizations Black Student Union, Black/Hispanic/Asian Societies of Engineers, Hispanic and Caribbean Student Association (HCSA), Society of Women Engineers (SWE), LGBTQIA+ Alliance

AFFORDABILITY

Cost of Attendance

tuition	$47,988
required fees	$840
room and board	$14,218

Financial Aid

total institutional scholarships/grants	$83,685,241
% of students with financial need	67
% of students with need awarded any financial aid	99
% of students with need awarded any need-based scholarship or grant aid	97
% of students with need whose need was fully met	55
% Pell Grant recipients among first-years	12
average aid package	$35,814
average student loan debt upon graduation	n/a

ADMISSIONS

# of applicants	10,331
% admitted	48
SAT Critical Reading	600-700
SAT Math	630-730
ACT Composite	30
SAT/ACT optional	yes
average HS GPA	3.8

DEADLINES

regular application closing date	2/1
early decision plan	n/a
application closing date	n/a
early action plan	yes
application closing date	11/1 and 1/1
application fee	$65
application fee online	$65
fee waiver for applicants with financial need	yes

Ferris State University

Ferris State University prepares students for successful careers, responsible citizenship, and lifelong learning. Through its many partnerships and its career-oriented, broad-based education, Ferris serves our rapidly changing global economy and society.

Pre-College Prep & Outreach **GEAR UP**

The GEAR UP/College Day Program's mission is to provide an opportunity for underrepresented students to discover first- hand the potential of a college education and to expose students to the information, knowledge and skills they need to complete high school and prepare themselves adequately for college entry and success.

First-Year Experience & Transition **First Year Experience**

The First Year Experience (FYE) Program is a unique opportunity for first year FSU students who would like to improve and gain leadership skills, form lasting relationships with other students, prepare for a lifetime of learning, connect with campus and community resources, live in an amazing community, and participate in service-learning initiatives.

Scholars & Leadership **T.O.W.E.R.S.**

T.O.W.E.R.S. stands for Teaching Others What Establishes Real Success and is a leadership development program coordinated by the Office of Multicultural Student Services.

TOWERS aims to assist underrepresented students at Ferris State University, but is open to all Ferris students to participate! The program encourages, motivates, and inspires Ferris students to become leaders, by providing opportunities for student engagement, learning and development outside of the classroom!

Academic Courses & Service Learning **Structured Learning Assistance**

Structured Learning Assistance courses goal is to give Ferris State University students a high level of academic support while reducing course withdrawal/failure rates and increasing the number of students who pass some of the most challenging and highest risk-for-failure university courses.

Ferris State University
1201 South State Street CSS 201
Big Rapids, MI 49307
Ph: (800) 433-7747
admissions@ferris.edu
www.ferris.edu

Fast Facts

STUDENT DIVERSITY

# undergraduates	13,798
% male/female	46/54
% first-generation college	26
% American Indian or Alaskan Native	1
% Asian	2
% Black or African American	7
% Hispanic/Latino	5
% Native Hawaiian or Pacific Islander	<1
% White	77
% two or more races	3
% race and/or ethnicity unknown	3
% International/nonresident	2

STUDENT SUCCESS

% first-to-second year retention	73
% six-year graduation	49
% six-year graduation for underrepresented minority groups	27
% first-years who live on campus	78
% undergraduates who live on campus	25
full-time faculty	590
full-time minority faculty	48
student-faculty ratio	16:1

Popular majors Pharmacy, Optometry, College of Health Professions, College of Engineering, College of Business

Multicultural student clubs and organizations Asian Student Organization, Black Leaders Aspiring for Critical Knowlege, Black Student Union, Circle of Tribal Nations, Diverse Sexuality & Gender Alliance, Hispanic Student Organization, Alpha Kappa Alpha Sorority, Inc., Alpha Phi Alpha Fraternity Inc., Kappa Alpha Psi Fraternity, Inc., Sigma Lambda Gamma, Inc.

AFFORDABILITY

Cost of Attendance

tuition	in-state: $11,368; out-of-state: $17,052
required fees	n/a
room and board	$9,894

Financial Aid

total institutional scholarships/grants	$26,326,757
% of students with financial need	74
% of students with need awarded any financial aid	83
% of students with need awarded any need-based scholarship or grant aid	62
% of students with need whose need was fully met	n/a
% Pell Grant recipients among first-years	41
average aid package	$8,145
average student loan debt upon graduation	$35,660

ADMISSIONS

# of applicants	10,279
% admitted	78
SAT Critical Reading	n/a
SAT Math	n/a
SAT Writing	n/a
ACT Composite	22
SAT/ACT optional	no
average HS GPA	3.26

DEADLINES

regular application closing date	rolling
early decision plan	no
application closing date	rolling
early action plan	no
application closing date	rolling
application fee	$0
application fee online	$0
fee waiver for applicants with financial need	n/a

Grand Valley State University

Grand Valley State University is a comprehensive, four-year public institution located near Grand Rapids, Michigan, that has established a reputation for preparing its more than 25,000 students to excel in virtually every field. As a relatively young state university, Grand Valley has a rich history of educating first-generation students. Today, 38% of our undergrads are first-generation students. Our first-year retention rate for first-generation students is 79% and our six-year graduation rate is 62% for first-generation students who entered as freshmen, and 62% for those who came as transfer students. We have programs in place to help serve first generation students and ensure their academic success. In addition, our liberal education focus emphasizes critical thinking, creative problem solving, and cultural understanding—preparing all students for life in a fast-changing world. It also fosters a commitment to economic, social, and environmental sustainability and an inclusive campus that values diversity.

Scholarship & Financial Aid **The Frederik Meijer First Generation Honors College Student Scholarship**

This award is a full-tuition scholarship for a select number of extraordinary freshmen who are the first in their immediate family to pursue a college degree. Eligible incoming freshmen who compete in the Scholarship Competition and are accepted into the Meijer Honors College by mid-February will automatically be considered—there is no additional application. The scholarship is renewable up to a maximum of eight semesters. Recipients must stay in good standing in the Honors College to renew this scholarship.

Scholars & Leadership **McNair Scholars Program**

The McNair Scholars Program is designed to help academically talented students from traditionally underserved backgrounds reach their potential by earning a doctoral degree.

Academic Advising & Support **Oliver Wilson Freshman Academy & Academic Success Institute**

The Oliver Wilson Freshman Academy Program is an academic support program for students who have demonstrated a strong potential to be successful at Grand Valley State University, and are first-generation, low-income, and/or students of color. The Freshman Academy Program works to increase retention and promote academic performance among its participants by providing support in the areas of academic support and personal development. The Academic Success Institute (ASI) is a pre-semester program that is designed to give Freshman Academy participants a head start on their first year. The ASI is a free five-day program designed to empower Freshman Academy participants to develop a sense of responsibility for their own education and learning. Participants will earn one credit towards graduation.

Student Life & Support **First Gen Scholars**

First Generation Scholars is a student organization focusing on first-generation college students. Through community service, cultural exposure and professional development, students are invited to challenge themselves during their undergraduate years to get involved and give back to the community.

Mentoring **Laker Connections**

Laker Connections Programs (Brothers: *Black Male Scholars*, *Laker Familia*, and *Niara*) are designed to help students of color achieve personal and academic success by creating a sense of belonging and connecting students to resources and specifically, faculty, staff and peer mentors. A majority of participants are first-generation college students.

Grand Valley State University
1 Campus Dr.
Allendale, MI 49401
Ph: (616) 331-2025
www.gvsu.edu

Fast Facts

STUDENT DIVERSITY

# undergraduates	21,937
% male/female	40/60
% first-generation college	38
% American Indian or Alaskan Native	<1
% Asian	2
% Black or African American	5
% Hispanic/Latino	5
% Native Hawaiian or Pacific Islander	<1
% White	82
% two or more races	3
% race and/or ethnicity unknown	<1
% International/nonresident	2

STUDENT SUCCESS

% first-to-second year retention	83
% six-year graduation	66
% six-year graduation for underrepresented minority groups	52
% first-years who live on campus	86
% undergraduates who live on campus	28
full-time faculty	1,184
full-time minority faculty	196
student-faculty ratio	17:1

Popular majors Business, Management, Marketing and related support services, Health Professions and related programs, Social Sciences, Biological and Biomedical Sciences, Psychology

Multicultural student clubs and organizations Arab Culture Club, Asian Student Union, Black Student Union (BSU), Japanese Culture Association, Korean Intercultural Society, Latino Student Union (LSU), Minorities Interested in Business, Native American Student Association (NASA), Out N' About (LGBTQ student organization), Vietnamese Interests, Education & Traditions

AFFORDABILITY

Cost of Attendance

tuition	$11,994
required fees	n/a
room and board	$8,600

Financial Aid

total institutional scholarships/grants	$84,000,000
% of students with financial need	62
% of students with need awarded any financial aid	99
% of students with need awarded any need-based scholarship or grant aid	90
% of students with need whose need was fully met	10
% Pell Grant recipients among first-years	33
average aid package	$10,870
average student loan debt upon graduation	$29,675

ADMISSIONS

# of applicants	17,104
% admitted	82
SAT Critical Reading	n/a
SAT Math	n/a
SAT Writing	n/a
ACT Composite	24
SAT/ACT optional	yes
average HS GPA	3.58

DEADLINES

regular application closing date	5/1
early decision plan	n/a
application closing date	n/a
early action plan	n/a
application closing date	n/a
application fee	$30
application fee online	$30
fee waiver for applicants with financial need	yes

Kalamazoo College

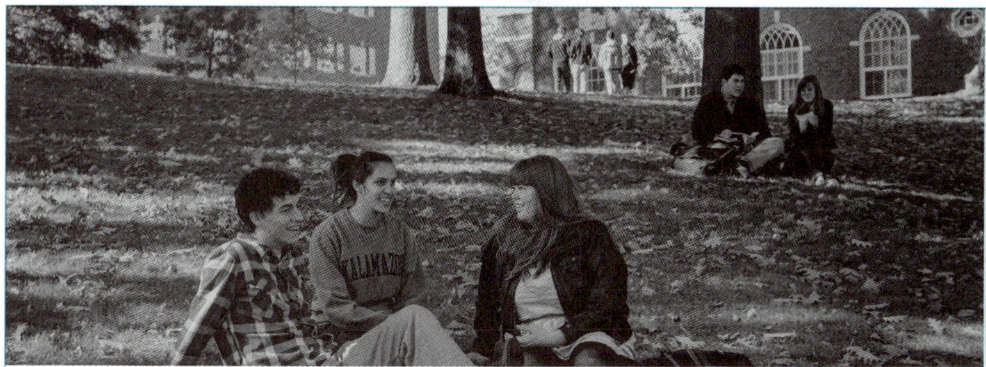

Kalamazoo College is a nationally renowned liberal arts college with a highly individualized and experiential curriculum. All students create their own unique K-Plan, combining scholarship, civic engagement and international study. K is one of the 100 oldest colleges in the country and has an established tradition of academic excellence. The faculty are committed teachers who challenge and support students, and introduce them to global perspectives and intercultural awareness in all programs of study. Located in the city of Kalamazoo, Michigan, K is an increasingly diverse institution; part of the mission of the college is to enroll talented students from varied backgrounds who seek both academic and personal challenges in their college experience. Kalamazoo College does more in four years, so students can do more in a lifetime.

Scholars & Leadership **Sisters in Science**

Kalamazoo College has award-winning service-learning partnerships with local public schools to help K-12 students prepare for college. Through "Sisters in Science," K's female science majors partner with elementary school girls to encourage pursuit of math and science interests. Mentors encourage students to learn and explore through weekly enrichment activities.

Scholars & Leadership **Helping Youth Through Personal Empowerment (HYPE)**

In partnership with many community-based organizations, K students lead weekly reading, writing and math programs, as well as arts, language, health/wellness and environmental education initiatives, at the Kalamazoo County Juvenile Home. The HYPE program is dedicated to promoting restorative, community-based justice by building meaningful relationships with local youth and through advocacy in the Kalamazoo community.

Scholarship & Financial Aid **William Randolph Hearst Endowed Scholarship**

All first-generation students at the College are considered for this Hearst Foundation-funded scholarship. Two recipients are chosen each year. There are numerous other scholarships – even scholarships in fine arts for non-majors. Some 98 percent of students receive some form of financial aid.

First-Year Experience & Transition **First Year Experience (FYE)**

The award-winning First-Year Experience (FYE) program at K combines hands-on activity, experiential learning and mentorship within the context of rigorous academics. FYE fosters academic success, intercultural understanding and balance through seminars, forums, academic advising and peer leaders. First-Year Forums feature interactive learning sessions and structured conversations that help first-year students achieve academic and personal success.

Academic Courses & Service Learning **Cultivating Community**

The College cultivates community throughout its curriculum with service-learning opportunities that allow students to address compelling social issues like food justice, health equity, sustainability, restorative justice, girls' empowerment and using art as a tool for social change.

Kalamazoo College
1200 Academy Street
Kalamazoo, MI 49006
Ph: (269) 337-7166
admission@kzoo.edu
www.kzoo.edu

Fast Facts

STUDENT DIVERSITY

# undergraduates	1,436
% male/female	43/57
% first-generation college	17
% American Indian or Alaskan Native	0
% Asian	8
% Black or African American	8
% Hispanic/Latino	13
% Native Hawaiian or Pacific Islander	<1
% White	56
% two or more races	4
% race and/or ethnicity unknown	3
% International/nonresident	8

STUDENT SUCCESS

% first-to-second year retention	88
% six-year graduation	81
% six-year graduation for underrepresented minority groups	80
% first-years who live on campus	100
% undergraduates who live on campus	53
full-time faculty	105
full-time minority faculty	29
student-faculty ratio	13:1

Popular majors Biology, Business, Chemistry, Economics, English, Political Science

Multicultural student clubs and organizations Arabic Club, Arcus Center for Social Justice Leadership, Asian-Pacific Islander Student Assoc., Black Student Org., Fellowship of Christian Students, Hillel, International Students Org., K Desi, KalamAfrica, Kaleidoscope (GLBTQ), Latinx Student Org., M.E.Ch.A., Muslim Student Assoc., Queer Trans People of Color, Refugee Outreach, Women of Color Alliance, Young Men of Color Alliance

AFFORDABILITY

Cost of Attendance

tuition	$44,418
required fees	$339
room and board	$9,174

Financial Aid

total institutional scholarships/grants	$39,360,263
% of students with financial need	68
% of students with need awarded any financial aid	100
% of students with need awarded any need-based scholarship or grant aid	99
% of students with need whose need was fully met	41
% Pell Grant recipients among first-years	26
average aid package	$37,979
average student loan debt upon graduation	$27,653

ADMISSIONS

# of applicants	3,626
% admitted	66
SAT Critical Reading	540-670
SAT Math	560-680
SAT Writing	550-660
ACT Composite	26-30
SAT/ACT optional	yes
average HS GPA	3.81

DEADLINES

regular application closing date	2/15
early decision plan	yes
application closing date	11/1
early action plan	yes
application closing date	11/1
application fee	n/a
application fee online	n/a
fee waiver for applicants with financial need	n/a

Northern Michigan University

Northern Michigan University, located in Marquette, Michigan along Lake Superior, is a four-year, public, comprehensive university with award-winning leadership programs, cutting-edge technology initiatives and nationally recognized academic programs. More than 75 percent of NMU's 300-plus full-time faculty members have doctorates or the highest degree in their fields, and full-time faculty members teach at all levels—freshmen through graduate courses. Northern is one of about 300 colleges and universities nationwide to have the Carnegie Foundation's "community-engaged campus" designation. NMU is one of the largest notebook computer campuses in the United States, with all full-time students receiving either a ThinkPad or MacBook as part of tuition.

Pre-College Prep & Outreach **Upward Bound**

The six-week Upward Bound Math-Science program exposes students to various career fields, improves their problem-solving skills and enriches their appreciation for science and math. Students will experience adventure and develop lasting friendships.

First-Year Experience & Transition **First Year Experience**

First Year Experience (FYE) is designed to help students successfully manage the transition to college. FYE is a learning community initiative that helps students develop strategies to maximize academic success, become familiar with campus resources, and cultivate positive relationships with faculty and other students.

Academic Advising & Support **Academic and Career Advisement Center (ACAC)**

ACAC is responsible for student orientation, first year student advising, academic proficiency, tutoring and the freshman probation program. Advisers help students with choosing the best academic path for success and navigating options to be successful after graduation.

Student Life & Support **First Generation Student Office**

The Dean of Students Office has a staff member dedicated to assisting first generation students with any issues or concerns and serves as an advocate for first generation students on campus. The office sponsors programs, social events, and a first generation awareness month.

Student Life & Support **Leadership Programs and Center for Student Enrichment**

The Student Leader Fellowship Program (SLFP) is a two-year, nationally recognized leadership program which is committed to developing competent, ethical, and community-centered leaders. Superior Edge is a student development program encompassing a wide range of experiential activities complementing classroom instruction to provide students with a distinct advantage by preparing them for lifelong learning, graduate school, careers and life as engaged citizens.

Mentoring **First Wildcats Student Organization**

First Wildcats student organization builds and strengthens connections between first generation college students and other NMU students, faculty, staff and campus resources. This organization provides first generation students with a support system of other students going through the same things, ways to make sure they succeed at Northern, and lifelong connections.

Mentoring **Jump Start**

Jump Start, a King*Chavez*Parks Initiative of Michigan, aims to improve retention rates of academically and economically disadvantaged students through academic and career workshops and networking opportunities. Jump Start students are teamed up with upperclassmen peer mentors. Peer mentors design programs to meet the specific needs of their students, including study sessions, career exploration sessions and social activities.

Northern Michigan University
1401 Presque Isle Ave.
Marquette, MI 49855
Ph: (906) 227-2650
www.nmu.edu

Fast Facts

STUDENT DIVERSITY

# undergraduates	7,168
% male/female	45/55
% first-generation college	35
% American Indian or Alaskan Native	2
% Asian	1
% Black or African American	2
% Hispanic/Latino	3
% Native Hawaiian or Pacific Islander	0
% White	86
% two or more races	4
% race and/or ethnicity unknown	n/a
% International/nonresident	2

STUDENT SUCCESS

% first-to-second year retention	71
% six-year graduation	45
% six-year graduation for underrepresented minority groups	n/a
% first-years who live on campus	n/a
% undergraduates who live on campus	41
full-time faculty	294
full-time minority faculty	31
student-faculty ratio	21:1

Popular majors Health Professions and Related Programs, Business, Management, Marketing, and Related Support Services, Biological and Biomedical Sciences, Visual and Performing Arts, and Education
Multicultural student clubs and organizations First Wildcats, Black Student Union, All Nations Club, Latino Student Union, OUTLook, Q&A, Native Americal Student Association, Many Shades of Sisterhood, Social Justice Committee

AFFORDABILITY

Cost of Attendance

tuition	in-state: $10,170; out-of-state: $15,666
required fees	$712
room and board	$10,328

Financial Aid

total institutional scholarships/grants	n/a
% of students with financial need	65
% of students with need awarded any financial aid	n/a
% of students with need awarded any need-based scholarship or grant aid	n/a
% of students with need whose need was fully met	16
% Pell Grant recipients among first-years	40
average aid package	$13,569
average student loan debt upon graduation	$31,257

ADMISSIONS

# of applicants	5,346
% admitted	76
SAT Critical Reading	350
SAT Math	590
SAT Writing	n/a
ACT Composite	25
SAT/ACT optional	n/a
average HS GPA	3.16

DEADLINES

regular application closing date	rolling
early decision plan	n/a
application closing date	rolling
early action plan	n/a
application closing date	rolling
application fee	$35
application fee online	$35
fee waiver for applicants with financial need	yes

University of Detroit Mercy

University of Detroit Mercy
4001 W. McNichols Road
Detroit, MI 48221-3038
Ph: (313) 993-1245
admissions@udmercy.edu
www.udmercy.edu

University of Detroit Mercy is Michigan's largest and most comprehensive Catholic university. Detroit Mercy offers more than 100 academic degrees and programs through seven schools and colleges, which include nationally recognized programs in the liberal arts, architecture, business, engineering, nursing, and pre-medical fields. Our educational mission is to integrate the intellectual, spiritual, ethical and social development of students, and our faculty is committed to a classroom environment that promotes educational excellence and academic exchange.

Pre-College Prep & Outreach **Pre-College Workshop**

The Pre-College Workshop is for students starting their senior year in high school. This program provides students with the tools necessary to make the right college choice and includes topics such as selecting an academic program or major, preparing for college admission, applying to college and learning about financial aid and scholarships.

Pre-College Summer Experience **Summer Camps**

University of Detroit Mercy offers a variety of summer programs that allow participants to explore science, technology, engineering and math through the most current methods of innovation with fun, hands-on and engaging activities. A variety of camps are offered including STEPS, Innovation Summer Program, Robotics Challenge for Young Men, Architectural Design, Product Development Innovation and Camp Infinity.

Special Admissions Policy **AIME Program**

The Student Success Center sponsors a limited conditional admission program, Academic Interest and Major Exploration (AIME), for students not meeting regular admission criteria but who show potential. AIME includes academic exploration for both conditional and general admission students. AIME students are linked to support services and developmental advising.

Scholars & Leadership **Institute for Leadership and Service**

Courses across the University incorporate Service Learning , resulting in course-related, direct services to the poor and marginalized in our community. Each year, approximately 1,500 Detroit Mercy student volunteers provide about 12,000 hours of service in conjunction with more than 100 community service agencies. Students in the co-curricular Emerging Leaders Program (ELP) complete 250 hours of service in order to qualify for the Emerging Leaders' Medallion or 125 hours to qualify for the Emerging Leaders' Pin.

Scholars & Leadership **ReBUILD Detroit**

ReBUILDetroit is a first of its kind program offering intensive training for undergraduate scholars interested in pursuing academic, research or industry careers in biomedical, behavioral, clinical or social sciences. The program offers underrepresented scholars financial support; academic skill support; and peer-to-peer and faculty-to-student mentoring opportunities. Beginning in the freshman year, ReBUILDetroit scholars experience the excitement of scientific discovery through direct participation in research, preparing scholars for graduate school and in-demand careers in biomedical disciplines.

Mentoring **1stGen Network**

1stGen Network is a support group for all students whose parents did not graduate with a bachelor's degree. We meet regularly for lunch, conversation and field trips as well as host speakers from on and off campus who speak about topics relevant to the first-gen experience. Detroit Mercy faculty and staff members, many of whom are first-generation college graduates, serve as mentors to the group.

Fast Facts

STUDENT DIVERSITY

# undergraduates	2,843
% male/female	37/63
% first-generation college	30
% American Indian or Alaskan Native	<1
% Asian	5
% Black or African American	13
% Hispanic/Latino	5
% Native Hawaiian or Pacific Islander	<1
% White	58
% two or more races	3
% race and/or ethnicity unknown	7
% International/nonresident	8

STUDENT SUCCESS

% first-to-second year retention	87
% six-year graduation	62
% six-year graduation for underrepresented minority groups	45
% first-years who live on campus	49
% undergraduates who live on campus	29
full-time faculty	345
full-time minority faculty	51
student-faculty ratio	10:1

Popular majors Biology, Business, Engineering, Nursing, Architecture

Multicultural student clubs and organizations Muslim Student Association (MSA), Arab Cultural Society (ACS), Chinese Student Association (CSA), International Student Union (ISU), Chaldean American Student Association (CASA), Hispanic American Student Association (HASA), Indian Student Association, African-American Student Organization

AFFORDABILITY

Cost of Attendance

tuition	$41,158
required fees	n/a
room and board	$9,452

Financial Aid

total institutional scholarships/grants	$40,930,145
% of students with financial need	68
% of students with need awarded any financial aid	99
% of students with need awarded any need-based scholarship or grant aid	96
% of students with need whose need was fully met	37
% Pell Grant recipients among first-years	33
average aid package	$33,808
average student loan debt upon graduation	$35,259

ADMISSIONS

# of applicants	4,452
% admitted	78
SAT Critical Reading	545
SAT Math	571
SAT Writing	531
ACT Composite	24
SAT/ACT optional	n/a
average HS GPA	3.59

DEADLINES

regular application closing date	3/1
early decision plan	n/a
application closing date	n/a
early action plan	n/a
application closing date	n/a
application fee	n/a
application fee online	n/a
fee waiver for applicants with financial need	n/a

University of Michigan

An early president declared that the University of Michigan would provide "An Uncommon Education for the Common Man." Today, 200 years after our founding in 1817, we remain committed to academic excellence, diversity, and serving the public good. We are recognized as a leader in higher education due to the outstanding quality of our 19 schools and colleges, internationally recognized faculty and departments with 275 degree programs. U-M students come from all 50 states and 122 foreign countries. More than 575,000 living alumni make a difference around the world and provide a valuable network for graduates. We are committed to actively recruit and encourage prospective first-generation students; to make financial aid resources known and provide financial aid based on demonstrated financial need; and, once enrolled, to provide appropriate academic and cultural support that will help ensure first-generation student success.

Pre-College Prep & Outreach **University of Michigan Detroit Center**

The University of Michigan Detroit Center mutually enriches University and Detroit communities through service, education, research and the exchange of culture. Among its initiates are the Semester in Detroit Program, a unique urban immersion program; Michigan Engineering Zone, a College of Engineering robotics program for high school students; the School of Social Work partnership in Good Neighborhoods; the University Health Systems' Project Healthy Schools; and the School of Public Health's community walking program, which aims to improve the cardiovascular health of Detroit citizens.

Academic Advising & Support **Summer Bridge Scholars and Comprehensive Studies Program**

The Comprehensive Studies Program is a comprehensive program of academic support for students with outstanding potential for success at the University of Michigan. CSP is a Michigan Learning Community that is an academic unit within the College of Literature, Science, and the Arts and which offers a variety of academic support services, including the Summer Bridge Scholars Program, academic year course instruction, advising, tutoring, and freshmen interest groups. The program's aim is to develop self-directed, successful students.

Student Life & Support **First Generation Student Gateway**

The First-Generation Student Gateway serves as a central hub of information and support for students who are the first in their families to pursue a bachelor's degree. The office serves as a welcoming space for students and as a starting point to connect them with resources and support. The gateway provides resources on financial aid, programs, grants, and scholarships, study abroad opportunities, career advice and community building activities. It also serves as a launching point for several partner offices, including Multi-Ethnic Student Affairs, the Comprehensive Studies Program, the Office of New Student Programs, and the Office of Academic Multicultural Initiatives.

Mentoring **Peer Mentors**

The Mentorship Program is designed to help new students transition easily into campus life, creates events to build a supportive network of students, faculty and staff, and find resources to succeed at Michigan. Peer Mentors are undergraduate students (sophomores, juniors and seniors) who volunteer to offer advice, respond to questions, and provide information about campus and community resources to incoming freshmen (mentees).

University of Michigan
Office of Undergraduate Admissions
515 E Jefferson, 1220 SAB
Ann Arbor, MI 48109
Ph: (734) 764-7433
www.umich.edu

Fast Facts

STUDENT DIVERSITY

# undergraduates	29,821
% male/female	50/50
% first-generation college	12
% American Indian or Alaskan Native	<1
% Asian	15
% Black or African American	5
% Hispanic/Latino	6
% Native Hawaiian or Pacific Islander	<1
% White	65
% two or more races	2
% race and/or ethnicity unknown	5
% International/nonresident	7

STUDENT SUCCESS

% first-to-second year retention	97
% six-year graduation	91
% six-year graduation for underrepresented minority groups	82
% first-years who live on campus	98
% undergraduates who live on campus	34
full-time faculty	2,791
full-time minority faculty	641
student-faculty ratio	15:1

Popular majors Economics, Psychology, Engineering, English, Business, Education, Nursing, Music, Biology, Neuroscience

Multicultural student clubs and organizations
n/a

AFFORDABILITY

Cost of Attendance

tuition	in-state: $14,982 out-of-state: $46,676
required fees	$328
room and board	$10,872

Financial Aid

total institutional scholarships/grants	n/a
% of students with financial need	38
% of students with need awarded any financial aid	100
% of students with need awarded any need-based scholarship or grant aid	85
% of students with need whose need was fully met	82
% Pell Grant recipients among first-years	17
average aid package	$24,323
average student loan debt upon graduation	$25,712

ADMISSIONS

# of applicants	55,504
% admitted	29
SAT Critical Reading	n/a
SAT Math	n/a
SAT Writing	n/a
ACT Composite	31-34
SAT/ACT optional	no
average HS GPA	3.87

DEADLINES

regular application closing date	2/1
early decision plan	n/a
application closing date	n/a
early action plan	yes
application closing date	11/1
application fee	$75
application fee online	$75
fee waiver for applicants with financial need	yes

University of Michigan-Flint

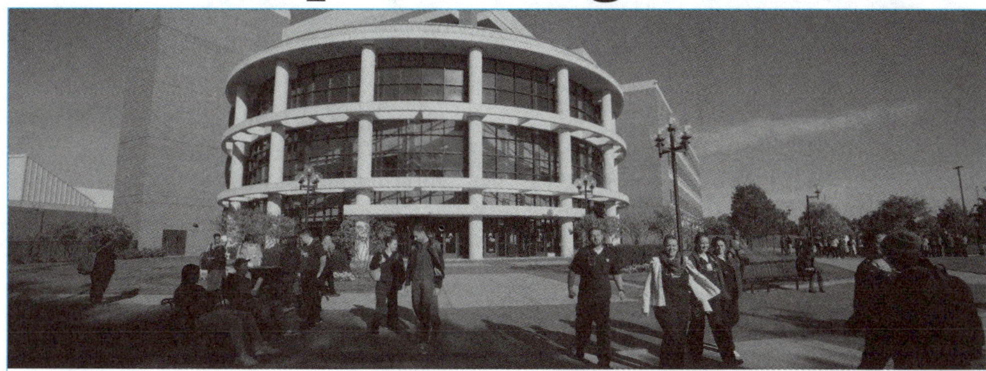

University of Michigan-Flint
303 E Kearsley St.
245 University Pavilion
Flint, MI 48502
Ph: (810) 762-3300
admissions@umflint.edu
www.umflint.edu

The University of Michigan-Flint is a regional campus of the University of Michigan located in the heart of a dynamic American city with an important history—and future. With a growing enrollment of over 8,000 students, UM-Flint has played a key role in the resurgence of downtown Flint. UM-Flint has become a global leader in engaged learning by encouraging students to apply what they learn in class to solve problems in Flint and beyond. Many UM-Flint students are the first in their family to attend college. Full-time freshman self-reported that over 40% are first generation college students. Over 60% of UM-Flint students are women—many who are raising families—and nearly 21% are from minority populations. UM-Flint is committed to the success of all students by addressing the unique needs of each student.

Special Admissions Policy **Promise Scholars Program**

Students who have demonstrated academic achievement and success yet do not meet one or more of the traditional freshman admissions criteria, are offered contractual admission to the University of Michigan-Flint through the Office of Admissions. Participation in the EOI Promise Scholar Program is intended as a means of providing students with a good high school to college transition experience and a foundation for success at the University.

Scholarship & Financial Aid **First-Generation Scholarships**

The Office of Financial Aid offers several scholarships specifically for first generation students, including Sylvester Broome Scholarship, Annie Mae Pointer Scholarship, Dr. Douglas L. Wright Memorial Scholarship and the Floyd J. McCree Scholarship.

First-Year Experience & Transition **Transitions Program**

The Transitions Program is designed to facilitate and increase the diversity and numbers of educationally or economically disadvantaged students who transfer from Mott Community College to UM-Flint. The Transitions Program also has an office on the Mott Community College Campus through the Counseling and Student Development Office. The Program provides a series of intervention and outreach services that encourages persistence at MCC, directs students through the transfer process and continues with follow-up services to support academic achievement and graduation from the University of Michigan-Flint. Program participants receive comprehensive academic and developmental advising, transfer credit evaluation, financial aid and scholarship workshops, and attend transfer student orientation.

Academic Advising & Support **College Student Inventory (CSI)**

Following orientation, new students return to campus to meet with their academic advisor/ career counselor to review results of the "College Student Inventory" survey. The goal of the CSI appointment is to create an individualized action plan for social, academic, and career development.

Mentoring **ACCESS Program**

The ACCESS Program features a unique concept entitled the Posse component. The program has adapted the concept to accommodate our largely commuter student body. Students are identified, recruited, and selected to form teams called "Posses." Students are grouped into teams according to academic majors and other interest areas as one means to promote peer mentoring and strong networking. A second component of the program is Workshops on Wednesday (WOW) initiative. WOW is directed to incoming first-year college students and rising high school seniors as an introduction and initial/brief immersion in a simulated college classroom. The workshops are led by UM-Flint professors in key academic areas with an emphasis on English, mathematics and the sciences.

Fast Facts

STUDENT DIVERSITY

# undergraduates	6,434
% male/female	39/61
% first-generation college	40
% American Indian or Alaskan Native	<1
% Asian	2
% Black or African American	13
% Hispanic/Latino	4
% Native Hawaiian or Pacific Islander	<1
% White	69
% two or more races	3
% race and/or ethnicity unknown	4
% International/nonresident	4

STUDENT SUCCESS

% first-to-second year retention	77
% six-year graduation	44
% six-year graduation for underrepresented minority groups	35
% first-years who live on campus	19
% undergraduates who live on campus	2
full-time faculty	316
full-time minority faculty	72
student-faculty ratio	14:1

Popular majors Nursing, Health Care Administration, Psychology, Business Programs, Computer Science, Mechanical Engineering, Biological/Life Sciences

Multicultural student clubs and organizations n/a

AFFORDABILITY

Cost of Attendance

tuition	In-state: $10,902; Out-of-state: $21,222
required fees	$432
room and board	$8,437

Financial Aid

total institutional scholarships/grants	$7,106,843
% of students with financial need	74
% of students with need awarded any financial aid	94
% of students with need awarded any need-based scholarship or grant aid	74
% of students with need whose need was fully met	1
% Pell Grant recipients among first-years	54
average aid package	$6,781
average student loan debt upon graduation	$27,358

ADMISSIONS

# of applicants	4,558
% admitted	65
SAT Critical Reading	420-710
SAT Math	400-670
SAT Writing	430-600
ACT Composite	22.99
SAT/ACT optional	no
average HS GPA	3.41

DEADLINES

regular application closing date	8/21
early decision plan	no
application closing date	n/a
early action plan	no
application closing date	n/a
application fee	$30
application fee online	$0
fee waiver for applicants with financial need	yes

Missouri State University

Missouri State University
901 S. National Ave.
Springfield, MO 65897
Ph: (417) 836-5517
info@missouristate.edu
www.missouristate.edu

Missouri State University is a public, comprehensive metropolitan system with a statewide mission in public affairs, whose purpose is to develop educated persons. The University's identity is distinguished by its public affairs mission, which entails a campus-wide commitment to foster expertise and responsibility in ethical leadership, cultural competence and community engagement.

Scholarship & Financial Aid **Inclusive Excellence Leadership Scholarship**

Value: $5,000 per year with a potential value of $20,000 over four years. Non-Missouri residents will also receive a full waiver of non-resident fees for fall and spring semesters. In addition to receiving the scholarship, recipients will participate in the Missouri State Inclusive Excellence program.

Summer Bridge & Orientation **New Student and Family Programs**

The mission of Missouri State parent and family programs is to provide parents and family members an opportunity to play an active supporting role in the education of their student, to provide forum for fellowship and networking with other parents, and to further the educational goal of Missouri State University by improving communication between parents and the University community. Services: 1. We inform members about Missouri State programs, services, and events through our Family Connection blog, our webpage, our Facebook page, Twitter, special emails, and other communication channels. 2. We invite members to attend special parent and family events such as our annual Family Weekend. 3. We provide opportunities to participate in Missouri State programs, assume leadership roles, and support important Missouri State parent and family programs initiatives. 4. We help serve as a first point of contact for parents and family members, help them answer questions, and direct them to appropriate departments and resources for further assistance. The family orientation program at our SOAR (Student Orientation and Registration program) runs alongside, but separately from, the student program. Family members attend some portions of the program with their student but will spend most of their time in sessions designed to meet their specific needs. There is a breakout session for families of first generation students to learn about services and opportunities at MSU.

First-Year Experience & Transition **First Year Programs**

First-Year Programs is committed to assist new students in achieving a successful transition. GEP 101 is an integrative and interdisciplinary experience which addresses public affairs issues and individual choices promoting academic success. We have dedicated sections of GEP 101 to first generation students taught by faculty and staff dedicated to improving overall retention and the college experience of those students.

Student Life & Support **Career Center**

The mission of the Career Center is to prepare students to make responsible career decisions, and this preparation begins at the freshman level. Students learn career-planning and job-search techniques that they will use not only during college and immediately after graduation, but throughout their career life.

Student Life & Support **MSU: I'm First**

The goal of MSU: I'm First is to provide resources and support for first generation college students, to assist in their transition to university life and to help them succeed through graduation.

Fast Facts

STUDENT DIVERSITY

# undergraduates	20,364
% male/female	42/58
% first-generation college	30
% American Indian or Alaskan Native	1
% Asian	1
% Black or African American	4
% Hispanic/Latino	4
% Native Hawaiian or Pacific Islander	1
% White	81
% two or more races	4
% race and/or ethnicity unknown	1
% International/nonresident	4

STUDENT SUCCESS

% first-to-second year retention	77
% six-year graduation	55
% six-year graduation for underrepresented minority groups	49
% first-years who live on campus	85
% undergraduates who live on campus	20
full-time faculty	753
full-time minority faculty	136
student-faculty ratio	21:1

Popular majors Business, Psychology, Education, Health Services

Multicultural student clubs and organizations Advocates, African Student Association (ASA), American Indian Student Association (A.I.S.A), Asian American Pacific Islander Organization, Association of Black Collegians (ABC), MSU: I'm First (I'm First), Spectrum, Leading in Education to Approach Latinos (L.E.A.L), Sister Circle

AFFORDABILITY

Cost of Attendance

tuition	$7,306 in-state; $14,746 out of state
required fees	$910
room and board	$8,537

Financial Aid

total institutional scholarships/grants	$46,952,925
% of students with financial need	60
% of students with need awarded any financial aid	95
% of students with need awarded any need-based scholarship or grant aid	78
% of students with need whose need was fully met	13
% Pell Grant recipients among first-years	32
average aid package	$9,171
average student loan debt upon graduation	$25,499

ADMISSIONS

# of applicants	9,453
% admitted	84
SAT Critical Reading	565
SAT Math	558
SAT Writing	n/a
ACT Composite	24
SAT/ACT optional	n/a
average HS GPA	3.63

DEADLINES

regular application closing date	n/a
early decision plan	n/a
application closing date	n/a
early action plan	n/a
application closing date	n/a
application fee	$35
application fee online	$35
fee waiver for applicants with financial need	yes

Missouri University of Science and Technology

Founded in 1870, Missouri University of Science and Technology is one of the nation's top technological research universities, with award-winning faculty and small classes. S&T students pursue degrees in high demand fields like engineering, math, science, business and computing. Through co-ops and internships, design projects, research and student organizations, students can build upon their interests to get the experience they need to excel in today's job market. S&T offers the career guidance, student support, academic assistance and mentoring programs that one might expect from a premier university, but with a personal touch. As one of the nation's top 10 best value public universities and as a top 5 public university for highest starting salaries, S&T provides students with an outstanding and affordable education.

Pre-College Prep & Outreach **Pre-College Initiative (PCI)**

Pre-College Initiative prepares students for careers in math and science, especially those who may never have considered that option and need help achieving their dream career. PCI is an overnight visit program for African-American students that focuses on success in high school, tutoring and college preparation.

Open House, Fly-In, Visit **¡Sí Se Puede!**

¡Sí Se Puede! is an overnight visit program for Hispanic and Latino students to explore a future career in math and science. The program allows students to explore careers and get an inside look at college life.

Summer Bridge & Orientation **Hit the Ground Running**

Hit the Ground Running is a three-week summer learning program that offers new students an exciting opportunity to sharpen and enhance their academic skills, work with teams on design projects, make new friends, develop leadership skills and learn about college-level coursework expectations. This program is intended to prepare students for college life by letting them know what to expect from their college experience.

First-Year Experience & Transition **Opening Week**

During Opening Week, new students arrive on campus a week before classes start to begin the transition to college life. This allows students to get to know the campus, meet new friends, compete in a team design project, learn about campus resources and attend academic workshops.

Academic Advising & Support **On-Track Academic Success Program**

The On-Track Academic Success Program supports students that need extra help with time-management, study skills and getting involved on campus. Through group activities, networking and study sessions, On-Track participants make important connections that will help them succeed and study more effectively.

Student Life & Support **Career Opportunities and Employer Relations**

Missouri S&T hosts one of the largest technological career fairs in the country. More than 900 employers recruit S&T students each year. COER offers individual career advising, job negotiation, help with interviews and guidance on internship and co-op programs.

Missouri University of Science and Technology
Parker Hall 300 West 13th Street
Rolla, MO 65409
Ph: (573) 341-4165
admissions@mst.edu
www.mst.edu

Fast Facts

STUDENT DIVERSITY

# undergraduates	6,920
% male/female	76/24
% first-generation college	21
% American Indian or Alaskan Native	<1
% Asian	4
% Black or African American	3
% Hispanic/Latino	4
% Native Hawaiian or Pacific Islander	<1
% White	73
% two or more races	3
% race and/or ethnicity unknown	2
% International/nonresident	5

STUDENT SUCCESS

% first-to-second year retention	83
% six-year graduation	64
% six-year graduation for underrepresented minority groups	49
% first-years who live on campus	95
% undergraduates who live on campus	47
full-time faculty	373
full-time minority faculty	120
student-faculty ratio	19:1

Popular majors Engineering, Computer Science, Business, Biological Sciences, Psychology

Multicultural student clubs and organizations Miner Mentors, Society of Hispanic Professional Engineers, National Society of Black Engineers, Missouri S&T Student Ambassadors, Chancellor's Leadership Academy, Joe'SS Peers (student mentoring program), Engineers Without Borders, Miner Challenge

AFFORDABILITY

Cost of Attendance

tuition	$24,146 or in-state: $7,896
required fees	$1,559
room and board	$10,094

Financial Aid

total institutional scholarships/grants	$43,345,145
% of students with financial need	94
% of students with need awarded any financial aid	100
% of students with need awarded any need-based scholarship or grant aid	95
% of students with need whose need was fully met	19
% Pell Grant recipients among first-years	22
average aid package	$17,252
average student loan debt upon graduation	$28,299

ADMISSIONS

# of applicants	4,166
% admitted	79
SAT Critical Reading	583-678
SAT Math	603-698
SAT Writing	n/a
ACT Composite	28
SAT/ACT optional	no
average HS GPA	3.61

DEADLINES

regular application closing date	7/1
early decision plan	n/a
application closing date	n/a
early action plan	n/a
application closing date	n/a
application fee	$50
application fee online	$50
fee waiver for applicants with financial need	yes

Truman State University

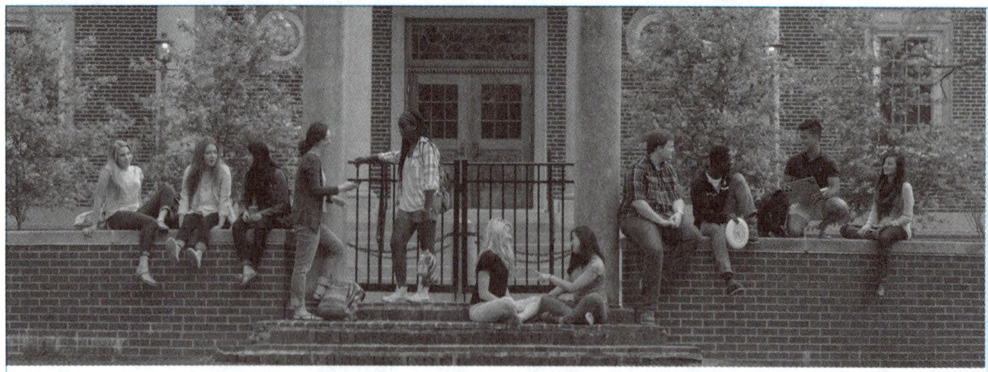

A welcoming community, where professors know students by name, committed to connecting knowledge from various subjects to tackle life's big questions. That's what students find at Truman State University. It is an approach that has been recognized repeatedly for quality and value. In fact, for 21 years in a row, *U.S. News & World Report* has ranked Truman State University as the #1 master's-level public institution in the Midwest. It is the University's mission to provide an affordable education and to maintain a student centered living and learning environment that will attract, nurture, and challenge diverse, outstanding students.

Pre-College Prep & Outreach **Upward Bound**

Truman was among the first five institutions in the country to sponsor Upward Bound, a program that assists high school students in building skills and motivation necessary for college success. Upward Bound provides students with academic skill development, tutoring and college career assistance.

Summer Bridge & Orientation **SEE Scholars Program**

The SEE Scholars Program is a two-week summer program for incoming, under-represented college freshman that takes place on the campus of Truman State University. Through SEE Scholars, students are introduced to college life, resources, and support systems in ways that will help them succeed at the university level.

First-Year Experience & Transition **The Multicultural Affairs Center**

Culturally, the Multicultural Affairs Center (MAC) provides comprehensive programming to help foster an inclusive environment committed to social justice and equity. Our goal is to empower global leaders through education, leadership, and service. Each year we host or cosponsor between 50 and 75 culturally enriching programs for the campus and local communities. In addition to monthly programs, the MAC also provides support to more than 10 Multicultural Student Organizations (Greek and non-Greek). There are a wealth of opportunities for students to get involved on campus starting the first year.

Scholars & Leadership **McNair Program**

The McNair Program was designed to provide disadvantaged college students with effective preparation for doctoral studies. McNair Scholars are matched with faculty mentors who supervise research and assist students in achieving their individual post-baccalaureate educational goals. Students participate in pre-research internships during their sophomore year and summer research internships during their junior year. During their senior year, the focus is on graduate school placement.

Academic Advising & Support **Student Success Center**

The Student Success Center is a multi-faceted academic support program that provides a range of services to enhance both a student's individual learning and in-class performance. The center provides tutoring services, collaborative group study for specific courses, peer mentoring and learning and study skills workshops.

Mentoring **Peer Mentor Program**

The Peer Mentor Program is a program that pairs students with upperclassmen mentors. These mentors advise students on picking classes, joining organizations, and becoming engrained in the campus community.

Truman State University
Ruth W. Towne Museum & Visitors Center
100 E Normal Ave
Kirksville, MO 63501
Ph: (800) 892-7792
admissions@truman.edu
www.truman.edu

Fast Facts

STUDENT DIVERSITY

# undergraduates	6,039
% male/female	40/60
% first-generation college	15
% American Indian or Alaskan Native	<1
% Asian	3
% Black or African American	4
% Hispanic/Latino	3
% Native Hawaiian or Pacific Islander	<1
% White	79
% two or more races	5
% race and/or ethnicity unknown	2
% International/nonresident	7

STUDENT SUCCESS

% first-to-second year retention	87
% six-year graduation	72
% six-year graduation for underrepresented minority groups	70
% first-years who live on campus	98
% undergraduates who live on campus	46
full-time faculty	332
full-time minority faculty	40
student-faculty ratio	16:1

Popular majors Business, Biology, English, Psychology

Multicultural student clubs and organizations
African Students Organization, Association of Black Collegians, Hablantes Unidos/United Speakers, Hispanic American Leadership Organization (HALO), International Club, Minority Ambassador Program, National Association of Black Accountants, National Pan-Hellenic Council, Unique Ensemble Gospel Choir

AFFORDABILITY

Cost of Attendance

tuition	in-state: $7,352; out-of-state: $14,136
required fees	$654
room and board	$8,630

Financial Aid

total institutional scholarships/grants	$22,095,438
% of students with financial need	52
% of students with need awarded any financial aid	99
% of students with need awarded any need-based scholarship or grant aid	94
% of students with need whose need was fully met	84
% Pell Grant recipients among first-years	24
average aid package	$12,437
average student loan debt upon graduation	$24,811

ADMISSIONS

# of applicants	5,178
% admitted	68
SAT Critical Reading	550-680
SAT Math	520-650
SAT Writing	n/a
ACT Composite	27
SAT/ACT optional	no
average HS GPA	3.79

DEADLINES

regular application closing date	rolling
early decision plan	n/a
application closing date	n/a
early action plan	n/a
application closing date	n/a
application fee	$0
application fee online	$0
fee waiver for applicants with financial need	yes

University of Central Missouri

The University of Central Missouri is a public institution where the experience transforms students into lifelong learners, dedicated to service, with the knowledge, skills and confidence to succeed and lead in the region, state, nation and world.

First-Year Experience & Transition **First Year Experience**

At UCM, your education stretches beyond the classroom. From challenging yourself on our rock-climbing wall to competing with the Talking Mules in England, you'll have the opportunity to expand your world.

Scholars & Leadership **Scholarships**

UCM has many financial assistance programs that can help you bring your total educational and living expenses well within reach. Each year, nearly $7 million in merit-based scholarships are awarded to students who demonstrate academic excellence, leadership, special talents or potential in a specific field of study.

Student Life & Support **Academic Advising**

Academic advising is critical to the success, satisfaction, retention, and graduation of the University of Central Missouri students. Advisors will assist students in their intellectual and personal development toward academic success and lifelong learning.

Academic Advising & Support **Multicultural Center**

The University of Central Missouri takes great pride in the diversity of its students and the many programs offered by the Center for Multiculturalism and Inclusivity to promote their success.

Scholarship & Financial Aid **TRIO**

TRIO supports student success by offering tuition-free courses, personalized advising, academic tutoring and mentoring.

University of Central Missouri
208 E. South Street
Warrensburg, MO 64093
Ph: (660) SAY UCMO
admit@ucmo.edu
www.ucmo.edu

Fast Facts

STUDENT DIVERSITY

# undergraduates	9,786
% male/female	44/56
% first-generation college	46
% American Indian or Alaskan Native	<1
% Asian	<1
% Black or African American	10
% Hispanic/Latino	4
% Native Hawaiian or Pacific Islander	<1
% White	76
% two or more races	4
% race and/or ethnicity unknown	1
% International/nonresident	2

STUDENT SUCCESS

% first-to-second year retention	71
% six-year graduation	53
% six-year graduation for underrepresented minority groups	44
% first-years who live on campus	87
% undergraduates who live on campus	35
full-time faculty	521
full-time minority faculty	105
student-faculty ratio	19:1

Popular majors Health Professions, Education, Business/Marketing, Homeland Security, Engineering Technologies

Multicultural student clubs and organizations
SoL - Student Org. of Latinos, PRISM - The student org. for LGBTQ, ABC - Assoc. of Black Collegians, UCM Muslim Org., MSO - Multicultural Student Outreach, FAMEous - Modeling Team, SAGE - students advocating for gender equality, NPHC - National Pan Hellenic Council - the African American Greek system, BMI - Black Male initiative

AFFORDABILITY

Cost of Attendance

tuition	$6,446
required fees	$876
room and board	$8,318

Financial Aid

total institutional scholarships/grants	$16,234,665
% of students with financial need	73
% of students with need awarded any financial aid	100
% of students with need awarded any need-based scholarship or grant aid	60
% of students with need whose need was fully met	15
% Pell Grant recipients among first-years	41
average aid package	$9,072
average student loan debt upon graduation	$26,369

ADMISSIONS

# of applicants	6,922
% admitted	74
SAT Critical Reading	n/a
SAT Math	n/a
SAT Writing	n/a
ACT Composite	22
SAT/ACT optional	no
average HS GPA	3.4

DEADLINES

regular application closing date	rolling
early decision plan	no
application closing date	n/a
early action plan	no
application closing date	n/a
application fee	$30
application fee online	$30
fee waiver for applicants with financial need	yes

Washington University in St. Louis

Washington University, a medium-sized research university, is internationally known for academic excellence. Here you'll find the broad educational resources of a much larger university, but our size and our friendly, supportive community combine to make faculty, staff, and students open and approachable. Washington University creates an environment to encourage and support wide-ranging exploration. Our community members strive to enhance the lives and livelihoods of students, the people of the greater St. Louis community, the country, and the world. To this end, we welcome students, faculty, and staff from all backgrounds to create an inclusive community that is welcoming, nurturing, and intellectually rigorous. While they explore their passions in our five undergraduate divisions of architecture, art, arts & sciences, business, and engineering, our students develop the attitudes, skills, and habits of lifelong learning and leadership, which prepare them to be productive members of a global society.

Pre-College Summer Experience **High School Summer Scholars Program**

The High School Summer Experiences at Washington University offer participants the opportunity to experience the independence of college life the summer after their sophomore or junior year in high school. Take advantage of the unique Washington University experience: the excitement of a world-class research institution, with faculty who are leaders in their fields, plus the encouragement of teachers committed to teaching well.

Open House, Fly-In, Visit **Admissions Visit Programs**

We invite students to visit for a variety of special experiences including our WashU Preview each fall, Multicultural Celebration Days each spring, and Open House and Discover WashU Days throughout the year. We are happy to talk to you and help plan an individual visit tailored just for you.

Scholarship & Financial Aid **Scholarships and Financial Aid**

Our financial assistance counselors are here to work with your family one-on-one. Families with incomes of $75,000 and less receive packages up to the full cost of attendance and are not required to take loans. We meet 100% of demonstrated financial need for all admitted students. Our merit-based scholarships bring deserving students to WashU each year.

Summer Bridge & Orientation **Freshman Summer Academic Program (FSAP)**

FSAP gives first-year students admitted to Washington University an introduction to the undergraduate academic life at the University. The intensive five-week academic program provides students the opportunity to earn six college credits, make friends, become familiar with the campus and surrounding neighborhoods, and register for fall courses.

First-Year Experience & Transition **First Year Center**

Washington University's First Year Center serves as the official welcome center for incoming students and families. In addition to coordinating Orientation and Parents Welcome activities, the First Year Center has a staff of current undergraduates, called WUSAs (Washington University Student Associates), who volunteer to serve as mentors throughout the first year.

Academic Advising & Support **Advising**

Students have four-year advisors who work with them throughout the undergraduate experience. In addition, students have major advisors, pre-professional advisors, study abroad advisors, and peer advisors. Cornerstone, the Learning Center, provides academic support, peer mentoring, and a writing center.

Washington University in St. Louis
Campus Box 1089
One Brookings Drive
St. Louis, MO 63130
Ph: (800) 638-0700
admissions.wustl.edu
www.wustl.edu

Fast Facts

STUDENT DIVERSITY	
# undergraduates	6,863
% male/female	48/52
% first-generation college	6
% American Indian or Alaskan Native	<1
% Asian	18
% Black or African American	8
% Hispanic/Latino	7
% Native Hawaiian or Pacific Islander	0
% White	53
% two or more races	4
% race and/or ethnicity unknown	2
% International/nonresident	8
STUDENT SUCCESS	
% first-to-second year retention	96
% six-year graduation	94
% six-year graduation for underrepresented minority groups	94
% first-years who live on campus	100
% undergraduates who live on campus	77
full-time faculty	935
full-time minority faculty	219
student-faculty ratio	8:1

Popular majors Business, Engineering, Art/ Architecture, Humanities, Biology/Natural Science
Multicultural student clubs and organizations Association of Black Students, Association of Latin American Students, Mixed, Asian American Association, African Students Association, ASHOKA South Asian Students Association, National Society of Black Engineers, Black Anthology, Black Pre-Med and Pre-Law Societies, Korean Students Association

AFFORDABILITY	
Cost of Attendance	
tuition	$50,650
required fees	$883
room and board	$16,006
Financial Aid	
total institutional scholarships/grants	$106,650,048
% of students with financial need	42
% of students with need awarded any financial aid	99
% of students with need awarded any need-based scholarship or grant aid	97
% of students with need whose need was fully met	100
% Pell Grant recipients among first-years	13
average aid package	$43,722
average student loan debt upon graduation	$23,577
ADMISSIONS	
# of applicants	29,197
% admitted	17
SAT Critical Reading	690-770
SAT Math	710-800
SAT Writing	690-770
ACT Composite	33
SAT/ACT optional	no
average HS GPA	n/a
DEADLINES	
regular application closing date	1/2
early decision plan	yes
application closing date	11/1
early action plan	n/a
application closing date	n/a
application fee	$75
application fee online	$75
fee waiver for applicants with financial need	yes

Dartmouth College

Dartmouth students and faculty are filled with an adventuresome spirit, embracing opportunities and challenges with curiosity, courage, and tenacity. At Dartmouth, a unique fusion of a renowned liberal arts college and leading research university takes place, and students and faculty partner to take on the world's great challenges. Consistently recognized for scholars at the forefront of their fields who work closely with undergraduates, both in the classroom and through independent study and research, Dartmouth offers you a rare opportunity to pursue your studies to the horizon of your aspirations and beyond. With a profound sense of place, Dartmouth's setting in the college town of Hanover, New Hampshire encompasses extraordinary natural beauty that fosters a close-knit and diverse community, deep academic engagement, and lifelong bonds. Dartmouth is committed to the success of all of its students, particularly its segment of historically underrepresented and first-generation students.

Open House, Fly-In, Visit **Native American Community Program**

This is an opportunity for some of the most promising and talented students in the country with an interest in Dartmouth's Native community and/or Native American Studies to experience life at the College. The program provides opportunities for students to visit campus and learn more about the academic programs and student life at Dartmouth, as well as the admissions and financial aid processes.

Open House, Fly-In, Visit **Dartmouth Bound: Summer Program**

This program is designed to provide talented, college-bound rising high school seniors from historically underrepresented backgrounds and communities with an opportunity to preview college by immersion in student life at Dartmouth. Participants will live in a Dartmouth residence hall, learn about the academic programs offered through attending classes, enjoy meaningful conversations with current students and staff about social engagement and campus life, and attend workshops on the admissions and financial aid processes.

Scholarship & Financial Aid **Full-Funding Financial Aid**

Offering nearly $87 million in scholarship to its students, Dartmouth's need-based financial aid program is among the most generous in the country. Dartmouth guarantees to meet 100 percent of the demonstrated financial need for all admitted students, including free tuition for students who come from families with annual incomes below $100,000 and with typical assets. Student financial aid packages provide a combination of scholarships and grants, with small loans and employment eligibility.

First-Year Experience & Transition **First Year Student Enrichment Program**

The First Year Student Enrichment Program (FYSEP) empowers first-generation students at Dartmouth to thrive academically and in the greater college community. Through a six day pre-orientation program and ongoing support throughout their first year, FYSEP students gain a broad array of skills designed to help them make the most of their experiences both inside and outside of the classroom. FYSEP works with students throughout their time at Dartmouth through advising, activities, and workshops to continue to provide access to resources at the College.

Dartmouth College
6016 McNutt Hall
Hanover, NH 03755
Ph: (603) 646-2875
www.dartmouth.edu

Fast Facts

STUDENT DIVERSITY

# undergraduates	4,410
% male/female	51/49
% first-generation college	14
% American Indian or Alaskan Native	2
% Asian	15
% Black or African American	7
% Hispanic/Latino	10
% Native Hawaiian or Pacific Islander	n/a
% White	50
% two or more races	3
% race and/or ethnicity unknown	3
% International/nonresident	9

STUDENT SUCCESS

% first-to-second year retention	97
% six-year graduation	97
% six-year graduation for underrepresented minority groups	85
% first-years who live on campus	100
% undergraduates who live on campus	86
full-time faculty	606
full-time minority faculty	100
student-faculty ratio	7:1

Popular majors Economics, Government, Computer Science, Engineering Sciences, History, Biology, Psychology & Brain Sciences

Multicultural student clubs and organizations Afro-American Society, Dartmouth Asian Organization, Dartmouth Chinese Culture Society, La Alianza Latina, MOSAIC, Native Americans at Dartmouth, Women of Color Collective, CoFired

AFFORDABILITY

Cost of Attendance

tuition	$51,468
required fees	$1,675
room and board	$15,384

Financial Aid

total institutional scholarships/grants	$97,217,754
% of students with financial need	49
% of students with need awarded any financial aid	100
% of students with need awarded any need-based scholarship or grant aid	98
% of students with need whose need was fully met	100
% Pell Grant recipients among first-years	15
average aid package	$51,231
average student loan debt upon graduation	$19,135

ADMISSIONS

# of applicants	20,034
% admitted	10
SAT Evidence-Based Reading & Writing	710-770
SAT Math	720-790
ACT Composite	32
SAT/ACT optional	n/a
average HS GPA	n/a

DEADLINES

regular application closing date	1/1
early decision plan	yes
application closing date	11/1
early action plan	n/a
application closing date	n/a
application fee	$80
application fee online	$80
fee waiver for applicants with financial need	yes

Keene State College

At Keene State College, we value each member of our college community and foster an environment of diversity, civility, and respect. Our student-centered approach supports the intellectual and personal growth of every individual and allows our students to focus on their educational, personal, and career aspirations. Academic success, community involvement, and the development of character, combined with the strong mentoring relationships that our faculty develop with Keene State students, contribute greatly to their success. As the public liberal arts college of New Hampshire, we are dedicated to the development of knowledge and skills that meet the challenges of our changing world.

Pre-College Prep & Outreach **Upward Bound**

This federally funded, year-round college preparatory program is designed to prepare students for success in high school and enrollment in college. Students attend weekly sessions to work on grades, college planning, career choices, and personal goals. High school seniors receive assistance throughout the college application and financial aid process.

Summer Bridge & Orientation **The Links Program**

The Links Program is a six-week summer program designed to introduce first-time students to the academic and social aspects of the college experience. The supportive learning community enhances college level skills in reading, writing, critical thinking, and communication. Learning takes place in classrooms, residence halls, campus locations, and in the City of Keene with the goal of providing students with the skills to become active, contributing members of the Keene State College community.

First-Year Experience & Transition **College Success Strategies**

College Success Strategies – The transition from high school to college is one of the most significant changes that students will experience in their lifetimes and can often be complex and difficult to navigate. This two-credit course, offered by Aspire and the Office of Diversity and Multiculturalism, provides insight into the new living environment, the sense of independence inside and outside of the classroom, and the academic expectations that accompany the college experience.

Academic Advising & Support **ASPIRE**

ASPIRE provides Keene State students with academic support services that have been designed to improve their performance and enhance their success. Students gain the skills they need to thrive in their academic environment. Through Aspire, students access peer tutoring and workshops on a variety of relevant topics including study skills, time management, and organizational support.

Academic Advising & Support **Tutoring**

Tutoring is available through the Center for Writing and the Math Center. In addition, Keene State College offers individual and small group tutoring through the Aspire program. The college hires and trains over 100 tutors each semester and financially supports the tutoring program. Students and tutors meet weekly to review course materials and assignments.

Keene State College
229 Main Street
Keene, NH 03435
Ph: (800) KSC-1909
www.keene.edu

Fast Facts

STUDENT DIVERSITY

# undergraduates	3,688
% male/female	45/55
% first-generation college	39
% American Indian or Alaskan Native	1
% Asian	2
% Black or African American	2
% Hispanic/Latino	4
% Native Hawaiian or Pacific Islander	<1
% White	86
% two or more races	2
% race and/or ethnicity unknown	4
% International/nonresident	<1

STUDENT SUCCESS

% first-to-second year retention	75
% six-year graduation	63
% six-year graduation for underrepresented minority groups	51
% first-years who live on campus	94
% undergraduates who live on campus	53
full-time faculty	217
full-time minority faculty	17
student-faculty ratio	15:1

Popular majors Education, Safety & Occupational Health Applied Science, Health Sciences, Management, Psychology, Film Studies, Communication, Criminal Justice

Multicultural student clubs and organizations Brothers/Big Sisters, Common Ground, Feminist Collective, Global Culture Club, Hillel, Interfaith Voices, KSC Pride, Newman Student Organization

AFFORDABILITY

Cost of Attendance

tuition	$19,934 or in-state: $11,188
required fees	$2,680
room and board	$10,736

Financial Aid

total institutional scholarships/grants	$18,483,574
% of students with financial need	78
% of students with need awarded any financial aid	99
% of students with need awarded any need-based scholarship or grant aid	70
% of students with need whose need was fully met	11
% Pell Grant recipients among first-years	n/a
average aid package	n/a
average student loan debt upon graduation	n/a

ADMISSIONS

# of applicants	5,580
% admitted	83
SAT Evidence-Based Reading & Writing	500
SAT Math	500
ACT Composite	22
SAT/ACT optional	n/a
average HS GPA	3.0

DEADLINES

regular application closing date	5/1
early decision plan	n/a
application closing date	n/a
early action plan	n/a
application closing date	n/a
application fee	$50
application fee online	$50
fee waiver for applicants with financial need	yes

Georgian Court University

Georgian Court University
900 Lakewood Ave
Lakewood, NJ 08701
Ph: (732) 987-2700
admissions@georgian.edu
georgian.edu

Founded in 1908 and sponsored by the Sisters of Mercy, Georgian Court University is Central and South Jersey's only Catholic university. GCU is a comprehensive, coeducational university with a strong liberal arts core and a historic special concern for women. As a forward-thinking university that supports diversity and academic excellence, Georgian Court expands possibility for more than 2,300 students of all faiths, races and socioeconomic backgrounds. The university's commitment to diversity is broad, and it attracts a significant population of students who are first in their families to attend college. GCU aggressively raises funds to support scholarships and institutional aid, and in 2017, awarded more than $21 million to keep college affordable for students. GCU students and alumni go on to lead purposeful lives in corporate careers, entrepreneurship, social justice, civic engagement, and community leadership.

Summer Bridge & Orientation **Educational Opportunity Fund**

New Jersey students who meet specific criteria established by the state of New Jersey may qualify for GCU services provided through the Educational Opportunity Fund. The program, which often attracts first-generation students from some of New Jersey's most economically challenged areas, offers academic advisement, pre-college orientation, tutoring, leadership development, and modest grants.

Academic Advising & Support **Chart the Course to Graduation**

Chart the Course to Graduation supports students at risk of not earning 30 credits by the start of their sophomore year. Chart the Course is supported by a $1.99 million federal grant. Eligible students take a free winter or summer course with the intention of getting back on track to timely graduation. Courses are carefully created to take into account challenges faced by remedial students. Faculty, success coaches, and peer tutors monitor student progress.

Academic Advising & Support **GCU's Academic Development and Support Center**

GCU's Academic Development and Support Center offers students a range of support services and activities, including peer tutoring, study resources (math, writing, reading), disability services and more. It is also home to The Learning Connection, a fee-based support program for students with learning differences that impact academic performance. In addition, GCU offers peer tutoring and intense academic advising via its Persistence through Academic Coaching and Tutoring (PACT) program, intended for provisionally admitted students.

Student Life & Support **GCU Leadership Programs**

GCU's Women in Leadership Development (WILD) equips students with the knowledge, skills, and values for effective and engaged citizenship. Similarly, GCU's Emerging Leaders program helps men and women establish a personal leadership style as they work with leadership mentors. Living and Learning Communities provide additional opportunities for exposure and leadership growth as students work with faculty and staff in four communities—International Cultures, Gateway to the Arts, Outdoor Adventures, and Sustainability.

Mentoring **TRIO-Student Support Services**

TRIO-Student Support Services at Georgian Court provides academic tutoring, personal counseling, mentoring, financial guidance, and other services. About 160 students are served through GCU's TRIO-SSS program as they benefit from tutoring, basic skills instruction, financial literacy training, a walk-in writing lab, advocacy support and more. TRIO-SSS works to increase the number of disadvantaged low-income college students, first-generation college students, and students with disabilities to successfully complete postsecondary study.

Fast Facts

STUDENT DIVERSITY

# undergraduates	1,591
% male/female	28/72
% first-generation college	43
% American Indian or Alaskan Native	<1
% Asian	3
% Black or African American	11
% Hispanic/Latino	10
% Native Hawaiian or Pacific Islander	<1
% White	56
% two or more races	2
% race and/or ethnicity unknown	17
% International/nonresident	1

STUDENT SUCCESS

% first-to-second year retention	85
% six-year graduation	42
% six-year graduation for underrepresented minority groups	34
% first-years who live on campus	64
% undergraduates who live on campus	34
full-time faculty	85
full-time minority faculty	22
student-faculty ratio	13:1

Popular majors Undeclared, Nursing, Education, Biology, English, Business Administration, Psychology

Multicultural student clubs and organizations Black Student Union, Da Poetry Corner, LGTBQ, Latin American Student Organization, Global Lions Club, Residence Hall Association, Women's Esteem, WILD (Women in Leadership Development), Young Lions Brotherhood, Emerging Leaders

AFFORDABILITY

Cost of Attendance

tuition	$30,158
required fees	$1,460
room and board	$10,808

Financial Aid

total institutional scholarships/grants	$21,000,000
% of students with financial need	95
% of students with need awarded any financial aid	100
% of students with need awarded any need-based scholarship or grant aid	97
% of students with need whose need was fully met	21
% Pell Grant recipients among first-years	43
average aid package	$29,659
average student loan debt upon graduation	$40,267

ADMISSIONS

# of applicants	1,609
% admitted	74
SAT Critical Reading	420-510
SAT Math	430-530
SAT Writing	400-510
ACT Composite	17-23
SAT/ACT optional	yes
average HS GPA	3.27

DEADLINES

regular application closing date	rolling
early decision plan	n/a
application closing date	n/a
early action plan	yes
application closing date	n/a
application fee	$40
application fee online	$40
fee waiver for applicants with financial need	yes

*data taken from Quick Stats 2016-17

New Jersey Institute of Technology

Established in 1881, NJIT stands as a leader of excellence in higher-education instruction and research, and is one of only 32 public research polytechnic universities nationally. It is a multidisciplinary university serving a diverse student body and housing six schools: Newark College of Engineering, College of Architecture and Design, College of Science and Liberal Arts, Martin Tuchman School of Management, Ying Wu College of Computing and Albert Dorman Honors College. Talented students who are from low-income households and/or underrepresented populations and who are the first generation in their families to attend college benefit from all NJIT has to offer. Through a variety of programs, NJIT is able to provide these students with the necessary academic, financial and social support to enable them to reap the rewards of a college education and degree. The university is ranked among the top colleges and universities nationally for graduating minority students in engineering and computer science.

Pre-College Prep & Outreach **Center for Pre-College Programs (CPCP)**

CPCP offers a broad range of services to low-income, first-generation pre-college students to gain college access and have success in the STEM fields. The center also helps to improve the teaching of STEM in secondary and elementary schools. CPCP supports partnership programs that include the U.S. Department of Education's federally funded TRiO Programs (Talent Search, Upward Bound), Gaining Early Awareness and Readiness for Undergraduate Programs (GEAR UP), and Upward Bound for English Language Learners (UBELLs).

Pre-College Summer Experience **Early College Preparatory Programs**

Early College Preparatory Programs, through the Center for Pre-College Programs, include STEM summer programs for high-achieving students from post fourth to post 11th grades and college-credit courses for high school students through the Options for Advanced Academic Achievement program (Options) and the Academy College Courses for High School Students. Although these programs are not exclusively for underserved and underrepresented students, many first-generation college students are enrolled in these programs.

Scholarship & Financial Aid **Partnership with the Give Something Back Foundation**

NJIT's partnership with the nonprofit Give Something Back Foundation will enable talented students from low-income households and underrepresented populations, many of whom are first-gen, to attend the university at no cost for tuition, fees and room and board. Give Something Back provides mentoring and scholarships to students of modest means to help them realize their full potential by achieving a college education.

Scholars & Leadership **Ronald E. McNair Post-baccalaureate Achievement Program**

The NJIT Ronald E. McNair Post-baccalaureate Achievement Program is specifically designed to assist low-income and first-generation or underrepresented students majoring in STEM disciplines in completing their bachelor's degree and to enroll in post-baccalaureate degree programs toward ultimately obtaining doctoral degrees. McNair Scholars engage in research and other scholarly activities with faculty mentors and have the results of their research presented at professional conferences and published in professional journals.

Academic Advising & Support **Educational Opportunity Program (EOP)**

EOP at NJIT offers academic support along with career and personal counseling to first-time full-time freshman and transfer students who may be educationally and economically challenged. EOP at NJIT is the only program in the state of New Jersey to allow over-income students to participate in the New Jersey Educational Opportunity Fund (EOF), which provides financial assistance and support services (e.g., counseling, tutoring and much more) to qualifying students from educationally and economically disadvantaged backgrounds.

New Jersey Institute of Technology
323 MLK Boulevard, University Heights
Newark, NJ 07102-1982
Ph: (973) 596-3300
njit.edu

Fast Facts

STUDENT DIVERSITY

# undergraduates	8,211
% male/female	75/25
% first-generation college	34
% American Indian or Alaskan Native	<1
% Asian	21
% Black or African American	8
% Hispanic/Latino	20
% Native Hawaiian or Pacific Islander	<1
% White	32
% two or more races	3
% race and/or ethnicity unknown	13
% International/nonresident	4

STUDENT SUCCESS

% first-to-second year retention	88
% six-year graduation	61
% six-year graduation for underrepresented minority groups	48
% first-years who live on campus	53
% undergraduates who live on campus	22
full-time faculty	436
full-time minority faculty	138
student-faculty ratio	17:1

Popular majors Engineering, Computer and Information Sciences, Engineering Technologies, Architecture, Business/Marketing

Multicultural student clubs and organizations
African Student Assoc., Caribbean Student Org., Chinese Students and Scholars Assoc., Filipinos in Newark Engaging in Sociocultural Traditions, Muslim Student Assoc., National Org. of Minority Architect Students, National Society of Black Engineers, Sikh Student Assoc., Society of Hispanic Professional Engineers, Society of Women Engineers, Spectrum - NJIT's LGBTQ+ Org.

AFFORDABILITY

Cost of Attendance

tuition	in-state: $13,602; out-of-state: $28,206
required fees	$2,828
room and board	$13,700

Financial Aid

total institutional scholarships/grants	$21,800,000
% of students with financial need	70
% of students with need awarded any financial aid	100
% of students with need awarded any need-based scholarship or grant aid	67
% of students with need whose need was fully met	11
% Pell Grant recipients among first-years	30
average aid package	$14,168
average student loan debt upon graduation	$21,768

ADMISSIONS

# of applicants	7,222
% admitted	59
SAT Critical Reading	520-630
SAT Math	590-680
SAT Writing	500-620
ACT Composite	23-29
SAT/ACT optional	no
average HS GPA	3.55

DEADLINES

regular application closing date	3/1
early decision plan	n/a
application closing date	n/a
early action plan	n/a
application closing date	n/a
application fee	$75
application fee online	$75
fee waiver for applicants with financial need	yes

Princeton University

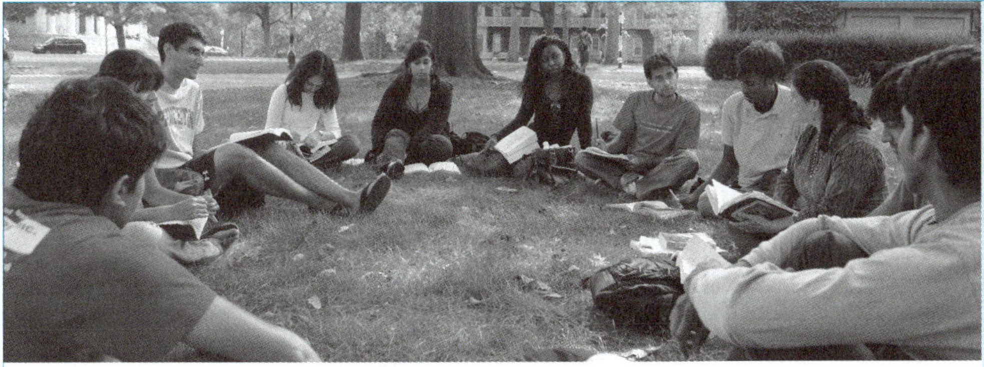

Princeton University is a private, four-year, research university with the heart and soul of a liberal arts college. Located in central New Jersey, the University's commitment to undergraduate education is unique among leading research universities. Princeton's 5,251 undergraduate students benefit from studying in one of the world's foremost research institutions, where faculty devote much of their time and energy to teaching and advising undergraduates. More than ever, through initiatives such as its generous financial aid program, Princeton's distinctive education is accessible to students from a broad range of cultural, ethnic and economic backgrounds. With 43% students of color and 13.4% the first in their families to attend college, Princeton is committed to building a diverse campus community where students pursue new interests and learn from each other. In addition, Princeton meets 100% of demonstrated need, and it is possible for students to graduate free of debt.

Pre-College Prep & Outreach **Princeton University Preparatory Program (PUPP)**

PUPP is a rigorous academic and cultural enrichment program that supports high-achieving, low-income high school students from local districts. The program helps students from ninth grade through high school graduation to build the academic skills, confidence and leadership abilities. Participants are also provided year-round academic and cultural enrichment opportunities. Program staff members assist students and their families with the college application process and encourage students through every step.

Scholarship & Financial Aid **QuestBridge**

Princeton participates in QuestBridge's National College Match program. Through one application, students can apply to partner colleges and be selected for admission and full scholarships to these schools. Most of the student participants in the program come from households earning less than $60,000 a year for a typical family of four, and more than 75 percent are in the top 5 percent of their high school class.

First-Year Experience & Transition **Freshman Scholars Institute**

Our Freshman Scholars Institute (FSI) is a seven-week summer program that allows a cohort of entering students from under-resourced backgrounds the chance to experience the intellectual, co-curricular and social life at Princeton prior to the beginning of the fall semester. During the program, Freshman Scholars engage in seminar-style courses and/or laboratory research experiences, participate in a variety of co-curricular, community-building activities, and work closely with faculty members from a range of academic disciplines and fields. The FSI program is designed as a fellowship opportunity and is free to students receiving grant aid from the University.

Student Life & Support **Princeton Hidden Minority Council**

The Hidden Minority Council is a student-run organization that works to create a community for first-generation and low-income students at Princeton by providing mentorship, networking, and resource accessibility.

Mentoring **Scholars Institute Fellows Program (SIFP)**

The Scholars Institute Fellows Program (SIFP) provides all first-generation and low-income students at Princeton with mentorship, academic enrichment and scholarly community throughout their undergraduate years. SIFP Fellows are part of a larger first-generation community of peers, staff and faculty at the University. The SIFP experience is composed of monthly mentorship group meetings, co-curricular workshops and programs, leadership opportunities, a summer enrichment experience and fully funded extracurricular activities.

Princeton University
P.O. Box 430
Princeton, NJ 08542
Ph: (609) 258-3060
uaoffice@princeton.edu
admission.princeton.edu

Fast Facts

STUDENT DIVERSITY

# undergraduates	5,251
% male/female	52/48
% first-generation college	13.4
% American Indian or Alaskan Native	<1
% Asian	21
% Black or African American	8
% Hispanic/Latino	10
% Native Hawaiian or Pacific Islander	<1
% White	44
% two or more races	4
% race and/or ethnicity unknown	1
% International/nonresident	12

STUDENT SUCCESS

% first-to-second year retention	98
% six-year graduation	97
% six-year graduation for underrepresented minority groups	97
% first-years who live on campus	100
% undergraduates who live on campus	96
full-time faculty	924
full-time minority faculty	235
student-faculty ratio	5:1

Popular majors Computer Science, Woodrow Wilson School of Public and International Affairs, Economics, History, Operations Research and Financial Engineering, Politics, Molecular Biology, Psychology, Ecology and Evolutionary Biology, English

Multicultural student clubs and organizations Asian American Students Association, Ballet Folklorico de Princeton, Black Arts Company - Dance, Black Student Union, DREAM team, Latinos y Amigos, Muslim Student's Association, National Society of Black Engineers, Pride Alliance, Princeton Association of Black Women

AFFORDABILITY

Cost of Attendance

tuition	$47,140
required fees	$850
room and board	$15,610

Financial Aid

total institutional scholarships/grants	$161,000,000
% of students with financial need	60
% of students with need awarded any financial aid	100
% of students with need awarded any need-based scholarship or grant aid	100
% of students with need whose need was fully met	100
% Pell Grant recipients among first-years	22
average aid package	$52,690
average student loan debt upon graduation	$8,900

ADMISSIONS

# of applicants	31,056
% admitted	6.4
SAT Evidence-Based Reading & Writing	680-760
SAT Math	700-780
ACT Composite	31-35
SAT/ACT optional	no

DEADLINES

regular application closing date	1/1
early decision plan	n/a
application closing date	n/a
early action plan	yes
application closing date	11/1
application fee	$65
application fee online	$65
fee waiver for applicants with financial need	yes

Ramapo College of New Jersey

Ranked by *U.S. News & World Report* as one of the Best Regional Universities North category for public institutions, Ramapo College of New Jersey is sometimes viewed as a private college. This is, in part, due to its unique interdisciplinary academic structure, its size of approximately 6,000 students and its pastoral setting in the foothills of the Ramapo Mountains on the New Jersey/New York border. Undergraduate students choose to concentrate their studies in more than 539 course offerings and 36 academic programs. Ramapo boasts an average student/faculty ratio of 18:1 and average class size of 23, affording students the opportunity to develop close ties to the College's exceptional faculty. In 2017, Ramapo was named among College Choice's ranking of the 20 Best College in New Jersey. More specifically, Ramapo ranks as #1 among nine of the public colleges in New Jersey. Ramapo College is also listed in *Kiplinger's Personal Finance Magazine* as among the "100 Best Values in Public Colleges" for 11 consecutive years.

Pre-College Prep & Outreach **Undergraduate Recruitment and Community Outreach**

The Office of Admissions participates in college information programs sponsored by community organizations working with first generation college students and their families. Admissions participates on college panels and facilitates workshops on navigating the college admissions process, understanding financial aid and scholarships as well as issues of diversity in higher education.

Summer Bridge & Orientation **Orientation**

Orientation for new Roadrunners is an exciting time for students and guests where Ramapo College staff, faculty and orientation leaders introduce the students to "Your First Year Experience!" Our mandatory orientation program provides students with access to faculty, staff and other academic offices. The orientation will assist students in the first semester registration and transition to college life whether a resident or commuter.

First-Year Experience & Transition **Academic Advising and First Year Experience**

First year students are introduced to Ramapo College through an integrated, and focused first-year experience program that includes peer mentoring, faculty connections, academic advising and transitional support services. Throughout their first year, students are introduced to their professional advisor within the Center for Student Success and First Year Experience. With mandatory academic advisement touch points, students are supported and mentored through their first-year.

Academic Advising & Support **Educational Opportunity Fund (EOF)**

The mission of the Educational Opportunity Fund (EOF) Program is to provide highly motivated students who exhibit the potential for success, but who come from families/communities disadvantaged by low income and a lack of quality educational preparation necessary to attend college, access to a four-year college degree. Students who qualify for EOF, receive extra academic and financial support. The six week EOF Pre-Freshmen Studies program starts in the last week of June and ends in the first week of August. All incoming EOF freshmen receive an EOF Peer Mentor for their freshmen year, as well as an EOF Student Development Specialist (advisor) who will work with them until they graduate from Ramapo.

Mentoring **Peer Facilitation Program (FYS)**

Peer facilitators work with FYS faculty to forge bonds with and among students in their classes. Peers attend the FYS course with their peer class. Through their presence and weekly class facilitation they help new students feel comfortable and provide them with tools to excel.

Ramapo College of New Jersey
505 Ramapo Valley Road
Mahwah, NJ 07604
Ph: (201) 684-7300
admissions@ramapo.edu
www.ramapo.edu

Fast Facts

STUDENT DIVERSITY

# undergraduates	5,618
% male/female	45/55
% first-generation college	n/a
% American Indian or Alaskan Native	<1
% Asian	7
% Black or African American	5
% Hispanic/Latino	15
% Native Hawaiian or Pacific Islander	<1
% White	64
% two or more races	1
% race and/or ethnicity unknown	5
% International/nonresident	2

STUDENT SUCCESS

% first-to-second year retention	86
% six-year graduation	74
% six-year graduation for underrepresented minority groups	n/a
% first-years who live on campus	75
% undergraduates who live on campus	47
full-time faculty	224
full-time minority faculty	66
student-faculty ratio	18:1

Popular majors n/a

Multicultural student clubs and organizations n/a

AFFORDABILITY

Cost of Attendance

tuition	in-state: $8,998; out-of-state: $17,998
required fees	$4,872
room and board	$11,640

Financial Aid

total institutional scholarships/grants	$2,645,580
% of students with financial need	53
% of students with need awarded any financial aid	82
% of students with need awarded any need-based scholarship or grant aid	53
% of students with need whose need was fully met	13
% Pell Grant recipients among first-years	27
average aid package	$12,143
average student loan debt upon graduation	n/a

ADMISSIONS

# of applicants	7,106
% admitted	53
SAT Critical Reading	480-590
SAT Math	500-610
SAT Writing	480-590
ACT Composite	n/a
SAT/ACT optional	n/a
average HS GPA	3.21

DEADLINES

regular application closing date	3/1
early decision plan	yes
application closing date	11/1
early action plan	n/a
application closing date	n/a
application fee	$60
application fee online	$60
fee waiver for applicants with financial need	yes

Rutgers University–Camden

A big-university education in a supportive setting: that's Rutgers University–Camden. Here you'll explore the superior academics of Rutgers, one of the nation's finest public research universities, in a close-knit community that connects you to opportunity. Rutgers–Camden offers a wide range of academic disciplines—nearly 40 majors and 50 minors and special programs—including the humanities, arts, social sciences, natural and physical sciences, computer science, business, and nursing. From courses that incorporate civic engagement into the curriculum and international experiences that take you across the globe, you'll receive a comprehensive, hands-on education that makes you stand out above the rest. And you'll find these extraordinary learning opportunities in a supportive environment where your education matters. Now, earning a Rutgers degree is more attainable than ever before. Our innovative Bridging the Gap program reduces tuition up to 100 percent for qualifying families.

Pre-College Prep & Outreach **Rutgers Future Scholars**

The Rutgers Future Scholars Program introduces economically disadvantaged, academically promising middle school students from Rutgers' four host communities—including Camden—to the opportunities of a college education. Each year, up to 200 students who are completing the seventh grade are accepted into the program. To ease the financial burden, Rutgers guarantees free tuition and fees to all who successfully complete the pre-college phase of the program, meet admission requirements, and choose to attend Rutgers.

Pre-College Prep & Outreach **Hill Family Center for College Access**

The Hill Family Center for College Access at Rutgers University–Camden seeks to create a more robust college-going culture in the city of Camden and the region by providing the support and guidance needed to students and their families to ensure access to and preparation for success in post-secondary education.

Scholarship & Financial Aid **Bridging the Gap**

The first of its kind among New Jersey's public four-year colleges and universities, Bridging the Gap closes the gap between federal and state sources of financial support and the balance of tuition and the general campus fee. Rutgers–Camden will then automatically apply the Bridging the Gap grant to remaining tuition.

Academic Advising & Support **EOF (Educational Opportunity Fund) Program**

The EOF program is a state-funded program that serves highly motivated first-generation students from educationally and economically disadvantaged backgrounds in New Jersey by providing access to higher education and the services and opportunities to achieve success in college and beyond. The Rutgers–Camden EOF staff provides services that focus on student learning and success, encourage civic engagement, promote leadership, and instill within students an appreciation for diversity and lifelong learning.

Academic Advising & Support **TRiO Student Support Services**

Rutgers University–Camden TRiO Student Support Services (SSS) is a federally funded program that provides programs specifically designed to increase the retention and graduation rates of first-generation and low-income students. Our services include one-on-one professional and peer tutoring, academic coaching, and academic enrichment and financial literacy workshops. We also provide grant aid/scholarships to eligible SSS participants.

Rutgers University–Camden
406 Penn Street
Camden, NJ 08102-1400
Ph: (856) 225-6104
admissions@camden.rutgers.edu
camden.rutgers.edu

Fast Facts

STUDENT DIVERSITY

# undergraduates	5,021
% male/female	41/59
% first-generation college	28
% American Indian or Alaskan Native	<1
% Asian	10
% Black or African American	17
% Hispanic/Latino	14
% Native Hawaiian or Pacific Islander	<1
% White	53
% two or more races	4
% race and/or ethnicity unknown	2
% International/nonresident	1

STUDENT SUCCESS

% first-to-second year retention	87
% six-year graduation	59
% six-year graduation for underrepresented minority groups	45
% first-years who live on campus	36
% undergraduates who live on campus	8
full-time faculty	315
full-time minority faculty	80
student-faculty ratio	10:1

Popular majors Business/Marketing, Health Professions and related programs, Psychology, Social Sciences, Criminal Justice/Safety Studies, Accounting, Nursing

Multicultural student clubs and organizations Latin American Students Organization, African Students Association, Asian Cultural Society, Muslim Students Association, Turkish Students Association, Campus Crusade for Christ, Students of Rutgers Volunteer Council, French Club, Black Students Union, Korean Students Association

AFFORDABILITY

Cost of Attendance

tuition	in-state: $11,750; out-of-state: $26,824
required fees	$2,817
room and board	$12,756

Financial Aid

total institutional scholarships/grants	$32,360,576
% of students with financial need	84
% of students with need awarded any financial aid	100
% of students with need awarded any need-based scholarship or grant aid	76
% of students with need whose need was fully met	5
% Pell Grant recipients among first-years	55
average aid package	$12,810
average student loan debt upon graduation	$29,624

ADMISSIONS

# of applicants	8,725
% admitted	57
SAT Critical Reading	440-550
SAT Math	450-570
SAT Writing	440-540
ACT Composite	n/a
SAT/ACT optional	n/a
average HS GPA	n/a

DEADLINES

regular application closing date	12/1
early decision plan	yes
application closing date	11/1
early action plan	n/a
application closing date	rolling
application fee	$70
application fee online	$70
fee waiver for applicants with financial need	yes

Rutgers University–New Brunswick

Established in 1766, Rutgers University–New Brunswick is the flagship campus of Rutgers, The State University of New Jersey. We are New Jersey's most comprehensive intellectual resource, as designated by the Association of American Universities. We are the region's most high-profile public research institution and a leading national research center with global impact. Smart, well-prepared, and economically and ethnically diverse, our students come from across the nation and around the globe. Down-to-earth and driven, they achieve both a level of academic scholarship and a mastery of practical skills, which earn them prestigious fellowships and the attention of top-corporate recruiters.

Pre-College Prep & Outreach **TARGET**

The Academy at Rutgers for Girls in Engineering and Technology (TARGET) is a summer program designed for middle- and high school girls to increase awareness about career opportunities in engineering. TARGET hosts six one-week commuter programs. Through a series of hands-on activities, team challenges, speakers, and mentorships, TARGET aims to familiarize girls with different engineering disciplines and to destroy negative stereotypes concerning their ability to do well in math and science. Visit precollege.rutgers.edu for additional programs.

Scholars & Leadership **Paul Robeson Leadership Institute**

The Paul Robeson Leadership Institute is an extension of Student Support Services. It provides first-generation students from historically underrepresented groups a range of experiences and support such as attending a summer bridge program, leadership workshops, financial support, post-graduation planning and opportunities to engage with distinguished faculty, staff and alumni.

Academic Advising & Support **Student Access and Educational Equity (SAEE)**

Student Access and Educational Equity (SAEE) houses a range of offices that provide resources and support for low-income, first-generation, and historically underrepresented students. Services range from: advising, summer bridge programs, opportunity to travel for conferences and/or study abroad and preparation for life after college. Please visit each program as resources vary at access.rutgers.edu. Some SAEE programs are:

• **Student Support Services (SSS)** provides undergraduate students with a host of services such as tutoring, workshops, and career and academic coaching in one-on-one and group workshop formats. SSS is a federally funded program, designed to increase the retention and graduation rates of first-generation and low-income students, as well as students with a disability.

• **Louis Stokes Alliance for Minority Participation (GS-LSAMP)**

• **Ronald E. McNair Post-Baccalaureate Achievement Program**

• **Educational Outreach** provides high impact programs that engage students' intellectual exploration and promotes community-building to foster an inclusive environment.

  • **Women of Color Initiatives (WOCI)** and **Rutgers University Male Empowerment Network (RU-MEN)**

  • **Access Week** (3rd Week of February) is a weeklong event connecting Rutgers and the surrounding communities on issues of access, equity, and race in higher education.

RU-1st provides programming and support for students who are first in their family to attend college to aid in their success and foster inclusive communities. Students may receive a host of school based academic and financial resources. Learn more about RU-1st at RU1.rutgers.edu or contact RU-1st at RU1st@rutgers.edu or 848.932.9988.

Rutgers University–New Brunswick
100 Sutphen Road
Piscataway, NJ 08854
Ph: (732) 445-4636
www.newbrunswick.rutgers.edu

Fast Facts

STUDENT DIVERSITY

# undergraduates	35,484
% male/female	50/50
% first-generation college	32
% American Indian or Alaskan Native	<1
% Asian	26
% Black or African American	8
% Hispanic/Latino	13
% Native Hawaiian or Pacific Islander	<1
% White	42
% two or more races	3
% race and/or ethnicity unknown	2
% International/nonresident	7

STUDENT SUCCESS

% first-to-second year retention	92
% six-year graduation	80
% six-year graduation for underrepresented minority groups	n/a
% first-years who live on campus	n/a
% undergraduates who live on campus	n/a
full-time faculty	2,731
full-time minority faculty	371
student-faculty ratio	12:1

Popular majors Business/Marketing, Engineering, Social Sciences, Biological/Life Sciences, Communication/Journalism

Multicultural student clubs and organizations Minority Engineering Education Task (MEET), National Society of Black Engineers (NSBE), Society of Hispanic Engineers (SHE), Society of Women Engineers (SWE), BLACK VOICE/CARTA LATINA, Black Student Union, West Indian Student Organization, Minority Association of Pre-Health Students (M.A.P.S.)

AFFORDABILITY

Cost of Attendance

tuition	in-state: $11,619; out-of-state: $27,560
required fees	$3,019
room and board	$12,452

Financial Aid

total institutional scholarships/grants	$70,933,910
% of students with financial need	53
% of students with need awarded any financial aid	53
% of students with need awarded any need-based scholarship or grant aid	37
% of students with need whose need was fully met	2
% Pell Grant recipients among first-years	28
average aid package	$13,292
average student loan debt upon graduation	$25,749

ADMISSIONS

# of applicants	36,677
% admitted	57
SAT Critical Reading	530-640
SAT Math	580-700
SAT Writing	540-660
ACT Composite	27
SAT/ACT optional	n/a
average HS GPA	3.76

DEADLINES

regular application closing date	12/1
early decision plan	n/a
application closing date	n/a
early action plan	yes
application closing date	11/1
application fee	$70
application fee online	$70
fee waiver for applicants with financial need	yes

Rutgers University–Newark

Rutgers University–Newark (RU-N) is a world-class urban research and teaching institution, with more than 12,800 students and over 500 faculty members. Since 1997, RU-N has been rated as the most diverse national campus by *U.S. News & World Report*. RU-N aims to be a national leader in 21st century higher education through a commitment to the values of educating a diverse citizenry, producing high impact scholarship, engaging in our community as an anchor institution, and drawing the connection between local and global, for the improvement of the economic and social well-being of society. Our campus has traditionally served as the place of educational opportunity for first-generation college students, for students whose home languages were not English, for students commuting to campus to save money, for students who work to stay in college and or support their families, and for students of diverse racial, ethnic, and religious backgrounds.

Scholars & Leadership **Honors Living-Learning Community**

Honors Living-Learning Community (HLLC) is a transformative college access and success program that fosters the academic, social, and personal development of talented students who have a desire to make a difference in their communities and beyond. With an innovative honors curriculum centered on a theme of "Local Citizenship in a Global World," HLLC students will live and learn at Rutgers University–Newark and receive a residential scholarship which covers room and board. To learn more, visit http://hllc.newark.rutgers.edu/

Scholarship & Financial Aid **RU-N to the TOP**

Rutgers University-Newark Talent and Opportunity Pathways program (RU-N to the TOP) provides a "last dollar" scholarship that covers the cost of in-state tuition and mandatory school fees after all federal, state and internal/external scholarships/ grants have been applied. This scholarship became effective for newly enrolling students entering in the fall 2016 semester or later, who meet all the eligibility requirements, and complete the FAFSA. To learn more, visit admissions.newark.rutgers.edu/paying-for-college/ru-n-top

Academic Advising & Support **The Academic Foundations Center (AFC)**

AFC provides academic opportunities, resources, and support programs primarily for underrepresented students including first generation, low income students to succeed through education. AFC provides strong instruction and tutorial services with the academic, personal, financial, and career advisement necessary for academic and social advancement for students ranging from the sixth grade through college graduation.

Academic Advising & Support **myRUN**

The myRUN portal (myrun.newark.rutgers.edu) is dedicated to providing first-generation students and families with easy online access to campus resources and information. Students can find quick answers on myRUN regarding issues covering, but are not limited to, academic advising, term bill payment, scholarships, registration, athletics, dining, and student life.

First-Year Experience & Transition **First Year Experience-Office of Student Life**

After attending a Student Orientation, Advising, and Registration (SOAR) Day, new students are invited to participate in a variety of programs and events specifically designed to support their transition into college. First-year students can attend "Welcome Week" events to learn about campus involvement and resources, join the "Peer Connection" program to build relationships with experienced student leaders, and participate in the "Emerging Leaders Institute" to develop the skills for leadership in one of RU-N's 90+ student organizations.

Rutgers University–Newark
Office of Graduate and Undergraduate Admissions
Newark, NJ 07102
Ph: (973) 353-5205
newark@admissions.rutgers.edu
newark.rutgers.edu

Fast Facts

STUDENT DIVERSITY

# undergraduates	8,170
% male/female	46/54
% first-generation college	30
% American Indian or Alaskan Native	<1
% Asian	20
% Black or African American	18
% Hispanic/Latino	27
% Native Hawaiian or Pacific Islander	<1
% White	24
% two or more races	3
% race and/or ethnicity unknown	4
% International/nonresident	4

STUDENT SUCCESS

% first-to-second year retention	83
% six-year graduation	66
% six-year graduation for underrepresented minority groups	61
% first-years who live on campus	33
% undergraduates who live on campus	15
full-time faculty	539
full-time minority faculty	58
student-faculty ratio	11:1

Popular majors Accounting, Finance, Criminal Justice, Biology, Psychology

Multicultural student clubs and organizations Black Organization of Students (BOS), Latino United Networking in America (LUNA), Indian Student Association (ISA), Haitian Association of students at Rutgers (HASAR), Muslim Student Association (MSA), Organization of African Students (OAS), Sikh Student Association

AFFORDABILITY

Cost of Attendance

tuition	in-state: $11,408; out-of-state: $27,059
required fees	$2,421
room and board	$13,059

Financial Aid

total institutional scholarships/grants	$13,511,576
% of students with financial need	78
% of students with need awarded any financial aid	100
% of students with need awarded any need-based scholarship or grant aid	83
% of students with need whose need was fully met	1
% Pell Grant recipients among first-years	53
average aid package	$14,141
average student loan debt upon graduation	$27,881

ADMISSIONS

# of applicants	13,435
% admitted	64
SAT Evidence-Based Reading & Writing	490-630
SAT Math	490-660
ACT Composite	24-29
SAT/ACT optional	n/a
average HS GPA	3.59

DEADLINES

regular application closing date	rolling
early decision plan	n/a
application closing date	rolling
early action plan	yes
application closing date	11/1
application fee	$70
application fee online	$70
fee waiver for applicants with financial need	yes

New Mexico Highlands University

New Mexico Highlands University
Box 9000
Las Vegas, NM 87701
Ph: (505) 454-3394
recruitment@nmhu.edu
www.nmhu.edu

Whether you're an undergraduate or graduate student, New Mexico Highlands is the right place for you. We consistently rate #1 in New Mexico for student satisfaction because of our attention to our highest priority: you. Our commitment to your success means we hire the best professors who care about your goals while making sure our tuition is one of the most affordable in the United States.

Academic Advising & Support **ARMAS in Education**

The ARMAS in Education center provides comprehensive support to science, technology, engineering and math students as they work toward their academic and professional goals. Our staff strives to create a caring community for our students and to empower them to realize their full potential through emphasis on critical thinking, teamwork, communication, effective study habits and setting and achieving goals. All students taking classes in STEM disciplines are welcome to participate in the services and programs offered by the center. Students do NOT have to be STEM majors to access Center services.

Academic Advising & Support **Peer Advisers**

Through the Peer Advisers program, students can get help from other students who know firsthand what it takes to succeed in college. Student advisers assist other students with academics, adjusting to college life and other areas.

Scholars & Leadership **Honors Program**

The Honors Program offers advanced and creative students an opportunity to develop their abilities and talents in classes and projects more challenging than those experienced by most undergraduates. In the final course, students design a semester- long research or creative project of professional quality related to their major field of study.

Pre-College Prep & Outreach **Student Support Services**

Incoming freshmen at New Mexico Highlands University participate in First-Year Experience Learning Communities. Highlands University understands the important role of community and prides itself on engaging programs focused on student success through community building and experiential learning. Students are placed in learning communities based on a variety of preference factors. Students provide information about their past experiences, preferences, interests, and goals in a survey, which is used to place students in the learning community that best fits them.

Scholarship & Financial Aid **Financial Aid**

The Office of Financial Aid at New Mexico Highlands is here to help students find ways to fund their college education through scholarships, work-study, grants and loans. Applying for financial aid is not a complicated process, but it does take time. So contact our office as soon as possible, so we can help you achieve your goals.

Fast Facts

STUDENT DIVERSITY

# undergraduates	2,181
% male/female	41/59
% first-generation college	n/a
% American Indian or Alaskan Native	8
% Asian	1
% Black or African American	5
% Hispanic/Latino	58
% Native Hawaiian or Pacific Islander	<1
% White	20
% two or more races	2
% race and/or ethnicity unknown	1
% International/nonresident	5

STUDENT SUCCESS

% first-to-second year retention	52
% six-year graduation	22
% six-year graduation for underrepresented minority groups	20
% first-years who live on campus	72
% undergraduates who live on campus	22
full-time faculty	138
full-time minority faculty	43
student-faculty ratio	15:1

Popular majors Education, Health, Business, Psychology, Social Sciences

Multicultural student clubs and organizations Association of Latino Professionals for America (ALPFA), Highlands Haciendas, Hispanic Culture and Language Association, NMHU International Club, Native American Club

AFFORDABILITY

Cost of Attendance

tuition	$7,581.60 or in-state: $4,248
required fees	$1,556.40
room and board	$7,696

Financial Aid

total institutional scholarships/grants	$8,348,539
% of students with financial need	69
% of students with need awarded any financial aid	96
% of students with need awarded any need-based scholarship or grant aid	84
% of students with need whose need was fully met	7
% Pell Grant recipients among first-years	n/a
average aid package	$1,827
average student loan debt upon graduation	n/a

ADMISSIONS

# of applicants	1,158
% admitted	100
SAT Critical Reading	360-470
SAT Math	360-478
SAT Writing	350-480
ACT Composite	15-20
SAT/ACT optional	yes
average HS GPA	2.99

DEADLINES

regular application closing date	rolling
early decision plan	n/a
application closing date	n/a
early action plan	n/a
application closing date	n/a
application fee	$15
application fee online	$15
fee waiver for applicants with financial need	yes

St. John's College (New Mexico)

At St. John's College, great books—and great discussions—are the heart of the college's distinctive liberal arts program. At the college's two campuses in Annapolis, MD and Santa Fe, NM, every class consists of 14-20 students discussing the greatest books of Western civilization across disciplines that include literature, philosophy, math, science, language, and music. The college's coeducational community, free of religious affiliation, takes an open-minded approach to ideas of all kinds. Rather than being told how and what to think about what they're reading, St. John's students are asked to reach their own conclusions through deep thinking, critical analysis, and intense discussion. Every part of the program aims to raise essential questions that have been the subject of human inquiry since the beginning of time. Most students live on campus in a socially and academically supportive community, where diversity of mind and thought are valued and encouraged.

Pre-College Summer Experience **The St. John's College Summer Academy**

The St. John's College Summer Academy is a pre-college, residential program that shows students the possibilities of a liberal arts education. Students explore works by some of the greatest thinkers of Western culture in discussion-based classes. They also participate in an array of extra-curricular activities—from poetry writing to improv techniques to yoga and pottery—and enjoy excursions to museums and historic sites. Financial assistance is available.

Open House, Fly-in, Visit **St. John's College Fly-In Program**

St. John's College encourages prospective students to visit campus to see our distinctive education in action. Students can schedule a campus tour or a day or overnight visit throughout the year, including during the summer. To make visiting accessible for accepted students, the college offers a fly-in program that covers travel expenses. Two admitted student events are scheduled in 2018: the first runs from Sunday, March 25 to Monday, March 26; the second from Sunday, April 22 to Monday, April 23.

First-Year Experience & Transition **First-Year Support**

St. John's hires student assistants in every subject studied at the college. These assistants, having experienced the program themselves, provide invaluable academic and social support to first-year students. Resident Assistants, current students trained to provide support in the dorms, also help students with their college transition. Through the Assistant Dean's office, academic tutoring and personal counseling can be arranged. Students are encouraged to build relationships with professors by participating in the college's "Take a Professor to Lunch" program.

St. John's College (New Mexico)
1160 Camino Cruz Blanca
Santa Fe, New Mexico 87505
Ph: (800) 331-5232
www.sjc.edu

Fast Facts

STUDENT DIVERSITY

# undergraduates (New Mexico campus)	339
% male/female	55/45
% first-generation college	12
% American Indian or Alaskan Native	<1
% Asian	2
% Black or African American	1
% Hispanic/Latino	9
% Native Hawaiian or Pacific Islander	<1
% White	54
% two or more races	5
% race and/or ethnicity unknown	1
% International/nonresident	26

STUDENT SUCCESS

% first-to-second year retention	75
% six-year graduation	64
% six-year graduation for underrepresented minority groups	n/a
% first-years who live on campus	94
% undergraduates who live on campus	85
full-time faculty	45
full-time minority faculty	1
student-faculty ratio	8:1

Popular majors Liberal Arts

Multicultural student clubs and organizations
Black Student Union, Inter-sectional Feminist Group, Pangea (International Student Club), Pink Triangle (LGBTQ+ Alliance Group), Shammai (Jewish Student Club), Chinese Teahouse (Eastern Authors study group)

AFFORDABILITY

Cost of Attendance

tuition	$51,200
required fees	$470
room and board	$11,486

Financial Aid

total institutional scholarships/grants	$3,942,772
% of students with financial need	75
% of students with need awarded any financial aid	100
% of students with need awarded any need-based scholarship or grant aid	100
% of students with need whose need was fully met	84
% Pell Grant recipients among first-years	23
average aid package	$37,870
average student loan debt upon graduation	$25,400

ADMISSIONS

# of applicants	1,175
% admitted	58
SAT Evidence-Based Reading & Writing	610-800
SAT Math	510-800
ACT Composite	22-35
SAT/ACT optional	yes
average HS GPA	3.5

DEADLINES

regular application closing date	rolling
early decision plan	n/a
application closing date	n/a
early action plan	yes
application closing date	11/15
application fee	n/a
application fee online	n/a
fee waiver for applicants with financial need	n/a

*Data reported is combined for St. John's College's two campuses in Maryland and New Mexico, unless otherwise noted.

Barnard College

Barnard College
3009 Broadway
New York, NY 10027
Ph: (212) 854-2014
admissions@barnard.edu
admissions.barnard.edu

Barnard is a small, highly selective liberal arts college for women located in New York City. Our students are part of a diverse and close-knit community and study with leading scholars who serve as dedicated, accessible mentors and teachers in small, intimate classes. Barnard also enjoys a unique partnership with Columbia University, situated directly across the street, providing students with additional course offerings, extracurricular activities, NCAA Division I Ivy League athletic competition and a fully coed social life. Our location in New York City grants students access to thousands of internship opportunities in addition to unparalleled cultural, intellectual and social resources. Barnard's diverse student body includes residents from nearly every state and more than 50 countries worldwide. 45 percent of the 2016 incoming class identifies as students of color, and 13 percent of the class comes from non-college backgrounds.

Pre-College Prep & Outreach **Science Pathways Scholars Program (SP)²**

The Science Pathways Scholars Program is a highly selective 4-year program designed to support talented young women from underrepresented backgrounds (Black, Latina, or Native American), or first-generation college students, who have a strong interest in biology, chemistry, environmental science, physics/astronomy or neuroscience. Scholar recipients will benefit from a personally matched faculty member in the sciences, a one-week, fully funded summer experience at Barnard for entering scholars, networking with Barnard alumnae working in the sciences, paid summer research positions and increased opportunities to conduct research during the academic year. To apply, students must indicate interest on the application and complete and additional short essay.

Open House, Fly-In, Visit **Barnard Bound**

Barnard Bound provides a taste of both Barnard College and New York City for promising female high school seniors from around the country. Barnard College is 100% need-blind in the review of applications and meets 100% of demonstrated need with need-based financial aid. Counselors from High Schools and Community-Based Organizations are asked to nominate students by mid-June and selected students will be notified of our decision in mid-August.

Scholarship & Financial Aid **The Arthur O. Eve Higher Education Opportunity Program (HEOP) and the Barnard Opportunity Program (BOP)**

For a select group of scholars, the Arthur O. Eve Higher Education Opportunity Program (HEOP) and Barnard Opportunity Program (BOP) offer additional pathway for admission to Barnard. A lending library, laptop computers, free tutoring, mentoring, and study skills workshops, and graduate school preparation and career guidance are available to all BOP and HEOP Scholars in addition to the resources and support they receive as Barnard students. To be considered for HEOP, students must be residents of New York State and meet other eligibility requirements. Additionally, a small number of students who are not New York State residents are identified by the office of admissions as BOP Scholars.

Academic Advising & Support **Academic Success and Enrichment Programs**

The Office of Academic Success and Enrichment Programs (ASEP) is committed to providing opportunities to enrich and support the intellectual life of students. Under the supervision of the Office of the Dean of Studies, ASEP works to engage students in rigorous academic experiences while providing services needed to meet academic challenges and to discover their own capabilities.

Fast Facts

STUDENT DIVERSITY	
# undergraduates	2,588
% male/female	0/100
% first-generation college	14
% American Indian or Alaskan Native	<1
% Asian	14
% Black or African American	6
% Hispanic/Latino	13
% Native Hawaiian or Pacific Islander	<1
% White	52
% two or more races	6
% race and/or ethnicity unknown	<1
% International/nonresident	9
STUDENT SUCCESS	
% first-to-second year retention	96
% six-year graduation	93
% six-year graduation for underrepresented minority groups	93
% first-years who live on campus	99
% undergraduates who live on campus	91
full-time faculty	214
full-time minority faculty	49
student-faculty ratio	10:1

Popular majors Psychology, English, Political Science, History, Economics

Multicultural student clubs and organizations Asian American Alliance (AAA), Barnard Organization of Soul Sisters (BOSS), Caribbean Students Association (CSA), Chinese Students Club (CSC), Grupo Quisqueyano (Dominican Students Organization), Haitian Students Association, Liga Flipina, Malama Hawaii, Organization of Pakistani Students (OPS), Club Zamana (South Asian Organization), etc.

AFFORDABILITY	
Cost of Attendance	
tuition	$48,614
required fees	$1,780
room and board	$15,598
Financial Aid	
total institutional scholarships/grants	$42,779,661
% of students with financial need	39
% of students with need awarded any financial aid	100
% of students with need awarded any need-based scholarship or grant aid	39
% of students with need whose need was fully met	100
% Pell Grant recipients among first-years	15
average aid package	$48,709
average student loan debt upon graduation	$23,450
ADMISSIONS	
# of applicants	7,716
% admitted	15
SAT Evidence-Based Reading & Writing	640-740
SAT Math	640-730
ACT Composite	30-33
SAT/ACT optional	no
average HS GPA	4.12
DEADLINES	
regular application closing date	1/1
early decision plan	yes
application closing date	11/1
early action plan	n/a
application closing date	n/a
application fee	$75
application fee online	$75
fee waiver for applicants with financial need	yes

Columbia University in the City of New York

Columbia maintains an intimate residential college campus within one of the world's most vibrant cities. The renowned Core Curriculum attracts free-minded scholars and connects all undergraduates. Ideas spill out from cutting-edge research labs and seminar-style classrooms, electrifying the campus and the neighborhood. Friendships formed in the residence halls solidify during a game of frisbee on the South Lawn or over bagels on the steps of Low Library. Columbia College and Columbia Engineering are proud to have nearly 900 undergraduates who are the first in their family to attend college. From your first day on campus, you will be part of our diverse community.

Pre-College Prep & Outreach **College Access Outreach**

The Office of Undergraduate Admissions collaborates with hundreds of community based and college access organizations nationwide, such as College Horizons, Chicago Scholars and Say YES, and is a QuestBridge partner institution. Students can take a virtual tour of campus and connect with current students in the Multicultural Recruitment Committee, a student volunteer group that assists Admissions to recruit a vibrant and dynamic first-year class.

Open House, Fly-in, Visit **Programs for Underrepresented Students**

Columbia offers a one-day Open House in the fall for underrepresented students of color and all students interested in diversity and multiculturalism. Underrepresented students interested in engineering are invited in August of their senior year to apply to Columbia Engineering Experience (CE2), a three-day overnight program on campus. Columbia also has a three-day program in April for admitted students; many students qualify for funding for travel to and from our campus.

Scholarship & Financial Aid **Need Based. Need Blind. Full Need. No Loans.**

Columbia meets 100 percent of the demonstrated financial need for all students admitted as first years, without loans and regardless of citizenship status. For students from families with incomes under $60,000 annually (and typical assets), parents are not expected to contribute to the cost of attendance. Additional funding is available for study abroad, research, internships and community service opportunities. Columbia awards more than $150 million annually in grants and scholarships.

Academic Advising & Support **Office of Multicultural Affairs**

The Office of Multicultural Affairs (OMA) aims to strengthen and support Columbia's richly diverse community. The OMA advises over 40 cultural and identity-based student organizations and oversees the Columbia Mentoring Initiative (CMI), a mentorship program that connects first-year students with returning student mentors and alumni. CMI focuses on participants' adjustment to college life and leadership and identity development, academic success, belonging and wellness.

Academic Advising & Support **Academic Success Programs (ASP)**

Advising at Columbia College and Columbia Engineering is multifaceted. Each student is paired with an academic Advising Dean as well as a major advisor from the corresponding academic department. The Academic Success Programs supplements this advising system for selected students by providing transitional programming, tutoring, skill-building seminars, educational and personal advising and mentoring.

Columbia University in the City of NY
212 Hamilton Hall MC2807
1130 Amsterdam Avenue
New York, NY 10027
Ph: (212) 854-2522
ugrad-ask@columbia.edu
undergrad.admissions.columbia.edu

Fast Facts

STUDENT DIVERSITY

# undergraduates	6,158
% male/female	52/48
% first-generation college	14
% American Indian or Alaskan Native	2
% Asian	23
% Black or African American	11
% Hispanic/Latino	12
% Native Hawaiian or Pacific Islander	n/a
% White	34
% two or more races	n/a
% race and/or ethnicity unknown	3
% International/nonresident	15

STUDENT SUCCESS

% first-to-second year retention	99
% six-year graduation	96
% six-year graduation for underrepresented minority groups	89
% first-years who live on campus	100
% undergraduates who live on campus	95
full-time faculty	1,678
full-time minority faculty	383
student-faculty ratio	6:1

Popular majors Political Science, Economics, Engineering, English, History, Biology

Multicultural student clubs and organizations African Students Association, Arab Students' Organization (Turath), Black Students Organization, Caribbean Students Association, Chicano Caucus, Chinese Students and Scholars Association, Korean Students Association, Native American Council, United Students of Color Council, Vietnamese Student Association

AFFORDABILITY

Cost of Attendance

tuition	$54,504
required fees	$2,704
room and board	$13,618

Financial Aid

total institutional scholarships/grants	$151,554,724
% of students with financial need	50
% of students with need awarded any financial aid	100
% of students with need awarded any need-based scholarship or grant aid	99
% of students with need whose need was fully met	100
% Pell Grant recipients among first-years	17
average aid package	$50,733
average student loan debt upon graduation	n/a

ADMISSIONS

# of applicants	36,292
% admitted	6
SAT Critical Reading	710-800
SAT Math	720-800
SAT Writing	710-790
ACT Composite	32-35
SAT/ACT optional	no
average HS GPA	n/a

DEADLINES

regular application closing date	1/1
early decision plan	yes
application closing date	11/1
early action plan	n/a
application closing date	n/a
application fee	$85
application fee online	$85
fee waiver for applicants with financial need	yes

Cornell University

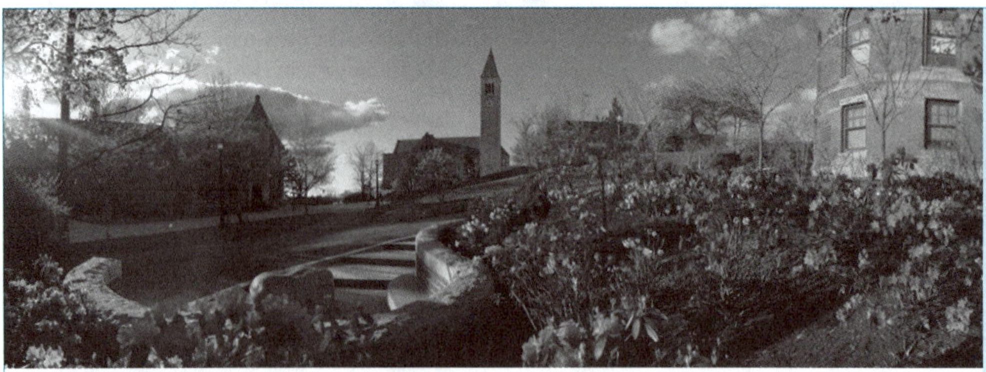

Cornell University
410 Thurston Avenue
Ithaca, NY 14850
Ph: (607) 255-7233
diversity@cornell.edu
www.admissions.cornell.edu

Founded in 1865 as both a private, co-educational university and the land-grant institution of New York State, Cornell University has a history of egalitarian excellence and diversity. Cornell educates leaders of tomorrow and extends the frontiers of knowledge in order to serve society. The university community fosters personal discovery, growth, scholarship, and creativity, and engages men and women from every segment of society. Valuing enrichment of the mind, Cornell pursues understanding and knowledge beyond the barriers of ideology and disciplinary structure.

Pre-College Prep & Outreach **Encourage Young Engineers and Scientists (EYES)**

EYES is a community-service organization committed to promoting engineering and the sciences as career fields and to increasing the math and science skills of elementary, middle, and high school students. Each year, teams of Cornell students create exciting, project-based math and science lessons and experiments that are taught at local schools and after-school programs.

Pre-College Prep & Outreach **Let's Get Ready!**

Cornell's Let's Get Ready! program mobilizes those who live and work around disadvantaged students to actively support education. It provides free SAT preparation courses and college/financial aid advising to underserved high school students, and it involves families, schools, churches, and businesses in offering these services. College students from surrounding communities run the programs and serve as instructors, role models and mentors to the students, helping them to navigate the college admissions process.

Open House, Fly-In, Visit **Diversity Hosting**

To encourage multicultural students to matriculate to Cornell, the University sponsors Diversity Hosting. This admitted student program occurs throughout April and offers students the chance to "get to know" Cornell. Diversity Hosting provides limited transportation to participants, and families are welcome.

Special Admissions Policy **New York State Opportunity Programs**

Cornell offers both a Higher Education Opportunity Program and an Education Opportunity Program. Both are programs for New York State residents who possess neither the traditional academic profile nor the financial means to afford college, but who do have the potential for success in a competitive academic environment. Students accepted under the EOP/HEOP programs receive academic counseling, assistance completing the financial aid application and a financial aid package to make a Cornell education affordable.

Academic Advising & Support **The Learning Strategies Center**

Providing tutoring and supplemental courses in biology, chemistry, economics, mathematics, and physics, the Learning Strategies Center is the central academic support unit for Cornell students. Semester long courses, workshops, individual consultations and website resources offer assistance in improving general study skills.

Academic Advising & Support **Office of Academic Diversity Initiatives (OADI)**

Cornell's Office of Academic Diversity Initiatives facilitates academic and personal adjustment to Cornell for the minority community. It encourages institutional change, when necessary, to ensure that the University embraces its diverse student population. The Office also offers referrals to campus-wide services, announcements of events and scholarships, and a student-produced yearbook. Additionally, OADI identifies and supports Cornell's first-generation students through the First-In-Class (FIC) program.

Fast Facts

STUDENT DIVERSITY

# undergraduates	14,907
% male/female	52/48
% first-generation college	14
% American Indian or Alaskan Native	<1
% Asian	19
% Black or African American	7
% Hispanic/Latino	13
% Native Hawaiian or Pacific Islander	<1
% White	38
% two or more races	5
% race and/or ethnicity unknown	8
% International/nonresident	11

STUDENT SUCCESS

% first-to-second year retention	97
% six-year graduation	94
% six-year graduation for underrepresented minority groups	92
% first-years who live on campus	100
% undergraduates who live on campus	54
full-time faculty	1,670
full-time minority faculty	309
student-faculty ratio	9:1

Popular majors Biological Sciences, Economics, Business, English, Engineering

Multicultural student clubs and organizations ALANA, Asian & Asian-American Forum, La Asociación Latina, Association of Students of Color, Baraka Kwa Wimbo Gospel Ensemble, Black Students United, Caribbean Students Association, Chinese Student Association, Filipino Association, Ghanaians at Cornell, Haitian Students Association, Multicultural Greek Letter Council, and more!

AFFORDABILITY

Cost of Attendance

tuition	$52,612
required fees	$241
room and board	$14,330

Financial Aid

total institutional scholarships/grants	$226,351,496
% of students with financial need	45
% of students with need awarded any financial aid	45
% of students with need awarded any need-based scholarship or grant aid	100
% of students with need whose need was fully met	100
% Pell Grant recipients among first-years	15
average aid package	$46,339
average student loan debt upon graduation	$23,389

ADMISSIONS

# of applicants	47,039
% admitted	14
SAT Evidence-Based Reading & Writing	690-760
SAT Math	700-790
SAT Writing	n/a
ACT Composite	31-34
SAT/ACT optional	no
average HS GPA	n/a

DEADLINES

regular application closing date	1/2
early decision plan	yes
application closing date	11/1
early action plan	no
application closing date	n/a
application fee	$80
application fee online	$80
fee waiver for applicants with financial need	yes

Fordham University

Fordham University
Duane Library, 441 East Fordham Road
Bronx, NY 10458
Ph: (718) 817-4000
enroll@fordham.edu
www.fordham.edu

Founded in 1841, Fordham University is an independent university rooted in the Jesuit tradition. Fordham's undergraduate student body reflects the diversity of the metropolitan area in which the university is located. Students from around the world are attracted to New York's cosmopolitan culture. Whether educated at the Rose Hill campus in the Bronx or the Lincoln Center campus in Manhattan, Fordham students benefit from close contact with distinguished faculty who teach at the undergraduate, graduate, and professional levels. At Fordham, students will acquire the knowledge, skills, confidence, and experience necessary to succeed in their chosen fields. Fordham offers a firm foundation and a competitive advantage that makes its students leaders at work and successful in life.

Pre-College Prep & Outreach **Federal TRIO Programs**

We participate in three federally funded TRIO programs—Upward Bound, Talent Search, and Student Support Services—that are designed to increase access and success for low-income, first-generation, and traditionally underserved college students.

Scholarship & Financial Aid **Merit Scholarships**

Fordham University participates in three primary scholarship programs: the UPS Foundation/LaFarge Endowed Fellowship program, the Metro Grant, and the National Merit and Hispanic Recognition Scholarship program. The UPS Foundation Fellowship assists resident students from underrepresented populations who show leadership and academic ability as well as financial need by providing an average annual award of $7,000 for four years. The Metro Grant is a $7,000 grant awarded to incoming freshmen commuting to Fordham from their permanent residences in New York City or the surrounding areas. Students who are designated National Merit Semifinalists, National Merit Finalists, or National Hispanic Recognition Scholars may qualify to receive a full-tuition scholarship if they are in the top of the admit pool.

Scholarship & Financial Aid **The Higher Education Opportunity Program (HEOP)**

The Higher Education Opportunity Program provides economically and educationally disadvantaged students from New York state with access to a Fordham education. The HEOP programs at Rose Hill and Lincoln Center provide support services for all incoming and continuing students enrolled in the program, including a pre-freshman summer program; tutorial services; academic advisement; career, personal, and financial aid counseling; and many other services.

Academic Advising & Support **Diversity Networking Career Fair**

Each Fall the Office of Career Services hosts a Diversity Networking Career Fair, where graduating seniors connect with employers seeking greater diversity in their workplace. Career Services also supports all undergraduate students and alumni with individual counseling, mock interviews, resume-writing workshops, and advice on graduate school preparation, dining etiquette, and other useful skills.

Fast Facts

STUDENT DIVERSITY

# undergraduates	9,258
% male/female	43/57
% first-generation college	22
% American Indian or Alaskan Native	<1
% Asian	10
% Black or African American	4
% Hispanic/Latino	14
% Native Hawaiian or Pacific Islander	<1
% White	56
% two or more races	3
% race and/or ethnicity unknown	2
% International/nonresident	8

STUDENT SUCCESS

% first-to-second year retention	91
% six-year graduation	80
% six-year graduation for underrepresented minority groups	n/a
% first-years who live on campus	77
% undergraduates who live on campus	51
full-time faculty	754
full-time minority faculty	115
student-faculty ratio	14:1

Popular majors Business Administration, Biological Sciences, English, Finance, Communications, Psychology, Marketing, History, International Political Economy, Accounting, Dance, and Theatre

Multicultural student clubs and organizations Insieme, Korean Student Association, Muslim Students' Association, PRIDE Alliance, Jewish Students Organization, Gaelic Society, Hellenic Society, Minority Association of Pre-Med Students, Polish Cultural Exchange, Sláinte: Fordham Irish Dance, ASCEND, Arabic Club, German Club, Student Organization of Latinos, Russian Forum

AFFORDABILITY

Cost of Attendance

tuition	$49,645
required fees	$1,341
room and board	$17,445

Financial Aid

total institutional scholarships/grants	$158,434,570
% of students with financial need	63
% of students with need awarded any financial aid	99
% of students with need awarded any need-based scholarship or grant aid	96
% of students with need whose need was fully met	29
% Pell Grant recipients among first-years	17
average aid package	$33,566
average student loan debt upon graduation	$25,069

ADMISSIONS

# of applicants	45,076
% admitted	46
SAT Reading & Writing	620-700
SAT Math	610-710
ACT Composite	28-32
SAT/ACT optional	no
average HS GPA	3.7

DEADLINES

regular application closing date	1/1
early decision plan	yes
application closing date	11/1
early action plan	yes
application closing date	11/1
application fee	$70
application fee online	$70
fee waiver for applicants with financial need	yes

Hamilton College

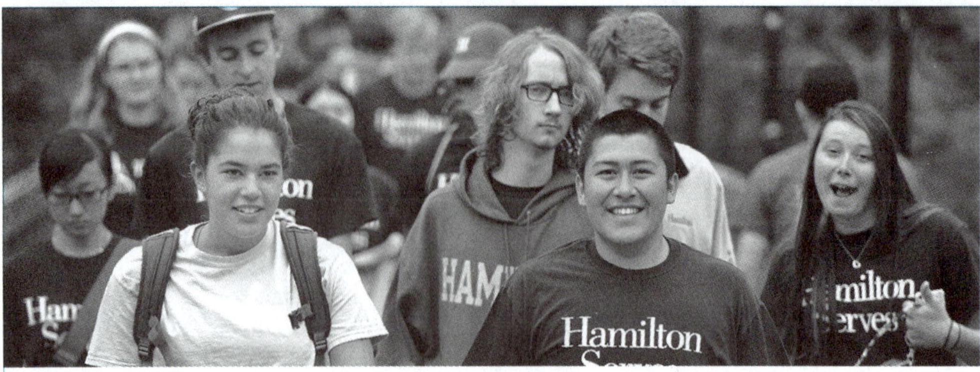

Founded in 1793 as the Hamilton-Oneida Academy, Hamilton has grown to become one of the nation's most highly regarded liberal arts colleges. The open curriculum gives students the freedom to shape their education within a research and writing-intensive framework, and with the close supervision of a faculty advisor. The Hamilton community welcomes and embraces students from diverse backgrounds and experiences, and we have a special affinity for first-year students who are among the first in their family to attend college. Hamilton has more than 300 members of the faculty, staff and student body who themselves represent the first generation in their families to attend college.

Open House, Fly-in, Visit **Diversity Overnight**

The Hamilton College Diversity Overnight Program is an opportunity for current seniors to visit campus and experience life on the College Hill. While all are welcome to apply, our selection process will prioritize the applications of students from ethnically diverse backgrounds as well as first-generation college students and those from families with limited financial resources.

Special Admissions Policy **Hamilton College Opportunity Programs**

The Hamilton College Opportunity Programs, HEOP and College Scholars, are designed to support students who present an alternate academic profile and who demonstrate the ability to compete successfully in an academically competitive environment. The Opportunity Programs staff provide a five-week summer program before the first year of college, academic counseling, financial assistance, and personal support.

Scholarship & Financial Aid **Posse University Partner**

Hamilton partners with the Posse Foundation, a four-year scholarship program that identifies public high school students with extraordinary academic and leadership potential who may be overlooked by traditional college selection processes. Posse students from the Boston and Miami areas are nominated by their high school and share a collaborative support system with a special mentor to adjust to campus and college life.

Scholarship & Financial Aid **QuestBridge Partner**

Hamilton celebrates its inaugural year as a QuestBridge Partner. Through this collaboration, QuestBridge recruits, develops, and motivates high-achieving, low-income students to increase the number of these students attending the nation's best colleges while continuing to support them in their careers and communities.

First-Year Experience & Transition **The First Year Experience (FYE)**

FYE creates opportunities for first-year students to feel connected to Hamilton from the moment they step on campus. A number of FYE core sessions are planned by the FYE leaders on topics such as wellness, the honor code, diversity and difference, and time management.

Student Life & Support **Student Emergency Aid Society (SEAS)**

The SEAS Fund provides emergency support to students whose financial barriers are extraordinary.

Mentoring **Multicultural Peer Mentoring Project**

This program facilitates relationships between first-year international, first generation, and historically underrepresented students with current students to support them through their initial year at Hamilton.

Hamilton College
198 College Hill Road
Clinton, NY 13323
Ph: (800) 843-2655
admission@hamilton.edu
www.hamilton.edu

Fast Facts

STUDENT DIVERSITY	
# undergraduates	1,850
% male/female	49/51
% first-generation college	15
% American Indian or Alaskan Native	n/a
% Asian	7
% Black or African American	4
% Hispanic/Latino	9
% Native Hawaiian or Pacific Islander	n/a
% White	64
% two or more races	4
% race and/or ethnicity unknown	6
% International/nonresident	6
STUDENT SUCCESS	
% first-to-second year retention	96
% six-year graduation	94
% six-year graduation for underrepresented minority groups	86
% first-years who live on campus	100
% undergraduates who live on campus	100
full-time faculty	199
full-time minority faculty	48
student-faculty ratio	9:1

Popular majors Economics, Mathematics, Psychology, Government, Biology, Neuroscience, Chinese

Multicultural student clubs and organizations Asian Student Association, Black and Latinx Student Union, Feminists of Color Collective, International Students Association, La Vanguardia, Rainbow Alliance (LGBT), Student Diversity Council

AFFORDABILITY	
Cost of Attendance	
tuition	$52,250
required fees	$520
room and board	$13,400
Financial Aid	
total institutional scholarships/grants	$40,000,000
% of students with financial need	50
% of students with need awarded any financial aid	100
% of students with need awarded any need-based scholarship or grant aid	100
% of students with need whose need was fully met	100
% Pell Grant recipients among first-years	18
average aid package	$47,003
average student loan debt upon graduation	$19,380
ADMISSIONS	
# of applicants	5,678
% admitted	24
SAT Evidence-Based Reading & Writing	680-740
SAT Math	670-760
ACT Composite	31-33
SAT/ACT optional	no
average HS GPA	n/a
DEADLINES	
regular application closing date	1/1
early decision plan	yes
application closing date	11/15
early action plan	n/a
application closing date	n/a
application fee	$60
application fee online	$60
fee waiver for applicants with financial need	yes

Hobart and William Smith Colleges

Hobart and William Smith Colleges are selective, residential, liberal arts colleges defined by a longstanding focus on educating across academic disciplines and the close work of research and creativity that connects faculty and students. With a strong commitment to diversity, the Colleges have a distinguished history of interdisciplinary teaching and scholarship, curricular innovation and exceptional outcomes. Sixty percent of HWS students study abroad and all participate in community service activities. Located in the heart of the Finger Lakes region in Geneva, N.Y., Hobart and William Smith enjoy a 320 acre campus on the shore of Seneca Lake. Originally founded as two separate colleges (Hobart for men in 1822 and William Smith for women in 1908), Hobart and William Smith students share the same campus, faculty, administration and curriculum. Each College maintains its own traditions, deans, student government and athletic department, providing students with a contemporary, 21st century construct to interrogate gender and difference.

Open House, Fly-in, Visit **Admissions and Open Houses**

Prospective students and families hear from current students and faculty, tour campus facilities, and learn more about the HWS community, student outcomes and life on campus. Our Diversity in Admissions Program is designed for prospective students from underrepresented populations. A Day in the Life at HWS is designed for prospective students to get a glimpse of what their life will be like as an HWS student. Attendees sit in on classes, meet with members of the HWS community and eat lunch in our dining hall.

Scholarship & Financial Aid **Posse**

In 2012, HWS established a partnership with Posse, one of the nation's most successful college access and youth leadership development programs. Ten students go to college together to act as a support system for one another, bolstering collegiate success and graduation rates. In 2017, a group of talented seniors from Los Angeles made history at HWS as the first cohort of Posse Scholars to graduate from the Colleges. The HWS partnership with Posse has created access for 50 students across five cohorts.

Academic Advising & Support **Higher Education Opportunity Program**

Academic Opportunity Programs, which includes HEOP and the HWS AOP program, is an access and academic support program that creates a web of support for first-generation and traditionally underrepresented populations in higher education. The HWS program population is made up of HEOP (90%) and HWS AOP students (10%) totaling approximately 80. Program students now enjoy a 90% or higher graduation and retention rate.

Student Life & Support **First Generation Initiative**

At HWS, our goal is to ensure that, to the extent individually desired by our first generation students, they: 1) are well-prepared to engage in many aspects of campus life—i.e., social and co-curricular, as well as academic; 2) as a group, have visibility on campus; 3) successfully persist to graduation; and 4) fully avail themselves of the resources and opportunities that HWS offers, both during and after their undergraduate years. There are also a number of information sessions for first-generation students that are specific to financial aid, career and internship opportunities, study abroad, residential education, etc. Each fall semester there is an annual mixer for students, faculty, and staff to get together and discuss their experiences about being first-generation with one another. In addition to the annual mixer, HWS has instituted a preorientation for students and their families to get to know one another. We also schedule events during Homecoming and Family Weekend, and have developed a Facebook page, which highlights the work we are doing on campus.

Hobart and William Smith Colleges
300 Pulteney St
Geneva, NY 14456
Ph: (315) 781-3622
www.hws.edu

Fast Facts

STUDENT DIVERSITY

# undergraduates	2,228
% male/female	41/59
% first-generation college	16
% American Indian or Alaskan Native	<1
% Asian	3
% Black or African American	6
% Hispanic/Latino	5
% Native Hawaiian or Pacific Islander	<1
% White	74
% two or more races	0
% race and/or ethnicity unknown	5
% International/nonresident	6

STUDENT SUCCESS

% first-to-second year retention	85
% six-year graduation	81
% six-year graduation for underrepresented minority groups	n/a
% first-years who live on campus	100
% undergraduates who live on campus	85
full-time faculty	221
full-time minority faculty	38
student-faculty ratio	10:1

Popular majors Economics, Media and Society, Political Science, Environmental Studies, Psychology, Biology

Multicultural student clubs and organizations
Latin American Organization, Asian Student Union, Sankofa, Caribbean Student Association, International Student Association, Pride Alliance, French and Francophone Club, Hillel, Project NUR, Women's Collective

AFFORDABILITY

Cost of Attendance

tuition	$52,345
required fees	$1,180
room and board	$13,525

Financial Aid

total institutional scholarships/grants	$55,576,570
% of students with financial need	57
% of students with need awarded any financial aid	100
% of students with need awarded any need-based scholarship or grant aid	100
% of students with need whose need was fully met	78
% Pell Grant recipients among first-years	18
average aid package	$36,758
average student loan debt upon graduation	$33,879

ADMISSIONS

# of applicants	4,409
% admitted	61
SAT Critical Reading	610-680
SAT Math	600-680
ACT Composite	28
SAT/ACT optional	yes
average HS GPA	3.37

DEADLINES

regular application closing date	2/1
early decision plan	yes
application closing date	12/15 & 2/15
early action plan	n/a
application closing date	n/a
application fee	n/a
application fee online	n/a
fee waiver for applicants with financial need	yes

Manhattan College

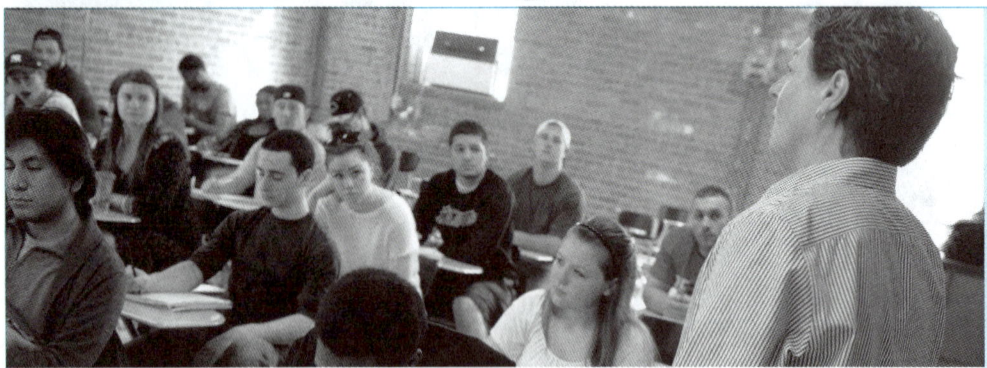

Manhattan College is a Lasallian Catholic college in Riverdale, NY, which offers more than 100 majors and programs in business, education and health, engineering, liberal arts and science. The mission of Manhattan College is to provide a contemporary, person-centered educational experience that prepares graduates for lives of personal development, professional success, civic engagement and service to their fellow human beings. Today Manhattan College maintains that tradition by providing scholarships and financial aid to many students who are the first in their family to attend college. Manhattan also has exceptional academic programs and a values-based Catholic education that nurtures the whole student. They also recognize that students sometimes need a more personal approach and have created The Center for Academic Success to keep students on track with a quiet place to study with their peer tutor, or engage in small group study sessions. It all adds up to a one of a kind education at Manhattan College.

Pre-College Prep & Outreach **Summer Literacy Institute (SLI)**

The Summer Literacy Institute provides teens with a weeklong residential college experience each July. Students experience campus life while studying with college professors. They also receive one-on-one guidance drafting admissions essays for the college applications. Many continue working with professors, students, and mentors during the school year to prep for the SAT.

Scholarship & Financial Aid **Scholarship Opportunities for First-Generation and Minority Students**

Manhattan College has a variety of scholarships available for first-generation and minority students. Among them are the Horan Family Scholarship, established by the late John Horan '40, former CEO and Chairman of Merck and Co., and his wife Julie; The Joseph E. Hanlon '58 Scholarship, founded by Joseph E. Hanlon '58; The Corr-Schmidt Scholarship for Engineering, founded by Mary Corr in member of her husband, Dr. Francis Corr B.EE. '54 and her father, John Schmidt B.E. '29; and the James Patterson Scholarship, established by famous author James Patterson '69. Admissions and financial aid counselors are always available to help prospective students with this process.

First Year Experience & Transition **The Arches and Common Interest Communities**

The Arches is a living-learning community within the college that houses roughly one hundred students in Lee Hall and facilitates these students' transition to college life. Students have access to a classroom and an academic office within their residence hall for a close relationship with their faculty. The program involves two freshmen liberal arts courses. This program also provides community service and cultural learning opportunities in New York City to allow the students to give back to and learn more about the New York City community. Students may also choose to live in Common Interest Communities which gathers students together in one residence hall based on a variety of common interests.

Manhattan College
4513 Manhattan College Parkway
Riverdale, NY10471
Ph: (800) 622-9235
admit@manhattan.edu
www.manhattan.edu

Fast Facts

STUDENT DIVERSITY

# undergraduates	3,664
% male/female	55/45
% first-generation college	10
% American Indian or Alaskan Native	<1
% Asian	5
% Black or African American	5
% Hispanic/Latino	22
% Native Hawaiian or Pacific Islander	<1
% White	55
% two or more races	2
% race and/or ethnicity unknown	8
% International/nonresident	3

STUDENT SUCCESS

% first-to-second year retention	85
% six-year graduation	71
% six-year graduation for underrepresented minority groups	62
% first-years who live on campus	70
% undergraduates who live on campus	51
full-time faculty	232
full-time minority faculty	37
student-faculty ratio	13:1

Popular majors Civil Engineering, Marketing, Communication, Dual Childhood/Special Education, Biology

Multicultural student clubs and organizations Italian Club, French Club, Gaelic Society, Polish Club, International Students Association, Muslim Student Association, Gamma Alpha Sigma, Society of Hispanic Professional Engineers, National Society of Black Engineers, Society of Women Engineers

AFFORDABILITY

Cost of Attendance

tuition	$38,200
required fees	$4,187
room and board	$15,600

Financial Aid

total institutional scholarships/grants	n/a
% of students with financial need	n/a
% of students with need awarded any financial aid	99
% of students with need awarded any need-based scholarship or grant aid	97
% of students with need whose need was fully met	12
% Pell Grant recipients among first-years	23
average aid package	$20,666
average student loan debt upon graduation	$39,371

ADMISSIONS

# of applicants	7,622
% admitted	75
SAT Critical Reading	480-580
SAT Math	490-610
SAT Writing	480-580
ACT Composite	22-26
SAT/ACT optional	no
average HS GPA	3.2-3.7

DEADLINES

regular application closing date	3/1
early decision plan	yes
application closing date	11/15
early action plan	n/a
application closing date	n/a
application fee	$75
application fee online	$75
fee waiver for applicants with financial need	yes

New York University

In 1831, NYU was founded with the vision of bringing education to all people. Today, in a world that is more interconnected than ever before, that vision extends to a network that spans six continents. You can begin at one of three campuses—New York City, America's cultural and financial center; Abu Dhabi, the cosmopolitan gateway of the Middle East; or Shanghai, China's largest and most international city—and continue at locations in 11 other cities. With NYU's more than 230 areas of study and over 3,900 courses to choose from, you can connect your interests as you build a multifaceted understanding of your chosen discipline. Students learn from award-winning faculty in small discussion-based classes and expand intellectually as they engage in thoughtful debate.

Open House, Fly-In, Visit **Diversity "Pathways" Open House**

Each fall NYU invites prospective students and their families to its Washington Square campus for Pathways Open House, an open dialogue on how inclusion and identity shape the NYU student experience--academically, culturally, and socially. Throughout the day, students engage with faculty, administrators, current students and alumni. Pathways Open House also provides students and their families with an opportunity to learn more about admissions and financial aid for NYU's undergraduate schools, colleges, and programs.

Scholarship & Financial Aid **Opportunity Programs**

NYU has two programs for qualified NYU undergraduates: the Arthur O. Eve Higher Education Opportunity Program (Arthur O. Eve HEOP) and the Collegiate Science Technology Entry Program (CSTEP), which provide a means for traditionally underserved, low-income students from New York State to obtain admission as well as academic and financial support.

Summer Bridge & Orientation **NYU Precollege Summer Program**

NYU Precollege Summer Program offers rising high school juniors and seniors the opportunity to experience academic and student life at NYU by taking college-level courses for academic credit which may be applied to a future degree. Participants take their credit-bearing courses with college students. Limited scholarships are available.

Scholars & Leadership **NYU College Access Leadership Institute (NYU-CALI)**

NYU College Access Leadership Insitute (NYU-CALI) is a precollege program offered to rising juniors and seniors in the New York Metro area who come from underrepresented communities or low income families or are the first in their family to attend a 4 year institution. This week-long residential program is designed to demystify the college application process at no cost to the students.

Academic Advising & Support **Academic Achievement Program (AAP)**

AAP is a multi-faceted program designed to develop and enhance the academic and leadership potential of Black, Latino and Native American students. AAP events include discussion sessions and a games day in which students can express their opinions and meet other AAP students. As part of the Big Brothers and Big Sisters Program the AAP freshmen are mentored by upperclassmen to help acclimate them to college life. AAP students also give back to the community by serving as mentors for students at a high school in the South Bronx.

Student Life & Support **Center for Multicultural Education and Programs (CMEP)**

CMEP produces intentional and sustained educational initiatives and campus-wide programs in the area of diversity and social justice. Through collaborations with a broad range of students, faculty, administrators and community partners, the Center's efforts are designed to make an institutional impact in enhancing intercultural awareness.

New York University
Office of Undergraduate Admissions
383 Lafayette Street
New York, NY 10003
Ph: (212) 998-4500
admissions@nyu.edu
www.admissions.nyu.edu

Fast Facts

STUDENT DIVERSITY	
# undergraduates	28,799
% male/female	42/58
% first-generation college	19
% American Indian or Alaskan Native	<1
% Asian	18
% Black or African American	7
% Hispanic/Latino	15
% Native Hawaiian or Pacific Islander	<1
% White	27
% two or more races	3
% race and/or ethnicity unknown	6
% International/nonresident	22
STUDENT SUCCESS	
% first-to-second year retention	93
% six-year graduation	85
% six-year graduation for underrepresented minority groups	n/a
% first-years who live on campus	86
% undergraduates who live on campus	44
full-time faculty	6,821
full-time minority faculty	n/a
student-faculty ratio	10:1

Popular majors Visual and Performing Arts, Business, Social Sciences, Liberal Arts and Sciences, Communications

Multicultural student clubs and organizations
Various

AFFORDABILITY	
Cost of Attendance	
tuition	$50,464
required fees	$2,472
room and board	$17,664
Financial Aid	
total institutional scholarships/grants	$337,858,522
% of students with financial need	53
% of students with need awarded any financial aid	97
% of students with need awarded any need-based scholarship or grant aid	89
% of students with need whose need was fully met	7
% Pell Grant recipients among first-years	21
average aid package	$37,000
average student loan debt upon graduation	~$30,000
ADMISSIONS	
# of applicants	63,921
% admitted	28
SAT Critical Reading	650-730
SAT Math	660-760
SAT Writing	630-730
ACT Composite	30-34
SAT/ACT optional	n/a
average HS GPA	3.56
DEADLINES	
regular application closing date	1/1
early decision plan	yes
application closing date	11/1
early action plan	n/a
application closing date	n/a
application fee	$80
application fee online	$80
fee waiver for applicants with financial need	yes

Purchase College

Purchase College
735 Anderson Hill Rd
Purchase, NY 10577
Ph: (914) 251-6300
www.purchase.edu

Nearly 25% of all Purchase students are first generation college students and just about all Purchase College students seek to charter unchartered paths. Purchase is uniquely qualified to offer such students an intense community with a deep respect for individuality and diversity and an unparalleled environment of creativity and innovation. The intimate classroom setting and engaged faculty inspire lively classroom discussion and debate, critical thinking, originality, discovery and invention. Students partner with faculty on scholarly research, public art, performances and academic presentations. Highly talented, motivated and entrepreneurial, Purchase students strive to impact our society through civic and cultural engagement. The dynamic residential community is ideal for fostering collaboration, fueling passions and getting students involved in campus life. Our proximity to New York City provides students access to outstanding cultural and career-related opportunities. Students see world-class performances at the PAC and notable exhibitions at the Neuberger Museum. "Think Wide Open" is more than just our motto. It's our way of teaching, learning and being.

Special Admissions Policy **Educational Opportunity Program (EOP)**

The Educational Opportunity Program (EOP) at Purchase College provides the opportunity for a college education for students who have not reached their full academic potential because of limited financial resources and inadequate academic preparation. EOP at Purchase has a committed, dedicated staff who are eager to assist students success. All first-time students must attend the EOP pre-freshman summer orientation program in addition to the college's regular summer orientation. The EOP summer program is one week in duration. Its primary focus is to orient the student to EOP and begin to formally introduce the student to Purchase College and its various supportive services.

First-Year Experience & Transition **Student Success Network/Student Success Fellows**

The Success Fellows program aims to orient students to different aspects of the college experience and provide an opportunity to become familiar with peers, upper class students, faculty, staff and with services on campus that are important to their academic success. Students are assigned a success mentor and set goals for first semester and beyond. The Summer Success Fellows Program is designed to equip students with the skills and confidence that will support success with the intention to have students pass on their knowledge and support to other incoming freshmen, helping others to navigate the college experience and support their success too.

Academic Advising & Support **MAP**

Merit Access Program (MAP) similar to EOP without the financial requirement or state funded support. Program students receive support services, such as academic, career, and personal counseling; tutoring and supplemental instruction.

Fast Facts

STUDENT DIVERSITY

# undergraduates	4,228
% male/female	43/57
% first-generation college	25
% American Indian or Alaskan Native	<1
% Asian	4
% Black or African American	12
% Hispanic/Latino	21
% Native Hawaiian or Pacific Islander	<1
% White	53
% two or more races	5
% race and/or ethnicity unknown	6
% International/nonresident	5

STUDENT SUCCESS

% first-to-second year retention	82
% six-year graduation	68
% six-year graduation for underrepresented minority groups	n/a
% first-years who live on campus	86
% undergraduates who live on campus	67
full-time faculty	80
full-time minority faculty	16
student-faculty ratio	16:1

Popular majors Biology, Theatre & Performance, Psychology, Journalism, Film

Multicultural student clubs and organizations Disabled Students' Union, Asian and Pacific Islander Heritage Club (HAPA), Hillel, Hip Hop Club, Latinos Unidos, LGBTQU, Organization of African People in the Americas (O.A.P.I.A.), Queer People of Color (QPOC), Students of Caribbean Ancestry (S.O.C.A.)

AFFORDABILITY

Cost of Attendance

tuition	$16,320 or in-state: $6,670
required fees	$1,828
room and board	$13,334

Financial Aid

total institutional scholarships/grants	$2,100,100
% of students with financial need	59
% of students with need awarded any financial aid	59
% of students with need awarded any need-based scholarship or grant aid	59
% of students with need whose need was fully met	n/a
% Pell Grant recipients among first-years	33
average aid package	$10,029
average student loan debt upon graduation	$25,707

ADMISSIONS

# of applicants	8,900
% admitted	45
SAT Critical Reading	510-610
SAT Math	490-580
SAT Writing	n/a
ACT Composite	25
SAT/ACT optional	yes
average HS GPA	3.33

DEADLINES

regular application closing date	3/1
early decision plan	n/a
application closing date	n/a
early action plan	yes
application closing date	11/15
application fee	$50
application fee online	$50
fee waiver for applicants with financial need	n/a

Rensselaer Polytechnic Institute

A world-class university reflects the world. Rensselaer strives to create an inclusive environment that develops true intellectual, geographic, gender, and ethnic diversity in its students, faculty and staff. RPI prides itself on providing an intellectually rigorous undergraduate education based on innovation in the laboratory, classroom, and studio. Its commitment to diversity is focused on engaging the best talent available and preparing students to work, communicate across cultural boundaries, and emerge as leaders in the global community.

Pre-College Prep & Outreach **STEP: Science & Technology Entry Program**

STEP is funded by the New York State Department of Education. It is designed to assist disadvantaged secondary students and those from minority groups under-represented in scientific, technical and health-related professions to acquire the skills, attitudes and abilities to pursue professional or pre-professional study in postsecondary degree programs. The program's initiatives focus on developing problem solving and critical thinking skills through a range of enrichment activities that include student development, leadership opportunities, career exploration, college preparation, internships and parent workshops. Rensselaer activities occur after school and Saturdays during the school year, and in the summer. RPI supports students entering grades 7 through 12 attending its partner schools, as well as students who live in neighboring communities as space permits.

Pre-College Summer Experience **ExxonMobil Bernard Harris Summer Science Camp**

The ExxonMobil Bernard Harris Summer Science Camp provides middle school students with an insider's look at engineering and other science careers. Former NASA astronaut Bernard Harris and ExxonMobil have partnered to provide academic enrichment camps on university campuses. Throughout the two-week residential program, students work side by side with ExxonMobil engineers and scientists as they conduct experiments, participate in highly interactive projects and demonstrations, attend classes, and weekly field excursions and interact with guest speakers.

Pre-College Summer Experience **The Rensselaer PREFACE Program**

PREFACE is a two-week residential summer experience for talented high school sophomores and juniors, who will enter 11th or 12th grade in the fall of the coming year and who have expressed a strong, early interest in pursuing a career in the engineering and technological professions. It is for high school students from groups that have been historically and traditionally under-represented or underserved in the fields of technology, science, and engineering.

Open House, Fly-In, Visit **Science, Technology, Arts at Rensselaer (STAR) Program**

STAR allows prospective students to experience life as a Rensselaer student- attend classes, tour campus, visit our laboratories and facilities and visit with current Rensselaer students. Academically talented, under-represented minorities and young women are invited to apply.

Student Life and Support **Under-Represented Minorities in Engineering**

Under-Represented Minorities in Engineering provides scholarships and resources for underrepresented minority students. Rensselaer believes that today's modern complex world requires exceptional multidisciplinary leaders to solve problems at home and abroad.

Rensselaer Polytechnic Institute
110 8th Street
Troy, NY 12180
Ph: (518) 276-6216
admissions@rpi.edu
www.rpi.edu

Fast Facts

STUDENT DIVERSITY

# undergraduates	6,314
% male/female	68/32
% first-generation college	n/a
% American Indian or Alaskan Native	<1
% Asian	12
% Black or African American	4
% Hispanic/Latino	9
% Native Hawaiian or Pacific Islander	<1
% White	53
% two or more races	7
% race and/or ethnicity unknown	1
% International/nonresident	14

STUDENT SUCCESS

% first-to-second year retention	93
% six-year graduation	83
% six-year graduation for underrepresented minority groups	67
% first-years who live on campus	100
% undergraduates who live on campus	57
full-time faculty	447
full-time minority faculty	125
student-faculty ratio	13:1

Popular majors Engineering, Computer and Information Science, Business, Architecture, Biology

Multicultural student clubs and organizations
Alianza Latina (AL), Black Students Alliance (BSA), National Society of Black Engineers (NSBE), Society of Hispanic Professional Engineers (SHPE)

AFFORDABILITY

Cost of Attendance

tuition	$51,000
required fees	$1,305
room and board	$14,960

Financial Aid

total institutional scholarships/grants	$142,000,000
% of students with financial need	61
% of students with need awarded any financial aid	100
% of students with need awarded any need-based scholarship or grant aid	100
% of students with need whose need was fully met	20
% Pell Grant recipients among first-years	16
average aid package	$38,742
average student loan debt upon graduation	$35,000

ADMISSIONS

# of applicants	19,506
% admitted	43
SAT Critical Reading	678
SAT Math	722
SAT Writing	n/a
ACT Composite	30
SAT/ACT optional	n/a
average HS GPA	n/a

DEADLINES

regular application closing date	1/15
early decision plan	yes
application closing date	11/1
early action plan	n/a
application closing date	n/a
application fee	$70
application fee online	$70
fee waiver for applicants with financial need	yes

Rochester Institute of Technology

Rochester Institute of Technology
60 Lomb Memorial Drive
Rochester, NY 14623
Ph: (585) 475-6631
admissions@rit.edu
www.rit.edu

Rochester Institute of Technology is one of the world's leading career-oriented, technological institutions. Students are from all 50 states and over 100 countries and have equally as diverse academic interests. More than 2,900 students of color have found a home in RIT's dynamic living-learning community. Rochester Institute of Technology's National Technical Institute for the Deaf supports over 1,200 deaf and hard-of-hearing students, adding a social and educational dynamic not found at any other university. The Institute's nine colleges offer more than 90 undergraduate programs in engineering, computing and information sciences, engineering technology, photography, business, science, visual arts, health sciences and the liberal arts.

Pre-College Prep & Outreach **The Upstate Louis Stokes Alliance for Minority Participation (ULSAMP)**

The Upstate Louis Stokes Alliance for Minority Participation was formed to attract and maximize the potential of students from underrepresented populations, specifically African-American, Latino American and Native American (AALANA) attending college in Upstate New York who are enrolled in STEM fields. Supported by a grant from the National Science Foundation, the ULSAMP program will work across the alliance of 7 Upstate colleges and universities to increase recruitment and the subsequent graduation rate of both first-time freshmen and transfer students, by enhancing academic experiences and opportunities.

Scholarship & Financial Aid **Hillside Work-Scholarship Connection (HWSC)**

Hillside Work-Scholarship Connection links urban adolescents to a support network of youth advocates and employers. Rochester Institute of Technology commits up to five, $10,000 per year renewable scholarships to students who successfully complete the program and enter the Institute as full-time freshmen, and up to five, $10,000 per year renewable scholarships for students who enter as full-time transfer students from Monroe Community College.

Scholarship & Financial Aid **National Action Council for Minorities in Engineering (NACME)**

RIT is a recipient of the National Action Council Minorities in Engineering block grant, which provides support for scholarships and academic support services for underrepresented students in STEM fields. In addition, RIT supports collegiate chapters of the National Society of Black Engineers (NSBE), Society of Hispanic Professional Engineers (SHPE) and the American Indian Science and Engineering Society (AISES), and many other organizations committed to student success.

Summer Bridge & Orientation **Multicultural Center for AcademicSuccess (MCAS)**

The Multicultural Center for Academic Success (MCAS) Summer Bridge Program is a four-week summer academic enrichment, confidence and community-building program that consists of credit-bearing courses, enrichment education, exposure to research, and community service programs. The Summer Bridge Program accepts 40 students and is available to first-year students who have been accepted by RIT and paid their deposit to the university. Once the academic year commences, students will meet with their MCAS academic advisor on a weekly basis to discuss academic progress and services available to support their success.

Fast Facts

STUDENT DIVERSITY

# undergraduates	13,515
% male/female	67/33
% first-generation college	n/a
% American Indian or Alaskan Native	<1
% Asian	8
% Black or African American	5
% Hispanic/Latino	7
% Native Hawaiian or Pacific Islander	<1
% White	63
% two or more races	3
% race and/or ethnicity unknown	8
% International/nonresident	6

STUDENT SUCCESS

% first-to-second year retention	90
% six-year graduation	70
% six-year graduation for underrepresented minority groups	60
% first-years who live on campus	95
% undergraduates who live on campus	68
full-time faculty	1,023
full-time minority faculty	196
student-faculty ratio	13:1

Popular majors Engineering, Computing, Engineering Technology, Visual Arts, Business Administration/Management, Information Technology

Multicultural student clubs and organizations Asian Culture Society, Korean Student Association, Latin American Student Association, Organization of African Students, Organization of the Alliance of Students from the Indian Subcontinent, Taiwanese Student Association, Vietnamese Student Association, Chinese Student Scholar Association

AFFORDABILITY

Cost of Attendance

tuition	$39,506
required fees	$562
room and board	$12,666

Financial Aid

total institutional scholarships/grants	$159,000,000
% of students with financial need	74
% of students with need awarded any financial aid	99
% of students with need awarded any need-based scholarship or grant aid	95
% of students with need whose need was fully met	80
% Pell Grant recipients among first-years	32
average aid package	$26,500
average student loan debt upon graduation	$27,000

ADMISSIONS

# of applicants	20,451
% admitted	57
SAT Reading & Writing	590-680
SAT Math	600-700
ACT Composite	29
SAT/ACT optional	no
average HS GPA	3.6

DEADLINES

regular application closing date	1/15
early decision plan	yes
application closing date	11/15
early action plan	n/a
application closing date	n/a
application fee	$65
application fee online	$65
fee waiver for applicants with financial need	yes

St. John Fisher College

St. John Fisher College is an independent, liberal arts institution in the Catholic tradition of American higher education. The College emphasizes liberal learning for students in traditional academic disciplines, as well as for those in more directly career-oriented fields.

The world has become more and more complex, and at St. John Fisher College, you'll grow both personally and academically to meet the challenges that will await you. As a Fisher student, you will acquire the tools and knowledge to live and learn independently, enabling you to reach your full potential. You'll get personal attention from our faculty, who are selected for their teaching excellence, scholarly initiatives, and commitment to students. They teach in one of the College's five schools, each of which is accredited by the highest national or international accrediting body in its discipline.

The College strives to enroll an increasingly diverse student body and one that is welcoming to all.

Academic Advising & Support **Arthur O. Eve Higher Education Opportunity Program (HEOP)**

The Arthur O. Eve Higher Education Opportunity Program (HEOP) provides a wide range of services for New York State students who have a strong desire to earn a college degree but would not otherwise be able to attend college due to economic or academic circumstances. The program provides academic, financial, personal, and career counseling support in order to guide students toward educational success.

Academic Advising & Support **Academic Opportunity Programs Office**

Through personalized guidance tailored to the needs of individual students, the Academic Opportunity Programs Office recruits, enrolls, and empowers academically under-prepared and economically disadvantaged students to overcome obstacles on their way to becoming informed, ethical, tolerant, self-reliant, and socially responsible citizens.

First-Year Experience & Transition **First-Year Program**

The First-Year Program is designed to assist students in the transition to college and orient them to the history and values of the Fisher community and the characteristics of successful Fisher students. The First-Year Program will give students the tools to navigate between their increased personal freedom and new responsibilities. It does more than help to adjust to their new surroundings; it provides the critical-thinking skills required to address the challenges of college life.

First-Year Experience & Transition **Freshman Seminar**

Freshman Seminar is a 1-credit course that serves as an orientation to college life and fosters academic success, personal growth, and career exploration. Together with about 18 peers, students discuss issues such as personal wellness, community, diversity, goal setting, study skills, time management, stress management, and the ins-and-outs of successfully navigating the academic world of St. John Fisher College.

St. John Fisher College
3690 East Avenue
Rochester, NY 14618
Ph: (585) 385-8064
admissions@sjfc.edu
www.sjfc.edu

Fast Facts

STUDENT DIVERSITY

# undergraduates	2,759
% male/female	40/60
% first-generation college	n/a
% American Indian or Alaskan Native	<1
% Asian	3
% Black or African American	5
% Hispanic/Latino	4
% Native Hawaiian or Pacific Islander	<1
% White	84
% two or more races	2
% race and/or ethnicity unknown	2
% International/nonresident	<1

STUDENT SUCCESS

% first-to-second year retention	85
% six-year graduation	71
% six-year graduation for underrepresented minority groups	n/a
% first-years who live on campus	88
% undergraduates who live on campus	51
full-time faculty	234
full-time minority faculty	41
student-faculty ratio	12:1

Popular majors Nursing, Business, Biology, Chemistry and Psychology

Multicultural student clubs and organizations Gay Straight Alliance, Asian Student Union, Black Student Union, Sustained Dialogue, Latino Student Union, Students of Multicultural Affairs

AFFORDABILITY

Cost of Attendance

tuition	$32,540
required fees	$580
room and board	$12,150

Financial Aid

total institutional scholarships/grants	$35,944,533
% of students with financial need	81
% of students with need awarded any financial aid	100
% of students with need awarded any need-based scholarship or grant aid	100
% of students with need whose need was fully met	29
% Pell Grant recipients among first-years	29
average aid package	$22,000
average student loan debt upon graduation	$38,639

ADMISSIONS

# of applicants	4,432
% admitted	65
SAT Reading & Writing	530-610
SAT Math	530-620
ACT Composite	22-26
SAT/ACT optional	no
average HS GPA	91

DEADLINES

regular application closing date	n/a
early decision plan	yes
application closing date	12/1
early action plan	no
application closing date	n/a
application fee	$0
application fee online	$0
fee waiver for applicants with financial need	n/a

Sarah Lawrence College

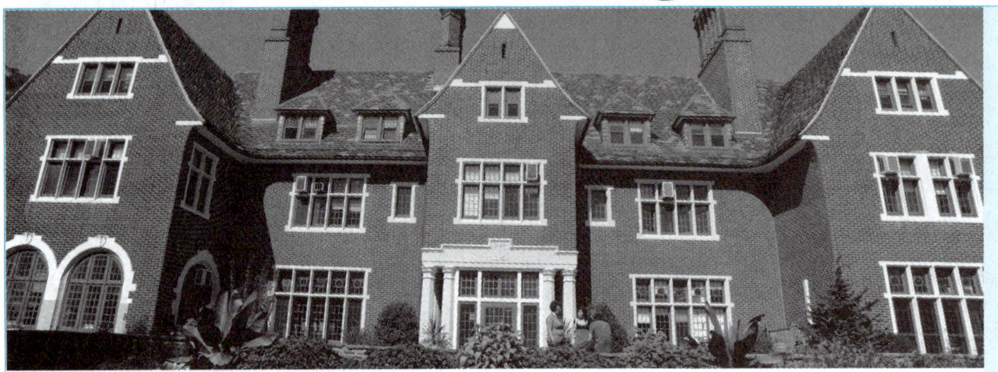

At Sarah Lawrence College our mission is to graduate world citizens who are diverse in every definition of the word, who take intellectual and creative risks, who cross disciplinary boundaries, and who are able to sustain exceptional academic discipline within a framework of humanistic values and concern for community. Our unique educational practices provide our students with the opportunity to study intensively in small classes, to engage in independent research, and to spend unparalleled amounts of time working one-on-one with an exceptional faculty of scholars and artists, creating a tailored academic program of students' own design. Our goal is to instill a lifelong intellectual curiosity and nimbleness, as well as the confidence and entrepreneurial spirit to embrace a broad range of personal, professional and creative pursuits. We thus prepare students to think and act independently so that they will tackle the problems of, and thrive in, a complex and rapidly evolving world.

Open House, Fly-in, Visit **Fall/Spring Collective**

Students who are interested in the topic of diversity on the SLC campus are encouraged to attend our Fall/Spring Collective. The Collectives provide an opportunity for prospective students to learn more about SLC from current students, faculty and staff of color as well as learn about our student of color identity groups and campus committees dedicated to diversity. The event is held in Common ground which is a student space on campus utilized primarily by our student of color identity groups as well as a place where dialog surrounding issues of multiculturalism and racial and ethnic diversity happens. It also serves as a place for programming including speakers, performances, discussions, movie nights, conferences, workshops, and other activities.

Student Life & Support **Office of Diversity and Inclusion**

The Office of Diversity & Campus Engagement plans and presents student-centered programs and events that focus on all aspects of diversity. These programs and events are organized by the Diversity & Activism Programming Subcommittee (DAPS).

Throughout each academic year, DAPS is proactive in its programming around issues related to enhancing visibility, examining prejudice, and addressing the exclusion of identities and communities represented on campus. It also looks at ways to enhance intercultural dialogue and understanding on our campus. DAPS plans and provides funding to campus-based programs focusing on issues of diversity, social justice, and inclusion related to personal identities defined by, but not limited to, race, economic status, sexual orientation, gender, gender identity and expression, ethnicity, religion, mental/physical ability.

In addition, The Office of Diversity & Campus Engagement sponsors a weekly dialogue group, Real Talk @ SLC, which focuses on understanding our intersecting social identities and experiences. Real Talk @ SLC is facilitated by students and was created to help break down the barriers that exist around talking about difficult topics such as race, class, sexuality, and other social identities.

Summer Bridge & Orientation **LEAD (Leadership Exploration and Discovery) Program**

The LEAD (Leadership Exploration and Discovery) Program gives first generation college students an opportunity to arrive on campus a few days before New Student Orientation and participate in four days of activities designed specifically to make the transition to SLC as seamless as possible. The objective of the program is to give first generation students a head start at acclimating to their new home and an introduction to the many resources and opportunities available on and around the Sarah Lawrence campus.

Sarah Lawrence College
1 Mead Way
Bronxville, NY 10708
Ph: (800) 888-2858
slcadmit@sarahlawrence.edu
www.slc.edu

Fast Facts

STUDENT DIVERSITY	
# undergraduates	1,400
% male/female	29/71
% first-generation college	16
% American Indian or Alaskan Native	<1
% Asian	4
% Black or African American	4
% Hispanic/Latino	9
% Native Hawaiian or Pacific Islander	<1
% White	50
% two or more races	7
% race and/or ethnicity unknown	9
% International/nonresident	13

STUDENT SUCCESS	
% first-to-second year retention	85
% six-year graduation	79
% six-year graduation for underrepresented minority groups	76
% first-years who live on campus	95
% undergraduates who live on campus	85
full-time faculty	108
full-time minority faculty	19
student-faculty ratio	9:1

Popular majors Students draft their own program of study within the liberal arts and sciences curriculum.

Multicultural student clubs and organizations Asian and Pacific Islander Coalition for Action and Diversity, Chinese Table, Dark Phrases, Harambee, International Students Union, Queer People of Color, Unidad, Women of Color Affinity Group

AFFORDABILITY	
Cost of Attendance	
tuition	$52,600
required fees	$1,410
room and board	$14,856
Financial Aid	
total institutional scholarships/grants	$32,000,000
% of students with financial need	61
% of students with need awarded any financial aid	98
% of students with need awarded any need-based scholarship or grant aid	97
% of students with need whose need was fully met	13
% Pell Grant recipients among first-years	15
average aid package	$38,476
average student loan debt upon graduation	$16,952

ADMISSIONS	
# of applicants	3,400
% admitted	50
SAT Critical Reading	n/a
SAT Math	n/a
SAT Writing	n/a
ACT Composite	n/a
SAT/ACT optional	yes
average HS GPA	3.6

DEADLINES	
regular application closing date	1/15
early decision plan	yes
application closing date	11/1, 1/2
early action plan	n/a
application closing date	n/a
application fee	$60
application fee online	$60
fee waiver for applicants with financial need	yes

Skidmore College

Skidmore College is a highly selective private liberal-arts university institution that attracts a diverse student body from all over the world. Due in part to its' nationally recognized Opportunity Program (HEOP/AOP), the College has long been dedicated to the outreach and support of talented students from New York and beyond who would otherwise be excluded from higher education due to academic and economic disadvantage. The College provides $44 million annually in financial aid, and is committed to meeting the full need of every accepted student. The graduation rates of first-generation students at Skidmore are consistently around 90%, a figure higher than the College's overall student population.

Special Admissions Policies **Opportunity Program (HEOP/AOP)**

For over 40 years, Skidmore's Higher Education Opportunity Program (HEOP) has been one of the most successful in New York State. HEOP recruits talented and motivated students from New York State whose academic and financial circumstances might make them otherwise unable to attend Skidmore. Skidmore's Academic Opportunity Program (AOP) recruits similar students who reside out of state and/or whose family income slightly exceeds HEOP guidelines.

Open House, Fly-in, Visit **Discovery Tour**

Each April, Skidmore invites accepted students from traditionally under-represented backgrounds and those who are first-generation students for a three-day campus program to really get to know Skidmore. Skidmore pays transportation costs for all invited students from across the country, including providing buses from New York City to campus and back.

Scholarship & Financial Aid **Scholarships**

Skidmore annually offers $44 million dollars in financial aid and supports the full financial need of those students it accepts. The average 2016-17 first-year aid package (grants/ loans/ work-study) is $39,900.

Student Life & Support **Intergroup Relations**

Skidmore College is the first college or university in the US to offer a minor in Intergroup Relations, a nationally recognized academic and social-justice program that originated at the University of Michigan to address racial tension. Its goal was to support student learning and competencies around inter- and intragroup relations, conflict, and social justice across a range of social identities, including race, gender, sexuality, social class, religion, and nationality.

Student Life & Support **Skidmore's Multicultural Speed-Networking Reception**

Skidmore's Career Development Center invites alumni and students of color to an annual speed-networking event in New York City. Students spent five minutes with each alumni/ae participant discussing post-Skidmore professional paths.

Academic Courses & Service Learning **Summer Funded Internships/Research Experiences**

The Skidmore Summer Funded Internship Awards Program provides up to 50 students an opportunity to participate in unpaid internships, volunteer, research, or community service projects over the course of the summer. Skidmore's SEE-Beyond Awards Program provides up to 25 students the opportunity to apply their academic-year learning to internships, experiences, and research projects. Skidmore's Faculty-Student Summer Research Program offers up to 80 students the chance to spend 5, 8, or 10 weeks in the lab or the classroom immersed in research, to gain a hands-on appreciation for scholarly work. All three programs are competitive and take into account students with true financial need.

Skidmore College
Eissner Admissions Center
815 North Broadway
Saratoga Springs, NY 12866
Ph: (800) 867-6007
admissions@skidmore.edu
www.skidmore.edu

Fast Facts

STUDENT DIVERSITY

# undergraduates	2,661
% male/female	40/60
% first-generation college	13
% American Indian or Alaskan Native	<1
% Asian	5
% Black or African American	4
% Hispanic/Latino	9
% Native Hawaiian or Pacific Islander	<1
% White	64
% two or more races	4
% race and/or ethnicity unknown	3
% International/nonresident	11

STUDENT SUCCESS

% first-to-second year retention	91
% six-year graduation	89
% six-year graduation for underrepresented minority groups	87
% first-years who live on campus	100
% undergraduates who live on campus	89
full-time faculty	279
full-time minority faculty	48
student-faculty ratio	8:1

Popular majors Business, Psychology, English, Economics, Art, Environmental Studies

Multicultural student clubs and organizations Asian Cultural Awareness, Chinese Cultural Association, HAYAT, Hip Hop Alliance, El Club Español, Frenchips, International Student Union, Lift Every Voice Gospel Choir, Raices, Ujima, Skidmore Pride Alliance, African Heritage Club

AFFORDABILITY

Cost of Attendance

tuition	$49,716
required fees	$1,118
room and board	$13,530

Financial Aid

total institutional scholarships/grants	$41,840,000
% of students with financial need	81
% of students with need awarded any financial aid	100
% of students with need awarded any need-based scholarship or grant aid	100
% of students with need whose need was fully met	100
% Pell Grant recipients among first-years	13
average aid package	$43,100
average student loan debt upon graduation	$25,001

ADMISSIONS

# of applicants	9,181
% admitted	27
SAT Critical Reading	560-670
SAT Math	560-660
SAT Writing	570-670
ACT Composite	28
SAT/ACT optional	yes
average HS GPA	n/a

DEADLINES

regular application closing date	1/15
early decision plan	yes
application closing date	11/15, 1/15
early action plan	no
application closing date	n/a
application fee	$65
application fee online	$65
fee waiver for applicants with financial need	yes

Syracuse University

Syracuse University is one of the top 65 universities in the United States and classified in the top tier for research activity among all doctoral universities in the nation. With more than 200 majors and 100 minors, Syracuse offers a rigorous private education within an inclusive, welcoming community of 15,000 diverse students and scholars from all 50 U.S. states and more than 130 countries. Syracuse University welcomes you. Thousands of students choose Syracuse every year for its blend of extraordinary academics, legendary spirit, and research, internship and extracurricular opportunities—all offered in a classic campus setting. As a first generation student you'll be supported by many services that help ensure a rich and productive experience, including the Office of First Year and Transfer Programs, the Gen One Scholars Learning Community, TheFirst program, faculty and peer advisors, tutoring and study centers, and more.

Pre-College Summer Experience **SummerStart**

SummerStart is a six-week program designed to ensure a smooth transition from high school to college for newly admitted students. This six-week program provides pre-freshmen with an opportunity to become familiar with the academic, social, and cultural life at Syracuse.

First-Year Experience & Transition **Gen-One Scholars Learning Community**

Join with other first-generation college students in taking a behind-the-scenes look at how the University works. Members of the Gen-One Scholars Learning Community will learn how to navigate SU and understand the keys to succeeding both in and out of the classroom. You will connect with students, faculty, and staff who identify as first-generation and meet people from offices all across campus who can help you during your college years.

Scholars & Leadership **fullCIRCLE Mentoring Program**

fullCIRCLE is a sustainable, multilayered program designed to assist its participants in effectively adjusting to the different challenges of college life, including those that are academic, social, professional and personal in nature, with the goal of building community. The program serves first-year and upper-class students with an emphasis on Black/African American, Asian American/Pacific Islander, Hispanic/Latinx American, and Indigenous/Native American students. fullCIRCLE promotes academic success, identity development, community leadership, and social responsibility. Mission: To support the holistic development of students of color through intentional relationships with peers, faculty, staff, alumni, and employers.

Scholars & Leadership **WellsLink**

The WellsLink Leadership Program is the nationally recognized academic and leadership excellence program for first-year students of color at Syracuse University. Through structured academic, social, and cultural enrichment activities, WellsLink scholars train for exceptional success at the University and beyond. The program is named after Barry L. Wells, former senior vice president and dean of student affairs at Syracuse University and founder of the University's Office Minority Affairs in 1976. Wells is currently a Special Assistant on Chancellor Kent Syverud's leadership team. The program is sponsored by the Office of Multicultural Affairs.

Student Life & Support **TheFirst**

Mission TheFirst (formerly known as The Story Project) is for those who are first in their families to attend college. TheFirst provides opportunities for first-generation students to describe their journeys to higher education. It is a space for dialogue and community/campus outreach where students who are first generation are encouraged to document their experience though journal writing, sharing, and videotaping their stories. They hope to put a face on various facets of diversity on this college campus while telling their stories of perseverance and determination.

Syracuse University
900 South Crouse Avenue
Syracuse, NY 13244
Ph: (315) 443-3611
orange@syr.edu
www.syr.edu

Fast Facts

STUDENT DIVERSITY

# undergraduates	14,600
% male/female	47/53
% first-generation college	21
% American Indian or Alaskan Native	<1
% Asian	6
% Black or African American	7
% Hispanic/Latino	8
% Native Hawaiian or Pacific Islander	<1
% White	54
% two or more races	3
% race and/or ethnicity unknown	3
% International/nonresident	12

STUDENT SUCCESS

% first-to-second year retention	91
% six-year graduation	82
% six-year graduation for underrepresented minority groups	79
% first-years who live on campus	100
% undergraduates who live on campus	70
full-time faculty	n/a
full-time minority faculty	n/a
student-faculty ratio	16:1

Popular majors Liberal Arts, Business, Engineering, Media/Communications, Performing & Visual Arts

Multicultural student clubs and organizations African Student Union, Chinese Students and Scholars, Caribbean Students Association, Black Reign Step Team, Latino Greek Council, African American Male Congress, Raices Dance Troupe, La LUCHA, National Pan-Hellenic Council, Asian Students in America

AFFORDABILITY

Cost of Attendance

tuition	$50,230
required fees	$1,637
room and board	$15,558

Financial Aid

total institutional scholarships/grants	$270,000,000
% of students with financial need	n/a
% of students with need awarded any financial aid	75
% of students with need awarded any need-based scholarship or grant aid	n/a
% of students with need whose need was fully met	n/a
% Pell Grant recipients among first-years	n/a
average aid package	n/a
average student loan debt upon graduation	n/a

ADMISSIONS

# of applicants	33,000
% admitted	48
SAT Evidence-Based Reading & Writing/Math	1250
ACT Composite	27
SAT/ACT optional	n/a
average HS GPA	3.6

DEADLINES

regular application closing date	1/1
early decision plan	yes
application closing date	11/15
early action plan	n/a
application closing date	n/a
application fee	$75
application fee online	$75
fee waiver for applicants with financial need	yes

University of Rochester

The University of Rochester, founded in 1850, is one of the nation's leading private, co-educational, nonsectarian universities. Located near downtown Rochester, the campus offers a balance between urban access and spacious comfort, thus creating a comfortable and unique learning environment. This environment no doubt contributes in part to the academic reputation of the institution. The university's 6,300 undergraduate students enjoy a well-rounded college experience, and 96 percent of freshmen return for their sophomore year. In maximizing retention and success among all community members, the University of Rochester offers a breadth of services targeted to the specific needs of minority and first-generation students.

Pre-College Summer Experience **Science and Technology Entry Program (STEP)**

STEP serves students enrolled in high school grades eight through twelve. In particular, participants come either from economically disadvantaged backgrounds or from groups that are historically underrepresented in scientific, technical, health-related, and licensed professions. The program works to raise participants' interest in the aforementioned fields, thereby encouraging them to join the professional workforce in medicine and the health care professions.

Open House, Fly-in, Visit **Multicultural Visitation Program**

University of Rochester's Multicultural Visitation Program brings together high school seniors from diverse backgrounds and allows them to experience Rochester on a more personal level. Admission to MVP is a competitive process that will consider your academic and personal qualities. Travel assistance is available; be sure to apply on time. Highlights include living and dining on campus, staying in a residence hall with a student host, participating in discussions with current students about the college experience and learning about the many opportunities available for undergraduates.

Special Admissions Policy **Higher Education Opportunity Program (HEOP) & Early Connection Opportunity (ECO)**

The University of Rochester's HEOP and ECO programs are designed to serve students of diverse racial, ethnic and cultural backgrounds. HEOP addresses the specific needs of students who have had economic or educational challenges in high school. For eligible students, the program provides a strong support network, academic advising, personal counseling and substantial financial assistance. Meanwhile, ECO is designed to help students positively and appropriately establish themselves within the academic setting.

Scholars & Leadership **McNair Program**

The objective of the McNair Program is to increase the numbers of low-income, first-generation and underrepresented undergraduates who pursue doctoral degrees and go on to careers in research and teaching at the university level. The program prepares students for the rigors of graduate study by providing the opportunity to conduct research under the guidance of faculty mentors. Students accepted to the program attend a series of colloquia, receive training for the Graduate Record Exam and are trained to present the results of their research at university-sponsored and national academic conferences.

University of Rochester
300 Wilson Blvd.
PO Box 270251
Rochester, NY 14627
Ph: (585) 275-3221
admit@admissions.rochester.edu
www.rochester.edu

Fast Facts

STUDENT DIVERSITY

# undergraduates	6,386
% male/female	50/50
% first-generation college	21
% American Indian or Alaskan Native	<1
% Asian	11
% Black or African American	5
% Hispanic/Latino	7
% Native Hawaiian or Pacific Islander	<1
% White	47
% two or more races	3
% race and/or ethnicity unknown	6
% International/nonresident	21

STUDENT SUCCESS

% first-to-second year retention	96
% six-year graduation	85
% six-year graduation for underrepresented minority groups	n/a
% first-years who live on campus	100
% undergraduates who live on campus	77
full-time faculty	649
full-time minority faculty	n/a
student-faculty ratio	10:1

Popular majors Psychology, Financial Economics, Economics, Biomedical Engineering, Business

Multicultural student clubs and organizations
National Society of Black Engineers, Society of Hispanic Professional Engineers, Black Students' Union, Chinese Students' Association, Filipino American Students' Association, Korean American Students' Association, Pan-African Students' Association, Spanish and Latino Students' Association, Student Assoc. for the Dev. of Arab Cultural Awareness, Student Organization for Caribbean Awareness

AFFORDABILITY

Cost of Attendance

tuition	$51,090
required fees	$930
room and board	$15,398

Financial Aid

total institutional scholarships/grants	$95,763,147
% of students with financial need	51
% of students with need awarded any financial aid	100
% of students with need awarded any need-based scholarship or grant aid	99
% of students with need whose need was fully met	99
% Pell Grant recipients among first-years	16
average aid package	$45,956
average student loan debt upon graduation	$30,507

ADMISSIONS

# of applicants	16,450
% admitted	38
SAT Critical Reading	600-700
SAT Math	650-760
SAT Writing	610-710
ACT Composite	29-33
SAT/ACT optional	yes
average HS GPA	3.8

DEADLINES

regular application closing date	1/5
early decision plan	yes
application closing date	11/1
early action plan	n/a
application closing date	1/5
application fee	$50
application fee online	$50
fee waiver for applicants with financial need	yes

Davidson College

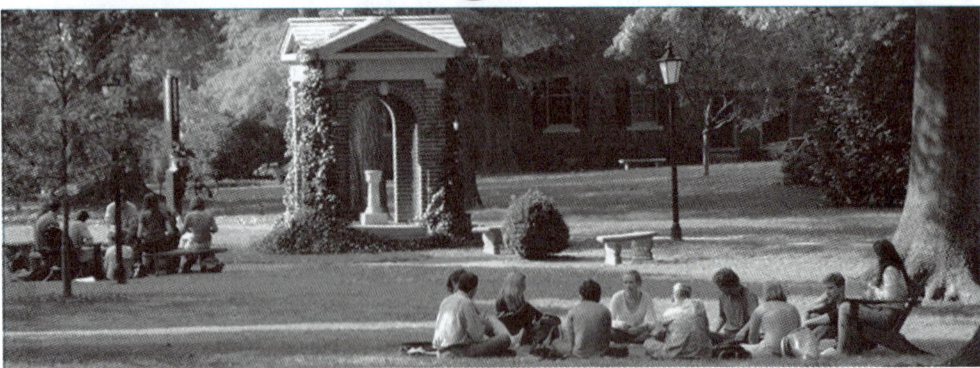

Davidson is a highly selective independent liberal arts college of approximately 2000 students located 20 minutes north of Charlotte in Davidson, North Carolina. Since its establishment in 1837, the college has been consistently regarded as one of the top liberal arts colleges in the country. Through The Davidson Trust, the college became the first liberal arts institution in the nation to replace loans with grants in all financial aid packages, giving students the opportunity to graduate debt-free. The college values diversity in all forms and the role it plays in creating a rich and meaningful experience for students and the campus community. A student-managed Honor Code is central to student life at the college.

Open House, Fly-in, Visit **Multicultural Visit Program**

Davidson's commitment to diversity extends to the entire Davidson community, but begins with admission. The Multicultural Visitation Program (MVP) provides students the opportunity to experience the Davidson community first-hand. Application for this program opens in August.

Special Admissions Policy **Need-Blind Admission**

Davidson practices a need-blind admission policy, which means an applicant's character, academic achievement, potential and talents are the factors considered for admission, not the family's bank balance. Davidson has also entirely replaced student loans with grants to ensure that all of their students are able to graduate without student loan debt.

Scholarship & Financial Aid **QuestBridge & POSSE Partner College**

These programs aim to increase the percentage of talented underrepresented students attending the nation's strongest colleges and universities, which meet full financial need.

Scholarship & Financial Aid **The Davidson Trust**

Through The Davidson Trust, the college meets 100 percent of demonstrated financial need through grants and students employment. Financial aid counselors are available to help families navigate the financial aid process. About 45 percent of the student body receives need-based aid, and more than half receive some form of aid.

First-Year Experience & Transition **Students Together Reaching for Individual Development & Education (STRIDE)**

STRIDE is a support program purposed to assist first-year ethnic minority students with their adjustment to Davidson College. A series of designed experiences offer academic, cultural and social support as well as vital information to aid students in understanding and working effectively within the college community. The program has five components: the Peer Mentoring Program, the Pre-College Enrichment Program, a Mid-Year Check Up, a Monthly Enrichment Series and the End of the Year Celebration.

Academic Courses & Service Learning **Exchange Programs**

Davidson College has cooperative Exchange Programs with Howard University and Morehouse College, which provide students opportunities for study at campuses with significant African-American student, faculty and staff populations. Study may be arranged for a full-year or a semester.

Davidson College
405 North Main Street
Davidson, NC 28036
Ph: (800) 768-0380
admission@davidson.edu
www.davidson.edu

Fast Facts

STUDENT DIVERSITY

# undergraduates	1,955
% male/female	50/50
% first-generation college	n/a
% American Indian or Alaskan Native	<1
% Asian	6
% Black or African American	7
% Hispanic/Latino	7
% Native Hawaiian or Pacific Islander	n/a
% White	65
% two or more races	5
% race and/or ethnicity unknown	2
% International/nonresident	7

STUDENT SUCCESS

% first-to-second year retention	97
% six-year graduation	95
% six-year graduation for underrepresented minority groups	n/a
% first-years who live on campus	100
% undergraduates who live on campus	100
full-time faculty	179
full-time minority faculty	38
student-faculty ratio	10:1

Popular majors Biology, History, Chemistry, English, Computer Science

Multicultural student clubs and organizations Multicultural House, Asian Culture & Awareness Association, Black Student Coalition (BSC), Curry Club, Davidson International Association, Hillel, Middle Eastern and North African Student Association, Muslim Students Association, Organization of Latin American Students, Shades of Brown

AFFORDABILITY

Cost of Attendance

tuition	$49,454
required fees	$495
room and board	$13,954

Financial Aid

total institutional scholarships/grants	$37,803,984
% of students with financial need	62
% of students with need awarded any financial aid	100
% of students with need awarded any need-based scholarship or grant aid	100
% of students with need whose need was fully met	100
% Pell Grant recipients among first-years	58
average aid package	$46,079
average student loan debt upon graduation	n/a

ADMISSIONS

# of applicants	5,666
% admitted	20
SAT Reading & Writing	650-730
SAT Math	640-730
ACT Composite	30-33
SAT/ACT optional	no
average HS GPA	n/a

DEADLINES

regular application closing date	1/5
early decision plan	yes
application closing date	11/15
early action plan	n/a
application closing date	n/a
application fee	$50
application fee online	$50
fee waiver for applicants with financial need	yes

Duke University

Duke University is a mid-sized, private, research university located in Durham, North Carolina. Duke offers a rigorous academic program with exceptional flexibility in course selection and degree program. Interdisciplinary study is central to the undergraduate experience. It challenges students to bridge varying interests and encourages them to take their academic interests beyond the classroom by studying abroad or engaging in research. Duke is among the most community-oriented of the nation's major universities. Due to its need-blind admissions policy for all U.S. citizens and lawful permanent residents, the student body represents all backgrounds. From orientation on, school spirit and a sense of belonging permeate Duke.

Pre-College Summer Experience **Pre Orientation Move-In**

Duke provides a pre-orientation program for first-generation students. This program assists students and their families as they transition from high school to college by giving them additional resources and support prior to Duke's First-Year Orientation.

Pre-College Summer Experience **The Talent Identification Program (TIP)**

Duke offers a number of Talent Identification Programs, summer academic camps ranging in focus from sciences to the arts. Financial aid is available for all of these programs, which take place on the Duke campus. These programs give high school students the opportunity to familiarize themselves with a college environment while broadening their academic and life experiences. TIP offers advanced summer studies courses, including creative writing, psychology, pre-law studies, and leadership, through eight different institutes.

Open House, Fly-In, Visit **Blue Devil Days, Black Student Alliance Invitational Weekend, and Latino Student Recruitment Weekend**

As students admitted to Duke University make their final college choices, Duke provides three major spring opportunities to visit the campus: Blue Devil Days, Black Student Alliance Invitational Weekend, and Latino Student Recruitment Weekend. These provide time for students to spend the night in a residence hall as the guest of a current student, to attend classes, to meet other prospective students and to see for themselves that Duke is the right match for them.

Mentoring **1G Network**

The 1G Network is a community of first-generation students and administrators that discuss academic, social and cultural issues relevant to students who are first in their family to attend college. All first generation college student support is managed by the Office of Access and Outreach in the Karsh Office of Undergraduate Financial Support.

Scholarship and Financial Aid **David M. Rubenstein Scholars Program**

The David M. Rubenstein Scholars program, established in 2016, is the first competitive merit scholarship at Duke that supports first-generation, low-income students financially, academically, personally and professionally. Scholars are selected for their outstanding achievements, resilience, and commitment to social engagement.

In addition to receiving a loan-free financial package that supports the full cost of attendance for all four years, David M Rubenstein Scholars also participate in a fully-funded, six-week summer academic experience on campus, which precedes the first academic year at Duke. Rubenstein Scholars receive one-on-one mentoring from Duke Faculty and older students, funding for summer professional opportunities, and a brand new laptop. Ongoing enrichment opportunities and professional development seminars are also part of the package.

Duke University
2138 Campus Drive
Box 90586
Durham, NC 27708
Ph: (919) 684-3214
undergrad-admissions@duke.edu
www.duke.edu

Fast Facts

STUDENT DIVERSITY

# undergraduates	6,810
% male/female	50/50
% first-generation college	10
% American Indian or Alaskan Native	1
% Asian	21
% Black or African American	10
% Hispanic/Latino	8
% Native Hawaiian or Pacific Islander	1
% White	46
% two or more races	2
% race and/or ethnicity unknown	2
% International/nonresident	14

STUDENT SUCCESS

% first-to-second year retention	97
% six-year graduation	95
% six-year graduation for underrepresented minority groups	95
% first-years who live on campus	100
% undergraduates who live on campus	82
full-time faculty	5,022
full-time minority faculty	1,155
student-faculty ratio	8:1

Popular majors Public Policy, Economics, Psychology, Biology, Biomedical Engineering, Neuroscience

Multicultural student clubs and organizations Center for Multicultural Affairs, Center for Race Relations, Black Student Alliance, Mi Gente, Native American Student Alliance, Asian Students Association, Diya - The South Asian Association of Duke, International House, Center for Sexual and Gender Diversity, Center for Muslim Life, Mary Lou Williams Center for Black Culture

AFFORDABILITY

Cost of Attendance

tuition	$53,744
required fees	n/a
room and board	$15,500

Financial Aid

total institutional scholarships/grants	$138,857,363*
% of students with financial need	42
% of students with need awarded any financial aid	100
% of students with need awarded any need-based scholarship or grant aid	96
% of students with need whose need was fully met	100
% Pell Grant recipients among first-years	13
average aid package	$50,312
average student loan debt upon graduation	$22,256

ADMISSIONS

# of applicants	34,448
% admitted	10
SAT (new)	1440-1570
ACT Composite	31-35
SAT/ACT optional	n/a
average HS GPA	n/a

DEADLINES

regular application closing date	1/1
early decision plan	yes
application closing date	11/1
early action plan	n/a
application closing date	n/a
application fee	$85
application fee online	$85
fee waiver for applicants with financial need	yes

*Includes need and non-need awards for merit recipients and athletes

Meredith College

Meredith College has grown to be one of the largest women's institutions in the U.S., educating strong, confident women for more than a century. We'll help you discover your strengths, we'll know what sparks your curiosity and even more important- when you're ready for even bigger challenges. Faculty will help you imagine and do more than you may have ever thought possible! First-generation students at Meredith won't get back papers with hastily-scratched grades from a teaching assistant. Instead, you're likely to be invited to find detailed feedback and an invitation to talk about it in person. Faculty are genuinely committed to your success! Academic advisers will ensure you're taking the courses you need to take, when you need to take them. At Meredith, our goal is helping you reach yours.

Scholarship & Financial Aid **Merit Scholarships and Tuition Grants**

Reward your strength - at Meredith, we recognize and reward outstanding ability and talent by sponsoring competitive scholarship programs for all students. Upon admission to the College, you're automatically considered for Meredith College Academic Merit Scholarships or tuition grants. Academic Merit Scholarships range from $17,500-$21,000. Tuition Grants range from $16,000-$17,000. Separate applications are required to be considered for additional first-year scholarships, which include: music, art, theatre, interior design, Teaching Fellows, The Honors Program, and Service Scholars.

The Meredith Legacy Scholarship (full ride plus study abroad stipend) and Presidential Scholarships (full tuition plus study abroad stipend) are awarded to students applying to the Honors program. A minimum 3.75 GPA, top 10% class rank, and 27 ACT/ / 1290 SAT (EBRW + M) is required to apply to the Honors program.

Summer Bridge & Orientation **Summer Symposium**

Summer Symposium is a two-day educational and transitional experience meant to foster a sense of community among incoming first-year and transfer multicultural students.

First-Year Experience & Transition **Meredith Hues Program**

The Meredith Hues Program is a student group sponsored by the Office of Admissions and allows multicultural freshmen the opportunity to assist in the recruitment of new multicultural students.

First-Year Experience & Transition **The First Year Experience Class (FYE)**

The FYE Class is a one-hour credit class taught by a faculty and staff across campus and is designed to help students make a successful transition from high school to college. Topics covered include: effective study skills for college, time management, communicating with professors and academic dialogue, critical thinking skills, diversity, learning about Raleigh and the Research Triangle Park area and dealing with independent living. Because FYE classes are small and interactive, they also provide a support group for new students, as well as the chance to develop strong relationships with faculty/staff.

Academic Advising & Support **StrongPoints**

A great college experience prepares you for a successful career and a satisfying life. That's why we developed StrongPoints®—an advising and personal coaching program found only at Meredith that's designed to help you make the most of college. Through this comprehensive initiative, you'll identify your strengths and then build on them. Explore academic and experiential activities. Increase your financial literacy. Examine potential career paths. And with the guidance of expert faculty and staff advisers, you'll develop a plan to achieve your goals in college—and throughout your life.

Meredith College
3800 Hillsborough Street
Raleigh, NC 27607
Ph: (919) 760-8581
admissions@meredith.edu
www.meredith.edu

Fast Facts

STUDENT DIVERSITY

# undergraduates	1,685
% male/female	0/100
% first-generation college	n/a
% American Indian or Alaskan Native	1
% Asian	3
% Black or African American	11
% Hispanic/Latino	3
% Native Hawaiian or Pacific Islander	<1
% White	73
% two or more races	3
% race and/or ethnicity unknown	2
% International/nonresident	4

STUDENT SUCCESS

% first-to-second year retention	80
% six-year graduation	64
% six-year graduation for underrepresented minority groups	55
% first-years who live on campus	88
% undergraduates who live on campus	61
full-time faculty	130
full-time minority faculty	12
student-faculty ratio	12:1

Popular majors STEM majors, Psychology, Biology, Health-Related Career field majors, Design - Interior Design, Fashion Design, and Graphic Design, Business/Marketing, Education, Visual and Performing Arts

Multicultural student clubs and organizations Association for Cultural Awareness, Meredith International Association, SGA Unity Council, Diversity Council, Meredith Hues, Muslim Student Association, Angelas Latinas, Black Student Union

AFFORDABILITY

Cost of Attendance

tuition	$35,816
required fees	$100
room and board	$10,718

Financial Aid

total institutional scholarships/grants	$19,000,000
% of students with financial need	74
% of students with need awarded any financial aid	100
% of students with need awarded any need-based scholarship or grant aid	60
% of students with need whose need was fully met	16
% Pell Grant recipients among first-years	33
average aid package	$26,713
average student loan debt upon graduation	$33,993

ADMISSIONS

# of applicants	1,920
% admitted	60
SAT Critical Reading	460-560
SAT Math	460-570
SAT Writing	n/a
ACT Composite	20-25
SAT/ACT optional	no
average HS GPA	3.4

DEADLINES

regular application closing date	2/15
early decision plan	yes
application closing date	10/30
early action plan	yes
application closing date	12/1
application fee	$40
application fee online	$40
fee waiver for applicants with financial need	yes

North Carolina State University

Founded in 1887, North Carolina State University is a comprehensive public university with a multicultural and diverse student body. NC State is widely renowned for its pioneering research in science and technology. Located in Raleigh, which has been ranked as one of the best places to live in the United States, NC State has also been ranked by the Princeton Review as one of the best value colleges in the country. Students can choose between more than 300 different undergraduate and graduate programs in 65 departments, and can begin taking classes in their major as soon as they come to campus.

Pre-College Prep & Outreach North Carolina Mathematics and Science Education Network Pre-College Program (NC-MSEN)

The mission of the North Carolina Mathematics and Science Education Network Pre-College Program is to prepare underserved students at the middle and high school levels (grades 6-12) for careers in education and science, technology, engineering and mathematics (STEM).

Pre-College Prep & Outreach Native Education Forum (NEF)

NEF is a six-day residential camp for high-achieving rising 11th and 12th grade students interested in NC State who identify with or would like to learn more about the Native American experience and culture. Students are exposed to a college classroom setting and learn more about the college application process while interacting with Native American faculty, staff and students.

Pre-College Prep & Outreach Emerging Scholars Academy (ESA)

ESA is residential camp for high-achieving rising 11th graders who have an interest in learning more about the African-American culture and experience at NC State. They will be exposed to college life and have a chance to participate in college preparation activities.

Open House, Fly-in, Visit Experience NC State Multicultural Admitted Student Day

For students who were admitted to NC State, the Multicultural Admitted Student Day is invitation-only and features representatives from student organizations, faculty from several academic departments, and admissions staff to answer questions specifically for students of various cultural and ethnic backgrounds.

Academic Advising & Support Multicultural Student Affairs

The Department of Multicultural Student Affairs (MSA) researches, designs and implements unique programs that promote the pursuit of academic success, retention and graduation of students, with an emphasis on African American, Native American and Hispanic students. Many of the programs and services expand students' cultural horizon while honoring their respective cultural experiences.

Student Life & Support TRIO Student Support Services, Student Support Services STEM (SSS and SSS-STEM), and McNair Scholars

TRIO Student Support Services Program (SSS) and Student Support Services STEM (SSS-STEM) are federally funded college retention and completion programs which provide academic and personal development opportunities including individualized coaching and academic tutoring at no cost to the student. The TRIO SSS and SSS-STEM Program serves 260 students annually. The Ronald E. McNair Post-baccalaureate Achievement Program is designed to prepare undergraduate students for doctoral studies through involvement in research and other scholarly activities and serves 25 students annually.

North Carolina State University
121 Peele Hall Campus Box 7103
Raleigh, NC 27695
Ph: (919) 515-2434
undergrad-admissions@ncsu.edu
www.ncsu.edu

Fast Facts

STUDENT DIVERSITY

# undergraduates	23,827
% male/female	55/45
% first-generation college	25
% American Indian or Alaskan Native	<1
% Asian	6
% Black or African American	6
% Hispanic/Latino	5
% Native Hawaiian or Pacific Islander	5
% White	72
% two or more races	4
% race and/or ethnicity unknown	3
% International/nonresident	5

STUDENT SUCCESS

% first-to-second year retention	94
% six-year graduation	76
% six-year graduation for underrepresented minority groups	64
% first-years who live on campus	100
% undergraduates who live on campus	41
full-time faculty	1,991
full-time minority faculty	410
student-faculty ratio	13:1

Popular majors Engineering, Business Administration, Psychology, Biological Sciences, Textiles, Animal Science, Communication

Multicultural student clubs and organizations There are 100+ organizations focused on culture/ multiculturalism including: Afrikan American Student Advisory Council, Asian Students in Alliance, Mi Familia, Multicultural Greek Council organizations, Muslim Students Association, Native American Students Association, National Panhellenic Council organizations, and many more.

AFFORDABILITY

Cost of Attendance

tuition	in-state: $9,058; out-of-state: $27,406
required fees	n/a
room and board	$10,854

Financial Aid

total institutional scholarships/grants	$106,560,507
% of students with financial need	67
% of students with need awarded any financial aid	98
% of students with need awarded any need-based scholarship or grant aid	91
% of students with need whose need was fully met	27
% Pell Grant recipients among first-years	20
average aid package	$12,567
average student loan debt upon graduation	$22,626

ADMISSIONS

# of applicants	26,160
% admitted	50
SAT Critical Reading	>600
SAT Math	>600
SAT Writing	n/a
ACT Composite	29
SAT/ACT optional	no
average HS GPA	3.68

DEADLINES

regular application closing date	1/15; College of Design 10/15
early decision plan	no
application closing date	1/15
early action plan	yes
application closing date	10/15
application fee	$85
application fee online	$85
fee waiver for applicants with financial need	yes

University of North Carolina Wilmington

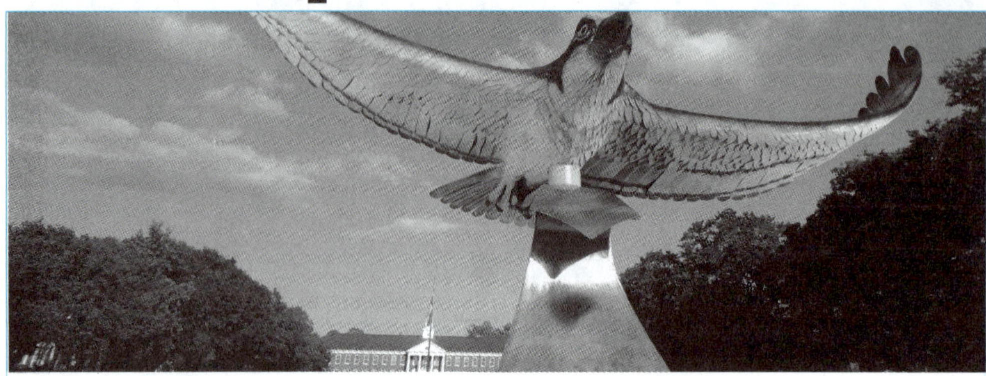

The University of North Carolina Wilmington, is dedicated to learning through the integration of teaching and mentoring with research and service. Our university is widely acknowledged for its superb faculty and staff and its powerful academic experience that stimulates creative inquiry, critical thinking, thoughtful expression and responsible citizenship. Continuously recognized at a national level for academic excellence and affordability, we remain committed to diversity and inclusion, global perspectives and enriching the quality of life through scholarly community engagement in such areas as health, education, the economy, the environment, marine and coastal issues, and the arts.

Scholarship & Financial Aid **Seahawk Admissions Network for Diversity (SAND)**

SAND members work with the UNCW admission staff in recruiting students. By leading campus tours, accompanying admission representatives on high school visits and attending other recruitment events, students are trained to use their leadership skills to encourage minority students to pursue a college education.

Scholarship & Financial Aid **Success Opportunities Aid and Responsibilities (SOAR)**

The SOAR Ambassador program is a financial assistance program that facilitates continued academic success and graduation for low-income students while limiting their accrual of student loan debt. SOAR Ambassadors are carefully selected based on a review of high school academic achievement and standardized test score performance. SOAR Ambassadors must maintain a 3.5 GPA cumulative GPA, complete a group community service project, complete 30 credit hours each year and attend several leadership-oriented workshops throughout the academic year to prepare them with relevant future skills.

Mentoring **Mi Casa (Mentors Initiating Community Action, Support, and Advocacy)**

MI CASA mentoring project is an innovative program designed to provide access to higher education to Hispanic/Latino high school students in North Carolina. The goal of this two-year program is to identify high achieving Hispanic students from local high schools who wish to further their education. MI CASA serves as a comprehensive support program that provides mentoring, college preparation seminars, tutoring, community service and cultural enrichment activities.

Mentoring **Teal Bridge Mentor Program**

The UNCW Teal Bridge program was designed to help newly enrolled transfer students during their time of transition from prior educational venues to UNCW. Teal Bridge Program events and Teal Bridge Mentors, volunteer transfer students, are designed to help transfer students navigate their new surroundings and make the most of their time at UNCW. Having recently been a new transfer student as well, Teal Bridge Mentors are ready to share their experiences and knowledge, as well as support each transfer student they mentor.

University of North Carolina Wilmington - Office of Admissions
601 S. College Rd.
Wilmington, NC 28403
Ph: (910) 962-3243
admissions@uncw.edu
www.uncw.edu

Fast Facts

STUDENT DIVERSITY

# undergraduates	14,496
% male/female	38/62
% first-generation college	n/a
% American Indian or Alaskan Native	<1
% Asian	2
% Black or African American	7
% Hispanic/Latino	7
% Native Hawaiian or Pacific Islander	<1
% White	77
% two or more races	3
% race and/or ethnicity unknown	3
% International/nonresident	1

STUDENT SUCCESS

% first-to-second year retention	87
% six-year graduation	72
% six-year graduation for underrepresented minority groups	n/a
% first-years who live on campus	94
% undergraduates who live on campus	30
full-time faculty	936
full-time minority faculty	104
student-faculty ratio	18:1

Popular majors Marine Biology, Business, Education, Film Studies, Nursing

Multicultural student clubs and organizations Seahawk Admissions Network for Diversity, Success Opportunities Aid and Responsibilities, Black Student Union, Caribbean Student Association, Gospel Choir: Voices of Praise, Mi Gente, NAACP, Student Veterans Organization, Turkish Student Association, Association of Diversity in Student Nursing, Minority Association of Pre-Health Students

AFFORDABILITY

Cost of Attendance

tuition	in-state $4,400; out-of-state $18,416
required fees	$2,648
room and board	$10,490

Financial Aid

total institutional scholarships/grants	n/a
% of students with financial need	56
% of students with need awarded any financial aid	97
% of students with need awarded any need-based scholarship or grant aid	92
% of students with need whose need was fully met	17
% Pell Grant recipients among first-years	30
average aid package	$8,932
average student loan debt upon graduation	$25,644

ADMISSIONS

# of applicants	13,550
% admitted	65
SAT Critical Reading	560-630
SAT Math	570-630
SAT Writing	n/a
ACT Composite	23-27
SAT/ACT optional	no
average HS GPA	3.9-4.4

DEADLINES

regular application closing date	2/1
early decision plan	no
application closing date	n/a
early action plan	yes
application closing date	11/1
application fee	$80
application fee online	$80
fee waiver for applicants with financial need	yes

Antioch College

Antioch College is a place for students who want a unique educational experience. Our academic programs encourage studying with purpose, engaging in community, and applying those lessons in the world at-large—becoming a catalyst for positive change wherever life leads. At Antioch, students alternate period of classroom study with full-time, and often paid, work experiences. Antioch's small size lets us support students through personalized attention from their professors. Our Center for Academic Success offers tutoring on study skills, time management, stress management and budgeting. The campus is also home to the Coretta Scott King Center for Cultural and Intellectual Freedom, a Writing Institute, Diversity Committee, and interest-based student groups. Antioch's transfer policy supports students who want to earn a bachelor's degree after completing an associate degree at a community college.

Academic Advising & Support **Writing Institute**

The Writing Institute provides opportunities for focused study of the writing craft. Our programs include writing assessment, weekly tutoring, cross-disciplinary consultations, and workshops that focus on various elements of academic writing. Additionally, through workshops and public readings, students have opportunities to learn from published authors in fiction, non-fiction, poetry, memoir, and journalism.

Student Life & Support **Coretta Scott King Center for Cultural and Intellectual Freedom (CSKC)**

The CSKC houses Friday Forums open to both the college campus and the local community, heritage month celebrations, the Martin Luther King, Jr. Day celebration and awards ceremony, and the Coretta Commemoration where a student is highlighted.

Student Life & Support **Diversity Committee**

The diversity committee was birthed out of the CSKC to bring diverse programming and awareness of social, national and international issues to light on our campus. The committee has since launched a book club on diverse issues, open to faculty, staff and students.

Mentoring **Peer Mentoring Program**

This is an academic and social support service for first-generation and other new Antioch students. Returning students serve as peer mentors for these first-year students, providing academic and social support to help them navigate college. Our Early Alert and First Watch programs also support students throughout their time at Antioch.

Antioch College
1 Morgan Place
Yellow Springs, OH 45387
Ph: (937) 319-6082
www.antiochcollege.edu

Fast Facts

STUDENT DIVERSITY

# undergraduates	223
% male/female	39/61
% first-generation college	32
% American Indian or Alaskan Native	2
% Asian	4
% Black or African American	8
% Hispanic/Latino	8
% Native Hawaiian or Pacific Islander	<1
% White	65
% two or more races	8
% race and/or ethnicity unknown	5
% International/nonresident	<1

STUDENT SUCCESS

% first-to-second year retention	67
% six-year graduation	59
% six-year graduation for underrepresented minority groups	60
% first-years who live on campus	100
% undergraduates who live on campus	65
full-time faculty	34
full-time minority faculty	7
student-faculty ratio	6:1

Popular majors Media Arts, Environmental Science, Psychology, Political Economy, History

Multicultural student clubs and organizations People of Color Group, Prison Justice Group, Queer Center, Coretta Scott King Center for Cultural and Intellectual Freedom

AFFORDABILITY

Cost of Attendance

tuition	$34,568
required fees	$1,000
room and board	$11,364

Financial Aid

total institutional scholarships/grants	$2,419,760
% of students with financial need	61
% of students with need awarded any financial aid	100
% of students with need awarded any need-based scholarship or grant aid	61
% of students with need whose need was fully met	34
% Pell Grant recipients among first-years	24
average aid package	$28,248
average student loan debt upon graduation	$34,500

ADMISSIONS

# of applicants	143
% admitted	71
SAT Critical Reading	n/a
SAT Math	n/a
SAT Writing	n/a
ACT Composite	n/a
SAT/ACT optional	yes
average HS GPA	2.89

DEADLINES

regular application closing date	rolling
early decision plan	yes
application closing date	rolling
early action plan	yes
application closing date	rolling
application fee	n/a
application fee online	n/a
fee waiver for applicants with financial need	n/a

Baldwin Wallace University

Baldwin Wallace University is a private, liberal arts-based, Methodist-affiliated college located in Berea, Ohio. Baldwin Wallace University is an academic community committed to the liberal arts and sciences as the foundation for lifelong learning. The University fulfills this mission through a rigorous academic program that is characterized by excellence in teaching and learning within a challenging, supportive environment that enhances students' intellectual and spiritual growth. Baldwin Wallace assists students in their preparation to become contributing citizens and their pursuit of personal and professional excellence.

Pre-College Prep & Outreach **BW Scholars Program**

As a pre-college access program, the primary purpose of the program is to ensure the Scholars' retention and graduation from high school, and ultimately their matriculation to higher education. The participants are expected to commit to the program for four years, earn their high school diploma, and enroll in a higher education institution. The program consists of four major elements: Academic Enrichment, Mentoring and Leadership Development, Community Engagement, & Career Preparation and Internships.

Pre-College Summer Experience **CSI: Conservatory Summer Institute**

The BW CSI: Conservatory Summer Institute is an intensive two-week program where high school students investigate college music study while exploring careers in music. Students participate in a quality pre-college experience led by faculty including members of the Cleveland Orchestra and BW Conservatory faculty while visiting Cleveland's major arts centers.

Pre-College Summer Experience **Gedanken Problem-Solving Institute**

Curious students between the ages of twelve (12) and seventeen (17) participate in a week long course working individually and in groups to solve real-world problems. The Institute includes topics such as risk management, pattern recognition, operations research, logic and a large variety of puzzles, including the Rubik's Cube. By participating in this program, students develop their abilities to tackle complex problems in an intellectually stimulating atmosphere.

Summer Bridge & Orientation **Jacket Link-BRIDGE**

Jacket Link- BRIDGE (JLB) is a year-long program that begins with a 4 day transition component just prior to the Week of Welcome for incoming students (particularly first generation and students of color) and continues throughout the academic year. The program provides an individualized package of tutoring, mentoring, and networking to ease the transition from high school to university life. Participants are assigned a JLB Peer Mentor who follows their progress throughout the first year.

Scholars & Leadership **Experience Honors Summer Program**

Rising high school juniors and seniors in this program get a leg up on the college admission process, sample academic subjects and experience campus life during a one week summer session. The goals include demystifying college choices and the application process. Students live on campus in the Honors Residence Hall and get to know a small group of their peers.

Academic Advising & Support **Freshmen in Reading Support Teams (BW FiRST)**

BW FiRST is a developmental reading pilot, taught by a literacy specialist. A major component of BW FiRST involves collaborative peer groups who come together to discuss complex texts, investigate multiple perspectives, and practice strategies under the direction of a literacy specialist. Emphasis is placed on vocabulary enhancement, analysis of college-level reading material, writing in the discipline and critical thinking.

Baldwin Wallace University
275 Eastland Road
Berea, OH 44017
Ph: (440) 826-2900
Info@bw.edu
www.bw.edu

Fast Facts

STUDENT DIVERSITY

# undergraduates	3,539
% male/female	46/54
% first-generation college	29
% American Indian or Alaskan Native	<1
% Asian	1
% Black or African American	9
% Hispanic/Latino	5
% Native Hawaiian or Pacific Islander	<1
% White	77
% two or more races	6
% race and/or ethnicity unknown	<1
% International/nonresident	2

STUDENT SUCCESS

% first-to-second year retention	81
% six-year graduation	68
% six-year graduation for underrepresented minority groups	n/a
% first-years who live on campus	84
% undergraduates who live on campus	62
full-time faculty	228
full-time minority faculty	16
student-faculty ratio	13:1

Popular majors Business/Marketing, Health Professions, Visual/Performing Arts, Education, Biological/Life Sciences

Multicultural student clubs and organizations Allies, Black Student Alliance, International Film Series, Men in Action, Middle Eastern Culture Club, People of Color United, Promoting our Women's Resources and Experiences, Spanish Club, Hispanic American Student Association

AFFORDABILITY

Cost of Attendance

tuition	$31,668
required fees	n/a
room and board	$10,796

Financial Aid

total institutional scholarships/grants	$48,222,808
% of students with financial need	86
% of students with need awarded any financial aid	100
% of students with need awarded any need-based scholarship or grant aid	100
% of students with need whose need was fully met	n/a
% Pell Grant recipients among first-years	33
average aid package	$24,408
average student loan debt upon graduation	$34,423

ADMISSIONS

# of applicants	4,515
% admitted	60
SAT Critical Reading	480-590
SAT Math	470-580
SAT Writing	460-570
ACT Composite	24
SAT/ACT optional	no
average HS GPA	3.4

DEADLINES

regular application closing date	rolling
early decision plan	no
application closing date	n/a
early action plan	no
application closing date	n/a
application fee	$25
application fee online	n/a
fee waiver for applicants with financial need	yes

Kent State University

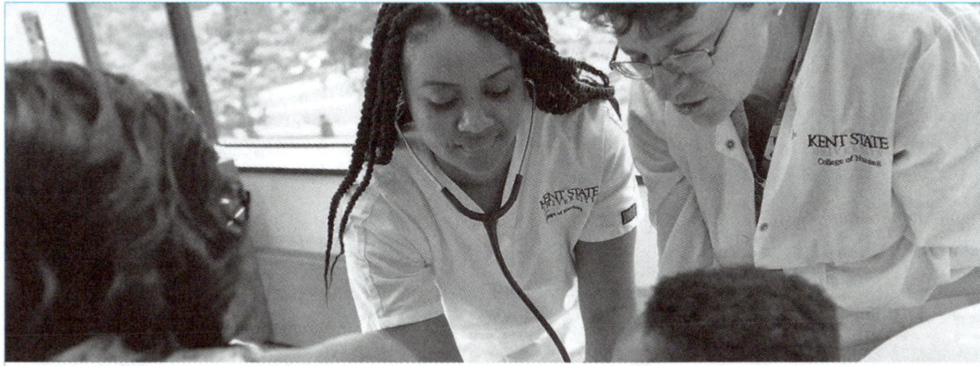

Located in Kent, Ohio, Kent State University features nearly 900 acres and 25 residence halls and enrolls more than 40,000 students across eight campuses. Kent State is ranked among the top research universities in the country, and has become a leader in economic, cultural, and workforce development locally and internationally. Kent State offers over 280 degree programs at the undergraduate level and engages students in diverse learning environments that expand their intellectual horizons and encourage them to become responsible citizens. The University provides a supportive community devoted to teaching excellence, first-tier scholarship and academic freedom.

Pre-College Summer Experience **Academic STARS (Students Achieving and Reaching for Success)**

Academic STARS is a retention program for African American, Latino and Native American freshmen who want to enhance their opportunities for academic success, to develop leadership and to enrich their college experience. The program kicks off with a five-week program during which participants will earn six credit hours to be applied toward graduation. Students also learn success strategies and skills through advising and workshops throughout the school year.

Summer Bridge & Orientation **Kupita/Transiciones**

Kupita/Transiciones is a four-day holistic enrollment management, orientation and retention program for newly admitted African American, Latino and American Indian freshmen and transfer students. It includes academic success workshops a week before the start of the semester.

Academic Courses & Service Learning **Department of Pan-African Studies**

The Department of Pan-African Studies encompasses the Center for Pan-African Culture and the Institute for African-American affairs. Its mission is to offer an Afrocentric academic curriculum grounded in the cultural traditions and experiences of people of African descent. Providing a major and minor that span the humanities, fine arts, and social sciences, the Department fosters tolerance for cultural diversity on campus and throughout the surrounding community. This is implemented through its African Community Theatre and Outreach Programs.

Student Life & Support **Student Multicultural Center**

The Student Multicultural Center seeks to ensure the successful enrollment, retention and graduation of underrepresented students. The Center develops and implements holistic retention programs and encourages mutual respect through cultural, educational and social programming. Their primary goals are to ensure the academic success of students of underrepresented groups and to provide information to help individuals embrace diversity.

Mentoring **The University Mentoring Program**

The University Mentoring Program is a transition and retention support program designed to enhance the college and life-management skills of underrepresented students by building a community of support around the freshman student.

Kent State University
Admissions Office
161 Schwartz Center
Kent, OH 44242-0001
Ph: (800) 988-KENT
admissions@kent.edu
www.kent.edu

Fast Facts

STUDENT DIVERSITY

# undergraduates	23,178
% male/female	40/60
% first-generation college	n/a
% American Indian or Alaskan Native	<1
% Asian	1
% Black or African American	9
% Hispanic/Latino	3
% Native Hawaiian or Pacific Islander	n/a
% White	75
% two or more races	2
% race and/or ethnicity unknown	3
% International/nonresident	6

STUDENT SUCCESS

% first-to-second year retention	80
% six-year graduation	55
% six-year graduation for underrepresented minority groups	35
% first-years who live on campus	84
% undergraduates who live on campus	28
full-time faculty	973
full-time minority faculty	128
student-faculty ratio	21:1

Popular majors Architecture, Business, Communication/Journalism, Education, Flight, Health and Human Services, Nursing, Psychology, Sciences, Visual and Performing Arts

Multicultural student clubs and organizations Association of International Students, Black Greek Council, Black United Studies, Harambee, Indian Student Association, Native American Student Association, Spanish and Latino Student Association

AFFORDABILITY

Cost of Attendance

tuition	$18,544 or in-state: $10,012
required fees	n/a
room and board	$10,916

Financial Aid

total institutional scholarships/grants	$82,812,454
% of students with financial need	89
% of students with need awarded any financial aid	99
% of students with need awarded any need-based scholarship or grant aid	86
% of students with need whose need was fully met	46
% Pell Grant recipients among first-years	33
average aid package	$23,127
average student loan debt upon graduation	$32,393

ADMISSIONS

# of applicants	16,145
% admitted	85
SAT Critical Reading	470-580
SAT Math	480-580
SAT Writing	440-560
ACT Composite	23
SAT/ACT optional	no
average HS GPA	3.4

DEADLINES

regular application closing date	3/1
early decision plan	n/a
application closing date	5/1
early action plan	n/a
application closing date	n/a
application fee	$50
application fee online	$50
fee waiver for applicants with financial need	yes

Miami University

Miami University, a student-centered public university founded in 1809, has built its success through an unwavering commitment to liberal arts undergraduate education and the active engagement of its students in both curricular and co-curricular life. It is deeply committed to student success, builds great student and alumni loyalty, and empowers its students, faculty, and staff to become engaged citizens and leaders who use their knowledge and skills with integrity and compassion to improve the future of our global society. As the tenth oldest public university in the country, Miami University has a long-standing tradition of providing first-generation college students with access to the life-altering benefits of a college degree and the opportunities and outcomes experienced as part of a college education.

Pre-College Prep & Outreach **Bridges Program**

The Bridges Program is an overnight visit experience for high-achieving high school seniors from historically underrepresented populations or who have a commitment to promoting a deeper understanding of and appreciation for diversity. Students representing different racial/ethnic, sexual orientation and gender identity, and socioeconomic backgrounds are encouraged to apply. Students will have the opportunity to meet current students, learn about academic areas of interest, experience campus life and interact with faculty and staff. Students who complete the Bridges Program, apply, are accepted for fall admission, and enroll full-time at Miami's Oxford, Ohio campus, will be eligible to receive scholarships ranging from $2,500 to full tuition annually.

Pre-College Summer Experience **Summer Scholars Program**

The Summer Scholars Program is an early college experience for academically-talented rising high school juniors and seniors from across the globe. This two-week program allows for students to participate in challenging and immersive academic modules centered on a specific topic or area of interest; reside in a living-learning community with other participants; attend special workshops on topics such as the college admission process, financial assistance, ACT/SAT test preparation and college fit; and participate in special excursions to local attractions, such as Kings Island and a Dayton Dragons game. Fall scholarships are available to students with financial need.

First-Year Experience & Transition **MADE@Miami**

MADE@Miami is a three-day pre-semester experience for first-year students of color, first-generation students, LGBTQ identified students, and Miami Access Fellows who are ready to make the most out of Miami. It is an opportunity for these students to connect with other first-year students and faculty and staff from a wide variety of cultural backgrounds. We promote qualities valued by the University community — Mentoring, Achieving, Diversity, and Excellence.

First-Year Experience & Transition **Miami, My Place (MMP)**

MMP is a new program created for students who are first in their family to earn a bachelor's degree and are recipients of the RedHawk Grant. Participants have typically had limited exposure to pre-college and professional enrichment experiences, and MMP ensures participants make a smooth transition to college. This specialized, interactive, and exclusive program allows participants to arrive early on Miami's campus and be part of a connected community of learners. Over the school year, students will engage in activities that will help them successfully acclimate to college life, continue on a path of academic success, and prepare them for a professional life following college.

Miami University
301 S. Campus Ave.
Oxford, OH 45056
Ph: (513) 529-2531
admission@MiamiOH.edu
MiamiOH.edu

Fast Facts

STUDENT DIVERSITY

# undergraduates	17,147
% male/female	50/50
% first-generation college	14
% American Indian or Alaskan Native	<1
% Asian	2
% Black or African American	3
% Hispanic/Latino	4
% Native Hawaiian or Pacific Islander	<1
% White	71
% two or more races	3
% race and/or ethnicity unknown	<1
% International/nonresident	15

STUDENT SUCCESS

% first-to-second year retention	91
% six-year graduation	79
% six-year graduation for underrepresented minority groups	70
% first-years who live on campus	98
% undergraduates who live on campus	45
full-time faculty	979
full-time minority faculty	192
student-faculty ratio	17:1

Popular majors Architecture, Biology, Engineering, International Studies, Kinesiology, Marketing, Psychology

Multicultural student clubs and organizations Historically Black and Latino-interest Greek Fraternities and Sororities, Spectrum, Miami Ambassadors Creating Change, International Student Organization, Association of Latin and American Students, Chinese Student and Scholar Friendship Association, Asian American Association, National Association for the Advancement of Colored People, Muslim Students' Organization

AFFORDABILITY

Cost of Attendance

tuition	$34,211 or in-state: $14,958
required fees	n/a
room and board	$13,202

Financial Aid

total institutional scholarships/grants	$82,825,454
% of students with financial need	34
% of students with need awarded any financial aid	97
% of students with need awarded any need-based scholarship or grant aid	84
% of students with need whose need was fully met	21
% Pell Grant recipients among first-years	11
average aid package	$14,415
average student loan debt upon graduation	$29,956

ADMISSIONS

# of applicants	30,255
% admitted	68
SAT Critical Reading	600-695
SAT Math	620-720
ACT Composite	29
SAT/ACT optional	n/a
average HS GPA	3.85

DEADLINES

regular application closing date	2/1
early decision plan	yes
application closing date	11/15
early action plan	yes
application closing date	12/1
application fee	$50
application fee online	$50
fee waiver for applicants with financial need	yes

Ohio University

Ohio University
1 Ohio University Drive
Athens, Ohio 45701
Ph: (740) 593-1000
admissions@ohio.edu
www.ohio.edu

Founded in 1804, Ohio University is the oldest public institution of higher education in the state of Ohio. A main campus in Athens offers students a residential learning experience in a picturesque academic setting. Additional campuses and centers serve students across the state, and online programs further advance the university's commitment to providing educational access and opportunity. OHIO's dual mission of access and excellence opens the doors to students from all backgrounds and then provides the support necessary for success. Students become scholars, leaders, and engaged citizens. They study abroad, volunteer, and form lifelong friendships.

Scholars & Leadership **OHIO First Scholars**

OHIO First Scholars is committed to supporting the success, persistence, and engagement of Ohio University's first-generation college students by providing proactive outreach and support programs. These programs include We Are First (first-generation student organization), a specialized living community, a seminar course, as well as a mentoring program that pairs Ohio University faculty and staff with first-generation students.

Academic Advising & Support **College Achievement Program (CAP)**

College Achievement Program (CAP) is a federal TRIO program that serves students who are low-income, first-generation, and/or have academic need. CAP provides opportunities for academic development, assists students with basic college requirements, and serves to motivate students towards the successful completion of an undergraduate degree. Between 2010 and 2015, the CAP persistence rate was 97 percent.

First-Year Experience & Transition **Learning Communities**

Learning Communities (LC) provide opportunities for small groups of students to take a common set of courses together or share a common experience built around their academic studies. Participants develop a deeper understanding of the courses' subject matter while they build relationships and learn together outside of the classroom. More than 230 LC options are available each year, with 3800+ students participating in them. LCs may be college-based, designed around student interests, or structured to serve a particular group of students.

Fast Facts

STUDENT DIVERSITY

# undergraduates	23,542
% male/female	40/60
% first-generation college	25
% American Indian or Alaskan Native	<1
% Asian	1
% Black or African American	5
% Hispanic/Latino	3
% Native Hawaiian or Pacific Islander	<1
% White	84
% two or more races	3
% race and/or ethnicity unknown	1
% International/nonresident	2

STUDENT SUCCESS

% first-to-second year retention	82
% six-year graduation	67
% six-year graduation for underrepresented minority groups	68
% first-years who live on campus	95
% undergraduates who live on campus	45
full-time faculty	944
full-time minority faculty	150
student-faculty ratio	18:1

Popular majors Health Professions, Business/Marketing, Communication/Journalism, Social Sciences, Education

Multicultural student clubs and organizations American Association of University Women, Black Student Cultural Programming Board, Black Student Union, Latino Student Union, Multicultural Leadership Ambassadors, International Student Union

AFFORDABILITY

Cost of Attendance

tuition	$21,208 or in-state: $11,744
required fees	n/a
room and board	$11,176

Financial Aid

total institutional scholarships/grants	$41,097,565
% of students with financial need	75
% of students with need awarded any financial aid	100
% of students with need awarded any need-based scholarship or grant aid	92
% of students with need whose need was fully met	42
% Pell Grant recipients among first-years	27
average aid package	$10,034
average student loan debt upon graduation	$27,880

ADMISSIONS

# of applicants	20,623
% admitted	75
SAT Critical Reading	490-600
SAT Math	500-600
SAT Writing	470-580
ACT Composite	24
SAT/ACT optional	no
average HS GPA	3.48

DEADLINES

regular application closing date	2/1
early decision plan	no
application closing date	n/a
early action plan	yes
application closing date	12/1
application fee	$50
application fee online	$50
fee waiver for applicants with financial need	yes

University of Cincinnati

Located 1.5 miles from the center of downtown Cincinnati, the University of Cincinnati is the second largest public institution in Ohio with more than 44,000 students. We invented cooperative education (co-op) in 1906; our focus on experiential learning is one unique—and well known—aspect of our university. With real-world experience implemented in all 300+ programs, Cincinnati is the perfect choice for students looking to graduate not only with a degree, but a resume filled with relevant, hands-on experience. Cincinnati students also benefit from small class sizes and an 17:1 student/teacher ratio, which allows students to build meaningful relationships with their professors and peers. Campus tours are offered most weekdays and Saturdays. Come see for yourself why Forbes says we are "One of the world's most beautiful campuses."

First-Year Experience & Transition **First Generation Theme Housing/Program**

Housed in the Division of Student Affairs, Gen-1 is a groundbreaking program that is the nation's first living-learning community to focus on first-generation college students. The Gen-1 Theme House is a residence hall providing freshmen and upperclassmen with a structured environment in which to live, learn, and work. The Gen-1 Program helps first-generation, Pell-eligible students transition from high school into college, increasing their likelihood of successfully completing their freshman year and earning a degree.

Student Life & Support **Ethnic Programs and Services**

EPS encourages academic excellence, positive social interaction, cultural enrichment, student leadership development and community service. EPS strives to actively promote the mission of the University by advancing the growth, matriculation, recruiting and retention of African American, Asian American, Hispanic American and Native American students. EPS provides a welcoming atmosphere where students can study, relax and experience a home away from home. We assist in educating the university community through innovative programming that embodies customs and traditions of students of color. EPS also offers the Darwin T. Turner Scholars Program, honoring an African American student who is the youngest person ever to graduate from the University of Cincinnati, to promote academic excellence, foster diversity and provide leadership opportunities to incoming students. In addition to providing full-tuition funding, Darwin T. Turner Scholars participate in programs and activities designed to improve their intellectual, personal and professional development.

Student Life & Support **African American Cultural and Resource Center**

AACRC supports the mission of the university by recruiting and retaining students of diverse identities. The AACRC's primary focus is to address the academic, social, spiritual, and cultural needs of the African American student population. Transitions is a first-year student experience that uses a "Rites of Passage" curriculum to increase retention and graduation rates for African American students at the University of Cincinnati. The program assists students with their adjustment to college by providing workshops, mentorships, and other social and academic activities to ensure that all participants successfully adjust to college.

University of Cincinnati
2600 Clifton Avenue
Cincinnati, OH 45221
Ph: (513) 556-1100
admissions@uc.edu
www.uc.edu

Fast Facts

STUDENT DIVERSITY

# undergraduates	26,608
% male/female	50/50
% first-generation college	27
% American Indian or Alaskan Native	<1
% Asian	3
% Black or African American	8
% Hispanic/Latino	4
% Native Hawaiian or Pacific Islander	<1
% White	71
% two or more races	3
% race and/or ethnicity unknown	6
% International/nonresident	5

STUDENT SUCCESS

% first-to-second year retention	88
% six-year graduation	66
% six-year graduation for underrepresented minority groups	n/a
% first-years who live on campus	80
% undergraduates who live on campus	n/a
full-time faculty	2,767
full-time minority faculty	n/a
student-faculty ratio	17:1

Popular majors Marketing, Psychology, Criminal Justice, Nursing, Communications, Accounting, Finance, Mechanical Engineering, Chemical Engineering, Biological Sciences, Industrial Design, Electrical Engineering, Civil Engineering

Multicultural student clubs and organizations African Student Assoc., Black Student Assoc., Cariba Caribbean Student Assoc., Colors of Pride, Latinos En Accion, Middle Eastern & Mediterranean Student Assoc., Shades of You, Society for Advancing Hispanics/Chicanos and Native Americans, South Asian American Student Assoc.

AFFORDABILITY

Cost of Attendance

tuition	$26,334 or in-state: $11,000
required fees	n/a
room and board	$11,000

Financial Aid

total institutional scholarships/grants	$47,911,904
% of students with financial need	79
% of students with need awarded any financial aid	75
% of students with need awarded any need-based scholarship or grant aid	62
% of students with need whose need was fully met	n/a
% Pell Grant recipients among first-years	23
average aid package	$11,889
average student loan debt upon graduation	$27,677

ADMISSIONS

# of applicants	20,155
% admitted	75
SAT Critical Reading	510-630
SAT Math	530-660
SAT Writing	n/a
ACT Composite	25
SAT/ACT optional	n/a
average HS GPA	3.6

DEADLINES

regular application closing date	12/1
early decision plan	n/a
application closing date	n/a
early action plan	yes
application closing date	12/1
application fee	$50
application fee online	$50
fee waiver for applicants with financial need	yes

University of Dayton

University of Dayton
Albert Emanuel Hall
Dayton, OH 45469-1669
Ph: (800) 837-7433
admission@udayton.edu
www.udayton.edu

Fast Facts

STUDENT DIVERSITY

# undergraduates	8,330
% male/female	53/47
% first-generation college	9
% American Indian or Alaskan Native	<1
% Asian	1
% Black or African American	3
% Hispanic/Latino	4
% Native Hawaiian or Pacific Islander	<1
% White	79
% two or more races	2
% race and/or ethnicity unknown	1
% International/nonresident	10

STUDENT SUCCESS

% first-to-second year retention	89
% six-year graduation	75
% six-year graduation for underrepresented minority groups	62
% first-years who live on campus	94
% undergraduates who live on campus	85
full-time faculty	612
full-time minority faculty	98
student-faculty ratio	15:1

Popular majors Business/Marketing, Engineering, Education, Communication/Journalism, Health Professions and Related Programs

Multicultural student clubs and organizations Black Action Through Unity, Hispanic Business Student Association, Multicultural Association of Pre-Med Students, Multicultural Programming Council, Multicultural Business Association, National Association for the Advancement of Colored People, National Association of Black Accountants, Society of Hispanic Professional Engineers, Women of Remarkable Distinction

AFFORDABILITY

Cost of Attendance

tuition	$41,750
required fees	n/a
room and board	$13,180

Financial Aid

total institutional scholarships/grants	$141,727,958
% of students with financial need	70
% of students with need awarded any financial aid	99
% of students with need awarded any need-based scholarship or grant aid	98
% of students with need whose need was fully met	37
% Pell Grant recipients among first-years	14
average aid package	$27,507
average student loan debt upon graduation	$37,571

ADMISSIONS

# of applicants	17,477
% admitted	60
SAT Critical Reading	500-610
SAT Math	520-630
SAT Writing	n/a
ACT Composite	27
SAT/ACT optional	n/a
average HS GPA	3.70

DEADLINES

regular application closing date	2/1
early decision plan	n/a
application closing date	n/a
early action plan	yes
application closing date	11/1
application fee	n/a
application fee online	n/a
fee waiver for applicants with financial need	n/a

The University of Dayton is a top-tier Catholic research university with offerings from the undergraduate to the doctoral levels. We are a diverse community committed, in the Marianist tradition, to educating the whole person—mind, body and spirit—and to linking learning and scholarship with leadership and service. As a Catholic, Marianist university, we are devoted to education for service, justice and peace, and we strive to develop critical minds and compassionate hearts.

First-Year Experience & Transition **Transitions Pre-Orientation Program**

Transitions is a free pre-orientation program for incoming first-year multicultural students, sponsored by the Office of Multicultural Affairs. Students are introduced to support services and resources through a series of presentations and activities. Students are also provided with an opportunity to network with fellow UD students, faculty, staff, and administrators.

Academic Advising & Support **Discover Programs**

As a member of the Discover Arts or Discover Sciences programs, students can explore the academic programs in the College of Arts and Sciences before finalizing a major. Through the Discover Arts and Discover Sciences programs, students take a seminar that covers the curriculum and careers of each program, as well as the multitude of complementary minors. With the help of this seminar, along with the assistance of an academic adviser, students discover the program that best suits their needs and goals.

Academic Advising & Support **Office of Learning Resources**

The Ryan C. Harris Learning Teaching Center's Office of Learning Resources is a learning resource for students, parents, faculty, and staff at the UD. OLR offers information and services to help everyone become a successful learner, including Tutoring services, Supplemental Instruction, Disability Services, Global Learning Support, and writing support.

Student Life & Support **Office of Multicultural Affairs**

The Office of Multicultural Affairs provides staff, facilities, services and special programs to support the academic experience of students. OMA staff members work closely with academic deans, faculty and administrative offices to provide a supportive campus environment based on the academic, social, and cultural needs of a diverse community of scholars. This office serves as a resource for the entire campus community, while providing multicultural students and their families with an additional connection to the University.

Student Life & Support **Success Professionals in Enrollment Management**

Directors of Student Enrichment and Academic Outcomes; and, College Access, Success and Transitions serve as co-pilots to support and retain undergraduate students at UD. Whether making the transition from high school to college or even to graduation, the success professionals provide excellent support and care to help you –and your family--make the most of your collegiate journey. We can help you: identify resources to support your classroom activities; develop your own "flight" (success) plan; or simply be the resource to help you discover the best of YOU and UD!

Mentoring **P.E.E.R.S. Mentor Program**

PEERS stands for "Program to Engage and Exchange Resources for Students." Participants of the program will: have access to a community of support and resources during key stages of their academic career; receive support that aids in their personal and leadership development; develop a greater sense of belonging to UD by engaging in the PEERS community; be exposed to diverse perspectives and experiences that affirms their cultural identity.

Walsh University

Walsh University is a place for discovery. With nearly 70 undergraduate majors, more than 50 student organizations, a campus just outside of Rome, Italy, and numerous other study abroad opportunities in places like Uganda, Tanzania and beyond, Walsh prepares students for well-rounded, global success. In addition, Walsh remains dedicated to its mission of developing leaders in service to others. At Walsh, volunteer work isn't simply encouraged—it is part of the core curriculum. Walsh also offers a test-optional admissions path for students whose potential for academic success is not accurately measured by standardized test scores.

First-Year Experience & Transition **GE100: FIRST YEAR INSTITUTE**

Each first generation student participates in this program specifically designed to ease the transition from high school to college. All freshman students are required to complete these credit-bearing courses. Instructors are trained on presenting topics related to time-management, self-care, connecting to campus resources, developing strategies for academic success, etc. Walsh offers lunch forums for students who need extra assistance to discuss their concerns and help provide the assistance that they need.

Academic Advising & Support **Structured Education Program (SEP)**

Walsh University offers a variety of programs for first generation college students. Among them is our Structured Education Program (SEP) in which students remain in a learning community triad for study skills, freshman comp, and math throughout the year. Each small group has a designated tutor/mentor who can help guide them every step of the way and provide 24/7 support.

Student Life & Support **Multicultural Affairs Support Services**

Walsh also offers special programs for our multicultural first generation students. These programs and services are dedicated to the success of the Walsh multicultural student population and provide various support services and collaborate with many other departments. For example, through the iMODEL program, peer mentors help connect incoming students to academic and social support.

Walsh University
2020 E. Maple Street
North Canton, OH 44720
Ph: (800) 362-9846
admissions@walsh.edu
www.walsh.edu

Fast Facts

STUDENT DIVERSITY

# undergraduates	2,009
% male/female	41/59
% first-generation college	26
% American Indian or Alaskan Native	<1
% Asian	<1
% Black or African American	7
% Hispanic/Latino	3
% Native Hawaiian or Pacific Islander	0
% White	68
% two or more races	2
% race and/or ethnicity unknown	15
% International/nonresident	5

STUDENT SUCCESS

% first-to-second year retention	74
% six-year graduation	58
% six-year graduation for underrepresented minority groups	n/a
% first-years who live on campus	72
% undergraduates who live on campus	n/a
full-time faculty	132
full-time minority faculty	n/a
student-faculty ratio	13:1

Popular majors Nursing, Business, Education, Biology, Exercise Science

Multicultural student clubs and organizations Black Student Union, International Club

AFFORDABILITY

Cost of Attendance

tuition	$27,650
required fees	$1,515
room and board	$10,530

Financial Aid

total institutional scholarships/grants	$29,482,336
% of students with financial need	86
% of students with need awarded any financial aid	99
% of students with need awarded any need-based scholarship or grant aid	67
% of students with need whose need was fully met	n/a
% Pell Grant recipients among first-years	32
average aid package	n/a
average student loan debt upon graduation	n/a

ADMISSIONS

# of applicants	1,665
% admitted	79
SAT Critical Reading	520
SAT Math	520
SAT Writing	n/a
ACT Composite	23
SAT/ACT optional	yes
average HS GPA	3.49

DEADLINES

regular application closing date	rolling
early decision plan	no
application closing date	n/a
early action plan	no
application closing date	n/a
application fee	$0
application fee online	$0
fee waiver for applicants with financial need	n/a

Oklahoma Baptist University

Oklahoma Baptist University
500 W. University
Shawnee, OK 74804
Ph: (800) 654-3285
admissions@okbu.edu
www.okbu.edu

Fast Facts

STUDENT DIVERSITY

# undergraduates	1,933
% male/female	40/60
% first-generation college	n/a
% American Indian or Alaskan Native	5
% Asian	1
% Black or African American	5
% Hispanic/Latino	2
% Native Hawaiian or Pacific Islander	n/a
% White	67
% two or more races	12
% race and/or ethnicity unknown	4
% International/nonresident	4

STUDENT SUCCESS

% first-to-second year retention	68
% six-year graduation	57
% six-year graduation for underrepresented minority groups	45
% first-years who live on campus	96
% undergraduates who live on campus	84
full-time faculty	125
full-time minority faculty	20
student-faculty ratio	13:1

Popular majors Education, Nursing, Business, Ministry, Pre-Med

Multicultural student clubs and organizations International Student Organization, Alpha Mu Gamma- Foreign Language, Council of First Nations Students, International Justice Mission, International Student Union

AFFORDABILITY

Cost of Attendance

tuition	$25,138
required fees	$3,120
room and board	$7,350

Financial Aid

total institutional scholarships/grants	$27,928,695
% of students with financial need	74
% of students with need awarded any financial aid	99
% of students with need awarded any need-based scholarship or grant aid	74
% of students with need whose need was fully met	24
% Pell Grant recipients among first-years	54
average aid package	$23,506
average student loan debt upon graduation	$25,262

ADMISSIONS

# of applicants	4,123
% admitted	65
SAT Critical Reading	489-661
SAT Math	517-559
SAT Writing	n/a
ACT Composite	23
SAT/ACT optional	no
average HS GPA	3.66

DEADLINES

regular application closing date	8/1
early decision plan	n/a
application closing date	n/a
early action plan	n/a
application closing date	n/a
application fee	n/a
application fee online	n/a
fee waiver for applicants with financial need	yes

As a Christian liberal arts university, Oklahoma Baptist University's mission is to transform lives by equipping students to pursue academic excellence, integrate faith with all areas of knowledge, engage a diverse world, and live worthy of the high calling of God in Christ. Toward that goal, the university offers ten bachelor's degrees in 88 areas of study. Driven by Christian values, OBU intends to provide the knowledge, skills, and preparation to prepare students for whichever career path they are called to, while maintaining their dedication to truly make a difference. OBU also embraces a diverse environment for their students, with 2,093 coming to OBU from 37 states and 41 other countries in the fall of 2017.

Scholarship & Financial Aid **Bison Grants and OBU Endowed Scholarships**

For students whose need is not met by federal student aid, scholarships, grants, or loans, OBU offers the OBU Bison Grants and OBU Endowed Scholarships. Amounts of these scholarships vary based on students' academic qualifications, demonstrated need, and financial aid packages. OBU guarantees every first-time freshmen at least $5,000 in student aid. Full tuition scholarships are available for those who qualify as University Scholars, Allen Scholars, or Martin Scholars.

Scholars & Leadership **Honors Program**

The Honors Program is meant to enhance students' studies, to give them more chances to ask questions, more time to pursue special issues, and more ways to learn and use what they know. As a member of the Honors Program, students will have the opportunity to explore unique aspects of academics through study abroad experiences, independent research opportunities, and engaging diverse intellectual perspectives.

Academic Courses & Service Learning **Intensive English Program**

OBU offers the Intensive English Program for students who would like to improve their English language proficiency in a variety of contexts. With a focus on English comprehension through practice in reading, writing, conversation and listening, the program enables students to succeed at English-speaking colleges, universities, or professional environments and meet the English qualifications required for admission to OBU. Students must be at least 16 years of age, have completed secondary school, and qualify as non-native speakers of English in order to apply.

Academic Courses & Service Learning **Milburn Student Success Center**

The Student Success Center offers help with writing assignments and academic support in core subjects as well as mathematics, chemistry, physics, accounting, and economics. The Student Success Center also provides aid in research, organizing study groups, and academic feedback. In addition, the Center provides academic advising to those undeclared or in the process of changing their majors.

Reed College

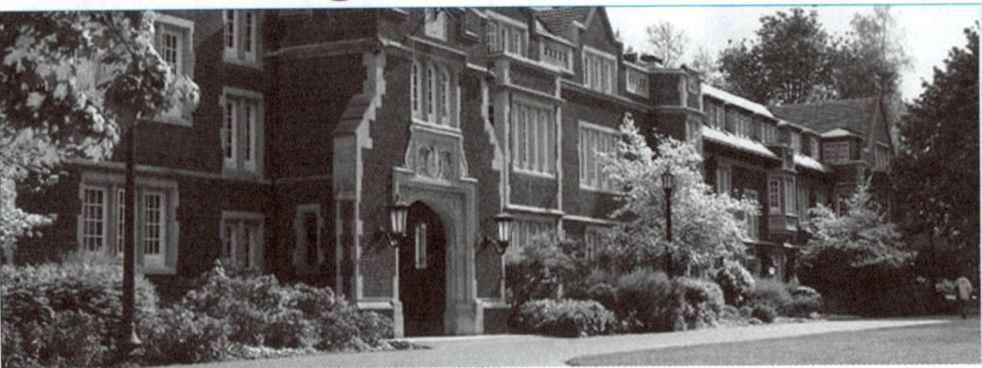

Reed is a college for intellectual, passionate, authentic, and unconventional students to pursue academic excellence in an extraordinary environment. Reedies share a love of learning, a spirit of friendship and independence, a commitment to responsibility and integrity, and a capacity for insight and intellectual growth. All of these qualities combine to form a top-notch population of liberal arts students. With a student-to-faculty ratio of 10:1 and all classes taught by professors rather than by teaching assistants, undergraduate education at Reed comes first. The conference method of learning brings together small groups of students to discuss great ideas, to read primary texts by leading thinkers, and to form opinions and defend them with skill and nuance. Guided by a thoughtfully constructed sequence of topics and architecture of ideas, students map an academic course that culminates in the senior thesis. Reedies also lead a full and exciting social life. There are currently over 100 student-led organizations on campus, ranging from the usual, like a student-run newspaper, to the completely unique, like DxOxTxU, a club in which students build huge play structures for the community at large to enjoy. Likewise, Reedies have always balanced development of mind and body, often pursuing physical activities that utilize the environmental treasures of the Pacific Northwest such as skiing, kayaking, and mountaineering. As for traditions and lore, Reed has plenty, including the Doyle Owl, Thesis Parade, and Paideia (among many others).

Open House, Fly-in, Visit **Discover Reed Fly-in Program and Junior Scholars Program**

Each year, the Reed Admission Office offers domestic high school seniors and juniors from historically underrepresented racial and ethnic backgrounds an opportunity to apply for a fly-in program. The program introduces students to life at Reed and in Portland. For more information and to apply, visit reed.edu/apply/visit/multicultural-programs.

Scholarship & Financial Aid **100% of demonstrated financial need met**

Reed College is committed to making a world-class liberal arts and sciences education affordable for all admitted and continuing students. Reed offers need-based financial aid, using both the FAFSA and the CSS Profile to evaluate each family's financial resources and determine eligibility for financial aid. Reed meets 100% of demonstrated need for admitted students. Over half of the student body receives aid. Reed keeps loan debt low—lower than the national average. Financial aid packages include a moderate loan and work-study expectation, and a student's remaining need is met with grant aid, which is not repaid after graduation.

First-Year Experience & Transition **Peer Mentor Program**

Reed's Peer Mentor program assists first-year students with their college transition by pairing them with an experienced Reedie, who can provide everything from tutoring to moral support to camaraderie. Mentees and mentors participate in both group and one-on-one activities. Administered through the Office for Inclusive Community, this program helps to foster a sense of multiculturalism and community at Reed.

Reed College
3203 SE Woodstock Boulevard
Portland, OR 97202
Ph: (503) 777-7511
admission@reed.edu
www.reed.edu

Fast Facts

STUDENT DIVERSITY

# undergraduates	1,410
% male/female	45/55
% first-generation college	11
% American Indian or Alaskan Native	<1
% Asian	6
% Black or African American	2
% Hispanic/Latino	11
% Native Hawaiian or Pacific Islander	<1
% White	59
% two or more races	8
% race and/or ethnicity unknown	4
% International/nonresident	8

STUDENT SUCCESS

% first-to-second year retention	87
% six-year graduation	78
% six-year graduation for underrepresented minority groups	73
% first-years who live on campus	100
% undergraduates who live on campus	67
full-time faculty	160
full-time minority faculty	30
student-faculty ratio	10:1

Popular majors English, Biology, Math, Physics, Psychology

Multicultural student clubs and organizations Multicultural Resource Center (MRC), Queer Alliance, Black and African Student Union, Latinx Student Union, DiversifY, Low SES/First Gen Students, Feminist Student Union, Students of Color, Bulding Connections: women of color, Trans & Gender Non-Conforming Peer Group, Students with Learning Differences/Disabilities, Asian and Pacific Islander Student Union, Women for Women

AFFORDABILITY

Cost of Attendance

tuition	$53,900
required fees	$300
room and board	$13,670

Financial Aid

total institutional scholarships/grants	$27,976,542
% of students with financial need	53
% of students with need awarded any financial aid	100
% of students with need awarded any need-based scholarship or grant aid	100
% of students with need whose need was fully met	100
% Pell Grant recipients among first-years	13
average aid package	$44,798
average student loan debt upon graduation	$19,528

ADMISSIONS

# of applicants	5,652
% admitted	36
SAT Evidence-Based Reading & Writing	670-750
SAT Math	670-750
ACT Composite	30-33
SAT/ACT optional	n/a
average HS GPA	3.9

DEADLINES

regular application closing date	1/15
early decision plan	yes
application closing date	ED1: 11/15; ED2: 12/20
early action plan	yes
application closing date	11/15
application fee	$0
application fee online	n/a
fee waiver for applicants with financial need	n/a

Southern Oregon University

SOU provides career-focused, comprehensive educational experiences to over 6,200 students. Along with an emphasis on student success and intellectual growth, SOU is committed to diversity, inclusion and sustainability. Theoretical and experiential learning programs provide quality, innovative experiences for students. At SOU, students build strong community connections through internships, mentorships, field studies, capstone projects, volunteer opportunities and civic engagement.

Scholarship & Financial Aid **Success at Southern**

Success at Southern/Student Support Services is a federally-funded TRIO grant program that helps eligible students (low-income or first-generation students, as well as those with disabilities) succeed in college and eventually graduate. Success at Southern provides a range of services, including college success classes; tutoring; academic advising; mentoring; assistance with completing scholarship applications; access to cultural activities; and career, personal, and financial counseling.

First-Year Experience & Transition **American Association of State Colleges and Universities (AASCU)**

SOU was selected by the American Association of State Colleges and Universities (AASCU) to be part of the Re-Imagining the First Year of College project. This is a national project aimed at ensuring success for all students, particularly those who have historically been underserved by higher education: low income, first generation, and students of color. With support from the Bill & Melinda Gates Foundation and USA Funds, AASCU created a coalition of 44 member institutions, including SOU, that will work together for three calendar years (2016-2018) to develop comprehensive, institutional transformations that redesign the first year of college and creates sustainable change for student success.

Academic Courses & Service Learning **The Bridge Program**

The Bridge Program is designed to invest in the strengths of Oregon college students, especially underrepresented populations: first-generation college students, second language learners, students from low-income families, and under-served minority groups. Oregon high school seniors with strengths such as leadership, active citizenry, creativity, innovations, passion, or other characteristics that may not be recognized by a SAT score or a borderline GPA may be nominated for this program.

Southern Oregon University
1250 Siskiyou Boulevard
Ashland, OR 97520
Ph: (855) 470-3377
admission@sou.edu
www.sou.edu

Fast Facts

STUDENT DIVERSITY

# undergraduates	6,100
% male/female	40/60
% first-generation college	23
% American Indian or Alaskan Native	1
% Asian	2
% Black or African American	2
% Hispanic/Latino	12
% Native Hawaiian or Pacific Islander	1
% White	48
% two or more races	7
% race and/or ethnicity unknown	28
% International/nonresident	2

STUDENT SUCCESS

% first-to-second year retention	73
% six-year graduation	38
% six-year graduation for underrepresented minority groups	38
% first-years who live on campus	78
% undergraduates who live on campus	16
full-time faculty	160
full-time minority faculty	23
student-faculty ratio	23:1

Popular majors Theatre, Criminology, Communication, Business, Psychology, Outdoor Adventure Leadership, Music, Education

Multicultural student clubs and organizations Black Student Union, Hawaii Club, Spanish Club, Latino Student Club, Tango Club, International Student Association, The Women's Resource Center, Queer Resource Center, Multicultural Resource Center

AFFORDABILITY

Cost of Attendance

tuition	$7,425
required fees	$1,860
room and board	$13,764

Financial Aid

total institutional scholarships/grants	$13,987,154
% of students with financial need	78
% of students with need awarded any financial aid	97
% of students with need awarded any need-based scholarship or grant aid	73
% of students with need whose need was fully met	23
% Pell Grant recipients among first-years	30
average aid package	$13,266
average student loan debt upon graduation	$26,590

ADMISSIONS

# of applicants	4,095
% admitted	80
SAT Critical Reading	460-590
SAT Math	450-560
SAT Writing	430-550
ACT Composite	22
SAT/ACT optional	n/a
average HS GPA	3.31

DEADLINES

regular application closing date	rolling
early decision plan	yes
application closing date	2/28
early action plan	n/a
application closing date	n/a
application fee	$60
application fee online	$60
fee waiver for applicants with financial need	yes

Warner Pacific College

Located in the heart of southeast Portland, Warner Pacific is dedicated to seeing individuals, families, and communities flourish. As an urban college designed to serve students from diverse backgrounds, Warner Pacific knows that for a city to thrive, its leaders must be prepared to engage actively in a constantly changing world.

Our Christ-centered, liberal arts approach invites you to seek answers to difficult questions and will challenge you to expand your comfort zone in order to explore the ways in which you understand society, community, and faith. A student-faculty ratio of 12:1 means that you will have professors who know you by name, and are dedicated to guiding you throughout your college experience.

Scholarship & Financial Aid **City Builder Scholarship**

Every year, groups of students from the same city head together to the same colleges. **Warner Pacific is intentionally developing these naturally occurring cohort here in the Portland-metro area.** Equipped with a strong cohort, a clearly defined sense of purpose, and practical college success skills, our City Builder students will come to college with a built-in support network, ready to engage the campus and persist through adversity. Many of our City Builder students are first-generation college scholars. Nationally, first generation college students graduate from an undergraduate program in six years at an 11% rate, or from a community college at a 4% rate.

Students who receive the City Builders scholarship ($1,500 per year) are required to attend weekly leadership training seminars throughout the summer leading up to the start of their first year at Warner Pacific College.

Scholarship & Financial Aid **Urban Service Track of the Act Six Leadership & Scholarship Initiative**

The Act Six Leadership and Scholarship Initiative is Oregon's only full-tuition, full-need scholarship for emerging urban leaders who want to use their college education to make a difference on campus and in their communities at home. Act Six Scholars are chosen for their distinctive leadership, academic potential, and commitment to serving local communities. Warner Pacific and Act Six staff provide ongoing leadership development, internships and preparation in a wide variety of areas necessary for success.

First-Year Experience & Transition **First-Year Learning Communities**

First-Year Learning Communities (FYLCs) at Warner Pacific are groups of 12-15 students who participate together in linked courses that include learning activities that extend outside the traditional classroom setting.

FYLCs focus on issues relevant to incoming students including; transitioning to college, social support, study skills, and community building. Dedicated faculty, co-curricular educators and upper-division peer mentors provide a strong framework while building a sense of community that encourages mutual academic, social, emotional, and spiritual support.

Student Life & Support **Diversity Council**

The Student Diversity Council oversees all student multicultural organizations and is a driving force on campus for diversity education, programs and social justice initiatives. Their primary role is to create an inclusive network between the Student Body and all student multicultural organizations. The Student Diversity Council partners with OCCV (the Oregon Center for Christian Values) in actively seeking social justice for marginalized populations both on and off campus.

Warner Pacific College
2219 SE 68th Avenue
Portland, OR 97215
Ph: (503) 517-1020
www.warnerpacific.edu

Fast Facts

STUDENT DIVERSITY	
# undergraduates	482
% male/female	45/56
% first-generation college	57
% American Indian or Alaskan Native	1
% Asian	1
% Black or African American	10
% Hispanic/Latino	17
% Native Hawaiian or Pacific Islander	3
% White	48
% two or more races	20
% race and/or ethnicity unknown	5
% International/nonresident	n/a
STUDENT SUCCESS	
% first-to-second year retention	69
% six-year graduation	66
% six-year graduation for underrepresented minority groups	n/a
% first-years who live on campus	78
% undergraduates who live on campus	45
full-time faculty	28
full-time minority faculty	4
student-faculty ratio	12:1

Popular majors Education, Social Work, Biological Science, Christian Ministries, Business Administration

Multicultural student clubs and organizations Local Connect volunteering, Campus Ministries activities, Student Diversity Council, and an active College Activities Board dedicated to diversity

AFFORDABILITY	
Cost of Attendance	
tuition	$22,710
required fees	$660
room and board	$8,320
Financial Aid	
total institutional scholarships/grants	$2,548,037
% of students with financial need	85
% of students with need awarded any financial aid	99
% of students with need awarded any need-based scholarship or grant aid	93
% of students with need whose need was fully met	12
% Pell Grant recipients among first-years	60
average aid package	$16,136
average student loan debt upon graduation	$28,773
ADMISSIONS	
# of applicants	1,523
% admitted	50
SAT Critical Reading	456
SAT Math	466
SAT Writing	428
ACT Composite	18
SAT/ACT optional	no
average HS GPA	3.23
DEADLINES	
regular application closing date	rolling
early decision plan	n/a
application closing date	rolling
early action plan	n/a
application closing date	rolling
application fee	$25
application fee online	$25
fee waiver for applicants with financial need	yes

Willamette University

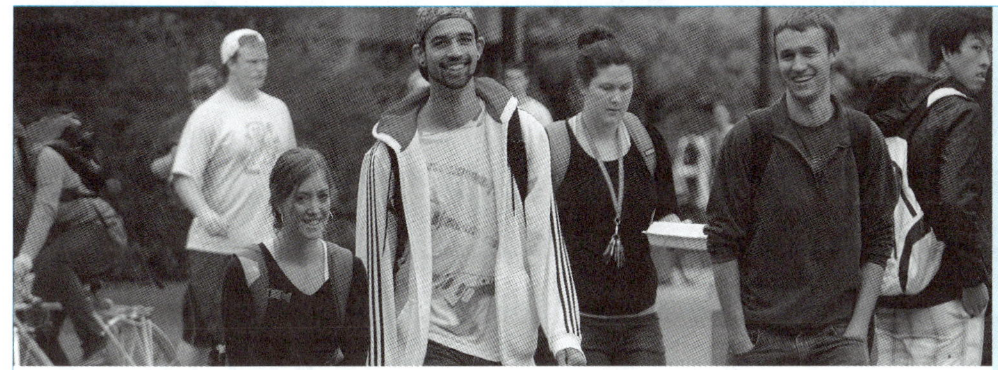

Willamette University is the first university established in the western U.S. and has earned a national reputation for its academic standards and leadership in sustainability and civic engagement. The university motto, "not unto ourselves alone are we born," was a founding principle for such engagement and continues to help foster a community dedicated to service and exemplary citizenship. Students and faculty at Willamette maintain this culture on campus by continually teaching and learning from one another, connecting life experiences in many forms—educationally, communally, culturally, as well as spiritually—in an effort to understand and alleviate injustices in our local communities and around the world.

Pre-College Prep & Outreach **Willamette Academy**

Willamette Academy reaches out to historically underrepresented communities by empowering youth who have the desire and potential to advance to higher education. This academic program is designed to address a number of factors that may discourage certain students from attending college or otherwise impede their academic progress. We are committed to helping our students achieve at a level that will enable them to attend the four-year college or university of their choice.

Summer Bridge & Orientation **Ohana Jump Start Program**

Led by current WU students who have successfully integrated into the campus community, Ohana is a time to learn about Salem, Willamette, academic life and cultural resources. During Ohana, students will also have an opportunity to meet key staff who will provide information regarding financial aid, living in residence halls, health services, and academic support services.

First-Year Experience & Transition **Opening Days**

Opening Days is a student-run, five-day program of activities which not only challenges students both academically and socially but also gives parents the opportunity to learn more about the university and the transition their child will be making.

Academic Advising & Support **Academic Support**

Academic Support cultivates the academic efforts, engagement, and achievements of College of Liberal Arts students by providing the following services: individual consultations, tutoring, and study groups.

Student Life & Support **Office of Multicultural Affairs**

We promote multiculturalism throughout the campus community by delivering a variety of educational programs and services advocating for social justice and diversity.

Open House, Fly-in, Visit **Access to Excellence**

On Campus Diversity Preview Programs bring together motivated, high-achieving high school seniors from underrepresented groups. These events provide an opportunity for prospective students of color who are very interested in Willamette University as a possible college choice to visit campus and experience life as a Bearcat.

Willamette University
900 State Street
Salem, OR 97301
Ph: (503) 370-6303
bearcat@willamette.edu
www.willamette.edu

Fast Facts

STUDENT DIVERSITY

# undergraduates	1,785
% male/female	42/58
% first-generation college	24
% American Indian or Alaskan Native	1
% Asian	9
% Black or African American	2
% Hispanic/Latino	13
% Native Hawaiian or Pacific Islander	1
% White	61
% two or more races	9
% race and/or ethnicity unknown	3
% International/nonresident	1

STUDENT SUCCESS

% first-to-second year retention	86
% six-year graduation	78
% six-year graduation for underrepresented minority groups	76
% first-years who live on campus	99
% undergraduates who live on campus	68
full-time faculty	217
full-time minority faculty	47
student-faculty ratio	10:1

Popular majors Economics, Biology, Psychology, Politics, History

Multicultural student clubs and organizations Alianza, Asian Coalition for Equality, Black Student Union, CAUSA, Chinese Taiwanese Culture Association, Hawaii Club, Japan Studies Student Leaders, Native and Indigenous Student Union, Rainbow Alliance

AFFORDABILITY

Cost of Attendance

tuition	$47,840
required fees	$317
room and board	$11,880

Financial Aid

total institutional scholarships/grants	$48,453,709
% of students with financial need	63
% of students with need awarded any financial aid	100
% of students with need awarded any need-based scholarship or grant aid	99
% of students with need whose need was fully met	15
% Pell Grant recipients among first-years	24
average aid package	$35,895
average student loan debt upon graduation	$29,958

ADMISSIONS

# of applicants	6,181
% admitted	78
SAT Critical Reading	560-680
SAT Math	550-650
SAT Writing	540-660
ACT Composite	25-30
SAT/ACT optional	yes
average HS GPA	3.93

DEADLINES

regular application closing date	1/15
early decision plan	yes
application closing date	11/15
early action plan	yes
application closing date	11/15
application fee	$0
application fee online	$0
fee waiver for applicants with financial need	n/a

Arcadia University

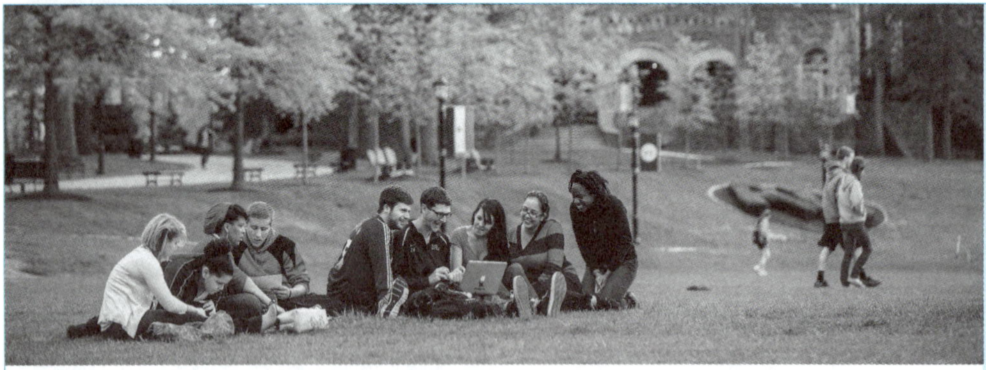

The Arcadia Promise affirms that students will have a distinctively global, integrative and personal learning experience that prepares them to contribute to and prosper in a diverse and dynamic world. The Arcadia Promise sums up the collective experiences of generations of alumni and provides a distinguished learning environment. Arcadia students are challenged to recognize their ability and responsibility to make choices that affect the future. Whether they pursue an undergraduate, graduate or further education path, they are part of a mutually supportive community. Through interactions with faculty, staff and peers representing a diversity of cultural backgrounds, they gain self-confidence and respect for others, learn by using the latest technologies, and acquire essential skills and knowledge that prepare them for a rich and meaningful life.

Pre-College Prep & Outreach **Meet the MAC**

Meet the MAC is a series of programs sponsored by a consortium of Pennsylvania colleges and universities that share common bonds in providing academic excellence. The members of this consortium will sponsor programs which give students who have historically been underrepresented in higher education the opportunity to interact with admissions professionals dedicated to increasing awareness of the opportunities available at small liberal arts institutions.

Special Admissions Policy **Gateway to Success Program**

Through the Gateway to Success Program, the Office of Enrollment Management offers admission to certain students who are identified as having the potential to succeed at Arcadia University despite some modest elements in their credentials. The program then provides a variety of services designed to help develop the levels of academic proficiency and social and leadership skills necessary for achieving academic success.

Academic Advising & Support **Act 101**

The ACT 101 Program is intended for economically and educationally disadvantaged first generation college students who are residents of Pennsylvania. The program offers tutoring, mentoring, counseling, curricular innovation and cultural enrichment activities to support these students.

Student Life & Support **Office of Institutional Diversity**

The Office of Institutional Diversity provides outreach, supplemental academic advisory support services and direct mentoring and advocacy for students identifying as being of African American, Latino, Asian or Native American descent (ALANA), and/or Lesbian, Gay, Bi-sexual, Transgender or Queer.

Student Life & Support **Common Cent$**

Designed for Arcadia students, Common Cent$ is a Financial Literacy Program that offers students a series of workshops and seminars throughout the year on topics such as: Budgeting, Dealing with Debt, Credit (Protecting Your Credit and Dealing With Credit Cards), Money Potholes: 10 Things to Avoid!, Getting Ahead on the Job, Budgeting for Life After College, Avoiding Identify Theft.

Arcadia University
450 S Easton Road
Glenside, PA 19038
Ph: (215) 572-2910
admiss@arcadia.edu
www.arcadia.edu

Fast Facts

STUDENT DIVERSITY

# undergraduates	2,390
% male/female	32/69
% first-generation college	29
% American Indian or Alaskan Native	<1
% Asian	5
% Black or African American	10
% Hispanic/Latino	9
% Native Hawaiian or Pacific Islander	<1
% White	65
% two or more races	4
% race and/or ethnicity unknown	4
% International/nonresident	3

STUDENT SUCCESS

% first-to-second year retention	78
% six-year graduation (2010 Cohort)	61
% six-year graduation for underrepresented minority groups (2010 Cohort)	52
% first-years who live on campus	83
% undergraduates who live on campus	49
full-time faculty	179
full-time minority faculty	28
student-faculty ratio	11:1

Popular majors Biology, Education, Business, Fine Arts, Psychology

Multicultural student clubs and organizations Arcadia Hindu Cultural Society, AU Muslim Student Association (AUMSA), Asian Students in American (ASIA), Black Awareness Society, Hillel (Jewish Student Organization), International Club, Latino Association, PRIDE Gay and Straight Alliance, Puro Ritmo

AFFORDABILITY

Cost of Attendance

tuition	$41,630
required fees	$700
room and board	$13,660

Financial Aid

total institutional scholarships/grants	$51,875,390
% of students with financial need	78
% of students with need awarded any financial aid	99
% of students with need awarded any need-based scholarship or grant aid	99
% of students with need whose need was fully met	43
% Pell Grant recipients among first-years	39
average aid package	$32,337
average student loan debt upon graduation	n/a

ADMISSIONS

# of applicants	8,909
% admitted	62
SAT Critical Reading	500-600
SAT Math	500-600
SAT Writing	490-600
ACT Composite	22-27
SAT/ACT optional	no
average HS GPA	3.63

DEADLINES

regular application closing date	rolling
early decision plan	n/a
application closing date	n/a
early action plan	n/a
application closing date	n/a
application fee	$30
application fee online	n/a
fee waiver for applicants with financial need	yes

Bucknell University

Bucknell University is a private, selective residential university with 3,600 undergraduates and a small graduate program. At Bucknell, you will join a close-knit community of students, faculty and alumni who think, act, create and engage with the world. We offer more than 50 majors and 65 minors in the arts, engineering, humanities, management, sciences and social sciences. Your professors will mentor and challenge you, take the time to get to know you personally, and provide opportunities to become involved in their research and creative projects. Bucknell educates students for a lifetime of intellectual exploration, creativity and leadership. All of your learning, in class and out, will give you the knowledge and skills that employers seek, and that you will need to create your future.

Open House, Fly-in, Visit **Journey to Bucknell**

Journey to Bucknell is an overnight program designed to expose high-achieving, traditionally underrepresented high school seniors to Bucknell. Participants stay in one of our residence halls, attend open house, and meet students, faculty and staff. Counselors can nominate students or they can fill out an application on their own. The program is free for students who are chosen to attend (trav el expenses, including flights and shuttles to and from campus, overnight accommodations with a current student and all meals while on campus).

Scholarship & Financial Aid

At Bucknell, we work to make the benefits of a Bucknell education accessible to families from many different economic circumstances. Financial aid and financing options include need-based grants, merit scholarships, federal and state grants, loans and payment plans, and student employment. Campus Enrichment Scholarships recognize the perspectives of first-generation college students, those outside the university's geographic area and those committed to bringing cultural and intellectual diversity to campus. Other scholarship programs include: Arts Merit, Bucknell Women in Science & Engineering, Dean's, FIRST and Mathematics Scholarships, Presidential Fellowships and PwC Scholarships. The Bucknell Community College Scholars Program provides full-tuition scholarships and mentorship for select transfer students from five partner community colleges.

Student Life & Support **Career Development Center**

The Career Development Center at Bucknell provides advising, networking, mock interviews, internship support and employer fairs. The placement rate for recent graduates is consistently high: 97% of the Class of 2016 was employed, in graduate school, both employed and in graduate school or volunteering within nine months of graduation. Bucknell is ranked #3 among best-value liberal arts colleges for alumni mid-career salary (PayScale 2016).

Mentoring **GenFirst!@BU**

At Bucknell, many of our faculty, staff and alumni are the first in their families to graduate from a four-year college or university. The GenFirst!@BU Mentoring Program facilitates relationships between first-generation students and first-generation faculty and/or staff who have offered to provide assistance and support throughout your years at Bucknell. You'll have opportunities to connect and network with your mentor and other mentees at campus programs. Plus, at least twice a semester, you'll share a meal with your mentor to touch base about your Bucknell transition, academics, social life, etc. Mentors know a lot about Bucknell, and they know what it's like to be a first-generation student.

Bucknell University
Admissions Office
One Dent Drive
Lewisburg, PA 17837
Ph: (570) 577-3000
admissions@bucknell.edu
www.bucknell.edu

Fast Facts

STUDENT DIVERSITY

# undergraduates	3,611
% male/female	49/51
% first-generation college	11
% American Indian or Alaskan Native	<1
% Asian	5
% Black or African American	4
% Hispanic/Latino	7
% Native Hawaiian or Pacific Islander	<1
% White	74
% two or more races	4
% race and/or ethnicity unknown	<1
% International/nonresident	6

STUDENT SUCCESS

% first-to-second year retention	94
% six-year graduation	90
% six-year graduation for underrepresented minority groups	88
% first-years who live on campus	100
% undergraduates who live on campus	91
full-time faculty	361
full-time minority faculty	65
student-faculty ratio	9:1

Popular majors Biology, Engineering, Economics, English, Management, Pol. Science, Psychology

Multicultural student clubs and organizations Black Student Union, Africa Student Assoc., Burmese Cultural Assoc., Caribbean Students Assoc., Chinese Culture Assoc., Common Ground, Essential, Filipino Club, Gender & Sexuality Alliance, Japan Society, Latinx Alliance for Community & Opportunity, National Society of Black Engineers, Russian Culture Society, Society of Hispanic Prof. Engineers, South Asian Students Assoc., Students for Asian Awareness, Ubuntu

AFFORDABILITY

Cost of Attendance

tuition	$53,692
required fees	$294
room and board	$13,150

Financial Aid

total institutional scholarships/grants	$57,000,000
% of students with financial need	62
% of students with need awarded any financial aid	100
% of students with need awarded any need-based scholarship or grant aid	52
% of students with need whose need was fully met	n/a
% Pell Grant recipients among first-years	11
average aid package	$37,500
average student loan debt upon graduation	$22,600

ADMISSIONS

# of applicants	10,253
% admitted	31
SAT Evidence-Based Reading & Writing	620-700
SAT Math	630-720
ACT Composite	28-31
SAT/ACT optional	no
average HS GPA	3.77

DEADLINES

regular application closing date	1/15
early decision plan	yes
application closing date	11/15, 1/15
early action plan	no
application closing date	n/a
application fee	$40
application fee online	$40
fee waiver for applicants with financial need	yes

Carnegie Mellon University

Carnegie Mellon University
5000 Forbes Avenue
Pittsburgh, PA 15213
Ph: (412) 268-2082
www.cmu.edu

The Carnegie Mellon community is made up of highly talented students, faculty, staff, alumni, and parents from all over the world. As individuals, we have many kinds of creative talents and intellectual strengths; as a community, we are widely regarded as a place where people connect and collaborate across disciplines to solve critical societal challenges. Attracting and retaining a diverse community remains a significant challenge for Carnegie Mellon. We continue to work to recruit and retain students from under-represented backgrounds, including those who seek to be the first in their family to graduate from a four-year institution. The university is also focused on inclusive policies and practices that build a sense of community among people with many backgrounds, skills, and strengths.

Pre-College Prep & Outreach **Summer Academy for Math and Science**

The Summer Academy for Mathematics and Science is a rigorous residential summer experience for students who have a strong interest in computer science, engineering and/or natural sciences. Students who are entering their senior year and are considering careers in engineering, science and other math-based disciplines are eligible to apply. The summer academy's goal is to help students achieve essential skills necessary to pursue and complete majors in the STEM fields.

Open House, Fly-in, Visit **Celebration of Diversity Weekend**

Celebration of Diversity weekend is a three day program in which prospective students visit the university to experience the diverse community and academic, extracurricular and cultural facets of campus. The weekend activities include campus tours, student panels, information sessions and college/department open houses or tours, and an evening social activity on Saturday night, during which prospective students and any accompanying family members meet with academic faculty, staff, and other members of the university community to learn about their respective departments and programs.

Student Life & Support **The Center for Student Diversity & Inclusion**

The Center, in its inaugural year, offers resources to enhance an inclusive and transformative student experience in dimensions such as access, success, campus climate and intergroup dialogue. Additionally, The Center supports and connects historically underrepresented students and those who are first in their family to attend college in a setting where students' differences and talents are appreciated and reinforced.

First-Year Experience & Transition **ORIGINS**

ORIGINS is an overnight, pre-orientation retreat designed for underrepresented students at Carnegie Mellon to connect and create community with other incoming and upperclass students, faculty, staff and alumni.

Academic Advising & Support **Summer (re)CHARGE**

Summer (re)CHARGE is a campus-wide initiative designed to ensure that all students are able to take advantage of all that Carnegie Mellon University has to offer. This program is the perfect option for rising sophomores and juniors who are exploring a new major that might be a better fit, needing to enhance their academic profile, longing for a greater connection with the university community, interested in re-taking a pre-requisite course, or planning a return to the university after a leave of absence.

Fast Facts

STUDENT DIVERSITY	
# undergraduates	6,100+
% male/female	53/47
% first-generation college	n/a
% American Indian or Alaskan Native	<1
% Asian	28
% Black or African American	4
% Hispanic/Latino	8
% Native Hawaiian or Pacific Islander	<1
% White	28
% two or more races	4
% race and/or ethnicity unknown	5
% International/nonresident	23
STUDENT SUCCESS	
% first-to-second year retention	96
% six-year graduation	90
% six-year graduation for underrepresented minority groups	80
% first-years who live on campus	100
% undergraduates who live on campus	65
full-time faculty	1,260
full-time minority faculty	163
student-faculty ratio	13:1

Popular majors Engineering, Computer Science, Business, Visual & Performing Arts, Statistics, Mathematical Sciences, Interdisciplinary Studies

Multicultural student clubs and organizations SPIRIT - African-American awareness organization; SALSA - Spanish and Latin Students Association; MAPS - Minority Association of Pre-Med Students; NSBE - National Society of Black Engineers; SHPE - Society of Hispanic Professional Engineers; SWE - Society of Women Engineers; Women@SCS - Women in the School of Computer Science; Black and Latino Business Association; Colors@CMU; YALA - Young African Leaders Association

AFFORDABILITY	
Cost of Attendance	
tuition	$52,732
required fees	$1,178
room and board	$13,784
Financial Aid	
total institutional scholarships/grants	$85,686,658
% of students with financial need	42
% of students with need awarded any financial aid	99
% of students with need awarded any need-based scholarship or grant aid	45
% of students with need whose need was fully met	27
% Pell Grant recipients among first-years	14
average aid package	$40,347
average student loan debt upon graduation	$30,866
ADMISSIONS	
# of applicants	20,497
% admitted	22
SAT Critical Reading	660-760
SAT Math	690-790
ACT Composite	33
SAT/ACT optional	no
average HS GPA	3.78
DEADLINES	
regular application closing date	1/1
early decision plan	yes
application closing date	11/1
early action plan	n/a
application closing date	n/a
application fee	$75
application fee online	$75
fee waiver for applicants with financial need	yes

Cedar Crest College

Cedar Crest College
100 College Drive
Allentown, PA 18104
Ph: (610) 740-3780
www.cedarcrest.edu

Since its founding in 1867, Cedar Crest College has taken a bold approach to education—creating a college and a curriculum designed for women who want to achieve at the highest levels! Recognizing the multi-dimensional nature of students, Cedar Crest College is dedicated to the education of the next generation of women leaders by preparing the whole student for life in the global community.

First-Year Experience & Transition **First Year Experience (FYE)**

FYE is a program for all traditional first-year students, created to help you prepare for a successful life during and after college. With a focus on women's leadership, global connectivity, civic engagement, and health and wellness, the experience as a whole will help you make a smooth transition into the Cedar Crest College community of scholars. The program also helps you explore your career options, get involved with campus clubs and groups, build a network of resources, and establish healthy habits that add up to a well-balanced life.

Academic Advising & Support **4 Year Guarantee (4YG)**

At Cedar Crest, we are committed to making an exceptional education affordable. The 4YG program provides a clear path to graduation by eliminating costly excess credits. Academically qualified first-year students that are enrolled full-time in a four-year bachelor's degree program, with the exception of Nuclear Medicine Technology, work closely with an advisor and follow an academic plan that ensures they graduate in four years.

Academic Advising & Support **Academic Services and the Student Success Center**

Academic Services and the Student Success Center serve as a resource to empower all students to become independent learners and active members of their community by providing holistic guidance in a creative and safe environment. We are committed to delivering inclusive, comprehensive, and free of charge resources and services that foster self-directed learning, confidence, and academic success.

Academic Courses & Service Learning **The Carmen Twillie Ambar Sophomore Expedition**

Studying abroad is a high-impact experience that invokes a new way of thinking.Cedar Crest makes it a priority to provide each student with a global experience. The Carmen Twillie Ambar Sophomore Expedition allows full-time traditional students (with a 2.5 GPA and in good judicial and financial standing) the opportunity to spend 7-10 days abroad in her sophomore year, with travel, lodging and meals fully funded by the college. The spring 2018 destination is Rio de Janeiro, Brazil, and the 2019 destination is Athens, Greece. Where will you go?

Mentoring **Student Employment Center**

The Student Employment Center (SEC) allows students to earn money while gaining valuable work experience during their college journey. The SEC strives to place students in campus departments and positions that align with their major and/or future career aspirations and help them develop soft skills that are critical when applying for internships and job opportunities.

Student Life & Support **Center for Diversity and Inclusion (CDI)**

The CDI supports Cedar Crest College's diversity statement through its educational programming and services. The CDI will provide resources that foster awareness as well as empower students with knowledge, tools and experiences that promote global citizenship and a more inclusive campus. The CDI also serves as an advocate for our diverse student population.

Fast Facts

STUDENT DIVERSITY

# undergraduates	1,433
% male/female	13/87
% first-generation college	37
% American Indian or Alaskan Native	0
% Asian	3
% Black or African American	8
% Hispanic/Latino	14
% Native Hawaiian or Pacific Islander	0
% White	59
% two or more races	1
% race and/or ethnicity unknown	7
% International/nonresident	8

STUDENT SUCCESS

% first-to-second year retention	82
% six-year graduation	50
% six-year graduation for underrepresented minority groups	n/a
% first-years who live on campus	74
% undergraduates who live on campus	32
full-time faculty	77
full-time minority faculty	n/a
student-faculty ratio	10:1

Popular majors Nursing, Forensic Science, Biology, Genetic Engineering, Art Therapy, New Media

Multicultural student clubs and organizations Black Student Union (BSU), Cultural Connections Club, FADED, International Student Organization (ISO), OutThere, Spanish Club

AFFORDABILITY

Cost of Attendance

tuition	$37,492
required fees	$950
room and board	$11,208

Financial Aid

total institutional scholarships/grants	$5,091,251
% of students with financial need	94
% of students with need awarded any financial aid	100
% of students with need awarded any need-based scholarship or grant aid	78
% of students with need whose need was fully met	22
% Pell Grant recipients among first-years	46
average aid package	$33,646
average student loan debt upon graduation	$38,726

ADMISSIONS

# of applicants	1,208
% admitted	63
SAT Critical Reading	480-600
SAT Math	460-570
SAT Writing	n/a
ACT Composite	19-26
SAT/ACT optional	n/a
average HS GPA	3.44

DEADLINES

regular application closing date	rolling
early decision plan	n/a
application closing date	n/a
early action plan	n/a
application closing date	n/a
application fee	n/a
application fee online	n/a
fee waiver for applicants with financial need	n/a

Chatham University

Founded in 1869, Chatham University is a fully coed institution with an enrollment of over 2,200 students and over 60 undergraduate and graduate programs in our areas of excellence: sustainability; health & lab sciences; business & communication; and the arts & humanities. Chatham has historically served a high percentage of first generation and Pell eligible students and continues to focus on access and affordability for all students. Chatham University's mission is to prepare women and men to be world ready: to build lives of purpose and value and fulfilling work. In addition to appropriate professional skills and liberal arts learning, Chatham believes that world readiness means being an informed and engaged citizen in one's communities; recognizing and respecting diversity of culture, identity and opinion; and living sustainably on the planet.

Pre-College Prep & Outreach **College Counseling & Support**

The Chatham University Office of Admission and Financial Aid partners with schools and Community Based Organizations to support early awareness and education about college access and affordability. Financial FAFSA workshops are provided and on-campus FAFSA filing resources are offered throughout the academic year and by appointment. Admission officers provide educational presentations to middle school through high school audiences, incorporating parents in the college readiness conversation.

First-Year Experience & Transition **SDE101 – Strategies for Successful Transition to College**

All new first year students take a 1 credit course, taught by a student affairs professional, which focuses on college transition skills, resiliency, major exploration and career preparation. In 2017, a specific section designated for first generation students will be available.

Academic Advising & Support **Academic Support, Advising and Supplemental Instruction**

PACE Center PACE academic skill–building services are based on two core beliefs: Chatham University is an intellectual community committed to empowering each of its members; Students are individuals with unique needs and preferences. As a result, we make available an array of resources and strategies including learning–skills coaching in the following areas: Goal–setting, including motivation and planning; Note–taking methods; Procrastination management; Study strategies training; Textbook reading strategies; Time management skills; Transitions: Essential Skills for Success at Chatham course; and Writing academic papers.

Academic Advising & Support **The Chatham Plan**

The Chatham Plan is a four year plan that student's design in collaboration with their academic advisor and the career development office. The Chatham Plan ensures that "day one - year one" students are thinking about and planning for their career. The Chatham Plan helps students to stay on track for graduation and have a solid plan for developing their career aspirations.

Student Life & Support **RISE: Retain. Involve. Strengthen. Excel**

RISE is a retention program designed to increase the academic success, professionalism and leadership skills of students of color at Chatham University. This is a two-year program that provides new students of color a mentor, institutional support and a series of co-curricular programming throughout a two-year transition period into college. Through regular monthly meetings, special events as well as semester retreats, members of RISE have the opportunity to learn and grow as contributing members of the Chatham community.

Chatham University
1 Woodland Road
Pittsburgh, PA 15232
Ph: (412) 365-1825
admissions@chatham.edu
www.chatham.edu

Fast Facts

STUDENT DIVERSITY

# undergraduates	1,208
% male/female	17/83
% first-generation college	30
% American Indian or Alaskan Native	<1
% Asian	2
% Black or African American	7
% Hispanic/Latino	3
% Native Hawaiian or Pacific Islander	n/a
% White	51
% two or more races	2
% race and/or ethnicity unknown	25
% International/nonresident	10

STUDENT SUCCESS

% first-to-second year retention	85
% six-year graduation	63
% six-year graduation for underrepresented minority groups	40
% first-years who live on campus	91
% undergraduates who live on campus	50
full-time faculty	114
full-time minority faculty	27
student-faculty ratio	11:1

Popular majors Biology, Chemistry, Exercise Science, Business & Accounting, Sustainability, Psychology, History & Political Science

Multicultural student clubs and organizations Asian Culture Association Black Student Union (BSU) Chabad House at Chatham Chatham Chinese Scholar Student Association (CSSA) Feminist Activists Creating Equality (F.A.C.E.) Gateway Student Association (GSA) - for students 23 years and older Girl Up Muslim Student Association R.I.S.E student club This is me! – Gay Straight Alliance

AFFORDABILITY

Cost of Attendance

tuition	$35,220
required fees	$1,290
room and board	$10,834

Financial Aid

total institutional scholarships/grants	$9,451,857
% of students with financial need	60
% of students with need awarded any financial aid	99
% of students with need awarded any need-based scholarship or grant aid	77
% of students with need whose need was fully met	5
% Pell Grant recipients among first-years	31
average aid package	$28,239
average student loan debt upon graduation	$25,292

ADMISSIONS

# of applicants	2,950
% admitted	47
SAT Critical Reading	485-585
SAT Math	470-560
SAT Writing	460-580
ACT Composite	24
SAT/ACT optional	yes
average HS GPA	3.69

DEADLINES

regular application closing date	rolling
early decision plan	n/a
application closing date	n/a
early action plan	n/a
application closing date	n/a
application fee	n/a
application fee online	n/a
fee waiver for applicants with financial need	n/a

Dickinson College

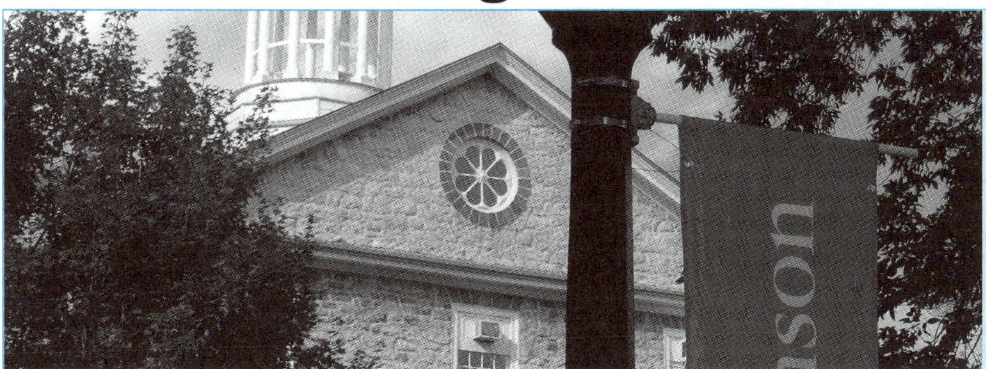

Dickinson is a nationally recognized liberal-arts college chartered in 1783 in Carlisle, Pa. Devoted to its revolutionary roots, the college maintains the mission of founder Benjamin Rush to provide a useful education for the common good. Dickinson offers 43 majors plus minors and certificate programs, and our global curriculum includes 13 languages and a variety of globally oriented courses. Dickinson is a diverse community—including individuals from majority populations, historically under-represented populations, international students and scholars, as well as those from various socioeconomic levels—bringing a wide variety of ideas, attitudes and beliefs, all thriving on the exchange of opinions, individual expression and celebration of our backgrounds and experiences.

Open House, Fly-in, Visit **Discover Diversity**

Discover Diversity is a three-day overnight program designed for promising high-school seniors who self-identify as students of color and/or will be first-generation college students. Participants will stay with a student host, attend classes, meet members of Dickinson's renowned faculty, collaborate with staff in workshops and connect with current students. Participants will also join visiting families during the fall open house prior to our first application deadline (Nov. 15).

Scholarship & Financial Aid **Financial Aid Access, Need-Based Aid and Merit Scholarships**

Dickinson is committed to affordability ensuring our students are able to access programs to make a Dickinson education possible. Dickinson offers need-based aid and academically competitive merit scholarships regardless of financial need as we seek to assemble a class that will contribute to our distinctive community. Special opportunities include the Posse Foundation, Yellow Ribbon Program, Public Service Fellowship and Community College Partnership.

First-Year Experience & Transition **First-Year Program**

Dickinson's First-Year Program is designed to help students make the transition from high school to college by supporting them while encouraging independence. The academic cornerstone of the first semester is the First-Year Seminar. Taught by the professor who will be your academic advisor, this class is designed to help you develop habits of mind that are essential to liberal learning, including critical thinking, analytical writing and information literacy skills. First-Year Groups (FYGs), run by a first-year mentor, provide experiences out of the classroom that help students connect with upper level students who share their interests and a staff mentor. Optional Pre-Orientation Adventure programs actively engage students in exciting student-run outdoor activities, community service or a theater project, just to name a few.

Academic Advising & Support **College Deans**

Dickinson is committed to providing both a rigorous, liberal-arts education and a generous, welcoming community. All students have a consistent faculty advisor and a college dean for all four years at Dickinson. The college dean helps students make the most of their Dickinson experience, whether by finding your niche or expanding beyond it, addressing your concerns or celebrating your accomplishments. One of the best ways the deans offer assistance is by helping students connect—with a professor who shares their interests, with other students who share their goals, or with members of the community with whom they can share their concerns.

Mentoring **Mentoring & Support**

Students benefit from one-on-one mentoring opportunities inside and outside the classroom. Faculty advisors form strong bonds with their advisees, a peer tutoring program provides ways to meet students' individual needs and a writing center and other support services are available.

Dickinson College
P.O. Box 1773
Carlisle, PA 17013
Ph: (800) 644-1773
admissions@dickinson.edu
www.dickinson.edu

Fast Facts

STUDENT DIVERSITY

# undergraduates	2,420
% male/female	41/59
% first-generation college	13
% American Indian or Alaskan Native	<1
% Asian	3
% Black or African American	5
% Hispanic/Latino	7
% Native Hawaiian or Pacific Islander	<1
% White	69
% two or more races	4
% race and/or ethnicity unknown	1
% International/nonresident	10

STUDENT SUCCESS

% first-to-second year retention	90
% six-year graduation	84
% six-year graduation for underrepresented minority groups	84
% first-years who live on campus	100
% undergraduates who live on campus	94
full-time faculty	225
full-time minority faculty	28
student-faculty ratio	9:1

Popular majors Economics, International Business & Management, Biology, Psychology, Political Science

Multicultural student clubs and organizations
Anwar Bellydance, Asian Pacific Assoc, Black Student Union, Chinese Students & Scholars Assoc, Greek (Kappa Alpha Psi, Sigma Lambda Beta, Sigma Lambda Gamma), Hypnotic Hip Hop Team, Kingdom Builders, Kpop Club, Latin Amer & Caribbean Club, Muslim Educ & Cultural Assoc, She's the First Dickinson, Sister Circle, We Introduce Nations

AFFORDABILITY

Cost of Attendance

tuition	$52,480
required fees	$450
room and board	$13,236

Financial Aid

total institutional scholarships/grants	$49,620,750
% of students with financial need	55
% of students with need awarded any financial aid	100
% of students with need awarded any need-based scholarship or grant aid	98
% of students with need whose need was fully met	85
% Pell Grant recipients among first-years	14
average aid package	$43,737
average student loan debt upon graduation	$26,908

ADMISSIONS

# of applicants	6,172
% admitted	43
SAT Critical Reading	590-680
SAT Math	610-705
SAT Writing	600-690
ACT Composite	29
SAT/ACT optional	yes
average HS GPA	n/a

DEADLINES

regular application closing date	1/15
early decision plan	yes
application closing date	11/15
early action plan	yes
application closing date	12/1
application fee	$65
application fee online	$65
fee waiver for applicants with financial need	yes

Elizabethtown College

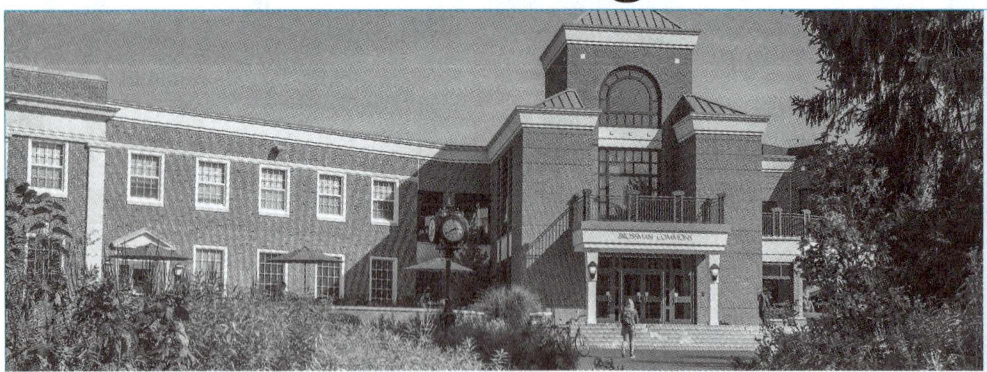

Since 1899, Elizabethtown College has been focused on educating first-generation students. With a mission to provide higher education for first-generation students who would return to the community as civic leaders, College founders adopted "Educate for Service" as its motto. Presently, about 34 percent of students are first-generation and represent a range of racial, ethnic, religious, socio/ economic and LBGTQA diversity. E-town's programming reflects this diversity and support students in their academic and personal development. With history rooted in peace, social justice and community service, commitment to inclusive excellence is evident in recruitment and retention of administrators, faculty, staff and students. E-town's curriculum, academic advising, mentoring philosophy and student life programming is consistently tailored to first-generation students.

Summer Bridge & Orientation **Momentum**

The Momentum program helps students learn how to navigate the curriculum requirements, think critically, develop research and writing skills, engage in creative expression, and find a balance between curricular and co-curricular involvement.

Summer Bridge & Orientation **First Year Experience**

During the First-Year Experience program students embark on a common learning experience with others in the incoming class. The First-Year Experience has three components: first year seminar, first-year advising and first-year honor society.

Scholars & Leadership **Global Scholars Program**

The Global Scholars Program allows students, supervised by a faculty mentor, to study international and peace related issues, and to participate in relevant co-curricular opportunities.

Scholars & Leadership **Summer Scholarship, Creative Arts and Research Projects Program (SCARP)**

The SCARP is an experiential learning program designed to enhance professional skills and provide a competitive advantage in the pursuit of career opportunities and graduate studies.

Academic Courses & Service Learning **Social Enterprise Institute (SEI)**

The SEI brings together faculty members, industry fellows of the Institute and students, to collaborate on social enterprise development initiatives that create sustainable social and economic value both domestically and internationally. These social enterprises are revenue-generating businesses with a mission to maximize improvements in human and environmental well-being, rather than maximizing profits for external shareholders.

Academic Courses & Service Learning **Sophomore Year Experience**

The Sophomore Experience program helps each student determine his or her distinct path in terms of career goals, life aspirations, and the practical steps (such as engaging in undergraduate research, internships, and study abroad) that will render those objectives achievable.

Mentoring **Eight Mentoring Programs**

We offer eight mentoring programs: (1) First Year Seminar Student Peer Mentors for acclimation to college life; (2) Momentum Student Peer Academic Advisors for academic support; (3) Sophomore student mentors for vocational discernment; (4) Student mentors for first generation students in the Honors program; (5) Student athlete mentors for first generation student athletes; (6) Student mentors for international students; (7) Faculty/Staff mentors for purposeful life work; (8) Alumni mentors for first generation students from diverse backgrounds.

Elizabethtown College
One Alpha Drive
Elizabethtown, PA 17022
Ph: (717) 361-1400
admissions@etown.edu
www.etown.edu

Fast Facts

STUDENT DIVERSITY

# undergraduates	1,647
% male/female	38/62
% first-generation college	34
% American Indian or Alaskan Native	<1
% Asian	3
% Black or African American	3
% Hispanic/Latino	4
% Native Hawaiian or Pacific Islander	<1
% White	85
% two or more races	2
% race and/or ethnicity unknown	<1
% International/nonresident	2

STUDENT SUCCESS

% first-to-second year retention	87
% six-year graduation	75
% six-year graduation for underrepresented minority groups	70
% first-years who live on campus	96
% undergraduates who live on campus	84
full-time faculty	128
full-time minority faculty	21
student-faculty ratio	13:1

Popular majors Occupational Therapy, Business Administration, Biology, Engineering, Education

Multicultural student clubs and organizations NOiR, Allies, Queer Student Union, CRU, Hillel, Neumann Club, Intervarsity Christian Fellowship. In addition, the Democrats club also has a lot of diversity-related programming.

AFFORDABILITY

Cost of Attendance

tuition	$45,350
required fees	n/a
room and board	$10,990

Financial Aid

total institutional scholarships/grants	$36,081,267
% of students with financial need	76
% of students with need awarded any financial aid	100
% of students with need awarded any need-based scholarship or grant aid	100
% of students with need whose need was fully met	23
% Pell Grant recipients among first-years	22
average aid package	$33,166
average student loan debt upon graduation	$27,000

ADMISSIONS

# of applicants	3,033
% admitted	74
SAT Reading & Writing	540-640
SAT Math	530-640
ACT Composite	22-27
SAT/ACT optional	n/a
average HS GPA	n/a

DEADLINES

regular application closing date	3/1
early decision plan	yes
application closing date	rolling
early action plan	n/a
application closing date	n/a
application fee	n/a
application fee online	n/a
fee waiver for applicants with financial need	yes

Gettysburg College

Gettysburg College, a historic institution with a reputation for academic excellence, provides students with a liberal arts education characterized by academic intensity and learning by getting involved. Founded in 1832 by anti-slavery theologian Samuel Simon Schmucker, Gettysburg College prides itself on a 9:1 student-faculty ratio that fosters close relationships and spirited class discussions. As champions for independent thinking and public action, Gettysburg students graduate with a love of learning, knowledge and skills they need for success and new insight into the world, their place in it, and their obligations to it. Gettysburg College engages highly motivated students in a comprehensive educational experience that prepares them for lives of personal fulfillment, career success and responsible, engaged citizenship.

Scholarship & Financial Aid **Making College Affordable for All Students**

Gettysburg College is committed to working with students and their families to ensure that one's ability to pay not become an obstacle to a Gettysburg education. Approximately 66 percent of all students receive some form of financial aid, and the average aid package exceeds $41,000 a year. Most aid is awarded based on financial need, but academic merit and music talent scholarships are also available.

First-Year Experience & Transition **First-Year Residential College Program**

First year students' residence hall assignments are linked to First-Year Seminar and College Writing courses, which help extend class discussions into the less formal arena of the living environment and promotes the open exchange of ideas. The First-Year Residential College Program benefits new students by easing their transition to college life, introducing them to the kind of thoughtful conversation that is characteristic of a great liberal arts education, enriching their learning and serving as a kind of academic ice-breaker, and helping them to build relationships with hallmates. The program also offers opportunities for peer tutoring, faculty counseling and mentoring with upper-class students.

Student Life & Support **Office of Multicultural Engagement (OME)**

OME celebrates Gettysburg's diversity by providing a warm and affirming home on campus for students from all backgrounds and by sponsoring activities that build mutual respect and understanding. OME brings speakers to campus who address topics related to diversity, provides services such as tutoring and mentoring, runs discussion groups to foster open conversation on important issues and offers a variety of other services to create a welcoming atmosphere on campus. It has a particular commitment to the development of African American, Asian American, Latino and American Indian students as well as providing support for International students.

Gettysburg College
300 N. Washington St.
Gettysburg, PA 17325
Ph: (800) 431-0803
admiss@gettysburg.edu
www.gettysburg.edu

Fast Facts

STUDENT DIVERSITY

# undergraduates	2,384
% male/female	47/53
% first-generation college	n/a
% American Indian or Alaskan Native	<1
% Asian	2
% Black or African American	3
% Hispanic/Latino	6
% Native Hawaiian or Pacific Islander	<1
% White	77
% two or more races	3
% race and/or ethnicity unknown	2
% International/nonresident	7

STUDENT SUCCESS

% first-to-second year retention	90
% six-year graduation	87
% six-year graduation for underrepresented minority groups	85
% first-years who live on campus	100
% undergraduates who live on campus	94
full-time faculty	223
full-time minority faculty	38
student-faculty ratio	9:1

Popular majors Organization and Management Studies, Political Science, Psychology, Biology, English, Economics, History

Multicultural student clubs and organizations Office of Multicultural Engagement, Black Student Union, Asian Student Alliance, LASA (Latin American Students' Association), International Club, China Club, Slavic Club, Vietnamese Student Association, Gettysburg African Student Association, Muslim Student Association, Hillel

AFFORDABILITY

Cost of Attendance

tuition	$52,640
required fees	n/a
room and board	$12,570

Financial Aid

total institutional scholarships/grants	$48,246,964
% of students with financial need	56
% of students with need awarded any financial aid	98
% of students with need awarded any need-based scholarship or grant aid	95
% of students with need whose need was fully met	88
% Pell Grant recipients among first-years	15
average aid package	$41,554
average student loan debt upon graduation	$22,221

ADMISSIONS

# of applicants	6,816
% admitted	43
SAT Critical Reading	600-680
SAT Math	610-680
SAT Writing	n/a
ACT Composite	26-30
SAT/ACT optional	yes
average HS GPA	n/a

DEADLINES

regular application closing date	1/15
early decision plan	yes
application closing date	11/15
early action plan	no
application closing date	n/a
application fee	$60
application fee online	$60
fee waiver for applicants with financial need	yes

Juniata College

One of the 40 colleges featured in the book *Colleges That Change Lives*, Juniata is a cohesive community of interesting, inquisitive, hardworking, and fun individuals who think deeply about who we are meant to be. We come to this place of stunning natural beauty—this oasis in the woods—because it provides for us the perfect backdrop for reflecting upon, deciding upon, and designing our individual pathways to rewarding careers and lives of meaning and happiness. Those who share this experience with us are compelling, talented, and inevitably surprising. Each of us has our own story and way of looking at the world. And yet we meet as friends—and partners—whether we are students, professors, staff, alumni, or community members. We support each other's journeys. We learn from and with each other. We enjoy one another. And we take Juniata with us no matter where we go. We believe there is no better place on the planet for discovering your passions, developing your intellect and your heart, and ultimately becoming the author of your own powerful story.

Summer Bridge Orientation **Plexus Inbound**

Juniata's Plexus Inbound retreat is an orientation event held just prior to the start of the school year in August. Plexus is designed to allow new students with concerns about multiculturalism to meet other new and returning students and share friendship, support, and guidance.

The event will not only give students insight into the ways in which diversity is being integrated into college life, but also will highlight the opportunities for cultural experiences and the resources available both here on campus as well as within the surrounding communities.

Student Life & Support **Beyond Tolerance Series**

Innovative, informative, and interactive. Juniata's commitment to inclusion goes public each year with BeyondTolerance—a series of lectures, workshops, screenings of films, and travel opportunities designed to help us learn more about one another and better discuss challenging issues. Whether discussing cultural differences or expanding the varied meanings of diversity, the Beyond Tolerance series helps move all of us beyond simply tolerating one another and toward challenging what we think we know about one another.

Student Life & Support **Commitment to Diversity**

In 2015 Juniata was awarded *Insight into Diversity Magazines* Higher Education Excellence in Diversity Award for our level of achievement and intensity of commitment in regard to broadening diversity and inclusion on campus.

Mentoring **Plexus**

The word "plexus" is taken from the Latin plectere, which means to weave or braid and is literally a network of interwoven parts. This name was chosen not only to be symbolic of the physical support network that is comprised of peer mentors, faculty and staff members with whom our mentees will interact but also the holistic approach we have taken in caring for students' well-being. At Juniata, Plexus is the umbrella that overarches the Plexus Inbound group, the Plexus RSO (registered student organization), and the Plexus Fellowship Program.

Juniata College
1700 Moore Street
Huntingdon, PA 16652
Ph: (814) 641-3420
www.juniata.edu
think.juniata.edu

Fast Facts

STUDENT DIVERSITY

# undergraduates	1,573
% male/female	44/56
% first-generation college	23
% American Indian or Alaskan Native	<1
% Asian	2
% Black or African American	3
% Hispanic/Latino	9
% Native Hawaiian or Pacific Islander	<1
% White	84
% two or more races	4
% race and/or ethnicity unknown	2
% International/nonresident	11

STUDENT SUCCESS

% first-to-second year retention	86
% six-year graduation	79
% six-year graduation for underrepresented minority groups	77
% first-years who live on campus	99
% undergraduates who live on campus	88
full-time faculty	105
full-time minority faculty	7
student-faculty ratio	13:1

Popular majors Education, Chemistry, Psychology, Biology, Health Professions, Environmental Science, Business

Multicultural student clubs and organizations African American Student Alliance, Burmese Club, UBUNTU, Chinese Club, French Club, German Club, Plexus Club, Otaku Cultural Club

AFFORDABILITY

Cost of Attendance

tuition	$44,770
required fees	$825
room and board	$12,520

Financial Aid

total institutional scholarships/grants	n/a
% of students with financial need	82
% of students with need awarded any financial aid	100
% of students with need awarded any need-based scholarship or grant aid	100
% of students with need whose need was fully met	90
% Pell Grant recipients among first-years	29
average aid package	$33,000
average student loan debt upon graduation	$36,500

ADMISSIONS

# of applicants	2,350
% admitted	70
SAT Critical Reading	540-650
SAT Math	540-640
SAT Writing	n/a
ACT Composite	25-28
SAT/ACT optional	yes
average HS GPA	3.72

DEADLINES

regular application closing date	2/15
early decision plan	yes
application closing date	11/15
early action plan	yes
application closing date	1/5
application fee	n/a
application fee online	n/a
fee waiver for applicants with financial need	n/a

Lafayette College

For more than 175 years, Lafayette has been known for a spirit of exploration that ignores boundaries, where faculty work with students across disciplines to tackle challenges and solve problems. The ability to make connections and think critically is paramount: on campus, off campus, and after graduation.

Open House, Fly-in, Visit **Our Beloved Community**

Lafayette College invites you to apply to the Annual Our Beloved Community (OBC) Symposium. Our Beloved Community is named for Dr. Martin Luther King Jr.'s vision of a society that embraces each of its members, not merely putting aside but rather understanding and celebrating their differences. We seek a limited number of students nationwide to join the Lafayette community in this celebratory event that will feature interactive discussions on a variety of social justice topics. If you have any questions or would like additional information, please contact Alex Bates at batesa@lafayette.edu.

First-Year Experience & Transition **Summer Program to Advance Leadership (SPAL)**

Summer Program to Advance Leadership (SPAL) is a comprehensive six-week program that exposes students to Lafayette and college courses. Students in the program take a math course and a writing course, participate in lab modules in the sciences and engineering, and visit local employers of scientists and engineers. Through the program students begin their career counseling, learn about study abroad, and find out about all the other academic opportunities available to them at Lafayette.

Academic Advising & Support **The Academic Tutoring and Training Information Center (ATTIC)**

The Academic Tutoring and Training Information Center (ATTIC) provides academic services to enhance student success in an educational environment that can be demanding and challenging. ATTIC programs include peer tutoring, study skills workshops, academic counseling, disability services, academic support services for student athletes, and supplemental instruction.

Academic Courses & Service Learning **President's McDonogh Lecture Series**

The President's McDonogh Lecture Series brings scholars to campus who have gained prominent attention for their work with multicultural education and diversity issues. Speakers invited to campus may participate in events that can include a campus lecture, student leadership development, course teach-in, and discussion with administration and interested faculty.

Student Life & Support **Kaleidoscope**

Kaleidoscope encourages students to take an active role in promoting intercultural exchange and exploring issues of multiculturalism, equity and social justice. Through the facilitation of critical conversations, Kaleidoscope leaders are uniquely poised among their peers to raise awareness, promote inclusiveness and prompt genuine celebration of differences across campus. Student Coordinators of Peer Education (SCOPEs) are invited into various spaces on campus to facilitate in-depth dialogue on a particular social justice related topic.

Student Life & Support **Multicultural Competency Training**

Lafayette College believes all of our graduates should possess multicultural Awareness, Skills and Knowledge. Many of Lafayette's student leaders take part in our Multicultural Competency Training (MCT) program to develop or enhance their cultural awareness, skills and knowledge. The MCT program consists of three independent, but progressive tracks, and student leaders advance through the program as their campus leadership continues.

Lafayette College
730 High Street
Easton, PA 18042
Ph: (610) 330-5100
admissions@lafayette.edu
www.lafayette.edu

Fast Facts

STUDENT DIVERSITY

# undergraduates	2,565
% male/female	49/51
% first-generation college	14
% American Indian or Alaskan Native	0
% Asian	4
% Black or African American	5
% Hispanic/Latino	7
% Native Hawaiian or Pacific Islander	<1
% White	66
% two or more races	3
% race and/or ethnicity unknown	6
% International/nonresident	10

STUDENT SUCCESS

% first-to-second year retention	95
% six-year graduation	90
% six-year graduation for underrepresented minority groups	86
% first-years who live on campus	100
% undergraduates who live on campus	93
full-time faculty	237
full-time minority faculty	46
student-faculty ratio	10:1

Popular majors Economics, Biology, Engineering, Psychology, International Affairs, English

Multicultural student clubs and organizations ACACIA (African Consciousness), Global China Connection, International Students Association, NIA (Multicultural Women's Support Group), Portlock Black Cultural Center, Minority Scientists and Engineers, English as a Second Language (ESL), C.H.A.N.C.E. (Creating Harmony and Necessary Cultural Equality), H.O.L.A. (Heritage of Latin America), and more!

AFFORDABILITY

Cost of Attendance

tuition	$52,415
required fees	$1,215
room and board	$15,640

Financial Aid

total institutional scholarships/grants	$39,929,294
% of students with financial need	30
% of students with need awarded any financial aid	100
% of students with need awarded any need-based scholarship or grant aid	100
% of students with need whose need was fully met	100
% Pell Grant recipients among first-years	13
average aid package	$49,361
average student loan debt upon graduation	$21,700

ADMISSIONS

# of applicants	8,469
% admitted	31
SAT Evidence-Based Reading & Writing	630-710
SAT Math	630-730
ACT Composite	28-31
SAT/ACT optional	no
average HS GPA	n/a

DEADLINES

regular application closing date	1/15
early decision plan	yes
application closing date	ED1: 11/15, ED2: 1/15
early action plan	n/a
application closing date	n/a
application fee	$65
application fee online	$65
fee waiver for applicants with financial need	yes

Lycoming College

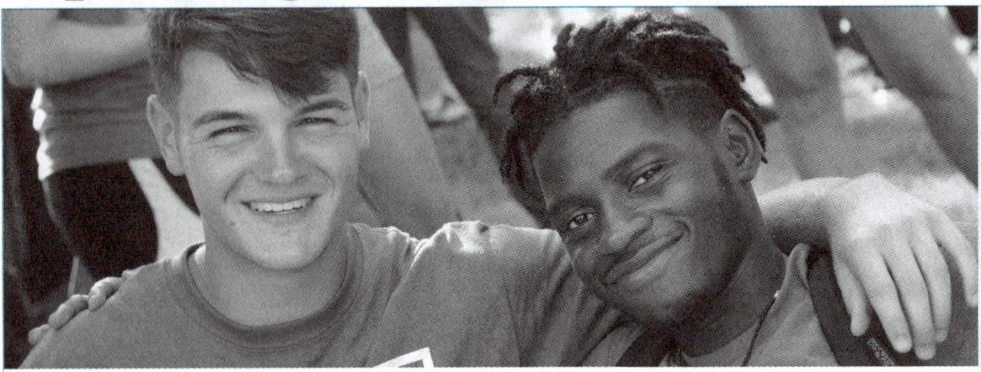

Lycoming College is a four-year, private liberal arts institution dedicated to the undergraduate education of 1,300 students. By design, Lycoming is focused exclusively on undergraduate education and offers a vibrant, residential community where 87 percent of students live on campus in a welcoming and supportive environment with nurturing faculty and staff that help to foster successful student outcomes. At Lycoming, we are not just teaching skills, we are teaching students to learn and to gain valuable hands-on experience through shared research with faculty members, as well as through internships, both on and off campus, through global travel. That difference means a graduate who is prepared for the careers of the future.

After four years at Lycoming, graduates are equipped with a 21st-century education—the knowledge, skills and adaptability to walk confidently into an ever-changing world as citizens dedicated to service, leadership and achievement, and to lead lives of meaning.

Pre-College Summer Experience **Lycoming College Prep**

"Opening eyes and minds to the possibilities" is the spirit of Lycoming College Prep, a pre-collegiate enrichment program that brings high-achieving, first-generation rising seniors from across the nation at our partnership schools to Lycoming College for two weeks in the summer. We invite both partnership and local school students to "imagine the possibilities," with a goal of providing a rich and diverse hands-on introduction to the liberal arts and to college life at our beautiful campus nestled near the banks of the Susquehanna River in Williamsport, Pa.

First-Year Experience & Transition **First-Year Experience & Transitioning**

New students need time to adjust to different surroundings, recover from jet lag and begin building new friendships before they feel ready to start classes. Lycoming can help with all of these things. The College's first-year student transition program—separate from traditional June orientation—invites students to campus for a series of academic and first-year transition programs one week prior to the start of the academic year. The program is offered to entering international students, partnership and United States outer-territory students, a high-majority of whom are first-generation students. For those living in the United States for the first time, a small group of international students will be available to answer questions, show students around and help them acclimate to life on an American college campus.

Scholars & Leadership **Lycoming Scholars Program**

The Lycoming Scholars Program is specially designed to meet the needs and aspirations of high-achieving students. Lycoming Scholars satisfy the College's distribution requirements with more challenging courses, and Lycoming Scholars participate in interdisciplinary seminars, as well as in an independent study culminating in a senior presentation.

Academic Advising & Support **Academic Support**

The Academic Resource Center exists to support students' goals of achieving academic success. Any student can take a paper to the Writing Center, get a subject tutor or seek assistance in forming a study group for a class. Support systems include the Math and Writing Centers, Academic Coaching, Resident Student Mentoring or even Study Group Support. Under the guidance of a peer facilitator who has been hand-picked by faculty and trained by the Academic Resource Center, students in traditionally (and newly) challenging courses at Lycoming College have the opportunity to engage with classmates outside of the classroom. A kind of supplemental instruction, study groups provide students with a regular time and place to review course content, prepare for exams and develop academic success skills.

Lycoming College
700 College Place
Box 164
Williamsport, PA 17701
Ph: (800) 345-3920
admissions@lycoming.edu
www.lycoming.edu

Fast Facts

STUDENT DIVERSITY	
# undergraduates	1,223
% male/female	50/50
% first-generation college	24
% American Indian or Alaskan Native	<1
% Asian	1
% Black or African American	12
% Hispanic/Latino	10
% Native Hawaiian or Pacific Islander	<1
% White	62
% two or more races	3
% race and/or ethnicity unknown	6
% International/nonresident	5
STUDENT SUCCESS	
% first-to-second year retention	80
% six-year graduation	67
% six-year graduation for underrepresented minority groups	41
% first-years who live on campus	91
% undergraduates who live on campus	87
full-time faculty	89
full-time minority faculty	4
student-faculty ratio	12:1

Popular majors Psychology, Business, Biology, Criminal Justice & Criminology, Art

Multicultural student clubs and organizations Black Student Union, Circle K, International Japanese Culture Club, L.A.C.E.S., Multicultural Awareness Group, United Campus Ministries

AFFORDABILITY	
Cost of Attendance	
tuition	$37,888
required fees	$1,027
room and board	$11,980
Financial Aid	
total institutional scholarships/grants	$32,579,899
% of students with financial need	85
% of students with need awarded any financial aid	100
% of students with need awarded any need-based scholarship or grant aid	100
% of students with need whose need was fully met	n/a
% Pell Grant recipients among first-years	44
average aid package	$35,481
average student loan debt upon graduation	n/a
ADMISSIONS	
# of applicants	1,924
% admitted	64
SAT Evidence-Based Reading & Writing	490-600
SAT Math	498-600
ACT Composite	21-25
SAT/ACT optional	yes
average HS GPA	3.37
DEADLINES	
regular application closing date	rolling
early decision plan	yes
application closing date	11/15
early action plan	yes
application closing date	12/1
application fee	n/a
application fee online	n/a
fee waiver for applicants with financial need	yes

Mount Aloysius College

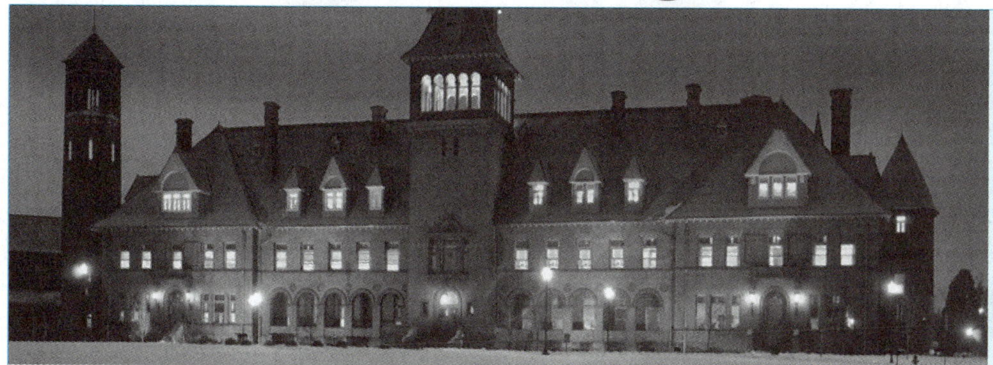

Mount Aloysius College
7373 Admiral Peary Hwy
Cresson, PA 16630
Ph: (888) 823-2220
www.mtaloy.edu

Mount Aloysius College is a private, comprehensive, Catholic liberal arts college sponsored by the Sisters of Mercy. Established in 1853, Mount Aloysius offers students undergraduate and graduate education. Since the founding of the College, nearly 17,000 men and women have become proud Mount Aloysius College graduates. The College is committed to providing students with small class sizes, dedicated faculty and a supportive learning community. There are over 2,500 students enrolled. Mount Aloysius sits in a beautiful rural setting, nestled on 193-acres in the southern Allegheny Mountains. The main building is an architectural marvel dating to 1897. Mount Aloysius offers 14 NCAA Division III sports. Sports include baseball, women's and men's basketball, cross-country, golf, soccer, tennis, women's bowling, softball and volleyball. Teams complete in the 10-member Allegheny Mountain Collegiate Conference (AMCC).

Pre-College Prep & Outreach **Accepted Student Day**

This takes place at the end of March to help bridge the gap between committing to Mount Aloysius College and starting your Orientation before classes begin. Accepted Student Day is fun – a full day with useful information, lots of focus on campus-life and introductions to every service provided on campus, each academic major, clubs, and athletics. Accepted Student Day is a great day to meet future classmates too, and learn even more about Mount Aloysius College.

Pre-College Summer Experience **Mount Aloysius Academic Preparation Program (MAAPP)**

Mount Aloysius Academic Preparation Program (MAAPP) is an academic preparatory program structured for first semester freshmen. MAAPP is aimed at giving program participants refresher courses to help them better prepare for college. MAAPP is a residential early entrance opportunity offering students an additional prep week aimed at easing the transition from high school to college. The ultimate goal is student success.

Open House, Fly-In, Visit **Open House and Horizon Days**

Mount Aloysius Open Houses are great opportunities for students and families to get a first-hand look at the College. Open House events are fun and activities take place throughout campus. Mount Aloysius President Tom Foley welcomes attendees to the Cresson, Pennsylvania campus. Campus tours are available all day, courtesy of Mount Aloysius students. Be sure to visit the College's gorgeous Athletic Convocation and Wellness Center situated on the western edge of our campus. Visit faculty during our Research Fair and learn more about great careers and academics from the professors who can take you through to Graduation Day. Have a question? Ask anyone. They will make it their business to get you to the right person with the answers you need.

Fast Facts

STUDENT DIVERSITY

# undergraduates	2,500
% male/female	32/68
% first-generation college	70
% American Indian or Alaskan Native	1
% Asian	2
% Black or African American	8
% Hispanic/Latino	2
% Native Hawaiian or Pacific Islander	<1
% White	87
% two or more races	n/a
% race and/or ethnicity unknown	1
% International/nonresident	7

STUDENT SUCCESS

% first-to-second year retention	72
% six-year graduation	n/a
% six-year graduation for underrepresented minority groups	n/a
% first-years who live on campus	75
% undergraduates who live on campus	36
full-time faculty	175
full-time minority faculty	n/a
student-faculty ratio	12:1

Popular majors Nursing, Medical Imaging, Business Administration, Criminology, Biology - Pre-Med
Multicultural student clubs and organizations

AFFORDABILITY

Cost of Attendance

tuition	$22,430
required fees	n/a
room and board	$9,880

Financial Aid

total institutional scholarships/grants	n/a
% of students with financial need	94
% of students with need awarded any financial aid	n/a
% of students with need awarded any need-based scholarship or grant aid	n/a
% of students with need whose need was fully met	n/a
% Pell Grant recipients among first-years	60
average aid package	$10,000
average student loan debt upon graduation	$25,000

ADMISSIONS

# of applicants	1,275
% admitted	65
SAT Critical Reading	425-535
SAT Math	420-525
SAT Writing	400-535
ACT Composite	20
SAT/ACT optional	no
average HS GPA	3.0

DEADLINES

regular application closing date	rolling
early decision plan	n/a
application closing date	n/a
early action plan	n/a
application closing date	n/a
application fee	$30
application fee online	$30
fee waiver for applicants with financial need	yes

Saint Francis University

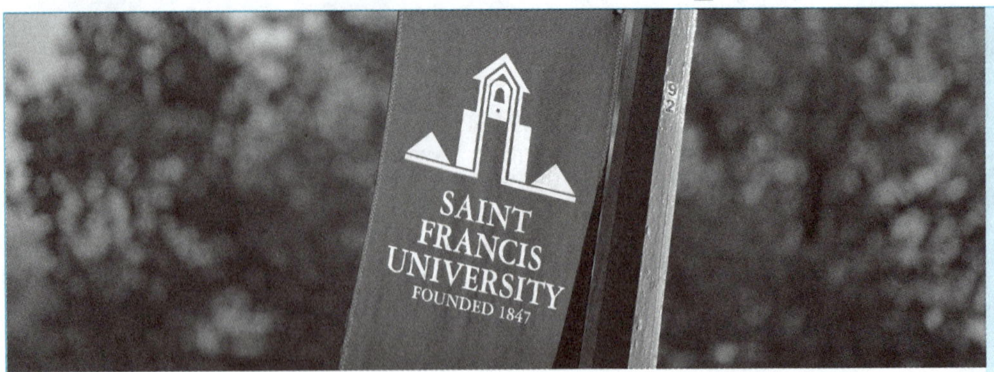

As a Franciscan institution located in rural Pennsylvania, Saint Francis University strives to imbue its students with "a mind for excellence, a spirit for peace and justice, and a mind for service." To this end, the university has opened the state-of-the-art DiSepio Institute for Rural Health and Wellness, an education and research center featuring physical training, conference, clinical, human performance laboratory and meditation spaces. It is used both to foster the science and health programs at the university and to help the school serve those suffering from illnesses common to rural areas. The oldest Franciscan institution of higher learning in the United States, Saint Francis University offers 25 undergraduate majors to nearly 2,000 students, and is an inclusive community that welcomes all people. By emphasizing values, skills and knowledge, each of its academic programs provides an understanding of Franciscan heritage, values and traditions.

Pre-College Prep & Outreach **Upward Bound**

Provided at no cost to participants, Upward Bound offers a wide variety of academic, career, cultural, and social development activities for high school students from Blair and Cambria counties. Each participant must come from a low-income family and/or be a potential first-generation college student. From September through May, the students participate in follow-ups held on campus and tutorials held after-school in their communities. Additional academic year activities include college visits, SAT sessions, and college fairs. During a six-week residential summer program, students attend academic classes each day and participate in a wide variety of cultural and recreational activities. Each summer Upward Bound Bridge students take Saint Francis University courses for credit.

Scholarship & Financial Aid **Scholarship Opportunities**

Saint Francis University believes every person who desires higher education has the right to pursue it. The university offers a variety of awards to supplement families' funds whenever possible, and aggressively seeks financial aid for those demonstrating need. The university offers a comprehensive program of merit-based scholarships, institutional grants, loans, part-time employment and federal and state financial assistance.

First-Year Experience & Transition **Opportunities for Academic Success in Studies Program**

Students are expected to meet with their counselor on a monthly basis through the Opportunities for Academic Success in Studies program, which is designed to assist first-year students who have not yet fully developed their academic potential. The program provides academic assistance and support services to enhance student growth, success, and persistence towards attaining a college degree. Although the support programming and services are important factors for success, the motivation to take advantage of these workshops and tutorials comes from within the student.

Saint Francis University
117 Evergreen Drive
Loretto, PA 15940
Ph: (814) 472-3100
admissions@francis.edu
www.francis.edu

Fast Facts

STUDENT DIVERSITY

# undergraduates	1,745
% male/female	39/61
% first-generation college	n/a
% American Indian or Alaskan Native	1
% Asian	1
% Black or African American	6
% Hispanic/Latino	2
% Native Hawaiian or Pacific Islander	1
% White	82
% two or more races	1
% race and/or ethnicity unknown	5
% International/nonresident	4

STUDENT SUCCESS

% first-to-second year retention	86
% six-year graduation	67
% six-year graduation for underrepresented minority groups	n/a
% first-years who live on campus	83
% undergraduates who live on campus	76
full-time faculty	130
full-time minority faculty	4
student-faculty ratio	14:1

Popular majors Accounting, Aquarium & Zoo Science, Chemistry, Computer Science, Digital Media, Environmental Studies, Fermentation Arts, Management Information Systems, Natural Gas & Petroleum Engineering, Public Health, Physical Therapy

Multicultural student clubs and organizations ASL Club, Center for International Education and Outreach, International Student Union, Student Government Association, Student Activities Organization

AFFORDABILITY

Cost of Attendance

tuition	$33,856
required fees	$1,100
room and board	$11,928

Financial Aid

total institutional scholarships/grants	$18,867,341
% of students with financial need	80
% of students with need awarded any financial aid	100
% of students with need awarded any need-based scholarship or grant aid	56
% of students with need whose need was fully met	20
% Pell Grant recipients among first-years	33
average aid package	$22,918
average student loan debt upon graduation	$27,113

ADMISSIONS

# of applicants	1,548
% admitted	75
SAT Evidence-Based Reading & Writing	510-610
SAT Math	510-610
SAT Writing	n/a
ACT Composite	23
SAT/ACT optional	no
average HS GPA	3.57

DEADLINES

regular application closing date	rolling
early decision plan	n/a
application closing date	n/a
early action plan	n/a
application closing date	n/a
application fee	$0
application fee online	$0
fee waiver for applicants with financial need	yes

Saint Vincent College

Saint Vincent College is a private, co-educational liberal arts college rooted in the tradition of the Catholic faith, the heritage of Benedictine monasticism and a liberal approach to life and learning. Founded to educate the children of immigrants, Saint Vincent takes a special interest in first-generation college students and offers a $2,000 First-Generation Grant, renewable for four years, to assist them with their education. Saint Vincent also encourages diversity; more than 20 percent of the incoming freshman class is made up of students of color. With a welcoming hospitality and an attention to individual needs, Saint Vincent teaches students to integrate their professional aims with the broader purposes of human life.

Pre-College Prep & Outreach **Step-Up Program**

The Step-Up Program offers homeschooled students from local communities, ranging from preschool age to grade 12, the opportunity to participate in one-hour enrichment courses held on the Saint Vincent campus. The program offers homeschoolers the opportunity to interact with other students with common interests, and to choose courses that specifically meet their interests while meeting curriculum requirements. It also assists older students with the transition to a college classroom setting.

Pre-College Prep & Outreach **The Challenge Program**

The Saint Vincent College campus transforms into a themed epic program for middle and high school students interested in an opportunity to explore academic enrichment courses, activities and evening events. While this program is being presented to students as Challenge, an "epic" enrichment program, the courses and activities are soundly based in academics, engaging activities and content-deepening experiences. Saint Vincent College Education Department is committed to bringing back the spirit of youth experiences while encouraging our young people to enjoy investigation, problem-solving, the arts and social activities in an accepting and safe environment.

Special Admissions Policy **The Opportunity SVC/ACT 101 Student Support Services (SSS)-TRiO Program**

The Opportunity SVC/Act 101/Student Support Services (SSS)-TRiO Program is an academic support system funded, in part, by the Commonwealth of Pennsylvania through Act 101 and by the U.S. Department of Education. Placement in the program is determined by the Admission Committee which evaluates the applicant's grades, test scores and recommendations. Program participants are required to complete a three-week, credit-bearing summer component where tutoring is provided by professional and peer tutors. In addition, a fall transitional semester is an added benefit of the program and provides ongoing academic support and counseling to the student throughout his or her college years.

Student Life & Support **Office of Multicultural and International Student Life**

The Office of Multicultural Student Life helps to connect the many national, ethnic and cultural groups of the Saint Vincent College community. The office offers special programming, activities such as the Dr. Martin Luther King Jr. Day of Remembrance, International Week, cultural workshops and community service trips, mentoring, on-campus employment opportunities and a special multicultural orientation.

Saint Vincent College
300 Fraser Purchase Road
Latrobe, PA 15650
Ph: (742) 805-2500
admission@stvincent.edu
www.stvincent.edu

Fast Facts

STUDENT DIVERSITY

# undergraduates	1,646
% male/female	52/48
% first-generation college	24
% American Indian or Alaskan Native	<1
% Asian	2
% Black or African American	5
% Hispanic/Latino	3
% Native Hawaiian or Pacific Islander	<1
% White	85
% two or more races	1
% race and/or ethnicity unknown	4
% International/nonresident	1

STUDENT SUCCESS

% first-to-second year retention	83
% six-year graduation	73
% six-year graduation for underrepresented minority groups	49
% first-years who live on campus	86
% undergraduates who live on campus	72
full-time faculty	102
full-time minority faculty	4
student-faculty ratio	12:1

Popular majors Biology, Communication, Education, Management, Psychology

Multicultural student clubs and organizations Visionaries of H.O.P.E. Club, and any of more than 50 clubs and organizations

AFFORDABILITY

Cost of Attendance

tuition	$33,516
required fees	$1,516
room and board	$11,136

Financial Aid

total institutional scholarships/grants	$30,909,377
% of students with financial need	76
% of students with need awarded any financial aid	100
% of students with need awarded any need-based scholarship or grant aid	64
% of students with need whose need was fully met	16
% Pell Grant recipients among first-years	27
average aid package	$30,476
average student loan debt upon graduation	$38,493

ADMISSIONS

# of applicants	2,494
% admitted	67
SAT Evidence-Based Reading & Writing	510-620
SAT Math	500-600
ACT Composite	23
SAT/ACT optional	no
average HS GPA	3.55

DEADLINES

regular application closing date	5/1
early decision plan	n/a
application closing date	n/a
early action plan	no
application closing date	n/a
application fee	$25
application fee online	n/a
fee waiver for applicants with financial need	yes

University of Pennsylvania

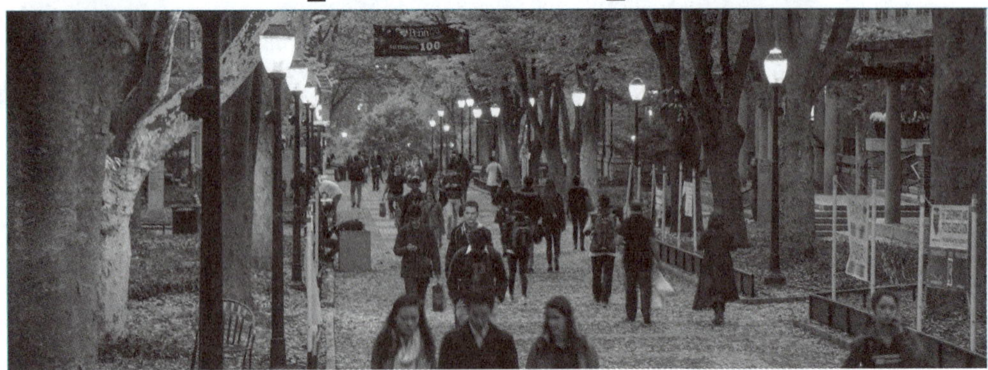

University of Pennsylvania
Office of Undergraduate Admissions
1 College Hall
Philadelphia, PA 19104
Ph: (215) 898-7507
info@admissions.upenn.edu
www.admissions.upenn.edu

Founded by Benjamin Franklin in 1740, the University of Pennsylvania is the nation's oldest university and a member of the Ivy League. The university offers undergraduate programs in the College of Arts & Sciences, the School of Engineering & Applied Science, the School of Nursing, and the Wharton School (Business). Penn is a popular choice among high achieving students who are the first in their families to attend college. Family income is not considered in the admissions process, making it need-blind for all citizens and permanent residents of the U.S., Mexico, and Canada. The University is committed to meeting demonstrated financial need with our grant-based aid packages. More than 270 years after its founding, Penn remains faithful to Franklin's spirit of limitless intellectual inquiry, and his adage that "The great aim and end of all learning is service to society."

Pre-College Summer Experience **Pre-Freshman Program (PFP) and Pennsylvania College Achievement Program (PENNCAP)**

The Pre-Freshman Program, a rigorous four-week long residential summer academic experience, gives invited participants comprehensive support services that begin with PFP and continue throughout the students' undergraduate experience. PFP participants build lasting bonds of friendships through social and cultural activities. PFP is hosted by PENNCAP, an umbrella organization which offers coaching, counseling, academic support, and assistance to Penn students throughout the year so that they can more confidently move towards their personal and academic goals.

Scholarship & Financial Aid **Grant-based Financial Aid for Qualifying Students**

Financial aid at Penn is based solely on financial need, and Penn is committed to meeting a student's demonstrated need. Student financial aid awards include grants (which means you do not have to pay them back after graduation) and a work-study job. All undergraduate applicants who are eligible for financial aid at Penn receive these grant-based aid packages, regardless of family income level.

Scholarship & Financial Aid **Partner College with QuestBridge, KIPP, and Say Yes to Education**

Penn partners with the QuestBridge program to offer students from low-income backgrounds the opportunity to attend Penn on a full scholarship. Penn's partnerships with Say Yes to Education and the KIPP Foundation also further our mission of admitting and engaging a freshman class that draws from every economic segment of society.

Open House, Fly-in, Visit **Multicultural Preview Programs**

Penn offers two overnight fly-in programs: the Penn Early Exploration Program (PEEP) for prospective applicants in the fall, and the Multicultural Scholars Preview (MSP) for admitted students in the spring. Both programs showcase Penn's academic and cultural vitality for students who may not otherwise have a chance to visit campus. Penn covers transportation costs for all students invited to PEEP, and for a limited number of students coming to MSP.

Student Life & Support **Cultural Resource Centers**

Penn's six Cultural Resource Centers—and their dedicated, full-time staff—inspire campus involvement, support cultural student organizations, and facilitate communication within and among groups. The Greenfield Intercultural Center, The Center for Hispanic Excellence: La Casa Latina, Makuu: The Black Cultural Center, the Pan Asian American Community House, the Penn Women's Center, and the Lesbian Gay Bisexual Transgender Center provide mentorship and a valuable support network to help ensure that students thrive at Penn.

Fast Facts

STUDENT DIVERSITY

# undergraduates	10,468
% male/female	49/51
% first-generation college	13
% American Indian or Alaskan Native	<1
% Asian	20
% Black or African American	7
% Hispanic/Latino	10
% Native Hawaiian or Pacific Islander	<1
% White	44
% two or more races	4
% race and/or ethnicity unknown	2
% International/nonresident	12

STUDENT SUCCESS

% first-to-second year retention	98
% six-year graduation	95
% six-year graduation for underrepresented minority groups	93
% first-years who live on campus	100
% undergraduates who live on campus	58
full-time faculty	4,346
full-time minority faculty	1,079
student-faculty ratio	6:1

Popular majors History, Psychology, Biology, International Relations, Business, Computer Science Engineering, Nursing

Multicultural student clubs and organizations
Various organizations with a focus on cultural identity including social clubs, performing arts groups, fraternities & sororities, pre-professional societies, and more.

AFFORDABILITY

Cost of Attendance

tuition	$47,416
required fees	$6,118
room and board	$15,066

Financial Aid

total institutional scholarships/grants	$214,000,000
% of students with financial need	47
% of students with need awarded any financial aid	100
% of students with need awarded any need-based scholarship or grant aid	100
% of students with need whose need was fully met	100
% Pell Grant recipients among first-years	13
average aid package	$50,644
average student loan debt upon graduation	$24,536

ADMISSIONS

# of applicants	40,413
% admitted	9
SAT Evidence-Based Reading & Writing	680-750
SAT Math	690-770
SAT Writing	n/a
ACT Composite	32-35
SAT/ACT optional	no
average HS GPA	n/a

DEADLINES

regular application closing date	1/5
early decision plan	yes
application closing date	11/1
early action plan	no
application closing date	n/a
application fee	$75
application fee online	$75
fee waiver for applicants with financial need	yes

College of Charleston

Founded in 1770, the College of Charleston is a nationally recognized, public liberal arts and sciences university located in the heart of historic Charleston, South Carolina. Students from 51 states and territories and nearly 61 countries choose the College for its small-college feel blended with the advantages and diversity of an urban, mid-sized university. The College provides a creative and intellectually stimulating environment where students are challenged by a committed and caring faculty of distinguished teacher-scholars. The city of Charleston serves students as a learning laboratory for experiences in business, science, teaching, the humanities, languages and the arts. For multicultural and first-generation college students, the College of Charleston is a particularly strong match.

Pre-College Summer Experience **Senior Project**

This summer college-prep program for rising high school seniors brings first-generation or multicultural students to the College for six days. Participants interact with current students, attend a College class, take a test-strategies class and a practice SAT/ACT exam, learn time-management skills and experience the city and university.

Summer Bridge & Orientation **Speedy Consolidation and Transition Program (SPECTRA)**

SPECTRA is a challenging transitional summer academic program for African American, Latino, Asian, and Native American (AALANA) high school graduates who are enrolling at the College for the fall semester. During a five-week, on-campus experience, students learn to develop successful academic and social networks; bridge the gap between stereotypical barriers that students of color face on predominantly white campuses; and understand the academic rigors of college life. Students are further supported through academic advising, mentoring, college skills workshops, financial aid advising and special seminars.

Scholars & Leadership **Gateway to Success**

The Gateway to Success Scholarship was established to increase enrollment of first-generation, underserved, and economically disadvantaged students with strong competitive academic credentials.

Scholars & Leadership **Bonner Leader Program**

Bonner Leaders are outstanding students who commit themselves to leadership through service and making positive change across campus and in the Charleston community. This four-year, service-based leadership and scholarship program allows students to apply theory to practice through real-life work experience at area nonprofit organizations. The program also facilitates students' transition from being volunteers to becoming leaders in their community. Scholarship recipients receive a graduated scholarship for participation in the program.

Scholars & Leadership **South Carolina Alliance for Minority Participation (SCAMP)**

SCAMP is a four-year, academic enrichment program for underrepresented minorities planning to major in STEM-related fields within the College's School of Sciences and Mathematics. Our program is designed to increase and retain these students through mentoring, counseling, networking, tutoring, and special access to professional and community development opportunities.

College of Charleston
66 George Street
Charleston, SC 29424
Ph: (843) 953-5670
admissions@cofc.edu
www.cofc.edu

Fast Facts

STUDENT DIVERSITY

# undergraduates	9,895
% male/female	37/63
% first-generation college	n/a
% American Indian or Alaskan Native	<1
% Asian	2
% Black or African American	8
% Hispanic/Latino	5
% Native Hawaiian or Pacific Islander	<1
% White	77
% two or more races	4
% race and/or ethnicity unknown	2
% International/nonresident	1

STUDENT SUCCESS

% first-to-second year retention	78
% six-year graduation	69
% six-year graduation for underrepresented minority groups	67
% first-years who live on campus	89
% undergraduates who live on campus	31
full-time faculty	531
full-time minority faculty	74
student-faculty ratio	15:1

Popular majors Business/Marketing, Biological/Life Sciences, Visual and Performing Arts, Communication/Journalism, Psychology

Multicultural student clubs and organizations Arabic Club, Asian Student Association, Black Student Union, Chinese Club, Collegiate Curls, Graduate Students of Color Association, Hispanic Latino Club, Japanese Club, International Students Club, Portuguese Club, Russian Club, Spanish Club

AFFORDABILITY

Cost of Attendance

tuition	$30,386 or in-state: $11,998
required fees	$320 first year or $460 UG
room and board	n/a

Financial Aid

total institutional scholarships/grants	$14,849,035
% of students with financial need	51
% of students with need awarded any financial aid	96
% of students with need awarded any need-based scholarship or grant aid	67
% of students with need whose need was fully met	16
% Pell Grant recipients among first-years	24
average aid package	$13,505
average student loan debt upon graduation	$26,203

ADMISSIONS

# of applicants	11,899
% admitted	80
SAT Critical Reading	550-630
SAT Math	520-600
SAT Writing	n/a
ACT Composite	22-27
SAT/ACT optional	n/a
average HS GPA	3.9

DEADLINES

regular application closing date	2/15
early decision plan	yes
application closing date	11/1
early action plan	yes
application closing date	12/1
application fee	$50
application fee online	$50
fee waiver for applicants with financial need	yes

Belmont University

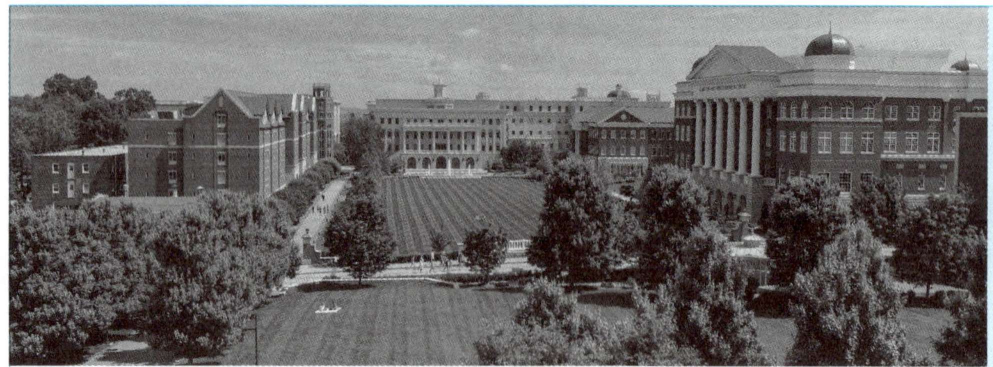

Founded in 1890, Belmont University is a private, Christian, coeducational university in Nashville, Tennessee, at the heart of Music Row. As one of the fastest growing Christian universities in the nation, Belmont University is a student-centered community providing an academically challenging education that empowers men and women of diverse backgrounds to engage and transform the world with disciplined intelligence, compassion, courage and faith. Ranked No. 5 in the Regional Universities South category and named as a "Most Innovative" university by *U.S. News & World Report*, Belmont University consists of more than 8,080 students who come from every state and more than 25 countries. Belmont offers undergraduate degrees in more than 90 programs of study in areas including the liberal arts, sciences, business, health sciences, religion, music and music business.

Scholarship & Financial Aid **Merit Scholarships**

Belmont offers several substantial merit scholarships in addition to generous need-based aid. The William Randolph Hearst Endowed Scholarship is offered annually to an incoming freshman from a diverse background with outstanding academic and leadership records. It covers full tuition, room, board, books and fees. The Ingram Diversity Leadership Scholarship, offered to four incoming freshmen with diverse backgrounds from the Nashville area, covers the full amount of tuition and is also awarded based on outstanding academic and leadership records.

Summer Bridge & Orientation **Towering Traditions New Student Orientation**

The Towering Traditions Orientation Program, founded more than 20 years ago, is designed to welcome new students to Belmont University. The program includes Summer Orientation and Welcome Week. Summer Orientation includes academic orientation, institutional orientation and registration sessions. Students have the opportunity to meet administration, faculty, and fellow students in preparation for their first days on campus in August.

Scholars & Leadership **Enactus**

Enactus students devote six weeks each summer, and every other Saturday during the school year, to the 100 Kings program. Sponsored by 100 Black Men of Middle Tennessee, the program supports 150 African-American students in Metro Nashville Public Schools. The seven-year program provides these students with English and math tutoring, personal finance counseling and vocational orientation in interests such as Business, Law and Engineering. The program offers preparation for the SAT and ACT exams, college counseling and an introduction to Belmont University. In 2012, Belmont won its second Enactus national championship, followed by the World Cup title.

Student Life & Support **Black Student Association (BSA)**

Belmont's Black Student Association promotes cultural awareness through campus events and forums. Open to students of all races, BSA strives to reach out to the Belmont and Nashville community through its involvement in the university's Martin Luther King Week, Diversity Week, and community service projects in the Metro Nashville area.

Student Life & Support **Office of Multicultural Learning and Experience (MLE)**

The newly established Office of Multicultural Learning and Experience (MLE) serves Belmont's student-centered community by providing academic and experiential multicultural learning opportunities that supports the university's mission to engage and transform the world. Focusing on creating culturally diverse conversations, the MLE permeates all aspects of campus life as it supports awareness events across campus, establishes programming surrounding key diversity and inclusivity topics and creates new initiatives and opportunities for diverse experiences.

Belmont University
1900 Belmont Blvd.
Nashville, TN 37212
Ph: (615) 460-6785
admissions@belmont.edu
www.belmont.edu

Fast Facts

STUDENT DIVERSITY

# undergraduates	6,569
% male/female	40/60
% first-generation college	n/a
% American Indian or Alaskan Native	<1
% Asian	3
% Black or African American	5
% Hispanic/Latino	4
% Native Hawaiian or Pacific Islander	<1
% White	79
% two or more races	3
% race and/or ethnicity unknown	3
% International/nonresident	1

STUDENT SUCCESS

% first-to-second year retention	85
% six-year graduation	69
% six-year graduation for underrepresented minority groups	n/a
% first-years who live on campus	95
% undergraduates who live on campus	60
full-time faculty	400
full-time minority faculty	39
student-faculty ratio	13:1

Popular majors Music Business, Nursing, Business Administration, Music, Biology

Multicultural student clubs and organizations Black Student Association, Delta Sigma Theta Inc., Rumi Club, Hispanic Student Alliance, Black Law Student Association, Minority Health Science Association, Chinese Cultural Club, Belmont Japan America Relations

AFFORDABILITY

Cost of Attendance

tuition	$31,300
required fees	$1,520
room and board	$11,680

Financial Aid

total institutional scholarships/grants	$23,683,916
% of students with financial need	52
% of students with need awarded any financial aid	72
% of students with need awarded any need-based scholarship or grant aid	65
% of students with need whose need was fully met	11
% Pell Grant recipients among first-years	15
average aid package	$15,499
average student loan debt upon graduation	$28,477

ADMISSIONS

# of applicants	7,737
% admitted	81
SAT Critical Reading	530-630
SAT Math	510-620
SAT Writing	n/a
ACT Composite	26
SAT/ACT optional	no
average HS GPA	3.6

DEADLINES

regular application closing date	7/1
early decision plan	n/a
application closing date	n/a
early action plan	n/a
application closing date	n/a
application fee	$50
application fee online	$50
fee waiver for applicants with financial need	yes

Fisk University

Founded in 1866, shortly after the end of the Civil War, Fisk University is a historically black university, and is the oldest institution of higher learning in Nashville, Tennessee. Fisk's outstanding faculty and students continue to enhance the University's national reputation for academic excellence, which is validated year after year by the leading third party reviewers, as well as by the pool of talented applicants and the large percentage of alumni who complete graduate or professional degrees and become leaders and scholars in their fields. Fisk University produces graduates from diverse backgrounds with the integrity and intellect required for substantive contributions to society. Our curriculum is grounded in the liberal arts. Our faculty and administrators emphasize the discovery and advancement of knowledge through research in the natural and social sciences, business and the humanities. We are committed to the success of scholars and leaders with global perspectives.

Pre-College Prep & Outreach **Talented Tenth Leadership Development Summer Program**

The Office of Recruitment and Admission, Office of Student Activities, Office of Student Support, Office of Residence Life and Campus Service have developed a program to create hope and opportunities for young men of color, develop leadership skills and roles across multiple industries and sectors, meet the growing demands of the U.S. and global knowledge based economy, and ultimately increase male enrollment at Fisk to 50% of the new student class. The goal of the TTP program is to target a select group of 30 national and international 10th to 12th grade high school young men and incoming freshmen to college with high aptitude who are interested in higher education at Fisk University. Finally, the program seeks to collaborate with influential Fisk University male alumni and men of the community to provide the network necessary to meet the multiple professional readiness and college planning needs.

Pre-College Prep & Outreach **Pre-College Summer Program (PCP)**

The goal of the PCP is to increase the number of students who successfully matriculate through the undergraduate curriculum by enhancing their reading, writing, analytical and critical thinking skills, while heightening their cultural and social readiness. The restructured program not only provides academic support during this six-week summer experience, but provides tutoring, academic counseling and mentoring throughout the freshman year.

Pre-College Summer Experience **Mini-College**

Mini-College, established around 1980 as the brainchild of Mrs. Ingrid Collier, surrounds children with Fisk culture and encourages them to think of college attendance at a young age and perhaps even consider matriculating at Fisk. The curriculum, for children from ages 5-12, is still centered on cultural arts, math, science, speech, music, dance, computer programing, Spanish, Life's Little Lessons, Black History, Field trips, etc.

Academic Advising & Support **Leadership Enrichment and Academic Development Program (LEAD)**

LEAD is a Student Support Services (SSS) initiative funded by the U.S. Department of Education, Office of Trio Programs. The LEAD Program provides personal, career and academic counseling, tutorial services, academic skills enrichment, workshops and cultural activities to qualified students. Targeted to first-generation, economically challenged and/or differently abled students, LEAD is funded to serve 200 students each year and provides services throughout their enrollment at Fisk University.

Fisk University
1000 Seventeenth Avenue North
Nashville, TN 37208
Ph: (615) 329-8666
admit@fisk.edu
www.fisk.edu

Fast Facts

STUDENT DIVERSITY

# undergraduates	750
% male/female	38/62
% first-generation college	n/a
% American Indian or Alaskan Native	n/a
% Asian	n/a
% Black or African American	83
% Hispanic/Latino	<1
% Native Hawaiian or Pacific Islander	n/a
% White	1
% two or more races	n/a
% race and/or ethnicity unknown	10
% International/nonresident	4

STUDENT SUCCESS

% first-to-second year retention	79
% six-year graduation	38
% six-year graduation for underrepresented minority groups	45
% first-years who live on campus	91
% undergraduates who live on campus	64
full-time faculty	65
full-time minority faculty	n/a
student-faculty ratio	8:1

Popular majors Biology, Business Administration, Psychology, Physical Sciences, Social Sciences, Visual and Performing Arts,Foreign Languages, Literature and Linguistics

Multicultural student clubs and organizations Campus Ministries, Choral Groups, Dance, Drama/Theater, Fraternities, Government or Political Activity, Jazz Band, Literary Magazine, Music Ensembles, Radio Station, Sororities, Student Newspaper, Television Station, Yearbook

AFFORDABILITY

Cost of Attendance

tuition	$19,624
required fees	$1,618
room and board	$10,160

Financial Aid

total institutional scholarships/grants	n/a
% of students with financial need	n/a
% of students with need awarded any financial aid	84
% of students with need awarded any need-based scholarship or grant aid	70
% of students with need whose need was fully met	n/a
% Pell Grant recipients among first-years	55
average aid package	n/a
average student loan debt upon graduation	n/a

ADMISSIONS

# of applicants	7,250
% admitted	83
SAT Critical Reading	410-540
SAT Math	400-570
SAT Writing	400-570
ACT Composite	21
SAT/ACT optional	n/a
average HS GPA	3.27

DEADLINES

regular application closing date	2/1
early decision plan	n/a
application closing date	n/a
early action plan	yes
application closing date	11/1
application fee	$25
application fee online	$25
fee waiver for applicants with financial need	yes

Maryville College

Maryville College is ideally situated in Maryville, Tenn., between the Great Smoky Mountains National Park and Knoxville, the state's third largest city. Known for offering its students a rigorous and highly personal experience, Maryville College is a nationally ranked institution of higher learning that successfully joins the liberal arts and professional preparation in partnership with others. Founded in 1819, Maryville is the 12th oldest college in the South and maintains an affiliation with the Presbyterian Church (USA).

Open House, Fly-in, Visit **Fly Maryville Program**

Maryville College offers tours three times a day Monday - Friday and some Saturdays. The College offers the Fly Maryville Program for out-of-state prospective students. The program is available for any high school junior, senior or college transfer who flies to campus for an official visit from September through April. Upon enrolling full-time at MC, the College will credit $300 to the student's first semester tuition.

Open House, Fly-in, Visit **Meet Maryville Open Houses**

Open to all high school students from freshmen to seniors and college transfer students! This is your chance during the academic year to attend a Meet Maryville preview day. Take a tour, meet our faculty and students, and discover where you could spend the best four years of your life. You and your parents are invited to attend and learn more about the Maryville College experience. Call (800) 597-2687 for more information.

Summer Bridge & Orientation **Scots Science Scholars**

Students who are interested in science, technology, engineering or math (STEM) fields are encouraged to apply for the Scots Science Scholars Program at MC. The four-year program includes an all-expenses paid, on-campus summer bridge program prior to start of your freshman year; $1,150 stipend for attending the program; and research opportunities at Oak Ridge National Lab and Great Smoky Mountains National Park.

Maryville College
502 E. Lamar Alexander Parkway
Maryville, TN 37804
Ph: (800) 597-2687
admissions@maryvillecollege.edu
www.maryvillecollege.edu

Fast Facts

STUDENT DIVERSITY

# undergraduates	1,181
% male/female	46/54
*We have transgender students	
% first-generation college	26
% American Indian or Alaskan Native	1
% Asian	1
% Black or African American	13
% Hispanic/Latino	4
% Native Hawaiian or Pacific Islander	<1
% White	73
% two or more races	5
% race and/or ethnicity unknown	<1
% International/nonresident	3

STUDENT SUCCESS

% first-to-second year retention	72
% six-year graduation	54
% six-year graduation for underrepresented minority groups	57
% first-years who live on campus	86
% undergraduates who live on campus	72
full-time faculty	78
full-time minority faculty	3
student-faculty ratio	13:1

Popular majors Management, Finance/Accounting, Psychology, Biology, Exercise Science

Multicultural student clubs and organizations Black Student Alliance, Global Citizenship Organization, LGBTQ+ Alliance, iMentor Program, Latino Student Alliance, MC Step Team, Voices of Praise

AFFORDABILITY

Cost of Attendance

tuition	$33,402
required fees	$794
room and board	$11,144

Financial Aid

total institutional scholarships/grants	$26,100,256
% of students with financial need	86
% of students with need awarded any financial aid	100
% of students with need awarded any need-based scholarship or grant aid	100
% of students with need whose need was fully met	26
% Pell Grant recipients among first-years	49
average aid package	$32,660
average student loan debt upon graduation	$21,535

ADMISSIONS

# of applicants	2,791
% admitted	49
SAT Critical Reading	460-580
SAT Math	470-580
SAT Writing	n/a
ACT Composite	24
SAT/ACT optional	no
average HS GPA	3.55

DEADLINES

regular application closing date	rolling
early decision plan	n/a
application closing date	rolling
early action plan	n/a
application closing date	rolling
application fee	n/a
application fee online	n/a
fee waiver for applicants with financial need	n/a

Vanderbilt University

Consistently ranked among the top 20 universities in the country, Vanderbilt is a private research university that features ten schools including four undergraduate schools and eight graduate or professional schools and programs. Each year, 1,600 first-year students join the University, bringing the total undergraduate population to approximately 6,900. Vanderbilt consistently challenges some of America's most talented students to expand their intellectual horizons in an inclusive environment based on open inquiry and respect. Recently earning Reuters' 10th Most Innovative University in the world, Vanderbilt offers myriad research opportunities for undergraduate students. The University's interdisciplinary approach to education allows students to pursue a wide array of interests outside their main focus of study, and its progressive financial aid policies assure that it is often cited among the country's best values among private universities.

Pre-College Prep & Outreach **QuestBridge**

Vanderbilt is a partner college with QuestBridge, which "connects the world's brightest low-income students to America's best universities and opportunities."

Pre-College Summer Experience **Vanderbilt Summer Academy (VSA)**

VSA invites highly talented students (grades 7-12) to a residential summer program on campus. VSA offers engaging and challenging curricula in math, science and the humanities. The program integrates resources from the University's many research programs.

Open House, Fly-In, Visit **MOSAIC Weekend**

Held in mid-March, MOSAIC Weekend is designed to introduce admitted students from diverse backgrounds to Vanderbilt's vibrant campus life. The weekend features academic sessions, student activities and performances by a variety of student groups.

Open House, Fly-In, Visit **Vandy Fan for a Day**

Vandy Fan for a Day provides high school sophomores and juniors of diverse socioeconomic backgrounds with information about selective college admissions and Vanderbilt's need-based aid, and a chance to enjoy an SEC football game. High school counselors nominate students for this program held in the fall each year.

Open House, Fly-In, Visit **Counselor Conference: Partners in College Success**

Designed for domestic and international high school counselors, and leaders of community-based organizations, Counselor Conference provides an opportunity to get to know our campus and our community, and to interact with current students, faculty, deans, and key members of the admissions staff. This program is one of the ways Vanderbilt builds and maintains partnerships with organizations focusing on low- and middle-income and first-generation college students.

Scholarship & Financial Aid **Chancellor's Scholarship Program**

The Chancellor's Scholarship Program selects students with outstanding leadership, strength of character, academic achievement and a deep-seated commitment to social justice to receive full-tuition plus a one-time stipend and programmatic support.

Scholarship & Financial Aid **Posse University Partner-Founding Collegiate Partner**

Vanderbilt is the founding collegiate partner in the Posse Foundation. Each year since 1989, Vanderbilt has recruited ten students from New York City through the Posse program to join our campus community.

Vanderbilt University
2305 West End Avenue
Nashville, TN 37203
Ph: (615) 322-2561
admissions@vanderbilt.edu
admissions.vanderbilt.edu

Fast Facts

STUDENT DIVERSITY

# undergraduates	6,885
% male/female	49/51
% first-generation college	n/a
% American Indian or Alaskan Native	<1
% Asian	14
% Black or African American	10
% Hispanic/Latino	10
% Native Hawaiian or Pacific Islander	<1
% White	48
% two or more races	5
% race and/or ethnicity unknown	5
% International/nonresident	8

STUDENT SUCCESS

% first-to-second year retention	97
% six-year graduation	92
% six-year graduation for underrepresented minority groups	90
% first-years who live on campus	99
% undergraduates who live on campus	90
full-time faculty	956
full-time minority faculty	158
student-faculty ratio	8:1

Popular majors Economics; Human and Organizational Development; Medicine, Health, and Society; Political Science; Mathematics; Neuroscience; Psychology; Mechanical Engineering

Multicultural student clubs and organizations Asian American Student Association, Black Student Association, Vanderbilt Undergraduate Chinese Association, Vanderbilt Association of Hispanic Students, Latin American and Caribbean Vanderbilt Student Association, Multicultural Leadership Council, Muslim Students Association, South Asian Cultural Exchange

AFFORDABILITY

Cost of Attendance

tuition	$46,500
required fees	$2,029
room and board	$15,584

Financial Aid

total institutional scholarships/grants	$164,929,757
% of students with financial need	50
% of students with need awarded any financial aid	99
% of students with need awarded any need-based scholarship or grant aid	98
% of students with need whose need was fully met	100
% Pell Grant recipients among first-years	15
average aid package	$49,242
average student loan debt upon graduation	$23,973

ADMISSIONS

# of applicants	31,462
% admitted	11
SAT Evidence-Based Reading & Writing	700-760
SAT Math	700-790
ACT Composite	32-35
SAT/ACT optional	no
average HS GPA	n/a

DEADLINES

regular application closing date	1/1
early decision plan	yes
application closing date	11/1; 1/1
early action plan	no
application closing date	n/a
application fee	$50
application fee online	$50
fee waiver for applicants with financial need	yes

Texas State University

Texas State values diversity in its classrooms, residence halls, dining venues and recreational events. The university offers 98 bachelor's, 91 master's and 13 doctoral degree programs in a supportive, academically challenging environment. Bobcats hail from across Texas and the United States, as well as from countries as far away as India, China and Israel. No matter where they come from, students find countless campus organizations that serve as enclaves of activity and support for those searching for familiar faces and customs or wanting to discover new ones. More than 52% of the 34,206 undergraduates are racial or ethnic minorities; about 36 percent are of Hispanic/Latino origin. Texas State's investment in students results in freshman-to-sophomore retention and graduation rates that rank among the highest in the state. As an Emerging Research University, Texas State offers opportunities for discovery and innovation for both students and faculty.

Open House, Fly-In, Visit **Come visit Texas State on Bobcat Days**

It's a great day to be a Bobcat! Come see for yourself. Texas State holds Bobcat Days four times a year to bring prospective and admitted students to campus and allow them to visit and explore the academic and cultural environment of Texas State University. During the day students can speak with faculty and staff about majors, attend information sessions, speak with students from a student panel about campus life, take a campus tour and dine at the university's student food court. Representatives from Student Diversity and Inclusion are available to visit personally with first-generation students. Learn more at www.admissions.txstate.edu/visit.

Scholarship & Financial Aid **The Bobcat Promise**

To increase access to higher education, Texas State University offers the Bobcat Promise. This program guarantees free tuition and mandatory fees for 15 credit hours per semester (not to exceed your demonstrated need) to new entering freshmen with a family adjusted gross income that does not exceed $35,000. Under the Bobcat Promise, tuition and mandatory fees will be paid (up to a student's demonstrated need) through a combination of federal, state and institutional funds. Learn more at www.finaid.txstate.edu/bobcatpromise.

Scholarship & Financial Aid **Freshman Scholarships Overview**

Texas State offers three categories of academic scholarships for incoming freshmen. The National Scholarships and Assured Scholarships are automatically awarded to you upon admission, provided you meet certain minimum academic requirements. We also offer a number of Competitive Scholarships, which are awarded on the basis of the overall strength of your scholarship application. To be considered for competitive freshman scholarships, you must meet Assured Admission standards, meet the minimum criteria for the scholarship, be admitted to Texas State and complete a Texas State scholarship application via the Bobcat Online Scholarship System (BOSS). Students are encouraged to apply for scholarships through BOSS and also view opportunities with their respective departments or colleges, including scholarships with a preference for first-generation applicants. Additional information is online at www.finaid.txstate.edu/scholarships.

Student Life & Support **Student Affairs & Supportive Community**

The university celebrates the diversity of the campus and strives to make the educational experience at Texas State positive and fulfilling. Students find that a culture of care exists as they interact with the departments within the Division of Student Affairs (www.dos.txstate.edu). Student Support Services assists eligible first-generation college students, low-income students and students with disabilities from all racial and ethnic backgrounds who have a need for academic and other support services in order to successfully complete their college education.

Texas State University
429 N. Guadalupe Street
San Marcos, TX 78666
Ph: (512) 245-2364
admissions@txstate.edu
www.txstate.edu

Fast Facts

STUDENT DIVERSITY

# undergraduates	34,206
% male/female	43/57
% first-generation college	39
% American Indian or Alaskan Native	<1
% Asian	2
% Black or African American	10
% Hispanic/Latino	37
% Native Hawaiian or Pacific Islander	<1
% White	46
% two or more races	4
% race and/or ethnicity unknown	0
% International/nonresident	1

STUDENT SUCCESS

% first-to-second year retention	78
% six-year graduation	54
% six-year graduation for underrepresented minority groups	51
% first-years who live on campus	92
% undergraduates who live on campus	20
full-time faculty	1,419
full-time minority faculty	342
student-faculty ratio	21:1

Popular majors Business/Marketing, Interdisciplinary Studies in Education, Visual and Performing Arts, Social Sciences, Communication/Journalism

Multicultural student clubs and organizations African Student Organization, Latino Student Organization, South Asian Student Association, First Generation Student Organization, Indian Student Association, Japanese Language and Culture, League of United Latin American Citizens, Native American Student Association, International Student Association, Bobcat Equality Alliance

AFFORDABILITY

Cost of Attendance

tuition	$20,537 or in-state: $8,087
required fees	$2,524
room and board	$8,100

Financial Aid

total institutional scholarships/grants	$122,511,369
% of students with financial need	56
% of students with need awarded any financial aid	96
% of students with need awarded any need-based scholarship or grant aid	84
% of students with need whose need was fully met	17
% Pell Grant recipients among first-years	38
average aid package	$11,281
average student loan debt upon graduation	$26,568

ADMISSIONS

# of applicants	24,277
% admitted	73
SAT Reading & Writing	510-600
SAT Math	510-590
ACT Composite	23
SAT/ACT optional	n/a
average HS GPA	n/a

DEADLINES

regular application closing date	5/1
early decision plan	n/a
application closing date	n/a
early action plan	n/a
application closing date	n/a
application fee	$75
application fee online	$75
fee waiver for applicants with financial need	yes

University of Texas at Arlington

The University of Texas at Arlington is a growing research powerhouse committed to life-enhancing discovery, innovative instruction, and caring community engagement. An educational leader in the heart of the thriving North Texas region, UTA nurtures minds within an environment that values excellence, ingenuity, and diversity. Guided by world-class faculty members, the University's more than 51,000 students in campus-based and online degree programs represent about 100 countries and pursue more than 180 bachelor's, master's, and doctoral degrees in a broad range of disciplines. Being the 5th most diverse college in the nation, our students increase their knowledge of the world, enhance their own self-awareness, and expand their horizons here.

Scholarship & Financial Aid **McNair Scholars Program**

The McNair Scholars Program is designed to prepare qualified undergraduates from low socio-economic and/or minority backgrounds for graduate study culminating in the Ph.D. McNair Scholars benefits from a considerable array of services ranging from free UTA transcripts for program-related use to a summer research internship with $3,000 stipend. The program particularly encourages science, technology, engineering and mathematics majors to apply.

Scholarship & Financial Aid **Scholarships**

Michele Bobadilla Bridge to Excellence Scholarship encourages deserving first-generation entering freshmen to bridge the gap between dreams and reality through education.

Centennial Endowed Scholarship, jointly sponsored by the UTA Alumni Association and the Student Affairs Division, provides support for deserving and academically promising first-generation college students who are entering freshmen or new transfers to UTA.

Shalyn & Al Clark Academic Achievement Scholarship, established by entrepreneurs and active community supporters, Shalyn and Al Clark, is a need-based scholarship supporting first-generation students. Sophomores who excel academically in the freshman year and who enter UT Arlington without a general scholarship will be eligible to apply.

The Shirlee J. and Taylor Gandy First Generation Scholarship is designed to provide support to rising UT Arlington sophomores on the basis of merit and financial need.

Simmons-Blackwell Scholarship, established by alumni Tom ('72) and Linda Simmons ('77), encourages first-generation college students.

James D. Spaniolo First Generation Scholarship Endowment was established to honor UT Arlington President James D. Spaniolo's commitment to college awareness and accessibility.

First-Year Experience & Transition **FIRST for First Generation College Students**

FIRST is a hands-on workshop for first-generation college students that covers time management, study skills, stress management, learning styles, major exploration, and more. Topics covered will include success skills, cultural awareness, building leadership skills, learning more about financial aid, and examining the transition into college. FIRST is designed to provide first-generation college students the tools they need to manage their college experience, the support to work through the stress of being the first from your family in college, and the words to explain the experience to those who may not understand the expectations that the university has of you.

University of Texas at Arlington
University Recruitment
Arlington, TX 76019
Ph: (817) 272-2090
recruitment.frontcounter@uta.edu
www.uta.edu/uta/

Fast Facts

STUDENT DIVERSITY

# undergraduates	30,633
% male/female	40/60
% first-generation college	n/a
% American Indian or Alaskan Native	1
% Asian	11
% Black or African American	15
% Hispanic/Latino	25
% Native Hawaiian or Pacific Islander	1
% White	40
% two or more races	1
% race and/or ethnicity unknown	1
% International/nonresident	12

STUDENT SUCCESS

% first-to-second year retention	71
% six-year graduation	46
% six-year graduation for underrepresented minority groups	46
% first-years who live on campus	41
% undergraduates who live on campus	11
full-time faculty	1,086
full-time minority faculty	254
student-faculty ratio	20:1

Popular majors Engineering, Architecture, Nursing, Business, Education

Multicultural student clubs and organizations
Arabic Language and Culture Organziation (ALCO), Bilingual Education Student Organization (B.E.S.O.), Delta Alpha Omega Multicultural Fraternity Inc. (ΔΑΩ), Delta Alpha Sigma Multicultural Sorority, Inc. (ΔΑΣ), Delta Xi Nu Multicultural Sorority, Inc. (ΔΞΝ), EXCEL Campus Activities (EXCEL), Indian Cultural Council, National Society of Black Engineers (NSBE), Sigma Lambda Beta Fraternity (ΣΛΒ), Vietnamese Student Association (VSA)

AFFORDABILITY

Cost of Attendance

tuition	$7,350
required fees	$2,266
room and board	$8,397

Financial Aid

total institutional scholarships/grants	$6,892,930
% of students with financial need	65
% of students with need awarded any financial aid	85
% of students with need awarded any need-based scholarship or grant aid	54
% of students with need whose need was fully met	7
% Pell Grant recipients among first-years	n/a
average aid package	$12,535
average student loan debt upon graduation	$21,456

ADMISSIONS

# of applicants	11,196
% admitted	64
SAT Critical Reading	460-590
SAT Math	490-610
SAT Writing	440-560
ACT Composite	23
SAT/ACT optional	yes
average HS GPA	n/a

DEADLINES

regular application closing date	rolling
early decision plan	n/a
application closing date	rolling
early action plan	n/a
application closing date	rolling
application fee	$60
application fee online	$60
fee waiver for applicants with financial need	yes

The University of Texas at Austin

The University of Texas at Austin leads the world in education, research and public service, and offers unparalleled resources to the Longhorn community. Our undergraduate students choose from more than 130 areas of study and over 1,000 student clubs and organizations. More than 55 percent of our 39,676 undergraduate students identify as racial or ethnic minorities, and 22 percent are first-generation college students. UT Austin supports students' educational and personal success, and empowers them to improve their lives and communities, through a high-quality, transformative and affordable education. At Texas, what starts here changes the world.

Academic Advising & Support **360 Connections**

Entering a university alongside more than 8,000 classmates can be overwhelming. That's why every UT Austin freshman joins a 360 Connection, a small community of students who meet regularly and start their college experience with plenty of support from each other, a faculty or staff member and a peer mentor.

Scholarship & Financial Aid **First Abroad**

UT Austin's Study Abroad office offers a special scholarship to remove financial barriers for first-generation students interested in studying abroad. Through the First Abroad initiative, 25 first-generation freshman students each year are selected to receive a $3,000 study abroad scholarship to use any time during their four years at UT Austin.

Special Admissions Policy **Fee Waivers**

UT Austin automatically waives the admission application fee for students attending partner high schools and for applicants who request a waiver. Applicants receiving an admissions application fee waiver also have their housing application fee, admission deposit and orientation fees waived or deferred.

Pre-College Prep & Outreach **Texas OnRamps**

OnRamps offers Texas high school students the opportunity to earn three core credit hours from UT Austin that are guaranteed to transfer to any public college or university in Texas. By taking OnRamps courses, students become more prepared for academic success in college, earn college credit for free and start working toward their college degree while still in high school.

Scholarship & Financial Aid **Presidential Scholars Program**

The Presidential Scholars program is one of the university's most prestigious student communities. Presidential Scholars are students with excellent academic credentials and significant financial need. In addition to a $20,000 scholarship, students benefit from a strong intellectual network and special academic opportunities. 51 percent of Presidential Scholars are first-generation college students.

Scholarship & Financial Aid **University Leadership Network**

The University Leadership Network (ULN) is a nationally recognized scholarship program for students with demonstrated financial need. The $20,000 ULN scholarship is paid monthly over a student's four years at UT Austin. ULN's comprehensive four-year plan includes leadership development, internships and academic support for over 500 students in each class. 71 percent of ULN students are first-generation college students.

The University of Texas at Austin
2400 Inner Campus Drive
Austin, TX 78712
Ph: (512) 471-3434
reply@austin.utexas.edu
www.utexas.edu

Fast Facts

STUDENT DIVERSITY

# undergraduates	39,676
% male/female	47/53
% first-generation college	22
% American Indian or Alaskan Native	<1
% Asian	21
% Black or African American	4
% Hispanic/Latino	23
% Native Hawaiian or Pacific Islander	<1
% White	42
% two or more races	4
% race and/or ethnicity unknown	1
% International/nonresident	5

STUDENT SUCCESS

% first-to-second year retention	95
% six-year graduation	80
% six-year graduation for underrepresented minority groups	71
% first-years who live on campus	61
% undergraduates who live on campus	18
full-time faculty	2,562
full-time minority faculty	543
student-faculty ratio	18:1

Popular majors Engineering, Business/Marketing, Communication/Journalism, Biological/Life Sciences, Public Administration and Social Services

Multicultural student clubs and organizations
Over 200 including Afrikan American Affairs, Asian Desi Pacific Islander American Collective, Black Student Alliance, Hispanic Student Association, Latino Community Affairs, National Society of Black Engineers, Native American and Indigenous Collective, Queer People of Color and Allies, Texas Hillel, Texas Latinos in Engineering and Sciences

AFFORDABILITY

Cost of Attendance

tuition	$35,766 or in-state: $10,136
required fees	n/a
room and board	$10,070

Financial Aid

total institutional scholarships/grants	$68,042,514
% of students with financial need	54
% of students with need awarded any financial aid	100
% of students with need awarded any need-based scholarship or grant aid	77
% of students with need whose need was fully met	20
% Pell Grant recipients among first-years	25
average aid package	$11,349
average student loan debt upon graduation	$25,338

ADMISSIONS

# of applicants	45,511
% admitted	40
SAT Critical Reading	560-680
SAT Math	580-730
SAT Writing	550-680
ACT Composite	29
SAT/ACT optional	no
average HS GPA	n/a

DEADLINES

regular application closing date	12/1
early decision plan	no
application closing date	n/a
early action plan	no
application closing date	n/a
application fee	$75
application fee online	$75
fee waiver for applicants with financial need	yes

Old Dominion University

Old Dominion University (ODU) is a forward-focused research university with rigorous academics and a commitment to student success at every level. The University is composed of individuals with varied backgrounds and experiences, nationalities, ethnicities, and religions, physical, political, intellectual and emotional differences. ODU actively supports diversity and inclusion through our programming, including a campus-wide campaign to support diversity and inclusion called #1ODU. At ODU, diversity and inclusion are celebrated and part of what makes our campus thrive.

Mentoring **First-Gen to Faculty Mentorships**

The main goal of the 'First-Gen to Faculty' mentor opportunity is to encourage faculty-student interaction outside of the classroom through mentoring relationships that help to build a sense of belonging for both first generation faculty and first generation students. Through this program, students can build their personal and professional network, get advice on achieving their goals, and socialize with ODU faculty at special lunches, dinners, and events.

Academic Advising & Support **Mane Connect Student Success Coaching**

Mane Connect is a success-coaching program offered to a select group of first-year students, many of whom are first generation students. Participating students will attend regular one-on-one meetings and workshops. Mane Connect will provide personal, educational, academic and career guidance.

Summer Bridge & Orientation **Monarch Summer Advantage Program**

Monarch Summer Advantage Program provides a group of incoming freshmen the opportunity to stay on-campus during the summer before enrolling and earn six academic credits in six weeks. This program also helps students build strong academic and life skills to become successful in a college environment.

Student Life & Support **First-Gen Fridays**

The first generation community at ODU meets once a month on Fridays to participate in socials and other activities. This is a great way to meet fellow first gen students, as well as first gen faculty and staff.

Student Life & Support **First-Gen Voices**

First Generation Voices is an ODU blog dedicated to highlighting the experiences of first generation students. Students can share stories, original works, images, and more.

Mentoring **Monarch 2 Monarch First Generation Edition**

Monarch 2 Monarch First Generation Edition is a new extension of the mentorship program, Monarch 2 Monarch, specifically designed for incoming first generation and transfer students. This program pairs freshmen and sophomores with a specific upperclassmen who can identify the challenges and opportunities of a first generation student. This group meets monthly and engages in enriching experience around financial literacy, balancing life demands, getting involved, and navigating campus.

Student Life & Support **ODU F1RST**

ODU F1RST is a student organization whose main purpose is to create a long-term relationship between first generation students, their mentors, and the University. These mentorships derived from the organization will help the first generation students adjust to their new college experience and connect with campus resources to increase opportunities for college success.

Old Dominion University
5115 Hampton Boulevard
Norfolk, VA 23529
Ph: (757) 683-3000
admissions@odu.edu
www.odu.edu

Fast Facts

STUDENT DIVERSITY

# undergraduates	19,606
% male/female	46/54
% first-generation college	21
% American Indian or Alaskan Native	<1
% Asian	4
% Black or African American	29
% Hispanic/Latino	8
% Native Hawaiian or Pacific Islander	<1
% White	46
% two or more races	7
% race and/or ethnicity unknown	3
% International/nonresident	1

STUDENT SUCCESS

% first-to-second year retention	78
% six-year graduation	n/a
% six-year graduation for underrepresented minority groups	51
% first-years who live on campus	75
% undergraduates who live on campus	23
full-time faculty	835
full-time minority faculty	174
student-faculty ratio	18:1

Popular majors Health Profession and Related Programs, Business/Marketing, Social Sciences, Psychology, Interdisciplinary Studies

Multicultural student clubs and organizations Muslim Students Assoc., ODU Bangladeshi Students' Assoc., Saudi Student Assoc., Chinese Student and Scholar Assoc., Persian Students International Assoc., Vietnamese Student Assoc., South Asian Student Assoc., Filipino American Student Assoc., Global Student Friendship Club, African Student Assoc.

AFFORDABILITY

Cost of Attendance

tuition	$26,730 or in-state: $9,750
required fees	$296
room and board	$10,864

Financial Aid

total institutional scholarships/grants	$14,011,575
% of students with financial need	83
% of students with need awarded any financial aid	97
% of students with need awarded any need-based scholarship or grant aid	81
% of students with need whose need was fully met	18
% Pell Grant recipients among first-years	34
average aid package	$11,895
average student loan debt upon graduation	$30,410

ADMISSIONS

# of applicants	11,352
% admitted	85
SAT Critical Reading	450-570
SAT Math	440-570
SAT Writing	n/a
ACT Composite	18-25
SAT/ACT optional	no
average HS GPA	3.28

DEADLINES

regular application closing date	2/1
early decision plan	no
application closing date	n/a
early action plan	yes
application closing date	12/1
application fee	$50
application fee online	$50
fee waiver for applicants with financial need	yes

University of Mary Washington

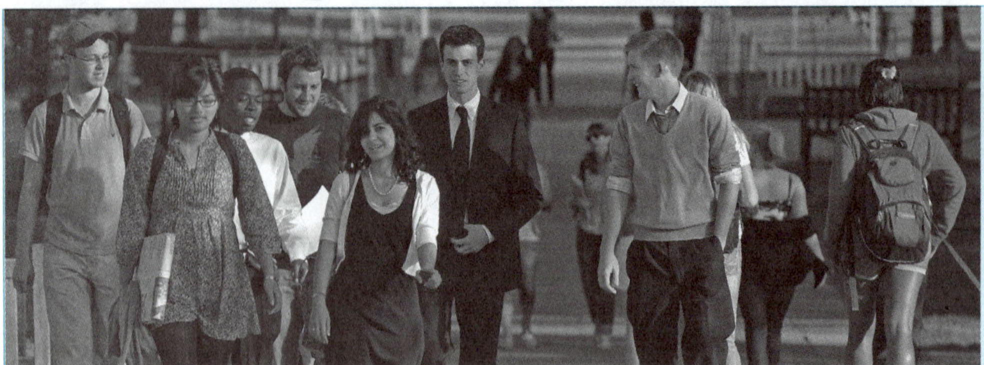

The University of Mary Washington is a mid-sized, public university that combines rich history and tradition with academic achievement. Nationally ranked as one of the top liberal arts colleges in the country, Mary Washington's academic program is rigorous, focusing on preparing students for success after college. The University's focus on diversity outreach is noteworthy, especially with the Rappahannock Scholars Program, a program aimed at college preparation and guaranteed admission for local high school students of underrepresented groups. The University of Mary Washington campus is located in the picturesque, culturally active city of Fredericksburg, Virginia, only a short drive from Washington, D.C., and Richmond, Virginia.

Pre-College Prep & Outreach **Rappahannock Scholars Program**

In participation with local high schools in the Northern Neck region of Virginia, the Rappahannock Scholars Program guarantees admission to the University of Mary Washington when program criteria are met. The Rappahannock Scholars Program also provides support, guidance and encouragement throughout high school for prospective students preparing for success in college. Students who attend participating high schools and exhibit promising academic, economic and leadership skills may be nominated by guidance counselors. Preference is given to students of underrepresented groups who will add cultural diversity to the university campus, first-generation students and students from economically disadvantaged backgrounds.

Summer Bridge & Orientation **Student Transition Program**

The Student Transition Program supports the University's mission of encouraging engagement among diverse communities. The program is an academic enrichment and bridge program that allows underrepresented and first-generation, first-year college students to take college classes during the summer in a supportive environment that prepares them for the rigors of academic life. This support continues into the first-year experience and gets students, faculty and staff involved in classes and programs based on academic excellence, honor and integrity. How to Succeed in College is a two semester, 1-credit course sequence designed to teach students how to develop, use and assess effective and efficient learning strategies with the goal of developing a personal system of study, and to encourage students to be reflective in identifying personal strengths and weaknesses and to place emphasis on team-building with fellow students.

Academic Advising & Support **Focus Seminars/Study Skills Workshops "Learning to Focus: Strategies for Success!"**

The Academic Services Office offers a series of workshops designed to build study skills and focus on topics such as time management, note taking and test preparation that provide strategies for academic success. The office also offers a Peer Tutor Program, designed to assist students in developing strategies that will help strengthen their knowledge of content material and develop study strategies.

Student Life & Support **James Farmer Multicultural Center**

The James Farmer Multicultural Center welcomes students from all ethnic and cultural backgrounds. The center works to enhance the educational experience by increasing awareness and knowledge of cultural, ethnic, intellectual and social diversity issues that impact individuals as well as the community as a whole. University of Mary Washington students involved in the center are strongly encouraged to take part in these initiatives through participation in clubs, programs, and other activities outside the classroom. The University is focused on helping students develop democratic principles and critical thinking skills that are key to becoming a successful leader.

University of Mary Washington
1301 College Avenue
Fredericksburg, VA 22401
Ph: (540) 654-2000
admit@umw.edu
www.umw.edu

Fast Facts

STUDENT DIVERSITY

# undergraduates	4,398
% male/female	35/65
% first-generation college	23
% American Indian or Alaskan Native	<1
% Asian	4
% Black or African American	7
% Hispanic/Latino	8
% Native Hawaiian or Pacific Islander	<1
% White	70
% two or more races	5
% race and/or ethnicity unknown	5
% International/nonresident	1

STUDENT SUCCESS

% first-to-second year retention	83
% six-year graduation	72
% six-year graduation for underrepresented minority groups	68
% first-years who live on campus	88
% undergraduates who live on campus	57
full-time faculty	251
full-time minority faculty	43
student-faculty ratio	14:1

Popular majors Social Sciences, Business, Psychology, English, Multi/Interdisciplinary Studies

Multicultural student clubs and organizations African Student Union, Asian Student Association, Black Student Association, Brothers of a New Direction, Islamic Student Association, Jewish Student Association, Latino Student Association, Native American Student Association, Students Educating and Empowering for Diversity, Women of Color

AFFORDABILITY

Cost of Attendance

tuition	$20,362 or in-state: $6,032
required fees	$6,156
room and board	$10,216

Financial Aid

total institutional scholarships/grants	$5,657,973
% of students with financial need	45
% of students with need awarded any financial aid	42
% of students with need awarded any need-based scholarship or grant aid	46
% of students with need whose need was fully met	5
% Pell Grant recipients among first-years	17
average aid package	$8,596
average student loan debt upon graduation	$18,029

ADMISSIONS

# of applicants	5,985
% admitted	73
SAT Critical Reading	500-620
SAT Math	500-590
SAT Writing	480-590
ACT Composite	25
SAT/ACT optional	yes
average HS GPA	3.52

DEADLINES

regular application closing date	2/1
early decision plan	yes
application closing date	11/1
early action plan	yes
application closing date	11/15
application fee	$50
application fee online	$50
fee waiver for applicants with financial need	yes

University of Virginia

Founded by Thomas Jefferson, the University of Virginia sustains the ideal of developing, through education, leaders who are well-prepared to help shape the future of the nation. Today the University values accessibility, diversity and affordability. The University of Virginia boasts strong undergraduate programs in engineering, nursing, architecture, leadership and public policy, commerce and education, as well as the liberal arts and sciences. At 88.9%, the University of Virginia holds the highest graduation rate among major public institutions in the country for African-Americans. Students are encouraged to take ownership of the University community and to become leaders not just at the University of Virginia, but also in the world.

Pre-College Prep & Outreach **The Outreach Office**

The Outreach Office is a unit within the Office of Admission created specifically to work with minority, first-generation and low-income students. The office oversees multicultural weekends (assisting students and families with visitations to the University), offers college counseling, and works with the financial aid office and scholarships programs specifically to encourage diversity. Their mission is to make sure all students have access to the same opportunities when they get to college.

Scholarship & Financial Aid **Access UVA**

Access UVA is a comprehensive financial aid plan that has pledged to meet 100 percent of demonstrated financial need for all eligible undergraduate students with grants, loans and work-study. The University caps the amount of need-based loans offered so that no student leaves with an excessive amount of debt upon graduation. We will provide comprehensive financial education to prospective and current students and their families.

First-Year Experience & Transition **Office of the Dean of Students**

Access UVA & First Generation Student Support works to provide comprehensive support services and programs to create equitable educational opportunities for all students across Grounds. This includes all students participating in the Access UVA financial aid program, first-generation college students, independent students, and non-traditional students. Our goal is to strengthen the University's commitment to promoting excellence and affordable access by ensuring all students have the support needed to overcome barriers to access and success while they attend the University. A few ways that we accomplish this are through one-on-one meetings with students, educational workshops, regular newsletters with important information for first-generation and high financial need students, emotional and academic support for students, and the newly created Hoos First Program, which connects the University's more than 1,700 first-generation faculty, staff and students.

Student Life & Support **Peer and Faculty Mentor Programs**

There are Peer and Faculty Mentor Programs specifically for minorities and low-income students coming to the University. Each student who enrolls at the University is assigned a Peer and/or Faculty Mentor to help them with their transition to college and advise them throughout their first year.

University of Virginia
PO Box 400160
Charlottesville, VA 22904
Ph: (434) 982-3200
undergradadmission@virginia.edu
www.virginia.edu

Fast Facts

STUDENT DIVERSITY

# undergraduates	16,034
% male/female	46/54
% first-generation college	12
% American Indian or Alaskan Native	<1
% Asian	14
% Black or African American	7
% Hispanic/Latino	7
% Native Hawaiian or Pacific Islander	<1
% White	58
% two or more races	4
% race and/or ethnicity unknown	6
% International/nonresident	5

STUDENT SUCCESS

% first-to-second year retention	97
% six-year graduation	95
% six-year graduation for underrepresented minority groups	85
% first-years who live on campus	100
% undergraduates who live on campus	40
full-time faculty	1,631
full-time minority faculty	366
student-faculty ratio	15:1

Popular majors Economics, Business/Commerce, English, Biology, Foreign Affairs, Psychology, History

Multicultural student clubs and organizations Black Student Alliance, Asian Pacific American Leadership Training Institute (APALTI), Latino Student Alliance, American Indian Student Union, Brothers United Celebrating Knowledge and Success (BUCKS), Association of African and Caribbean Cultures, National Society of Black Engineers (NSBE) and Hispanic Engineers (NSHE)

AFFORDABILITY

Cost of Attendance

tuition	$45,058 or in-state:$15,714
required fees	n/a
room and board	$11,220

Financial Aid

total institutional scholarships/grants	$63,575,107
% of students with financial need	32
% of students with need awarded any financial aid	100
% of students with need awarded any need-based scholarship or grant aid	100
% of students with need whose need was fully met	100
% Pell Grant recipients among first-years	13
average aid package	n/a
average student loan debt upon graduation	$12,852

ADMISSIONS

# of applicants	36,779
% admitted	27
SAT Critical Reading	650-730
SAT Math	640-740
SAT Writing	n/a
ACT Composite	29-33
SAT/ACT optional	n/a
average HS GPA	n/a

DEADLINES

regular application closing date	1/1
early decision plan	n/a
application closing date	n/a
early action plan	yes
application closing date	11/1
application fee	$70
application fee online	$70
fee waiver for applicants with financial need	yes

*Data and program information from 2016-17

Virginia Commonwealth University

Situated in Richmond, Virginia's capital city since 1779, Virginia Commonwealth University (VCU) continues to grow in size, programs and students. With more than 31,000 undergraduate, graduate and professional students, the university offers prestigious programs that have developed the university into an institution with an international reputation. The university enrolls students in 208 certificate and degree programs in the arts, sciences and humanities. Sixty-five of the programs are unique in Virginia, many of them crossing the disciplines of Virginia Commonwealth University's 13 schools and one college. Since its founding, the university has combined the traditional and nontraditional, creating diversity in our academic programs, campus events, students, faculty and staff.

Pre-College Prep & Outreach **Primeros Pasos (First Steps)**

Primeros Pasos is a one-day program designed to provide Latino high school students and their families with an overview of the college experience and opportunities in higher education. VCU students, parents, administrators, faculty and alumni participate throughout the day sharing their experiences. Activities include a bilingual workshop for parents regarding financial aid and scholarships, a panel discussion with university students from the Latino community, admissions counselors, and campus tours.

Scholars & Leadership **Acceleration Program**

Students admitted into the Acceleration Program begin college with a four-week summer enrichment program which exposes them to a pre-health-specific math and science curriculum. Students participate in internships in various clinical health service provider settings and receive a stipend. Students are expected to commit to 50 hours of volunteer work per year in community health provider settings and receive specialized, career-related academic advising and support services throughout the program.

Academic Advising & Support **University Academic Advising**

University Academic Advising provides all first-year students with a common advising experience to ensure they receive the exposure and support needed to excel in their first year of study at the university. Academic advisors will help students learn about the academic requirements of their majors as well as help them explore new majors if they are undecided or interested in changing their current major. University Academic Advising also provides professional program advising for students who are interested in pursuing future careers in medicine, dentistry, pharmacy, law, or other professional health degrees.

University Academic Advising offers courses which are designed to provide tools to help students with the critical transition from high school to college, to improve their academic success, or for those who are seeking a more structured experience to explore majors and future career paths.

Academic Advising & Support **Campus Learning Center**

The Campus Learning Center provides quality academic support to all Virginia Commonwealth University undergraduates. From one-on-one tutoring, academic coaching and drop-in tutoring to Supplemental Instruction sessions, the CLC offers a variety of ways to help students do well in their classes and reach their academic goals.

Student Life & Support **Office of Multicultural Student Affairs (OMSA)**

A resource for students, faculty and staff, the VCU Office of Multicultural Student Affairs works toward the primary mission of assisting traditionally underserved and/or underrepresented student populations through advising, support, program development, retention, and mentoring.

Virginia Commonwealth University
821 West Franklin Street
PO Box 842526
Richmond, VA 23284
Ph: (804) 828-1222
ugrad@vcu.edu
www.vcu.edu

Fast Facts

STUDENT DIVERSITY

# undergraduates	24,212
% male/female	41/59
% first-generation college	n/a
% American Indian or Alaskan Native	<1
% Asian	12
% Black or African American	16
% Hispanic/Latino	7
% Native Hawaiian or Pacific Islander	<1
% White	50
% two or more races	5
% race and/or ethnicity unknown	4
% International/nonresident	3

STUDENT SUCCESS

% first-to-second year retention	87
% six-year graduation	62
% six-year graduation for underrepresented minority groups	n/a
% first-years who live on campus	83
% undergraduates who live on campus	25
full-time faculty	2,274
full-time minority faculty	627
student-faculty ratio	18:1

Popular majors Visual and Performing Arts, Psychology, Business, Health Professions, Homeland Security

Multicultural student clubs and organizations
African Student Union, Black Caucus, Filipino Americans Coming Together, Indian Student Association, Latino Student Association, NAACP at VCU, Vietnamese Student Association, Persian American Students, Caribbean Student Organization

AFFORDABILITY

Cost of Attendance

tuition	in-state: $13,684; out-of-state: $33,716
required fees	$1,142
room and board	$10,187

Financial Aid

total institutional scholarships/grants	$71,859,955
% of students with financial need	71
% of students with need awarded any financial aid	59
% of students with need awarded any need-based scholarship or grant aid	48
% of students with need whose need was fully met	6
% Pell Grant recipients among first-years	29
average aid package	$15,203
average student loan debt upon graduation	$32,512

ADMISSIONS

# of applicants	16,848
% admitted	74
SAT Critical Reading	500-610
SAT Math	500-600
SAT Writing	n/a
ACT Composite	25
SAT/ACT optional	yes
average HS GPA	3.6

DEADLINES

regular application closing date	1/16
early decision plan	n/a
application closing date	n/a
early action plan	n/a
application closing date	n/a
application fee	$65
application fee online	$65
fee waiver for applicants with financial need	yes

Virginia Polytechnic Institute and State University

Virginia Tech takes a hands-on, engaging approach to education, preparing scholars to be leaders in their fields and communities. As the commonwealth's most comprehensive university and its leading research institution, Virginia Tech offers 240 undergraduate and graduate degree programs to more than 31,000 students and manages a research portfolio of more than $513 million. The university fulfills its land-grant mission of transforming knowledge to practice through technological leadership and by fueling economic growth and job creation locally, regionally, and across Virginia. Through a combination of its three missions of learning, discovery, and engagement, Virginia Tech continually strives to accomplish the charge of its motto Ut Prosim (That I May Serve).

Pre-College Prep & Outreach **College Access Collaborative**

Virginia Tech's College Access Collaborative is an organizational unit dedicated to college access. Consistent with Virginia Tech's land-grant mission, institutional motto (Ut Prosim, That I May Serve), and InclusiveVT initiative, the university is committed to supporting and enhancing a more diverse undergraduate student body. The Virginia Tech College Access Collaborative aims to increase academic preparation, access and affordability for first-generation, low-income, underrepresented minorities (Black, Latino, and Native American), women and students from rural and inner city communities.

Pre-College Summer Experience **Upward Bound**

Upward Bound at Virginia Tech is dedicated to encouraging and preparing low-income and potential first-generation students to pursue a college education.

Summer Bridge & Orientation **Virginia Tech Summer Academy**

The Virginia Tech Summer Academy (VTSA) is designed to ease your transition from high school to college by coupling required course work with opportunities to become familiar with university expectations, making new friends, and finding your way around campus and the Blacksburg community.

Academic Advising & Support **The Student Success Center and Other Academic Support**

The Student Success Center offers free academic support, such as tutoring and study skills seminars to undergraduate students. Programs and activities for students who are already succeeding academically, and simply want to enrich their educational experiences are also available. Dozens of college and department-based academic support programs are available along with specific diversity support and engagement opportunities.

Academic Advising & Support **University Academic Advising Center**

Academic advising at Virginia Tech is a collaborative process between student and advisor leading to the exchange of information that encourages the individual student to make responsible academic and career decisions.

Virginia Polytechnic Institute and State University
925 Prices Fork Road
Blacksburg, VA 26061
Ph: (540) 231-6267
www.vt.edu

Fast Facts

STUDENT DIVERSITY

# undergraduates	25,741
% male/female	57/43
% first-generation college	n/a
% American Indian or Alaskan Native	<1
% Asian	9
% Black or African American	4
% Hispanic/Latino	5
% Native Hawaiian or Pacific Islander	<1
% White	63
% two or more races	4
% race and/or ethnicity unknown	3
% International/nonresident	11

STUDENT SUCCESS

% first-to-second year retention	93
% six-year graduation	82
% six-year graduation for underrepresented minority groups	73
% first-years who live on campus	98
% undergraduates who live on campus	38
full-time faculty	4,206
full-time minority faculty	630
student-faculty ratio	14:1

Popular majors General Engineering University Studies Biology Business Human Nutrition, Foods, & Exercise

Multicultural student clubs and organizations
Asian American Student Union, Black Organizations Council, Black Student Alliance, Latino Association of Student Organizations, Jewish Student Union, Council of International Student Organizations, Latin Link, Native at VT, Student Hip Hop Organization, African Student Association

AFFORDABILITY

Cost of Attendance

tuition	in-state: $11,093
required fees	$2,137
room and board	$8,690

Financial Aid

total institutional scholarships/grants	n/a
% of students with financial need	67
% of students with need awarded any financial aid	90
% of students with need awarded any need-based scholarship or grant aid	79
% of students with need whose need was fully met	20
% Pell Grant recipients among first-years	n/a
average aid package	$18,334
average student loan debt upon graduation	$28,000

ADMISSIONS

# of applicants	27,178
% admitted	69
SAT Critical Reading	540-640
SAT Math	560-680
SAT Writing	530-630
ACT Composite	n/a
SAT/ACT optional	yes
average HS GPA	3.96

DEADLINES

regular application closing date	12/1
early decision plan	yes
application closing date	11/1
early action plan	n/a
application closing date	n/a
application fee	$60
application fee online	$60
fee waiver for applicants with financial need	yes

Whitman College

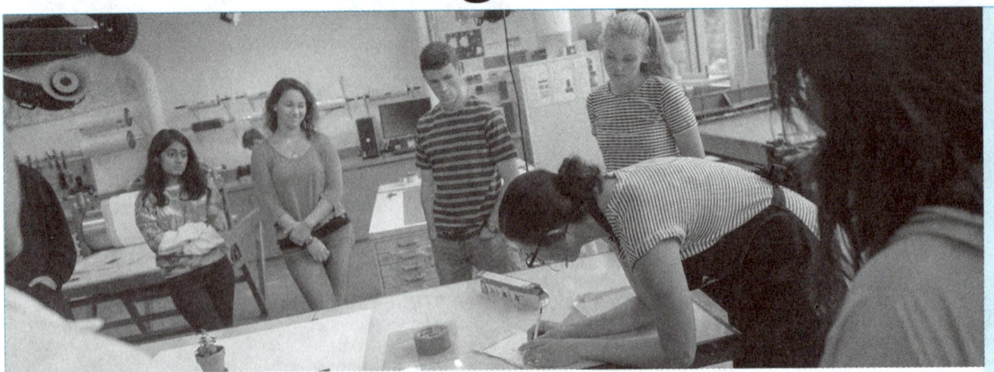

Whitman College
345 Boyer Avenue
Walla Walla, WA 99362
Ph: (877) 462-9448
admission@whitman.edu
www.whitman.edu

Founded in 1882, Whitman College is a private, co-educational liberal arts institution. Located in Walla Walla, Whitman offers an ideal setting for rigorous learning in a collaborative, non-competitive environment encouraging creativity, character and responsibility. Through the study of humanities, arts and social and natural sciences, Whitman's students develop capacities to analyze, interpret, criticize, communicate and engage. A comprehensive learning environment is supported by residential and student life programs that are intended to foster intellectual vitality, confidence, leadership and the flexibility to succeed in a changing technological, multicultural world.

Pre-College Summer Experience **Whitman Institute for Summer Enrichment (WISE)**

WISE is an expenses-paid, program for local middle school students who show academic promise from diverse backgrounds. WISE aims to generate interest in pursuing a college education for these students, who stay on campus, and attend classes taught by Whitman professors and college prep workshops. Current students act as Resident Assistants and mentors. The program includes a workshop for parents offering guidance on financial aid, academic choices in high school and other concerns about college.

Student Life & Support **Glover Alston Center (GAC)**

The GAC is a resource to facilitate Whitman's commitment to sustaining a diverse community. By providing a safe space for meaningful conversation and interaction, the GAC welcomes and supports differences, collaborates with academic departments, encourages input from divergent perspectives, enhances intercultural and international awareness, and models respect for all.

Student Life & Support **First Generation/Working Class (FG/WC) Mentorship Program**

The goal of the FG/WC Mentorship Program is to build a strong and lasting relationship between incoming and current FG/WC identified students. Current students support assist, and act as a resource on campus for their mentee through frequent interactions and open communication. The Mentorship Program puts on workshops and activities specifically to support a successful college transition for FG/WC students.

Summer Bridge & Orientation **Summer Fly-In**

Whitman's Summer Fly-In aims to ease the transition to college life for students from underrepresented backgrounds. Students are familiarized with Whitman's campus, faculty and staff members, as well as the range of resources available, such as financial aid, the writing center, health services and student activities. They have the chance to preview Whitman academics by taking part in small classroom discussions led by their future professors.

Open House, Fly-In, Visit **Visit Scholarship Program (VSP)**

Approximately 85 high school seniors from underrepresented backgrounds are invited for an expenses-paid visit to Whitman. Visiting students stay with a current student in a residence hall, visit up to two classes, meet with coaches, faculty, staff and student leaders and interview with an admission officer.

Scholarship & Financial Aid **Lomen-Douglas Scholarships**

Students whose backgrounds and experiences demonstrate the ability to contribute to increasing socioeconomic, racial or ethnic diversity awareness at Whitman are chosen to receive the Lomen-Douglas Scholarship. Scholarships range from $2,000 to $55,000 and vary depending on achievement and financial need.

Fast Facts

STUDENT DIVERSITY

# undergraduates	1,493
% male/female	43/57
% first-generation college	11
% American Indian or Alaskan Native	1
% Asian	4
% Black or African American	2
% Hispanic/Latino	7
% Native Hawaiian or Pacific Islander	1
% White	70
% two or more races	7
% race and/or ethnicity unknown	3
% International/nonresident	5

STUDENT SUCCESS

% first-to-second year retention	96
% six-year graduation	87
% six-year graduation for underrepresented minority groups	84
% first-years who live on campus	100
% undergraduates who live on campus	64
full-time faculty	165
full-time minority faculty	19
student-faculty ratio	9:1

Popular majors Biology, English, History, Environmental Studies, Psychology, Politics, Biochem/Biophysics & Molecular Biology

Multicultural student clubs and organizations American Indian Assn., Asian Cultural Assn., Black Student Union, Club Latino, First -Gen/Working-Class Students, Beyond Borders Club, South Asian Students Assn., China at Whitman, Coalition for Gender and Sexuality Awareness, Feminists Advocating Change and Empowerment, Whitman African Students Assn.

AFFORDABILITY

Cost of Attendance

tuition	$49,780
required fees	$390
room and board	$12,524

Financial Aid

total institutional scholarships/grants	$25,000,000
% of students with financial need	50
% of students with need awarded any financial aid	100
% of students with need awarded any need-based scholarship or grant aid	100
% of students with need whose need was fully met	70
% Pell Grant recipients among first-years	11
average aid package	$36,400
average student loan debt upon graduation	$18,000

ADMISSIONS

# of applicants	3,749
% admitted	47
SAT Critical Reading	610-730
SAT Math	600-690
SAT Writing	600-700
ACT Composite	30
SAT/ACT optional	yes
average HS GPA	3.72

DEADLINES

regular application closing date	1/15
early decision plan	yes
application closing date	1/1
early action plan	n/a
application closing date	n/a
application fee	$50
application fee online	$50
fee waiver for applicants with financial need	yes

Marshall University

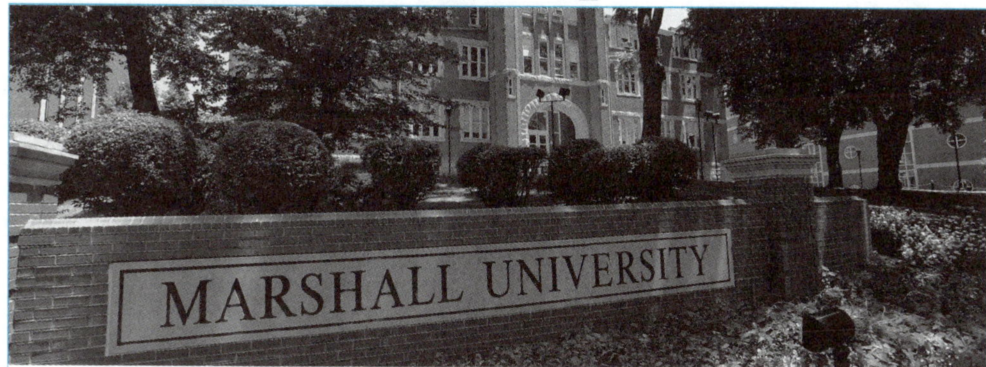

Marshall University is a historic public university located in Huntington, WV with over 13,000 students from 49 states and 56 foreign countries. We strive to provide a diverse in-depth real-world learning environment; 14 percent of our full-time institutional faculty are minorities and 83 percent of our faculty have Ph.D. or terminal degrees. An average class size is 21 students, which provides for one-on-one attention with professors that's unmatched. With over 230 recognized student organizations there are many opportunities for learning outside of the classroom. Founded in 1837 as Marshall Academy and named for John Marshall, 4th Chief Justice of the United States, we are all Sons or Daughters of Marshall.

First-Year Experience & Transition **First Year Experience**

The First Year Experience at Marshall is a compilation of activities and opportunities for our freshman students. Among the programs are New Student Orientation, First Year Seminar, First Year Residential Experience, Living Learning Communities and the Week of Welcome. All aimed at helping freshman integrate into the MU community and jumpstart a successful academic experience. http://www.marshall.edu/uc/fye/

Academic Advising & Support **Tutoring Services**

The University College provides tutoring services to help students stay on track by providing help in subjects such as business, science, math and modern language. http://www.marshall.edu/uc/tutoring-services/

First-Year Experience & Transition **Week of Welcome**

The program is offered during that pivotal first week of the college experience. It is a collaborative, introductory, effort to welcome, educate and socialize freshmen to the Marshall University campus, academic expectations, personnel, resources and traditions during the first few weeks of the fall semester. http://www.marshall.edu/wow/

Student Life & Support **Counseling Center**

The Counseling Center provides students with somewhere to sit down and talk to professionals about any concerns or issues they are dealing with. We offer services to help you attain both personal and academic goals. Services may include, but are not limited to, counseling focused on mental health symptoms such as depression and anxiety, including test anxiety, stress management, conflict resolution, anger management, and relationship concerns. http://www.marshall.edu/counseling/

Pre-College Prep & Outreach **TRiO Program**

TRiO programs are federally-funded initiatives to help support low-income and first-generation college students enter college, graduate and move on to participate more fully in America's economic and social life. The Student Support Services TRiO program at Marshall helps students improve their reading, learning and study skills. We work individually helping students to achieve academic goals. Student Support Services provides help to 200 eligible participants. http://www.marshall.edu/trio/

Student Life & Support **Office of Student Advocacy and Success**

The Office of Student Advocacy and Success is committed to helping Marshall University students with their needs. The office will work with the student, their family, the campus community and faculty to help assist in the learning environment. The office can help guide students through: academic appeals, student conduct decisions and providing accountability plans to ensure academic success. http://www.marshall.edu/student-affairs/advocacy/

Marshall University
1 John Marshall Drive
Huntington, WV 25755
Ph: (304) 696-3170
admissions@marshall.edu
www.marshall.edu

Fast Facts

STUDENT DIVERSITY

# undergraduates	9,615
% male/female	43/57
% first-generation college	n/a
% American Indian or Alaskan Native	<1
% Asian	<1
% Black or African American	7
% Hispanic/Latino	2
% Native Hawaiian or Pacific Islander	<1
% White	84
% two or more races	3
% race and/or ethnicity unknown	1
% International/nonresident	1

STUDENT SUCCESS

% first-to-second year retention	75
% six-year graduation	45
% six-year graduation for underrepresented minority groups	34
% first-years who live on campus	59
% undergraduates who live on campus	24
full-time faculty	500
full-time minority faculty	97
student-faculty ratio	19:1

Popular majors Health Professions, Business/ Marketing, Liberal Arts/General Studies, Education, Psychology

Multicultural student clubs and organizations Campus Activities Board (CAB), Student Government Association, Black United Students, International Student Organization, Native American Student Organization, Muslim Student Association, National Panhellenic Council, Intercultural Hispanic Organization

AFFORDABILITY

Cost of Attendance

tuition	in-state: $7,798; out-of-state: $17,856
required fees	$1,122
room and board	$10,126

Financial Aid

total institutional scholarships/grants	$7,975,547
% of students with financial need	77
% of students with need awarded any financial aid	99
% of students with need awarded any need-based scholarship or grant aid	78
% of students with need whose need was fully met	33
% Pell Grant recipients among first-years	45
average aid package	$11,418
average student loan debt upon graduation	$27,121

ADMISSIONS

# of applicants	4,891
% admitted	89
SAT Critical Reading	450-575
SAT Math	430-560
SAT Writing	420-550
ACT Composite	22
SAT/ACT optional	no
average HS GPA	3.40

DEADLINES

regular application closing date	rolling
early decision plan	no
application closing date	n/a
early action plan	no
application closing date	n/a
application fee	$40
application fee online	$40
fee waiver for applicants with financial need	yes

Marquette University

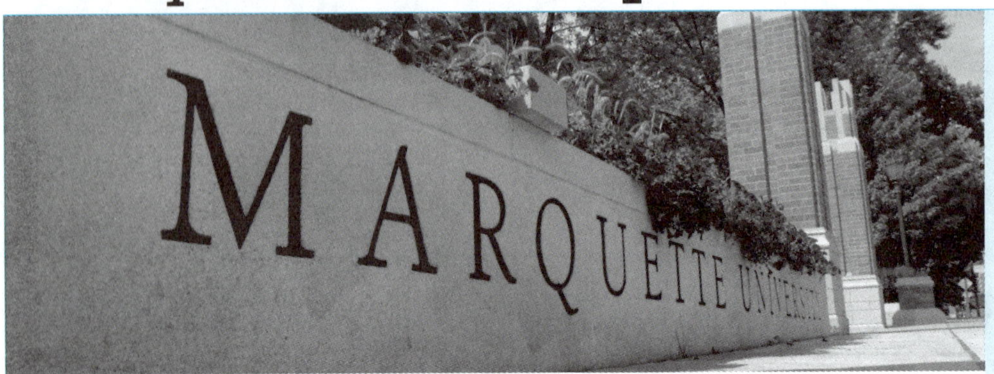

Marquette University is a private, Jesuit university consistently named one of the top 5 Catholic universities. Marquette is dedicated to fostering excellence, faith, leadership and service in all of its students and offers strong support to first generation and underserved students. Our Urban Scholars program provides full-tuition scholarships to talented, economically-disadvantaged students. The university runs four unique programs under The Educational Opportunity Program (EOP). Marquette's Multicultural Center works hard to promote diversity awareness and cultural inclusiveness within the diverse student body, and the Office of Student Educational Services supports every individual student's educational goals. With an urban campus located in downtown Milwaukee, Marquette students take advantage of the many educational, cultural and social outlets the city has to offer.

Pre-College Prep & Outreach **Upward Bound Math and Science**

Local high school students who come from low-income families in which neither parent holds a bachelor's degree can benefit from Marquette's Upward Bound Math and Science, a pre-college program that provides a group of students with the right tools to pursue their dreams of earning a college degree. This program is intended for students with a strong interest in math, science, computer technology, or engineering. Students benefit from weekly tutoring, field trips, workshops and a six-week summer enrichment program.

Scholarship & Financial Aid **Goizueta Foundation Scholarship Award**

The Goizueta Foundation Scholarship Award is for Hispanic/Latino high school seniors who demonstrate financial need. The award covers half of the Marquette tuition.

Scholarship & Financial Aid **Boys & Girls Clubs / Urban Scholars Scholarship Program**

Marquette's Urban Scholars Program provides ten full-tuition awards to low-income students, including undocumented students, who show great academic promise. The award guarantees that a student's federal, state and Marquette gift assistance cover tuition costs for a four-year undergraduate program, provided the student maintains a 2.0 GPA. Students are selected for this award based on academic merit, leadership and financial need. The ten awards are granted to graduates from Milwaukee area high schools and the Cristo Rey High School network.

Scholarship & Financial Aid **Opus Scholars Award**

The Opus Scholars Award (a full-tuition scholarship) recognizes a combination of outstanding academic achievement as well as financial need for two incoming engineering freshmen. Priority consideration is given to first-generation students who have participated in organizations that serve low-income youth, such as the Cristo Rey Network and the Boys & Girls Clubs.

Marquette University
1250 W Wisconsin Avenue
Milwaukee, WI 53233
Ph: (414) 288-7302
admissions@marquette.edu
www.marquette.edu

Fast Facts

STUDENT DIVERSITY

# undergraduates	8,334
% male/female	48/52
% first-generation college	24
% American Indian or Alaskan Native	<1
% Asian	7
% Black or African American	4
% Hispanic/Latino	12
% Native Hawaiian or Pacific Islander	<1
% White	70
% two or more races	4
% race and/or ethnicity unknown	<1
% International/nonresident	4

STUDENT SUCCESS

% first-to-second year retention	89
% six-year graduation	81
% six-year graduation for underrepresented minority groups	74
% first-years who live on campus	96
% undergraduates who live on campus	54
full-time faculty	1,128
full-time minority faculty	167
student-faculty ratio	15:1

Popular majors Biomedical Sciences, Nursing, Marketing, Engineering, Speech Pathology

Multicultural student clubs and organizations African Students Association, Arab Student Association, Black Student Council, Chinese Student Association, Cuban American Student Association, Global Village, Indian Student Association, Latin American Student Organization, Pacific Islands Student Organization, Society of Caribbean Ambassadors

AFFORDABILITY

Cost of Attendance

tuition	$39,330
required fees	$285
room and board	$11,370

Financial Aid

total institutional scholarships/grants	$105,609,831
% of students with financial need	62
% of students with need awarded any financial aid	99
% of students with need awarded any need-based scholarship or grant aid	98
% of students with need whose need was fully met	26
% Pell Grant recipients among first-years	18
average aid package	$22,399
average student loan debt upon graduation	$35,204

ADMISSIONS

# of applicants	20,486
% admitted	74
SAT Critical Reading	530-640
SAT Math	540-660
SAT Writing	510-640
ACT Composite	27
SAT/ACT optional	n/a
average HS GPA	n/a

DEADLINES

regular application closing date	12/1
early decision plan	n/a
application closing date	n/a
early action plan	n/a
application closing date	n/a
application fee	n/a
application fee online	n/a
fee waiver for applicants with financial need	n/a

University of Wisconsin–Milwaukee

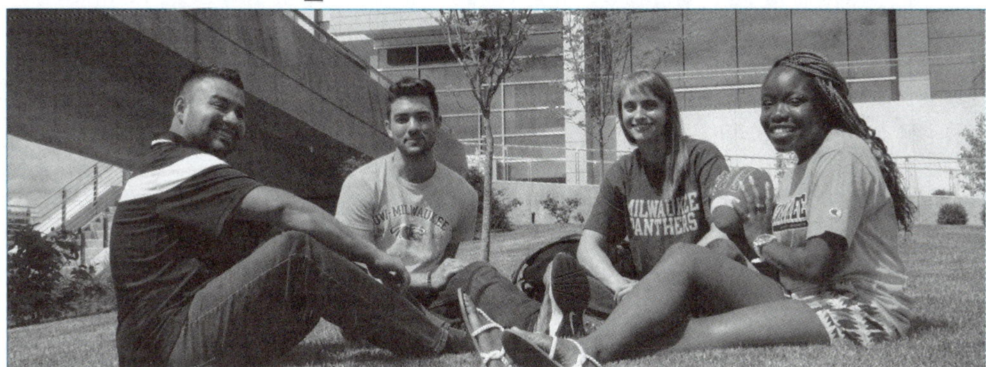

University of Wisconsin–Milwaukee
3253 N. Downer Ave
Milwaukee, WI 53211
Ph: (414) 229-2222
www.uwm.edu

Recognized as one of the nation's 115 top research universities, UW–Milwaukee provides a world-class education to more than 25,000 students from 91 countries. Its 14 schools and colleges include Wisconsin's only schools of architecture, freshwater sciences and public health, and it is a leading educator of nurses and teachers. UW–Milwaukee partners with leading companies to conduct joint research, offer student internships and serve as an economic engine for southeastern Wisconsin. The *Princeton Review* named UW–Milwaukee a 2018 "Best Midwestern" university based on overall academic excellence and student reviews, as well as a top "Green College."

Scholarship & Financial Aid **U1.0 Biweekly Workshops**

The U1.0 biweekly workshops are opportunities for first-generation college students at UWM to meet other first-generation college students, and engage in interactive workshops facilitated by distinguished faculty and staff. The workshops are designed to help students explore campus resources and learn skills they don't necessary learn in the classroom (i.e. study skills, financial literacy, applying for scholarships, leadership, stress management, and community building) to succeed at UW–Milwaukee.

First-Year Experience & Transition **U1.0 Kickoff, Fall Welcome**

The U1.0 Kick Off is a welcome reception for both new and returning first-generation students at UW–Milwaukee. The purpose of the event is to provide first-generation college students information about U1.0, campus resources, and the opportunity to meet other faculty and staff who are first-generation.

Academic Courses & Service Learning **U1.0: I'm First Living Learning Community (LLC)**

Students in this LLC will live together in the residence halls and take a class together. Students learn and lead through service learning with and for each other, share perspectives and get to the core of Multicultural America. Be a pioneer to make a difference … just one, maybe the first.

Student Life & Support **First Gen Week (September)**

First Generation Week is an awareness week to educate others about first-generation college students, and to celebrate the strengths and successes of UW–Milwaukee's first-generation community. The week includes a panel discussion, a film screening, and video recordings of first-generation college students sharing their personal success stories to encourage and inspire others.

Mentoring **U1.0 Monthly Spotlight**

The U1.0 monthly spotlight is to highlight a first-generation faculty/staff/student at UW–Milwaukee. The purpose of the spotlight is to create an opportunity for the UWM community to gain insight through the lenses of a first-generation via comments from the individual:

- First Generation Defined
- First Generation Advice
- Proudest Accomplishment
- Best Thing About UWM
- Favorite Resource on Campus
- Best Place to Study on Campus.

Fast Facts

STUDENT DIVERSITY

# undergraduates	20,777
% male/female	48/52
% first-generation college	39
% American Indian or Alaskan Native	<1
% Asian	5
% Black or African American	7
% Hispanic/Latino	3
% Native Hawaiian or Pacific Islander	0
% White	66
% two or more races	13
% race and/or ethnicity unknown	1
% International/nonresident	4

STUDENT SUCCESS

% first-to-second year retention	74
% six-year graduation	41
% six-year graduation for underrepresented minority groups	26
% first-years who live on campus	74
% undergraduates who live on campus	18
full-time faculty	1,010
full-time minority faculty	223
student-faculty ratio	19:1

Popular majors Finance, Marketing, Education, Psychology, Nursing

Multicultural student clubs and organizations Better Together Interfaith, Brazilian Cultural Club, Desi Student Association, Geek Culture Club, Hmong Student Association, Out in the Sciences, Tech, Engineering, & Mathematics, Signing Student Association, Sisters in Solidarity, Youth Empowered in the Struggle, and Zeta Sigma Chi Multicultural Sorority

AFFORDABILITY

Cost of Attendance

tuition	$9,565
required fees	$1,337
room and board	$10,140

Financial Aid

total institutional scholarships/grants	$3,601,594
% of students with financial need	78
% of students with need awarded any financial aid	83
% of students with need awarded any need-based scholarship or grant aid	57
% of students with need whose need was fully met	19
% Pell Grant recipients among first-years	36
average aid package	$7,501
average student loan debt upon graduation	$36,945

ADMISSIONS

# of applicants	10,000
% admitted	72
SAT Critical Reading	n/a
SAT Math	n/a
SAT Writing	n/a
ACT Composite	22
SAT/ACT optional	no
average HS GPA	3.658

DEADLINES

regular application closing date	8/1
early decision plan	yes
application closing date	3/1
early action plan	n/a
application closing date	rolling
application fee	$50
application fee online	$50
fee waiver for applicants with financial need	yes

University of Wisconsin–Platteville

The University of Wisconsin-Platteville is a comprehensive, four-year public institution of higher education and is the fastest growing UW System school. Founded in 1866, UW-Platteville has been excelling in higher-education for over 150 years thanks to a determined Pioneer attitude that has enriched Southwest Wisconsin and the tri-state region.

First-Year Experience & Transition **Academic Support Programs**

The Mission of the First Year Experience (FYE) program: 1. A student's first year at UW-Platteville is an opportunity to explore and develop an individual's identity and future direction. 2. The university is committed to creating a safe environment conducive for learning, engagement, and personal growth. To chart a pathway for success, each student will embark on an individual journey to explore and complete a degree. 3. The Academic Support Program (ASP) is dedicated to creating opportunities for students to develop academic and social skills that are necessary to successfully complete this journey.

Academic Advising & Support **Academic Support Programs**

Academic Support Programs is here to help you! The mission of Academic Support Programs is to equip students for academic success by providing innovative learning strategies and connections to campus resources. All UW-Platteville students can choose from a comprehensive range of services, including tutoring, writing assistance, collaborative learning through a Peer Assisted Learning program, academic coaching, peer workshop instruction, and a first year experience course. The department also coordinates academic intervention for students experiencing grade-related and class attendance issues and provides grade recovery resources for students on academic probation. We are dedicated to helping students refine and strengthen the academic skills necessary for success in college.

Academic Advising and Support **Student Support Services**

Student Support Services (SSS) offers free, one-on-one, scheduled, course-based tutoring for its participants. In order to become a participant in SSS, a student must meet at least one of the eligibility requirements.

Scholarship & Financial Aid **New Freshmen Scholarships**

New Freshman Scholarships are a series of general university and specific college/major scholarships. Students must apply and be admitted to UW-Platteville by Jan. 15 to receive a scholarship letter and instructions on how to apply for NFS. Deadline: February 1

Pre-College Summer Experience **Pre-College**

Pre-College Programs is brought to you by the Office of Multicultural Student Affairs. We are excited for a start to another productive summer for our students and are ready to take on the challenge of bringing opportunities to students everywhere!

Summer Bridge & Orientation **Summer Bridge**

The SUCCEED Summer Bridge Program is a residential summer program that starts 3 weeks before classes. During this 3-week program students will get a jump start on becoming a college student. Students will enroll and start three required courses during this program: First Year Experience Course, Public Speaking and Fitness Assessment. Also included during the program are math workshops, writing skill enhancement workshops and a variety of other opportunities to help students prepare and adjust to college life.

University of Wisconsin–Platteville
1 University Plaza
Platteville, WI 53818
Ph: (608) 342-1125
admit@uwplatt.edu
www.uwplatt.edu

Fast Facts

STUDENT DIVERSITY

# undergraduates	7,520
% male/female	65/35
% first-generation college	43
% American Indian or Alaskan Native	<1
% Asian	1
% Black or African American	1
% Hispanic/Latino	3
% Native Hawaiian or Pacific Islander	<1
% White	89
% two or more races	2
% race and/or ethnicity unknown	<1
% International/nonresident	2

STUDENT SUCCESS

% first-to-second year retention	74
% six-year graduation	53
% six-year graduation for underrepresented minority groups	22
% first-years who live on campus	99
% undergraduates who live on campus	47
full-time faculty	347
full-time minority faculty	81
student-faculty ratio	21:1

Popular majors Engineering, Business/Marketing, Agriculture, Education, Criminal Justice

Multicultural student clubs and organizations Asian Students in Action Club, Black Student Union, French Club, Hmong Club, International Club

AFFORDABILITY

Cost of Attendance

tuition	in-state: $6,298; out-of-state: $14,149
required fees	$1,190
room and board	$7,160

Financial Aid

total institutional scholarships/grants	$1,378,757
% of students with financial need	88
% of students with need awarded any financial aid	100
% of students with need awarded any need-based scholarship or grant aid	77
% of students with need whose need was fully met	24
% Pell Grant recipients among first-years	27
average aid package	$6,227
average student loan debt upon graduation	$19,856

ADMISSIONS

# of applicants	4,401
% admitted	77
SAT Critical Reading	n/a
SAT Math	n/a
SAT Writing	n/a
ACT Composite	23
SAT/ACT optional	no
average HS GPA	n/a

DEADLINES

regular application closing date	rolling
early decision plan	n/a
application closing date	n/a
early action plan	n/a
application closing date	n/a
application fee	$50
application fee online	$50
fee waiver for applicants with financial need	yes

University of Wisconsin–River Falls

The University of Wisconsin–River Falls is a public university located in River Falls, Wisconsin. Situated on the Kinnickinnic River, our beautiful, mid-sized campus spans across 303 acres and is home to 11 residence halls, a state-of-the-art student center and a soon-to-be $63.5 million health and human performance center. As a leader in providing academic excellence, UW–River Falls enrolls nearly 6,000 students in four distinct colleges with undergraduate and graduate degrees in 60 majors. In addition to dynamic learning experiences in the classroom, UW–River Falls offer a variety of programming allowing you to take part in research, cultural, leadership and recreational opportunities. Falcon Athletics has 16 NCAA varsity teams that compete in the Wisconsin Intercollegiate Athletic Conference (WIAC), regarded as the strongest Division III conference in the country.

Open House, Fly-In, Visit **College Visit Day**

We strongly encourage all high school juniors, seniors and their guests to attend our College Visit Day, a half-day program to gain an overview of what it's like to live and learn at UWRF.

Special Admissions Policy **UWRF Pathways Program**

The UWRF Pathways Program is designed to support first-year students for whom English is not their first language. The Pathways Program assists students as they adjust to university academic expectations, while taking into consideration their English language proficiencies. In this two-semester program, students take three general education courses and two Academic Support courses each semester. The credits earned in the Academic Support courses count toward students' cumulative GPAs but not toward their degrees.

Students who are non-native speakers of English and who have a lower ACT score due to English proficiency will be evaluated for admission into the Pathways Program. Visit our website for more information about admission into the Pathways Program.

Scholarship & Financial Aid **Scholarships**

UWRF awarded more than $1.3M in scholarships in 2015-2016. UW–River Falls also provides a Scholarship Guarantee to every new freshmen who demonstrates strong academic potential.

Scholars & Leadership **Honors Program**

The UW–River Falls Honors Program is designed to meet the educational needs of students who have an outstanding record of academic achievement and a true sense of intellectual adventure by allowing students to experience a variety of course types and educationally related experiences while gaining academic credit. Honor students benefit from priority registration, honors advising community atmosphere, connections with dedicated faculty, Collegiate Honors Society membership, and use of students, staff and faculty interaction space.

Academic Advising and Support **Academic Advising**

Advising resources are available to admitted, pre-admitted and prospective undergraduate and graduate candidates. A faculty member or a full time advisor will guide and mentor you as you progress in your program. Advising programs are active year-round programs where advisors assist students with academic affairs such as reviewing progress, plans for future semesters, and course registration.

Academic Advising and Support **Student Support Services**

SSS is funded by a federal TRIO grant and serves 200 students at UWRF. SSS seeks to improve the retention and graduation of its students through committed coaches, academic and study skill support as well as many other program benefits.

University of Wisconsin–River Falls
410 S. Third Street
112 South Hall
River Falls, WI 54022
Ph: (715) 425-3500
admissions@uwrf.edu
www.uwrf.edu

Fast Facts

STUDENT DIVERSITY

# undergraduates	5,507
% male/female	38/62
% first-generation college	47
% American Indian or Alaskan Native	1
% Asian	3
% Black or African American	2
% Hispanic/Latino	3
% Native Hawaiian or Pacific Islander	1
% White	87
% two or more races	2
% race and/or ethnicity unknown	1
% International/nonresident	5

STUDENT SUCCESS

% first-to-second year retention	74
% six-year graduation	65
% six-year graduation for underrepresented minority groups	n/a
% first-years who live on campus	88
% undergraduates who live on campus	40
full-time faculty	210
full-time minority faculty	11
student-faculty ratio	22:1

Popular majors Business, Animal Science, Biology, Psychology, Elementary Ed.

Multicultural student clubs and organizations Asian American Student Association, Black Student Union, Chinese Culture Club, French Club, German Club, Global Programming Society, Korean Student Association, Latino Student Organization, Native American Council, Sister and Brothers of Islam

AFFORDABILITY

Cost of Attendance

tuition	in-state: $8,150; out-of-state: $15,722
required fees	n/a
room and board	$6,424

Financial Aid

total institutional scholarships/grants	$11,577,268
% of students with financial need	45
% of students with need awarded any financial aid	85
% of students with need awarded any need-based scholarship or grant aid	60
% of students with need whose need was fully met	n/a
% Pell Grant recipients among first-years	29
average aid package	$10,994
average student loan debt upon graduation	$27,134

ADMISSIONS

# of applicants	3,236
% admitted	72
SAT Critical Reading	n/a
SAT Math	n/a
SAT Writing	n/a
ACT Composite	22
SAT/ACT optional	no
average HS GPA	3.3

DEADLINES

regular application closing date	rolling
early decision plan	none
application closing date	rolling
early action plan	none
application closing date	rolling
application fee	$50
application fee online	$50
fee waiver for applicants with financial need	yes

Glossary of Terms

The Glossary of Terms is printed with permission from First in the Family, an initiative of What Kids Can Do. We've updated and added a few additional terms that we think are helpful. Visit www.firstinthefamily.org to find videos, planning checklists, helpful links, and more resources from and for first-generation college students.

The college application process is filled with special terms, forms, deadlines, requirements, standardized tests, college "searches" and visits—and more. It is daunting, especially for students who are the first in their family to go to college. On these pages, we offer a list of terms and definitions students, parents, and community mentors will encounter along the way. We have grouped the terms, alphabetically, in these categories: (1) applying; (2) college entrance exams; (3) types of institutions; (4) college acceptance terms; (5) some college lingo; (6) types of post-secondary degrees.

We've created a separate section for the financial aid process.

APPLYING

Applicant: Any student who has completed the college application process at a particular institution.

Application: A college application is part of the competitive college admissions system. Admissions departments usually require students to complete an application for admission that generally consists of academic records, personal essays, letters of recommendation, and a list of extracurricular activities. Most schools require the SAT or ACT. Deadlines for admission applications are established and published by each college or university.

Application Deadline: The date, set by college admissions offices, after which applications for admission will not be accepted.

Advanced Placement (AP): AP courses are college-level classes taught in the high school following guidelines and covering material that will instruct students in AP subject areas and should prepare them to take Advanced Placement tests offered by The College Board.

"Best Fit": The college search is not about getting into the best college. There is no school that is best for all students. Some students do best at large public universities; others excel in small liberal arts colleges; still others want to study far from home. If you want to make the most of college, don't just apply to the big–name schools or the ones your friends are excited about. Do your own research to find schools that are the best fit for you.

Campus Interview: This is a personal, face-to-face interaction between an admissions applicant and an institutional representative (admissions officer, alumnus, faculty, etc.). Interviews are rarely required.

Campus Visit/Tour: A service by the college admissions office for prospective students, allowing them to visit various campus buildings, meet key institutional personnel, and get a firsthand look at campus life.

Catalogue: A catalogue is a comprehensive publication that provides a detailed overview of an institution, including its mission, programs, costs, admissions requirements, faculty and administration, etc.

College Fair: An event at which colleges, universities, and other organizations related to higher education present themselves in an exposition atmosphere for the purpose of attracting and identifying potential applicants.

College Rep Visit: This is when a college or university admissions representative visits a high school or community site for the purpose of recruiting students for admission to the institution.

College Search: These are the steps you take in the early phases of college planning in order to identify, locate, and investigate college-level programs that meet your individual interests, abilities, and needs as a student.

Common Application: The Common Application (informally known as the Common App) makes it possible for students to use one admissions application to apply to over 750 member colleges and universities. There is a Common Application for First-Year Admission and a Common Application for Transfer Admission. Both versions allow the application to be filled out once online and submitted to all schools with the same information going to each.

Course Rigor: Course rigor is how challenging your high school classes are, and they help admissions officers to see whether or not you are prepared for college-level coursework. For example, AP, Honors, IB, and dual enrollment courses are all academically rigorous courses.

Demonstrated Interest: This includes a student's expression of his or her desire to attend a particular college through campus visits, contact with admissions officers, and other actions that attract the attention of college admissions personnel. While not all institutions use this as a factor in accepting students for admissions, studies have shown that more than half of schools do consider demonstrated interest in their admissions decisions.

Dual Enrollment: Dual enrollment students are in high school but taking college courses, and are receiving both college and high school credit.

Extracurriculars: Extracurricular activities are simply anything you do that is not a high school course or paid employment (but note that paid work experience is of interest to colleges and can substitute for some extracurricular activities). You should define your extracurricular activities in broad terms—many applicants make the mistake of thinking of them solely as school-sponsored groups such as yearbook, band or football. Not so. Most community and family activities are also "extracurricular."

GPA (Grade Point Average): Quantitative measure of a student's grades. The GPA is figured by averaging the numerical value of a student's grades. It is cumulative, starting freshman year: grades count every year. A poor GPA in ninth grade can drag down the overall average, despite, for example, good grades junior year.

Honors Classes: The difference between a regular class (such as English 1) and the honors class (English 1 Honors) is not necessarily the amount of work, but the type of work required and the pace of studying. Honors courses are not advanced in the same sense that high school Advanced Placement and International Baccalaureate courses are. Rather, honors courses are enriched; they offer the same material in greater depth and with a faster pace.

In-state (Resident) Student: A student whose permanent residence is in the same state as the college or university he or she attends or hopes to attend. In-state students pay lower tuition than do out-of-state students.

Personal Statement: Also referred to as "the college essay," this is a brief narrative essay on a single subject, required by many colleges as part of the application process for admission.

Prospective Student: Any student who is a potential applicant for admission, particularly those who have shown interest in attending the institution or in which the institution has shown interest.

Out-of-State (Non-Resident) Student: Student whose permanent residence is in a different state than that of the college or university which he or she attends or hopes to attend. Out-of-state students generally pay higher tuition than do instate students.

"Reach School": A college or university that you have a chance of getting into, but your test scores, GPA and/or class rank are a bit on the low side when you look at the school's profile. The top U.S. colleges and top universities should always be considered reach schools.

Recommendations: Statements or letters of endorsement written on a student's behalf during the college application process.

"Likely School": A college or university where you clearly meet the admission requirements: minimum GPA, test scores, etc. It's important, though, that the school also be one that you would want to attend, should you not gain admission to more selective colleges.

School Profile: This is an overview of your high school's program, grading system, course offerings, and other features that your school is submits to admissions offices along with your transcript. For better or worse, admissions offices use this information to weigh your GPA, placing a student's GPA against the academic reputation of the school she or he attends.

Selectivity: Selectivity is the degree to which a college or university admits or denies admission based on the individual student's record of academic achievement. In general, a highly selective school admits 25% of applicants, a very selective school admits 26% to 49% of applicants, a selective school admits 50% to 75% of applicants and a school with open admission admits applicants based on space availability.

Supplement: Many schools which accept the Common Application also require a supplement, or addition to the general application, which is specific to the school. Generally, this supplement will include an additional essay.

Transcript: This is the official document containing the record of a student's academic performance and testing history. The school at which a student is or has been officially enrolled must issue the transcript, certified by the signature of an authorized school administrator. The school's official seal or watermarked school stationery may also be used to authenticate the transcript.

Virtual Tour: This is an online feature offered by some colleges and universities to allow prospective students to view various aspects of campus life without visiting the institutions in person.

COLLEGE ENTRANCE EXAMS

ACT: A two-hour-and-55-minute examination that measures a student's knowledge and achievement in four subject areas—English, mathematics, reading and science reasoning—to determine the student's readiness for college-level instruction. There is also an optional writing test that assesses students' skills in writing an essay. The ACT is scored on a scale of 1 to 36 for each of the four areas. The four subject area scores are averaged to create a Composite Score.

PLAN Test: This test is usually taken in the sophomore year to prepare the student for the ACT.

PSAT Test: This exam prepares students for the SAT and is used to qualify students for the National Merit Scholarship semifinals and other academic awards.

SAT: This is a widely used college entrance examination program administered by the College Board. The SAT test prioritizes content that reflects the kind of reading and math students will encounter in college and their future work lives. It is a 3-hour exam measuring verbal and mathematical skills, as well as grammar/conventions and the ability to write a brief essay. Students may earn a total of up to 1600 points on two sections Evidence-Based Reading and Writing (200-800) and Math (200-800), with an optional essay scored separately.

SAT Subject Test: SAT subject tests (also known as SAT II tests) are offered in many areas of study including English, mathematics, many sciences, history, and foreign languages. Some colleges require students to take one or more SAT subject tests when they apply for admission.

Test Optional School: A college or university which does not require applying students to submit ACT or SAT scores.

TYPES OF POST SECONDARY INSTITUTIONS

Art School (Arts College, Art Institute, Conservatory): An institution specializing in the visual, performing, and/or creative arts.

College: An institution of higher learning, often referred to as a "four-year" institution, which grants the bachelor's degree in liberal arts or science or both.

Community College: Community colleges, sometimes called junior colleges, technical colleges, or city colleges, are primarily two-year public institutions providing higher education and lower-level courses, granting certificates, diplomas, and associate's degrees. Many also offer continuing and adult education. After graduating from a community college, some students transfer to a four-year liberal arts college or university for two to three years to complete a bachelor's degree.

Faith-Based Institution: Faith-based colleges and universities are those institutions of higher learning related to a faith tradition.

Graduate School: Usually within universities, these schools offer degree programs beyond the bachelor's degree.

Hispanic-Serving Institution: Hispanic-Serving Institutions are institutions of higher education which serve a student body that includes at least 25% Hispanic/:atino students.

Historically Black College: Historically black colleges and universities (HBCUs) are institutions of higher education in the United States that were established before 1964 with the intention of serving the black community. There are 105 HBCUs today, including public and private, two-year and four-year institutions, medical schools and community colleges. Almost all are in former slave states.

Liberal Arts College: A degree-granting institution where the academic focus is on developing the intellect and instruction in the humanities and sciences, rather than on training for a particular vocational, technical, or professional pursuit.

Military Service Academy: Military service academies are institutions which prepare students to become leaders in a specific branch of the armed forces.

Private Institution: This is a college or university funded by private sources without any control by a government agency. The cost of attending a private institution is generally higher than the cost at a public institution.

Proprietary Institution: This is a term used to describe postsecondary schools that are private and are legally permitted to make a profit. Most proprietary schools offer technical and vocational courses.

Public Institution: A college or university that receives public funding, primarily from a local, state, or national government that oversees and regulates the school's operations is considered a public institution.

Tribal Colleges and Universities: Tribal Colleges and Universities (TCUs) are institutions chartered by tribal governments to serve and support American Indian students (along with other students as well).

University: A "post-secondary institution" that consists of a liberal arts college, a diverse graduate program, and usually two or more professional schools or faculties, and that is empowered to confer degrees in various fields of study.

Vocational or Technical School: This type of institution is similar to a community college in that it offers specific career-oriented programs that last from a few months to a couple of years. Most are specialized and offer intense training in one specific skill area.

Single-Sex (or Single-Gender) College: This is a college that accepts either women only or men only.

COLLEGE ACCEPTANCE TERMS

Acceptance: The decision by an admissions officer or committee to offer the opportunity for enrollment as a student at a particular institution.

College Selection: The act of choosing and making the decision to enroll in and attend a particular higher-education program.

Deferred Admission: A category of admission used in conjunction with early (action, decision, notification, or acceptance) plans to indicate that a student has not been admitted early but will in the applicant pool for reconsideration during the review of applications for regular admissions.

Deferred Enrollment: This is a category of admission available at some institutions for fully accepted students who wish—for a justifiable reason—to take a semester or year off before enrolling in college.

Denial: The decision by an admissions officer or committee to not offer a student admission to a particular institution.

Early Action: Early action is when a prospective student applies for admission by early deadline (before the regular admission deadline) and receives notice of acceptance, denial, or deferment with no obligation to the university to enroll, if accepted for admission.

Early Admission: Through this program, qualifying high school juniors with outstanding academic records may forego their senior year in high school and enroll in a college or university.

Early Decision: Through this program offered by many post-secondary schools, students willing to commit to a school if accepted submit their application by a date well before the general admission deadline. If accepted, the student must enroll in that school, so students should only apply early decision to their first choice school.

Gap-Year Programs: Year-long programs designed for high school graduates who wish to defer enrollment in college while engaging in meaningful activities, such as academic programs, structured travel, community service, etc.

Notification Date: The date by which applicants who are accepted for admission are expected to notify the institutions of their intent to enroll and make enrollment deposits. That date is often on or around May 1st.

Rolling Admissions: This is a practice used by some institutions to review and complete applications as they arrive, rather than according to a set deadline.

Waitlist: An applicant is put on the waitlist when an admissions officer or committee decides to offer the applicant the opportunity to enroll in the institution only if there is space available in the incoming class after fully admitted students have responded to their offers to enroll. This category of admissions is reserved for students whose profiles are strong, but who are marginally qualified in comparison to the overall strength of others in the pool of applicants.

SOME COLLEGE LINGO

Alumni: This is a group of people who have graduated from a college or university.

Audit: To attend a class without receiving credit for the class.

Commuter students: Full-time students who live with their parents, part-time students who live in off-campus apartments, parents with children at home, and full-time workers—in sum, students for whom campus residency is not an option. Work or family obligations often mean that commuter students are unable to spend additional time outside of the classroom on campus. More than 85 percent of college and university students do not live in university-owned housing.

Course Numbers: Numbers assigned to specific classes.

Credit (or Semester) Hour: Credit given for attending one lecture hour of class each week for 15 weeks or equivalent. Most college classes are three credit hours, meaning their total meeting time for a week is three hours.

Developmental Education: Instructional and support activities designed to keep unprepared students in college and help them improve their basic skills so that they can successfully complete a program and achieve their educational goals.

Enrollment: The action of enrolling or being enrolled. The number of people enrolled, typically at a school or college.

First-Generation Student: A student whose parents have no college experience.

First-Year Student: A college freshman.

Matriculation: The payment of deposits, tuition, fees, and other charges to enroll in a program of studies at an educational institution. A university might make a distinction between "matriculated students," who are actually accumulating credits toward a degree, and a relative few "non-matriculated students" who may be "auditing" courses or taking classes without receiving credits.

Major: A student's concentrated field of study.

Minor: A student's secondary field of study.

Orientation: Orientation is generally held for first-year students during the summer or immediately before the fall semester begins, and is designed to help new students adjust to their new community.

Placement Tests: Colleges and universities use these examinations to place students in courses—most often mathematics and foreign languages—that match their proficiency. In some cases, a student's level of competency on the test may exempt them from having to take a course required for graduation.

Prerequisite: A course that must be taken prior to enrollment in another course.

Registration: Enrollment in classes.

Residence Halls: Dormitories, apartments, houses, and other living quarters provided for students by the college or university in which they are enrolled.

Student Persistence: This is the act of working, progressing, and earning credits toward graduation in an academic environment.

Student Retention: This is the degree to which students remain enrolled as members of the college or university community and persist toward graduation.

Study Abroad: A program through which a college student spends an extended period of time studying in another country, organized through their college.

Undergraduate Student: A student enrolled in a 4- or 5-year bachelor's degree program, an associate's degree program, or a vocational or technical program below the baccalaureate.

Underrepresented Minority: Students who come from ethnic backgrounds underrepresented on a particular college campus.

TYPES OF POST-SECONDARY DEGREES

A.A.: This stands for an "associate of arts" degree, which can be earned at most two-year colleges.

A.A.S.: This refers to an "associate of applied science" degree, which can be earned at some two-year colleges.

B.A. or B.S.: B.A. stands for "bachelor of arts," and B.S. stands for "bachelor of science." Both degrees can be earned at four-year colleges.

Graduate Degrees: These degrees are earned beyond the bachelor's degree when the student completes graduate school curriculum requirements. Common examples include the MA (master's degree), PhD (doctoral degree) MBA (master's degree in business administration), MD (medical doctor).

Certificates: In an economy that increasingly rewards specialization, more and more institutions are offering certification programs, typically a package of five or six courses, for credit or not, taken over three to 18 months. Some cost a few thousand dollars, others much more.

FINANCIAL AID TERMS

The financial aid terms offered here are intended for high school students, their families, and mentors. Applying for financial aid for college may seem overwhelming, like a maze. But the payoff can be substantial. Ask for help from those who know the process. Keep an eye out for free workshops—at school and in the community—where you can get hands-on assistance filling out the FAFSA.

SOME BASICS

Average Loan Debt Upon Graduation: This is the average amount which students are responsible for repaying to their college or university after their graduation.

Award Letter: An award letter from a school states the type and amount of financial aid the school is willing to provide the student, if s/he accepts admission and registers as a full-time student.

Cost of Attending College: This is the total cost of going to college, including tuition, room and board, books, transportation, fees, and personal expenses.

CSS Profile: The CSS Profile, similar to the FAFSA, is a tool through which individual colleges and universities (usually private) determine how much financial need a student has in order to decide how much aid to award them.

Demonstrated Need: This is the difference between the cost of attending a college and your expected family contribution.

Expected Family Contribution (EFC): The EFC is the amount of money you and your family could be expected to pay for one year of college costs, based on the data gathered from the FAFSA and determined by a federal formula applied to that data. This figure often differs from the actual amount you will be required to pay.

FAFSA: This is the Free Application for Federal Student Aid, a federal form required as the application from all students who wish to apply for need-based financial aid, including grants, loans and work-study awards.

Fees: These are charges that cover costs not associated with the student's course load, such as costs of some athletic activities, clubs, and special events.

Financial Aid Gap: The gap appears when the student's expected family contribution (EFC) plus the school's financial aid package don't equal the cost of attendance.

Financial Aid Package: The total amount of financial aid a student receives. Federal and nonfederal aid—such as grants, loans, or work-study—are combined in a "package" to help meet the student's need. Using available resources to give each student the best possible package of aid is one of the major responsibilities of a school's financial aid administrator.

Need-Blind Admission: Full consideration of an applicant and his or her application without regard to the individual's need for financial aid.

Room & Board: This is the cost of living and eating at a school. Only residential students have to pay this fee.

Sticker Price: The sticker price for a college or university is the total cost of attending, however does not represent the actual amount a student will have to contribute after financial aid.

Tuition: This is the amount of money that colleges charge for classroom and other instruction and use of some facilities such as libraries.

Work-Study: This is a program through which students hold a part-time job on their college campus in order to pay off part of their school fees.

SCHOLARSHIPS

A scholarship is a sum of money given to a student for the purposes of paying at least part of the cost of college. Scholarships can be awarded to students based on students' academic achievements or on many other factors. Scholarships do not need to be repaid.

Academic Scholarships: Academic scholarships are based upon academic achievement as reflected in your college application.

Athletic Scholarships: These scholarships are based upon athletic ability and your prospective college's departmental needs. Division I, II, and III college athletic scholarships are very difficult to receive because of fierce competition.

Corporate Scholarships: These scholarships are awarded to help employees and their families, show community support and to encourage future job seekers toward a career in the company's area of business. Corporate scholarships are much less competitive than other types of scholarships because of geography, employment and the relatively low number of applicants. Start with your family's employers, check out the newspaper and see which companies in your area are awarding scholarships, and then contact these businesses to find out how to apply.

Private Organization Scholarships: These scholarship opportunities number in the millions. Places of worship, labor unions, school districts, chambers of commerce and philanthropic organizations are all excellent sources for college scholarships. Sit down with your family and make a scholarship search list of potential sources (you may be amazed at what's right in your own backyard).

LOANS

A loan is a type of financial aid that is available to students and to the parents of students. An education loan must be repaid. In many cases, however, payments do not begin until the student finishes school.

Federal Perkins Loans: These loans are similar to Stafford loans in that no interest accrues while you are in college. The interest rate is lower, and the repayment grace period is longer than that of a Stafford subsidized loan. The need-based standards are more stringent for the Perkins loan and funds are awarded based on the FAFSA Student Aid Report.

Institutional Loan: Any student loan administered by the college or university using the institution's funds as the source of funding. Perkins Loans may also be considered institutional loans.

PLUS Loan: The Federal Parent Loan for Undergraduate Students (PLUS) allows parents, regardless of income, to borrow up to the total cost of education minus the amount of any other financial aid awarded by the institution or the government.

Stafford Loan: This is a federal student loan for college students used to supplement personal and family resources, scholarships, grants, and work-study. A Stafford Loan may be subsidized or unsubsidized, depending on whether it is need-based.

Subsidized Loans: These loans are need-based loans with interest paid by the government and payments deferred as long as the student is enrolled in a post-secondary program of studies.

William Ford Direct Loan Program: The William Ford Direct Loan Program is administered by the U.S. Department of Education to provide loans that help students pay for their postsecondary education.

GRANTS

Grants, like loans and most scholarships, are based on financial need. A grant may be provided by federal or state governments, an institution, a foundation, or some other nonprofit funding source and does not have to be repaid.

Federal Pell Grant: This grant is a form of financial aid provided by the Federal government to students whose FAFSA indicates a high level of financial need.

Institutional Grant: This is a need-based grant provided by an institution and offered to students whose families are unable to pay the full cost of college. Institutional grants do not have to be repaid.

Merit-Based Grant: A form of gift aid (does not require repayment) based upon your grade point average, academic excellence and extracurricular involvement with some attention to your financial need.

Need-Based Grant: This grant is offered, as a part of the financial aid package, when a student and his or her family are unable to pay the full cost of attending an institution. The grant does not need to be repaid.

LINKS

College Goal Sunday
www.collegegoalsundayusa.org
This free on-site service for filling out the FAFSA service typically takes place in January, in cities and towns across the country.

FAFSA (Free Application for Federal Student Aid)
www.fafsa.ed.gov
Learn all about the FAFSA, the Free Application for Federal Student Aid, usually the first step in seeking financial aid for higher education.

FastWeb
www.fastweb.com
This free service from Monster.com allows users to search over 1.3 million scholarships worth more than $3 billion.

The Student Guide
www.studentaid.ed.gov
Available in English and Spanish, the Student Guide is a comprehensive resource on student financial aid from the U.S. Department of Education.

Notes

Notes

Notes